PRODUCING
USEFUL KNOWLEDGE
FOR ORGANIZTIONS

PRODUCING
USEFUL KNOWLEDGE
FOR ORGANIZATIONS

Edited by
Ralph H. Kilmann, Kenneth W. Thomas,
Dennis P. Slevin, Raghu Nath,
and S. Lee Jerrell, all of the
Organizational Studies Group
Graduate School of Business
University of Pittsburgh

PRAEGER SPECIAL STUDIES • PRAEGER SCIENTIFIC

New York • Philadelphia • Eastbourne, UK
Toronto • Hong Kong • Tokyo • Sydney

Library of Congress Cataloging in Publication Data
Main entry under title:

Producing useful knowledge for organizations.

   Includes bibliographies and indexes.
   1. Research, Industrial—Addresses, essays, lectures.
2. Social sciences—Research—Addresses, essays,
lectures. I. Kilmann, Ralph H.
HD30.4.P76   1983   607'.2   83-13980
ISBN 0-03-063199-8

Published in 1983 by Praeger Publishers
CBS Educational and Professional Publishing
A Division of CBS, Inc.
521 Fifth Avenue, New York, New York 10175 U.S.A.

© 1983 by Praeger Publishers

3456789   052   987654321

Printed in the United States of America on acid-free paper.

FOREWORD

Over the years there has been much criticism of academia generally, but specifically of business schools for failing to use relevance of the problem addressed a prime criterion for deciding what issues to research. The charge of abstract, unfocused research has been leveled frequently as a reason why so little of the published results of business academic scholarship finds itself implemented into business practice. This is as true in the organizational sciences as it is in other fields of business. The papers represented in this book provide an effort to address this issue in an organizational setting by suggesting the problem is much better addressed by producing useful knowledge in the first place rather than by encouraging implementation of results which ignore the standard of usefulness.

The use of a research conference to address such issues has been a tradition at the Pitt Graduate School of Business for some years. We have attempted to identify a crucial issue every few years and to invite the major scholars in that field to focus on advancing creative approaches to the problems inherent in that issue within the context of a research setting. *Producing Useful Knowledge for Organizations* follows the pattern we have established. The issue was judged by our faculty in this area as at the cutting edge of importance in terms of making significant progress possible and as an area where there was insufficient literature to provide the basis for solutions to the complex questions involved.

Under the leadership of our senior scholar in organizational studies, Dr. Ralph Kilmann, the faculty identified those scholars whose prior contributions in this and related fields would suggest they were most likely to provide new thrusts to moving the field forward. The enthusiasm with which those invited to make the major presentations viewed the opportunity was further testimony to the centrality of the questions posed. The quality of the papers produced justifies our confidence that the conference might yield a significant incremental addition to the literature of the field. By bringing the major scholars in the field together in one setting and producing the resultant interactions in a single volume, we hope to crystalize the major facets of the area in a more organized, cohesive, and coherent fashion. If the following material provides a summary of what the current thinking is in the area of producing useful knowledge for organizations and sets the agenda for what research is needed in the future, we will have achieved our major goals. We believe the contributions included do indeed move the field forward in a meaningful way and are grateful for the willingness of not only the University of Pittsburgh faculty to participate so intensely but for the dedicated efforts of all of the scholars who came so far to join with like-minded researchers.

We are pleased with the opportunity to disseminate the findings of this conference to a wider audience. So often the contributions of academic conferences are available only to the participants and others in an unorganized manner depending on which of the papers are accepted for publication and whether the interested reader locates that particular publication. A benefit of a conference of this type is that the major scholars in the field are invited to prepare papers which are carefully reviewed by a peer group. Those accepted for presentation can be selected so as to provide a comprehensive and organized approach to the totality of the subject matter. When brought together in a format such as this volume, these papers provide a way of creating a watershed statement of the current status of the field and a roadmap for the next stage of development. Hopefully they do so in a way which provides useful knowledge for both researchers and practitioners.

H. J. Zoffer, Dean
Graduate School of Business
University of Pittsburgh

LIST OF CONTRIBUTORS

Chris Argyris (Harvard University)
Vincent P. Barabba (Eastman Kodak Company)
Mary Elizabeth Beres (Temple University)
Janice M. Beyer (State University of New York at Buffalo)
Rabi S. Bhagat (University of Texas at Dallas)
Jacob G. Birnberg (University of Pittsburgh)
David G. Bowers (University of Michigan)
Douglas W. Bray (American Telephone and Telegraph Company)
C. West Churchman (University of California, Berkeley)
Thomas G. Cummings (University of Southern California)
Tim R. V. Davis (Cleveland State University)
André L. Delbecq (University of Santa Clara)
Liam Fahey (Northwestern University)
Dan Farrell (Western Michigan University)
Stewart D. Friedman (University of Michigan)
Sue M. Gordon (Boston University)
Raymond G. Hunt (State University of New York at Buffalo)
Mariann Jelinek (McGill University)
William D. Kane, Jr. (Western Carolina University)
Ralph H. Kilmann (University of Pittsburgh)
Harvey F. Kolodny (University of Toronto)
James M. Kouzes (University of Santa Clara)
Edward E. Lawler, III (University of Southern California)
Joseph A. Litterer (University of Massachusetts)
Meryl Reis Louis (Naval Postgraduate School)
Tom Lupton (University of Manchester)
Kenneth D. Mackenzie (University of Kansas)
Harry J. Martin (Cleveland State University)
Peter F. Mathias (General Foods Corporation)
John B. Miner (Georgia State University)
Ian I. Mitroff (University of Southern California)
Susan Albers Mohrman (University of Southern California)
V. K. Narayanan (University of Kansas)
James C. Petersen (Western Michigan University)
Robert F. Rich (Carnegie-Mellon University)
Thomas L. Saaty (University of Pittsburgh)
Roy Serpa (Gulf Oil Chemicals Company)
Nirmal Sethia (University of Southern California)
Dennis P. Slevin (University of Pittsburgh)

Kenneth W. Thomas (University of Pittsburgh)
Noel M. Tichy (University of Michigan)
Harrison M. Trice (Cornell University)
Lawrence Turopolec (University of Pittsburgh)
Mary Ann Von Glinow (University of Southern California)
Robert J. Waller (University of Northern Iowa)
David J. Webber (West Virginia University)
William H. Weekes (Deakin University)
Karl E. Weick (Cornell University)
S. Mark Young (University of Pittsburgh)
Gerald Zaltman (University of Pittsburgh)

PREFACE

On October 28-30, 1982, a research conference was held in Pittsburgh, Pennsylvania, sponsored by the Organizational Studies Group, Graduate School of Business, University of Pittsburgh. The topic of this three-day affair was: Producing Useful Knowledge for Organizations. Nearly 150 individuals attended this conference, about 30 practitioners and the remainder academics. The audience heard and discussed presentations that were given by a distinguished group of both academics and practitioners. These papers were later revised to comprise the chapters in this book. Perhaps the reader would find it helpful for us to trace the background of this conference, what our immediate objectives were, and what we hoped would develop as a result of this project.

Regarding the background of the conference, in the fall of 1981 the Organizational Studies Group formed around five faculty members whose research had evolved into the macro (systems) view of organizational theory and analysis. The dean of the school gave us the support and encouragement to conduct a major research conference as our first group effort. In January 1982, we met to consider what sort of conference could have a major impact on the field and, particularly, what the topic of the conference might be.

Several topics were considered: Organizational Politics, Strategic Organizational Behavior, Organizational Conflict, Organizational Culture, Productivity and Innovation, and Organizational Change and Development. While each of these was seen as potentially directing the efforts of research in the 1980s, we identified a theme that was central to all these topics and others as well. In fact, this theme seemed so fundamental that if we did not address it, then the contributions from any of these topical areas would be in jeopardy.

The fundamental theme we focused on was whether *any* research in the organizational sciences is going to contribute knowledge to managing real organizational problems. What we did not want to do was to have a conference that continued to develop a topical area like politics, culture, conflict, innovation, etc., and yet the knowledge developed would not help practitioners define and solve their many problems in these areas. In short, we felt that we might have a major impact by questioning the very purpose of the organizational sciences, and by challenging the field to do something useful and meaningful for the practice of management.

We believe that the initial intent of the organizational sciences, as the field emerged in the 1960s, was to be an *applied science*. In most cases, academics in the field were based in professional schools of business, management, and administration, rather than in the more basic social science disciplines. Our perception was and still is, however, that the methodology, the rigor, and the purpose of the disciplines have had an undue influence on the development of this applied science. Perhaps the training of most of our colleagues in the 1960s was in the basic disciplines, and they wanted the initial status and recognition given with membership in the basic disciplines. Perhaps they were not sure of what an applied science was and felt that attaining scientific respectability as a new field was a primary objective. In any case, we sensed that the field needs to shift back to its original purpose.

The worst scenario is that this topic of producing useful knowledge simply provides academics with another reason to publish articles in academic journals for academic recognition, tenure, and promotion. It is our hope that we can do something more than that. We want to do something useful, something meaningful.

The best scenario is that, as a result of the conference and this volume of original papers, researchers will seek to examine what knowledge organizations and practitioners really need; that researchers will spend a little more time finding out what these needs are from practitioners themselves; that researchers will make a special effort to communicate the results of their research in ways that help practitioners realize the usefulness of the knowledge; that researchers will put some pressure on their administrators and deans to include the criteria of usefulness in the formal reward system; that editors and reviewers of academic journals will require not only a statement of how the research results are useful, but will demand that the problems being addressed really matter and are not just theoretically interesting.

There is a need for basic research and the study of interesting theoretical problems. There is also a dire need for research that will make a difference in solving organizational problems. We should not have to remind anyone of the state of the economy, the failure of thousands of businesses, the decrease in funding from public agencies and private institutions, and increased competition in world markets. The stage of these problems is critical. We feel that the organizational sciences should do something about these problems, or perhaps we should not be.

The conference was designed to bring together the presenters who have the knowledge, the experience, and the stature to make a difference. We invited those individuals whom we considered to be the "opinion leaders" of the organizational sciences. We also invited a number of practitioners who have made a habit of going to academia and finding something useful despite our efforts to remain mostly scholarly, as opposed to practical. In addition, we conducted a research paper competition. We attracted over 130 submissions on the topic of producing useful knowledge, from which we selected 22. The total set of 38 papers is therefore very selective, very focused, and we believe, very, very good.

The major burden for change we place on the academic community. It is simply too easy to say: "Let's wait for the practitioners to realize how much they need us and how much we can do for them." We are willing to say that the major obstacle to change is the structure and functioning of the academic system. While we have included some discussion on the utilization of existing knowledge in our introductory chapter, the material in this book focuses on the producing side of the problem. This is what we, as academics, are in control of, and this is why our book concentrates on: general perspectives (Part 1), conceptual approaches (Part 2), research strategies (Part 3), and redesign of academic institutions (Part 4), for making scientific-based knowledge more useful.

There were many people who helped us conduct the conference and prepare the final manuscripts for publication. The seven organizational studies doctoral students made us very proud of our program. We wish to thank: Jeff Covin, Jeff Kravitz, Young Doo Lee, Jeff Pinto, Jackie Rider, Bob Russell, and Mary Jane Saxton. Skip Gross and Jeanette Engel, from the Executive Development Division, superbly managed the conference and hotel arrangements. Karen Hoy, from the Communications Department, was essential in the development and printing of the conference literature. Kathy Robbins, an excellent secretary, handled the conference registration, as well as correspondence and numerous details. Mary Jane Saxton contributed to the paper review process and to coordinating our doctoral students. Finally, we wish to express our appreciation to Dean Jerry Zoffer for his active support and encouragement throughout this endeavor.

RHK
KWT
DPS
RN
SLJ

TABLE OF CONTENTS

1

THE PROBLEM OF PRODUCING USEFUL KNOWLEDGE

Ralph H. Kilmann, Dennis P. Slevin, and Kenneth W. Thomas

The organizational sciences are generally recognized as a field of study distinct from the basic social science disciplines. While psychology, sociology, political science, and economics all examine aspects of organizational phenomena, only the organizational sciences are dedicated to this study exclusively. What seems to be a major issue in this field, however, is whether the objectives are primarily to develop theories of organizations or to produce knowledge that will solve organizational problems. It is not that this is an either/or issue, but that this distinction seems to bring out very strong arguments by both academics and practitioners.

The organizational sciences assumed their present form in the late 1950s and in the 1960s, when schools of business and management were growing rapidly. The tremendous growth spurt of the field was encouraged by the American Association of Collegiate Schools of Business (AACSB). Their new accreditation standards mandated coursework in organization theory, behavior, interpersonal communications, and administrative processes.

Of necessity, researchers/teachers in the organizational sciences were recruited largely from the basic social science disciplines. Housing social scientists in these professional schools put some pressure on them to apply themselves to the problems of business and management. The initial expectation, apparently, was to rely upon the social science disciplines as a base for knowledge to predict, explain, and control organizational behavior—but the focus was to be more applied than the basic disciplines. The purpose of the organizational sciences was to produce knowledge that would help practitioners define and solve real world problems. The root disciplines were expected to continue the development of knowledge that would be translated, adapted, and modified for the organizational arena.

For a number of reasons, it does not seem that this purpose has been sufficiently realized. Perhaps the social scientists who first were associated with the business schools retained their major identity with their discipline. It might have been natural for these individuals to desire the status and recognition that came from disciplinary ties rather than commit themselves to the uncertain status of the new business schools. Alternatively, it may not have been evident to them at the time what an applied science really was.[1] Whatever the reasons, for many organizational scientists it seems that today's field is more concerned with theory development than with the application of knowledge to organizational problems.

It is not surprising to find that the practitioner/manager is also perplexed as to the mission of the organizational sciences. Practitioners may well wonder why professional schools of business focus on research for which they see little immediate use. While the faculty of these schools teach courses leading to undergraduate and graduate degrees in business administration, the research is perceived to be geared to other academics and not to practicing managers. This contrasts strongly with the orientation of other professional schools within universities (such as law, medicine, and dentistry), where research and publications are more directly aimed at practitioners.

Managers need knowledge to solve their many complex problems. However, in order to obtain this knowledge, they are more likely to contact consulting firms with some track record in helping organizations than to seek out researchers housed in the business schools for methods and solutions to their problems. Practitioners often find that academics do not seem to understand the language, problems, and concerns of managers. To practitioners, academics seem to be in their own isolated world with little interest or inclination to work outside in the "real world." While these characterizations may seem unduly harsh or extreme, they do capture the stereotypes we have heard regarding these two rather distinct communities.

This introductory chapter attempts to put these issues and stereotypes into perspective. We wish to sort out what seems to divide the two communities so that we can work to bring them together. Our basic assumption is that they need one another: the organizational sciences are irrelevant without a client to serve, and the practitioner community is apt to pay a steep price for relying on the slow process of trial-and-error learning in such very turbulent times.

VALIDITY AND USEFULNESS CRITERIA

Contrary to some of the stereotypes cited above, it is apparent that organizational scientists as well as managers are concerned with both the validity and usefulness of knowledge. A survey of organizational scientists reported in this volume (Thomas and Kilmann, Chapter 4) indicates that organizational scientists place a high personal value on both the "rigor" and "relevance" of research in their field. Likewise, Summer (1959) noted two decades ago that managers value precise and valid information in pursuit of their objectives.

The difference between these two groups seems to lie in how systematically they have attended to these two criteria. Managers and their organizations are geared to performance criteria. A great deal of emphasis is given to methods and procedures "that work"—the usefulness issue.

In contrast, elaborate philosophies and methodologies for determining the truthfulness or validity of theories and hypotheses have been the foundation of science. For example, Campbell (1957) and Campbell and Stanley (1963) have emphasized the centrality of internal and external validity to social science research. Internal validity concerns whether the particular "treatment" in any study or experiment was the true cause of the measured differences, in contrast to a variety of alternative explanations. External validity concerns the extent that the reported findings are generalizable to other populations and settings. While both internal and external validity are often cited as equally important, an observation of the research that gets published in scholarly academic journals shows that internal validity is the primary objective. It seems that the training of social scientists, their cognitive preferences included, and the norms and reward systems of most research-oriented universities very much favor research studies that concentrate on internal validity (Kilmann, 1979) at the expense of generalizability to the larger world.

In order to improve the overall production and utilization of the knowledge process, both communities should augment their shadow sides: the criteria that get underplayed and even ignored. Just as academics have greatly emphasized internal validity over external validity and other prerequisites of usefulness, practitioners are guilty of focusing on one side of the equation. Pressures for short-term results and immediate decision making and action taking result in practitioners being more concerned with usefulness than validity. This is not to say that practitioners are concerned with only expediency and ignore the accuracy and truthfulness of information, but these time pressures impose deadlines that can preclude research, experimentation, search procedures, and extensive analysis. While some problems can be solved with commonsense knowledge, some decisions and actions can and should wait for a more thorough, scientific study. This is when organizational science research and concern with validity and rigor can be utilized more effectively.

The Concept of Usefulness

Our focus is primarily upon a more systematic understanding of usefulness within the organizational sciences. Elsewhere in this volume,

TABLE 1.1. Two Key Distinctions Involved in Concepts Related to the Usefulness of Knowledge

| | | Distinction 1: Actual vs. Potential Events or Outcomes | |
		Actual: accessible after the fact	*Potential:* assessed before the fact
Distinction 2: Descriptive vs. Evaluative Concepts	*Descriptive:* not directly related to investigator's values	Knowledge *Use*	Knowledge *Usability*
	Evaluative: must be assessed with respect to a set of values or goals	Knowledge *Effectiveness*	Knowledge *Usefulness*

Louis (Chapter 2) discusses the ambiguous use of this concept and provides important distinctions between related terms. As she notes, a number of related words (usefulness, relevance, use, usableness) have been used interchangeably in recent organization science treatments of this area. According to Louis, this lack of differentiation marks the newness of this topic as a field of systematic study in the organizational sciences, and is understandable in view of the fact that all these terms have been offered primarily to provide contrasting terms to the more traditional concepts of validity and rigor. Differentiation among these terms will be needed to enable the more precise nomological networks that can provide guides and standards of usefulness in the organizational sciences.

Table 1.1 offers some of the terms cited by Louis to show several key distinctions. It is intended as a framework to help clarify some of the differences between those terms, but also to suggest the complexities involved in operationalizing "useful" research.

As shown in Table 1.1, differences between the concepts involve two important sets of distinctions. The first distinction is between *actual* events and outcomes and the *potentialities* to produce those events and outcomes.

Thus, knowledge use and the effectiveness of knowledge use are variables that relate to actual occurrences and can be assessed by investigators after the fact. In contrast, the usability of knowledge and its usefulness are judgments of the potentialities or capabilities of knowledge, and must be assessed *before* the fact. Louis, for example, defines "useful" as "*capable* of being used advantageously or beneficially" (italics added).

The second distinction is between concepts that are relatively *descriptive* from the researcher's point of view and those that are more *evaluative*. Knowledge use and usability are relatively descriptive in the sense that they do not rely directly upon the investigator's value system. Given adequate data and definitions of these constructs, it would be possible in principle for researchers with different value systems to reach agreement on whether a given piece of knowledge had been used in one situation and whether it has the capacity for use in another. In contrast, the effectiveness of knowledge use and the usefulness of a given piece of knowledge are evaluative in that they must be compared to a set of values or goals. The investigator must answer the implicit question, "Effective or useful with respect to what (or whose) standards?"

Use is thus the most straightforward of the terms. Here we think of knowledge use in terms of influence—some change in the user's decision processes or behavior. Complexities arise in that knowledge can be used to different degrees and in different ways (Dunn, 1980; Weiss, 1980). Nevertheless, the concept of use relates to an actual, measurable process or outcome. Moreover, it is descriptive in that it says nothing about the goodness or badness of the outcome.

Effectiveness adds to use an evaluative dimension, denoting that the outcome of use was desired. The focus here is upon the outcomes of use and its goodness/badness relative to the user's (or someone else's) goals. By knowing the goal, the effectiveness of the outcome remains measurable in principle. However, more complex operations and choices are involved in that the effects of use must be identified, a goal system selected, and the two compared.

Usable, as Louis notes, means "capable of being used." Rather than an observable process or outcome, usability refers to the *potentiality* of knowledge. Once knowledge is used, its past potentiality for use in that one situation is determined. The problem comes in attempting to assess the usability of knowledge in some future sense. Thus, determining the usability of knowledge requires projections of groups of users and their situation, their probable acceptance of the knowledge, and their probable ability to use it in some fashion.

Usefulness is the most complex of the four terms since it denotes the potentiality of knowledge for producing outcomes that will be evaluated as effective in terms of a set of goals. It involves the sum of the sets of difficulties involved in the concepts of effectiveness and usability: anticipating a group of users and their situation, their probable acceptance and use of the knowledge, the probable outcome of that use, and a set of goals or values by which to assess that outcome.

Our discussion highlights the difficulties involved in operationalizing *usefulness*. Elsewhere in this volume, Beres (Chapter 19) and Louis (Chapter 2) comment on the ethical issues involved in selecting potential users and their value systems. Yet we argue that the concept of usefulness remains extremely important for our field. To focus upon knowledge use, although it is easier to assess, involves a somewhat arrogant assumption that our knowledge will be helpful or beneficial. Likewise, studying the effectiveness of past knowledge use will not be helpful in shaping current or future research efforts unless we make questionable assumptions that the future will duplicate the past.

This analysis suggests that usefulness is easiest to project in the short term, when users, their situations, and their goals can be relatively well known by interested researchers. Along these lines, Thomas and Tymon (1982) recently reviewed a large number of criticisms of the organizational sciences to identify five necessary properties of "relevant" research—which should be relabeled "useful" research in this context. These five properties are: descriptive relevance (external validity to the user's situation), goal relevance (correspondence of outcome variables to those desired by the user), operational validity (usableness, ability of the user to implement the theory), nonobviousness (adds something to what the user already knows), and timeliness (availability to user in time to deal with problems). Clearly, more work is needed to conceptualize further and operationalize the notion of research usefulness in the short and intermediate terms. However, this task does seem manageable.

Over the longer term, usefulness becomes more difficult to project, given probable changes in users and their situations. It is here that we necessarily rely heavily upon basic research to provide new ideas that may yield useful research in the future. However, to rely only upon the autonomous directions of basic research is to rely largely upon serendipity to produce useful knowledge. It is vital to our field that basic research be part of a mix that contains a large portion of research directed at foreseeable usefulness.

To understand more fully the complexity of forces surrounding the conduct of research and its use and to put these issues in perspective, we now turn to a systems model that outlines the processes and structures within and between the two communities of researchers and practitioners (users). This model will help to locate and interrelate the contributions of chapters in this book, and will also serve to suggest implications and strategies for change.

A SYSTEMS MODEL OF RESEARCH PRODUCTION AND USE IN THE ORGANIZATIONAL SCIENCES

The view adopted here is that the production of knowledge in the organizational sciences cannot be understood in isolation of the use of such knowledge. Rather, it is an outcome of the complex system in which both researchers (knowledge producers) and practitioners (knowledge users) are embedded.

The skeleton of the model is shown in Figure 1.1. The level of analysis chosen is the community of organizational science researchers and of practitioners. These two communities are treated as focal subsystems of the larger knowledge production and utilization system in our field. The two are distinguished as separate subsystems since interactions within these communities are regarded as more frequent than between them (Caplan, 1979).

As portrayed in Figure 1.1, the model focuses upon the principal processes and structures of this system, which are identified in their most abstract or generic form. The arrows represent the four central *processes* of the system. Arrows 1 and 2 represent focal processes within the two communities: (1) knowledge production within the organizational science research community, and (2) knowledge utilization within the practitioner community.[2] Arrows 3 and 4 represent key processes between the communities: (3) the dissemination or provision of scientific knowledge by the research community to the practitioner community problems, and (4) the solicitation of knowledge by the practitioner from the research community and the giving of feedback on its value or usefulness. The rectangles represent the central social system *structures* within which these processes occur. Rectangles 5 and 6 represent the culture and organization of the two communities or subsystems. Rectangle 7 represents the structural features of the larger system, including the interfaces that link the two subsystems together.

For convenience, the seven causal factors of the model are presented in Table 1.2. The two dichotomies used are processes versus structures and systems level (subsystem versus system). These have been used elsewhere to describe causal factors of conflict behavior (Kilmann and Thomas, 1978), and theories of organization design (Van de Ven and Astley, 1981),[3] although the level of analysis used here (communities) is different.

As noted above, a key feature of the systems viewpoint is the essential interrelatedness of the processes and structures of the model. One cannot fully understand the utilization process without knowing the culture and organization within which the practitioner is located. The practitioner's utilization processes, in turn, have an impact upon that culture and

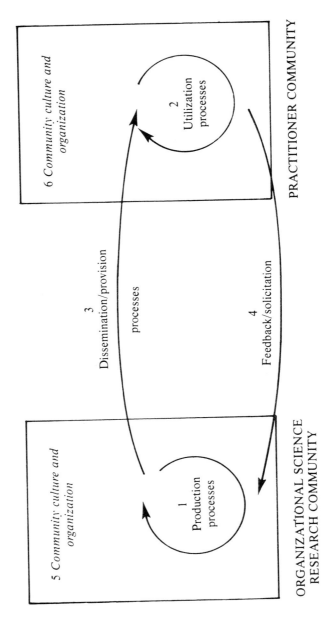

FIGURE 1.1. Overview of the Production/Utilization System for Scientific Research

TABLE 1.2. Tabular Presentation of Causal Factors in the Model, by Systems Level and by Process versus Structure.

	Processes		*Structures*	
System-level (inter- and extra-community) factors	(3)* Dissemination/ provision processes		(7a) Interfaces	
	(4) Feedback/solicitation processes		(7b) External forces	
Subsystem-level (intracommunity) factors	(1) Production processes	(5)	Research community culture and organization	
	(2) Utilization processes	(6)	Practitioner community culture and organization	

*Factors are numbered to correspond to Figure 1.1.

organization. The same is true for production processes within the research community. The four central processes are also strongly interrelated: utilization depends upon what is provided, which depends upon what is produced, which is influenced by feedback and solicitation from practitioners, which is influenced by their utilization experiences, and so on. Likewise, one cannot understand the interaction processes between communities without understanding relevant structural features of the larger system (that is, the interfaces and external forces that shape the two communities and their interdependencies).

Thus, all of the processes and structures of the model play a significant role in shaping research use and the production of useful research in our field. In essence, the seven factors of the model provide a set of generic categories for grouping more specific variables which organizational scientists have proposed as causes and remedies of research use and nonuse and for producing useful/nonuseful research. Stated in other terms, descriptive work by individual researchers on knowledge production and use consists largely of identifying subprocesses or substructures of these generic factors and discussing their effects upon knowledge production/utilization.

To illustrate this point, Table 1.3 lists variables asserted by contributors to this book as central to understanding these research/utilization issues. The variables are organized under the major headings of the seven factors in the model. Major implications of this model will be presented below. At this point, however, it is important to note that the model serves to put existing

TABLE 1.3. Specific Processes and Structural Features that Impact on the Production/Utilization of Organizational Science Knowledge

Processes	Structures
Inter- and Extra-Community Factors	
(3)* *Dissemination/provision processes*	(7) *Interfaces and External Forces*
	A. Interfaces
Direct presentation to decision makers (Webber)	
Translation (Petersen & Farrell; Mackenzie)	Interface types:
Transmission across boundaries (Bowers)	
Training processes (Delbecq & Kouzes; Kane)	Linking roles (Beyer & Trice; Petersen & Farrell)
Writing and publishing (Webber)	Institutes (Birnberg, Turopolec & Young; Tichy & Friedman)
Consulting (Lupton)	Collaborative research structures (Bowers)
	Exchanges of personnel (Martin; Mathias)
(4) *Feedback/solicitation processes*	Advisory boards (Petersen & Farrell)
	Executive seminars (Delbecq & Kouzes)
	Practitioner roles in faculty reviews (Petersen & Farrell)
Cooptation processes (Beres; Beyer & Trice)	MBA and undergraduate business program (Martin; Waller)
Feedback processes (Von Glinow & Sethia; Petersen & Farrell)	Interface forces:
Joint provision/solicitation or dissemination/feedback processes:	Researcher dependence upon access to settings (Narayanan & Fahey)
Action research (Lupton; Hunt; Bowers; Tichy & Friedman)	Researcher dependence upon business funds (Lupton)
Dialogues (Beres)	Social pressures of practitioners upon researchers (Bhagat; Lupton)
Other joint or collaborative projects (Lupton)	Power balances (Beres)

10

(7) continued

B. External forces

Research dependence upon reduced nonbusiness funding sources (Narayanan & Fahey)

Political dependence of organizational researchers upon other academic departments (Tichy & Friedman; Gordon)

Intra-Community Factors

(1) *Production Processes*

Observing organizational phenomena firsthand (Tichy & Friedman)

Conducting practitioner needs assessments (Petersen & Farrell; Delbecq & Kouzes)

Selecting significant topics (Litterer & Jelinek; Bray)

Conceptualizing in a systems or wholistic manner (Weekes; Churchman)

Defining terms (Louis)

Selecting research methods (Lupton; Hunt)

Applied research processes (Mackenzie; Argyris; Bowers)

Assessing the usefulness of theories (Miner; Tichy & Friedman)

Cycling between applied and basic research (Bowers; Mackenzie)

Interaction between applied and basic researchers (Kolodny)

Building theory (Martin; Weick)

(5) *Research community culture and organization*

A. Culture (Serpa; Beyer & Trice)

Philosophies and paradigms of science (Rich; Martin; Bhagat)

Assumptions (Rich; Mackenzie)

Argument (evidentiary) styles (Webber)

Writing styles (Bowers)

Attitudes and orientations (Mathias)

Values and norms (Tichy & Friedman; Thomas & Kilmann)

Priorities (Saaty)

Ethics (Louis)

Archetypes (Mitroff & Kilmann)

B. *Organization*

Business school and research structures (Lupton; Tichy & Friedman; Kolodny; Mohrman, Cummings, & Lawler)

(continued next page)

11

TABLE 1.3 *(continued)*

Processes	Structures
Intra-Community Factors (continued)	
(2) *Utilization Process* (Louis; Rich)	Institutional goals (Tichy & Friedman)
	Evaluation and reward systems (Birnberg, Turopolec, & Young; Serpa; Von Glinow & Sethia; Beres; Tichy & Friedman; Martin; Bhagat; Thomas & Kilmann)
Problem perception (Mackenzie)	Editorial policies and standards (Beres)
Search processes (Webber; Rich)	Doctoral curricula (Gordon; Waller; Martin; Mathias; Mackenzie; Beres)
Screening and evaluation processes (Webber; Mackenzie; Zaltman)	
Knowledge synthesis (Waller)	
Problem solving (Hunt)	
Adaptation (Davis)	
The adoption process (Mackenzie)	
Learning processes (Argyris)	
Emotional processes (Davis)	
Monitoring and evaluation of change (Tichy & Friedman)	(B) *Practitioner community culture and organization*
	A. Culture (Beyer & Trice; Serpa)
	Theories in use (Argyris)
	Argument (evidentiary) styles (Webber)
	Priorities (Saaty)
	Evaluation of results (Barabba)
	B. Organization
	Role demands from technical and political systems (Kane; Tichy & Friedman)
	Structures for information search and utilization in user organizations (Rich)

*Factors are numbered to correspond with Figure 1.1.

12

work on research use into perspective by providing generic constructs for identifying related clusters of more specific concepts, and by emphasizing the fundamental interdependencies of these concepts in shaping research use. Equally important for our purposes, however, they also serve to identify major strategies for improving research usefulness and the interdependencies among those strategies.

IMPLICATIONS OF THE MODEL FOR CHANGE

We shall attempt to use the systems model presented above to describe the current functioning of the research production/utilization system, to identify forces for change and resulting disequilibria in that system, and to identify structural changes that would be required to reach a new state of equilibrium. Our purpose is not a detailed treatment of specific structures and processes in the model, most of which are discussed in depth in subsequent chapters. Rather, our purpose is to provide an overview of major inter-relations at work and their general implications for change.

Intracommunity and Intercommunity Processes

We begin with the intracommunity and intercommunity processes (numbered 1 to 4 in Figure 1.1). Based upon our own experiences and the views of the remaining chapters of this book, there appears to be a working consensus on a number of points. First, knowledge production processes appear to be focussed much more clearly upon issues of internal validity than upon external validity and other requirements of useful research. Second, there is relatively little systematic effort by most researchers to contact practitioners to identify needs and problems or to solicit feedback on the usefulness of existing theory. Third, dissemination is mostly limited to academic journals intended for other researchers, to teaching potential managers (and writing textbooks for them), and to occasional consulting. Fourth, practitioners draw heavily upon other practitioners, their own experiences, and upon consulting firms for knowledge, relying only to a minor degree upon academic research, which is not generally regarded as useful. Finally, practitioners rarely solicit inputs from academic researchers. In short, the knowledge production/utilization system operates currently as a very loosely linked system.

To understand the loosely coupled functioning of the system, it is necessary to understand the structural forces that bear upon it. As in a Lewinian force-field analysis, these structures (numbered 5 to 7 in Figure 1.1) can be viewed as exerting driving and restraining forces on process and as setting up disequilibria that require change. We will now consider their impacts one at a time.

Environmental Forces

Much of the driving force for change in the knowledge production/ utilization system can be traced to changes in the structure of the larger environment. These changes have the cumulative impact of making both communities more dependent upon each other.

The practitioner side has been strongly affected by the economic focus of the late 1970s and early 1980s, as pressures for short-term results and survival are more pronounced in unfavorable conditions. One could argue in general that the amount of organizational slack (resources in reserve) has declined over the last two decades, resulting in practitioners feeling environmental pressures more acutely. At the same time, foreign competition has increased dramatically such that the United States is not the leader in productivity in world markets as once was the case. Lastly, since the 1960s a major cultural change has developed in this country: members of organizations now expect a more challenging, involving, and meaningful experience at the workplace.

In the face of these changes, the practitioner world can no longer rely primarily or exclusively on its own short-term, largely commonsense methods to solve its organizational problems. These formerly tried-and-true methods are no longer working. Different methods and approaches are needed. This need makes the practitioner world more dependent upon academe as a source of new approaches and ideas. However, because of the critical short-term problems facing practitioners, their demands are even more vocally centered on useful research findings, technologies, and theories.

On the academic side, the research community has also encountered diminishing munificence in its environment. Universities as a whole have projected decreases in enrollment to the leveling of the birth rate. These projections have materialized in shrinking resources for many university departments. Already, the pressures for change have been felt on the "less applied" areas of the university (such as schools of philosophy, humanities, languages, theology, and classics); some schools have even had to close their doors. Professional schools, which have been perceived as providing more useful knowledge and methods, have fared better, but the environmental changes noted above are catching up with these schools as well. Certainly, the business schools that house most of the organizational scientists have been feeling the environmental pressures more and more strongly.

In contrast to the physical sciences, there has recently been a widespread disenchantment on the part of the public and the government with the usefulness of social science research (Fishman and Neigher, 1982). This disenchantment and the general scarcity of funds in the economy have resulted in dramatic decreases in government grants for basic faculty research in the organization sciences. Policy changes have thus forced researchers to compete for a reduced number of grants that increasingly emphasize applied concerns. Declining support from government and nonprofit foundations has also made researchers more in need of research funds controlled by private sector organizations, with their strongly applied concerns.

It appears that it will be increasingly difficult for the organizational sciences to maintain an isolated posture with regard to changes in their environment. The organizational sciences, like other "industries," will have to devote more effort to proving to its environment (that is, to government policy makers, private foundations, and organizational decision makers) that it has a useful product to offer.

In short, environmental forces have made both communities more dependent upon each other. In the extreme case, one might argue that the prosperity or even survival of parts of the two communities may be threatened if more interaction and exchange do not take place between them. As noted above, this increasing interdependency is a driving force for change and appears to have created a disequilibrium between current processes and the new needs of both communities. Some efforts at change have already taken place. However, to understand the restraining forces that resist change, it is necessary to appreciate the role of other structural factors, most notably the cultures and organizations of the two communities themselves.

Cultural Differences

Cultural differences between academics and practitioners are inevitable to some degree because of the differences in their daily tasks and activities. Academics are persons of science—they use the scientific method in the pursuit of knowledge. Whether the knowledge is used or not has been less central to their concerns. Managers are persons of affairs—they spend most of their time interacting with others, collecting data, communicating information, motivating, analyzing, in short, *doing* (Schultz and Slevin, 1983).

Academic norms place more emphasis on basic research that is high on internal validity than research that is relevant to solving problems for practitioners. The journals most valued for publication by academics are the ones least likely to be read by practitioners. Academic cultures appear to downgrade the practitioner community as "anti-intellectual" and seem to encourage the myth that academics have little to gain or learn from practitioners. To protect this myth, academics reinforce the use of jargon, abstractions, and behavioral styles that further distance even the most sympathetic practitioners.

Likewise, practitioners also have a culture that is counter to the concerns of the other community. Crisis management and the rewarding of short-term results can drive out a more thorough and systematic analysis of the problem. Practitioners and their organizations often lack patience when it comes to careful, thorough problem analysis. Rather, the practitioner asks, "What should be done now?" Practitioner cultures also have their particular language and their business literature. They expect others to be aware of business news just as academics expect others to be aware of their literature.

These different cultures make it difficult for processes to occur across the boundaries. Processes take place rather well, relatively speaking, within each community as opposed to between the two communities. Thus, academics have their conferences, conventions, editorial processes, journal communications, and so on; practitioners have their newspaper and magazine communications, and are able to interact with each other across company lines quite easily. It is the dissemination and provision processes as well as the feedback and solicitation processes between the communities that are most affected (see Figure 1.1).

Here, we will focus on the barriers from the academic side.[4] In most research-oriented universities, not only is textbook writing discouraged as a form of dissemination, but minimal recognition is given for taking a complex set of ideas and presenting them in a clear-cut, down-to-earth article for a practitioner magazine. The latter process is often referred to in academic circles as mere "popularizing" and not research. Academics assume that some other person will realize the significance of their research and will translate it into usable ideas and methods. This expectation is seen by us as wishful thinking.

Even if the dissemination process were improved by academics who wished to see their work reach a larger audience, the ultimate relevance and usefulness of their research must still be questioned. To us, the enhancement of dissemination processes must coincide with the enhancement of feedback processes, as a total systems effort. Unless the feedback and solicitation processes are improved, academics may become guilty of pushing their useless research onto practitioners. The notion of practitioner input into research conception has often been labeled "cooptation," or when it occurs in lesser degrees, "contamination." This viewpoint denies the objectives of an applied science and its need for outside inputs. To us, the occurrence of inbreeding by academics appears to be as much a threat to useful knowledge as is cooptation by practitioners.

Research Community Organization

Again, we shall focus primarily upon the research community here, emphasizing the two structural features most often cited by chapters in this volume: evaluation and reward systems and doctoral programs (see Table 1.3). Both of these structures currently serve to reinforce and perpetuate the current academic culture, and both are potentially powerful strategies for realigning the culture to better fit the environmental demands upon the field.

Along these lines, the findings presented by Thomas and Kilmann (Chapter 4) seem especially important. In their survey of organizational scientists in the Academy of Management, they found that researchers placed high personal value on both research relevance (defined as usefulness) and rigor (validity), although they reported that the norms of the field and academic reward systems strongly favored rigor. Thus, it appears that there may be significant sentiment on the part of researchers that would support changes toward greater usefulness.

Reward Systems

With respect to reward systems, it is unclear whether schools of business or management would prefer to support separate applied and basic research tracks or a single research track with a stronger applied focus than most current schools. In either case, there is a need for systems that explicitly reward the development of scientific knowledge that will aid the definition and solution of complex problems. The focus, therefore, would not be on theory development and hypothesis testing per se, but on the development, translation, and modification of knowledge to solve real world problems.

To encourage more fully usefulness (and use), academic reward systems would also need to encourage the dissemination of knowledge to the practitioner community. Traditional criteria of publish or perish would have to be modified to include an assessment of knowledge development and dissemination with explicit usefulness criteria. For example, trade journal publications would be encouraged, valued, and rewarded; publications that concentrate on theory development and hypothesis testing for internal validity primarily would not be encouraged.

To get explicit evidence of usefulness, reward systems may also formalize feedback processes from the practitioner community. Such feedback provisions would further motivate researchers to solicit practitioner input with respect to needs, problems, settings, and criteria for success *before* conducting their research. The effect would be to make it more likely that research results that were disseminated would be seen as useful, and in fact used by practitioners.

Doctoral Programs

Since the 1970s, most organizational scientists have been trained in doctoral programs within professional schools. These programs provide the organizational sciences some control over both the provision of skills and the socialization of new organizational scientists into the culture of the field.

To provide more useful research to meet practitioner needs, present curricula would require a marked change. Rather than focusing almost entirely on basic research skills (and philosophies borrowed from basic social science disciplines and in some cases even the physical sciences), it would be necessary to focus explicitly upon applied skills as well, and upon a true philosophy of applied science. The producer of useful knowledge would require the clinical skills of diagnosis and change of organizations, as well as data collection and theory construction and testing. The program would also need to provide students opportunities to move back and forth across community boundaries to learn the realities of practitioner cultures and problems.

In designing such a program, all the assumptions that underlie our traditional doctoral teaching and evaluation methods would have to be questioned explicitly so that the new program would be based on a congruent set of assumptions. This new set of assumptions would necessarily address the concept of usefulness, its relation to validity, the nature of real world problems, the context of real, complex organizations, the culture of the practitioner world as distinct from the academic setting, the reward system of either, and the mechanisms that motivate each community to engage with one another.

Interfaces

Initially, some of the necessary interactions between communities may have to take the form of informal contacts between individual researchers and practitioners. But a wide variety of more formal interfaces would be required to accommodate the sort of high-volume interaction needed if the organization sciences as a field are to make a strong commitment to producing useful knowledge.

For example, to develop an effective organizational clinician program, a formal mechanism would have to be devised that brings the students and the faculty back and forth across community boundaries. Perhaps the faculty should include a certain proportion of full-time practitioners who serve as part-time faculty, or full-time faculty who have served a significant amount of time in a nonacademic setting. It is very difficult to imagine such a program being taught by faculty who have spent most of their career in a traditional research setting. In any event, there would have to be a variety of interfaces that bring students to the world of practitioner problems and bring practitioners into academe to examine and discuss problem-solving material.

Likewise, if reward structures change to assess both the uefulness of research in business schools and the journal-reviewing processes, some need may exist for formal representation of practitioners in the review processes. It seems problematic that academics should take the full burden of proving usefulness by themselves. This would be like practitioners being responsible for demonstrating the validity of their theories.

In addition, practitioners could be more visible and involved in professional associations like the Academy of Management (where practitioner membership is now restricted to a small percentage) and the Institute of Management Sciences. This seems like the perfect opportunity for interaction across the boundaries. Linkages between organizational science associations and practitioner (industry or trade) groups might also be formed to discuss mutual interests and activities.

Back to Processes

At present, there are sufficient forces for change to motivate isolated individual attempts at dissemination and feedback between communities, occasional changes in journal-reviewing policies, and structural experimentation by research groups. The conference on which this book is based was intended to share information on these experiments and the conceptual frameworks that underlie them. Our hope was both for consciousness raising within the organizational sciences and for dialogue between the two communities.

The best general strategy we can offer at this time is to develop numerous opportunities for academics and practitioners to interact over these issues. This may seem oversimplified, but it is a necessary first step. Our own impression is that the stereotype that each community has of the other is a major obstacle to change. We do not believe that many efforts will ensue to establish changed cultures and organizations until these stereotypes break down. Inviting practitioners to review boards, conferences, seminars, classrooms, and so on, is a step in the right direction. Holding workshops that include equal representation of both communities for active discussion and debate of the issues in this book would keep the dialogue going. These joint workshops also could be the basis for planning more formal interfaces to foster further interaction in the future and to set the stage for the formal processes of dissemination and feedback. We are confident that such discussions could go a long way toward bringing the two communities together. In this effort, we would like to charge practitioners with taking their share of initiative as well. Only by soliciting academic input can practitioners learn what new ideas organizational scientists do have to offer; only by actively providing feedback can they help fit academic research to their needs. This is the essential method of organizational and transorganizational development: opening up communications so that problem solving, decision making, and action taking can occur. As the dialogue continues, steps can be taken to change the culture and organization of each community. Interfaces can be established once trust and the need for these interfaces have been developed.

CONCLUSION

The remaining chapters in this book provide in-depth discussions of the points made in this introductory chapter. They are organized into four parts. Part I presents viewpoints by both academics and practitioners on the general topic of this volume. Part II includes the chapters that focus on different conceptual approaches to the problem, while Part III includes the chapters that discuss and advocate particular research approaches that are more likely to produce useful knowledge. Finally, Part IV contains the chapters that present either a general discussion of redesigning academic institutions or argue for a specific form of research organization that would foster the development of useful knowledge.

NOTES

1. Interestingly, the field of management information systems (MIS) appears to be going through a similar identity crisis as it emerges in the 1980s.

2. The focus of the model is the applied use of scientific knowledge by practitioners. Thus, theoretical use of research within the organizational science community is not included; neither is the production of everyday or commonsense knowledge within the practitioner community.

3. Kilmann and Thomas (1978) focused upon individuals as subsystems of interaction systems within organizations, while Van de Ven and Astley (1981) focused upon organizations and their components as subsystems of environments composed of networks of organizations.

4. It should be apparent that we are placing the major burden for the impetus to change on the academic community. This is only because we are most aligned with this community and do not have much leverage in the other community. However, the change strategy would be facilitated if the practitioner community realized that it could benefit from more useful knowledge in the future by planning for better interfaces now with the academic community. But this would necessitate changes in the culture and reward systems in the practitioner world so that practitioners would be encouraged to plan their knowledge needs for the future. Only the most enlightened firms seem to consider the question of what new knowledge they need to identify and to solve their future problems. This would include the development of a research solicitation and provision plan in order to obtain this knowledge. Many firms seem to be captivated entirely with trying to survive today.

REFERENCES

Beres, M. E.
1983   "Usefulness as a research criterion: reflections of a sympathetic critic." In R. H. Kilmann, K. W. Thomas, D. P. Slevin, R. Nath, and S. L. Jerrell (eds.), Producing Useful Knowledge for Organizations. New York: Praeger. Chapter 19.

Campbell, D. T.
1957   "Factors relevant to the validity of experiments in social settings," Psychological Bulletin, 54: 297–312.

Campbell, D. T., and J. C. Stanley
1963   Experimental and Quasi-Experimental Designs for Research. Chicago: Rand McNally.

Caplan, N.
1979   "The two-communities theory and knowledge utilization," American Behavioral Scientist, 22: 459–470.

Dunn, W. N.
1980   "The two-communities metaphor and models of knowledge use: an exploratory case survey," Knowledge: Creation, Diffusion, Utilization, 1: 515–536.

Fishman, D. B., and W. D. Neigher
1982   "American psychology in the eighties: who will buy?" American Psychologist, 37: 533–546.

Kilmann, R. H.
1979   "On integrating knowledge utilization with knowledge development: the philosophy behind the MAPS Design Technology," Academy of Management Review, 4: 417–426.

Kilmann, R. H., and K. W. Thomas
1978   "Four perspectives on conflict management: an attributional framework for organizing descriptive and normative theory," Academy of Management Review, 3: 59–68.

Louis, M. R.
1983   "Useful knowledge and knowledge use: toward explicit meanings." In R. H. Kilmann, K. W. Thomas, D. P. Slevin, R. Nath, and S. L. Jerrell (eds.), Producing Useful Knowledge for Organizations. New York: Praeger. Chapter 2.

Schultz, R. L., and D. P. Slevin
1983   "Science and affairs," Interfaces, 13, No. 2.

Summer, C. E., Jr.
1959   "The managerial mind," Harvard Business Review, 37, No. 1, 69–78.

Thomas, K. W., and R. H. Kilmann
1983   "Where have the organizational sciences gone? A survey of the Academy of Management membership." In R. H. Kilmann, K. W. Thomas, D. P. Slevin, R. Nath, and S. L. Jerrell (eds.), Producing Useful Knowledge for Organizations. New York: Praeger. Chapter 4.

Thomas, K. W., and W. G. Tymon, Jr.
1982   "Necessary properties of relevant research: lessons from recent criticisms of the organizational sciences," Academy of Management Review, 7: 345–352.

Van de Ven, A. H., and W. G. Astley
1981   "Mapping the field to create a dynamic perspective on organization design and behavior." In A. H. Van de Ven and W. F. Joyce (eds.), Perspectives on Organization Design and Behavior. New York: Wiley, 427–468.

Weiss, C. H.
1980   "Knowledge creep and decision accretion," Knowledge: Creation, Diffusion, Utilization, 1: 381–404.

PART I

GENERAL PERSPECTIVES FROM THE TWO COMMUNITIES

Section A:
The Academic Perspective

2

USEFUL KNOWLEDGE AND KNOWLEDGE USE: TOWARD EXPLICIT MEANINGS

Meryl Reis Louis

The production of useful knowledge has become a concern among organizational scientists, particularly during the past five years. Witness the special issues of *Administrative Science Quarterly* (December 1982, March 1983) and the growing number of conference sessions on the subject. However, in my view basic terms are not being adequately articulated. My purpose here is to identify fundamental issues underlying current discourse on usefulness and use of knowledge produced among organizational scientists.

I do not mean to suggest that either the issues or their individual articulation among applied social scientists is new. On the contrary, my reading of current works indicates that there is a need once again to make explicit fundamental issues contributing to the framing of inquiry into organizational science knowledge use and usefulness. The types of issues raised here are as follows: semantic issues, ontological issues, pragmatic issues, ethical/political issues, and ideological/strategic issues.

Each issue offers the inquirer a set of potential choices. The inquirer takes a stand on each basic issue—whether by design or drift, explicitly or implicitly. The *explicit* consideration of basic issues by the inquirer during the framing, conduct, and dissemination of results of inquiry will yield knowledge that is far more useful and rigorous.

What does this explicit consideration of basic issues entail? Beyond enumerating critical issues cum premises of the usefulness of knowledge debate, I will argue that scholarly practice necessarily encompasses: recognizing each issue as a choice point; examining alternative choices associated with each issue; articulating alternatives selected and rationale for their selection; and outlining potential limitations/qualifications of results stemming from choices on basic issues. The broader purpose of this chapter is to help enhance both the usefulness and use of organizational science knowledge by identifying means to strengthen the quality of future argument.

SEMANTIC ISSUES

Is there any difference in meaning between useful and relevant knowledge; between useful and usable knowledge; between used and useful knowledge? What is meant by each?

The *American Heritage Dictionary* (1976) defines the terms as follows:

> *usable*—capable of being used; in a fit condition for use; intact or operative
> *useful*—capable of being used advantageously or beneficially
> *used*—employed for some purpose
> *relevant*—related to the matter at hand; to the point; pertinent

The dictionary definitions reveal a qualitative distinction between usable and useful—useful knowledge offers "advantage" over and above usable knowledge. The definitions indicate a change in state from potentiality in the case of usable and useful knowledge to activation in knowledge that is used. *Used, useful*, and *usable* are grounded in purpose and direction—toward some end—and hence convey a sense of futurity; *relevant* connotes an immediacy, a connection with a present situation in both time and space.

With respect to knowledge per se, Weiss and Bucuvales (1980) have demonstrated that *useful* and *relevant* are conceptually and empirically distinct. They identified three frames of reference used by decision makers in mental health agencies to screen the stream of social science research flowing across their desks. The frames were: *relevance* of the content of the study to the person's job situation; *direction* (or utility) the study provided in helping move toward a given end or purpose ("action orientation") or in altering the purpose ("challenge status quo"); *trustworthiness* (or truth) of the study in terms of quality and/or conformity to one's expectations (1980: 311). Thus, the terms useful and relevant with respect to knowledge had different meanings for decision makers.

Despite such differences in meaning, the adjectives relevant, useful, and usable have been employed almost interchangeably to refer to a common quality of knowledge produced in the organizational sciences (for example, by Boehm, 1981; Evered and Louis, 1981; Thomas, 1982). One likely reason for equating and interchanging these terms for describing knowledge may be that the meanings seem very similar in comparison with meanings of the terms with which they are frequently contrasted in the current debate:

such as valid, reliable, rigorous, precise, scientific knowledge. In view of the formal denotative differences among the adjectives and the empirically documented differences in the use of the terms by policy makers to describe knowledge, our inquiry and discourse ought to reflect the more subtle semantic shadings among relevant and useful, useful and usable, and useful and used.

Enough among us now appreciate the need to move beyond preoccupation with the traditional criteria for knowledge and purposes of inquiry— beyond "truth tests" (Weiss and Bucuvales, 1980) and "scientifically meaningful" research (Selltiz and Cook, 1948). Attention can be shifted away from drawing large contrasts between "scientistic" and "pragmatic/ use-oriented" inquiry that previously may have been necessary in order to sell others on the need for both. Attention can be directed toward implementing more comprehensive research aims, toward carrying out the work of determining what multipurpose inquiry might mean and how we might accomplish it. These activities require greater semantic precision than in the past.

In the future we will need to specify which adjectives (relevant or useful) apply to the "knowledge" in question and in what ways. What assumptions, if any, are made about the other sorts of knowledge? For instance, is it assumed that knowledge considered useful by policy makers is used by them? Is the assumption warranted? On what basis? Such assumptions when unexplicated may result in research that produces knowledge that fails both truth tests and utility tests.

ONTOLOGICAL ISSUES

What aspects of a piece of knowledge lead to it being considered "useful"? Where does the quality "usefulness" reside: In knowledge as product? In the packaging of the knowledge? In the choice of issue to study? In the knowledge-generating process? In the knowledge-using process?

Properties of relevant research corresponding to practitioner needs have been identified by Thomas and Tymon (1982). They invoke the term *relevant* to encompass meanings of relevant and useful, as defined in the previous section. The properties were derived from a review of recent criticisms or organizational science research. According to Thomas and Tymon, practical relevance results from (that is, the quality of usefulness resides in): the relevance to a practitioner of a theory's dependent variables (goal relevance); the ease with which a practitioner can implement a theory's action implications (operational validity); the availability of a theory in time to deal with problems at hand (timeliness); and the simultaneous correspondence between research findings and a practitioner's experiences (descriptive relevance) and the extension of theory beyond a practitioner's common sense (nonobviousness) (1982: 346–50). Thomas and Tymon have focused on characteristics of and the fit between the product of inquiry and the practitioner as potential user.

An alternative view is taken by Dunn (1980), who proposes five "models of knowledge use," identifying alternative determinants of policy makers' knowledge use. For purposes of this discussion, we will assume some carryover between what leads policy makers to use particular knowledge and what leads policy makers to view particular knowledge as useful. Dunn proposes that the scope of knowledge used by policy makers is determined by, alternatively:

> the characteristics of products of social science research (form, content, language, length, reliability, validity, timeliness)—PRODUCT CONTINGENT
>
> differences in modes of inquiry used to acquire, process, and interpret information (research design, analytic techniques, observational methods, sampling)—INQUIRY CONTINGENT
>
> the characteristics of policy problems (levels of conflict, uncertainty, and risk associated with attempts to satisfy needs or realize opportunities)—PROBLEM CONTINGENT
>
> variations in the structure of organizations (authority, responsibility, power, and incentive systems)—STRUCTURE CONTINGENT
>
> the nature of interaction (authoritarian, delegative, collaborative) among products and potential users and beneficiaries of knowledge—PROCESS CONTINGENT (1980: 517).

Although no definitive, empirically derived answers are yet available, it is reasonable to assume that usefulness reflects some combination in a wide set of possibilities such as those listed by Dunn, Thomas and Tymon, and at the beginning of this section. In the meantime, care must be taken not to lose sight of the answers we of necessity assume in order to get on with inquiry and action. Assumptions channel energies and shape questions and research designs. For instance, the assumption that usefulness is primarily a function of the choice of issue to study leads to different research and action strategies than the assumption that usefulness is a reflection of the packaging of the knowledge produced in the inquiry.

The assumption that research done in organizational settings is necessarily useful has long been commonly adopted. It underlies the arguments of Selltiz and Cook (1948), Boehm (1981), and Evered and Louis (1981). Yet in and of itself, the organizational location of inquiry constitutes neither necessary nor sufficient condition of usefulness of knowledge generated through the inquiry. In many respects, this assumption may undermine ultimate usefulness of knowledge. For instance, Frost argues most persuasively that appropriate detachment from organizational settings is essential to "avoid becoming co-opted by any organizational group" (1980: 505) and thus to avoid producing knowledge of questionable truth and overall utility.

PRAGMATIC ISSUES

How and by whom is organizational science knowledge presently used? Answers to such pragmatic questions are being sought through a number of empirical and conceptual endeavors. For instance, Weiss and her colleagues have observed that research is used by policy makers in mental health agencies in a wide variety of ways (Weiss and Bucuvales, 1980; Weiss, 1980). As a result, they argue for a much broader formulation of the concept of knowledge utilization than is typically found in the literature. In their formulation, knowledge use refers to "taking research into account in the work of one's office." It encompasses

> generating awareness of needs, problems, and shortcomings in service;
> providing news about strategies that are proving effective;
> alerting people to environmental changes and emerging issues;
> reducing the uncertainties that inevitably attend complex issues;
> justifying current policies;
> offering ideas and concepts for making sense of experiences;
> constituting a language for communication with other actors in the public
> arena. (Weiss and Bucuvales, 1980: 312)

They conclude that our view of utilization must reflect how social science knowledge is being used by policy makers. It must

> encompass the assimilation of social science information, generalizations,
> and ideas into agency perspectives as a *basis for making sense of
> problems* and *pondering strategies of action.* (1980: 312) (emphasis
> added)

An approach to the broader question of how knowledge is used is provided by Alfred Schutz. In 1945 Schutz developed a framework for distinguishing among systems or categories of relevance or usefulness that a thing, idea, or piece of information (an item) may have for an individual. Notes on the framework were put into manuscript form in 1970. Categories are interrelated and come into play in a hierarchical or chronological sequence during one's experience of an item. The first and most fundamental category is "topical relevance": that relevance "by virtue of which something is constituted as problematic in the midst of the unstructuralized field of unproblematic familiarity—and therewith the field into theme and horizon" (1970: 26). Simply put: we notice; our attention is drawn to an item as figure or theme against ground or horizon in a perceptual or conceptual field. Something is topically relevant by virtue of standing out, of being noticed.

A second category is "interpretative relevance," in which the task is "to grasp the meaning of what is now within the thematic kernel of his conceptual field" (1970: 36). That which was previously noticed must now be interpreted. A final category is "motivational relevance," through which actions are selected in response to the noticed and (partially) interpreted item (1970: 50). In part, interpretations are formed through one's motivational orientation, illustrating one area of interrelationship among categories of relevance.

The resemblance between Schutz's general categories of relevance and the Weiss and Bucuvales findings about how social science research is screened and used by policy makers is striking. Schutz's topical relevance parallels Weiss's generation of awareness or consciousness-raising function; Schutz's category of interpretative relevance translates into Weiss's sense-making function; and motivational relevance embodies an action-selection function such as Weiss notes.

Another subtle use of knowledge has been considered by Giddens (1976) and Moch (1983). Moch (1983) (after Giddens, 1976) argues that social science theories are interventions; that by virtue of being believed they are "used" by their proponents, including social scientists themselves. He urges the development of a metatheory to aid scientists and practitioners in recognizing theories as schemata, rather than continuing to tacitly enact theories as reality. Moch's argument raises two points of particular interest here: that social scientists may "use" the knowledge that they produce; and that they may do so without explicit awareness that or how they are using the knowledge.

Other pragmatic assumptions that result in problems have been noted by Dunn and Thomas. "If the study of knowledge use is to prove relevant to practical problems it must move beyond implicit assumptions that quality research is used research" (Dunn, 1980: 534). Similarly, we must move beyond assumption that "qualitative" research or "field" research inherently is more useful (Thomas, 1982).

A final issue here is the extent to which one conceptually and empirically separates and believes in the separability of knowledge generation and knowledge utilization. This constitutes a critical choice in the framing of thought and inquiry on knowledge use. Consider, for example, the positions of Selltiz and Cook (1948) and Beyer and Trice (1982). The former draw very little distinction between the production of socially useful knowledge and the facilitation of its use. Instead, they focus on what it would take to produce that knowledge. In contrast, Beyer and Trice focus on knowledge utilization as though it were largely independent of knowledge characteristics and generation processes. Neither view is sufficient; each requires supplementing, grounding, and bounding in order for the arguments in which they are embedded and for which they provide frames to convince and endure.

ETHICAL/POLITICAL ISSUES

In what context is usefulness to be assessed? Knowledge as useful toward what ends? For whom? In what temporal frame?

Usefulness has no meaning when considered outside of a particular context. Usefulness is a judgment made about knowledge from a particular vantage, from the perspective of some user or set of users. It is a judgment made from a temporal/historical perspective as well. What is useful in the immediate situation may not help in the long term. What is useful to managers may be antithetical to the needs of customers or employers. Useful in meeting whose needs in what time frame? Assumptions about answers to such questions underlie efforts to enhance usefulness of organizational science knowledge. Therefore, it is incumbent upon researchers to explicate assumptions concerning which constituencies in what time frames they seek to aid and reevaluate larger political and ethical positions those assumptions may reflect.

Who is and ought to be our client? Until this point in our history, organizational scientists have worked primarily to provide knowledge of use to managers and policy makers. Some researchers may feel they have "a social mandate to try to help managers," as a result of working in schools of management or business (Thomas, 1982). Others may not have made such an explicit choice. In either case, this has been the situation until recently. Whether we continue primarily to serve managers *is* a matter of choice.

Frost (1980) and Nord (1978) among others are telling us that managers and policy makers do not represent the realities of all or even most organizational members, though they typically represent the power. Nord's two Golden Rules summarize his view of the political realities of organizational life.

> Do unto others as you would have them do unto you.
> Them that has the gold makes the rules. (1978: 678)

Frost reflects on current organizational science practice and offers a set of guides for broadening our approach. In his "radical framework" for practicing organizational science, he urges us to:

> try to understand how others in the organizational arena perceive and construct their realities . . .
> work toward a greater awareness . . . of our assumptions . . . about what constitutes organizational reality . . .
> adopt an historical perspective to organizational events . . .
> attend to data, to meaning, to criticism . . . [through developing] an attitude of partnership in our relations with organizational members . . .
> become much more knowledgeable about and sensitive to political realities within which organizational events take place . . .
> avoid participation . . . where we clearly contribute to . . . manipulative practical decision-making, where we cater to only . . . one group at the expense of others. (1980: 504–5)

On considering knowledge use, a traditional concern with inquiry as intervention has been expanded in recent years to encompass theory as intervention. Giddens best articulates the point:

> Social theory must incorporate a treatment of action as rationalized conduct ordered reflexively by human agents. . . . Anyone who recognizes that self-reflection, as mediated linguistically, is integral to the characterization of human social conduct, must acknowledge that such holds also for his own activities as a social "analyst," "researcher." . . . Theories produced in the social sciences are not just "meaning frames" in their own right, but also constitute moral interventions in the social life whose conditions of existence they seek to clarify. (1976: 8)

How many of us give deep consideration to the potential influence our theories and research results as framed may have on readers' experiencings of their lives in organizational settings?

IDEOLOGICAL/STRATEGIC ISSUES

How might usefulness of social and organizational knowledge be enhanced? How might use of knowledge be increased? What, if any, relation might there be between these two aims? Are these aims inherently desirable?

Mitroff and his colleagues (1974) have proposed a model of a cycle of scientific inquiry in which usefulness and use concerns are incorporated. The cycle moves through "perception of a real-world problem situation, broad conceptualization of the phenomenon, formulation of a scientific model [theory], and the derivation of implications . . . [which] then are implemented to try to remedy the problem situation, resulting in a change or reinforcement of conceptualization" (as summarized in Thomas and Tymon, 1982: 346). Usefulness derives in part from the real-world source of the problem situation under study. Use completes the cycle and in turn fuels subsequent inquiry. Implicit in this model is an assumption that the scientist shares responsibility for insuring the social usefulness and actual use of the knowledge generated through scientific inquiry. Before Mitroff, Selltiz and Cook (1948) concluded that research must be both socially useful and scientifically meaningful. Lewin argued that for any field of action, the study of general laws and the diagnosis of a specific situation must be joint aims of scientific research (1948: 204).

In contrast, Lindbloom and Cohen state: "We do not assume that social science and social research should always—or even most often—be designed for or tested by their usefulness for social problem solving" (1979: 4–5).

Early work describing means of doing research such that it is socially useful as well as scientifically meaningful was carried out by Selltiz and Cook. Here is their list of essential characteristics of research that is socially useful:

> Research must deal with problems that have present social consequence or that are likely to demand solutions within the near future. . . . Results of research must be applicable in concrete social situations. . . . Investigations must be carried out in such a way as to stimulate application of their results in practical social situations. [Studies must be] part of a coordinated research plan. (1948: 456–59)

Toward the same ends, Lewin (1948) proposed an "action research model" wherein planning and execution of the first step in the plan are followed by fact finding in order to evaluate the first action and to give the planners a chance to learn, to plan the next step correctly, and to modify the overall plan as needed. The cycle continues, according to Lewin, in another iteration of the planning, action, fact-finding circle of activity.

Thomas and Tymon (1982) recommend a two-pronged strategy for enhancing knowledge usefulness. First, we must find out about practitioners' experiences of, goals in, and skills in coping with organizational situations. Second, we need to develop a two-way interaction between researchers as knowledge producers and practitioners as knowledge users. Knowledge per se is not directly addressed in their approach.

It is commonplace to hear the argument that if knowledge generated by our research were more useful it would be more widely used. I wish to propose the reverse: that the increased use of knowledge, particularly by those who produce it, will enhance the usefulness of knowledge produced

over time. A cynic might say I am adopting the Gilbert and Sullivan ploy—
"let the punishment fit the crime." That is not my intention. Instead, I am
suggesting a kind of role integration for researchers in which we consciously
yoke or harness our roles as members of various organizational units (school,
department, committees, academies, and so on) to our roles as organizational
researchers.

Such a linking could be accomplished through a variety of activities and
serve multiple functions. One could observe how the unit in which one is a
member functions, comparing what is seen with academic descriptions of
similar phenomena; this could also identify phenomena of practical consequence in need of research or new ways of framing old research questions.
One could try out action implications of research findings, one's own and
others'. This could be conceived of as an informal test and could also reveal
the psychological and time costs as well as the pure feasibility or operational
validity of results. Finally, in linking roles one would have a clear
opportunity for a dual self-reflection in the roles of organizational member
and organizational researcher. Reflecting on each role from the perspective
of both roles is more likely than is "single role self-reflection" to reveal
otherwise tacit assumptions concerning political, pragmatic, ontological, and
moral/value issues—with respect both to one's research frames and to one's
organizational participation.

Researchers' attempts to thus employ social science knowledge in
understanding and acting in organizational situations may in many ways
contribute to enhancing the usefulness of social science knowledge and the
researchers' abilities to generate useful knowledge.

Certainly in the organizational units in which we participate there are
endless opportunities to examine close up bureaucratic structures and
processes—some gone awry, some well-functioning; to try to facilitate
improved administrative practices and policy procedures; to work with
comparable group-level phenomena in varied contexts; and so on. I am not
suggesting that any one of us become preoccupied with studying oneself,
one's colleagues, or one's organizational settings. But since we are there, why
not make use of the resources at hand? Needless to say, good judgment
concerning ethical issues of "manipulating" or "observing" others and
courtesy on such matters are essential. We are, as Giddens (1976) reminds
us, intentional agents seeking to achieve purposes. I am suggesting that we
expand our purposes and the arenas in which we pursue them; that we
incorporate trying out in our home organizational settings that which we
would have others do. There could be no better first judge of the extent to
which research helps make sense of problems and helps one ponder strategies
of action than each of us struggling to cope as actors in our own
organizational lives.

CONCLUSION

My purpose has been to identify fundamental issues underlying discussions of the usefulness of social and organizational science knowledge, to highlight choices associated with various issues, to point out how assumptions unexplicated may undermine usefulness and scientific meaningfulness of inquiry, and to review choices made tacitly or explicitly in exemplary works on the topic.

My personal position is that organizational science inquiry is meaningful to the extent that it jointly pursues aims of scientific quality and social usefulness. Inquiry oriented toward only one of the two aims is inadequate from the outset.

Usefulness is gaining widespread support among organizational scientists as an appropriate, even essential, criterion for evaluating research products. Recent trends in the prominence of various topics and subfields may be interpreted in part as manifestations of this new orientation. For instance, there appears to be a dramatic increase in interest in the policy/strategy subfield and a cooling of interest in both the micro- and macro-organization subfields (organization behavior and organization theory). Central to policy strategy is a clear sense of constituencies in organizational settings and purposes of organizational units. The core topics tackled within the policy sciences derive directly from real-world organizational problems. Change management and organization design are areas in which there has been a substantial increase in work being done; both are areas concerned with organizational purpose and movement in selected directions toward pursuit of purposes.

Though organizational scientists now seem to recognize the need to consider usefulness of knowledge issues in designing and assessing research, we have a long way to go before we have adequately investigated the territory. In the meantime, it is important that we conduct investigations in a scholarly manner. We must endeavor to become aware of the assumptions we have made. We must assess the extent to which they have influenced our inquiry. We must explicate our assumptions and qualify results accordingly. And we must examine alternatives and choose among assumptions as explicit frames of inquiry.

REFERENCES

American Heritage Dictionary of the English Language. Boston: Houghton Mifflin, 1976.

Beyer, Janice M., and Harrison M. Trice. "The utilization process—a conceptualization, review, and analysis," *Administrative Science Quarterly*, December 1982.

Boehm, Virginia R. "Conditions for useful research in organizations: 3 mysteries and some clues," a paper presented at the Academy of Management Meetings, San Diego, August 1981.

Dunn, William N. "The 2-communities metaphor and models of knowledge use," *Knowledge Creation, Diffusion, Utilization*, 1, 515–536, 1980.

Evered, Roger, and Meryl Reis Louis. "Alternative perspectives in the organizational sciences: 'Inquiry from the inside' and 'inquiry from the outside,' " *Academy of Management Review*, 6, 385–395, 1981.

Frost, Peter. "Toward a radical framework for practicing organizational science," *Academy of Management Review*, 5, 501–507, 1980.

Giddens, Anthony. *New Rules for Sociological Method: A Positive Critique of Interpretative Sociologies*. London: Hutchinson, 1976.

Lewin, Kurt. "Action research and minority problems," in G. W. Lewin (ed.), *Resolving Social Conflict*. New York: Harper, 1948.

Lindbloom, Charles E., and David K. Cohen. *Usable Knowledge: Social Science and Social Problem Solving*. New Haven: Yale University Press, 1979.

Mitroff, I. I., Betz, F., Pondy, L. R., and Sagasti, R. "On managing science in the systems age: Two schemas for the study of science as a whole systems phenomenon," *Interfaces*, 4, 46–58, 1974.

Moch, Michael K. "Toward a theory of administrative practice: For what? For whom? And for how long?" in Ralph H. Kilmann et al. (eds.), *Producing Useful Knowledge for Organizations*. New York: Praeger, 1983.

Nord, Walter R. "Dreams of humanization and the realities of power," *Academy of Management Review*, 3, 674–679, 1978.

Schutz, Alfred. *Reflections on the Problem of Relevance*. New Haven: Yale University Press, 1970.

Selltiz, Claire, and Stuart W. Cook. "Can research in social science be both socially useful and scientifically meaningful?" *American Sociological Review*, 13, 454–459, 1948.

Thomas, Kenneth W. Personal correspondence, September 1982.

Thomas, Kenneth W., and Walter G. Tymon, Jr. "Necessary properties of relevant research: Lessons from recent criticisms of the organizational sciences," *Academy of Management Review*, 7, 345–352, 1982.

Weiss, Carol H. "Knowledge creep and decision accretion," *Knowledge: Creation, Diffusion, Utilization*, 1, 1980.

Weiss, Carol H. and Michael J. Bucuvales. "Truth tests and utility tests: Decision-makers' frames of reference for social science research," *American Sociological Review*, 45, 302–313, 1980.

3

THE UNPAVED ROAD FROM THEORY:
OVER THE MOUNTAINS TO APPLICATION

John B. Miner

The title of this chapter is intended to emphasize theory, application, and the relationship between the two. It suggests that this relationship is uncertain and unstable at best; that we have failed as yet to forge a solid, proven route from good theories to useful applications. Most would agree with that conclusion. Yet it may be helpful to take a systematic look at established theories in the field to determine what they have contributed by way of useful knowledge for organizations. By identifying instances where we have failed and where we have succeeded, it should be possible to gain some insights into how theory might contribute more effectively to improved organizational practice, and thus to make the route over the mountains somewhat more passable.

IDENTIFYING ESTABLISHED THEORIES

The first step in such a systematic analysis of the theories in organization science, and their applications, is to identify a set of theories for consideration. A survey related to this purpose was carried out during the first half of 1977. The objective was to determine which theories might be most appropriately considered in a book dealing with the major theories of the field. This book subsequently became two: *Theories of Organizational Behavior* (Miner, 1980a) and *Theories of Organizational Structure and Process* (Miner, 1982a). Although the survey is somewhat dated, it is unlikely that significant changes in what constitutes our major, established theories have occurred in the interim. Because of the need for a sufficient body of research tests, theories simply do not become established very rapidly; once established, they appear to take on a self-perpetuating quality.

37

In fact there is a distinct risk of their remaining viable long beyond what might be scientifically justified.

The Survey Sample

Initially, 100 individuals were contacted to obtain their views. These people were selected as they were among the most knowledgeable in the field. The great majority were known personally to the author. Their names were obtained from lists of the editorial review boards of major professional journals and of past and present officers of relevant professional associations.

Replies of some kind were obtained from 47 of the 100. A total of 35 provided usable responses. Of these, seven turned out to be strongly identified with the origins of one of the theories ultimately nominated. There is no reason to believe that this fact exerted a meaningful influence on the results, however. The respondent group does not appear to differ significantly from the nonrespondents in any way that might be related to knowledgeability. This, however, is an impressionistic conclusion. There is every reason to believe that the data were obtained from people who have a solid knowledge of organization science.

Nomination Procedure

The letter contained in Figure 3.1 was sent out during February 1977 and replies were received during the ensuing five months. Attached to this letter was a nomination form that asked for a theory name, important contributor(s), and comments for each theory. Space was provided to nominate up to 30 theories, although most respondents noted considerably less. The form was headed with the following statement:

> The term theory is understood to include conceptual formulations which are not strictly speaking theories such as theoretical models, definitional systems, analytical schemeta, and powerful constructs.

Survey Results

Table 3.1 lists the theories most frequently nominated, their actual frequencies (out of 35), and the individuals considered in the discussions of these theories in the two theoretical volumes (Miner, 1980a, 1982a). These latter include the theorists mentioned most frequently in the survey questionnaire, but are not limited to that source. At least 110 distinct theories were noted, of which the most frequently nominated 24 appear in Table 3.1. Table 3.2 is based entirely on the important contributors'

Dear _____:

I am winding up to start work on a book tentatively entitled *Theories of Organizational Behavior and Design* and I would very much appreciate your help. My intention is to consider some 25 or 30 theories (models, definitional systems, analytical schemata, powerful constructs) in our field broadly defined. My goal is to emphasize those theories that are considered most important in the field by its knowledgeable scholars. To do this I need to find out what theories are considered important, and that is the reason for this letter. Would you be willing to spend a few minutes noting those theories you feel should be covered in such a book on the enclosed sheets?

The criteria that I have in mind for selecting theories to be included are the following:

1. The theory should have proved useful in understanding, explaining, and predicting the functioning of organizations or the behavior of people in them.
2. The theory should have generated significant research.
3. The theory should have clear implications for practice and application in some area of management or organizational functioning.

Please nominate as many theories as you feel appropriate. It would be helpful if you would indicate the name of each theory and then list the names of the one or more individuals you consider to be most closely associated with it. Some sort of ranking would be useful, but this is not essential; also any comments you might want to make on your choices would be very much appreciated.

Thank you for your help.

Sincerely yours,

John B. Miner
Research Professor

FIGURE 3.1. Letter Used to Solicit Nominations

notations without reference to the particular theory involved. Well over 300 names were given; the top 26 are listed in Table 3.2. All 26 are included in Table 3.1 as indicated.

The theories and theorists of Tables 3.1 and 3.2 were all considered in the theory volumes. These volumes also contain discussions of certain

TABLE 3.1. Theories Nominated Most Frequently and Theorists Considered

Number of Nominations	Name of Theory	Theorists
24	Contingency theory of organization	*Paul R. Lawrence *Jay W. Lorsch
24	Expectancy theories	Basil S. Georgopoulos *Victor H. Vroom Jay Galbraith Larry L. Cummings *Lyman W. Porter *Edward E. Lawler George Graen Edward L. Deci
20	Contingency theory of leadership	*Fred E. Fiedler
17	Decision-making concepts and constructs	*Herbert A. Simon *James G. March Richard M. Cyert
16	Need hierarchy theory	*Abraham H. Maslow Clayton P. Alderfer
16	Psychological open systems theory	*Daniel Katz *Robert L. Kahn
15	Technological determinism	*Joan Woodward
15	Job characteristics theory	*J. Richard Hackman
15	Behavior modification and operant learning	*B. F. Skinner W. Clay Hamner Fred Luthans Arnold P. Goldstein Melvin Sorcher
15	Path-goal theory	*Robert J. House Martin G. Evans
14	Sociological open systems theory	*James D. Thompson
14	Equity theory	*J. Stacy Adams
14	Theory of System 4 and 4T	*Rensis Likert
14	Motivation-hygiene theory	*Frederick Herzberg
12	Technology in a comparative framework	*Charles Perrow

TABLE 3.1 *(continued)*

Number of Nominations	Name of Theory	Theorists
12	Goal congruence theory	*Chris Argyris
12	Goal-setting theory	*Edwin A. Locke
11	Achievement motivation theory	*David C. McClelland John W. Atkinson Bernard Weiner
11	Sociotechnical systems theory	Eric L. Trist
10	Mechanistic and organic systems theory	*Tom Burns *G. M. Stalker
10	Theory X and theory Y	*Douglas McGregor Raymond E. Miles
10	Decision tree theory of participative leadership	*Victor H. Vroom
10	Theory of bureaucracy	Max Weber Peter M. Blau Victor A. Thompson
10	Theory of bureaucratic demise	Warren G. Bennis

*Included in the individual nomination list of Table 3.2.

theories which, although not nominated with sufficient frequency, appear in the author's judgment to be worthy of consideration. In the absence of supporting evidence, these inclusions must be considered as judgment calls:

Influence-power continuum theory (Frank A. Heller)
Leadership pattern choice theory (Robert Tannenbaum and Warren H. Schmidt)
Vertical dyad linkage theory (George Graen)
Control theory (Arnold S. Tannenbaum)
Group-focused systems theory (Ralph M. Stogdill)
Theory of strategy and structure (Alfred D. Chandler)
Classical management theory (Henri Fayol)

TABLE 3.2. Individuals Nominated Most Frequently

Number of Nominations	Individual
25	Jay W. Lorsch
24	Paul R. Lawrence
24	Victor H. Vroom
21	Fred E. Fiedler
18	Lyman W. Porter
18	Edward E. Lawler
18	Frederick Herzberg
17	Herbert A. Simon
17	Rensis Likert
16	James G. March
16	Abraham H. Maslow
16	Robert L. Kahn
16	Joan Woodward
16	Robert J. House
15	James D. Thompson
15	J. Stacy Adams
14	Chris Argyris
13	Daniel Katz
13	Charles Perrow
12	J. Richard Hackman
11	B. F. Skinner
11	Edwin A. Locke
11	David C. McClelland
11	Douglas McGregor
10	Tom Burns
10	G. M. Stalker

A number of these theories probably have become more salient in recent years, although this is not true of all. The author's role-motivation theory is similar in status and would have been included in one or the other volume except for the conflict of interest problem that dictated its omission. In any event, these 32 theories provide the framework within which the analyses of this chapter have been carried out.

ANALYSIS OF THEORETICAL APPLICATIONS

The following discussion considers each of the 32 theories in terms of their contributions to "useful knowledge for organizations." Some make no pretense of contributing, some do so well, and some poorly. The treatment draws heavily on the previously noted volumes (Miner, 1980a, 1982a). Although the underlying theories themselves are not considered in detail, it should be apparent that a theory's validity can be a major factor in evaluating applications derived from it.

Underlying the discussion is the supposition that for most purposes research detached from theory is unlikely to be scientifically rewarding. There are literally millions of research questions that could be addressed, and we must somehow focus our limited efforts on what is most likely to yield a substantial knowledge payoff. Theory, with its value-added characteristic, seems best calculated to achieve this result. Furthermore, there is no shortcut to finding useful applications, discouraging as that may seem. We simply have to carry out the hard research to see if our applications work. One of the best demonstrations of this proposition is to be found in the equal employment opportunity area, where legal considerations now mandate this research (Ledvinka, 1982; Arvey, 1979; Miner and Miner, 1979). There is good reason to believe that society, and its legal processes, may intervene in other areas of organization science in much the same way in years to come. Any social science field that emphasizes practical applications is likely to face legal constraints as it moves toward maturity. Kurt Lewin's early statement that "nothing is so practical as a good theory" remains equally viable today. Good theory continues to mean theory that is validated by an adequate body of sound research.

In the following discussion usefulness is specified in terms of three categories: useful knowledge theories, question mark theories, and not-so-useful theories. For the purposes of this classification, usefulness is defined in terms of verified successful application. Research has been conducted that indicates that theoretically anticipated affects do in fact occur. This usefulness criterion says nothing about how widespread applications are; only that applications have occurred and have been shown by research to produce the results predicted. It is assumed that for numerous reasons applications might be widespread and still fail the test of research justification.

Placement in the three categories is relative. Useful knowledge theories have in fact generated applications, and at least some of these applications have met the applied research tests. Question mark theories are associated with applications, but some uncertainties exist—as to the degree to which the applications derive from the theory, as to the amount of research support, as to the appropriateness of the research conducted. Not-so-useful theories often simply have not generated applications; in other cases the difficulty is that the applications associated with the theory have failed to yield evidence of the needed research support. In either case there is no basis for assuming that the theory can be applied effectively at the present time.

Theories of Motivation in Organizations

One of the most fruitful theoretical areas from an applications viewpoint has been employee motivation, extended to include the motivation of members of organizations of all types. Yet even here application has not been a universal concern.

Useful Knowledge Theories

Job characteristics theory is not so much a theory or organizational behavior that has spawned an application as a theory of the application itself: job enrichment. The theory specifies when job enrichment is likely to work and when it is not, and measures have been developed to aid in applying these concepts in practice (Hackman and Oldham, 1980). The theory is quite explicit about how one should go about harnessing the motivational potential of job enrichment; on the evidence, although it may not yet be perfectly on target, it appears to be very close. Job enrichment programs often fail, and that may very well represent a major problem for the continued use of the approach, but it is also true that job characteristics theory would anticipate these failures—if the employees involved and the procedures used are not those the theory advocates (Hackmann, 1975).

Behavior modification builds upon Skinner's theory of operant learning. Yet in its organizational applications it does not always follow the basic theory closely, and Skinner himself has not been involved in these developments at all. His contributions to industrial applications are limited to a belief that the principles of operant conditioning have the potential for making an important contribution there (Skinner and Dowling, 1973). Organizational behavior modification has evolved through the efforts of a number of individuals. Specific statements giving details of application include Hamner and Hamner (1976), Luthans (1975), and Goldstein and Sorcher (1974). These statements do not always follow Skinner closely and certain hypotheses, such as the universal superiority of variable ratio reinforcement, have not been supported in the organizational context (Latham and Dossett, 1978). In addition, there is some reason to believe that certain other theoretical positions might better predict the research outcomes. Nevertheless, the emergent theory of organizational behavior modification has produced useful knowledge. It is not easy to teach managers to use the approach, and there clearly are many situations where it cannot be applied effectively. However, it can work to improve performance under certain circumstances as has been demonstrated often.

Goal-setting theory has its primary application in an approach to the superior-subordinate relationship that results in the subordinate accepting specific, difficult performance goals (Locke, 1970). When these goals are accepted, whether they are assigned or developed on a participative basis, performance should improve. Although the theory was initially tested in a laboratory setting, it has now been extended into a variety of organizational contexts with impressive results (Latham and Baldes, 1975; Latham and Locke, 1975). Whether in fact a true motivational theory underlies these results is something on which even Locke has been uncertain. In many respects the theory is one of a motivational technique, and thus of the same basic type as job characteristics theory. In any event, the theory and the application are very closely aligned.

Goal-setting theory has been extended to a number of other applications such as incentive pay systems and knowledge of results with varied outcomes. In these instances, the theory has been used to explain the effects of the applications rather than to generate them. A prime example of this process occurred with respect to management by objectives (MBO) (Locke, 1968). MBO antedates goal-setting theory by some years. Its recent popularity dates from discussions by Drucker (1954) and McGregor (1957). Yet it appears best understood in terms of goal-setting theory. The problem is that MBO often does not work very well, tends to lose what effects it does have rather quickly, and frequently incorporates a whole bag of techniques of which goal setting is only one. All in all, this particular theory-application marriage has not worked out as well as might have been expected. It is goal setting within a circumscribed dyadic relationship that produces the most consistent results, and even then there appears to be some variation with individual differences.

Achievement motivation theory narrowly defined is a limited domain theory of entrepreneurial performance and performance in positions of an essentially entrepreneurial nature in larger bureaucratic contexts. Thus defined, the theory has generated achievement motivation training, which follows the theory closely in its format. This training has proved effective in stimulating entrepreneurial activity in a variety of settings (McClelland and Winter, 1969; Miron and McClelland, 1979). Several other management development approaches, with different names, are clearly modeled on the McClelland procedure.

A more expanded definition of the theory includes not only achievement motivation, but power and affiliation motivation as well (McClelland, 1975). To these have been added certain related concepts such as fear of failure and fear of success. A training program to develop socialized power motivation of the kind said to be needed by most managers has been designed, although evidence of its effectiveness is much less extensive than for achievement motivation training (McClelland and Burnham, 1976). In addition to the training applications, the expanded theory provides a useful set of working hypotheses regarding motivation and behavior to the manager. The theory appears to be of much greater value in dealing with males than females, however, and it considers only a specific, circumscribed set of motives and organizational contexts.

This relating of specific motive patterns to organizational contexts also characterizes role motivation theory (Miner, 1980b). In fact, what is involved is a set of theories for different organizational systems. Of these, the most fully developed by far in terms of its applications is managerial role motivation theory (Miner, 1965, 1977). This was developed in close conjunction with the design of a management development program intended to stimulate higher levels of managerial motivation. A considerable body of research supports the effectiveness of this training. In addition, the theory has guided the development of measures that appear to be useful means of selecting people for organizational positions and assisting in career development.

Question Mark Theories

In contrast with the motivational theories considered to have made contributions to useful knowledge for organizations, there are several others where on one ground or another considerable uncertainty exists. Expectancy theory has proved to possess requisite validity and a substantial body of research support has been developed, building in larger part on Vroom's (1964) propositions. The theory appears to work only in highly rationalized organizational contexts, but within those contexts it works well. The problem is that most proponents of expectancy theory, in its various versions, have given little attention to applications. Potentially, guidelines both for creating the type of organization in which expectancy theory would prove effective and for implementing the theory could be developed and the techniques taught to others. But this has not happened.

The one real exception to this generally anti-application orientation has been a continuing series of statements related primarily to pay and compensation emanating from the Porter and Lawler (1968) version of the theory. In recent years Lawler has been the one who has developed these ideas primarily, and he has tended increasingly to cast them in an organization development framework (Lawler, 1981). Probably the best known applications are cafeteria benefit plans, where employees can select their benefits in accordance with valences and expectancies, and open pay policies, where pay secrecy is curtailed to permit needed perceptions of existing contingencies. These approaches have met considerable resistance, however, both from practitioners and scholars. It cannot be said that their status as useful knowledge has been definitely established. Thus, we are faced with the unusual situation of a good theory that has produced relatively little by way of applications, and what it has produced remains at this time of uncertain quality.

The situation with regard to motivation-hygiene theory is much different. In this case, the basic theory has suffered from a continuing series of attacks of both a logical and empirical nature, to the point where its validity must be seriously questioned. Accordingly, one must also question the use of these ideas as managerial working hypotheses, and proposals such as the organization of industrial relations departments into two formal divisions—one to deal with hygiene matters such as benefits and one to deal with motivators such as job enrichment (Herzberg, 1966).

But the emphasis on job enrichment per se is another matter. Orthodox job enrichment is said to have been stimulated by the theory, has been associated with it for many years, and its application can prove effective although not with everyone (Ford, 1969; Herzberg, 1976). There are two problems in addition to those inherent in the theory itself. First, job characteristics theory appears to provide a more comprehensive and precise understanding of the same phenomena. Second, orthodox job enrichment emphasizes motivators only, not hygienes; thus it is concerned with only half of the theory at best. Furthermore, it emphasizes the work itself, responsibility, opportunity for growth, and advancement at the expense of achievement and recognition, even though the latter two factors are by far the most strongly supported in the type of research Herzberg (1966) considers appropriate to the theory. In short, the logical tie between motivation-hygiene concepts and orthodox job enrichment is distinctly tenuous. The theory does not appear to have contributed much to the application, but in view of the theory's current status that may be just as well.

Not-So-Useful Theories

Need hierarchy theory has been widely extolled in management development courses and appears to have won frequent managerial acceptance. It has provided working hypotheses for many managers as they deal with motivational problems. Maslow (1965) argues strongly that companies should provide the highest level of need satisfaction possible, and that in itself is a type of application. Beyond this, however, the only specific approach generated by the theory is a type of sensitivity training that focuses on developing self-actualization and growth needs (Bugental and Tannenbaum, 1965). This latter did not prove particularly effective and is no longer a viable application. The real problem, however, is that need hierarchy theory was accepted for many years on faith, because of its intuitive appeal. Now, as evidence has accumulated, its validity is more and more in doubt. Except for the prepotency of certain needs at the very lowest level, the idea of a fixed, biologically rooted need hierarchy for all mankind is highly unlikely. People seem to develop their own valences and motive hierarchies on an individual basis. The simplicity of need hierarchy theory has proved seductive, but the theory has not produced valid, useful applications.

Equity theory, on the other hand, simply has not produced much by way of applications. The theory was formulated to indicate changes in the workplace that would result in improved quality or quantity of work (Adams,

1965). Yet the research itself has never moved beyond a laboratory-type setting. Compensation specialists have been concerned with equity considerations for years, but not necessarily with the specific formulations of equity theory in mind. The theory has tremendous potential insofar as applications are concerned, but these have not been realized, even though the theory itself has stood the test of research well. The only clear attempt to extend equity theory into the compensation field is the work of Belcher and Atchison (1976). In this instance, it has been shown that inputs and outcomes do vary in different groups and for different individuals so that organizations may well provide outcomes that lack relevance for a particular employee. Yet even these ideas have not been stated in a form that would constitute a specific application of the theory.

Summary

In the field of motivation, applications have been most useful when the gap between the theory governing the applications and the applications themselves is small. This does not mean that the theory involved does not draw upon a conceptual framework of a more general nature as in the case of organizational behavior modification; but even in these instances, the broader theory has been redefined and specialized to deal with a much more limited set of problems. In short, useful motivation theories have dealt with a limited domain that is not far removed from the application itself; they are not grand theories of motivation, but specific theories of organizational behavior and technique. The road from theory to application may be paved, but it is short and it moves over rolling hills rather than precipitous mountains. Perhaps this type of restricted approach is necessary in beginning to chart an unknown landscape. In any event, it is what has proved most practically useful in dealing with employee motivation.

Theories of Leadership and Supervision

The distinction between leadership and supervision is that the leadership concept arose out of group dynamics and assumes no more than an isolated group. Supervision, on the other hand, assumes a hierarchic flow of power or authority in an organizational context. The two types of theories are closely intermingled, but the distinction is important, as Graen and his coworkers have shown (see Dansereau, Graen, and Haga, 1975 for instance). Irrespective of which type of theory is involved, sound applications have not been a frequent outgrowth. This seems surprising given the numerous claims regarding the "best way" to lead or supervise and the tremendous body of research (Bass, 1981). However, the field has suffered from its long-term domination by a group dynamics paradigm (Miner, 1982b).

Question Mark Theories

Contingency theory of leadership has long advocated situational engineering whereby leader-member relations, task structure, and position power are adjusted so as to yield an optimum fit with the individual (Fiedler, 1965). More recently, the leader match concept has been developed so that it may be possible to learn how to engineer one's own situation appropriately (Fiedler, Chemers, and Mahar, 1976). Research on leader match has indicated that this type of training often is effective in producing change (Fiedler and Mahar, 1979).

There are certain problems that cast the theory into the question mark category. LPC, (Least Preferred Co-Worker) the underlying individual personality dimension, is not always stable as the situational engineering concept requires; it can change over time, especially with exposure to any type of management development. Furthermore, performance levels are not equal across the octants created by various combinations of contingency variables, even though situational engineering assumes equality; accordingly, one could follow the theory and engineer lower rather than higher productivity. Even more important, hypothesized relationships have been supported by research for only half of the theoretical octants at best. Finally, studies of leader match itself indicate that performance changes are not necessarily accompanied by the anticipated learning; situation engineering could not have been the cause of change, because those involved had not in fact achieved the conditions necessary for such engineering to work (Csoka and Bons, 1978). It is apparent that a great deal more needs to be known before these applications of contingency theory can be fully endorsed.

McGregor (1960, 1967), in writing about applications of the theory X and theory Y concepts, advocates a management style that is based on theory Y assumptions. Accordingly, he endorses psychotherapy for managers, sensitivity training, team building, job enlargement, and the Scanlon Plan. None of these derives directly from the theory X-theory Y formulations, although they are consistent with the theory's hypotheses. Goal setting within the management appraisal context in a manner comparable to MBO did derive from the theory, however, and represents its major direct contribution to practice. Yet McGregor's (1957) emphasis was on a highly participative approach to goal setting. The theory cannot account for the successes that have subsequently been obtained using assigned goals.

The advocacy of a theory Y-based management style also raises questions. It is predicted on the validity of the need hierarchy concepts, a validity that now seems unlikely. Furthermore, the theory appears to call for an advisory, consultant, or teaching relationship with subordinates— something approaching the professional-client situation. This is appropriate for professional systems, but not for bureaucratic systems, as McGregor himself seemed to recognize on occasion. In any event supervising, or more correctly leading, from a theory Y set of assumptions is only likely to work if these assumptions are valid in a particular situation. The theory is one of managerial stereotypes. Since subordinates are likely to reflect a wide range of individual differences, universal theory Y assumptions are probably going to be wrong more often than right. This is a problem with any "best way" approach to supervision.

Decision tree theory of participative leadership recognizes that different situations and subordinates may require different styles, and it spells out in considerable detail what styles are preferable under given circumstances (Vroom and Yetton, 1973). From the viewpoint of theoretical elegance and specificity of guidelines for applications it represents a major advance. A management development program has been designed and marketed to teach the use of the approach (Vroom, 1976). The major problem is that neither the normative approach to style choices nor the training program has been effectively validated as yet (Vroom and Jago, 1978). There is some research but design problems make conclusions difficult, and in any event the results are mixed. There is no evaluation on the management development program. It is quite possible that the theory has spawned very useful knowledge, but we do not know for sure. If ultimately the applications do prove valid, they should be supplemented with skill training in the actual use of the varied styles.

Influence-power continuum theory is in large part descriptive. It specifies conditions under which upper level managers will and will not share decisions (Heller, 1971). Theory of this kind generates applications only to the extent it becomes normative. The position taken in this regard is that power-sharing methods are to be preferred because they utilize more of the existing reservoir of skills in the organization, thus contributing to increased performance. The theory is not one of management-worker power sharing; it deals only with relationships among managers all of whom are at high levels. There is some evidence, however, that more successful managers share decisions more (Heller and Wilpert, 1981). The correlations are not large and the direction of causality has not been established. A great deal more needs to be known, including how various contingency variables moderate these relationships. The theory cannot be said to have created useful knowledge as yet, but the promise is there.

Not-So-Useful Theories

In the early years path-goal theory appeared to offer the prospect of producing useful contributions to practice (Evans, 1970). However, to date it has been even less successful in this regard than its parent, expectancy theory. A statement by House and Mitchell (1974) suggests that the theory is more likley to serve as a tool for directing research and stimulating insight than as a guide to managerial action. This remains the case today.

The leadership pattern choice theory of Tannenbaum and Schmidt (1958) lacks the precision needed for direct application. In fact, it was this deficiency that prompted Vroom and Yetton (1973) to construct their decision tree theory of participation. Leadership pattern choice theory does provide an inventory of managerial, subordinate, and situational factors that may condition decision sharing, but beyond this it appears to have been superseded by other theories.

Vertical dyad linkage theory represents a reaction against the tendency to consider leader behaviors as averages that apply to all subordinates—the kind of approach utilized in developing constructs such as consideration and initiating structure, and inherent in the theory Y assumptions. Basically it is a descriptive theory, although there is the possibility that it could be extended to normative prescriptions, and training and coaching techniques developed from it (Graen and Cashman, 1975). None of these extensions and applications has as yet appeared; there is no road to applications at all.

A final point needs to be made regarding the consideration and initiating structure constructs themselves. In recent years this approach has come upon very hard times, and "best way" formulations related to it have suffered equally, if not even more (Larson, Hunt, and Osborn, 1976). There are major problems of both causality (Mitchell, Larson, and Green, 1977) and measurement (Rush, Thomas, and Lord, 1977). Given the research findings, applications derived from this source do not appear to constitute useful knowledge at the present time. To the extent other theories, such as path-goal theory at a point in time, have relied on these formulations they appear to have been affected adversely.

Summary

It is difficult to generalize in the leadership-supervision area because of the lack of clearly successful applications. One view is that leadership theory simply cannot stand alone and produce useful knowledge. This would suggest that some formulation regarding the effects of different organizational contexts and systems would have to be built into the theories on one end and some motivational constructs on the other. In this way the leadership-supervision formulations would become more specific and circumscribed. Theories like those of Vroom and Heller clearly move in this direction, in one regard or the other, and these theories do appear to be relatively close to shifting from the question mark category to that of useful knowledge.

A second point also extends back to the motivational theories. A number of theories have generated training procedures that produce definite changes in those exposed to them: achievement motivation training, role motivation training, leader match, and perhaps decision tree training. Sensitivity training and behavior modeling might well be added to this list. In many of these instances it is not at all clear exactly how the changes are brought about. One possibility is that these approaches produce a degree of role sensitization in certain participants, through either behavioral or mental modeling. The roles may vary—managerial, entrepreneurial, good group member—but the processes are the same. In this view the theory that generated the training does not in fact account for its success. Rather, the training stimulates interest in and knowledge of a role that the person is predisposed toward in any event. The results are motivational and behavioral changes.

Organization Development-Oriented Theories

Theories of this type contain constructs dealing with structures and processes above and beyond the single work group. In addition, they emphasize humanistic values and/or group processes. Often they utilize typologies of organizations, but among the various types those that are more humanistic or more group based are the ones on which applications are modeled.

Useful Knowledge Theories

Two theories definitely have produced useful applications, although in neither case is the road paved all the way over the mountains. One is the theory of system 4 and 4T, and the other is sociotechnical systems theory. To some extent these may be considered U.S. and European counterparts of one another, although there are differences in both the theories themselves and their applications, if not in their value positions.

The applications developed from system 4 theory were designed to assist in moving an organization from more authoritative structures and processes to participative ones. There are a number of them: human resource accounting (Likert, 1967, 1973), cross-functional teams (Likert, 1975), management by group objectives (Likert and Fisher, 1977), and the survey feedback or survey-guided approach to organization development (Mann and Likert, 1952; Nadler, 1977). Of these, two did not originate from the theory, although they fit well with it. Cross-functional teams were transported from project management generally and from sociotechnical systems theory, while management by group objectives is of course an elaboration of MBO. Neither has been given a great deal of attention or researched adequately. Human resource accounting, designed as a method of preventing managers from squandering human assets through the use of authoritative methods, is another matter. Likert and others have devoted considerable attention to the subject, and various demonstration projects have been initiated. The system 4 approach is characterized by a heavy reliance on survey data. Yet here too evaluative research has been minimal, and adoptions have been sparse. Much more needs to be known.

The survey feedback approach to organization development, on the other hand, has been researched, it can move organizations toward system 4 and also to greater effectiveness, and accordingly it does represent useful knowledge. However, it is necessary to add several qualifications. System 4 theory is of the "best way" type—participative processes should always yield the more positive outcomes; they do not. Similarly, survey feedback works sometimes, and sometimes it does not. It does not always yield changes on the variables measured, and when it does the organization is not always better off. Furthermore, system 4 theory being "best way" cannot help in specifying contingency conditions. To obtain more useful knowledge in this area we need another theory.

The case of sociotechnical systems theory is analogous in a number of respects. The essential application is the introduction of autonomous or self-managing work groups (Emery and Trist, 1978; Herbst, 1976; Cherns, 1977). The underlying theory would call for other organizational forms based on the particular status of its contingency variables—technological process and environmental turbulence—but only this one type of application has emerged. Sometimes it has worked, but there have been major failures also.

Autonomous work groups appear to function most effectively when well isolated from bureaucratic systems—whether company or union—and where the culture or prior traditions support them. They also appear to require a particular kind of person: someone who likes group interaction and is responsive to group controls. Thus start-up situations and volunteer participation are most conducive to success. More needs to be known about why and when autonomous work groups are successful and perpetuate themselves—the underlying theory is not very helpful in this regard—but there is no question that the approach can work.

In both of these cases the applications have now outdistanced their theoretical underpinning. In both cases the applications have their major effects at the work group level, even though the theoretical intent is to deal with a wider arena. The theories sparked the applications, but the need for new theoretical rudders is now apparent.

Question Mark Theories

The most widely endorsed single theory in the organizational field, the contingency theory of organization, has produced one application—a particular approach to organization development (Lawrence and Lorsch, 1969; Lorsch, 1977)—and endorsed another—matrix structure (Davis and Lawrence, 1977, 1978). In both cases, however, research support for the application is practically nonexistent. It is not at all clear whether we have useful knowledge or not.

The theory itself has suffered badly under the looking glass of research tests. Environmental uncertainty does not seem to matter much, differentiation may not be a key consideration, and integration is important no matter what. Confrontation is important but probably for the same reason as bureaucracy—an emphasis on rationality. The organization development approach does appear to produce structural change, but largely through the use of hierarchic authority. The theory asserts that changes to both less and more differentiation and integration may be required, depending on uncertainty levels, but only the "more" side has been addressed in applications. The endorsement of matrix structures is consistent with this focus, but contingency theory did not create this approach. Nevertheless, the theory has stimulated an explication and understanding of matrix systems that is useful. We seem to have a situation where an intriguing, but ultimately not really valid, theory has produced applications of unknown value. In this case the uncertainty moderator has come to shroud the applications as well as drive the theory.

Organization development in all of its forms owes something of a debt to sensitivity training and T-groups. All of the approaches considered so far incorporate this approach to some degree or its modern equivalent, team building, but goal congruence theory and the theory of bureaucratic demise have given it the most central role in bringing about change itself. Other theories often view sensitivity training as a means of consolidating change once it has been achieved by other methods. In the process of co-opting sensitivity training, both goal congruence theory and bureaucratic demise theories have contributed to the technology of and provided rationales for various family group approaches within an organization development framework.

Goal congruence theory envisages an ultimate movement from bureaucratic forms to group-based, highly participative systems via the T-group interventions (Argyris, 1970). More recently the theoretical base has been expanded to include concepts such as double-loop learning, and the term *learning seminar* has been invoked, but the debt to sensitivity training approaches remains strong (Argyris and Schön, 1978). These approaches have not fared as well at the hands of research as some of the other organization development approaches (Porras and Berg, 1978). In most cases the entrenched bureaucratic structures are modified very little. Practitioners have become increasingly skeptical about the use of sensitivity training. All in all, the future of applications tied closely to traditional types of sensitivity training appears rather cloudy.

Much of what has been said with regard to goal congruence theory applications applies to bureaucratic demise theory as well. Bennis (1966) emphasizes temporary systems of a professional nature as the ultimate goal, but replacing bureaucratic forms and using T-groups to do it remains the central focus. Again also, successes have been liberally mixed with failures (Mirvis and Berg, 1977). Bureaucracy appears to be more resistant to this type of application than originally anticipated.

Not-So-Useful Theories

Theories that have followed the systems paradigm closely tend not to yield much by way of useful applications. A case in point is psychological open systems theory (Katz and Kahn, 1978). The theory's authors do recommend a number of applications that would tend to democratize organizations in various respects, but these applications were created elsewhere and often do not follow logically from the theory. The theory itself is value neutral; it could lead logically to a wide range of organizational actions. But only applications of a democratic nature are endorsed (Katz and Georgopoulos, 1971). There have been some developments, using the theory to more fully understand organizational actions such as the provision of government services (Katz, Gutek, Kahn, and Barton, 1975), which suggest psychological open systems theory might serve as a basis for managers' working theories. This type of application has not been pursued, however, and suitable methods of teaching such an approach have not been devised.

Mechanistic and organic systems theory has relatively little to say about specific applications. It simply advocates a switch to more organic forms under conditions of technological and market change (Burns and Stalker, 1961). Research to test the hypothesis of the theory directly has been surprisingly lacking. What has been done has not been consistently supportive. There is a body of related research that suggests that the simplicity of mechanistic-organic theory, which makes it so appealing, is also its undoing. More complex explanations appear to be needed.

Control theory has produced a sizable amount of research demonstrating that anything that can be done to increase the amount of control in an organization, or the perception of it, should be done (Tannenbaum, 1968; Tannenbaum and Cooke, 1979). This is one of the best documented findings in organizational science. Yet the theory has not moved on to generate techniques for increasing control, nor has it endorsed other means to this end. At one point there was some endorsement of participative management and democratic systems. However, as it became increasingly apparent that democratic control structures were not consistently associated with organizational effectiveness, this endorsement has paled.

A final theory within the organization development framework is the group-focused systems theory of Stogdill (1959). In this instance the categorization is based primarily on the group orientation of the theory. The theory has not been as strongly committed to humanistic values as most of the others, nor has it endorsed humanistic applications. In fact, in tune with its systems emphasis, it has little to say about applications at all. Stogdill indicated at an early point that good theories do not need to develop applied technologies. That is true, but when they do not, their contribution to *useful* knowledge, as we are using the term here, is nil.

Summary

Two major problems are apparent from the analysis of organization development-oriented theories. One is that a number of these theories, often those of a systems nature, have not been concerned with application. It is not surprising that some theorists are more concerned with understanding the organizational world than influencing it. But in these cases, when the theory obviously has value, there should be some mechanism so that others take up the application slack. There is a place in organization science for those who would serve as application theorists, extending the concepts of others so that they may meaningfully be put to use. This kind of theoretical extension work might well turn out to be as demanding of creativity and intellect as the original theory formation.

The second problem relates to the "best way" stance of the organization development-oriented theories. Even the most useful of these theories work only part of the time. Yet "best way" assumptions discourage looking for contingency variables and applicable, limited domains. On the evidence it would appear that the kind of group-based systems typically espoused require a certain constellation of personality characteristics, motives, values—a particular type of person—to function well. Also, these systems need to be isolated or protected against bureaucratic encroachment as they tend to be fragile. Theoretical extensions to deal with such matters are badly needed if applications are to be introduced in ways that will have a maximal probability of success.

Structuring Theories

Structuring theories are the most difficult to create because they operate at a macrolevel and thus must deal with the greatest complexity. Theories of an organization development-oriented nature can deal with the same broad domain, but they have tended to gravitate to the less complex work group level, especially insofar as their applications are concerned. The structuring theories have little choice but to deal with the organization as a whole. None of those considered can be truly said to have *produced* applications that represent useful knowledge, although several *deal with* applications of this kind.

Question Mark Theories

Max Weber's (1968) theory of bureaucracy did not create bureaucratic structures. It set out to describe something that already existed. Yet ultimately Weber endorsed bureaucracy as the most effective form of organization, although not necessarily as the most attractive from the viewpoint of the members. Further, he formulated certain critical dimensions that would make it easier to structure and operate an organization along bureaucratic lines. Most of these formulations have met the test of research, although the statements of the theory are not adequate to handle either the introduction of professional knowledge into bureaucratic systems or decentralization of authority within bureaucracies (Blau, 1974). In general more rationalized, standardized, formalized, and specialized bureaucracies—those that more closely approximate the theoretical ideal—function better. But comparative research that would pit bureaucracy at its best against other forms at their best—professional organizations, for instance—has not been conducted. Thus, it is not possible to respond to Weber's claims for the normative superiority of the bureaucratic form.

The theory of strategy and structure emerged out of historical analyses. Thus, both the growth strategy and the divisionalized structure that are its major concerns existed before the theory was stated (Chandler, 1962, 1977). Even so, there is reason to believe that the theory served to stimulate a number of consultants to recommend multidivisional structures to their clients, and to specify when these structures should be introduced (Franko, 1976). The theory did not create the structure, but it almost certainly fostered it. A question may be raised, however, as to whether this particular structural response to a diversification strategy is desirable. Is the application a good one? The answer is strong and positive insofar as growth is concerned; the multidivisional form fosters growth. But this particular type of structural implementation shows little relationship to profits (Rumelt, 1974; Grinyer, Yasai-Ardekani, and Al-Bazzaz, 1980). Thus, at present the value of the application must be considered in question.

There is little doubt that classical management theory has influenced practice. Beginning with Fayol (1949), principles of management have guided managerial behavior for over half a century. In fact, Fayol (1937, 1970) himself put these principles to use in the role of chief executive and as a consultant. The basic question is not whether the theory contributed to practice, but whether it contributed well. Insofar as the theory represents a "best way" approach, it clearly needs qualification. Principles of management can no longer be considered universal. They make for absolute chaos when applied strictly in a professional organization, for instance. Furthermore, there is sufficient ambiguity so that application is often difficult (Simon, 1976), and there has been very little reseach focused directly on these principles.

In many areas theory and practice have moved beyond the classical concepts. Role theory formulations, for instance, are much more powerful than unity of command. Yet historically the theory appears to have contributed something useful to some (primarily bureaucratic) organizations at a time when nothing else was available. Theories are made to be superseded and this one has been, but it would not be correct to say that the classical views never represented a useful knowledge theory. If one averages it all out over time, the question mark classification appears most descriptive. Some of the principles remain valid even now, in certain contexts, but there are better and more precise ways of stating these ideals.

Not-So-Useful Theories

The decision-making concepts and constructs of the Carnegie theorists are stated in largely descriptive, rather than normative, terms (Simon, 1976; March and Simon, 1958; Cyert and March, 1963). There was never any intention of developing applications. Hierarchy is viewed as a natural outgrowth of the limitations of human intelligence (Simon, 1977). Decentralization serves the same end, although to the extent computers can help overcome these limitations, it becomes less necessary. Thus, the structuring of organizations is viewed as a consequence of their decision processes, but the theory remains concerned only with understanding existing structures. There is at various points an implicit endorsement of rationality, by Simon in particular. On the other hand, March has moved in the opposite direction. There are even some guidelines for behavior under the not-so-rational conditions of the garbage can model (Cohen and March, 1974). But this whole concept of decision making under conditions of organized anarchy needs much more research before useful applications are possible.

Technological determinism of the kind proposed by Woodward (1965) has never gotten to a point where applications seem feasible. The original research was undertaken to test certain of the principles of classical theory. Positive results presumably would have resulted in more precise and specific formulations that could be taught and used. But the research results were not of a kind that could be used in this manner. Accordingly, efforts to reanalyze the data were initiated, seeking to develop from them a new theoretical perspective. The technological imperative was the result, but the focus never shifted back to developing applications. The problems of formulating and testing the new theory became all-consuming (Woodward, 1970).

Sociological open systems theory owes a considerable debt to the Carnegie theorists. It is also stated within the formal framework of the systems paradigm. These two factors should almost certainly doom it to failure insofar as applications are concerned, and it has not disappointed these expectations. The theory deals with practical matters of structuring and operating organizations, and it is capable of interpretation in normative terms (Thompson, 1967). However, its high level of abstraction has stymied not only the development of applications, but in large part research as well. Thompson himself had little interest in organizational practice and preferred to leave the creation of technologies for implementing his ideas to others. No one else has met this challenge.

Viewing technology in a comparative framework, as Perrow (1967) has done, appears to have been of little help in making the technological imperative operational. Apparently the potential value of the evolving theory for developing applications was recognized by the author at an early point (Perrow, 1966). However, as conceptual difficulties and research problems mounted, he came to have serious questions about the theory (Perrow, 1972). The Woodward and Perrow situations seem to be analogous: both authors appear never to have become sufficiently satisfied with their theories per se to move on to matters of application.

Summary

Theory, at the level of total organizational functioning, has not been very successful in spawning applications. Those who design organizations in the role of organization planners or consultants rarely operate from a specific theoretical base. We noted with the organization development-oriented theories a tendency to move toward more manageable smaller units of analysis (in that case, work groups). The same type of tendency is apparent with regard to structuring theories (Pierce and Dunham, 1978). This microshift is not usually an intentional process; it appears to be a response to the natural limits of finite human intelligence (Simon, 1977). Given this, it might be best to focus deliberately on more delimited problem areas: ways of organizing temporary project teams, or top level decision making, or sales offices. Then out of a solid base of knowledge in relation to limited domain and middle range theories, it may be possible to make the conceptual leap to organizational issues of greater complexity that we do not seem to be able to make very effectively right now (Pinder and Moore, 1980). In terms of the title analogy, this would mean paving several roads over the foothills and then using these as a jumping-off place to tackle the mountains themselves.

CONCLUSION

Various conclusions related to the specific areas of theory development have been noted already. One overall conclusion that seems to emerge from these separate analyses is that if applications are to emerge from theory, someone has to work directly on the applied problems. Applications do not

TABLE 3.3. Frequency of Nomination for Theories Related to Estimated Scientific Validity

Frequency of Nomination	Estimated Validity		
	Low	Mixed	High
20–24	1	1	1
15–19	2	3	2
10–14	6	3	5
5–9	1	0	1
0–4	1	3	2
Total	11	10	11

just pop out, even from very good theories; they have to be dug out, and that can be hard theoretical work in its own right. Furthermore, limited scale applications focused on specific problems appear to be much more likely than broad solutions to complex problems, at least at this stage in the development of organizational science.

In the letter to those who nominated the theories considered (Figure 3.1), certain criteria for nomination were set forth. These included usefulness in understanding, explaining, and predicting organizational functioning (that is, scientific validity) and usefulness in practice for purposes of application. If these criteria were in fact utilized, then the more frequently nominated theories should be more valid, and they should be more closely tied to applications. Tables 3.3 and 3.4 relate to these matters.

The validity estimates in Table 3.3 were developed at the time the macrotheories book manuscript was completed in order to make certain comparisons between micro- and macrotheories (Miner, 1982a: 455–456). No doubt many would disagree with them. Ideally, reliability analyses would be carried out to see whether agreement could be obtained in classifying the theories into the three categories. To do this well, however, additional people would have to carry out the same extensive analysis of theoretical statements and research that the author attempted to do. Such a time commitment can hardly be justified, or obtained, for purposes of reliability study alone. However, the reasoning behind the classification of each theory is clearly stated in one or the other of the two theories books. For role-motivation theory, it may be found in two papers (Miner, 1978, 1981). Thus, readers may carry out impressionistic reliability analyses on their own. The data in Table 3.3 indicate no relationship between frequency of nomination and estimated validities for the theories.

In these validity analyses, three categories are employed: high, mixed, and low. Relatively, the theories rated high are those that have produced a sizable body of research that on balance is supportive of the theory. The mixed rating is applied where the research results remain inconsistent even though a substantial research output has been elicited. Theories rated low on scientific validity either have not been supported by the research done on them or, less frequently, have been the subject of very little research. Since very recent theories, which have not yet had time to receive an adequate research test, are not included in the study sample, it can be assumed that failure to generate sufficient research represents some type of theoretical failure. Typically, this relates to the abstractness and difficulty of operationalizing the theoretical variables.

The usefulness criteria in application estimates in Table 3.4 are those employed throughout this chapter. They were made at the time the chapter was written, working directly from the theories books (Miner, 1980a, 1982a) and without reference to the validity estimates made approximately a year and a half before. The same kinds of disclaimers as for the validity estimates hold. Others may not care for my conclusions, and they may be more correct than I, but the rationales for what was done are available. It is hoped that some will find this type of study using theories as the unit of analysis helpful. The data in Table 3.4 again indicate no relationship between frequency of nomination and validity of the theory.

Assuming that unreliability of the data is not responsible for these results, one is left with a serious question as to what bases are used to define established theories in organization science—if not scientific validity and usefulness in application. One might consider value positions, overall reputation of the theory's author, amount of publication stimulated by the theory, the size of the interpersonal network surrounding the theory, and so on. I really do not know and do not have the data to take the issue further, but the results are a surprise.

TABLE 3.4. Frequency of Nomination for Theories Related to Estimated Usefulness in Application

Frequency of Nomination	Estimated Usefulness in Application		
	Low	Questionable	High
20–24	0	3	0
15–19	5	0	2
10–14	4	6	4
5–9	1	1	0
0–4	3	2	1
Total	13	12	7

TABLE 3.5. Estimated Usefulness in Application and Estimated Scientific Validity of Each Theory

Estimated Usefulness in Application	Estimated Validity		
	Low	Mixed	High
High	Theory of system 4 and 4T (OD)	Behavior modification and operant learning (M) Sociotechnical systems theory (OD)	Job characteristics theory (M) Goal-setting theory (M) Achievement motivation theory (M) Role motivation theory (M)
Questionable	Motivation-hygiene theory (M) Theory X and theory Y (L/S) Contingency theory of organization (OD) Theory of bureaucratic demise (OD) Classical management theory (S)	Contingency theory of leadership (L/S) Influence-power continuum theory (L/S) Goal congruence theory (OD) Theory of strategy and structure (S)	Expectancy theories (M) Decision tree theory of participative leadership (L/S) Theory of bureaucracy (S)
Low	Need hierarchy theory (M) Leadership pattern choice theory (L/S) Mechanistic and organic systems theory (OD) Technological determinism (S) Technology in a comparative framework (S)	Path-goal theory (L/S) Psychological open systems theory (OD) Group-focused systems theory (OD) Sociological open systems theory (S)	Equity theory (M) Vertical dyad linkage theory (L/S) Control theory (OD) Decision-making concepts and constructs (S)

(M)   Theories of Motivation
(L/S) Theories of Leadership and Supervision
(OD) Organization Development-Oriented Theories
(S)   Structuring Theories

Table 3.5 gives specific data on each theory with reference to estimated validity and usefulness in application. Several conclusions seem warranted. One is that the two criteria are not perfectly correlated. Useful applications can emerge from theories that in the end turn out not to be very valid. There are a rather large number of theories that rate higher on their applications than their validities: one-quarter of the total. In several of these cases one may observe a gradual detaching of the application from its theory, so that it achieves an independent identity of its own. It would appear very important, therefore, at this stage of the development of the science to evaluate theories and applications separately. This is particularly true of organization development-oriented theories. Others have also noted that practice is outstripping theory in this area (Burke, 1977).

There are also a large number of theories with better validities than applications: 11 to be exact. Most striking are the four theories that do very well in terms of scientific validity, but fail almost completely insofar as applications are concerned. These four would seem to represent a gold mine for those who might wish to develop applications from them. The need for applied theorists as opposed to basic theorists becomes apparent here. This assumes of course that there are good theorists who really care little about application per se—something I believe to be as true in the organization field as it is in other sciences. Not unexpectedly, theories that have not fulfilled their validity potential in practice come about equally from all four areas.

A final point that stands out is the total control over the good theory— good application sector exerted by motivation theorists. Even if one does not like the author's placement of his own theory there, the result remains the same. These are narrow, limited domain theories, at least as defined by the research on them, if not by their authors. If we are to find the road over the mountains from theory to application, and pave it so that the crossing becomes easy, a close look at these theories seems warranted. They should provide guides that can be used not only with regard to other motivation theories, but in the remaining three areas of organization science as well.

REFERENCES

Adams, J. Stacy.
1965   "Inequity in Social Exchange." In Leonard Berkowitz (ed.), Advances in Experimental Social Psychology. Vol. 2. New York: Academic Press.
Argyris, Chris.
1970   Intervention Theory and Method: A Behavioral Science View. Reading, Mass.: Addison-Wesley.
Argyris, Chris, and Donald A. Schön.
1978   Organizational Learning: A Theory of Action Perspective. Reading, Mass.: Addison-Wesley.

Arvey, Richard D.
1979   Fairness in Selecting Employees. Reading, Mass.: Addison-Wesley.
Bass, Bernard M.
1981   Stogdill's Handbook of Leadership. New York: Free Press.
Belcher, D. W., and T. J. Atchison.
1976   "Compensation for Work." In Robert Dubin (ed.), Handbook of Work, Organization, and Society. Chicago: Rand McNally.
Bennis, Warren G.
1966   Changing Organizations. New York: McGraw-Hill.
1969   Organization Development: Its Nature, Origins, and Prospects. Reading, Mass.: Addison-Wesley.
Blau, Peter M.
1974   On the Nature of Organizations. New York: Wiley.
Bugental, J. F. T., and Robert Tannenbaum.
1965   "Sensitivity Training and Behavior Motivation." In Edgar H. Schein and Warren G. Bennis (eds.), Personal and Organizational Change Through Group Methods: The Laboratory Approach. New York: Wiley.
Burke, W. Warner.
1977   Current Issues and Strategies in Organization Development. New York: Human Sciences Press.
Burns, Tom, and G. M. Stalker.
1961   The Management of Innovation. London: Tavistock.
Chandler, Alfred D.
1962   Strategy and Structure: Chapters in the History of the American Industrial Enterprise. Cambridge, Mass.: MIT Press.
1977   The Visible Hand: The Managerial Revolution in American Business. Cambridge, Mass.: Harvard University Press.
Cherns, Albert R.
1977   "Can Behavioral Science Help Design Organizations?" Organizational Dynamics, 5 (4):44–64.
Cohen, Michael D., and James G. March.
1974   Leadership and Ambiguity: The American College President. New York: McGraw-Hill.
Csoka, Louis S., and Paul M. Bons.
1978   "Manipulating the Situation to Fit the Leader's Style: Two Validation Studies of Leader Match." Journal of Applied Psychology, 63:295–300.
Cyert, Richard M., and James G. March.
1963   A Behavioral Theory of the Firm. Englewood Cliffs, N.J.: Prentice-Hall.
Dansereau, Fred, George Graen, and William J. Haga.
1975   "A Vertical Dyad Linkage Approach to Leadership within Formal Organizations: A Longitudinal Investigation of the Role Making Process." Organizational Behavior and Human Performance, 13:46–78.
Davis, Stanley M., and Paul R. Lawrence.
1977   Matrix. Reading, Mass.: Addison-Wesley.
1978   "Problems of Matrix Organizations." Harvard Business Review, 56 (3):131–142.
Drucker, Peter F.
1954   The Practice of Management. New York: Harper.
Emery, Fred E., and Eric L. Trist.
1978   "Analytical Model for Sociotechnical Systems." In William A. Pasmore and John J. Sherwood (eds.), Sociotechnical Systems: A Sourcebook. La Jolla, Calif.: University Associates.
Evans, Martin G.

1970   "Leadership and Motivation: A Core Concept." Academy of Management Journal, 13:91–102.

Fayol, Henri.
1937   "The Administrative Theory in the State." In Luther Gulick and Lyndall F. Urwick (eds.), Papers on the Science of Administration. New York: Institute of Public Administration.
1949   General and Industrial Management. London: Pitman.
1970   "The Importance of the Administrative Factor." In Ernest Dale (ed.), Readings in Management: Landmarks and New Frontiers. New York: McGraw-Hill.

Fiedler, Fred E.
1965   "Engineer the Job to Fit the Manager." Harvard Business Review, 43 (5):115–122.

Fiedler, Fred E., and Linda Mahar.
1979   "The Effectiveness of Contingency Model Training: A Review of the Validation of Leader Match." Personnel Psychology, 32:45–62.

Fiedler, Fred E., Martin M. Chemers, and Linda Mahar.
1976   Improving Leadership Effectiveness: The Leader Match Concept. New York: Wiley.

Ford, Robert N.
1969   Motivation Through the Work Itself. New York: American Management Association.

Franko, Lawrence G.
1976   The European Multinationals: A Renewed Challenge to American and British Big Business. Stamford, Conn.: Greylock.

Goldstein, Arnold P., and Melvin Sorcher.
1974   Changing Supervisor Behavior. New York: Pergamon Press.

Graen, George, and James F. Cashman.
1975   "A Role-Making Model of Leadership in Formal Organizations: A Developmental Appraoch." In James G. Hunt and Lars L. Larson (eds.), Leadership Frontiers. Kent, Ohio: Kent State University Press.

Grinyer, Peter H., Masoud Yasai-Ardekani, and Shawki Al-Bazzaz.
1980   "Strategy, Structure, the Environment and Financial Performance in 48 United Kingdom Companies." Academy of Management Journal, 23:193–226.

Hackman, J. Richard.
1975   "On the Coming Demise of Job Enrichment." In E. L. Cass and F. G. Zimmer (eds.), Man and Work in Society. New York: Van Nostrand Reinhold.

Hackman, J. Richard, and Greg R. Oldham.
1980   Work Redesign. Reading, Mass.: Addison-Wesley.

Hamner, W. Clay, and Ellen P. Hamner.
1976   "Behavior Modification on the Bottom Line." Organizational Dynamics, 4 (4):3–21.

Heller, Frank A.
1971   Managerial Decision-making: A Study of Leadership Styles and Power-sharing Among Senior Managers. London: Tavistock.

Heller, Frank A., and Bernhard Wilpert.
1981   Competence and Power in Managerial Decision-Making. New York: Wiley.

Herbst, P. G.
1976   Alternatives to Hierarchy. Leiden, the Netherlands: Martinus Nijhoff.

Herzberg, Frederick.
1966   Work and the Nature of Man. Cleveland, Ohio: World.
1976   The Managerial Choice: To Be Efficient and To Be Human. Homewood, Ill.: Dow-Jones-Irwin.

House, Robert J., and Terence R. Mitchell.
1974   "Path-Goal Theory of Leadership." Journal of Contemporary Business, 3 (4): 81–97.

Katz, Daniel, and Basil S. Georgopoulos.
1971   "Organizations in a Changing World." Journal of Applied Behavior Science, 7: 342–370.

Katz, Daniel, Barbara A. Guteck, Robert L. Kahn, and Eugenia Barton.
1975   Bureaucratic Encounters: A Pilot Study in the Evaluation of Government Services. Ann Arbor, Mich.: Institute for Social Research, University of Michigan

Katz, Daniel, and Robert L. Kahn.
1978   The Social Psychology of Organizations. New York: Wiley.

Larson, Lars L., James G. Hunt, and Richard L. Osborn.
1976   "The Great Hi-Hi Leader Behavior Myth: A Lesson from Occam's Razor." Academy of Management Journal, 19:628–641.

Latham, Gary P., and J. James Baldes.
1975   "The Practical Significance of Locke's Theory of Goal Setting." Journal of Applied Psychology, 60:122–124.

Latham, Gary P., and Dennis L. Dossett.
1978   "Designing Incentive Plans for Unionized Employees: A Comparison of Continuous and Variable Ratio Reinforcement Schedules." Personnel Psychology, 31:46–61.

Latham, Gary P., and Edwin A. Locke.
1975   "Increasing Productivity with Decreasing Time Limits: A Field Replication of Parkinson's Law." Journal of Applied Psychology, 60:524–526.

Lawler, Edward E.
1981   Pay and Organization Development. Reading, Mass.: Addison-Wesley.

Lawrence, Paul R., and Jay W. Lorsch.
1969   Developing Organizations: Diagnosis and Action. Reading, Mass.: Addison-Wesley.

Ledvinka, James.
1982   Federal Regulation of Personnel and Human Resource Management. Boston, Mass.: Kent.

Likert, Rensis.
1967   The Human Organization. New York: McGraw-Hill.
1973   "Human Resource Accounting: Building and Assessing Productive Organizations." Personnel, 50 (3):8–24.
1975   "Improving Cost Performance with Cross-Functional Teams." Conference Board Record, 12 (9):51–59.

Likert, Rensis, and M. Scott Fisher.
1977   "MBGO: Putting Some Team Spirit into MBO." Personnel, 54 (1):40–47.

Locke, Edwin A.
1968   "Toward a Theory of Task Motivation and Incentives." Organizational Behavior and Human Performance, 3:157–189.
1970   "The Supervisor as Motivator: His Influence on Employee Performance and Satisfaction." In Bernard M. Bass, R. Cooper, and J. A. Haas (eds.), Managing for Task Accomplishment. Lexington, Mass.: Heath.

Lorsch, Jay W.
1977   "Organizational Design: A Situational Perspective." Organizational Dynamics, 6 (2):2–14.

Luthans, Fred, and Robert Kreitner.
1975   Organizational Behavior Modification. Glenview, Ill.: Scott, Foresman.

Mann, Floyd C., and Rensis Likert.
1952   "The Need for Research on the Communication of Research Results." Human Organization, 11 (4):15–19.

March, James G., and Herbert A. Simon.
1958   Organizations. New York: Wiley.

Maslow, Abraham H.
1965   Eupsychian Management. Homewood, Ill.: Irwin.

McClelland, David C.

1975   Power: The Inner Experience. New York: Irvington.
McClelland, David C., and David H. Burnham.
1976   "Power is the Great Motivator." Harvard Business Review, 54 (2):100–110.
McClelland, David C., and David G. Winter.
1969   Motivating Economic Achievement. New York: Free Press.
McGregor, Douglas.
1957   "An Uneasy Look at Performance Appraisal." Harvard Business Review, 35 (3): 89–94.
1960   The Human Side of Enterprise. New York: McGraw-Hill.
1967   The Professional Manager. New York: McGraw-Hill.
Miner, John B.
1965   Studies in Management Education. Atlanta, Ga.: Organizational Measurement Systems Press.
1977   Motivation to Manager: A Ten Year Update on the "Studies in Management Education" Research. Atlanta, Ga.: Organizational Measurement Systems Press.
1978   "Twenty Years of Research on Role Motivation Theory of Managerial Effectiveness." Personnel Psychology, 31:739–760.
1980a   Theories of Organizational Behavior. Hinsdale, Ill.: Dryden.
1980b   "Limited Domain Theories of Organizational Energy." In Craig C. Pinder and Larry F. Moore (eds.), Middle Range Theory and the Study of Organizations. Boston, Mass.: Martinus Nijhoff.
1981   "Theories of Organizational Motivation." In George W. England, Anant R. Negandhi, and Bernhard Wilpert (eds.), The Functioning of Complex Organizations. Cambridge, Mass.: Oelgeschlager, Gunn, and Hain.
1982a   Theories of Organizational Structure and Process. Hinsdale, Ill.: Dryden.
1982b   "The Uncertain Future of the Leadership Concept: Revisions and Clarifications." Journal of Applied Behavioral Science, 18:293–307.
Miner, Mary G., and John B. Miner.
1979   "Employee Selection within the Law." Washington, D.C.: BNA Books.
Miron, David, and David C. McClelland
1979   "The Impact of Achievement Motivation Training on Small Business." California Management Review, 21 (4):13–28.
Mirvis, Philip, H., and David N. Berg.
1977   Failures in Organization Development and Change: Cases and Essays for Learning. New York: Wiley.
Mitchell, Terence R., James R. Larson, and Stephen G. Green.
1977   "Leader Behavior, Situational Moderators, and Group Performance: An Attributional Analysis." Organizational Behavior and Human Performance, 18:254–268.
Nadler, David A.
1977   Feedback and Organization Development: Using Data-Based Methods. Reading, Mass.: Addison-Wesley.
Perrow, Charles.
1966   "Technology and Organizational Structure." Industrial Relations Research Association Proceedings, 156–163.
1967   "A Framework for the Comparative Analysis of Organizations." American Sociological Review, 32:194–208.
1972   Complex Organizations: A Critical Essay. Glenview, Ill.: Scott, Foresman.
Pierce, Jon L., and Randall B. Dunham.
1978   "An Empirical Demonstration of the Convergence of Common Marco- and Micro-organization Measures." Academy of Management Journal, 21:410–418.
Pinder, Craig C., and Larry F. Moore.
1980   Middle Range Theory and the Study of Organizations. Boston, Mass.: Martinus Nijhoff.
Porras. Jerry L., and Per O. Berg.

1978   "The Impact of Organization Development." Academy of Management Review, 3:249–266.
Porter, Lyman W., and Edward E. Lawler.
1968   Managerial Attitudes and Performance. Homewood, Ill.: Irwin.
Rumelt, Richard P.
1974   Strategy, Structure, and Economic Performance. Boston, Mass.: Harvard Business School.
Rush, Michael C., Jay C. Thomas, and Robert G. Lord.
1977   "Implicit Leadership Theory: A Potential Threat to the Internal Validity of Leader Behavior Questionnaires." Organizational Behavior and Human Performance, 20:93–110.
Simon, Herbert A.
1976   Administrative Behavior: A Study of Decision-Making Processes in Administrative Organization. New York: Free Press.
1977   The New Science of Management Decision. Englewood Cliffs, N.J.: Prentice-Hall.
Skinner, B. F., and William Dowling.
1973   "Conversation with B. F. Skinner." Organizational Dynamics, 1 (3):31–40.
Stogdill, Ralph M.
1959   Individual Behavior and Group Achievement. New York: Oxford University Press.
Tannenbaum, Arnold S.
1968   Control in Organizations. New York: McGraw-Hill.
Tannenbaum, Arnold S., and Robert A. Cooke.
1979   "Organizational Control: A Review of Studies Employing the Control Graph Method." In C. J. Lammers and D. Hickson (eds.), Organizations Alike and Unlike. London: Routledge and Kegan Paul.
Tannenbaum, Robert, and Warren H. Schmidt.
1958   "How to Choose a Leadership Pattern." Harvard Business Review, 36 (2):95–101.
Thompson, James D.
1967   Organizations in Action. New York: McGraw-Hill.
Vroom, Victor H.
1964   Work and Motivation. New York: Wiley.
1976   "Can Leaders Learn to Lead?" Organizational Dynamics, 4 (3):17–28.
Vroom, Victor H., and Arthur G. Jago.
1978   "On the Validity of the Vroom-Yetton Model." Journal of Applied Psychology, 63:151–122.
Vroom, Victor H., and Philip W. Yetton.
1973   Leadership and Decision-making. Pittsburgh, Pa.: University of Pittsburgh Press.
Weber, Max.
1968   Economy and Society. New York: Bedminster Press.
Woodward, Joan.
1965   Industrial Organization: Theory and Practice. London: Oxford University Press.
1970   Industrial Organization: Behavior and Control. London: Oxford University Press.

4

WHERE HAVE THE ORGANIZATIONAL SCIENCES GONE? A SURVEY OF THE ACADEMY OF MANAGEMENT MEMBERSHIP

Kenneth W. Thomas and Ralph H. Kilmann

INTRODUCTION

Momentum seems to be building up for the view that the organizational sciences have gotten off-track or have become misdirected. Comments to this effect are heard more and more frequently at professional meetings when academics have a chance to discuss the ultimate purpose of their work. Disenchantment with the impact of academic journals on the practice of management, and questions of one's own personal meaning regarding research effort, also raise the question of utility. The simple fact that practitioners are unlikely to read and take note of the articles in our most prestigious journals leaves one wondering if academics are just writing to one another to maintain their own existence.

The basic argument centers on the question of scientific rigor versus practical relevance. Those who are satisfied with the field seem to argue for the continued attention and further emphasis of the validity criterion in organizational research. In fact, this side, when dissatisfied, argues that the research in the field is not rigorous enough and that journals should use the higher standards of the traditional scientific method for accepting articles for publication. Those who question both the purpose of the organizational sciences and the meaning of their work tend to argue that the validity criterion has been overemphasized to the exclusion of a relevance criterion. They seem to wonder how managers will make use of our scientifically based knowledge if it is not initially conceived and then communicated in a form that speaks to their problems and setting.

The authors have been struggling with this issue for some time and have presented some of these issues in the literature (Kilmann, 1979; Mitroff and Kilmann, 1978; Thomas and Tymon, 1982). What has concerned us, however, is whether or not our impressions of this issue derive from a biased sample of colleagues who seem to share our views, or if these issues are really quite widespread throughout the field. Specifically, what is the prevailing mood on the rigor versus relevance debate as determined by a more rigorous assessment?

The purpose of the present study was to survey the sentiments and perceptions of organizational scientists on these issues. Questions addressed the basic purpose of organizational science research, the perceived importance of relevance vis-á-vis rigor, and perceptions of the emphases of academic reward systems and the norms of the field as a whole. The last was included since we felt that the incentive systems and the culture of university departments must be playing a role in determining the directions of the field.

The authors also were interested in the perceived need for change. Thus, the study seeks to assess organizational scientists' ideal state of the field, to identify perceived gaps or deficiencies relating to these ideals, and to assess some important causal factors that may contribute to these gaps.

METHOD

Population and Sample

It was not possible to survey all organizations that contain organizational science researchers. Therefore, for economic and convenience reasons, the Academy of Management was selected as the focal population for study. The Academy was attractive for the study because its divisional structure explicitly identifies three major subfields of the organizational sciences: organizational behavior, organization and management theory, and organization development. The sample for the survey consisted of 1,000 randomly selected members of these three divisions of the Academy.

Survey Instrument

A mail survey was used as the data-gathering device. To be able to draw credible conclusions about the opinions of Academy members, a high response rate was considered essential. To encourage responses, the survey questionnaire was kept relatively brief, was printed rather than typed, was sent by first-class mail in a hand-addressed envelope, and was accompanied by a cover letter from the researchers that stressed the importance of the topic. After a month, a second copy of the questionnaire was mailed with a follow-up cover letter urging respondents who had not yet completed the questionnaire to do so. A copy of the questionnaire is included in the appendix of this chapter.

Response Rate

The resulting response rate was 75 percent—unusually high for a mailed questionnaire (Selltiz, Wrightsman, and Cook, 1976: 277). Of the 750 usable responses, 576 were from academics, and the remainder from Academy members who classified themselves as practitioners. Since our primary interest in the present chapter is in academic researchers, data analysis is confined to these 576 respondents.

RESULTS AND DISCUSSION

Purpose of Organizational Science Research

A two-part item on the purpose of organizational science research (shown, with response distributions, in Table 4.1) was intended to capture researchers' values and perceptions concerning the basic versus applied nature of the field. The response categories, in fact, were paraphrased from descriptions in several organizational behavior textbooks regarding the purpose of research in this field. These brief descriptions progress from producing knowledge for its own sake (basic research) through a succession of progressively more applied aims.

Responses indicate that the sample sees the organizational sciences as, ideally, a fairly applied field. Only 9 percent of respondents indicate a belief that the fundamental purpose of the field should be the pure "basic-research" goal of producing knowledge of organizational phenomena for its own sake. At the other extreme, only 9 percent endorse the purely "developmental" role of the organizational sciences as generating ways to improve practice. The remaining 82 percent indicate an ideal purpose combining the production of knowledge of organizational phenomena with some contribution to practice. For 49 percent of respondents, the contribution to practice is a "hoped-for" characteristic of the knowledge sought. For 33 percent, it is the essential feature of the knowledge sought.

In contrast, ratings of the actual purpose of published research are considerably less applied, with 61 percent of all respondents indicating that the apparent purpose underlying most research in academic journals has been to develop knowledge of organizational phenomena for its own sake. The difference between the mean responses to these two questions is highly significant ($z = 22.74$, $p < .001$).

In sum, respondents appear to see the organizational sciences as ideally a fairly applied research area, but see a significant gap between that ideal and the apparently less applied research actually published in academic journals.

TABLE 4.1. Ideal and Actual Purpose of Organizational Science Research, with Response Percentages

A. Ideal Purpose[a]

In my opinion, the fundamental purpose of the organizational sciences should be to develop:

9% knowledge of organizational phenomena

49% knowledge of the above, with the hope that it will be of use to organizational practice

33% knowledge that will be of use to organizational practice

9% ways to improve organizational practice

B. Actual Purpose[b]

In fact, the apparent purpose underlying most research published in academic journals during the past decade has been to develop:

61% knowledge of organizational phenomena

34% knowledge of the above, with hope that it will be of use to organizational practice

4% knowledge that will be of use to organizational practice

1% ways to improve organizational practice

[a]$N = 550$; when coded 1–4, mean = 2.42, s.d. = .787.
[b]$N = 528$; when coded 1–4, mean = 1.45, s.d. = .620.
Means on these items are significantly different ($z = 22.74$) at $p < .001$.

Perceptions of Rigor and Relevance

The remaining items in the questionnaire asked respondents to respond separately to the rigor and relevance of organizational science research. The questionnaire explicitly defined these terms as follows:

Rigor: the methodological and logical properties of a study that give one confidence in its findings.
Relevance: The usefulness of a study's findings for a practitioner's decisions and actions.

The first such item (see Table 4.2) asked for an assessment of the adequacy of the rigor and relevance of published research. The responses to part B of this question show that members of the sample see the relevance of current research as insufficient. Only 20 percent of respondents rate organizational science research as "relevant enough," and only 1 percent rate it as "too relevant." The remaining 79 percent of these academics, then, rate current research as being at less than satisfactory levels. For 12 percent, the research is viewed as simply "irrelevant." But for the majority (67 percent), research is rated as being "of some, but insufficient relevance."

In comparison, responses to part A of this item reveal a general acceptance of the rigor of current research, with 67 percent of all respondents indicating that research is "rigorous enough." The difference between mean responses to the two parts of the question is highly significant ($z = 20.97$, $p < .001$).

Thus, the results indicate a relatively widespread perception that the relevance or practical usefulness of research is less than desired. This is not the case with rigor. This gap is consistent with the differences reported earlier between the ideal purpose of the organizational sciences as an applied field versus the perception that most research is actually done for its own sake.

Perceived Importance of Rigor and Relevance

The remaining three sets of items used the same basic response format to ask respondents to rate the importance of rigor and relevance from three

TABLE 4.2. **Perceptions of Rigor and Relevance of the Organizational Sciences, with Response Percentages**

How would you assess the adequacy of most research in the organizational sciences appearing in academic journals?

A. with respect to *rigor*[a]

    1%   nonrigorous

   23%   of some, but insufficient rigor

   67%   rigorous enough

    9%   too rigorous

B. with respect to *relevance*[b]

   12%   irrelevant

   67%   of some, but insufficient relevance

   20%   relevant enough

    1%   too relevant

[a]$N = 559$; when coded 1–4, mean $= 2.83$, s.d. $= .590$.
[b]$N = 561$, when coded 1–4, mean $= 2.09$, s.d. $= .583$.
Means on these items are significantly different ($z = 20.97$) at .001.

TABLE 4.3. Importance of the Rigor and Relevance of Organizational Science Research, from Viewpoint of Own Beliefs and Values

A. *rigor*[a]

0%	not at all important
2%	of minor importance
25%	moderately important
58%	very important
15%	of paramount importance

B. *relevance*[b]

1%	not at all important
3%	of minor importance
22%	moderately important
51%	very important
23%	of paramount importance

[a]$N = 574$; when coded 1–5, mean = 3.85, s.d. = .694.
[b]$N = 574$; when coded 1–5, mean = 3.91, s.d. = .812.
Means on these two items are *not* statistically different ($z = 1.46$).

different perspectives: from the viewpoint of their personal beliefs and values, their academic reward system, and the norms and values of organizational science researchers as a group. (Responses to these items are shown in Tables 4.3, 4.4, and 4.5.)

Whereas earlier questions have shown a gap between desired and actual levels of relevance, question 3 was intended to indicate the importance of this gap to the individual by assessing the absolute and relative importance of relevance in the individual's value system. Specifically, the item asked: "From the viewpoint of *your own beliefs and values*, how important is it that a research study is (a) *rigorous*? (b) *relevant*?" The results (shown in Table 4.3) indicate that the relevance of a research study tends to be "very important" to this sample. This is the mean, median, and modal response, accounting for 51 percent of respondents. Only 4 percent of respondents indicate that relevance is "not at all important" or "of minor importance." While 22 percent rate relevance as "moderately important," 23 percent of respondents see relevance as being "of paramount importance."

In comparative terms, Table 4.3 shows that the relevance of research is of equal importance to research rigor for this group of organizational scientists. In fact, the mean for relevance is somewhat higher, though nonsignificantly so ($z = 1.46$, n.s.).

The importance of relevance or practical usefulness to this sample is consistent with one set of findings reported by Duncan (1974). Duncan

TABLE 4.4. Importance of the Rigor and Relevance of Organizational Science Research, from Viewpoint of Academic Reward System

A. *rigor*[a]

7%	not at all important
15%	of minor importance
31%	moderately important
36%	very important
12%	of paramount importance

B. *relevance*[b]

18%	not at all important
31%	of minor importance
33%	moderately important
15%	very important
4%	of paramount importance

[a]$N = 563$; when coded 1–5, mean $= 3.13$, s.d. $= 1.08$.
[b]$N = 564$; when coded 1–5, mean $= 2.56$, s.d. $= 1.06$.
Means on these two items are statistically different ($z = 11.93$, $p < .001$).

TABLE 4.5. Importance of the Rigor and Relevance of Organizational Science Research, from Viewpoint of Other Organizational Science Researchers

A. *rigor*[a]

1%	not at all important
4%	of minor importance
33%	moderately important
47%	very important
16%	of paramount importance

B. *relevance*[b]

10%	not at all important
39%	of minor importance
37%	moderately important
12%	very important
1%	of paramount importance

[a]$N = 561$; when coded 1–5, mean $= 3.73$, s.d. $= .793$.
[b]$N = 563$; when coded 1–5, mean $= 2.55$, s.d. $= .880$.
Means on these two items are statistically different ($z = 23.60$, $p < .001$).

surveyed random samples of the Academy of Management and a practitioner group. Questions concerned perceptions of various aspects of the knowledge utilization process. The analysis highlighted differences between researchers and practitioners, and was used as evidence of a gap between these two groups. However, there was relatively strong agreement between the two groups on the issue of the most important criteria for management theory and research. Both groups considered "practicality and usefulness" as the most important characteristic in comparison with other criteria, including "logical preciseness" and "empirical validity."

In summary, these results suggest that the gap or deficiencies in the applied relevance of organizational science research reported by respondents are felt to be quite significant. These results are also clearly at variance with traditional characterizations of scientists as concerned with theory as an end in itself, and indicate that this myth has been inaccurate in the organizational sciences.

Academic Reward Systems

Questions 4 and 5 were directed at potential *sources* of the "relevance gap" perceived by respondents. As noted above, both were stated in formats that allowed comparison with respondents' own beliefs and values regarding the importance of rigor and relevance.

Question 4 concerned the emphases on rigor and relevance in academic reward systems. Respondents were asked: "From the viewpoint of *the reward system in your own academic department*, how important is it that faculty research is (a) *rigorous*; (b) *relevant*?" The results (displayed in Table 4.4) show that the reward system is seen as placing less emphasis upon both rigor and relevance than the individual's own value system (Table 4.3). The mean responses to rigor and relevance items for academic reward systems are both significantly lower than for own values. For rigor, the difference between means is .72 ($z = 9.94$, $p < .001$). For relevance, the difference is 1.35 ($z = 24.27$, $p < .001$). To some extent, this lowered emphasis on both properties may reflect the fact that some reward systems are more concerned with publication per se than the qualities of the published research, that research is given lower priority in some institutions, and that rigor and relevance are not always recognized accurately or rewarded by a given reward system.

Nevertheless, the lower emphasis upon relevance is especially pronounced. Whereas only 4 percent of respondents had indicated that relevance was "not at all" or "of minor importance" to themselves, a full 49 percent indicate that relevance is this unimportant to their academic reward system. Likewise, whereas 74 percent had indicated that relevance was "very important" or "of paramount importance" to themselves, only 19 percent report that relevance is this important to their academic reward system. Moreover,the results in Table 4.4 clearly show that academic reward systems are seen as emphasizing rigor over relevance ($z = 11.93$, $p < .001$).

Other Researchers' Norms and Values

The last question involved respondents' perceptions of the "research culture" of the organizational sciences. Respondents were asked: "From the viewpoint of the existing values and norms of *most organizational science researchers outside your institution*, how important is it that a research study is (a) *rigorous*, (b) *relevant*?" The intent of this question was to determine the perceived expectations (Katz and Kahn, 1966) that researchers experienced from colleagues in the larger field.

Responses to the question (displayed in Table 4.5) show that relevance is clearly seen as less valued than rigor. Whereas only 5 percent of respondents see rigor regarded as "not at all important" or "of minor importance," 49 percent see relevance as receiving this small a level of emphasis. Likewise, while 63 percent of respondents report that rigor is regarded as "very important" or "of paramount importance," only 13 percent state that relevance is emphasized this highly. Differences between the mean responses to rigor and relevance are highly significant ($z = 23.60$, $p < .001$).

What is especially interesting, however, is the *fact* of the difference between own beliefs and values, on the one hand, and the perceived norms and values of other researchers on the other. Comparisons between the response distributions in Tables 4.3 and 4.5 show only a slightly lower perceived emphasis on rigor by other researchers (mean difference $= 0.12$, $z = 2.60$, $p < .01$), but a very large drop in perceived emphasis on relevance (mean difference $= 1.36$, $z = 27.05$, $p < .001$). Collectively, then, our respondents are indicating that they place a much higher value on relevance than they appear to show to each other.

DISCUSSION AND CONCLUSIONS

The most dramatic finding is the strong belief that the organizational sciences should be an applied rather than a basic science. A full 91 percent of the sample surveyed felt that the *ideal* purpose of the organizational sciences should contribute to practice, either as a "hoped-for" characteristic (49 percent), as an essential feature of the knowledge sought (33 percent), or in a purely "developmental" role of generating ways to improve practice (9 percent). In contradistinction, only 9 percent endorsed a pure "basic-research" goal of producing knowlege of organizational phenomena for its own sake. However, when asked of the *actual* purpose of published research, 61 percent of all respondents indicated that most research in academic journals has been directed at developing knowledge of organizational phenomena for its own sake. This gap between the actual and ideal purpose of the field is also supported by the view that although current research is rigorous enough (67 percent), it is of some, but insufficient relevance (also 67 percent).

Another important finding is the apparent pluralistic ignorance that exists concerning these sentiments and perceptions. Specifically, respondents' own beliefs and values do not distinguish rigor and relevance as one being more important than the other. Yet when asked to consider *other* organizational science researchers, they perceive that these others rate rigor significantly more important than relevance. Since respondents perceive the same differential rating of their academic reward systems, perhaps each researcher feels that others' values coincide with these reward systems, while presumably theirs do not. As these perceptions are shared, we will have a basis for altering the reward systems to weigh the criteria of rigor and relevance according to the agreed-upon purpose of the organizational sciences.

What will it take to bring about this awareness of purpose and recognition that the means (that is, the weighing of rigor over relevance criteria in academic reward systems) have become misdirected? Will academic institutions and the mechanisms they use to reward and promote individuals (for example, criteria for accepting articles in prestigious journals and presentations at professional meetings) be altered to emphasize the relevance criterion equally with the rigor criterion? Will researchers and practitioners turn their attention to developing a more sophisticated understanding of what constitutes relevance and how one measures it, just as elaborate treatment has been given to developing methodologies for assessing rigor?

It is one thing to recognize these issues and needs for change; it is quite another to enact the behavior to bring about the change. We hope that our colleagues with whom we have been discussing the issues of purpose, direction, and meaning will join with us to promote the necessary change in research criteria. It must start at home, with one's own colleagues, department, and university. Otherwise, the misdirections will persist and may become more problematic.

APPENDIX

A Brief Questionnaire on Rigor and Relevance*

This brief questionnaire attempts to assess some general impressions concerning research rigor and relevance in the organizational sciences—specifically, Organizational Behavior, Organization Theory, and Organization Development.

Please keep the following definitions in mind as you respond to the questionnaire items:

Rigor—the methodological and logical properties of a study which give one confidence in its findings.

Relevance—the usefulness of a study's findings for a practitioner's decisions and actions.

Academic journal—a scholarly report of theories and/or research findings, for example, *Administrative Science Quarterly, Academy of Management Journal, Academy of Management Review, Journal of Applied Psychology, Human Relations,* and the like.

For each question, please check the answer that is closest to your perception or opinion.

1. How would you assess the adequacy of most research in the organizational sciences appearing in academic journals?

   (a) with respect to **rigor**
   ____non-rigorous
   ____of some, but insufficient rigor
   ____rigorous enough
   ____too rigorous

   (b) with respect to **relevance**
   ____irrelevant
   ____of some, but insufficient relevance
   ____relevant enough
   ____too relevant

2. Consider the purpose of organizational science research.

   (a) In my opinion, the fundamental purpose of the organizational sciences should be to develop:
   ____knowledge of organizational phenomena

---

*Selected items. Demographic items not relevant to the present analysis are not shown.

_____knowledge of the above, with the hope that it will be of use to organizational practice
_____knowledge which will be of use to organizational practice
_____ways to improve organizational practice

(b) In fact, the apparent purpose underlying most research published in academic journals during the past decade has been to develop:
_____knowledge of organizational phenomena
_____knowledge of the above, with the hope that it will be of use to organizational practice
_____knowledge which will be of use to organizational practice
_____ways to improve organizational practice

3. From the viewpoint of **your own beliefs and values,** how important is it that a research study is:

(a) **rigorous:**
_____not at all important
_____of minor importance
_____moderately important
_____very important
_____of paramount importance

(b) **relevant:**
_____not at all important
_____of minor importance
_____moderately important
_____very important
_____of paramount importance

4. (Answer only if your primary employment is academic.) From the viewpoint of **the reward system in your own academic department,** how important is it that faculty research is:

(a) **rigorous:**
_____not at all important
_____of minor importance
_____moderately important
_____very important
_____of paramount importance

(b) **relevant:**
_____not at all important
_____of minor importance
_____moderately important
_____very important
_____of paramount importance

5. From the viewpoint of the existing values and norms of **most organizational science researchers outside your institution,** how important is it that a research study is:

(a) **rigorous:**
_____not at all important
_____of minor importance
_____moderately important
_____very important
_____of paramount importance

(b) **relevant:**
_____not at all important
_____of minor importance
_____moderately important
_____very important
_____of paramount importance

Please respond to the following demographic question by placing a checkmark in the appropriate space.

6. Your primary employment is:

_____ an academic
_____ a practitioner

REFERENCES

Duncan, W. J.
1974   "Transferring management theory to practice." Academy of Management Journal, Vol. 17, 4:724–738.
Katz, D., and Kahn, R. L.
1966   The Social Psychology of Organizations. New York: Wiley.
Kilmann, R. H.
1979   "On integrating knowledge utilization with knowledge development: the philosophy behind the MAPS design technology." Academy of Management Review, Vol. 4, 3:417–426.
Mitroff, I. I., and Kilmann, R. H.
1978   Methodological Approaches to Social Science. San Francisco: Jossey-Bass.
Selltiz, C., Wrightsman, L. S., and Cook, S. W.
1976   Research Methods in Social Relations, 3rd edition. New York: Holt, Rinehart & Winston.
Thomas, K. W. and Tymon, W. G., Jr.
1982   "Necessary properties of relevant research: lessons from recent criticisms of the organizational sciences." Academy of Management Review, Vol. 7, 3:345–352.

5

KNOWLEDGE UTILIZATION: ESTIMATING GAPS BY THE ANALYTIC HIERARCHY PROCESS

Thomas L. Saaty

INTRODUCTION

As a nonexpert in the field of knowledge utilization who had been invited to contribute a chapter, I found myself dealing with two trends of thought. The first is of a philosophical nature whose basic query is: Does the study of knowledge utilization really make sense? The second line of thinking is more pragmatic and seeks to make a quantitative evaluation of the differences between researchers and practitioners as one way of getting a hold on the subject.

While preparing this chapter I consulted my colleague, Ralph Kilmann, about knowledge utilization. He told me that it can be regarded as a debate between publish-or-perish researchers and diehard practitioners. That reminded me of a story I once heard about cooperative ventures.

While wandering near the fence of a farm not very far from its coop, a hen came upon a very bored looking pig lying in its mud bath. The hen started up a conversation. "Hey, Piggy," she said, "Why don't we go into a business venture together?" The pig, wallowing deeper in his mud, said, "What would we do, Henny?"

Henny replied, "We could sell ham and eggs."

"My dear," said the pig, "for you it is only a daily effort, but for me it is a total commitment."

To do knowledge utilization you have to be something of a diplomat who persuasively matches good ideas to user needs. As I see it, knowledge utilization is like matchmaking. That reminds me of a story told about a former secretary of state who was the original shuttle diplomat.

Kissinger once counseled a bachelor friend of his to get married. The friend said that he had no money to support a wife and that it would tie him down too much anyway. Kissinger said, "Would you marry a rich girl like Rockefeller's daughter?" The friend said, "I might." So Kissinger went off to see Rockefeller. He said, "Rocky, you have a beautiful daughter—sensible, intelligent—who needs a husband and I know just the man."

Rockefeller said, "You know, Henry, she has to marry in our social class or she will be unhappy."

Kissinger said, "What if the man is a World Bank vice-president?"

Rockefeller said, "I might consider him."

Kissinger went off to see McNamara at the World Bank. He said, "Bob, do you have openings for vice-presidents?"

"No, I am fed up with them and don't feel that I need any," said McNamara.

Kissinger said, "What if the man were Rockefeller's son-in law?"

McNamara said, "Oh, in that case, yes, I would consider him."

THE NONUTILIZATION OF KNOWLEDGE UTILIZATION

The law of supply and demand here seems to be a bootstrap operation, and I suspect that this is also the case with knowledge utilization. The potential users are not much involved in the process—their own story may remain unknown. It should be clear to most of us that why we do not use knowledge is because we do not understand it, it does not fit our idiosyncrasies, we are jealous, fearful, stupid, too supercilious and conceited to listen to others, too busy making our own noise and tooting our horns or those of someone we like. Creative people by their nature cannot spend too much time on what other people have to say. They want to make it obsolete with new discoveries. They also want to be famous and immortal and need to be constantly trying out new ideas.

We pass through periods of fashions, cliques, and jargon that generate little whirlpools of change in knowlege and tradition. In the end much knowledge is ignored and refuted, or discarded before it has a chance to germinate. Refutation is more likely to be on political grounds than on truth and understanding. It is fashionable to take a dim view of the lust for fame. But remember Newton? Newtonian physics was not only fascinating but Newton promoted it with demonic energy. Our system of professional recognition contributes both to generating new knowledge and to the neglect of knowledge that has just been invented and not used much. I see a danger in piling up new knowledge before the old has been absorbed.

Up to a point, the knowledge we acquire at a certain time must integrate coherently with what we already know. But scientific revolutions are responses to crises, and sometimes we have to throw out or rework large amounts of old knowledge within the new framework. Knowledge that may appear useless when viewed from one angle may be seen to be useful from another. However, an effort to cling onto and promote old knowledge past its natural life is counterproductive.

A problem we face in knowledge utilization is the idea that what we are capable of learning must be linked to what we already know. If it does not fit in the context of what we know, it may not make sense.

One way to solve this problem is to create a new tradition to broaden the base of knowledge so that a new idea can be presented from different vantage points: mathematical, cultural, scientific, humanist, and the like. In this manner what we want to learn would be broadly mixed with what we already know. The question now is: What knowledge is worthy of this elaborate treatment? I expect that this is a central question in the field.

In an article called "Resistance by Scientists to Scientific Disovery" (*Science*, vol. 134, pp. 596–602, 1961), Bernard Barber made several useful observations about why scientists resist new ideas. He quotes Wilfred Trotter: "Change from without . . . seems in its very essence to be repulsive and an object of fear," and Max Planck: "A new scientific truth does not triumph by convincing its opponents and making them see the light, but rather because its opponents eventually die, and a new generation grows up that is familiar with it."

Among the variety of causes of resistance to new ideas on which he elaborates are: cultural blinders that serve as idols threatened by distortion with new ideas; an unwillingness to believe that better theories can arise from new theories; methodological grooves that keep people holding on to what is becoming obsolete; preference for the evidence of the senses, which have been conditioned in certain ways; a tendency to think in terms of established models; depending too much or too little on mathematics rather than using it objectively along with other methods of discovery; religious beliefs of scientists serve as cultural barriers; patterns of social interactions among scientists serve as sources of resistance to discovery; specialization, which is necessary, often causes insiders to resist outsiders; and domination of academies and learned societies by the older foofoos who are slow and reluctant to react to new ideas.

Although some resistance is inevitable, there are positive aspects to the scientific method that encourage one to believe that the system is working well. The powerful norm of openmindedness in science, the objective tests by which concepts and theories often can be validated, and the social mechanisms for ensuring competition among ideas new and old, all make up a social system in which objectivity is greater than it is in other social areas with a little less resistance.

Since I am a mathematician, I am particularly interested in how mathematicians view the utility of their knowledge. There seems to be substantial divergence of opinion. I have here two statements by two great mathematicians of the twentieth century. The first is proud not to have made contributions useful in applications, and the second is concerned about staying useful. G. H. Hardy, the first, was a British number theorist who spent his life teaching at Cambridge University. John von Neumann, the second, was a creative Hungarian mathematician of great versatility. He was a creator of game theory and contributed to the development of the modern computer.

Pride in Not Being Useful (G. H. Hardy)

I have never done anything "useful". No discovery of mine has made, or is likely to make, directly or indirectly, for good or ill, the least difference to the amenity of the world. I have helped to train other mathematicians, but mathematicians of the same kind as myself ... Judged by all practical standards, the value of my mathematical life is nil ... that I have created something is undeniable: the question is about its value. [The things I have added to knowledge do not differ from] ... the creations of the great mathematicians, or of any of the other artists, great or small, who have left some kind of memorial behind them.
—*A Mathematician's Apology*, 1967, p. 150–151

Concern about Being Useful (John von Neumann)

I think that it is a relatively good approximation to truth ... that mathematical ideas originate in empirics, although the genealogy is sometimes long and obscure. But, once they are so conceived, the subject begins to live a peculiar life of its own and is better compared to a creative one, governed by almost entirely aesthetical motivations, than to anything else and, in particular, to an empirical science ... As a mathematical discipline travels far from its empirical source ... it is beset with very grave dangers. It comes more and more purely aestheticizing, more and more purely l'art pour l'art. ... whenever this stage is reached, the only remedy seems to me to be the rejuvenating return to the source ...
—*The Mathematician*, 1956, p. 2063

NARROWING THE GAP

In the past few years I have developed a new theory for planning, setting priorities, and resource allocation in complex situations. It is called the analytic hierarchy process, with a book by this title published by McGraw-Hill in 1980. It occurred to me that it would be the perfect approach to use in exploring the conflict between researchers and practitioners in the field of knowledge utilization. I have included a brief discussion of this process at the end of this chapter.

To use the analytic hierarchy process, we decompose a complex problem hierarchically; we pairwise compare the elements in a given level with respect to the elements in the next higher level using the judgments of experts. For example, if one is buying a car, cost and style would be among the criteria of an upper level used to compare makes of cars in the immediately lower level. To give the judgments one asks, for example, when comparing cars A and B, which car is preferred for style and how strongly.

One goes through this for each criterion on the upper level for each pair of cars on the lower level. The priorities derived from the judgments are then synthesized to obtain global priorities in the form of a ratio scale estimate.

In "Organization Design for Knowledge Utilization," R. H. Kilmann develops a nontraditional knowledge utilization design that I have borrowed and adapted for my example. The hierarchy of knowledge utilization as I have structured it in Figure 5.1 has four actions on its bottom level.

The focus of the hierarchy is the question: What are the motives that cause a scientist to enter the knowledge utilization field? In the end we want to use what we find out to determine the relative importance of the actions available to the knowledge utilization specialist of either persuasion to promote his interest.

The focus divides into benefits to the knowledge utilization specialist and obligations expected of him. We thought that the benefits fell into three types and obligations into four types (see objectives level in the hierarchy under the benefits and obligations).

Next we identified three criteria clusters involved in knowledge utilization. They are problem formulation, problem analysis, and solution and implementation. Problem formulation is divided into two subcriteria: definition and modeling. The other two have no subcriteria. Remember, I am still using Kilmann's classification. (In some cases I have his branchings titles, for example, in naming the subcriteria of definition and modeling.) Each is followed by a set of activities that pertain to it, which I call Kilmann functions. These functions are tied to the bottom level of utilization controlling actions. Here we have the bottom line. What we want to do is to prioritize conscientiously this bottom level, which consists of the actions the knowledge utilization specialist can take to promote his purposes identified in the objectives level.

Many pairwise comparison matrices were involved in the process. This hierarchy is incomplete since it branches off independently in parts only to regroup on lower levels. The judgments I did with my colleague, Luis Vargas, were our own, but we did debate them carefully. Of course, this is only an illustration and if it were to be pursued one should consult experts in the field for the judgments. Still, we feel that there are many lessons to be learned.

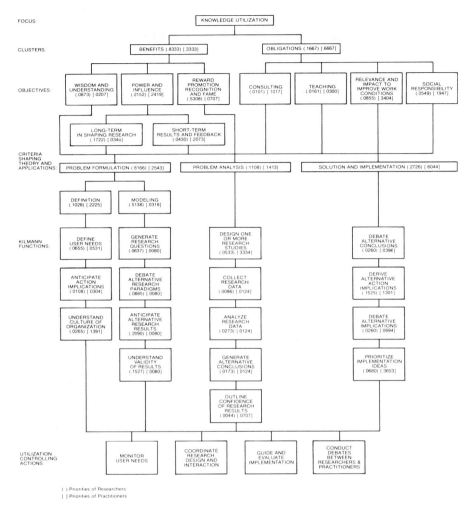

FIGURE 5.1. A Hierarchy of Interactions Used to Set Priorities

For example, there seems to be a distinction worth noting at the level of the Kilmann functions between researchers and practitioners. Researchers focus more on modeling and on solution and implementation. Practitioners focus on the defintion of the problem and on the solution and implementation. Under modeling, researchers are more interested in anticipating research results and their validity; under solution and implementation, they are interested in devising alternative schemes to address the implications of the model.

Practitioners give higher priority to understanding the culture of the organization in the definition of the problem, since this is the interface between model and user. Under solution and implementation, practitioners are interested in the steps of the implementation process, highlighted by the high priority of "prioritize implementation ideas."

Note that not all Kilmann functions are of equal priority to each group. Thus, not all such functions were used to prioritize the controlling actions. Some had to be chosen in such a way that the priorities of the controlling actions reflect a need for interaction between researchers and practitioners. Only those high priority functions whose cluster priority was also sufficiently high for either type were selected. For example, we did not select a Kilmann function from the cluster "definition" for the researchers because its priority was not high enough. However, because this cluster has high priority for the practitioners, one Kilmann function, "understand culture of organization," was selected from it. Since knowledge utilization is a problem for both types and we wish to provide useful guidelines as to which are the critical areas of disagreement or need, we prioritized only once the utilization controlling actions with respect to the selected Kilmann functions.

The overall priorities are shown in Figure 5.1 (in the parentheses for researchers and in brackets for practitioners). The final weights of the controlling actions for both groups of specialists are shown in Table 5.1.

TABLE 5.1. Priorities of Actions with Respect to Functions

	Understand cultural organization (practitioners)	Generate research questions (researchers)	Debate alternative research paradigms (researchers)
Monitor user needs	.4167	.0818	.2502
Coordinate describe, design, and Introduction	.0833	.5506	.2248
Guide and evaluate implementation	.0833	.1921	.1106
Conduct debates	.4167	.1755	.4143
Priorities			
Researchers	.0615	.0997	.1385
Practitioners	.2056	.0118	.0118

Each column in this table has been constructed according to the appropriate point of view as indicated under each Kilmann function.

These priorities differ by five $[(.22 - .17/.22) = 23\%;$ $(.16 - .12/.16) = 25\%]$ in two instances and by nine $[(.23 - .14/.23) = 39\%; (.48 - .39/.48) = 19\%]$ in the other two. It seems that practitioners place higher priorities than the researchers on activities in which they directly interact with clients' "monitor user needs" and "conduct debates," and the researchers tend to put more emphasis on what might be considered the theoretical aspects of "research design" and the "evaluation of implementation." The most important controlling action priority is given to "conducting debates" with each other—it has the smallest relative percentage difference.

Here we assumed that both groups would work jointly to set priorities on the actions in terms of the Kilmann functions regardless of which function was more important to a given group. The reason for this is that despite divergence on the functions, the differences in the actions they must take to improve knowledge utilization should converge. Our purpose was to identify and estimate the gap in the priorities of the actions as a result of differences higher up in the hierarchy. Had we prioritized the actions without assuming cooperation, we would have obtained two separate points of view without being able to point out what the best actions could be to close the gap.

For example, we believe that a meeting such as this one can be viewed as an important debate, which is the most relevant step toward improving knowledge utilization as indicated by the analysis.

Anticipate alternative research results (researchers)	Understand validity of results (researchers)	Outline confidence of research results (practitioners)	Derive alternative action implications (both)	Prioritize implementation ideas (practitioners)
.0952	.2459	.0952	.1176	.1869
.1905	.1639	.5714	.0980	.1121
.1629	.4918	.1095	.1961	.1402
.5714	.0984	.1629	.5882	.5607
.3272	.2390	.0069	.0407	.1064
.0118	.0118	.1045	.1026	.5400

TABLE 5.2. Overall Priorities of Actions For Researchers and for Practitioners

Actions	Researchers' Priorities	Practitioners' Priorities
Monitor user needs	.17	.22
Coordinate research, design, and interaction	.12	.16
Guide and evaluate implementation	.23	.14
Conduct debates	.39	.48

CONCLUDING REMARKS

It appears that the complexity involved in understanding and improving knowledge utilization must be systematized, debated, and developed by a structural process such as a hierarchy or a feedback system, which is an adaptive mechanism used to satisfy the needs of either group. This structure can then be used to assess the knowledge available about the preferences of people to set priorities, which are then used to take the necessary actions to bring about potential improvement in the field.

REFERENCE

Kilmann, Ralph H. "Organization Design for Knowledge Utilization." *Knowledge: Creation, Diffusion, Utilization*, Vol. 3, No. 2, December 1981, pp. 211–31.

APPENDIX

The Analytic Hierarchy Process

The analytic hierarchy process (AHP) is a problem-solving framework. It is a systematic procedure for representing the elements of any problem. It organizes the basic rationality by breaking down a problem into its smaller constituents and then calls for only simple pairwise comparison judgments to develop priorities in each level.

The analytic hierarchy process provides a comprehensive framework to cope with intuitive, rational, and irrational factors in making judgments. It is a method of integrating perceptions and purposes into an overall synthesis. The AHP does not require that judgments be consistent or even transitive. The degree of consistency of the judgment is revealed at the end of the AHP.

Human Reasoning

People generally provide subjective judgments based on feelings and intuition rather than on well worked out logical reasoning. Also, when they reason together, people tend to influence each other's thinking. Individual judgments are altered slightly to accommodate the group's logic and the group's interests. However, people have very short memories, and if asked afterward to support the group judgments, they instinctively go back to their individual judgments. Repetition is needed to effect deep-rooted changes.

People also find it difficult to justify their judgments logically and to explicate how strong these judgments are. As a result, they make great compromises in their thinking to accommodate ideas and judgments. In groups, there is a willingness to compromise. If truth is to be an objective reality, reality must be very fuzzy because the search for truth often ends in compromise. What is regarded as truth may often be essentially a social product obtained through interaction rather than by pure deduction.

Logical understanding does not seem to permeate judgment instantaneously. It apparently needs time to be assimilated. However, even when logical understanding has been assimilated, people still offer judgment in a spontaneous, emotional way without elaborate explanation. Even when there is time, explanations tend to be fragmentary, disconnected, and mostly without an underlying clear, logical foundation.

Outline of the Process

People making comparisons use their feelings and judgment. Both vary in intensity. To distinguish among different intensities, the scale of absolute numbers in Table 5A.1 is useful.

The analytic hierarchy process can be decomposed into the following steps. Particular steps may be emphasized more in some situations than in others. Also as noted, interaction is generally useful for stimulation and for representing different points of view.

1. Define the problem and determine what knowledge is sought.

2. Structure the hierarchy from the top (the objectives from a broad perspective) through the intermediate levels (criteria on which subsequent levels depend) to the lowest level (which usually is a list of the alternatives).

3. Construct a set of pairwise comparison matrices for each of the lower levels, one matrix for each element in the level immediately above. An element in the higher level is said to be a governing element for those in the lower level since it contributes to or affects it. In a complete simple hierarchy, every element in the lower level affects every element in the upper

TABLE 5A.1. Scale of Relative Importance

Intensity of Relative Importance	Definition	Explanation
1	Equal importance	Two activities contribute equally to the objective
3	Moderate importance of one over another	Experience and judgment slightly favor one activity over another
5	Essential or strong importance	Experience and judgment strongly favor one activity over another
7	Demonstrated importance	An activity is strongly favored and its dominance is demonstrated in practice
9	Absolute importance	The evidence favoring one activity over another is of the highest possible order of affirmation
2,4,6,8	Intermediate values between the two adjacent judgments	When compromise is needed
Reciprocals of above nonzero numbers	If an activity has one of the above numbers (e.g., 3) compared with a second activity, then the second activity has the reciprocal value (i.e., ⅓) when compared to the first.	

level. The elements in the lower level are then compared to each other, based on their effect on the governing element above. This yields a square matrix of judgments. The pairwise comparisons are done in terms of which element dominates the other. These judgments are then expressed as integers according to the judgment values in Table 5A.1. If element A dominates element B, then the whole number integer is entered in row A, column B, and the reciprocal (fraction) is entered in row B, column A. Of course, if element B dominates element A, the reverse occurs. The whole number is then placed in the B, A position with the reciprocal automatically being assigned to the A, B position. If the elements being compared are equal, a one is assigned to both positions. The numbers used express an absolute rather than an ordinal relation.

4. There are $n(n-1)/2$ judgments required to develop the set of matrices in step 3 (taking into account the fact that reciprocals are automatically assigned in each pairwise comparison), where n is the number of elements in the lower level.

5. Having collected all the pairwise comparison data and entered the reciprocals together with n unit entries down the main diagonal (an element is equal to itself, so a one is assigned to the diagonal positions), the eigenvalue problem $Aw = \lambda_{max}w$ is solved and consistency is tested, using the departure of λ_{max} from n (see below).

6. Steps 3, 4, and 5 are performed for all levels and clusters in the hierarchy.

7. Hierarchical composition is now used to weight the eigenvectors by the weights of the criteria, and the sum is taken over all weighted eigenvector entries corresponding to those in the next lower level of the hierarchy.

8. The consistency ratio of the entire hierarchy is found by multiplying each consistency index by the priority of the corresponding criterion and adding them together. The result is then divided by the same type of expression, using the random consistency index corresponding to the dimensions of each matrix weighted by the priorities as before. The consistency ratio should be about 10 percent or less to be acceptable. If not, the quality of the judgments should be improved, perhaps by revising the manner in which questions are asked in making the pairwise comparisons. If this should fail to improve consistency, it is likely that the problem should be more accurately structured; that is, similar elements should be grouped under more meaningful criteria. A return to step 2 would be required, although only the problematic parts of the hierarchy may need revision.

If the exact answer in the form of hard numbers was actually available, it would be possible to normalize these numbers, form their ratios as described above, and solve the problem. This would result in getting the same numbers back, as should be expected. On the other hand, if firm numbers were not available, their ratios could be estimated to solve the problem.

Example of the Process

In the following example, the analytic hierarchy process is used to assist a young family (a father, mother, and child) of specified income to buy a new car, either model A, B, or C. The choice will be determined through four important criteria.

The hierarchy of such a decision often takes the form shown in Figure 5A.1. In this hierarchy, level 1 is the single overall objective: best new car to buy. On level 2 are the criteria that are perceived to compose what is meant by best new car, such as price and running cost (operating and maintenance).

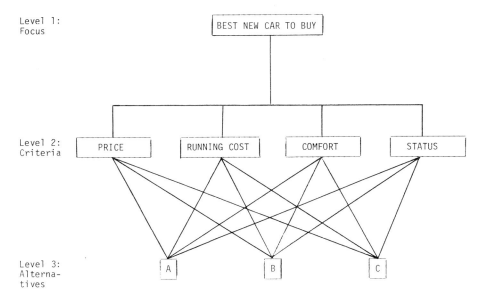

Level 1:
Focus

Level 2:
Criteria

Level 3:
Alterna-
tives

FIGURE 5A.1. A Hierarchy for Choosing a Best Car

On level 3 are the various alternative cars from which the family will choose.

This downward decomposition format can easily be used on a wide class of problems. In addition, a slight further modification to incorporate feedback loops will cover an even wider range.

The questions asked when comparing each criterion are of the following kind: Of the two alternatives being compared, which is considered more important by the family buying a car and how much more important is it? The comparison matrix of Table 5A.2 is then formed. Since price and running cost have the highest priorities, the other factors are discarded and only these two are used in continuing the process. Care must be taken in doing this. The original priorities are then normalized by dividing each by their sum to obtain the new relative priorities in equation (1):

$$0.67 = \frac{.58}{.58 + .28}$$

$$0.33 = \frac{.28}{.58 + .28}$$

(1)

TABLE 5A.2. Pairwise Comparison Judgments For Criteria

Decision to Buy a Car	Price	Running Cost	Comfort	Status	Priorities
Price	1	3	7	8	.582
Running Cost	⅓	1	5	5	.279
Comfort	$1/7$	$1/5$	1	3	.090
Status	⅛	$1/5$	⅓	1	.050
λmax = 4.198					
C.I. = .066					
C.R. = .073					

TABLE 5A.3. Pairwise Comparison Judgments For Alternatives

Price	Car A	Car B	Car C	Priorities
Car A	1	2	3	.540
Car B	½	1	2	.297
Car C	⅓	½	1	.163
λmax = 3.009				
C.I. = .005				
C.R. = .008				

Running Cost

	Car A	Car B	Car C	Priorities
Car A	1	$1/5$	½	.106
Car B	5	1	7	.745
Car C	2	1.7	1	.150
λmax = 3.119				
C.I. = .059				
C.R. = .103				

TABLE 5A.4. Overall Priorities

	Price (priority .67)	Running cost (priority .33)	Composite priority cars
Car A	.540	.106	.396
Car B	.297	.745	.445
Car C	.163	.150	.159

The process is then repeated for the third level, where each car is compared with respect to the two high-priority factors from the second level, as shown in Table 5A.3.

The two priority columns are then recorded as in Table 5A.4. All entries of the first column are then multiplied by .67, the priority of price, and those of the second column by .33, the priority of running cost, and added. This gives the third column. Thus, car B was selected for its efficient operation even though its initial price is considerably higher than car A. Car dealers in the income neighborhood of this family may find it profitable to stock up on the cars in the respective proportions.

One of the most powerful contributions that the analytic hierarchy process makes is to test out the degree of inconsistency or incompatibility of new ideas or new policies adopted with older, more familiar, better tried successful methods. For example, in doing the above problem, the participants were not sure whether the judgments for price over running cost should be 7, 5, or 3. Each one was tried separately, and it was found that 3 yielded the highest consistency. Those who voted for 3 won that argument.

Priorities and Consistency

An easy way to get a good approximation of the priorities is to use the geometric mean. This is done by multiplying the elements in each row and taking their *nth* root, where n is the number of elements. Then, normalize the column of numbers thus obtained by dividing each entry by the sum of all entries. Alternatively, normalize the elements in each column of the matrix and then average each row.

The consistency index can also be determined by hand calculations. Add the numbers in each column of the judgment matrix, multiply the first sum by the first priority, the second by the second, and so on, and add. For the first matrix the column sums (1.60, 4.40, 13.33, 17) are obtained, and multiplying by (.582, .279, .090, .050) gives 4.20. This number is denoted by λ_{max}. The consistency index is given thus:

$$C.I. = \frac{\lambda_{max} - n}{n - 1} \qquad (2)$$

The consistency is now checked by taking the ratio (C.R.) of C.I. with the appropriate one of the set of numbers in Table 5A.5 to see if it is about 10 percent or less (20 percent may be tolerated in some cases but not more). Otherwise the problem must be studied again and judgments revised. The

TABLE 5A.5. Random Consistencies

n:	1	2	3	4	5	6	7	8	9	10
Random consistency:	0	0	.58	.90	1.12	1.24	1.32	1.41	1.45	1.49

consistency of the hierarchy in the above example, as given by equation (3), is .06, which is good:

$$\frac{.066 \times 1 + .005 \times .67 + .059 \times .33}{.900 \times 1 + .580 \times .67 + .580 \times .33} = \frac{.089}{1.48} = .06 \qquad (3)$$

Judgment Formation

When several people participate, judgments are often debated. Sometimes the group accepts a geometric average of their combined judgments. If there is strong disagreement, the different opinions can each be taken and used to obtain answers. Those that subsequently display the highest consistency within the group are the ones usually retained.

The analytic hierarchy process incorporates equally both tangible factors, which require hard measurements, and such intangible factors as comfort, which require judgment. Eventually one finds that so-called hard numbers have no meaning in themselves apart from their utilitarian interpretations. In the above example, buying a $10,000 car is more than twice as "painful" as buying a $5,000 car.

The interdependence of criteria, such as comfort and price, have to be considered carefully since there may be some perceived overlap. For example, higher price buys more comfort, but it also buys other desirable attributes. Judging the relative importance of such things as price and comfort, therefore, must be done as independently as possible with avoidance of overlaps.

Validation by Physical Laws

Using the scale 1-9 has been justified and demonstrated by many examples. However, the following simple optics illustration, carried out with small children, shows that perceptions, judgments, and these numbers lead to results that can be validated by laws of physics. In this example, four identical chairs were placed at distances of 9, 15, 21, and 28 yards (1 yd. = 0.9144m) from a floodlight. The children stood by the light, looked at the line of chairs, and compared the first with the second, the third, and then with the fourth, and so on for the second, third, and fourth chairs. Each time the children said how much brighter one chair was when compared to the other.

Their judgments were entered in the matrix of Table 5A.6 to record the relative brightness of the chairs. The reciprocals were used in the transpose position.

The inverse-square law of optics is now used to test these judgments. Since the distances are 9, 15, 21, and 28 yards, these numbers are squared and their reciprocals calculated. This gives .0123, .0044, .0023, and .0013 respectively. Normalization of these values gives .61, .22, .11, and .06, which are very close to the brightness ratios obtained in the test using the analytic hierarchy process.

Structuring a Hierarchy

There are no rules for structuring a hierarchy. However, a typical analytic hierarchy for allocating resources—either by measuring costs or by measuring benefits—will often be stratified roughly as follows. The top level will include the overall objectives of the organization or system. Benefit-cost criteria may appear in the next level. A subordinate level may further clarify these criteria in the context of the particular problem by itemizing specific tasks that are to be accomplished at some level of performance. This is followed by the alternatives being evaluated.

Capabilities

Designing an analytic hierarchy—like the structuring of a problem by any other method—is more art than science. It necessitates substantial knowledge of the system in question. A very strong aspect of the analytic hierarchy process is that the knowledgeable individuals who supply judg-

TABLE 5A.6. Comparison Matrix Comparing Perceived Brightness of Chairs

	Chair 1	Chair 2	Chair 3	Chair 4	Brightness Ratios
Chair 1	1	5	6	7	0.61
Chair 2	$1/5$	¼	4	6	0.24
Chair 3	$1/6$	¼	1	4	0.10
Chair 4	$1/7$	$1/6$	¼	1	0.05

$\lambda_{max} = 4.39$
C.I. $= 0.13$
C.R. $= 0.14$

ments for the pairwise comparisons usually play a prominent role in specifying the hierarchy.

Although a hierarchy to be used in resource allocation will tend to have the vertical stratification indicated above, it can also be much more general. The only restriction is that any element on a higher level must serve as a governing element for at least one element (which can be the element itself) on the immediately lower level. The hierarchy need not be complete; that is, an element at an upper level need not function as a criterion for all the elements in the lower level. It can be partitioned into nearly disjoint subhierarchies sharing only a common topmost element. Thus, for instance, the activities of separate divisions of an organization can be structured separately. As suggested above, the analyst can insert and delete levels and elements as necessary to clarify the task or to sharpen a focus on one or more areas of the system.

The analytic hierarchy process has already been successfully applied in a variety of fields, including: planning the allocation of energy to industries; designing a transport system for the Sudan; planning the future of a corporation and measuring the impact of environmental factors on its development; designing future scenarios for higher education in the United States; selecting candidates and winners in elections; setting priorities for the top scientific institute in a developing country; solving a faculty promotion and tenure problem; and predicting oil prices.

For background information see *Decision Theory: Systems Engineering* in the *McGraw-Hill Encyclopedia of Science and Technology*.

REFERENCES

Hardy, G. H. *A Mathematician's Apology*, Cambridge, London: Cambridge University Press, 1967.

Saaty, T. L. *The Analytic Hierarchy Process*, New York: McGraw-Hill International Book Company, 1980.

Saaty, T. L. *Decision Making for Leaders*, Belmont, CA: Lifetime Learning Publications (A Division of Wadsworth Publications), 1982.

Saaty, T. L. "A Scaling Method for Priorities in Hierarchical Structures," *Journal of Mathematical Psychology*, 15 (3), 1977, pp. 234–281.

Saaty, T. L., and Vargas, L. *The Logic of Priorities*, Boston: Kluwer-Nijhoff, 1981.

Von Neumann, John. "The Mathematician," In James R. Newman (ed.), *The World of Mathematics*, 4:3:2053–2063. New York: Simon and Schuster, 1956.

6

SOME REAL WORLD ADVENTURES
OF A BENCH SCIENTIST

Kenneth D. Mackenzie

INTRODUCTION

From 1963 to 1976 this author spent all of his professional time in either research or teaching about organizational behavior. During this period he was involved with an extensive series of laboratory researches to develop and test a theory of group structures; his income from consulting was zero. All of his efforts were directed toward developing a theory of group structures that could be used to improve organizational performance. Despite several books, many papers, and numerous appearances at conferences of his peers, there seemed to be no interest in the knowledge being so carefully produced. His mailbox contained no offers and his telephone calls never had an eager manager at the other end who wanted to try out the new theories. In fact, at one conference in the United Kingdom he had the dubious distinction of being introduced as "the ultimate academic." That's like a blind date being described as "interesting."

Now in some sense the honor of being "the ultimate academic" was a testimonial to the inability to produce useful knowledge. For if he had produced useful knowledge he would at least be called an "expert." Apparently we ultimate academics are supposed to putter about our laboratories, produce arcane research, mumble in our beards, and be generally ineffectual. However, if one believes that the purpose of an experiment is to test a theory and the purpose of developing better theory is to improve the ability of others to apply the knowledge, then being ignored by managers was not a good sign. Consequently, the linkage between the development of good theory and its application was made stronger.

The lack of application and worse, the lack of interest by managers in application, was taken as a sign that somehow the theory was not yet good enough. It was time for the obscure bench scientist to venture forth from his laboratory and into the world for which the research was being conducted. So, in 1976, with high hopes, no previous experience, no business contacts, a well-tested laboratory theory, some capital, and dubious associates, an enterprise was created. The purpose of the enterprise was to develop the theory of organizational structures by direct application as a research-based management consulting firm.

One must conclude that the judgment of being the ultimate academic was reinforced by the overwhelming disinterest by managers. Revenues in 1976 were zero. Revenues in 1977 were only $1,500, and that was from a disorganized company trying to sell a product to this author. Our prospects began to change in 1978, and we have been compounding our growth ever since then. Looking back, the market was very perceptive about the theory and the ability to produce useful knowledge. Consequently, there was a strong incentive to being able to produce useful knowledge for organizations. Thus the Scot and the ultimate academic became united in purpose.

MAIN CONCLUSIONS

The years from 1963 to 1976 were spent solely to produce knowledge. The years since then have been devoted to producing both knowledge and useful knowledge for organizations. From the vantage point of this experience and the real need to produce useful knowledge for organizations, the lessons learned can be summarized in a very short list of conclusions. These conclusions are frankly utilitarian and perhaps, to some, trivial and simplistic.*

Knowledge and Its Assumptions

Knowledge is never complete.

All knowledge involves assumptions: some recognized and some unrecognized.

---

*A more thorough analysis of assumptions with particular relevance to the social sciences can be found in a stream of research articles and books emanating from a group of scholars having a tie with the University of Pittsburgh, C. W. Churchman and Russell Ackoff. The articles (Mitroff, Emshoff, and Kilmann, 1979; Kilmann, 1979, 1982) describe a process for uncovering critical assumptions. T. Saaty (1980) has developed a mathematical framework called belief-assessment analysis. Mason (1969), Mason and Mitroff (1973), Mitroff and Emshoff (1979), and many other publications have extended these ideas to the level of corporate strategy. The works by C. W. Churchman (cf. 1961, 1968, 1971) had much to do with the development of this line of inquiry. The 1961 publication by Churchman, read while taking a class from him, had major impact on the future research by this author. His work encouraged me to decide to become a bench scientist rather than a mathematician.

Assumptions represent unsolved problems.

Recognized assumptions are, in fact, recognized unsolved problems.

Unrecognized assumptions become revealed when the knowledge is applied.

Safe assumptions are those one can get away with.

The set of safe assumptions in knowledge generated in one context is usually not the same as that generated in another context.

The issue of assumptions is well recognized in the philosophy of science and is built into the formal logic of the explanans sentences in any deductive nomological explanation. However, the statements made here have special relevance to the theorist who wants to apply his theories in organizations. The problem of knowledge and its assumptions is illustrated by the assumptions in the author's own work on task processes.

Useful Knowledge and Real Problems

A problem is *real* when there is an information system that indicates a disadvantageous discrepancy between what is and what is desired by an organization.

Knowledge is *useful* to organizations only when it is *used* to solve a real problem.

Knowledge is used in an organization when its application is seen to solve a real problem.

The tautology that useful knowledge to an organization is that which the organization uses creates real problems to a knowledge vendor. If the knowledge has not been used before, the natural question is why. Few organizations desire to be guinea pigs. Furthermore, if the knowledge has not been used then there probably is not an information system to generate problems for its application, and thus the knowledge is not real. The situation is similar to the inexperienced job applicant applying for jobs requiring experience. Converting knowledge to useful knowledge is a difficult process.

The Decision to Use Knowledge Is an Adoption of Innovation Process

The decision to use a type of knolwedge in an organization is an adoption process.

Whenever the decision to use a type of knowledge in an organization involves more than one person, the adoption process for the organization is a diffusion process across the involved individuals.

Knowledge will be adopted by an organization if, after considering all perceived costs, there is net benefit.

The *usefulness* of a type of knowledge is directly proportional to the net benefit of using it.

The greater the usefulness of knowledge, the more costs the organization is willing to incur to obtain it.

The extensive literature on the adoption and diffusion of innovations (see Rogers and Shoemaker, 1971) is relevant to the issue of producing useful knowledge for organizations. Almost all decisions to make knowledge useful in an organization involve more than one person. Some of the costs are money costs. Many are political and emotional. Diffusion processes take time and the advocate of new knowledge must learn to initiate and manage the adoption-diffusion process if he hopes to convert his knowledge into useful knowledge for a particular organization. This adoption-diffusion process usually involves other organizations.

The Greater the Costs a User Is Willing to Incur to Obtain a Type of Knowledge, the Greater Its Value to Him

At first glance, this statement seems to contradict certain statements made above. There is no real contradiction when one understands that the decision to use a type of knowledge is not quite the same as the process of using it. A higher cost improves both the priority and the commitment to use it. On the other hand, high costs decrease the net benefits. So a knowledge vendor walks a very narrow line in converting knowledge into useful knowledge. For example, if one offers the knowledge gratis, one usually does not receive much cooperation. If one charges a very high price and is hired, the high price improves the priority and then, once incurred, the commitment to justify the expense. When the priority and commitment are low, the cooperation and support needed to make it useful are likely to increase the chances that it will not be useful.

To put this less delicately, when the "meter is running" at \$125/hour one is much more likely to obtain cooperation than if it is running at \$10/ hour. At \$125/hour times n hours the commitment to seeing the knowledge be useful is directly proportional to \$125n. Clearly \$10n involves less commitment. But, *ceteris paribus*, there is more net benefit for a type of knowledge being adopted at \$10n than at \$125n. However, once a decision to adopt a type of knowledge has been made, there is both greater priority and commitment at \$125n than at \$10n. This dilemma is usually solved by doing a pilot project at \$10n and then employing diffusion processes to convert the pilot project into a \$50n project, and so on. Marketing professors refer to this as "pricing to penetrate." One can use the diffusion process across organizations to increase the hourly rate *and* the size of n. Slowly, as one builds a reputation and enjoys the effects of learning curve productivity improvement in applying the knowledge, it becomes increasingly useful and valuable. For example, my firm is ten times as productive for banks in 1982 as it was in 1978. Hourly prices have only quadrupled. The price per hour is increasing at a rate where the total cost is decreasing, and hence the net benefit is increasing. Thus, the services are increasingly useful.

Knowledge and the Organizational Processes

Knowledge is made more useful to an organization by making it easier to use.

The application of knowledge in an organization involves its task processes and personnel.

The fewer changes in task processes in an organization, the easier it is to make knowledge useful.

The greater the changes in task processes involved in the application of knowledge in an organization, the greater its perceived costs and hence the less likely the knowledge will be useful.

In most cases, the introduction of useful knowlege involves changes in how the organization conducts its operations. Care taken to make it easy to use the knowledge increases its usefulness. For example, the wide use (and misuse) of statistical methods is a result of the availability of computers and good software that makes it easy for the user to apply statistics. A similar mechanism has helped diffuse methods of mathematical programming. It has been noted that both processes and personnel are involved in the application of knowledge in an organization. Knowledge will probably not become useful if the adopters feel threatened with a loss of employment or if they believe that they either cannot or will not be allowed to use it. For example, organizational design rearranges the power and authority relationships. Unless the CEO is behind the project, the application of this knowledge will probably not occur. My firm once had a bank holding company as a potential client, and our initial contact was with a staff vice-president who was in charge of organizational design. After volunteering the judgment that our methods were far superior to hers, she then concluded that if her bank made our knowledge useful, she would be out of a job. Not being a fool, she made it her task to block adoption. After over six years, we have *never* been successful in making our knowledge useful to a corporation when we tried to work up from a staff person to the CEO.

The Production of Useful Knowledge Is a Research Process

Knowledge is considered *strange* by an organization to the degree it is not recognized as solving a real problem.

Strange knowledge is not useful to an organization.

The production of useful knowledge for an organization is a research process to make it less strange.

The research process for producing useful knowledge is not different from the research process for producing knowledge.

One of the greatest shocks felt by "the ultimate academic" was the growing realization that his knowledge was very strange to businesspeople. While it did not seem so strange to his students and a subset of his colleagues, the knowledge was very strange to his potential adopters in organizations. Before he had any clients for his knowledge, he tried to get adoption by explaining his theory. Businesspeople were usually polite when they said no. Such strange knowledge was simply not useful. I later found out that even colleagues are not persuaded by a rigorous argument. Repeated rejections spurred the research necessary to make his knowledge less strange. This research process has been very fruitful both in improving and extending the theory and in making it less strange. Currently, the underlying research knowledge is only alluded to. Referrals are far more persuasive.

ASSUMPTIONS ABOUT TASK PROCESSES IN A THEORY OF GROUP STRUCTURES

The development of a theory of group structures by this author began as his dissertation. This was followed by a long sequence of laboratory experiments designed to test and improve the theory. It was only in 1976 that this research was extended to organizational design. While some laboratory work did take place since 1976 (cf. Luzi and Mackenzie, 1982 and Mackenzie and Bello, 1981), the emphasis since 1976 has been organizational design. The summary of the laboratory-based theory can be found in a two-volume work (Mackenzie, 1976a,b) and the first tentative extensions to organizations in Lippitt and Mackenzie (1976) and in Mackenzie (1978). While it would be inappropriate here to summarize almost two decades of research into a theory of group structures, one can illustrate the role of assumptions by selecting the critical subtopic of task processes.

Task processes are central to this author's *A Theory of Group Structures*. They are important to managers. They are virtually ignored by most organizational research. The purpose here is to illustrate the role of research in exposing recognized and unrecognized assumptions in the development of useful knowledge.

The principal problem in a theory of group structures is to predict and explain structural change. Earlier work had clearly established that organizations have multiple structures and that these structures can and do change.

Aside from numerous mathematical and methodological issues, a key subproblem is to connect the various structures to the task processes engaged in by the group. In a nutshell, the dictum that "form follows function" becomes "structures follow the task processes." A structure is an interaction pattern among members of a group. The structures form as a method for doing task processes. There are multiple task processes because there are multiple structures.

The early laboratory research produced useful knowledge for more laboratory research. Later field work in designing organizations produced useful knowledge for organizations. However, that which was useful knowledge for laboratory research was generally not useful knowledge for organizations. But useful knowledge for organizations produced useful knowledge for laboratory research.

The 1964 dissertation contained a lot of ideas that sparked a long program of research, but it was deficient in the explication of theory. For example, the text is unclear about the assumptions made about task processes. It did, however, propose an elementary mathematical apparatus for examining task processes and structure, and it did apply it to both a laboratory investigation (Mackenzie and Barron, 1970) and some field work in word products markets (Mackenzie and Frazier, 1966; Mackenzie, 1969). Consequently, in light of what is now "known," there appears to have been ten implicit major assumptions about task processes:

A1. The environment determines the work done by an organization.

A2. Organizations perform work and the work determines its task processes.

A3. Task processes can be determined independently of the positions involved.

A4. Task processes, once known, are considered fixed.

A5. Task processes have levels.

A6. Relationships among task processes are fully describable by set theoretic combinations.

A7. Task processes define structures and role matrices.

A8. Each position is fully identified by its structure and row in the role matrix.

A9. Task processes are independent of the goals and strategies of the organization.

A10. Task processes do not have task resource characteristics.

About 1967, laboratory experiments showed that assumption A3 was incorrect. It was learned that structures and task processes were *jointly determined*—that is, changes in task processes caused changes in structures and changes in structures caused changes in task processes. These findings also invalidated assumption A4. In retrospect, A3 and A4 are naive, but they certainly simplified the research. A3 took further knocks as a safe assumption when experiments from 1967 to 1972 showed that the selection of a task process by a laboratory group is dependent upon both the incentives given to the group and other influence processes. By this time, simple task-completion processes had become extended to the task processes involved in exercising influence. In fact, a special calculus for how influence processes work was developed, called behavioral constitutions. Assumption A4 was rocked in 1971 when it became clear that there were supervisory task processes (directing, controlling, and coordinating) taking place that arose out of a combination of the existing structures and the selection of task processes by a group.

The failure of assumptions A3 and A4 lead to new theoretical work on the nature of task processes. By 1971 a system for describing task processes and structural change involving milestones and task process graphs was invented to resolve these failures. This work meant that A6 was no longer tenable. Elementary set theory was inadequate to the task of describing task processes. The description of task processes became more behavioral. This in turn sparked new theoretical work.

The first foray of the bench scientist to organizations occurred in 1975 when the author worked with Mary Lippitt Nichols on the committee system at the University of Kansas. This work (Lippitt, 1975; Lippitt and Mackenzie, 1976, 1979) further hammered A3. We discovered a phenomenon known as authority-task gaps and problems— that is, there were large discrepancies among the actual organizational structures and processes, the official ones, and those sanctioned by legal authority. This work marked the beginning of research into producing useful knowledge for organizations. Of course, it was not useful to organizations yet. Committees kept being formed and no attempts were even considered to reconcile the reasons for the authority-task gaps. However, because the theory for the existence and the consequences for the authority-task gaps could be specifically derived from *A Theory of Group Structures* and because the predictions were so accurate, this intermediate step between useful laboratory knowledge and useful organizational knowledge stimulated extensions to real organizations. The stage was set for a more systematic program of research to produce useful knowledge for organizations out of the useful knowledge produced for laboratory experiments.

The early pilot work with real organizations quickly shot down assumption A7. Direct consulting experiences by 1977 had demonstrated that the type of business (bank, restaurant, hotel) and the relationships among the personnel influence the selection of both task processes and structures. Thus, it was no longer safe to assume that task processes define structures and role matrices. This meant that the carefully constructed models and measures for organizational structures and the existing computer programs had to be changed. This meant that an investment of approximately $100,000 suddenly depreciated. This is an example of the high cost of tuition in the school of hard knocks.

The unravelling of the theory so useful for laboratory research continued in 1978 when assumption A1 failed. A1 assumes that the environment determines the work. Actually, real managers can select their environments to suit their work. The choice of goals and strategies can be seen as representing the selection both of an environment and the direction the firm intends to follow through it. One day while looking at very depressing financial results, the author redefined his firm as one that is national in scope rather than local. This basic redirection altered most of OSI's (Organizational Systems, Inc.) task processes. By selecting a new environment, the work was changed. This led to a theory of organizational congruencies (Mackenzie, 1982).

Later in 1978 assumption A8 fell. The old role matrix had to be modified to what is called an organizational responsibility grouping (ORG). With this change, it was no longer safe to assume that each position is fully described by its structures and row in the role matrix. The ORG was a major breakthrough because it transferred the search for embedded role sets by the positions to a generalization that embedded the task processes directly. For example, the persons performing a task was given a P (for Perform) in the relevant column of the ORG. But this person usually had a supervisor who was given an entry of S_1 (first level). It turns out that there is an $S_2, S_3, \ldots$ up to the board of directors. This improved the flexibility of the design process and allowed direct negotiation of changes on a task-by-task basis. This small change in format was actually already incorporated into the earlier procedures for defining a role matrix. The rejection of A8 allowed a very powerful tool (the ORG) to be developed that made the knowledge more useful. It also meant more freedom from the obsolete computer programs. The author had been sitting on this idea since 1970.

Assumption A5 then began to break down and become unsafe. That task processes had levels was recognized explicitly in 1964, but the nature of the levels began to change from combinatorial relationships to more behavioral ones. By this time algebras began to evolve for task processes. These purely theoretical research issues flowed out of problems in the production of useful knowledge. A new idea, called an Organizational Logic (see Mackenzie, 1981), was developed that gave elegance to the notion of levels. There were two types of levels: levels by inclusion and levels by the type of processes. For example, there were execution task processes; directing, controlling, and coordinating task processes; and change in processes (planning) task processes. There was leveling by a hierarchy consisting of a macrologic, areas, group, bundles, modules, and activities. The work of M. E. Bird

(1981) followed the evolution of organizational changes in a community bank over a two-year period. This study demonstrated the theoretical and practical importance of a more complete framework for task processes.

The research into the algebra of task processes led this year to the uncovering of a major assumption that was now unsafe. A10 assumes that task processes do not have task resource characteristics. This is clearly incorrect. In fact, the understanding of task processes had to extend from the purely logical relationships among task processes to a consideration of what resources were involved. This led to a rethinking of the concept of management and then to the development of new services that make our knowledge more useful to organizations (see Mackenzie, 1983).

The real world adventures of this bench scientist have demonstrated that his knowledge was incomplete. His knowledge involved assumptions, some recognized and most unrecognized, and these assumptions represented unsolved problems. He learned that some assumptions are safe in one context but not in another. The exposure of laboratory-based knowledge to real problems in organizations was helpful in both uncovering and correcting the assumptions. The most rapid unravelling of the assumptions occurred in the early phases of the experimental work and in the application to real organizations. Of the ten assumptions made in 1964, only A2 has survived—and even it is suspect. The other nine were shown to be unsafe.

THE PROBLEM AND SOURCES OF STRANGENESS

The number of activities in an organization is very large. Each of these requires some specialized knowledge. Consequently, one must expect different strategies for producing useful knowledge that depend upon the knowledge itself, the characteristics and processes of the specific organization, and its needs. Producing useful knowledge about tax liability involves different people and processes than those that produce useful knowledge about a production technology or advertising copy. Because this bench scientist has been producing knowledge about organizational structures and trying to produce useful knowledge for designing corporations to be more productive, he thought that a discussion of the problem and sources of strangeness might be informative.

The previous section described one aspect of the issue by examining the fate of ten assumptions about one aspect of these problems—the task processes. In this section, the issue of strangeness that inhibits the production of useful knowledge for organizations is discussed in the context of real world adventures in designing corporations to be more productive. It is hoped that the discussion of the successive unfolding of incorrect assumptions has given the impression that the evolution of a laboratory theory to actual organizational design has been a sustained research process. The main result of this research has been to reduce its strangeness.

Organizational researchers have always been interested in understanding how organizations work and in developing theories about these phenomena. Unfortunately, most organizational researchers do research on the research, research on the methods, research on aspects of the problems, surveys on various practices, and so on. Rarely do they do research in situ and rarely do they study organizations. Consequently, the literature and the theories produced are inherently strange to managers. The typical researcher is a desk-top scientist and not a bench scientist. Many of the desk-top researchers would enjoy actually doing organizational research, but they lack access and incentive.

Collectively, those in organizational research present a confused picture to managers. There are many little theories, many approaches, and little agreement. Taken as a whole, we produce strange knowledge among our own schools. The knowledge is so fragmented that it can be taught in at least ten departments within one university with little overlap in the production of knowledge. Despite our efforts, we lack a dominant paradigm and perhaps are at the same stage in the development of a science of organizations as were those studying the phenomenon of electricity at the time of Benjamin Franklin. Consequently, it is no surprise that managers find us producing strange knowledge.

But the production of useful knowledge for an organization is seen as a research process to make knowledge less strange. There are at least four ways an academic researcher in organizational behavior appears strange to managers.

First, academic researchers and managers typically do not speak the same dialect of English. We confuse our theoretical problems with their real problems. We usually start our work with the assumption that the client is wrong and we are right. We often approach their real problems as an instance to justify our prior conceptions. We look more to justify our theories, regardless of the practical consequences to the client, than to honestly seek to improve them. Academic researchers are strange and will remain so until they sincerely desire to be serious scientists. The normative and prescriptive stance of many prevents them from even seeing organizational phenomena.

We must start the research process of producing useful knowledge by first changing ourselves. In the organizational area, one should start with the assumption that the client is an expert about his business and organization. No matter how we may believe that his organization is a mess, needs our help, and would really benefit from our expertise, we should never underestimate the client's knowledge, tenacity, and cunning. This author refrains from offering advice until both he and the CEO agree that he understands the client's organization well enough to run it. We can advise on the process of our work long before we have such in-depth understanding, but we should refrain from advising on specific changes until we have a deeper understanding of the problems as seen by the CEO. That means we do our homework and learn to listen. For example, we spent over two man years learning about banks before we engaged in the organizational design of a bank. Experience shows that the first step in the research process in producing useful knowledge for organizations is to change ourselves so that we are less strange to our clients. It helps to take them more seriously and ourselves less seriously. Second, academic knowledge about organizations is strange. For the reasons cited earlier, we must assume that our knowledge is strange to our clients. Our theoretical categories, our models and theories, and so on are generally derived from reading books and journal articles, lecturing, casual empiricism, and experimental studies whose purposes are to improve theory rather than organizations. For example, this author was an expert in five-man groups solving simple problems in a short period of time. Confronting a supermarket chain with 4,000 employees, 11,000 activities, fierce competition, a truculent labor union, and confused goals and strategies is hardly the same as a five-man group of mostly placid sophomores.

Our focus on exceptions and our theories that reduce complexity to laws should help us know what questions to ask and how to assemble and integrate the data. However good our theories are, common sense should tell us that just as there is a wide gap between the laws of physics and the construction of an offshore drilling rig, so too must we be prepared to learn that our theories, by themselves, are limited. Knowing that $f = ma$ is simply not enough to design, build, and operate a drilling rig in the North Sea. A physicist who only understands analytical mechanics would appear to possess strange knowledge to the man in charge of the drilling rig project. But analytical mechanics is more solid a theory than a theory of group structures. We must accept the premise that our knowledge is suspect and incomplete. We do not have the benefits of several centuries of theoretical and engineering development. We do not have agreed-on standards for measurement. We lack the assurance that our clients have even been exposed to our theories. In fact, if one has been exposed to the theories or organizational behavior, he might be actively suspicious. Our knowledge is strange, indeed.

An example of strangeness in knowledge occurred while writing this chapter. The author's wife was putting on a large dinner party and called the author at his downtown office and asked him to pick up 60 wine glasses. His office is only two blocks away from the glass vendor, and it would be very convenient for him to pick up the glasses. Good idea. The problem was that he pedaled his bicycle to work. So the suggestion to pick up the 60 wine glasses and carry them home on a bicycle was very strange even though it was good "in theory." Third, our techniques for producing knowledge are strange to managers. Desk-top research on research done by others, on methods for doing research, and on speculative theories or syllogisms designed to encourage someone else to do research is very strange to managers. Managers are successful if they produce good results. Desk-top researchers are successful when they entice someone to publish their work. Metaresearch techniques are foreign to results-and-action-oriented managers. Criteria of elegance, cuteness, and controversy are scary to persons whose careers may be riding on the results of the application to their organization.

Bench science, a more humble approach, is typified by the experimental scientist. His orientation is to develop a theoretical controversy and then attempt to ascertain which alternative is less likely to be wrong by means of an experiment. Most managers are experimenters at heart. Every time they invest in a new project, change a policy, make a personnel decision, set a price, write an ad, and so on, they are essentially conducting an uncontrolled experiment. The real difference lies in the manager's need to bet on the more likely outcome rather than run an experiment to eliminate the less likely one. Another difference is that a manager's unsuccessful experiment has more serious consequences to the organization.

The decision to bring in an organizational researcher to produce useful knowledge for an organization is essentially another uncontrolled experiment. The manager responsible for allowing such an experiment is taking a big risk. It is in his interest for it to be successful. He is more likely to incur such a risk if the knowledge offered is not strange. The knowledge offered is in the form of a search procedure for applying it in an organization. Consequently, the research process itself becomes a source of strangeness.

There are at least two aspects of the research process of a bench scientist in the organizational area that create strangeness: rigidity and the length of time required. Most experimental work in the organizational behavior area is focussed more on the research methodology than the ideas being tested. A great deal of effort is made to plan the experiment in terms of the instruments, the experimental tasks, and on the procedures for analysis of the data. It reminds one of an offensive play in football. All of the players have been trained in a set routine that is executed when the play is called. The planning of the play and the execution of it become important determinants of its success. So the experimenter lines up his instruments, his assistants, the laboratory setting, the data-recording and data-processing methods before he runs the experiment. Just as every offensive play theoretically ends up with either a first down or a score, so too is each experiment supposed to result in a success. However, managers are more like soccer players. The game is fluid and opportunistic and changing. A research process that does not seem flexible and contingent is strange.

Along with the rigidity of most bench science, and often as a result, the length of time taken may be too long for a manager. The manager really needs a research process that yields results faster than the time taken for the problem to change. If one designates by T_A the time taken to find, formulate, solve, and implement the solution to a problem, and designates by T_C the time during which the problem is not likely to change, then the manager will insist that $T_A < T_C$. So will the researcher. But the researcher presumably is dealing with problems that are stable and have large values of T_C. Because of the chance of error and the possible loss of esteem should it be published, bench scientists work with data for a long time before announcing a tentative result. Our data methods are essentially "rear-view mirror" methods. The data have been collected; they are behind us and we will work with them, sometimes for years, before reaching conclusions we are willing to publish. Hence, our T_A is also large. But the manager must use "windshield" methods. He is looking to the future. The data are ahead of him and he must maneuver through the data while they are being collected. The problems are changing while he works on them. For him, T_C is often short. Hence, he needs methods for which T_A is shorter.

For example, the author was once an observer in the purchase of 3 million pounds of cheese by a shrewd dairy buyer for a large wholesaler.* Negotiations with the supplier led to a possibility of saving 9¢ per pound by changing the shape of a stick of cheese. The problems faced by the buyer were how much of 9¢ could he get from the supplier and would consumers buy the new size of cheese. The buyer was able to get a consumer panel done in two weeks. Imagine an academic researcher buying cheese and how long it would take him to do the research. Since cheese prices change weekly, T_A had to be very short because T_C was short. The same dairy buyer once heard that the price of soybean futures was on the rise at 6:00 a.m. Since soybean future prices are the prime determinant in the price of margarine, such a shift will mean a rise in margarine prices. By about 10:30 a.m. the dairy buyer had verified the rumor (and not by statistical reasoning) by calling a few trusted insiders, had ordered 50 carloads of margarine at the current price, and had arranged their distribution throughout divisions across the United States. Can one even imagine an academic moving that fast with his research methods?

Organizational design work also can move very fast, and so the research methods must be changed if the researcher ever hopes to have $T_A < T_C$. To this author, organizational design is analogous to repairing a moving truck. The desideratum that $T_A < T_C$ has profound consequences on the research process for producing useful knowledge for organizations.

A fourth type of strangeness associated with a bench scientist attempting

---

*Robert S. Goodale, formerly director of dairy for Fleming Foods and currently senior vice-president of sales and merchandising at Harris-Teeter Supermarkets, Inc.

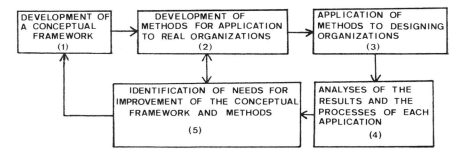

FIGURE 6.1. A Strategy for Development of Useful Knowledge for Organizations

to produce useful knowledge is the concept of an application of his knowledge. To the typical bench scientist, an application means that it could either be done in principle or if it were done it would yield data confirming his hypothesis. The manager, understandably, is less interested in the confirmation of a hypothesis in another world than he is in making a decision that benefits himself and the organization. For example, a banker undergoing an organizational design to improve productivity of his bank has to be worried more about the implementation of the changes and results than in whether or not the changes are verifications of a theory of group structures.

A STRATEGY FOR PRODUCING USEFUL KNOWLEDGE

The basic strategy is to view every organizational project as an experiment in the development of a theory. This strategy has five parts:

Develop the conceptual framework.
Develop methods for applications to actual organizations.
Apply these methods to an actual organization.
Analyze the results and processes in each application.
Identify needs for improving the conceptual framework and methods.

Figure 6.1 illustrates this strategy and the linkages among the five components.

This strategy is not dissimilar from normal bench research except that real organizations have replaced laboratory groups. The intention of the strategy is development of a new paradigm about a theory of group structures following the method described by Mackenzie and House (1978). Theory and its application are seen as mutually reinforcing processes. While it seems reasonable for organization theorists to study real organizations, examples of this are rare in the research literature. The benefits from the experience of producing useful knowledge in the development of theory are immense. This point has been made in other contexts (Sahal, 1981; Hersen and Barlow, 1976; Willems and Raush, 1969).

PROGRESS IN THEORY DEVELOPMENT

The various fields involved with organizational behavior and human resources management resemble Balkan states. The many fields and subfields have their own research agenda, power structure, research publications, curricula, and claims on public and private resources. Each of the separate schools comes complete with assumptions, methodologies, and public postures of rectitude and relevance.

The rigors of producing useful knowledge force one to discard the assumptions and stances of these contending factions. It is like riding in a balloon over thermal currents. As one rises the boundaries of the states become blurred and unimportant. Real problems must be solved. Techniques and ideas are combined. One acquires a new perspective as different types of knowledge become linked into a new network of theory. The process of producing useful knowledge across organizations becomes a research process that is cumulative and requires a continual effort to link new types of knowledge into the old and to rearrange the existing network to improve its logical coherence. While the process of producing useful knowledge is very similar to producing knowledge, the exciting feature is the loss of control of one's assumptions. The main problem with research within a narrow paradigm or within a specialized field is that one controls the definition of what is a safe assumption. The loss of control over the assumptions would eventually occur in laboratory research, but the process of producing useful knowledge speeds this up. This is especially true given the long lead time on publication and the low interest in the work in other schools. Facing the need for rejecting an old assumption is exhilarating to a theoretician because every time he can discard an assumption, he is making progress.

This chapter previously described how successive research caused most of the ten original assumptions about task processes to fail. These failures represent progress, and such theoretical molting is desirable. While there may be those who know they have the truth, the approach here is the more sensible one of acting on the belief that one's theory has flaws. The object then is to find flaws, correct them, and then rebuild the theory.

Table 6.1 is a quantitative summary of the progress of the author's research in producing useful knowledge for organizations since the founding of OSI. Rather than state the theories, since we are discussing producing useful knowledge, it seems more appropriate to enumerate the growth

TABLE 6.1. Service Growth at OSI

Year	1976	1977	1978	1979	1980	1981	1982
Number of Services	4	6	6	7	16	26	42

number of the four services available since OSI was founded in 1976 to the 42 that exist at the present time.

A service is a body of knowledge that has become useful to a client by application in a real organization to solve real organizational problems. Each service has distinct characteristics and methodologies. For example, the organizational audit has its own techniques, computer programs, and theory to support it. The service of career planning has its own technology and theory. Each of the services is linked back to the theory of group structures.

The growth of services in 1976 and 1977 was based on the direct conversion of laboratory methods. Since then, a combination of client problems and available R & D funds from consulting has sped the development of new services. Over the years the clients have grown in size and sophistication of services required. The development of services generally follows the need by clients for useful information, and the revenues generated permit further refinements and new developments. The process of developing useful knowledge has clearly been assisted by the capability of doing so. There are a number of new services being developed at the present time, including: strategic assessment programs, more software for existing services, financial and strategic planning packages, new methods for performance evaluation, linking of financial data and the organizational processes, computer graphics of structural information, and organizational positioning charts.

CONCLUSION

This chapter focussed more on the lessons learned and some of the processes for producing useful knowledge than it did on the adventures of a bench scientist. It did not describe the failures, rejections, dashed hopes, and foolish decisions that were made and are probably still being made. It also did not describe the great pleasure in a few hard-won successes and in the many people who have trusted this bench scientist with their futures. These many experiments have forced personal growth. They have also allowed a laboratory theory to become useful knowledge for organizations. The long process has changed the bench scientist and his theories.

The principal lesson learned is that the process of producing useful knowledge is essentially the same as producing knowledge. It is done in a different context where one loses control over safe assumptions and it is done for much greater stakes. It is a research process to make oneself and one's ideas less strange. Like all worthwhile research processes, it feeds on itself. Growth and change beget growth and change in ever-widening circles. It is challenging, fun, and exciting. It is also very hard work. It means giving.

Probably the greatest barrier for most academics in producing useful knowledge for organizations lies in themselves. The general desire, with a few notable exceptions, is to extract resources from their environment. As undergraduates they received scholarships. As graduate students they received fellowships. As faculty they seek grants. The production of useful knowledge requires the attitude of giving and serving others. The more you give, the more you receive. The more you care for the persons and organizations you produce knowledge for, the more they care about you and your knowledge.

REFERENCES

Bird, M. E., A Theory of Work: Application in a Community Bank. Ph.D. Dissertation, University of Kansas, 1981.

Churchman, C. W., *Prediction and Optional Decision: Philosophical Issues of a Science of Values.* Englewood Cliffs, NJ: Prentice-Hall, 1961.

Churchman, C. W., *Challenge to Reason.* New York, NY: McGraw-Hill, 1968.

Churchman, C. W., *The Design of Inquiring Systems.* New York, NY: Basic Books, 1971.

Hersen, M., and Barlow, J. H., *Single Case Experimental Designs: Strategies for Studying Behavior Change,* New York, NY: Pergamon Press, 1976.

Kilmann, R. H., "Problem Management: A Behavioral Science Approach," in *Management Principles for Non Profit Agencies and Organizations* (G. Zaltman, Ed.). New York, NY: AMACOM, 1979.

Kilmann, R. H., "A Dialectical Approach to Formulating and Testing Social Science Theories: Assumptional Analysis, *Human Relations,* 1982 (in press).

Lippitt, M. E., Development of a Theory of Committee Formation. Ph.D. Dissertation. University of Kansas, 1975.

Lippitt, M. E., and Mackenzie, K. D., "Authority-Task Problems," *Administrative Science Quarterly,* 1976, *21,* No. 4, pp. 643–660.

Lippitt, M. E., and Mackenzie, K. D., "A Theory of Committee Formation," in *Communication and Control in Social Processes* (K. Krippendorff, Ed.). New York, NY: Gordon and Breach Science Publishers, 1979, pp. 389–405.

Luzi, A., and Mackenzie, K. D., "An Experimental Study of Performance Information Systems," *Management Science,* 1982, *28,* No. 3, pp. 243–259.

Mackenzie, K. D., A Mathematical Theory of Organizational Structures. Ph.D. Dissertation, University of California (Berkeley), 1964.

Mackenzie, K. D., "The Structure of a Market," in *Management Science in Planning and*

Control (J. Blood, Jr., Ed.). New York, NY: TAPPI STAP No. 5, 1969, pp. 167–216.

Mackenzie, K. D., *A Theory of Group Structures, Volume I: Basic Theory*, New York, N.Y.: Gordon and Breach Science Publishers, 1976a.

Mackenzie, K. D., *A Theory of Group Structures, Vol. II: Empirical Tests*, New York, NY: Gordon and Breach Science Publishers, 1976b.

Mackenzie, K. D., *Organizational Structures*. Arlington Heights, Ill.: AHM Publishing Company, 1978.

Mackenzie, K. D., "Concepts and Measurements in Organizational Development," in *Dimensions of Productivity Research, Vol. 1* (John D. Hogan and A. Craig, Eds.). Houston, Texas: American Productivity Center, 1981, pp. 233–304.

Mackenzie, K. D., "Organizational Congruency Tests," *Journal of Enterprise Management*, 1982, *3*, No. 3.

Mackenzie, K. D., "Organizational Structures as the Primal Information System: An Interpretation." in *Management of Office Information Systems* (S. K. Chang, Ed.), New York, NY: Plenum, 1983.

Mackenzie, K. D., and Barron, F. H., "An Analysis of a Decision Making Investigation," *Management Science*, 1970, *17*, No. 4, pp. B224–B241.

Mackenzie, K. D., and Bello, J. A., "Leadership as a Task Process Uncertainty Control Process," *Human Systems Management*, 1981, *2*, No. 3, pp. 199–213.

Mackenzie, K. D., and Frazier, G. D., "Applying a Model of Organization Structure to the Analysis of a Wood Products Market," *Management Science*, 1966, *12*, pp. 340–352.

Mackenzie, K. D., and House R. J., "Paradigm Development in the Social Sciences: A Proposed Research Strategy," *Academy of Management Review*, 1978, *3*, No. 1, pp. 7–23.

Mason, R. O., "A Dialectical Approach to Strategic Planning," *Management Science*, 1969, *15*, pp. B403–B413.

Mason, R. O., and Mitroff, I. I., "A Program for Research on Management Information Systems," *Management Science*, 1973, *19*, pp. 475–487.

Mitroff, I. I., and Emshoff, J., "On Strategic Assumption-Making: A Dialectical Approach to Policy and Planning," *Academy of Management Review*, 1979, *4*, pp. 1–12.

Mitroff, I. I., Emshoff, J., and Kilmann, R. H., "Assumptional Analysis: A Methodology for Strategic Problem Solving," *Management Science*, 1979, *25*, pp. 583–593.

Rogers, E. M., and Shoemaker, F. F., *Communications of Innovations: A Cross Cultural Approach* (2nd Ed.). New York, NY: Free Press, 1971.

Saaty, T. L., *The Analytical Hierarchy Process: Planning, Priority Setting, Resource Allocation*. New York, NY: McGraw-Hill, 1980.

Sahal, D., *Patterns of Technological Innovation*. Reading, Mass.: Addison-Wesley, 1981.

Willems, E. P., and Raush, H. L., (Eds.), *Naturalistic Viewpoints in Psychological Research*. New York, NY: Holt, Rinehart and Winston, 1969.

PART 1

GENERAL PERSPECTIVES FROM THE TWO COMMUNITIES

Section B:
The Practitioner Perspective

7

CULTURE: THE OFTEN IGNORED FACTOR IN KNOWLEDGE UTILIZATION

Roy Serpa

During the past 35 years, corporate managers have not faced a greater challenge than they confront today: the need for improved organizational performance. The traditional managerial styles and organizational techniques emphasizing control and the downward flow of influence and direction are not working any more. Throughout U.S. industry the search is on for new methods to increase productivity. Top executives are recognizing that achieving success in goal-directed effectiveness is critical to the survival of their companies during the 1980s. To survive, many corporations will require the institution of major organizational development programs. In order for these programs to be implemented successfully, the corporate cultures of many companies must be evaluated and changed. Culture, the often ignored factor in the past, will be a key to knowledge utilization in the future. The need and the opportunity for managers and managerial scholars to contribute jointly to strengthening our free enterprise system by introducing knowledge to our corporations have never been greater. Their ability to understand corporate culture and to facilitate cultural change will determine to a great extent the level of knowledge utilization that will be achieved.

ANTICIPATED CHANGES

More than 20 years ago, Rensis Likert anticipated the following changes that he believed would require new organizational designs:

Increased competition from foreign countries with equal technology but relatively lower costs.

A trend in U.S. society toward greater individual freedom and initiative and, therefore, a need for less supervision.

A higher level of education resulting in increased expectations as to the amount of responsibility, authority, and income to be received.

An increasing concern about mental health and the growth of the individual.

The advent of increasingly complex technologies requiring expertise beyond the ability of any one person to comprehend. Consequently, there is a much greater need for cooperation and participation in managing subordinates who possess a greater knowledge of their specialty than their supervisor.[1]

These changes have occurred. They are among the critical issues challenging managers today. Our inability to cope with them is reflected to some extent by:

The loss of technological leadership by many U.S. industries.

A lack of loyalty and dedication on the part of a substantial number of U.S. workers.

The elimination of hundreds of thousands of jobs in the industrial sector.

A prolonged economic recession.

A bankruptcy rate among U.S. companies during the first six months of 1982 that exceeded the entire year of 1981.

Likert proposed what he called System 4 to enable organizations to be productive and profitable in this new environment.[2] The new environment has arrived and unfortunately few firms heeded Likert's warning. If System 4 were operating in many U.S. firms today, the current preoccupation with the Japanese style of management would not be as prevalent in the popular U.S. business press. Likert recommended communications, interactive, and control processes similar to those of the so-called Japanese style. Although most corporate managers have heard and perhaps read about the Japanese methods, how many have heard and taken advantage of the advice given by Likert and other managerial scholars?

Over the past 25 years, Peter Drucker, George Steiner, Chris Argyris, Douglas McGregor, and Frederick Herzberg have joined Likert and others to provide U.S. managers with excellent guidance and advice. Their presentations have been well received, and their books have been widely read and often quoted. Yet, when it comes to the implementation of their concepts and principles, how receptive have managerial practitioners been? How often have their proposed concepts been applied with conviction and continuity?

CAUSES OF RESISTANCE

The lack of receptivity to and implementation of the managerial technology developed during the past three decades has been, at least partially, the result of three major conditions:

A reward system that motivates managers to focus their efforts primarily on short-term financial performance.

A predominance of the theory X management style within U.S. industry.[3]

A lack of initiative on the part of management scholars to pursue strategies that will transfer their concepts and principles into practice.

Two of these conditions can be viewed as consequences of three interrelated cultures that exist within our free enterprise system: the industrial culture, the corporate culture, and the subordinate or group culture. The industrial culture encompasses all corporations within the U.S. free enterprise system. It is shaped by our position within the world economy and our governmental and regulatory environment, as indicated in Figure 7.1. The industrial culture influences each individual corporate culture. Each corporate culture is a product of its unique values, beliefs, and norms of behavior. Within each corporate culture exist subordinate cultures possessing distinctive characteristics. The subcultures are directly affected by the organizational culture and indirectly by the industrial culture. There is continual interaction among these related but distinct cultural entities.

The industrial culture in our country continues to place emphasis, for the most part, upon short-term problems and solutions, while new knowledge such as organizational development requires time and patience in order to become effective. Wendell French addressed this issue when he stated: "Successful organization development tends to be a total system effort; a process of planned change—not a program with a temporary quality; and aimed at developing the organization's internal resources for effective change in the future." However, most reward systems in our industrial culture are geared to short-term financial results; therefore, managers often neglect preparing today's business for the future. Part of this preparation must include organizational development as well as the application of other managerial knowledge, if improved performance is to be achieved over the long run.

The traditional style of management, which has been described as theory X, continues to be a strong influence within our industrial culture despite erroneous perceptions that theory Y (participative management) has become the norm.[4] As our economy grew rapidly after World War II and our

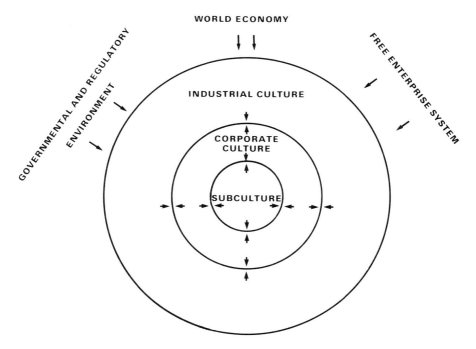

FIGURE 7.1. Cultural Spheres

companies benefited from this growth, there was little pressure for significant cultural change in spite of growing problems in effectiveness and efficiency. These problems, which were ignored or camouflaged by the prosperous environment of the past, are now emerging with a devastating impact upon our economic system.

The U.S. economic system is experiencing a legacy of ignoring the trends anticipated by Likert coupled with the resistance to creating corporate cultures that are adaptable and participative. As foreign competitive pressures increased and work processes became more complex, many corporations employed short-term "Band-Aid" type solutions. The classical approaches of reward, punishment, control, and top-down management continued as the norms in U.S. industry. A few enlightened companies have taken participative management seriously as a method to cope successfully with rapid and complex changes. Unfortunately, these companies were and are in the minority.

In 1971 Peter Drucker was asked if he thought corporations were headed in the direction of participation in management.[5] His answer was "Hell, no." He saw organizations remaining essentially autocratic. His perception continues to be accurate as we move through the 1980s. This autocracy and the short-term focus of U.S. managers have contributed to the suppression of useful managerial knowledge.

Rather than encouraging open communications, candid dialogue, and problem solving among employees, many managers continue to rely on obsolete policies and procedures to deal with critical, rapidly evolving challenges to their businesses. The expertise that exists at the lower levels of our corporations continues to be stifled by the autocratic position power existing at higher levels.

There is a perception that for knowledge to be used it must be managed from the top of an organization. This factor in itself is a testimony to the predominance of the theory X management style. It also implies that top management has defined the need for such knowledge. Yet in many cases a more accurate definition of problems can occur at the lower levels of the corporate hierarchy. Often the solutions can be conceived there also. When the participation of lower-level personnel is not considered, a situation can develop in which solutions to the wrong problems are introduced with resultant failure guaranteed. Experiences of this type discourage further initiatives by managers in considering and applying knowledge.

CULTURAL CHANGE

A reversal of the autocratic management style and the short-term focus will require major changes in industrial, corporate, and group cultures, and will therefore present a stiff challenge to practicing managers and managerial scholars. Without these cultural changes there will be limited knowledge utilization and performance improvement. Cultural issues must be recognized, confronted, and managed.

The National Science Foundation recently funded a study by the National Academy of Engineering. This study states: "In the case of productivity, product quality and the role of the work force, we are talking about something close to a cultural revolution, about fundamental changes in the way the business is managed and the ways people at all levels participate in the enterprise."

In discussing the Japanese management style, William H. Franklin, Jr., states "that successful, highly productive organizations are a cultural phenomenon; they give form and expression to what motivates the people and groups that work in them."[6]

Anthropologist Clyde Kluckhohn had defined culture as "the set of habitual and traditional ways of thinking, feeling, and reacting that are characteristic of the ways a particular society meets its problems at a particular point in time." The substitution of corporation for society in

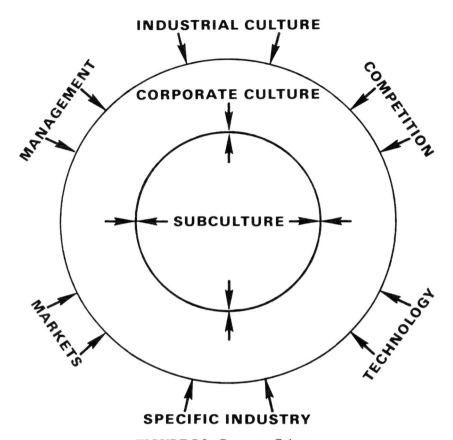

FIGURE 7.2. Corporate Cultures

Kluckhohn's definition is one approach to identifying corporate culture. In *The Competence Process*, Jay Hall defines corporate culture as "a fundamental character or spirit—which is revealed in a prevailing system of values, beliefs about the importance and basic nature of people, and norms of authority and influence."[7] Edwin L. Baker of McKinsey & Co. calls it, very simply, "the social glue holding a company together."[8]

This social glue has evolved over time and has been shaped by internal as well as external factors. The industrial culture, the specific industry, competition, technology, markets, and the style of past and present management all influence the individual corporate culture (see Figure 7.2). It is in a constant state of evolution, just as societal cultures adjust to the environment and to human influence. James L. Hayes, chairman of the American Management Association, has provided the following insight: "If it were possible to freeze an organization on a given day, we could identify the various management beliefs, theories, and practices to which its managers subscribe but changes would begin to occur the very next day."[9]

Certain traditional values, beliefs, and norms of behavior are difficult to change. However, a healthy organizational culture is supportive of adaptability, particularly when it comes to the traditional factors motivating behavior. A likely example of a healthy cultural response is unfolding at Texas Instruments. T.I. has been cited many times as a case history of a corporation that has fostered a culture that possesses the capability to undergo strategic change.[10] The challenges of the 1980s caught up with T.I., and now it appears that a major change in culture is underway.[11,12] If T.I. possesses a healthy culture, it will readily adapt to change. If not, it may well be that the weaknesses of T.I.'s culture were camouflaged by the prosperous economy of the 1970s.

The subordinate or group culture that exists within a corporation is molded by its management, function, discipline, work process, and relationships with other subcultures as well as the corporate culture (see Figure 7.3).

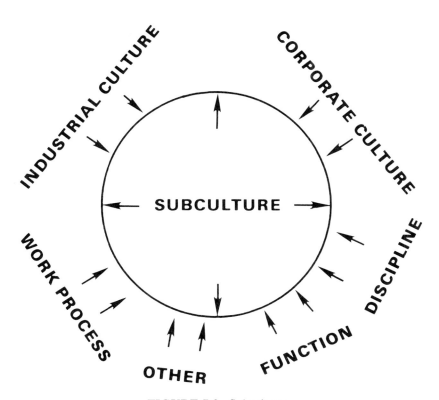

FIGURE 7.3. Subcultures

P. Singh of the Administrative Staff College of India contends that group culture is a powerful force in determining individual behavior.[13] However, from his studies on group problem solving in several Indian companies, he concludes that a group problem-solving culture will not be accepted in an organizational culture where an autocratic decision-making style is prevalent. He goes on to state that effective group problem solving can be achieved only if a supportive organizational culture is created.

In the application of new managerial concepts and techniques, just as in problem solving, the organizational culture is the key factor due to its predominant influence upon behavior. The group culture can facilitate or retard knowledge utilization, but because of its subordinate and subcomponent nature it is a secondary factor.

CULTURE IGNORED

The existence of corporate culture is often ignored when knowledge is introduced to corporations by managerial scholars. Due to the unwritten, intangible nature of each corporate culture, it is difficult for outsiders to define and to understand. Frequently, concepts and principles are proposed as universal prescriptions for organizational needs with the implicit assumption that all corporate cultures are alike and that validity insures applicability. Even a healthy culture, one that supports change, requires an intervention tailored to its individual cultural character. The fact that each corporation possesses a unique culture is especially relevant to organizational development, since most O.D. efforts are aimed directly at changing values, beliefs, and norms. The traditional cultural influences of a corporation must be identified and understood before modification can be accomplished. Scholars must make a special effort to understand the unique cultural phenomena within individual corporations. New concepts must be considered in a cultural context rather than in isolation. Concurrent modification of both culture and concept may be necessary to achieve successful knowledge utilization.

Too many of our corporations have allowed their cultures to deteriorate and to sustain the behavior of the past in spite of the critical need for change and new knowledge to maintain viability in the 1980s. These sick cultures are characterized by resistance to change, inadequate communications, lack of candor, resentment of criticism, and a completely task-oriented predilection. In a sick culture there is a reluctance to allow criticism from within as well as without. Criticism of existing practices and the suggestion of new concepts and principles are perceived as threatening and destructive. Such cultures may also lack pride in performance, discipline, and delegation of authority.

A healthy culture is receptive to knowledge and will support change. It will adapt to the needs of both the external and internal environment. It is eager to meet the challenges of the free enterprise system, not only to survive but to prosper, to strengthen its resources, and to eliminate its obsolete, nonproductive components. A healthy culture is one of pride and discipline. Employees are considered an investment and an asset—a creative resource. The July 5, 1982 issue of *Forbes* magazine described Lincoln Electric as a model of extraordinary productivity. It is not a coincidence that Lincoln Electric possesses many of the foregoing cultural attributes.

THE CHALLENGE

Derm Barrett states that "productivity and innovation require a special culture which, if non-existing, must be created and evolved." He proposes a new corporate culture with a higher level of awareness, curiosity, intelligence, thought, and imagination, which will nourish productivity.[14]

The productivity and performance crisis will persist well into the 1980s and will encourage practitioners to become more receptive to managerial principles, methods, and techniques ignored in the past. As our corporations move through the 1980s, there will be a growing awareness in the U.S. management community that significant changes in corporate cultures will be necessary. An indication of this growing awareness at the executive level within some large corporations is revealed in a recent statement made by Edward L. Hennessey, Jr., CEO at Allied Corporation. He intends to create "a new culture where there is freedom to fail without reprisal if the idea, suggestion, or project doesn't work." In addition, he has tied the reward system (bonuses) directly to clearly defined objectives with a five-year time period.[15]

The challenge to managerial scholars to contribute to healthy corporate cultural change is great. However, there will always be elements of resistance that will block knowledge utilization, particularly in an unhealthy culture. A common obstacle will be subculture managers who will support cultural change publicly while privately withholding resources needed for progress. Reluctance to change will occur because traditional values, beliefs, and norms of behavior have been the proven source of strength in the past and are thought to be adequate to meet the challenge of the present and the future. Some managers will feel threatened by cultural change since they have been comfortable in the traditional culture within their corporations. Others will be receptive but not patient enough to take the time to allow cultural change to be accomplished. In either case, the application of knowledge will be facilitated by assessing the corporate culture, defining what the new culture should be, and gradually moving toward the new culture with the assistance of those managers who are receptive to cultural change.[16]

An excellent example of how a corporate culture can be shaped by knowledge utilization exists at American General Corporation. Harold Hook, the CEO, has implemented a system called Model-Netics, which he designed in the 1960s to communicate his management experience. This system uses 151 symbols and catchwords and has been taught to two-thirds of American General's 9,000 employees. An executive at another insurance company recently commented that he did not believe in the system at first. However, he went on to say, Hook has "a whole army that thinks that way, and it works."[17]

THE THIRD CONDITION

If our free enterprise system is to become more productive, scholars and practitioners must direct their attention and efforts toward cultural change. It will be necessary for scholars to take the initiative to pursue strategies that will transfer their concepts and principles into practice. They must not assume that if there is a need for change that new models and methods will be warmly received and implemented with dedication. This is a rational expectation, but corporations and individual managers are greatly influenced by the existing industrial and corporate cultural values, beliefs, and norms. Change does not occur unless the organizational culture is motivated and prepared to change. Each culture must be understood before an environment can be created that will facilitate this motivation and preparedness.

Scholars must heed the statement by J. W. McGuire of the University of California: "The development of management theories that are helpful to managers, and that will improve the practice of management, should be more than an esoteric game played for purposes of promotion in academic careers."[18] Scholars must end the situation in which the majority of the business school academic community continues to be estranged from the mainstream of the practicing management community.[19]

To end this estrangement and to effect knowledge utilization, there are several initiatives that academics may consider:

Differentiating between the type and process of communication with practitioners and with academic peers and students.

Writing for and speaking to practitioners more frequently.

Identifying the problems and needs of our corporations and then developing concepts and principles to solve and satisfy them.

Anticipating obstacles to knowledge utilization and creating techniques to overcome them.

Seeking out practitioners who are receptive to new managerial knowledge to collaborate on presentations, publications, and research projects.

Developing information concerning the cultural contexts in which specific knowledge can be applied.

Assessing each corporate culture before intervention.

Dr. Edward Deming, the man who revolutionized industry in Japan, recently said of the United States, "Management has failed in this country." He believes we are not going to make it. Although time is running out, we can and must reverse the unfavorable trend in managerial performance and organizational productivity. The true test of our ability to modify the U.S. management style and to develop healthy corporate cultures is at hand. Academics and practitioners must join together to change our corporate and industrial cultures so that knowledge can be successfully utilized.

NOTES

1. R. Lickert, *New Patterns of Management* (New York: McGraw-Hill, 1961), pp. 1–3.

2. R. Lickert, *The Human Organization* (New York: McGraw-Hill, 1967).

3. D. MacGregor, *The Human Side of Enterprise* (New York: McGraw-Hill, 1960).

4. R. W. Bauer, "How to Make OD Work Better for Your Organization," *Management Review*, June 1982, pp. 56–61.

5. T. J. Murray, "Our Top-Heavy Corporations," *Dunn's*, April 1971, pp. 38–41.

6. William H. Franklin, Jr., "What Japanese Managers Know that American Managers Don't," *Administrative Management*, September 1981, pp. 36–39.

7. J. Hall, *The Competence Process* (Woodlands, Texas: Teleometrics, 1980), p. 72.

8. E. L. Baker, "Managing Organizational Culture," *Management Review*, July 1980, pp. 8–13.

9. L. Hayes, "The Excitement of Management," *Management Review*, October 1981, pp. 2–3.

10. "Texas Instruments Shows U.S. Business How to Survive in the 1980's," *Business Week*, September 18, 1978, pp. 66–92.

11. "An About-Face in T.I.'s Culture," *Business Week*, July 1982, p. 77.

12. B. Uttal, "Texas Instruments Regroups," *Fortune*, August 9, 1982, pp. 40–45.

13. P. Singh, "Group Problem-Solving: Pains And Pleasures," *Administration Staff College of India Journal of Management*, March 1981, pp. 71–96.

14. F. D. Barrett, "Productivity Programs: Nurturing the Climate for Creativity and Innovation," *Business Quarterly*, Autumn 1981, pp. 55–62.

15. "The Hennessy Style May Be What Allied Needs," *Business Week*, January 1982, pp. 126–127, 129.

16. H. Schwartz and S. M. Davis, "Matching Corporate Culture and Business Strategy," *Management Analysis Center's Concept-Paper Series*, 1981.

17. A. C. Brown, "The Profitable Pariah of Insurance," *Fortune*, August 1982, pp. 60–63.

18. J. W. McGuire, "Management Glory: Retreat to the Academy," *Business Horizons*, July–August 1982, pp. 31–37.

19. R. L. Hilgert, "Business Schools Fail to Communicate with Managers," *Business Horizons*, December 1972, pp. 59–63.

REFERENCES

Batten, Joe D. *Tough-Minded Management*, New York: Amacom, 1978.

Beckhard, R. *Organization Development–Strategies and Models*, Cambridge, Mass.: Addison-Wesley, 1969.

Deal, Terrence E., and Kennedy, Allen A. *Corporate Cultures*, Reading, Mass.: Addison-Wesley, 1982.

Gibson, James L., et al. *Organizations, Structure, Processes Behavior*, Dallas: Business Publications, 1973.

Hampton, David R., et al. *Organizational Behavior and the Practice of Management, Revised*, Glenview, Ill.: Scott Foresman, 1973.

Margulies, Newton, and Raia, Anthony P. *Organization Development: Values, Process and Technology*, New York: McGraw-Hill, 1972.

Michael, Stephen R., et al. *Techniques of Organizational Change*, New York: McGraw-Hill, 1981.

8

INTRODUCING CHANGE IN ORGANIZATIONS: MOVING FROM GENERAL THEORIES OF CONTENT TO SPECIFIC THEORIES OF CONTEXT

Peter F. Mathias

The past few years have been a time of significant change and agonizing reappraisal for many large corporations. It is difficult to read the business press without coming across frequent descriptions of plant shutdowns, widespread layoffs, and renegotiations of major labor contracts. Important sectors of our economy and some regions of the country are facing intense economic pressure. The slow economic growth and strong foreign competition have put U.S. management on trial.

Out of these circumstances has come a realization that the human side of the management equation has not been accorded as much attention and importance in the United States as it has received in some of our economic competitors, particularly Japan. The response to this deficiency has been a variety of corporate programs geared toward improving the effectiveness of management and people. Some of these programs have been well received. They include quality of work life, productivity programs, and organizational restructuring to reduce the number of levels in large corporations. This emphasis on the human element provides an opportunity for management researchers and management theorists to shape the agenda and guide the decisions of large corporations in this area. Unfortunately, management theories and management researchers have not been as effective as they could. This is a missed opportunity. Managers in industry have not benefited to the extent possible from the many insights of social scientists. While academics and researchers have missed out on a opportunity to test and refine their theories in the marketplace of ideas and practice. Needless to say, this will have a negative impact on the education of future managers in our business schools.

I believe that there are two basic sets of reasons for this gap: differences in beliefs, attitudes, and orientation between practitioners and researchers;

and differences between the needs of managers and the objectives of management theorists. This chapter describes my views and observations, based upon my experiences in applying research toward changing management practice in the business world. It attempts to: describe why the interaction between managers and management researchers has not been more productive: develop a set of concepts to understand better the difficulties of this interface; and propose some steps to improve the effectiveness of this interface between researchers and practitioners.

DIFFERENCES IN BELIEFS, ATTITUDES, AND ORIENTATION

I have been surprised by the differences between practitioners and academics in approaching a similar problem. These differences in attitudes and orientation are an important component of the problems and difficulties that managers and researchers have in interacting with each other. Both communities often look at the same data about a phenomenon, but then ask different questions, arrive at different answers, and have an entirely different set of priorities in proposing solutions. I have attempted to summarize these differences into five categories. These categories are to some extent oversimplifications as there is no one way in which all managers and all researchers approach a problem. The categories are designed to be illustrative and highlight the differences between the two communities. These differences are:

Managers often approach problems through thinking by analogy, whereas researchers are prone to specification, quantification, and model building.

Managers believe and accept the test of the marketplace, whereas researchers are more concerned about the fit with literature and research.

Managers, of course, are concerned with the practice of management, improvement in organization performance, and the management of change, whereas researchers are concerned with communicating with social scientists.

Implementation of a concept or program is critical to a manager's thinking, whereas researchers are concerned only with "application" of theories.

Managers are concerned with utility in any framework that they use, whereas academics and researchers are concerned with the rigor of construction.

Analogy versus Specification, Quantification, and Model Building

When senior managers face a complex and unstructured problem, they have a tendency to draw upon their own experiences where they were confronted with a similar type of problem. When there is no similar situation in their own experience base, they often consult the experience of other executives or other companies. It is for this reason that the business press—which carries numerous stories about companies coping with problems and seizing opportunities—has such an impact on the thinking of executives. These stories tend to provoke thinking and insight into executives' own situation, and often force executives to understand how the other company or the other executive defined the problem, what actions were taken, what were the circumstances surrounding the decision or action taken, and whether or not that action succeeded. At first glance, this may appear to be a somewhat undisciplined approach to important decisions and challenges. However, in my experience the use of analogies has been a powerful tool in dealing with unstructured, complex problems.

Many management researchers and academics I have worked with quite understandably approach the problem somewhat differently. Their first reaction is an attempt to conceptualize the problem in terms of the series of variables interacting with each other. In most cases, these variables are not easily understood by practitioners and are hence not perceived as being manageable or concrete. In many cases, these researchers prescribe the use of instruments and "technology" that seek to collect data on the variables that they have specified. This premature construction of models to describe a complex administrative situation results in losing sight of the manager and in oversimplifying the many complex, unstructured, and messy details of an administrative situation.

Test of the Marketplace versus Fit with Literature and Research

The fact that a program or an approach to a particular problem has been tried and has been found to be successful at another company is an important factor in gaining credibility with managers. Executives tend to have a greater respect for what has been tried elsewhere and shown to be effective than a program based on hypothesis or conjecture. A theory that has not been tested in the marketplace of ideas and practice has an unfinished quality to it with many rough edges. Most practitioners understand that there are significant differences between firms, but when something has worked in one company it provides a manager with hard data that can be helpful in understanding the totality of circumstances surrounding the use of that concept or theory and its implementation in the form of a program.

I have frequently asked researchers and academics for evidence that the particular program or concept that they espouse has been applied or tested at another company. I have been surprised by the number who have dismissed such questions as being irrelevant. It is far more important, I have been told, that the concept is consistent with a large body of literature and research in the social sciences. If I persist with the need for hard evidence, I have often been given articles that make superficial references to the application of this or that concept in a particular corporation. Upon closer examination, these applications are not at all what has been described in these articles. There is very little detail provided on why the concept was adopted, how the program was used, what problems were encountered in implementation, what were the results of this application, and the extent to which this resulted in significant and lasting change in the organization.

Improving the Practice of Management versus Orientation Toward the Social Science Community

The effective practice of management requires that managers communicate with other members of their organization in a clear, direct, and comprehensible manner. While there are some differences in the way in which language is used in different corporations and in different functions within a firm, most managers would have little difficulty in understanding other practitioners. On the other hand, management theorists have developed a jargon that is far removed from the world of the practitioner. This language, borrowed to a great extent from the social scientists, comes across to the practitioner as either forbidding or pretentious. The great majority of academic journals carry articles on business problems that most senior executives would find totally incomprehensible. The use of language associated with social scientists rather than with managers has created a significant gulf between practitioners and management researchers. This has had a negative effect both on the quality and relevance of theory developed by academics and the speed and effectiveness with which these theories have influenced practice.

Implementation versus Application of Theories

Managers seeking to make changes in the way in which the organization behaves are aware that this is a complex process. One has to be aware of how a new concept or program will be perceived by an organization's members, whether they will support change or resist it, and how one can get their commitment toward making the changes. There are many risks and pitfalls in managing such a complex process. Often the practitioner looks for help to those who have had a role in developing the concepts of the program. In my view, prior experience in managing the implementation of a concept or program is an important element in enhancing its total value.

When one looks to academics or researchers for such help in implementation, very little assistance is forthcoming. It seems that most researchers are far more interested in defining "the problem" and explaining the situation in terms that a social scientist would understand. Managing the complex and intricate processes associated with implementation and changing an organization's behavior are not considered part of theory construction and building. I often am sent articles by academics and researchers where at the end of the article there is a brief section on application and implications for practitioners. One is left with the impression that the purpose of the article is to discuss an elegant intellectual construct rather than the improvement of the practice of management in organizations.

Utility versus Rigor of Construction

For most managers, the value of a conceptual framework is utility in understanding, explaining, motivating, and communicating the need for action to change the social system of which he is a part. He is dealing with a very limited audience–members of his organization. As a result, he may employ concepts and terminology uniquely suited to his organization. Sometimes this may result in the use of a framework that has a greater degree of plausibility than precision. On the other hand, many management researchers are prone to sacrifice relevance to rigor. The result of this approach to theory construction is that the focus of the problem shifts away from the administrative situation and on to the definition of the variables and the relationship of those variables within a particular model. The result is that we lose sight of the manager, the dilemmas he faces, and the changing and impermament world he lives in.

THE NEEDS OF MANAGERS VERSUS THE OBJECTIVES OF THEORY CONSTRUCTION

The most important reason that organization and management theories have not had a greater impact on the practice of management has been the inconsistency between what has been perceived to be the objectives of good theory construction and the needs of management practice. I will attempt here to contrast managerial needs with what appears to have been the objectives of management researchers in theory construction. There are four major issues:

Management need for action versus research objective of explanation.
Management need for situational theory versus researcher objective of universal theory.

Management view of problems in the multidimensional versus researcher view as being one or few dimensional.

Management need to explain to other managers versus a researcher need to link up with the literature.

Action versus Explanation

The primary purpose of most management analysis is to gain a better understanding and insight into the social system of which the manager is a part. The manager seeks to understand the causes for substandard performance and to define alternative ways in which the performance of the organization can be improved. While the manager seeks to make changes in the organization, he is aware of the constraints facing him. These constraints may be the result of the organization's past history, its capability to accept new ways and ideas, and the wishes and expectations of its members. In my experience, most management researchers do not have action and change as their primary focus in theory construction. Their prime objective is to explain the phenomenon in language and terminology understandable to social scientists.

Situational versus Universal

Most of the problems managers face are situational in nature—that is, they are unique to one social system or a few social systems. The focus of the managers' analytical efforts is on understanding a particular problem in the short or near term, recognizing that the nature of the problem will be somewhat different over the years. For such types of problems, generic theories are of very little value. Most management theories tend to be universal in scope. They deal with a broad phenomenon over a longer time horizon. The researcher seeks to develop generalizable relationships, while the manager recognizes that relationships in his social system are probably not generalizable to many others. In the search for truth, the researcher often sacrifices relevance and utility. The number of variables that make a social system unique are multiple. It is often not sufficient to standardize data by size of company or technology, and hope that the results will be extremely relevant.

Multidimensional versus One or Few Dimensional

Few important management problems are simple. Most cut across disciplines and require the integration of many different theories and disciplines. This requires the practitioner to do a significant amount of translation through the application of many theories to a particular situation. The manager tends to look at the organization as a whole, while the researcher does research on one or a few dimensions of the problem. The primary focus of the researcher is on one set of variables, with the objective of establishing relationships among these variables to explain the behavior of the total system. This focus on one aspect of the whole social system decreases the utility of most management theories.

Communication with Managers versus Linkage with Literature

Managers use conceptual frameworks to understand and communicate within their social system. These conceptual frameworks are judged by social norms that include utility, simplicity, and consistency. Researchers have a greater tendency to standardize terminology, abstract data, and focus on general phenomena rather than the unique characteristics of a particular social system.

CONTENT AND CONTEXT

Typology for Management Theories and Concepts

In order to gain a better understanding of the different approaches to theory and concept utilization by management researchers and practitioners, I would like to propose two terms: content and context. Content will be defined as the refinement, testing, validation, and application of social science theory to management problems with a focus on universal validity and the explanation of general phenomena. Theories of context, on the other hand, focus primarily on the improvement of practice and understanding, recognizing that management problems are situational in nature and require credible action to deal with complex and uncertain administrative situations.

Table 8.1 outlines three types of theories and concepts: research-oriented theories, practitioner-oriented theories and concepts, and theories of context.

Research-Oriented Theories

These theories focus on application of the considerable learnings from economics, sociology, and psychology to the understanding of management problems. This is performed primarily through the formulation of hypotheses and their testing and validation through statistical analysis. The data used to

TABLE 8.1. Typology for Theories/Concepts/Methololologies

		Low	High
Relative Emphasis on Content	High	Practitioner-Oriented Concepts	Theories of Context
	Low		Research-Oriented Theories

Relative Emphasis on Context

validate these hypothesis are often secondary statistical data. This process puts the focus on the validity of the data, the techniques used to analyze the data, and on the relationship among the variables based on concepts borrowed from social scientists. In this process, we have lost sight of the manager, the administrative situation, and the direct impact of concept or theory on management practice.

Practitioner-Oriented Theories and Concepts

Many managers begin the analysis of a complex problem by researching how other practitioners or companies have approached the same problem. They start with what has worked in practice. The analysis is based on primary data and a careful analysis of all the situational details surrounding a particular decision or strategy. There is a recognition both of the operating dilemmas facing most managers and of the fact that not many observation points are available. One cannot conduct the kind of careful analysis and collect the primary data necessary to perform this analysis from many organizations. However, the few companies that are selected have some direct relevance to the problem and to the company for which the manager works. The analyst seeks to gain an understanding of why certain actions or organizations are perceived as being successful. The result of the analysis is often a list of "lessons" that a manager can apply to his situation. These concepts are grounded in the practice of management and the reality that most managers face.

Theories of Context

There is a need for theories that attempt to bridge the rigor of research-oriented theories with the relevance of practitioner-oriented theories and concepts. Such theories of context will have the following characteristics:

They will use as a starting point the careful analysis of successful and unsuccessful approaches to a particular problem using primary data.

They will place primary focus on the administrative situation and the operating dilemmas of the manager.

Focus on the organization as a whole rather than on one aspect of the social system.

Use concepts from economics, sociology, psychology, and other fields to explain successful action in managerial terms.

Develop a theory of action decisions that an executive can take to address a particular type of problem.

Test, validate, and refine these theories by application in other similar social systems, with the objective of gaining experience in implementation and improving practice.

A CASE STUDY

I would like to use a case study, based on my experiences, to demonstrate the meaning of some of the concepts I have outlined. A few years ago I was involved in efforts to improve organizational productivity in a large industrial corporation. The primary vehicle for improving productivity was to be changes in organization structure design to improve the allocation of resources to important activities and manage the interface between functions efficiently.

The company had been using a program developed by a consultant and had some success in achieving significant productivity gains. The program was simple, easily understood by all the managers involved, and resulted in gaining their commitment to making significant organization structure changes. The program defined all activities performed by all members of the organization, and then asked each manager to allocate to those activities the time spent by each of the people reporting to him. The salary of the individual was then multiplied by the time spent on that activity so that it was possible to get the cost of each activity performed within that organization. The managers were then given a list of other organizations at which a similar study had been undertaken and were then asked to select a small group of organizations from this list that would be directly comparable to their own organization. This would provide the basis for setting norms and standards for each one of the activity groups. In addition to the norms, there were other simple rules concerning span of control, number of levels, and so on, that were easily understood and were entirely in accordance with the experience of managers involved in the study. Because of the simplicity of the data and the fact that they were widely understood, the process acquired a great deal of credibility. There was consequently a greater commitment to make changes when significant negative variances were demonstrated. Often they would call managers in the units they were being compared to in order to find out how a particular activity was performed.

In order to improve the effectiveness of this process, I was able to track down a research-oriented program that I thought would be a superior vehicle for gaining understanding and making change within the organization. Like the practitioner-oriented method, this research-oriented program also defined activities performed within the organization. More important, it used concepts of task interdependence within organizations to group-related activities into management units. It also attempted to set norms for expenditure levels based on how important people within the organization thought each activity was to the accomplishment of their own objectives. Further, it used sophisticated multivariate statistical methodology to arrive at the establishment of activity groupings and people groupings based on their interest in those activities.

Initially, there was significant resistance to this methodology. First, there was a problem of comprehension. Most managers did not understand the methodology, and it was easy for them to attack something they did not understand. Second, the program put the focus of their analysis on the methodology rather than on the activity analysis and the underlying reality those numbers represented. Third, it lacked the experience base of application in other companies and other organizations that the practitioner-oriented model was based upon. Overall, the practitioner-oriented model resulted in superior "savings" due to its simplicity, its versatility, and its comprehension by managers.

As a result of using a practitioner-oriented model in conjunction with a research-oriented program, we were able to make significant improvements in both. For the research-oriented methodology we were able to: improve the focus on cost savings through changes in assumptions and methodology used in the model; simplify the format in which the data were presented to managers; and improve the program as a way to make significant structure changes in organizations through linking strategic objectives with operating tasks and people assignments.

IMPROVING THE INTERFACE BETWEEN THEORY AND PRACTICE

An improved interface between management researchers and practitioners will probably increase the number and quality of theories of context. The key to improving the efficiency and effectiveness of this interface is to initiate a series of changes in attitudes and orientation within the researcher and practitioner communities. This change in attitude and orientation can be brought about by improving communication and interaction between management researchers and practitioners. I would like to suggest two ways in which this can be brought about.

Greater use of adjunct professors at prestigious business schools. At present, most large business schools have a program of executive-in-residence. This executive is often a senior manager who spends a few months on campus. While I believe that this program has significant beneficial effects both on the facility and on the study body, it is not significant in scope and commitment to produce the kind of change required to produce more relevant theories. Most large business schools should have a small percentage of their faculty composed of adjunct professors who are also practitioners. These would be managers who have a long-term commitment to two worlds: the practitioner world and the world of the management researcher. Such executives are likely to occupy staff roles within large corporations and perceive themselves as having a vested interest in improving the quality of theories and the effectiveness with which they are applied within the business world. This would be a long-term career goal for many of these individuals. Having a greater number of adjunct professors on a business school faculty will increase the likelihood that there will be cooperative research projects between practitioners and management researchers. I recognize that at present most large business schools are not permitted to have more than a very small percentage of professors who are adjuncts. I feel that a business school that has a healthy mixture of research-oriented professors and adjuncts who are practitioners will be more effective in developing relevant theory and in educating future managers.

The recruitment of doctoral students. Teaching and research in management are significantly improved if an individual has had a body of management experience upon which he can draw. Hence I believe that an individual ought to work for a period of time after his MBA, say between five and ten years, before he returns to do his doctorate and teach. Such an individual is more likely to be able to balance the needs of both practitioners and reseachers and to appreciate the different realities of both worlds and combine the best of both. I also recognize that at present many graduate schools of business place great emphasis on attracting "young" doctoral students as opposed to those who have worked for a few years. This is a measure of the extent to which norms and reward systems may have to be changed.

A CAVEAT

In this chapter I have made many assertions concerning the interest of managers in improving organization performance and in the management of change. These observations are based on my experiences in the corporate world. As a result of my living in the practitioner world, I may be too much a part of events to distinguish between managers' perceptions and the reality. Some may argue that, when they are facing decisions that infringe on the survival of their firms, managers tend to implicitly use "theories" of practice, performance, and change.

Using Argyris's terminology, my arguments may be based more on managers' espoused theories of action rather than on their theories in use. On the other hand, my observations on the social scientist community are based on their theories in use rather than on their espoused theories in which they maintain that they are interested in implementation.

9

MAKING USE OF METHODOLOGIES DEVELOPED IN ACADEMIA: LESSONS FROM ONE PRACTITIONER'S EXPERIENCE

Vincent P. Barabba

Top management within the Eastman Kodak Company recognizes that today, more than ever, *relevant* information is a major factor in meeting its fundamental corporate objective. That objective can be summarized this way: "To sail ahead of the winds of change in an increasingly competitive environment" (*Advertising Age*, 1982).

Relevant information, as defined by Kodak management, is accurate, timely, and easy to use. Its value comes when it can have an impact on business decisions as they arise. It is the role of Market Intelligence to provide this critical marketplace information so that management, in turn, can make better marketing decisions on a worldwide basis.

WHAT IS KNOWLEDGE UTILIZATION?

To understand the conceptual framework for Market Intelligence within Kodak, it is useful to start with a simple definition of *knowledge utilization*: It is the conversion of raw data into an ultimate action. Professor Gerald Zaltman (1976) has provided a useful description of the critical factors involved in this process. First, research users or decision makers must determine their needs and communicate these clearly to researchers. This adds to the probability that the research activities will actually answer the needs of decision makers in terms of new knowledge. When this new knowledge is then communicated to decision makers and applied to the problem, the end result should be better decisions.

In support of this concept, the role of Market Intelligence is organized on a worldwide basis. In addition, a dedicated computer system is in place. A powerful data-base management tool, it is designed to support the functions

145

Kodak MAIN System

Organization's
Decision Process
What the organization
is capable. and
willing, to present
to the marketplace.
"PRODUCT/TECHNOLOGY
DRIVEN"

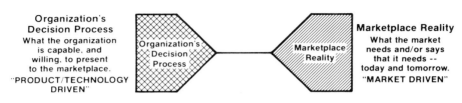

Marketplace Reality
What the market
needs and/or says
that it needs --
today and tomorrow.
"MARKET DRIVEN"

FIGURE 9.1

of tracking short-term market conditions and to look forward in the longer-term planning process.

THE KODAK MAIN SYSTEM

Let us take a close-up view of the functions of the Kodak MArket INtelligence System (or as we call it, the MAIN System). In describing the basic framework, we have again built on insights from the academic setting. This time, we draw on the work of James Meyers of the University of Southern California (1976), who put forth the concept of the "Organization-Forward vs. Market-Back" dimension.

The Basic Framework

At one end of the horizontal plane (see Figure 9.1) we have the organization's decision process. This reflects what the organization is capable and willing to present to the marketplace. At the other end we have marketplace reality. This reflects what the market needs—or says that it needs.

Now, let us look at the vertical dimension (see Figure 9.2). At one end is accountable management. These are the people responsible for the decisions about what the organization will present to the marketplace. Thus, accountable management comprises the people who determine what information is needed; in other words, doing the right things. At the other end of the vertical dimension is Market Intelligence. These are the people responsible for the reliability and validity of the information about the marketplace. Thus, it is Market Intelligence that determines how the information will be acquired and presented; in other words, doing things right.

Note that in Figure 9.2 the marketplace reality and the market intelligence function are shaded the same to signify the bond between them. Likewise, accountable management and organization decision making have similar shadings to reflect their link.

The Five Functions of Market Intelligence

Let us place four of the five primary Market Intelligence functions within this framework (see Figure 9.3). Again, we are grounded in ideas drawn from the academic setting—in particular, Zaltman and his guidelines on enhancing the utilization of research studies (1976).

Function 1 of the MAIN System is to assess market information needs. This involves determining market information requirements within a world-wide scope. In assessing market information needs, we must focus on priority assumptions that are uncertain. We must also monitor key factors that are critical to the success of selected marketing plans. Obviously, this is a function that, if done properly, increases the likelihood of successfully

Kodak MAIN System

Accountable Management

Responsible for the decisions about what the organization can -- and will -- present to the marketplace. Determine what information is needed.
"DOING THE RIGHT THINGS"

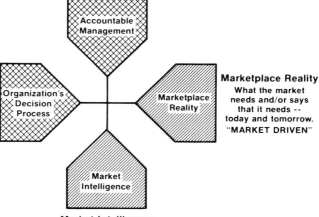

Organization's Decision Process

What the organization is capable, and willing, to present to the marketplace.
"PRODUCT/TECHNOLOGY DRIVEN"

Marketplace Reality

What the market needs and/or says that it needs -- today and tomorrow.
"MARKET DRIVEN"

Market Intelligence

Responsible for the reliability and validity of market information. Determine how the information will be acquired and presented.
"DOING THINGS RIGHT"

FIGURE 9.2

Kodak MAIN System

FIGURE 9.3

implementing the other functions. We will discuss this function in more detail later.

Function 2 of the MAIN System is to measure the marketplace. This means to gather relevant and valid data.

Function 3 is to store, retrieve, and display market data. This function utilizes the powerful computer data-base management system we mentioned earlier.

Function 4 is to analyze and describe market information for use by decision makers in developing business strategy for the company.

Now, we add a fifth function. This reflects all the ways we evaluate the

Kodak MAIN System

FIGURE 9.4

impact that the information has had on Kodak's decision-making process. This last function is represented by the diamond in the middle (see Figure 9.4). The fifth function is positioned central to the overall structure and the initial four functions. Its placement reflects the broad-based participation and interaction required to make the whole process work.

Market Intelligence in the Planning Framework

As we stated earlier, a major objective for the Kodak MAIN System is to provide forward-looking information. That means, in effect, a system that allows Kodak to anticipate and plan for change in the marketplace—rather than finding out about change after the fact, and then being forced to react.

Obviously, corporate commitment is needed to achieve this goal. It must be built on a planning framework that clearly states company objectives and their underlying assumptions. As a way to more fully understand this corporate planning framework, it is useful if we focus on Function 1 of the MAIN System: to assess market information needs.

The Challenge of Complex Problems

Let us begin by looking at what some practitioners see as the major challenge for knowledge utilization during the 1980s: to avoid coming up with the right solutions to the wrong problems (Kilmann, 1977; Mitroff, Barabba, and Kilmann, 1977). As the eminent statistician John Tukey once observed, "Far better an approximate solution to the right problem than an exact solution to the wrong problem." Or, as the author has noted from time to time: "Just as a problem well-defined is half-solved . . . so a problem ill-defined will never be solved!"

Two underlying factors merit special focus in the competitive marketplace of the 1980s: first, we are dealing with highly complex problems; and second, we must function in an environment where there is a diminishing margin for error in problem solving. Today's complex problems can often be recognized by their shared characteristics (Mason and Mitroff, 1981). They tend to be highly ambiguous; they lack definitive formulation; and they are marked by a large degree of uncertainty.

The Impact of Management Assumptions

Because there is so much uncertainty surrounding complex problems, managers must make many assumptions in order to develop solutions. However, it is unusual for decision makers to spend much time examining the particular set of assumptions they hold. It is easy to understand why: because assumptions are implicit, they can easily escape our attention. What is more, the planning activity in U.S. business is still aimed primarily at coming up with the right solution, not to "waste time" on examining whether or not we are asking the right question.

Indeed, when it comes to planning, it is increasingly clear that the real difficulty top management faces is to identify the underlying assumptions that have shaped the definition of the complex problem they are trying to solve. Once these assumptions can be surfaced and examined, decision-makers are in a better position to judge those assumptions that are subject to challenge, as well as those that can be taken as givens. Through this process, managers can identify those areas that require additional marketplace information. They can then determine whether or not to allocate resources to reduce the uncertainty of the business strategies under consideration.

The issue is critical: millions of dollars—even the future of the organization itself—can ride on these strategies. And, as we pointed out earlier, there is a diminishing margin for error.

PLANNING: TWO TRADITIONAL APPROACHES

For the purposes of discussion in this brief overview, it will be useful to simplify two traditional—and very complex—approaches to planning. Let's call them the Expert Approach and the Devil's Advocate Approach.*

With the Expert Approach, management utilizes a planning unit— sometimes outside consultants—to gain expert advice in determining a course of action. The drawbacks are that the experts are people with their own vision of what is right. Either consciously or unconsciously, it is likely that they will ignore (at best) or hide (at worst) some of the assumptions that underlie the recommended plan. In addition, the presented plan is more likely to be within the scope of the problem as articulated by management. In effect, depending on the breadth and depth of the vision—by management or by the consultants—this approach may or may not suggest new and perhaps more relevant assumptions related to the problem.

With the Devil's Advocate Approach, management receives a plan that is developed by an existing planning unit. The proposal is then turned over to selected staff members to determine what is wrong with it. The review is usually directed from the perspective that represents a special expertise (at best) or a special interest (at worst) of the devil's advocate group. While this approach does expose some underlying assumptions, it does so in the context of what is wrong with them, rather than what they should be. In essence, it tends to tear down assumptions rather than clarify them so they can be better understood. What is more, if the staff critics are successful and the plan is rejected, there is no new plan to replace it. Perhaps most worrisome of all, the planning unit's response to extended criticism could result in a tendency to play it safe. What we may wind up with are plans designed to "give management what it wants"—rather than innovative plans, admittedly with higher risk, but also with the potential of higher payoff.

---

*I do this with the understanding that *simplifying* is exactly what those of us in business always criticize the academic community for doing! By using this technique of simplification, however, I am *not* saying what these two planning approaches are *supposed* to do. Rather, my purpose is to share some observations, based on experience, about the ways these approaches have evolved in practice in the real world.

Once again, our purpose is not to say that these two approaches, properly applied, are wrong. Rather, given our experience with these two approaches, here are things to which we should be sensitive.*

Striving for the Best of Both Worlds

What we are developing at Kodak is a process that addresses the weaknesses inherent in the application of these two planning systems and, at the same time, utilizes their strengths. Why is Market Intelligence so interested and involved in developing a planning process? The answer is simple: we feel the need for a process that leads directly to Function 1 of the MAIN System; that is, a planning process that explicitly generates information needs directly related to critical underlying assumptions of the stated strategy.

At the core of the process we use at Kodak are elements of the essential steps found in the approach called Strategic Assumption Surfacing and Testing (SAST). There is a small but growing body of literature dealing with this concept (see Mason and Mitroff, 1981; Mitroff, Mason, and Barabba, 1983). We have also utilized a number of the concepts on group formation developed by Ralph Kilmann (1977).

To insure that we are starting from the same point, let us go very briefly through the five basic steps in the process as we use it at Kodak (see Figure 9.5).

The first step is group formation (Figure 9.5.1). We use this as the basis for bringing together the right mix of people to represent the full spectrum of views on a problem. Divergent groups are formed with people of similar beliefs or characteristics.

The second step in the process is to surface and rate assumptions (Figure 9.5.2). Each group, meeting separately, is encouraged to develop the strongest position possible from their own perspective—that is, their assumptions—about the situation. The assumptions are then differentiated by rating them, with a value on the importance and the certainty (and/or plausibility) of each one. Each group then presents the most pivotal of these assumptions to the other groups. The other groups, in turn, must identify those assumptions that are most damaging to their own position.

This forms the basis for the third step: debate (Figure 9.5.3). During debate, each group has the opportunity to challenge the other's assumptions while defending its own. From this debate arise the issues deemed critical to all positions.

---

*Readers will find a lively debate on the merits of the Devil's Advocate Approach in strategic planning in the series of articles that appeared in the *Academy of Management Review* (Cosier, 1981a, b; Mitroff and Mason, 1981).

S.A.S.T.

1. Group formation
2. Surface and rate assumptions
3. Debate
4. Analyze information requirements
5. Synthesis

FIGURE 9.5

Forming Groups

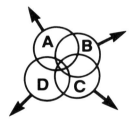

FIGURE 9.5.1

Assumption Surfacing & Rating

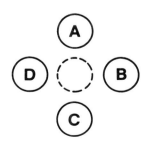

FIGURE 9.5.2

Debate

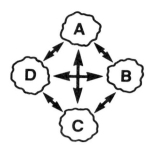

FIGURE 9.5.3

This leads to step four: the analysis of information requirements to resolve the important assumptions that carry high levels of uncertainty. In all likelihood, these will be the focus for the informational activities of Market Intelligence.

The fifth step is synthesis. Here, the objective is directed toward a linking of assumptions relative to each critical issue (see Figure 9.5.4). This step also forms the basis for attaining the information that will resolve the plausibility questions about critical assumptions.

Through this, we hope to get as much "buy-in" as possible among key participants with strongly competing viewpoints.

Evaluating the Process

We have utilized this process at Kodak to deal with several current and complex problems facing decision makers. For four of these, we have completed an evaluation process as well.

The key document used in evaluation is an eight-page questionnaire that includes both open-ended questions and a semantic differential scale measuring 15 attributes. The questionnaire is distributed to each person who participates. At the time of this writing, we have 94 responses. Our analyses of the results reveal an overwhelmingly positive reaction to the process: 93 percent of all respondents gave it an overall positive rating, while only 7 percent rated the overall conferences as less than favorable.

This evaluation procedure is important for a number of reasons. Obviously, the results demonstrate that, from the participants' viewpoint, the process is a valuable tool for dealing with complex problems in a real-life setting. However, the purpose of our evaluation efforts is not just to prove whether or not Kodak people like the approach. Our real focus is to identify the strengths and weaknesses within the process itself. Through this effort, we will continue to modify our approach and thus make the process as effective as possible. Further, we are measuring our outcomes both in terms of the resources required and in terms of results that will benefit decision makers.

Analytic Methods

At this point, it would be useful to touch briefly on the methodology we have used to conduct our analysis.

One of the more quantitative parts of our evaluation is comprised of a statistical analysis of the bipolar scale responses to 15 attributes, plus the overall rating of the conferences. These are included in the questionnaire as a semantic differential segment. Participants are asked to rank various features of the conference on a scale of 1 to 9, and then to rank the overall conference using the same scale.

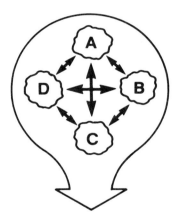

- **Develop Critical Issues**

- **Information - Gathering Projects**

FIGURE 9.5.4

S.A.S.T. Evaluation

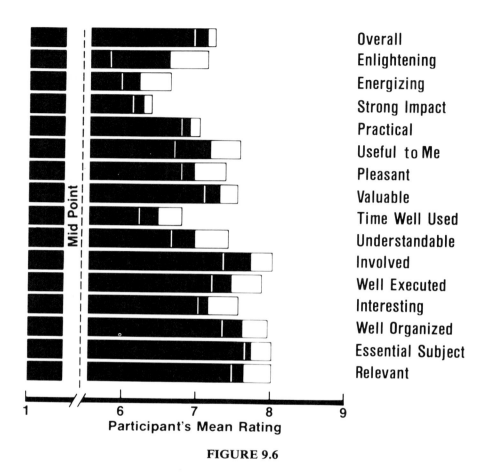

Overall
Enlightening
Energizing
Strong Impact
Practical
Useful to Me
Pleasant
Valuable
Time Well Used
Understandable
Involved
Well Executed
Interesting
Well Organized
Essential Subject
Relevant

Participant's Mean Rating

FIGURE 9.6

In Figure 9.6 you see one view of the results. Here, we have plotted the mean ratings for the key attributes from the four conferences, along with the high and low variations. The mean overall ratings from participants in the four conferences ranged from 6.9 to 7.2 on our 1 to 9 scale. This certainly shows that we are headed in the right direction. In addition, statistical tests proved there was virtually no difference among groups or within categories of working backgrounds, such as marketing, manufacturing, or research.

ADDITIONAL FINDINGS: A FUNCTIONAL MODEL

Let us look more closely at some of the additional findings we have made from our actual experiences. We can begin by building an abbreviated functional model of the major elements in the process (see Figure 9.7).

A major finding from our experience has been the underlying significance of the first phase: developing the process plan. What this means, in essence, is that we have found it valuable to spend more time than we had initially anticipated with the prime client group. We have described this step as "doing needs assessment on needs assessment."

During this phase, we have found that we must be flexible in applying the methodology. Our role is to be both problem-centered and client-centered. Thus, working closely with client management we can help develop a process plan that will meet mutually acceptable objectives. Just as important, it is against these objectives that the full process design will be evaluated.

In addition, this first phase—which requires the investment of up-front thinking and initial management involvement by the prime client—can facilitate the ultimate planning process through such factors as more careful selection of participants and support facilities. Further, by better assessing objectives, we have been able to determine what process designs are most suitable. In some instances, we have even been able to help the client greatly streamline the scope of the problem to be addressed through the process.

Building Diverse Groups

Next, we will examine the point in the process where we build diverse groups with different perspectives around a complex problem. This presupposes that we have given attention to the first step. It means putting into place such key factors as management sanction of the process as it is being applied to this particular problem, and the means to provide appropriate process support (see Figure 9.8).

Our purpose is to form diverse groups that meet three criteria. First, they should be as internally homogeneous as possible. We find that putting like-minded individuals in the same group has the general effect of strengthening a particular outlook. Thus, we can strengthen the surfacing of assumptions behind a particular viewpiont. Second, the groups should be as different from one another as possible. Third, the groups should cover, collectively, the total spectrum of diverse positions that can have an impact on the ultimate business strategy.

Unlike some planning processes, this one does not presuppose strong initial agreement among the parties. In fact, the process presupposes the

Function 1 of the MAIN System:
Assess Market Information Needs

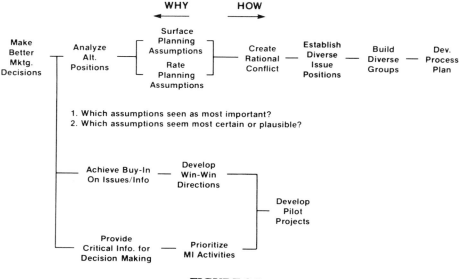

FIGURE 9.7

existence of strong differences. We want to insure that many viewpoints across all levels and perspectives are included. One of the most fruitful outcomes is for upper management to be willing to seek and work with the views of lower-level employees. When this is done, lower-level employees become more confident in stating their views in front of upper management. On one of the evaluation forms, a participant described it this way: "This procedure gave widely-opposed views equal airing . . . and forced those holding what will probably be the corporate view to think it through and vigorously defend it."

Establishing Diverse Positions

The next two elements on our functional model are closely linked: to surface and rate planning assumptions through the establishment of diverse issue positions. As far as possible, we want to structure the process so that what one group takes for granted does not go unchallenged by another group (see Figure 9.9). We also want to insure that important aspects of the strategy are not neglected by the need for consensus that often develops within groups. If anything, we wish to deliberately create rational conflict—and in

Establish Diverse Issue Positions —— Build Diverse Groups —— Dev. Process Plan

FIGURE 9.8

such a way that we can make constructive use of it. Indeed, the function is so important that we give it individual prominence on our functional model.

Some of the techniques we use to promote diverse issue positions include sanctioning role-play (or advocacy) behavior to encourage participants to go to extremes in promoting their positions. We also apply time pressure to concentrate the focus on this activity, a situation that often results in a heightened energy level among participants. One of our respondents viewed it this way: "Everyone seems to have an opportunity to get on their soap boxes and be heard. . . . The process developed a group spirit that generally raised the energy level!"

Stakeholder Analysis

After each group has worked for some time to develop in detail its unique perspective on the issue, the process moves into one of the most critical and difficult phases: the surfacing and rating of key assumptions that underlie each strategy.

In the process of surfacing assumptions, we utilize the "stakeholder" method (Mitroff and Emshoff, 1979). In brief, stakeholder analysis asks the participants to consider all the parties who have a stake in the position under consideration. This list is typically much broader than the three or four groups that first come to mind. The whole point about getting decision makers to identify the important stakeholders in their position is to help them confront the important question: What is it you have been assuming about

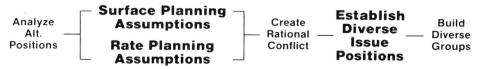

FIGURE 9.9

the stakeholders? Or, what is it that you have had to assume about them, so that starting from these assumptions you are able to derive your position?

As pointed out in earlier publications (see Mitroff, Kilmann, and Barabba, 1979), what is different is this: participants are not allowed to consider the problem at the level of the position they have already adopted. Instead, our process asks them to focus on the underlying assumptions and to regard the real problem as being at this level—to ask themselves: What assumptions have we been making and why? What is the effect of other assumptions? Can our position stand up to other assumptions?

Rating Assumptions

Once a group feels it has adequately identified its underlying assumptions, the process proceeds to a sorting of them by plotting on a two-dimensional scale. This in turn leads to an important step: the analysis of alternative positions. The procedure applies two basic questions: With respect to the set of critical assumptions for the position developed by the group, which are seen as relatively most important? Which assumptions does the group feel are most plausible?

A Closer Look at Plausibility

The concept of plausibility demands a closer look (see Figure 9.10). In effect, it acknowledges that decision makers must bring all they can to bear on the problem right now—and then move on. Plausibility helps managers avoid "paralysis by analysis." Best of all, plausibility allows managers to legitimately say "I think!" and to really mean it.

Why is plausibility such an important idea? It offers a test of the reasonableness of an argument and it keeps decision makers from getting bogged down because they cannot prove something. What we are saying, in effect, is that management can look at the available facts, determine whether these facts support or rebut the claim being made, and come to a judgment about the claim based on the available information.*

Recall the other reasoning models we touched on earlier: the Expert Approach and the Devil's Advocate Approach. We are convinced that our ability to cross-compare alternative strategies at this stage provides a framework for getting the best of each position—as opposed to the accept-or-not-accept position generally provided to decision makers under the other

---

*The particular use of the word "claim" reflects another facet of our experience as practitioners: namely, it is essential to pay attention to the uses of language as an instrument of exact thought and argument in critical analysis. Thus, we have designated the word "claim" to describe a particular kind of assumption. Interested readers will find many useful insights on the varied uses of language in *An Introduction to Reasoning* (Toulmin, Rieke, and Janik, 1979).

Assumption, Surfacing, and Rating

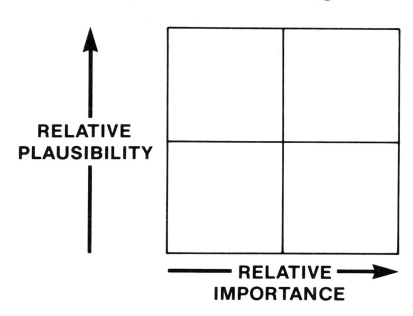

FIGURE 9.10

two reasoning models. The process we use attempts to insure that as many alternatives as possible will be examined more broadly and systematically than if they were regarded one at a time or in isolation from one another.

Two Key Criteria

Relative to each issue, we are most interested in the claims that meet two criteria: first, that the participants are clear that these claims are the most important; and second, the participants are either clear or not clear that these same claims are highly plausible or implausible. In other words, if participants feel certain that a claim surrounding an issue is highly plausible or implausible, we are now beginning to treat these as a "given."

In effect, we do not need original research about this claim right now. What we do need is the ability to monitor that claim and its underlying assumptions for continued certainty as to its high or low plausibility. What this says, in effect, is that we feel certain this claim is true today. However, if

Assumption, Surfacing, and Rating

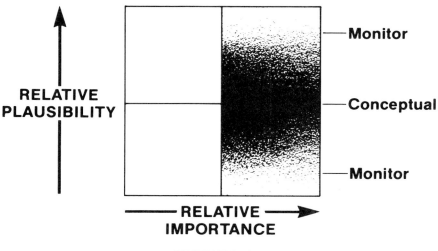

FIGURE 9.10.1

it should ever change—if, for example, public response shifts or there is new competitive activity—we want to know about it as early as possible. Stated another way, if something is at the extremes of plausibility or implausibility, it may be preferable to utilize monitoring techniques rather than conceptual research (see Figure 9.10.1).

There are times when we are clear that a claim is important, but—given the evidence—we are uncertain whether an argument is either plausible or implausible. It is at this point that we want to conduct conceptual-type research. This research would enable us to gather information to assist in determining more precisely the plausibility or implausibility of the associated claim. This, by the way, is the latest version of our attempt to deal with the rating of arguments. We are not convinced this is the last version. It is the one in which we currently have the most confidence.

DIALECTICAL DEBATE: SOURCE FOR NEW INSIGHTS

The prioritizing of arguments reveals the different emphasis held by diverse groups. This sets the stage for a dialectical debate among the proponents of different positions regarding their respective claims.

The primary purpose of this debate is not for each group to convince the other, but to show how each group views the situation and what its viewpoint entails. The various parties learn that there are different ways of viewing the situation—and that what each takes as a set of givens is not necessarily agreed upon by other groups. One of our participants described it this way: "First and foremost, I was introduced to valid divergent opinions from my own, which is always a healthy medicine to have to take."

The exercise is meant to demonstrate to all sides that there are really very few givens. Typically, we have found it is possible to reduce the number of pivotal assumptions for each group to several really critical ones. The technique we use is for each group to focus on the other groups' assumptions that are most damaging to its own position. This makes the debate much more manageable and productive.

It is important to note our use of creative adversarial thinking. Academic research has demonstrated the cultural and social norms toward compromise. The danger is not that the participants will *not* compromise—but rather that they will do so too soon, and for the wrong reasons. Only after each group has made its position known and debate has occurred do we enter the last phase: the move toward synthesis, or what we describe in our functional model as developing win-win directions (see Figure 9.11).

The integration of arguments at the issue level is the most difficult part of the process. It is even more difficult to come up with an entirely new, synthesized set of assumptions that bridge the established positions and go beyond them as well. Here, in contrast to our rational conflict, we seek a mood of collaboration to reach a consensus on an assumption. We are looking for a win-win direction as a way to resolve conflict.

Normally, when there is disagreement between two positions—for example, let us simplify the process to a disagreement between Group A and Group B—participants can deal with the problem several ways. First, they can avoid the conflict entirely. (It has been my experience that business and

FIGURE 9.11

government are very adept at doing this!) Second, they can accommodate. For example, Group B may let Group A win (and then work at "evening the score" later). Maybe Group A has the better idea, or perhaps A has the greater number of top management people. Therefore, Group B feels it is politically advantageous to give in. Third, the participants may compromise—especially if they are fairly equal in terms of group membership.

Going Beyond the Zero-Sum Game

Compromise, in fact, is an easy solution for A and B—if they assume a zero-sum game. This is an approach that says: "I'll start off by demanding twice as much as I really want. Then, by compromising from my extreme position, I'll be sure to get my half."

What A and B may not be aware of, however, is what—and how much—they are giving up in the compromise. For example, by using a collaborative approach rather than compromise, both A and B might each get more than half.

This is the foundation for the value of the process we use at Kodak. Through it, we can increase the chances that our participants no longer think in the limited sense of a zero-sum game.

In our streamlined example, Groups A and B have debated. B has had a chance to rebut A's damaging assumptions and vice versa, and A and B have had the opportunity to look at the reasonableness of the arguments and better understand each other's underlying assumptions.

Further, the probability of achieving the win-win objective is enhanced by forming synthesis teams with representatives from each of the original groups. We give these newly formed teams the job of finding elements of their original points of view that, when combined, allow them to go beyond the zero-sum game and adopt a win-win position.

ACHIEVING WIN-WIN: A CASE HISTORY

A case history drawn from the files of the Census Bureau—greatly simplified for our purposes here—is useful to illustrate this point. (For an in-depth discussion of the substantive issues involved in this case history, see Mitroff, Mason, and Barabba, 1983.)

In 1980, despite having counted a greater percent of the U.S. population than ever before, the Bureau was the subject of the greatest controversy in its history. A major reason, of course, is that census data are used not only to allocate congressional seats, but also to disburse an estimated $75 to $120 billion in federal monies. While it is now estimated that less than 1 percent of the nation's population was missed (undercounted) in 1980—as compared to 2.5 percent in 1970—it is not altogether surprising that a number of localities sued in the federal courts. Their objective was to have the Census Bureau adjust local population figures for the number of persons the Bureau supposedly failed to count.

In order to address various positions relative to this question, the Bureau held a major workshop to surface the critical assumptions and considerations that would either justify an adjustment or not. In the solution that emerged, the Bureau was able to address the positions held by two competing points of view. (In our streamlined case history, we will call them Group A and Group B.) Through this process, the participants were able to adopt a win-win position in the resultant plan.

Two Competing Positions

Group A held the position that "You can only adjust the count if you are certain that the adjustment is going to get you closer to the truth—in other words, the correct count." Group B, on the other hand, said that "You've got to remember that people get fed and sheltered from these numbers. We know there is inequity somewhere in these numbers . . . so if the people have to wait for us to adjust the numbers until we are certain, they'll have to wait another 10 years." Group B concluded: "It's not fair for us to put so much weight on the statistically pristine nature of the numbers. The Bureau ought to adjust now because we *think* it's going to be right." Those are certainly two valid positions for the Census Bureau—a statistical agency—to take.

The strategy that emerged from the SAST workshop satisfied the interests of both groups. The Bureau decided not to adjust the 1980 census, which satisfied those concerned with the quality of the count. However, that decision was conditioned by the proposition that the Bureau would consider an adjustment if later findings indicated that specific undercount adjustments would improve the Bureau's intercensal *estimate* of the population and its characteristics. (The intercensal count is done in years ending in numbers other than zero. It is an updated estimate of the count by the Bureau, based on births, deaths, emigration, and immigration.) Since these are clearly estimates, everyone recognizes that these "components of change" incorporate many assumptions.

The participants said: "We will now add a fifth component, which we will call 'the best understanding of the quality of the count.' Thus, if inequities could be proven, they could be addressed by adjustments in the intercensal estimates program, which is used for various allocation purposes." In this way, the Bureau would make adjustments using a value known to be an estimate. This, in turn, would increase the chances of the ultimate users of information being aware of the limitations of the adjustment. At the same time, this plan addressed Group B's concerns about inequities from an undercount.

An essential component of the decision process was keeping many vested interests (the stakeholders) informed and involved. For example, to enhance public awareness before making the decision on the adjustment, the Bureau published the assumptions it would address (*Federal Register*, U.S. Bureau of the Census, 1980) and sought public response. As more information about the census count became available, the Bureau published its evaluation of this new information and its impact on the critical assumptions. By doing this, the Bureau also tried to call attention to the fact that it was attempting to use new modes and methods of reaching decisions on complex issues. It thus hoped to serve as a model in this respect for other agencies and to highlight ways in which new knowledge was being brought to bear in dealing with complex issues.

THE SEARCH FOR SYNTHESIS

Once again, let me underscore the fact that this kind of win-win, collaborative mode is not easy to achieve. It is largely outside our social and cultural norms, especially in the corporate world.

Returning to the Kodak setting, the feedback on our evaluation questionnaire supports this finding. Results showed that this is the one area where Kodak participants felt most unsatisfied with the process. Here is a quote that typifies many of the respondents' concerns: "I'm not sure we came out with a commitment. Did the process in a sense artificially bring us to a consensus?" We think such responses are important for two reasons: first, they point up the need to examine the way we handle the process itself; second, they show the underlying doubt among participants that the "idealized" planning process will actually get translated into real-world action.

Among the procedures we are considering to address this concern is a plan for longer-term follow-up to keep participants informed of the progress that is being made on a problem. It has also occurred to us that this perceived lack of synthesis could result from a lack of awareness on the part of participants about what the process is supposed to achieve. In addition to our added attention to the first step (developing the process plan), we may design an introductory presentation for all participants to help develop more realistic expectations.

Another rationale for why people rated the synthesis concept as "low" may stem from the fact that the process is so different from the traditional decision-making methods they have used. Take a moment and think how difficult it must be for a person who is accustomed to being *the* decision

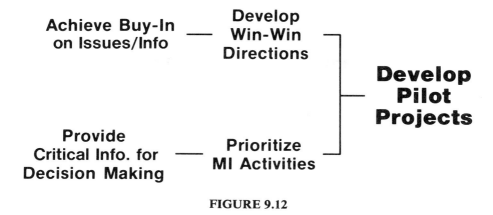

FIGURE 9.12

maker to become suddenly a peer of 23 other participants in a group process. This is the kind of issue that is not readily apparent until a textbook process, such as SAST, is implemented in a real-life situation.

If a win-win solution is not possible, we have found a useful technique to be the development of pilot projects as a way to get initial buy-in on key assumptions (see Figure 9.12). A major objective is to achieve broad-scale buy-in on key issues. Participants made some interesting points here. One said: "It may be that this process is most effective when employee 'buy-in' is essential and the question is not within management's absolute prerogative." Another observed: "Key people were involved and had an opportunity to air their views. Whatever the ultimate decision, there will be more ownership as a result."

THE MANAGER'S PLANNING BOOK

It is essential to emerge with a plan to provide the critical information that management needs to meet the ultimate corporate objective: better business decisions. Given the scarcity of limited resources, how do we determine what and how much critical information to provide?

An answer lies in what we call the "manager's planning book," a by-product of the process. This book contains a prioritized list of the most critical issues and a list of Market Intelligence activities designed to improve the state of knowledge relative to those issues. Figure 9.13 shows an example of one approach to this matrix.

The final decision, of course, is not made by this process. But management can use the results with a high degree of confidence because of the following conditions: first, a broad base of knowledge within the

The Manager's Plan Book Matrix

LIST OF CRITICAL ISSUES RELATED TO STRATEGY IN PRIORITY ORDER	ASSESSMENT OF CURRENT STATE OF KNOWLEDGE*	MARKET INTELLIGENCE ACTIVITIES (PRIORITY ORDER)				
		A $ Date	B $ Date	C $ Date	D $ Date	E $ Date
1.	Certain			§	★	
2.	Somewhat Certain	†				
3.	Very Certain				★	
4.	Somewhat Certain		†			
5.	Certain		§	★		
6.	Uncertain	†				
7.	Uncertain	§	†			
8.	Certain					†
9.	Very Certain		★			
10.	Uncertain	‡				

*Determined by analysis of existing data.

Very Certain — Supported by empirical evidence
Certain — Unanimous acknowledgment by respected observers
Somewhat Certain — Generally accepted opinion among respected observers
Uncertain — Disagreement among respected observers

§ Provides more insight to the issue
‡ Improves general knowledge of issue
† Provides empirical evidence
★ Monitors issue

FIGURE 9.13.

organization was brought to bear on the strategic issues; second, a thorough, systematic, and critical examination was conducted on the various strategic options and underlying assumptions; and third, all the participants understand—many for the first time—the critical assumptions that underlie the adopted strategy. While agreement among all of the parties is not probable, their awareness and mutual understanding are substantial elements in the successful implementation of the strategy.

SUMMARY

At Kodak, we are convinced of the importance of surfacing and testing our assumptions. The process we are developing is an exercise in tough, critical analysis. It has proven to be an effective way to help uncover the reality of strategic plans.

Indeed, if a strategy can survive the intensive process we apply, we are convinced it is in a far better position to survive in the competitive world in which we operate.

REFERENCES

Advertising Age, April 19, 1982, p. 54.

Cosier, Richard A. "Dialectical Inquiry in Strategic Planning: A Case of Premature Acceptance?" *Academy of Management Review*, Vol. 6, No. 4 (1981a), pp. 643–648.

Cosier, Richard A. "Further Thoughts on Dialectical Inquiry: A Rejoinder to Mitroff and Mason," *Academy of Management Review*, Vol. 6, No. 4 (1981b), pp. 653–654.

Federal Register. "Position on Adjustment of the 1980 Census Counts for Under-enumeration," Department of Commerce, Bureau of the Census, Federal Register 45:No. 243, December 16, 1980.

Kilmann, Ralph H. *Social Systems Design: Normative Theory and the MAPS Design Technology* (New York: Elsevier, 1977).

Mason, Richard O., and Mitroff, Ian I. *Challenging Strategic Planning Assumptions* (New York: Wiley & Sons, 1981).

Meyers, James H. "Benefit Structure Analysis: A New Tool for Product Planning," *Journal of the American Marketing Association*, October 1976, pp. 23–32.

Mitroff, Ian I., Mason, Richard O., and Barabba, Vincent P. *The 1980 Census, Policymaking Amid Turbulence* (Lexington, Mass.: D. C. Heath, 1983).

Mitroff, Ian I., and Emshoff, James. "On Strategic Assumption-Making," *Academy of Management Review*, Vol. 4, No. 1 1979, pp. 1–2.

Mitroff, Ian I., Kilmann, Ralph H., and Barabba, Vincent P. "Management Information Versus Misinformation Systems," in Gerald Zaltman, ed., *Management Principles for Nonprofit Agencies and Organizations* (New York: AMACOM, 1979).

Mitroff, Ian I., and Mason, Richard O. "The Metaphysics of Policy and Planning: A Reply to Cosier," *Academy of Management Review*, Vol. 6, No. 4 (1981), pp. 649–651.

Mitroff, Ian I., Barabba, Vincent P., and Kilmann, Ralph H. "The Application of Behavioral and Philosophical Technologies to Strategic Planning: A Case Study of a Large

Federal Agency," *Management Science*, September 1977, pp. 44–58.

Toulmin, Stephen, Rieke, Richard, and Janik, Allen. *An Introduction to Reasoning* (New York: Macmillan, 1979.)

Zaltman, Gerald. "Enhancing Research Utilization: Guidelines for a Funding Agency," prepared for the RANN Research Utilization Task Force, June 1976.

PART 2

CONCEPTUAL APPROACHES

10

KNOWLEDGE DISAVOWAL IN ORGANIZATIONS

Gerald Zaltman

INTRODUCTION

Ignorance is bliss.
What you don't know won't hurt you.
Curiosity killed the cat.
No news is good news.
A little knowledge is a dangerous thing.

The above is just a sample of sayings about the wisdom of being uninformed. There are still others, such as, "If you're so smart why aren't you rich?," "Don't be a know-it-all," and so forth that reflect less than positive attitudes toward those who acquire, possess, and display knowledge. Just in case we make the mistake of knowing, we are reminded that "Dead men don't speak" or, more gently, that "Silence is golden." Not knowing is even viewed as a basic right: "The right to know everything is a false slogan. People also have a right not to know, and it is a much more valuable one" (Solzhenitsyn, 1978).

The notion that we should not always know—that knowing is not always nice—might be referred to as knowledge disavowal. By knowledge disavowal I mean the avoidance of knowledge in order to preserve or maintain the status quo or to avoid a difficult choice or threatening situation. This does not include the avoidance of information or knowledge for reasons related to the relevance, timeliness, expected utility, or financial cost of knowledge. The two related themes of this chapter are that knowledge disavowal phenomena

This chapter was prepared with the support of National Institute of Mental Health Grant No. MH30537-03.

may be as systematic and pervasive as pro-knowledge phenomena, and that consequently their dampening effect on the accumulation of knowledge may rival the enhancing effect of knowledge production, dissemination, and application enterprises.

Despite the pervasiveness of knowledge disavowal phenomena, relatively little organized effort has been given to understanding them. There are, of course, some excellent investigations of various types and instances of knowledge disavowal. However, they largely exist in isolation of one another. This follows closely a pattern in the study of innovation. Most research in this area has focused on the development of innovations, their acceptance by individuals, and their general diffusion rather than on the failure of innovations to appear or resistance to them when they do appear. This is what Everett M. Rogers refers to as the "pro-innovation" bias (Rogers, 1976).

The significance of the two themes of this chapter and of the relative neglect of knowledge disavowal phenomena is this: unless we understand knowledge disavowal processes better, we cannot progress very far in understanding and improving upon pro-knowledge processes. Knowledge disavowal and pro-knowledge processes commingle in their functioning and their effects. Studying the creation, dissemination, and application of knowledge without studying the avoidance of these activities at the same time is roughly analogous to playing a piano concerto with many of the keys missing from the keyboard. The failure to consider the commingling of knowledge disavowal and pro-knowledge social processes may be one of the causes for the difficulties experienced in the design and implementation of management information systems noted by C. West Churchman (1983) and others (Huber, 1982).

A related reason for being concerned with knowledge disavowal is that knowledge creation, dissemination, and application are themselves not separable processes. While it is intellectually convenient to treat these as separable processes or activities, it is also misleading. For example, knowledge is created during dissemination and application processes and vice versa. This is one reason why it is so difficult to measure knowledge use, nonuse, and misuse. If I may use a statistical metaphor, we should be studying three-way interaction effects rather than so-called main effects. When the knowledge enterprise is viewed this way, the phenomenon of knowledge disavowal takes on added importance: knowledge disavowal is one of the reasons knowledge creation, dissemination, and application factors are inextricably interwoven. However, before this issue can be explored it is necessary to understand better the nature of knowledge disavowal phenomena. Most of this chapter is concerned with treatments of knowledge disavowal found in various literatures.

EXAMPLES OF RESEARCH ON KNOWLEDGE DISAVOWAL

Comfort Zones and the Law of the Lens

Individuals possess integrated sets of assumptions, expectations, and decision rules. These constitute their frames of reference, which together work with various reality tests to mediate responses to various stimuli (Holzner and Marx, 1979). Reality tests and frames of reference constitute a viewing lens. Viewing lenses are generally created on the basis of existing knowledge and usually lead us to find what we are looking for. This is the "Law of the Lens" (Zaltman, 1982). We view things in terms of what is comfortable for us. The Law of the Lens does not break down very often. As a result, we develop an intellectual comfort zone. One side of this zone is bounded by negative surprises; the other side is bounded by positive surprises. Information lying outside our comfort zone is likely to be greeted with surprise. In the several organizational contexts in which colleagues and I have been studying research use, we have found that surprising research results tend to be rejected (Deshpande and Zaltman, 1982). Based on our research thus far, it does not appear to matter greatly whether these surprises are positive or negative.

An example of the rejection of a so-called positive surprise appeared in recent interviews with personnel in a large industrial products firm. The firm was very concerned with obtaining an accurate estimate of its market share for a product it was introducing for the first time. The product was new to the firm, and hence its production capacity would be based on this estimate. For various reasons, scales of production could not be easily altered once established. Three different methods were used to estimate market share at specified periods of time, and all three methods produced roughly the same estimates. These estimates were nearly three times greater than management had expected. In this particular industry, this information can be labelled a very positive surprise. However, the research estimates were rejected and relevant decisions were based on the preresearch expected market share. By the end of the first six months after the firm's entry into the market, it had reached the sales level it anticipated at the 18-month point. The firm's best guess now is that its prior expectations were off by one-third. Unfortunately, it cannot alter production sufficiently to reach this potential market. The most relevant point to make is *not* the one that only hindsight permits: the firm should have accepted the estimates arising out of its market research. It is quite possible that its record of overall success when deliberately ignoring market research warranted its doing so in this instance. The important point is that no mechanism existed for challenging the decision to disavow the formal research when it fell outside the firm's comfort zone.

The Law of the Lens manifests itself in several ways. For example, new product management teams when assessing the feasibility of introducing new products tend to favor their introduction with a frequency that is unwarranted by subsequent commercial performance. Analyses of many new product failures point to a tendency to both design research and to interpret research results in a way that does not allow equal opportunity for evidence to arise that runs counter to a new product launch decision. Similarly, evaluations of educational programs, innovations in mental health delivery systems, and patient-counseling procedures have frequently been found to contain research design biases favoring research conclusions consistent with the attitudes of senior administrators in these settings, even though these administrators are often not involved in research design decisions. It can only be noted briefly here that the tendency to seek confirming rather than disconfirming evidence appears to be well rooted in individuals and organizations. A considerable literature already exists describing these tendencies in both the encoding and decoding of information (Wason and Johnson-Laird, 1972; Snyder and Swann, 1978). This issue will be raised again shortly.

Group Think

One of the more thorough examinations of group processes related to knowledge disavowal can be found in Irving L. Janis's analysis of group think (Janis, 1972). This concept refers to a mode of thinking in a group that is characterized in part by the systematic but largely unwitting avoidance of information that might question the wisdom of the apparent or emerging group consensus. Janis describes the various group pressures and "the emergence of self-appointed mind guards, members who protect the group from adverse information that might shatter their shared complacency about the effectiveness and morality of their decisions" (p. 198). This psychological contagion is most readily achieved in cohesive groups. It is basically a rapid diffusion of the resistance to or the rejection of new information. Group dynamics assist in avoiding the acquisition of certain information. If that information is somehow encountered, other group dynamics such as ridicule (Westrum, 1982) prevent careful processing of that information. Such deliberate failure to process information fully is a form of knowledge disavowal. Boje and Murnigham (1982) suggest that the presence of "group confidence pressures" may contribute to a form of group think. Members of a group may become more confident in and satisfied with iterative decisions as a result of the exchange of opinion among group members about the decision. This tends to occur even as the accuracy of their decision decreases.

Forbidden Research

Another manifestation of knowledge disavowal is called "forbidden research" (Nelkin, 1980). Nelkin observes that:

> Political convention, laws, and the availability of finding and social taboos have long placed many limits on both the ends and means of research in the social sciences. The choice of research areas, the acceptability of certain procedures are sometimes strongly, but more often subtly, constrained in ways that serve to protect prevailing social values and existing political relationships (p. 21).

There are many reasons why certain types of research and problems may be considered off limits. I would exclude from the term "knowledge disavowal" those inquiries that are discouraged to protect the rights of human subjects or where the conduct of the actual research poses some very clear danger or threat to the well-being of individuals. I would include within the term "knowledge disavowal" the avoidance of inquiries that might yield insights that in turn suggest major changes in existing social arrangements. Knowledge disavowal in response to threats to existing social arrangements and constructions of reality often occurs after some item of knowledge has already been developed to the point where it has been applied in an unacceptable way (Nelkin, 1978), or where the consequences if it were to be applied are quite clear and unacceptable to some group. Interviews we have conducted with professionals in social work and mental health service agencies as well as in private sector corporations strongly suggest that the perceived political unacceptability of an idea within an agency is a major factor influencing a therapist's or manager's decision not to introduce new research results. Thus, there are forbidden uses of research as well.

Half-Knowledge

Paul Lazarsfeld (1967) has made passing reference to the concept of "half-knowledge." This refers to a vague awareness of certain aspects of one's situation. There are positive as well as negative consequences of maintaining a state of half-knowledge. One reason for maintaining this state is the possibility that there may be more to know and that more complete awareness of matters might require difficult or unpleasant choices and actions.

Bernd Morin (1981) has developed this concept in a rather interesting and creative fashion. He described it as "a set of subtle devices for focusing organized selective political attention and institutional neglect. Half-knowledge, then, is something like a collective defense mechanism, an equivalent within organizations to processes like repression or perception in individual personalities" (p. 47). What is interesting here about this concept is not so much the "half" or portion that is known (although that too is interesting), but the response to the conscious or less-than-conscious suspicion that one has a knowledge deficit that ought to be maintained. The term "half-knowledge" seems to relate to less conscious knowledge disavowal tendencies, while the term "forbidden research" seems to cover more conscious, deliberate knowledge disavowal actions.

Common Sense

The several phrases with which this chapter began ("Ignorance is bliss" and so on) are outcroppings of commonsense culture. It might well be argued that these phrases reflect nothing more than idle and superficial ideas; that they are not outcroppings of anything significant, but merely a kind of surface debris on the plain of wisdom. I would caution against such quick dismissal of these notions. Clifford Geertz (1975) presents a very insightful evaluation of common sense as a cultural system. In this evaluation he makes two very important points.

The first point Geertz makes is that common sense is a "relatively organized body of considered thought, rather than just what anyone clothed and in his right mind knows." There is much more to common sense than ordinarily meets the eye. In fact, the modelling of common sense is proving to be one of the most difficult and challenging tasks facing researchers in the area of artificial intelligence (Waltz, 1982). Whatever one's attitudes toward common sense (and very conflicting attitudes exist), it does represent the most pervasive body of thought we possess (see also Campbell, 1979, especially pp. 69–70). The important second point Geertz makes is that "it is an inherent characteristic of common sense thought precisely to deny [that is a relatively organized body of thought] and to affirm that its tenets are immediate deliverances of experience, not deliberated reflections upon it" (p. 7).

The denial that we know as much as we do is itself an interesting form of knowledge disavowal. A claim that our common sense is "more than what anyone clothed and in his right mind knows" would only invite closer scrutiny of its underlying assumptions. Such a scrutiny may lead to challenges to our assumptions. Worse still, we may have to alter our assumptions and consequently alter social arrangements that we would rather have unchanged.

The notion that common sense may reflect organized, considered thought suggests that a theory-in-use approach might be fruitfully applied to the several sayings or folkisms mentioned at the outset. Each saying seems to be derived from a set of propositions. Moreover, there are relationships among the different sets of propositions. Collectively, they manifest a rather well-integrated theory of willful ignorance that can be displayed mechanically as a causal model. Such a model has sufficient face validity to suggest the presence of a deeply held *normative* theory of knowledge disavowal. The social actions giving rise to this theory have an imprint on or spillover effect upon our approach to traditional scientific inquiry. The effect is to establish limits to inquiry.

Biased Assimilation and Confirmation

Knowledge disavowal is a rather subtle, less-than-conscious process. Considerable evidence has accumulated to the effect that information that could lessen our confidence in an item of knowledge or require an alteration in that knowledge may actually have the opposite effect. When mixed or inconclusive evidence about a position is presented, biases in the assimilation of that information will reinforce a person's existing beliefs while also being seen as lending no support for an opposite position. "Through such biased assimilation even a random set of outcomes or events can appear to lend support for an entrenched position, and both sides in a given debate can have their positions bolstered by the same set of data" (Lord et al., 1979, p. 2099). If research findings do not agree with our theoretical predilection, we often only then question the methodology used in the study. In fact, Lord et al. suggest an interesting reasoning process that goes something like this: "If research results contradicting my position can only be produced by a faulty methodology then my own position must be correct." This appears true for both professional researchers and managers (Mahoney, 1977). An investigation of managers' use of research found that, when results were not consistent with the preferred or desired findings, managers often turned (for the first time) to the research methods section of a report to find out *what* was wrong with the research methodology as opposed to *whether* it was in error (Deshpande and Zaltman, 1982). This was most likely when research findings fell outside a comfort zone of knowledge. That is, the further away a particular research finding was from some core set of familiar understandings, the more likely disavowal processes were to occur. Mahoney's work suggests the same phenomena among scientists. The social and psychological dynamics of biased assimilation cannot be addressed here. The consequences of these dynamics, however, are that we systematically—if unwittingly—disavow knowledge or information that contradicts our positions. This is precisely the kind of information that may have the greatest impact on our frames of references.

Other evidence noted earlier suggests that people tend to seek evidence that confirms rather than disconfirms inferences even though a disconfirming approach may be the most efficient, that is, require the least number of tries for ultimate verification where a correct solution exists (Wason, 1960,

1969). The tendency to avoid disconfirming evidence even in very artificial, low involvement exercises is suggestive of a natural tendency to disavow knowledge. In fact, as Einhorn (1980) points out rather convincingly, we continually judge our judgments in rather biased ways that prevent us from learning fully or even accurately from feedback about the outcomes of our decisions. The persistent avoidance of knowledge about the outcomes of our action is significant. We can only evaluate judgments and decisions through an assessment of outcome-related feedback. That is the principal way of knowing. Yet, we tend to disavow such activity.

Vague-Specifics

Research concerning the use of research by managers in public and private sector agencies suggests a phenomenon that might be described as "vague-specifics" (Zaltman and Deshpande, 1980). The expression "vague-specifics" refers to an attribute of a research report or a set of research findings relating to a specific decision. An example would be research related to the decision to introduce a potentially important new product. From the users' standpoint, the research should be *specific* enough to be of value in that decision. For example, the research should address certain important issues such as which market segments will be most receptive to the product and what are the preferred attributes of the new product among these segments. At the same time, the research should be suitably *vague* about certain issues, even when greater specificity might be obtained at little or no extra cost. In other words, a number of managers did not want to know everything they might have been enlightened about. One reason given for this posture was that in a risky situation (most new products are market failures and hence are risky ventures) a scapegoat is necessary in the event of failure. An incomplete research report may serve as a scapegoat. If the new product fails, the absence of information related to one or more causes of failure can be cited by a manager as the cause. Blame is at least partially displaced. The incomplete report (and consequently the researchers) share the responsibility. In effect, the manager is able to say, "It wasn't so much my interpretation of the research and my recommendation that were in error, but rather it was the failure of the research to provide all the information I really needed."

There is another side to this. It was also found, as attribution theory predicts, that managers desired vagueness or incomplete knowledge for reasons more related to successful outcomes. When information is specific and complete, the nature of a decision becomes more obvious. There is correspondingly less opportunity for a decision maker to add his or her own value through interpretation and through the provision of insight and judgment based upon his or her experiences. A related reason encountered was found in response to the question: Are there situations where it is advantageous to disguise the amount or type of information you have concerning particular marketing decisions? When the completeness of a research report lessens the ability of managers to add their own special contribution, they may simply not attach all the information supporting a decision or recommendation. If the outcomes is favorable, that portion of their recommendation based on "absent" information will be credited to their insight. Of course, if the outcome is unfavorable, they may subsequently bring forth the "absent" data to justify their recommendation and hence lessen their individual culpability.

Half-Life Knowledge

An individual item of knowledge might be considered to have a half-life; that is, it is subject to change and is "good" only for a particular period of time before wear-out becomes evident. The determinants of half-life are rather varied and collectively probably produce an irregular rate of decay. When a qualifying condition is added to a generally accepted principle, that principle is changed in some degree. Its original form is less valid. When an item of knowledge is applied to a given population, that population may change and hence the original item of knowledge may be less useful. For example, when we estimate a certain level of awareness among a group about early signs of mental illness and attempt to alter that level of awareness through an educational program, that initial estimated level of awareness becomes less valid or accurate and hence less useful than it was prior to the educational program.

Disputes about scientific findings are clashes between persons who want a longer life for an idea versus those who want a much shorter life for that idea. It is a central tenet of the scientific community that the extension of certified knowledge by scientists be the major guideline in awarding them professional recognition. To the extent that this is true and that extensions of knowledge involve significant alterations in previous knowledge, then we reward colleagues for shortening the half-life of knowledge.

However, there is an "on-the-other-hand" lurking about. There appear to be many events that might plausibly be construed as efforts to establish a longer half-life of knowledge. Knowledge disavowal is one way of doing this. It may take many forms. One form is only to accept information that comes from highly credible sources. A provocative study by Peters and Ceci (1982) suggests that journal referees and editors may find "serious methodological flaws" in research papers ostensibly from nonprestigious institutions, even when these very same papers had already been published by authors from high prestige institutions. Thus, creative use of truth tests (Dunn, 1980) may extend the half-life of knowledge. We also may limit access to information or sources that could provide information, thereby lessening the risk that currently accepted beliefs will be found inaccurate or somehow less valid according to one or more truth tests. While they are often surmountable, the barriers to accessing data for research are numerous and substantial (Brown et al., 1976). These barriers exist within both the subject pool of individuals and agencies that researchers study as well as within the research community itself.

Accessing research results may be no easier. All of us have heard—perhaps have even made—complaints about the unnecessary use of technical language and jargon in research reports. Similarly, the distribution of knowledge may be restricted to prolong its half-life. Market research findings become outdated more quickly if all firms are aware of the results and act upon them. Certain journals in various fields will not publish an article if it has been widely distributed as a preprint. This practice, its merits aside, has the effect of prolonging the half-life of the research finding or concept since journal publication may take considerably longer to reach a given audience (which may then alter the idea) than does preprint distribution.

IMPLICATIONS

The notion of knowledge disavowal has several implications for the production of useful knowledge within organizations. At a general level, it is important to recognize that forces for the production of knowledge are also influenced by the forces that inhibit the collection and dissemination of information or influence its interpretation. For example, exploratory research intended by some stakeholders to provide a better understanding of a problem or to identify possible solutions may be unwittingly implemented in a way that confirms the preferred definition or solution of other stakeholders in the firm. Alternative problem definitions/solutions are less likely to surface when research is confirmatory rather than exploratory. Certain options are thus unlikely to arise for consideration by those who are expecting a relatively wider array of perspectives. Not knowing that a confirmatory orientation was pursued by persons implementing the research would create the possibly incorrect impression that there was only one appropriate definition of the problem and once feasible solution.

Much research is intended to be confirmatory by all stakeholders in a firm. However, in such circumstances outside research providers often believe that the intent is exploratory. Hence, more information is produced than is desired. Some of this information may also contradict the position that was to be confirmed, thereby creating defensive reactions among the research clients. These reactions may be expressed through criticism of the research methodology. Special efforts are needed to ensure that the users and producers of research, when they are separate entities, have a common understanding about the exploratory and confirmatory purposes of the research. This means, for example, that users should inform outside research suppliers that a decision has been tentatively reached or that one particular action is favored and that the research is intended to validate or invalidate that particular action. This disclosure permits a more thorough exploration of the action management is primarily concerned with. Unfortunately, this disclosure often does not occur in instances where it is warranted. Consequently less useful knowledge is produced, although it has all outward appearances of being highly relevant and technically sound.

Another important implication concerns the notion of comfort zones. The tendency to reject research results that are surprising and fall outside a potential user's comfort zone poses a special problem for knowledge users and producers. In different ways each party may suffer. One way of widening comfort zones is to increase the frequency of interaction between the knowledge producer and user groups at all stages of the knowledge production process. Involving managerial clients in the pretesting of instruments and in pilot study activities may alert them to a potential surprise if this becomes evident during this preliminary stage (as it often does). This preliminary finding is that much less surprising should it persist in the more comprehensive investigation. Thus, there is an inoculation against resisting surprising results. The increased interactions may also increase user confidence in the researcher and in the research methodology. This lessens the tendency of an unwarranted dismissal of a surprise on these grounds. The increased interactions will also familiarize the researcher with users' comfort zones and enable the researcher to introduce a surprising result in a way that is more commensurate with the user's frames of reference.

The tendency to seek confirming evidence and to interpret data in ways that are consistent with existing assumptions, expectations, and decision rules suggests the need for an advocacy approach to research. For example, a venture team may tend to identify with a decision to introduce a new product. Information produced relevant to go/no go decisions may be biased in a "go" direction. Even if it appears to another party to favor a "no go" decision, the venture team may still be unconsciously biased in its interpretation. In this situation it has sometimes been found appropriate to have a formal "go" advocate and a formal "no go" advocate. Both parties must agree on all phases of the knowledge production process. This ranges from problem definition through various data collection stages to the selection and use of data-analytic techniques and even the reporting format. A limitation of this approach is that the devil's advocate role is an unpopular one and should be rotated.

Perhaps the most important message in this chapter is that pro-knowledge and knowledge disavowal phenomena commingle and are equally prevalent and impactful. The design of management information systems must explicitly acknowledge both forces. Failure to consider knowledge disavowal processes in MIS design will result in a system with half its working parts missing. Moreover, the missing considerations may be the more interesting elements. Knowledge disavowal is not an undesirable process; it may be quite healthy and functional for the organization. For these reasons alone knowledge disavowal phenomena should be built into the design of management information systems.

One special consideration merits a concluding comment. Rewards for researchers tend to encourage the production of knowledge that is consistent with extant assumptions, expectations, and decisions. The Law of the Lens reinforces this tendency and works equally among researchers in academic and commercial settings. When hidden events are found, various social forces mentioned earlier inhibit communication about these events. The difficulties that tend to keep hidden events hidden are to be found in part in the reward systems that operate during and subsequent to the training of researchers. Current reward systems are of course quite functional. They do encourage the production of very usable knowledge. A central challenge the management community faces (in academic and industrial settings) is how to maintain present benefits while altering the reward system so that we may encounter hidden events more often and at the same time more discriminatingly disavow elements in our present frames of reference. A caution from Will Rogers is in order: "It's not what we don't know that gives us trouble. It's what we know that ain't so." We need the ability to disavow present "knowledge," as well as the ability to avoid the disavowal of new knowledge.

CONCLUSION

This chapter has attempted to highlight the pervasiveness of knowledge disavowal phenomena by identifying several scattered treatments of the issue. Collectively, these treatments suggest that the avoidance of knowledge is an important social process. The several factors contributing to knowledge disavowal—such as the avoidance of disconfirming evidence, forbidden research, group think, and the dismissal of common sense—are interrelated. They also interact with pro-knowledge social processes in organizations. Therefore, this chapter will conclude with a discussion of the commingling of pro-knowledge and knowledge disavowal forces. It is this topic that should have a high research priority.

The coexistence of pro-knowledge and knowledge disavowal tendencies raises several interesting issues with respect to the study of knowledge use.

For example, it is suggested that information systems in organizations tend to acquire more information than the organization can employ (Feldman and March, 1981). Substantial surplus information is often acquired on a routine basis (for example, subscription to data services), but seldom if ever used and yet never discontinued when renewal decisions are made (Clarke, 1980). The existence of surplus information may be only partially understood in terms of pro-knowledge explanations such as risk reduction and environmental scanning. The existence of knowledge disavowal phenomena allows substantial surplus information to be accumulated without causing information overload at the organizational level. In this instance, knowledge disavowal processes do not develop merely in response to information overload. Disavowal phenomena may develop initially to ensure knowledge deficits. Once in place for this purpose, they may serve the additional purpose of helping the organization cope with knowledge surplus. This point will be elaborated upon briefly below.

There is good documentation supporting the illusion of control phenomena in which skill factors cause individuals to feel unjustifiably more confident than chance factors warrant (see Langer, 1975). That is, when applying skills in a setting where chance is also important, people feel more confident than is objectively warranted. The very act of engaging in forecasting and planning activities may give managers a greater sense of control over events than is in fact justified (Hogarth and Makridakis, 1981). There is not only a disavowal of the role of chance, but also a disavowal of new information as unnecessary. This is caused by the confidence induced by engaging in planning activities. This disavowal tendency is stimulated when wishful thinking is involved since desired outcomes are likely to receive higher probability assignments independently of the planning process. The presence of surplus information may be tolerated more easily because of this or may even be required by phenomena such as these. Knowing that the organization subscribes to many data services that supply potentially relevant information may provide a sense of security to individuals involved in planning and forecasting: "If information that contradicts my assessment exists surely someone will have noted it, particularly since it is very likely to be in our data bank;" or: "Fortunately we have a substantial data bank I could consult if my estimate is challenged, or if I need to cover myself with further supporting evidence in the event of a mistake." Thus, surplus information may provide a false sense of security or a potentially false sense of opportunity for cover-up in the event of an error or challenge. It is important to have this sense of security and cover-up opportunity, and hence important to have knowledge surplus precisely because of the tendency to avoid information that may lessen one's sense of control or highlight the possibility of undesired outcomes.

REFERENCES

Boje, David M., and J. Keith Murnigham. "Group Confidence Pressures in Interactive Decisions," *Management Science*, Vol. 28, No. 10, October 1982, pp. 1187–1196.

Brown, Colin, Pierre Guillet de Montheux, and Arthur McCullough. *The Access-Casebook: Social Scientists Account for How to Get Data for Field Research.* Stockholm, Sweden: Teknisk Hogskolelitteratur i Stockholm AB, 1976.

Campbell, Donald T. "Assessing the Impact of Planned Social Change," *Evaluation and Program Planning*, Vol. 2, 1979, pp. 67–90.

Churchman, C. West. "On the Epistemology of Useful Information for Organizations," In R. H. Kilmann, K. W. Thomas, D. P. Slevin, R. Nath, and S. L. Jerrell (eds.), *Producing Useful Knowledge for Organizations.* New York: Praeger, 1983, Chapter 11.

Clarke, Darryl. Unpublished report to the Marketing Science Institute, Cambridge, Mass., 1980.

Deshpande, Rohit, and Gerald Zaltman. "Factors Affecting the Consumption of Market Research: A Path Analysis," *Journal of Marketing Research*, February 1982.

Dunn, William. "The Two-Communities Metaphor and Models of Knowledge Use," *Knowledge: Creation, Diffusion, Utilization*, Vol. 1, No. 4, June 1980.

Einhorn, Hillel J. "Overconfidence in Judgment," *New Directions for Methodology of Social and Behavioral Science*, No. 4, 1980, pp. 1–16.

Feldman, Martha S., and James G. March. "Information in Organizations as Signal and Symbol," *Administrative Science Quarterly*, Vol. 26, 1981, pp. 171–186.

Geertz, Clifford. "Common Sense as A Cultural System," *Antioch Review*, Vol. 33, No. 1, 1975.

Hogarth, Robin M., and Spyros Makridakis. "Forecasting and Planning: An Evaluation," *Management Science*, Vol. 27, No. 2, February 1981, pp. 115–138.

Holzner, Burkart, and J. Marx. *Knowledge Application: The Knowledge System in Society.* Boston: Allyn & Bacon, 1979, p. 3.

Huber, George. "Organizational Information Systems: Determinants of Their Performance and Behavior," *Management Science*, Vol. 28, No. 2, February 1982, pp. 138–155.

Janis, Irving L. *Victims of Groupthink: A Psychological Study of Foreign Policy Decisions and Fiascos.* New York: Houghton Mifflin, 1972.

Langer, Ellen, J. "The Illusion of Control," *Journal of Personality and Social Psychology*, Vol. 32, No. 2, August 1975, pp. 311–328.

Lazarsfeld, Paul F. *The Uses of Sociology*, P. Lazarsfeld, W. Sewell, and H. Wilensky (eds.). New York: Basic Books, 1967.

Lord, Charles G., Lee Ross, and Mark Lepper. "Biased Assimilation and Attitude Polarization: The Effects of Prior Theories on Subsequently Considered Evidence." *Journal of Personality and Social Psychology*, Vol. 37, No. 11, 1979, pp. 2098–2109.

Mahoney, M. J. "Publication Prejudices: An Experimental Study of Confirmatory Bias in the Peer Review Systems," *Cognitive Therapy and Research*, Vol. 1, 1977, pp. 161–198.

Morin, Bernd. "What Is 'Half-Knowledge' Sufficient For—And When? Theoretical Comment on 'Policymakers' Use of Social Science," *Knowledge*, Vol. 3, No. 1, 1981.

Nelkin, Dorathy. "Forbidden Research: Limits to Inquiry in the Social Sciences," paper presented at the Conference on Political Realization of Social Science Knowledge, Vienna, June 18–20, 1980.

Nelkin, Dorathy. *Science Textbook Controversies and the Politics of Equal Time*, Cambridge, Mass.: MIT Press, 1978.

Peters, Douglas, and Stephen Ceci. "Peer-Review Practices of Psychological Journals: The Fate of Published Articles, Submitted Again," *Behavioral and Brain Sciences*, Vol. 5, No. 2, June 1982, pp. 187–195.

Rogers, Everett M. "New Product Adoption and Diffusion," *Journal of Consumer Research*, Vol. 2, March 1976, pp. 290–301.

Snyder, M., and W. B. Swann. "Behavioral Confirmation in Social Interaction: From Social Perception to Social Reality," *Journal of Experimental Social Psychology*, Vol. 14, 1978, pp. 148–162.

Solzhenitsyn, A. I. Harvard Commencement Address, 1978.

Waltz, David L. "Artificial Intelligence," *Science*, Vol. 247, No. 4, 1982, pp. 118–133.

Wason, P. C. "On the Failure to Estimate Hypotheses in a Conceptual Task," *Quarterly Journal of Experimental Psychology*, Vol. 12, 1960, pp. 129–140.

Wason, P. C. "Reasoning About A Rule," *Quarterly Journal of Experimental Psychology*, Vol. 20, 1969, pp. 273–281.

Wason, P. C., and P. N. Johnson-Laird. *Psychology of Reasoning: Structure and Content.* Cambridge, Mass.: Harvard University Press, 1972.

Westrum, R. "Social Intelligence About Hidden Events," *Knowledge: Creation, Diffusion, Utilization*, Vol. 3, No. 3, March 1982.

Zaltman, Gerald. "Presidential Address," presented at the ACR 1982 Annual Conference, San Francisco, October 1982.

Zaltman, Gerald, and Rohit Deshpande. "The Use of Market Research: An Exploratory Study of Manager and Researcher Perspectives." Cambridge, Mass.: Marketing Science Institute, 1980.

11

ON THE EPISTEMOLOGY OF USEFUL INFORMATION FOR ORGANIZATIONS

C. West Churchman

In this chapter, I will discuss a technology for producing useful knowledge for organizations. The technology, a very old one, is called "counting." It is so natural a human function, even for the very young, that one is apt to forget its technical meaning. I will be using a very general meaning of counting, namely, the assignment of a number to a class of objects.*

EPISTEMOLOGY OF COUNTING

To a philosopher, a conference devoted to producing useful knowledge must surely be concerned with epistemology, though there may be some who assert that the title has a redundancy (knowledge that has no use is not knowledge). But for those who do not agree with the redundancy, it is interesting to note that in the history of modern epistemology—starting, say, in the seventeenth century—epistemologists did not emphasize "useful," but rather "accurate" or as near to accurate as possible.

It is probably worthwhile to review briefly the search for the criteria of accurate knowledge or, as some would say, objective knowledge. The criteria were to be found in the notion of very simple knowledge, either the simplicities of reason (such as logic) or sensation (for example, of the color red). All accurate knowledge was to be based on these simplicities. Of

---

*For those with formal minds, the numbers obey the following laws: (a) There is an object in the class that has the number 1; (b) For any object of the class having the number x, there exists an object in the class with the number $x + 1$, except the "last" object (there are none beyond the last). No two objects have the same number. The number of the last object is the count of the set.

course, the problem was to establish which kind of knowledge was truly simple. If I say "no proposition can be both true and false," that seems simple enough; but is it? What about the proposition that declares itself to be false? Or, it is obvious that this cloth is red. Is it? John Locke said that all would agree that it is because all would perceive it to be red without using any analytic argument, as might be required if we were asked whether this object is a chair. But the source of the universal agreement for very simple sensations remained a mystery.

What has all this to do for the task of providing organizations with useful knowledge? One example is counting. All organizations need to be able to count accurately. Counting is a combination of the simplicities of reason (elementary arithmetic) and sensation ("one," "two," and so on). There has been very little change in the counting process over the centuries: it is basic to accounting, inventory control, personnel records, and other areas, all of which provide useful knowledge for organizations.

One should note that "objectivity" in counting is based on some combination of reason and sensation.

In the Book of Numbers, the Lord tells Moses to count the young men, 20 and over, in each of the tribes: an early example of census taking. But Moses had no simple empirical way of taking the count so as to satisfy the laws of counting, especially the law that says no object in the class shall be missed, nor any two objects given the same number. Indeed, Moses seemed to have sensed the difficulties, because he rounds the count off to the nearest 50. I do not intend to go into modern methods of counting, since I am chiefly interested in the enrichment of the concept of "count."

COUNTING AND TIME

Is that all there is to it? Is all useful knowledge for organizations acquired basically by some process of counting? In the first place, there are the economies of counting, which often tend to be fairly complicated (for example, we often use sampling procedures). But there is a feature about counting that bothers many organizations: a count is meaningful only in the context of a specific time. How often should an organization count?

To obtain some perspective on this question, we should look at measurement, another process of producing accurate knowledge that was being developed at about the same time that professional accounting was invented. Measurement does involve some form of counting, but a great deal more. Galileo was not the first measurer, but he did provide in his writings the basic process that is still used. At one point he was interested in how a freely falling (or freely rolling) ball behaves with respect to velocity and acceleration. He had used reason to deduce that the acceleration should be constant and decided to test his conclusion empirically. By use of an ingenious water clock and a smooth panel with regular marks, he was able to time the distances covered by the rolling balls and found that his rational conclusion was emprically accurate. All this appears to be a case of counting, albeit rather sophisticated. But Galileo's method was a lot more than his empirical setup because he assumed, through his reasoning, that his result was independent of time: his measurement information is good for all smooth panels and balls. As we would say today, his result is based on the gravitational *constant*, meaning that the result is an invariant. Thus, the process of measurement overcomes the problems of simple counting. Someone who is counting inventory on the shelves of a retail store is not measuring inventory. But if he knew how to predict the changes in inventory over time by means of supply-demand constants, then he would be measuring inventory.

Through the efforts of such organizations as the National Bureau of Standards, we in the United States have become so used to the invariances in the measurements of consumer goods that we are often unaware of them. When I was in India, I was introduced to a ruler with inch markings of varying lengths. It has not always been the case that a pound of sugar at one store was approximately equal to a pound of sugar in another store. The fact that we use a wooden ruler rather than a rubber ruler is another example of the search for invariances over time and space.

It is strange how the intellectuals of our day concentrate their attention on the structure of the measurement results (asymmetry, transitivity, density, and additivity) rather than the essence of measurement, which is information that remains useful in different times and places. Measurement also has another advantage: very frequently its results can be estimated in terms of an error term (probable error, or some such).*

It is important to notice that, though counting may be analytic, measurement is not. By an analytic process I mean one that can be designed by putting together simple elements (such as counting objects in a row, adding, multiplying, and so forth). I suspect that counting may not really be analytic, but measurement surely is not. Every aspect of Galileo's experiment needed to be examined. His water clock was not accurate and, over the years, could only be improved by developing a more and more sophisticated kinematics and mechanics. In other words, calibration, the heart of the measurement process, unfolds into more complicated theories and not into simpler and simpler elements.

---

*For a fuller discussion, see C. West Churchman, "Why Measure?" in *Measurement: Definitions and Theories*, ed. C. West Churchman and Philburn Ratoosh (New York: Wiley, 1959, pp. 83–94).

COUNTING AND PURPOSE

Is that it? Is "useful knowledge" some form of counting or measurement? No, because we have not yet examined "useful." To do so, we have to turn to teleology, the study of purposive behavior. All organizations can be observed as goal-seeking entities, that is, teleologically. If so, "useful" has a fairly clear-cut meaning. Suppose you are lost in a strange city and want to find the hotel where you have reserved a room. You ask a knowledgeable native who tells you how to proceed. Assuming the native is knowledgeable and honest, his information will be "useful." This suggests that the definition of "useful" is based on first ascertaining organizational objectives and then determining whether a meaningful string of symbols improves the manner in which the organization strives to attain its objectives. Since survival is often a major objective of most organizations, "useful" information tells organizations where the dangers and resources are.

Because it is often difficult to determine the objectives of organizations and the information supplier is often uncertain about how information ties into the objectives, there has been a tendency in the computer age to overload the information system with data that appear to have some usefulness. But I am less interested here in overload than I am in a peculiar kind of information that seems essential for organizations and yet is very poorly understood.

COUNTING AND OPPORTUNITY COSTS

To understand this kind of information, I need to make the distinction between bounded problem solving and systemic management. In bounded problem solving, the objective can be clearly stated and its accomplishment taken as desirable in and of itself, as in the case of the lost tourist seeing his hotel. If one asks why the tourist chose to come to this town or chose this hotel, the bounds become more relaxed. As long as the problem is tightly bound, the meaning of "useful" information is fairly clear. As the bounds ease, its meaning becomes more and more obscure. If the tourist should really be elsewhere, responding, say, to an emergency, then learning how to get to the hotel may be the opposite of "useful" because he should be seeking the railway station. Thus, information that accurately solves the wrong problem in the unbounded sense is not useful.

This may sound obvious enough. But the obvious common sense hides the real difficulty of producing what I will call the "systemic" or "unbounded systemic" management information.

There is a common image of the decision maker that is found in many texts on decision making. He is supposed to be faced by a number of feasible alternatives that are depicted as though they were so many doors he can open. But the image tells us he can open only one and that is it: the tiger or the lady? Each door leads to a set of results that vary in their quality. Some results have very good features; some, bad. All have a mixture of values for the decision maker. All results need not occur at the same time. The image tells us how to find a unifying utility function over the results, which includes time and probabilities. Finally, the image tells us which door he should open.

For example, Reno and Las Vegas provide a large number of options for the gambler. If he brings a modern planner along, the planner can tell the decision maker where to gamble—perhaps.

The trouble is that for the managers of public or private organizations the image is wrong, and for a very good reason. One can begin to understand the reason if one compares slot machines and blackjack. For the sake of the innocents, I need to explain that slot machines operate by the gambler's inserting a coin and pulling down a handle. Usually three pictures of, say, different fruits appear in a window. Some sequences of the pictures pay money; some do not. Blackjack is a game of cards between the gambler and the dealer. Now, in the case of the slot machine, once the gambler has pulled the handle he has nothing to do but wait for the result. In the case of blackjack, however, once the gambler is dealt the initial cards he usually has to make another decision, namely, whether to ask for another card—he does *not* just wait for the outcome.

One should understand that there is quite a difference between these two gambling games. Perhaps, based on my own experience, I can put it this way: within reasonable limits, it really does not matter whether a gambler has had several drinks before playing a slot machine; but for most gamblers it matters a great deal when playing blackjack. In philosophical language, the slot machine is mechanical, ateleological, whereas blackjack is teleological. In management language, the slot machine needs no management once the handle is pulled, whereas blackjack requires management. In systems thinking, the slot machine and the gambler are a bounded system, but not the blackjack dealer and the gambler because the system of the dealer and the gambler unfolds into the system of the gambler and drinking, or of the gambler and fatigue, or of the gambler and intelligence and experience.

Most managers, in addition to opening the doors, have to manage the passage to the results. This means that the "management information" is totally different from a set of empirical data or management "principles." The needed information is information about how to manage the situation that each door opening demands. Hence, "management information" is incredibly difficult to obtain because it means knowing how to manage a plethora of other systems.

Consider inventory, for example, the "problem" of how many white shirts, size 15½, 33, to order for a men's store. The "doors" are the integers from 0 to n. Operations-research texts tell poor, unprepared students to use some sort of inventory model. The texts point out that if the students open door 20, they may have shirts that sit on the shelf for days earning no money at all for the store. If they had opened door 10, they would have had, in the form of cash, ten times the cost of a shirt. What could they do with the cash? Most texts tell them to use the current interest rate to measure the value of this "lost opportunity." But is that the best way to manage cash? In fact, the manager needs to have a cash flow model to solve the inventory problem.

Now, one can understand why the systems approach is more realistic than the "separate problem" approach. If I have some image (weltan-schauung) of the retail store, I may be able to make the necessary approximations of a measure like opportunity costs.

Consider demand on inventory. Most texts tell students how to make probability distributions of past demands, thereby assuming that there is no need to manage demand. But, of course, any wise manager knows that managing demand by pricing, advertising, and so forth is the heart of retailing.

Another way to explain the unusual aspect of the epistemology of useful organizational information is that the conclusion of the intellectual effort is an action and not a proposition. A mathematician who proves a theorem ends his task with a set of symbols on a piece of paper; writing the symbols appropriately is the only action he takes. An experimenter also writes symbols; the numbers he obtains from his observations and the analysis he performs of his results. But the planner has to consider the actions of humans. For example, he may derive from his method an instruction that reads "reduce manpower 25 percent in Division 1," but that instruction is *not* the action. The action consists of managing personnel reduction so that it does not harm the organization and the people who are to be fired.

Since I often write on the "systems approach," I am asked what "it" really is. My response is that one way to recognize a systems approach versus a nonsystems approach is to do pretty much what I did at the outset in distinguishing between elementary counting and measurement (the latter being an unfolding process into other domains of science). If the process of acquiring useful information for an organization simply ends in a set of data or graphs, then the process is not a systems approach. But if it unfolds into other domains of management, thereby showing, for example, that the problem of inventory always involves financial, marketing, and personnel management, then it may be a systems approach.

As I understand the state of the art of the systems approach today, we simply do not understand how to count opportunity costs. We might like to say that we can "approximate" them, but if we dared to say this we would have to show that one estimate is a closer approximation than another. I do not think we can do anything of the kind.

I regard the task of designing a defensible process of counting opportunity costs to be among the deepest mysteries of all human knowledge acquisition and a far more dangerous mystery than any other we face in this area. What does it cost us to maintain a huge military system rather than a smaller one or none at all?

"Give me liberty or give me death" is a statement about opportunity costs; it says that the option of some form of governmental control over a part of our lives against our wills costs far more than the option of more freedom and a dangerous and costly militaristic system. I do not see how we can have any assurance that this judgment is correct. An individual might feel personally that he by himself has confidence in the judgment, but the correct form of the judgment is not "Give *me* liberty or give me death," but rather "Give me and all future generations forever liberty or give us death."

There are a number of examples that show we design our lives by means of the wrong opportunity costs. Worldwide, we choose the option of starving a billion people. Why? Because the option of feeding everybody is too costly. Does anyone care to say that this way of estimating the opportunity cost is correct?

I know some of the difficulties we face. In our culture, intellectuals are trained in reductionism within bounded disciplines. Ph.D. candidates are told to "keep the problem within manageable limits." But the task of designing a process to count opportunity costs cannot be kept within manageable limits, nor does it belong to any discipline.

Of course, our government and corporate managers cannot hold on to their jobs if they confess that they cannot estimate opportunity costs in a reliable manner. At best, if they are honest, they have to occasionally say to themselves, "You know, you have no idea whatsoever that what you are doing makes sense."

I sent this chapter to my friend, Tom Cowan, to comment on, and he replied that it ended a bit abruptly, as though I had pushed the reader off the precipice. He then suggested the following ending:

"Ancient wisdom tells us that when setting out on any venture to be sure 'to count the costs' or, as we put it, 'count the opportunity costs.' Now, we know without being told that opportunity and costs are frightfully complex things, but one usually prefers not to raise the question of how to *count* them.

Perhaps, I have come full circle on myself. Not too long ago I was occupied with the 'stories' one tells on himself in attempting to understand his fundamental epistemological puzzles. Perhaps, I should pause to reflect on how near the word 'count' is to its relative 'recount.' A count is indeed a 'conte,' a story.* I have been playing with things deeper than I knew when I started out with what usually appears such a simple matter—the adventure known as counting."

---

*COUNT COUP of an American Indian: ... "to relate the story of one's coups." *Webster's Third New International Dictionary*, 1976, 518.

12

INTELLECTUAL PERFORMANCE AND UTILIZATION IN A TWO-PARADIGM ADMINISTRATIVE AND ORGANIZATIONAL SCIENCE: A PHILOSOPHY OF SCIENCE-BASED ASSESSMENT

Rabi S. Bhagat

From time to time, researchers pause from their data collection and theory-generation efforts to pursue an evaluation of the intellectual performance of their scientific discipline. Existing conceptual models and empirical research methodology are typically the subjects reviewed. However, fundamental questions regarding the intrinsic intellectual performance of a discipline, the significance and utility of its discoveries, and the effectiveness of its predominant paradigms are posed less frequently. When an inquiry is made into the effectiveness of administrative and science-based organizational theories, the traditional modes of evaluation are based on "understanding, prediction, and control" of the organizational phenomena. If one were to inquire further into what is meant by "understanding," the answer might well be framed in terms of the scientist's role in "apprehending clearly the character, nature or subtleties" or organizational life (Urdang, 1968). From this perspective, inquiry into the causes and consequences of social and behavioral phenomena is granted a preeminent ontological status in that it furnishes the essential mysteries for the social scientist to discover.

An earlier version of this chapter was presented at the symposium chaired by Rabi S. Bhagat and Kim Cameron entitled "New Directions in Organizational Behavior: A Young Turk Perspective" at the National Academy of Management Meetings, August 1979. Research on this chapter was made possible by a grant from the Division of Behavioral and Neural Sciences of the National Science Foundation (BNR: 8011859). Appreciation is expressed to Edward E. Sampson, Kenneth J. Gergen, H. Peter Dachler, and Louis R. Pondy for their encouragement in furthering my interest in the philosophy of science-based analyses of organizations. Helpful comments on an earlier draft were provided by Janice M. Beyer, Larry L. Cummings, Kenneth J. Gergen, Don Hellriegel, Sara J. McQuaid, Michael Moch, Lawrence H. Peters, Lyman W. Porter, and Harry C. Triandis.

The fundamental question posed in this philosophy of science-based inquiry focuses on the effectiveness of the existing state of knowledge in the field of administrative and organizational sciences (Roberts, Hulin, and Rousseau, 1978). Such examination has an important role in the development of the "science" of organizations. The criticisms thus generated regarding the fundamental nature, as well as the current intellectual performance, of a discipline, act as a guidance system, helping to establish firm theoretical footholds in the volumes of published empirical information and to offer directions for future research efforts (Gordon, Kleiman, and Hanie, 1978). Such examinations may also signal a need for renewed theoretical analysis along nontraditional avenues (Gergen, 1973, 1976, 1978, 1980, 1981) and may precipitate paradigm shifts (Sampson, 1978). Some incisive and critical evaluations of the performance of organizational behavior, and of behavioral science in general, already exist (see Dunnette, 1966, 1976; MacKenzie and House, 1978; Gordon, Kleiman, and Hanie, 1978; Behling, 1980; Morgan and Smircich, 1980; and Frost, 1980). But when compared to the amount of empirical work in the last two decades in the area of administrative and organizational analysis, such evaluations have been infrequent. However, we have witnessed a significantly larger number of evaluative research-related reviews, which were based on increasing the vigor with which research efforts are currently undertaken. Reviews on the empirical literature on sensitivity training by Campbell and Dunnette (1968), on job enlargement processes by Hulin and Blood (1968), on task redesign by Roberts and Glick (1981), on cross-cultural organizational research by Roberts (1970) and Child (1981), on organizational climates by Schneider (1975), and on organizational effectiveness research by Hannan, Freeman, and Meyer (1976), Steers (1975), and Cameron (1978), illustrate the general tenor of this approach. As evaluative and integrative reviews of topical research areas within the current paradigms for studying administrative and organizational science, they provide excellent blueprints of achievements and failures of the research efforts of organizational scholars. However, in order to understand the nature of the intellectual performance of administrative and organizational sciences, it is necessary to consider not only the theories, methods, and findings in several topical areas in the last three decades (Greiner [1979] recently traced the historical roots of organizational sciences to 1945), but also the adequacy of the paradigms within which such research traditions have typically been pursued. Evaluations of the paradigms are concerned with the fundamental nature of scientific inquiry itself, in contrast to research reviews within an established paradigm undertaken to enhance the technical performance as opposed to the philosophical efficacy of the inquiries.

There have been some important evaluations of this nature since the first editor of *Administrative Science Quarterly*, James D. Thompson, called for the "building of an administrative science" (1956:102). For Thompson, sound development of administrative science necessitated the assumption of identifiable regularities in organizational phenomena, use of abstract concepts, development of operational definitions, and systematic interpretation and assimilation of empirical findings. But perhaps after 26 years, as the call for a special issue of *Administrative Science Quarterly* signifies, the time has arrived to undertake a critical analysis of whether the promise Thompson saw in using the scientific paradigm has been fulfilled. Specifically, are we developing knowledge of a transtemporal and transhistorical nature (two fundamental objectives of the scientific method) to guide and enrich the quality of the applications of the discipline? If not, what are the major theoretical impediments to the development of our science? In this evaluative chapter, I draw upon my own experience as a student of administrative and organizational sciences and make some observations about the current state of the field and the challenges it faces. I will be speaking primarily from the perspective of a participant observer; hence, I have the strengths and weaknesses of this method of inquiry. Although my observations have the advantages of being derived from my firsthand encounters with the field, they also reflect my personal biases, values, and aspirations for the field. A more detached reviewer might analyze the intellectual performance of the field in a different light and so might very well reach different conclusions.

THE DISCIPLINE OF ADMINISTRATIVE AND ORGANIZATIONAL SCIENCE AS A SOCIAL SYSTEM

The typical researcher in our field would argue that the substantive content of knowledge that is attained is ultimately determined by the intrinsic nature of the phenomena under investigation. Since empirical research is essentially a process of discovery with an internal logic of its own, the quality of intellectual performance is ultimately determined by the intrinsic complexity of the phenomena being studied. The notion that the organizational scientist is confronted with an organization that is both sensitive to wide-ranging influences and capable of immense variations in behavior is widely accepted. Further, the individual's complex set of symbolic interactions with the organizational setting, the range and type of inputs to which he or she may be responsive, and the organizational norms governing these interaction may all be altered over time. Thus, patterns of human activity in organizational contexts may be in a continuous state of emergence, aleatoric in the sense that they may largely reflect prevailing contingencies (Gergen, 1977, 1980). The information-processing capabilities of humans place severe restrictions upon the administrative and organizational scientist's efforts to improve the intellectual performance of the discipline. In contrast, for example, astronomical theory continues to provide reasonably accurate predictions of the movement of celestial bodies because the movements of the specific entities are relatively reliable and hence can be mapped within the framework of existing theoretical models. It is now widely accepted that the complexity of organizational phenomena is at least partly responsible for the limited scope of applicability of the models of the discipline (Daft and Wiginton, 1979; Pinder and Moore, 1979; Frost, 1980) to real life organizational settings.

It is also quite true, as Cartwright (1979) and Gordon et al. (1978) have recently argued, that knowledge attained in a discipline is the product of the social system of that discipline and, as such, is basically influenced by the demand characteristics of that system and by its cultural, social, and political environments. Tracing the historical development of contemporary social psychology, Cartwright (1979) pointed out that there are certain pragmatic advantages to be gained from conceiving of the discipline as a social system. First, it helps to establish realistic standards for evaluating a field's rate of progress. In adopting this social system approach to a discipline, one does not seek to minimize the contributions made by individual scholars. But in order to understand how these scholars came to make their distinctive contributions and why their work continues to influence the present development of the field, we must examine the nature of the social system within which they functioned, its stage of paradigmatic development, and the demands made upon it by the larger social setting.

A second advantage of this point of view is that it helps us to recognize areas where efforts might be redirected in order to bring about some fundamental changes in the way the field operates—including perhaps the nature and quality of its intellectual performance. Cartwright (1979), in a critical appraisal of social psychology in a historical perspective, suggests that for the discipline to upgrade the quality of its performance, it is necessary not only to mend the existing theoretical and methodological ways of its current group of researchers, but also to bring about some drastic changes in the manner in which the discipline itself as a social system functions and distributes its rewards to these scholars. He also called for an examination of the historical, political (such as World War II), and social forces that affected the development of social psychology in its formative years and the influence of such forces on the intellectual performance of the discipline.

The expanded analysis that follows implies that a change in organizational science's intellectual performance, at the very minimum, will require focusing on: first, the functioning of the social system of the discipline; second, developing an alternative conception of proper science (Paradigm II) that is more inclusive and effective compared to the existing view (Paradigm I); and third, contrasting patterns of utilization of research outcomes in a two-paradigm organizational science.

FORCES IMPACTING DEVELOPMENT OF THE FIELD

Research in administrative and organizational science, especially industrial-organizational psychology (with the notable exception of work by organizational sociologists such as Perrow, Thompson, Burns and Stalker, Trist, and others), is characterized by an overwhelming engineering or managerial perspective. Despite our persistent attempts to establish a value-free and objective science, our scientific activities are primarily devoted to the service of solving "real-life" organizational problems; as Dubin (1976, p. 19) puts it, "the kind of problems to which an executive is willing to address himself." There can be little doubt that the single most important influence on the development of the science of organizations came from outside the system itself. I am referring, of course, to the demands industrial organizations and their managers made on the discipline to provide them with guidelines for practical issues such as personnel selection, validation, and testing. These demands came at a critical stage of the field's development and still are largely responsible for the one-sided growth that has characterized much of its development (Argyris, 1976). During the first two decades of its existence, organizational science was mainly concerned with establishing itself as a legitimate field of empirical research. Much of its substantive content was determined by what the industry wanted from the field in the way of recommendations for organizational policies regarding the selection and maintenance of their personnel systems (Argyris, 1976). Work on applied problems like these called for the sharpening of technical tools from related behavioral science disciplines. While much of this work was done by industrial/personnel psychologists, individuals trained in other disciplines—notably sociology and business administration—made important and extensive contributions as well. The result of these efforts, taken collectively, was a dramatic expansion of the empirical base of "the science of organizations." This expansion has not, however, been paralleled by a similar trend in the development of integrative theories of organizational functioning (Kimberly, 1976). Many explanations can be provided to account for the apparent gap between the body of data generated and the adequacy of accompanying theoretical frameworks. Although it is not the goal of this chapter to attempt to develop an elaborate argument on that issue, it does appear that at least part of this unfortunate state of affairs lies in the predominance and preeminence of the engineering or the managerial approach underlying most of the theoretical frameworks in the discipline.

This gap between theory and data is important for two reasons. First, it reflects an inadequate understanding of organizational phenomena based on research conducted within the present paradigm. Second, it reflects a lack of usefulness of organizational research despite its practical intent and engineering bias.

Dachler (1979) has argued that much of what are typically considered the basic cornerstones or explanations of organizational phenomena are nothing but predictive frameworks of a preestablished managerial problem in the real life of work organizations. For example, although leadership is one conceptualization of the basic social influence processes between two groups of individuals, we have reduced the study of leadership within organizational contexts to the narrowly conceived and predictive frameworks of leadership effectiveness. Similarly, while expectancy theory is one conceptualization of the basic phenomenon of human motivation, we have converted the theory into a predictive framework of productivity, turnover, and absenteeism. The ultimate goal behind much of this theorizing is to attempt to make immediately useful the fruits of our intellectual labors to pragmatic managers and hardlined practitioners. As a result of this need to be useful to managers, the "responses" that organizational scientists choose to study are few, compared with the whole range of human responses that are generally elicited within organizational settings. Rarely do we inquire, for example, into the sense-making processes of a minority female beginning to work in a traditionally masculine work role for a male-dominated, Protestant work ethic-oriented organization. Roberts, Hulin, and Rousseau (1978) make this point even more explicit:

> We look for responses that define organizations in terms of enduring patterns of social interactions. We therefore select for study measures reflecting the relative productivity or effectiveness of individuals, groups or organizations. We usually select for observation responses thought relevant to the efficient attainment of organizational goals consistent with high quality of worklife for organizational members. (p. 9)

Such an emphasis has opened up new areas of investigation within the discipline designed to supply applied knowledge to meet the needs of the ever-hungry group of industrial managers. This tendency has demonstrated the power of empirical research based on the survey techniques. It has resulted in the accumulation of a tremendous mass of new information but, I must add, not much in the way of what Gergen (1978) would call "generative theory." Generative theory is defined as that which is liberated from the pressure of immediate empirical verification and function to sustain personal value commitments of the researcher, thus facilitating the process of restructuring the character of social life.

At any rate, the emphasis on concrete as opposed to abstract problems of the discipline established the practical usefulness of what is called industrial/organizational psychology in the eyes of managers of work organizations. Most important, it fundamentally altered the insider's view of the field and its place in society, and established administrative and organizational science, once and for all, as a legitimate field of specialization and as a field worthy of large-scale public support.

No review of the historical forces that have shaped contemporary organizational behavior would be complete without a detailed consideration of such influences on how inquiry within the discipline is typically carried out. It can become apparent now why we pursue knowledge of the causes and consequences of work motivation and job satisfaction processes, of the antecedents and outcomes of effective leadership and managerial styles, of the determinants of organizational commitment and its attendant effects on system effectiveness. It will also explain why organizational intervention techniques such as work redesign, career development, stress management, and so forth are popular research topics within the discipline. Indeed, many of the conceptual frameworks of administrative and organizational science, including all of the unexamined assumptions about its proper subject matter and dominant methods of research, are largely the product of a group of academic professionals with a common interest (that of improving effectiveness of personnel development processes) and with a rather homogeneous point of view. Furthermore, because of the social conditions of the time in which they were developing the science of organizations, they are predominantly white, male, middle-class Americans, and thus reflect the interests and value biases of this segment of the population. As a result of World War II and the political events that followed, the scientific study of work organizations became, to a great extent, an American academic enterprise.

Important contributions have also been made by European and British scholars like Burns and Stalker, Trist, Woodward, and others at the Tavistock Institute of Human Relations. Organizational sociologists like Merton, Blauny, Lipset, Blau, Perrow, and Etzioni also made important contributions at this time. However, since they did not write from a managerial perspective, their intellectual efforts did not affect the growth of an applied reputation of the discipline. This turn of events has profound implications for evaluating the current intellectual performance of the field as we know it today. The study of organizations, more than any other branch of science (with the possible exception of anthropology), requires a breadth of intellectual perspective that can only be achieved by a truly international community of scholars. Organizational scientists are not merely students of organizations—they are also active participants in these work organizations. Despite their sincere and honest efforts to attain a detached participant observer-based objectivity in their research, their thinking and mode of pursuing research inquiries are strongly affected by the demands of the particular organizational and societal culture in which they live and do their work (Cartwright, 1979; Lambright and Teich, 1981).

The truth of the above assertion became apparent to me while I undertook the task of reviewing the empirical literature on the relations between work and nonwork. I found that we seem to know a great deal about the impact of work on nonwork, but almost nothing about the reverse effect (Bhagat, 1980). The institution of work is and has always been a valued one in the historical evolution of modern day industrial America; as such, the cultural conceptions of how work affects nonwork are likely to be pursued with much more vigor than the reverse. The academic researchers investigating this relationship are after all products of middle class Anglo-Saxon America, and despite their best efforts to attain a detached objectivity in their research, their thinking is shaped by the strong work-related and achievement-focused values of the American culture dominant in the universities in which they function. I am not suggesting that all of these cultural influences have been detrimental to the intellectual performance of the field, but I do feel that it would be a mistake to underestimate the magnitude of their effects upon the problems that have been chosen for investigation, how they have been approached, the research strategies employed, the way the research efforts have been organized, and the amount of time organizational scientists have devoted to thinking about alternative conceptions of what may be termed proper science.

Following Cartwright's (1979) and Gergen's (1978, 1981) incisive commentaries on the status of theory and intellectual performance of the field of social psychology, I would also like to suggest that much of what has been accomplished has been influenced by: the pragmatic demands of practitioners of the industry; the policies of journals and publishing houses; the monetary and symbolic reward system of the universities and of the discipline; the nature of the demographic composition of the profession; and the constraining effect of widespread acceptance of the "self-contained individualism" and "cognitivism" of Paradigm I science of organizations.

Paradigm I science is based on the natural law thought that eliminates the value-laden standpoint of the knower from the research process so that both increased objectivity and abstract, universally applicable, scientific truths in the form of nomothetic statements are made possible (Sampson, 1978).

In this analysis, I widen my thesis by arguing that unless we learn to grapple theoretically with this issue of Paradigm I science and its value-laden inquiries, the current intellectual performance of organizational science will merely continue to survive at its present level of commonsensicalness (Gordon et al., 1978) and will remain rather uninteresting (Davis, 1971).

SELF-CONTAINED INDIVIDUALISM, COGNITIVISM OF PURITAN PROTESTANTISM, AND THE PARADIGM I VIEW

A review of the intellectual and cultural history of Great Britain would reveal that both Protestantism and the emerging view of "proper science" were at their very core liberation movements. They both were efforts to break away from existing religious and social forms—including the inertia of tradition as embodied in the church and state. These liberation movements, in which the superiority of individualism was encouraged over former oppressive demands for autocratic, collective rule, slowly began to affect each other's intellectual growth (Merton, 1957; Israel, 1966). It should, therefore, come as no surprise to discover that the model of proper scientific thought that evolved at the intersection of these two social liberations sought to remove itself from any particularistic reference points (which had been formal tradition in the earlier era) and to seek laws of natural science that would be applicable to all persons, everywhere. In other words, efforts were redirected to discovering laws of human behavior with both transhistoric and transtemporal applicability. Sampson (1978) argued that the notion of evolving Puritan Protestantism affected the growth of the theories of social organization by assuming liberally the role of the individual as a significant causal entity. It stressed cognitive rather than emotional forms, orienting itself toward educating and instructing people rather than appealing to their emotional beings (Israel, 1966). Such emphasis facilitated the study of cognitive processes within organizational contexts as a commendable activity. It also oriented the central concern of organizational science toward developing a corresponding set of cognitive or rationally derived utilitarian and instrumental indexes for the study of micro- and macrolevel organizational phenomena. This emphasis on cognitive as contrasted with more *aesthetic, nonutilitarian,* but *integrative values* earmarked the period of the sharp departure of the Paradigm I science-based social inquiries from values that characterized the former pre-Protestant era. Sampson (1981) has recently characterized this intellectual movement as "cognitivism," and analyzed its antecedents in terms of the ideological roots inherent in the social history of the industrializing Western world. The essence of the spirit of Protestantism was also consonant with the rise of experimentally oriented cognitive social science that sought to unlock systematically the mysteries of God's handiwork through the rigorous application of positive rationale or logic (Rossides, 1978). Thus, the positive and empirical demands of a growing science were sustained in the fertile soil of Puritan Protestantism (see Rossides for a detailed discussion). The appeal to individualistic fervor in the service of mankind that Protestantism contained affected several other aspects of the patterning of social science-based inquiries. As Ratner (1973) and Merton (1957) suggested, the individualistic tone of this view of proper science placed the burden of responsibility on the individual's own analytical and cognitive skills—resulting in the development of extremely atomistic and analytic scientific models. Finally, the democratization and pursuit of equality that helped evolve the religious ethos also influenced the scientific paradigm by forcing it to search for general and universal laws.

A view of proper organizational science that is abstract, general, and universal seeks relatively permanent truth in organizational contexts. Immediate acceptance of this view would imply that there is little to be learned from examining the relationship between these "findings" and the nature of the particular sociohistorical context. Mannheim (1936, 1971) and Sampson (1978) have suggested that if social science theorists were to argue strongly for the transtemporality of their empirical findings, then they would become susceptible to the built-in blindness of their own sociohistorical position. The natural science conception of proper science makes it harder for organizational scientists to grasp the particularistic nature of social-psychological truths that are indeed embedded within the context of a given sociohistorical era. For example, theories of organizational effectiveness (Mott, 1972; Steers, 1975; Goodman, Pennings, and Associates, 1977) are pursued with the persistent belief that the development of a universally applicable theory of organizational effectiveness is simply awaiting the development of a set of measurement techniques to measure the concept across various types of organizations. In accepting this approach, organizational scientists ignore the possibility of studying the social and ideological bases of such organizational effectiveness theories (see Cameron's [1978] work on organizational effectiveness as an exception to this rule). The trend is to develop valid, value-free, objective, reliable measures of organizational effectiveness—even though what is considered "value-free" in terms of the accepted paradigmatic modes of organizational inquiry may indeed mirror the virtues of what Sampson (1978) has called the "self-contained individualism" and "cognitivism" of Puritan Protestantism.

This value orientation would succinctly favor the generation of only those theories of organizational effectiveness that are based on the notions of organizational survival and are in consonance with the themes of preservation of private property, market economy, political-legal equality, and above all faith in organizational progress and prosperity. In this view, a Paradigm I conception of both social and organizational science provides us with a limited perspective, one that we must carefully examine in terms of its potential for serving the interests of those who would like our theories of organizations to perpetuate the ethos and virtues of Protestant Puritanism in the conduct and execution of their favored organizational policies. Gergen (1978) noted that despite the traditional attempt to remain ethically neutral, the social science theorist is inevitably pursuing the desirability of certain forms of social activities over others, certain segments of society over others, and certain values over their antitheses. It is perhaps for this reason that hardly anyone within the discipline of organizational science would raise a debate concerning the suitability of the traditional indicators of organizational or even individual effectiveness in terms of their embeddedness in the social and intellectual history of the liberal Protestantism of nineteenth-century America. A given scientific paradigm can either invite or deter certain kinds of theoretical or conceptual schemes as opposed to others. Thus, the kinds of theorizing that a Paradigm I view would help sustain in the area of organizational inquiry may indeed act to prevent entry of alternative (and possibly radically different) modes of scientific inquiry. Such a trend would, of course, seek to maintain an ideally close relationship between canons of traditional theorizing and the generation of empirical data to validate and sustain these theories.

THE NEED FOR A PARADIGM SHIFT

From the traditional positivist standpoint, the scientist's task is to develop theories of transhistoric validity. Thus, in developing well-focused theoretical models and isolating major variables, theorists normally assume transtemporal applicability of their formulations (Gergen, 1978). Cognitive dissonance theory, Adams's equity theory, Locke's theory of job satisfaction and job performance (Locke, 1973), Mitchell, Green, and Wood's (1981) attributional theory of leadership, and so on are not generally viewed as merely reflections of contemporary social life-styles as reflected in ongoing organizational contexts. Theorists who develop and present these conceptual models in the field of administrative and organizational science and then subject them to rigorous empirical tests believe these models are transcendent and therefore possess, or at least are capable of possessing, transhistoric qualities. This is the classic view of empirical truth in natural and physical sciences, one that is still the dominant paradigm in the area of organizational sciences (Behling, 1980). This view of science is what Sampson (1978) calls the Paradigm I mode of natural inquiry, as contrasted with the romantic and historicist countermovement or as one that describes "the consciousness of an epoch" (Lichtheim, 1967, p. 31).

In the Paradigm II view of natural science, the images of society are reflected in the thought processes of scientific knowledge. To conceive of a paradigm as historical in this sense is to acknowledge its ultimate embeddedness in a particular culture and in its social and intellectual history. In this view, facts and truth emerge within "specific places and times"; the concrete context affects what we ultimately get to "know" about the processes we study. Mannheim (1936) and Sampson (1979) among others have noted that the influence of this sociohistorical standpoint of knowledge is not considered a source of error, as contrasted with the Paradigm I conception of science, but as an element that is intrinsic to all knowledge. Rather than something to be treated as "error variance" and therefore eliminated, it is something to be understood as part of the very process by which knowledge and facts are eventually generated. Even Kuhn (1970), while discussing the predominance of the epistemological mode of inquiry of Paradigm I in natural sciences, notes that "it no longer functions effectively" (p. 125). The concept of the existence of paradigms in sciences is the essence of a Paradigm II view of scientific inquiry (Sampson, 1978). However, for scientists socialized into accepting the dogmas of a Paradigm I view of science, it becomes difficult to come to terms with this notion of paradigm shift. For the purpose of the present analysis, I argue that it is essential to recognize the superiority of Paradigm II conceptions of administrative and organizational science. The Paradigm II view actually incorporates the Paradigm I view.

A Paradigm I view of proper science in the area of organizational inquiry has certainly contributed to the development of a vast body of empirical knowledge regarding various aspects of organizational functioning. But then, since Paradigm I endeavors to represent and reaffirm a particular cultural ideology and value orientation, it also places research findings within a particular sociohistorical context. Sampson (1978) argues that social values of liberalism, individualism, capitalism, and male dominance are the essential cornerstones of a Paradigm I view. Therefore, the findings and recommendations of the discipline of organizational behavior tend to reflect this nexus of values contained in the Paradigm I conception. Concepts like employee "growth need strength," "individual job involvement," "individual self-competence," and "organizational effectiveness" abound in our discipline and are indeed reflections of the abovementioned value nexus as embedded in Paradigm I. Merton (1957), in presenting his analysis of theories of social structure, argued that a particular society's value orientations help maintain and direct researchers into specific modes of scientific paradigms. Demonstrating the role of Puritan Protestantism in the development of both natural and social sciences, Merton showed the connection between the dominant paradigm of proper scientific inquiry and some important value orientations that exist within a given society. He noted that "the values embedded in the Protestant ethic pervaded the realm of scientific endeavor such that the why and wherefore of science bore a point-to-point correlation with the Puritan teachings on the same subject" (1957, pp. 575–576).

THE NEGOTIATED CHARACTER OF THEORIES

If we accept the proposition that a great majority of organizational theories are indeed pastiches of probably unrecognized expressions of "value," as embedded in the form of Puritan Protestantism, then some grave issues arise concerning the transhistoric, transtemporal, and universal validity and utility of these theories. It is at this juncture that I propose the negotiated character of organizational theories. For example, "actions" within or of organizations themselves carry little intrinsic meaning; the conceptual category that these "actions" are patterned after depends not on the intrinsic relevance of the categories themselves, but rather on the development and validation of an agreement as to the suitability of such a patterning among a community of active, empirically minded scholars. As a consequence, the conceptual labeling of any given "act" of or within the organization is continuously open to negotiation and renegotiation. (Pfeffer [1981] recently elaborated on this issue when he provided the framework for an analysis of the acts of management as symbolic actions.) According to Gergen's (1978, 1980) thesis, the present validity of the theoretical status of a concept may largely be viewed as a function of the social influence and academic prestige of the concept's originators.

In sharp contrast to this trend in the social and organizational sciences, the potential for challenging the adequacy of existing meaning systems does not appear to pose serious threats to internal validity in the natural sciences (Gergen, 1978). The major advantage of theorizing in the domain of the natural science lies in the extreme concreteness of the operational measures of such terms as *temperature, weight, mass, energy*, and so on. Given the wide acceptance and convergence of the operational formulations of the basic building blocks or conceptual units of natural science, the process of social negotiation and renegotiation and consequently the generation of a conflict of interest among theorists does not generally evolve.

Although Kuhn (1970) noted that such a state of affairs is likely to be a problem symbolic of the pre-paradigmatic state of social science disciplines, Gergen (1978) suggested that it may be intrinsic to the language of intellectual patterning of social/organizational events and their interactions. Thus, there is hardly any concept of organizational functioning that may be tied to its rigid empirical and operational formulation and could indeed be expected to possess transcontextual, transhistoric, and transtemporal qualities. The definitional and operational ambiguity relating to concepts such as "organizational commitment," "behavior modification," and "organizational effectiveness" perhaps illustrates Gergen's basic argument. Cameron's (1978) analysis of organizational effectiveness documents this sense of operational ambiguity.

Therefore, it follows that for scientists to "make sense" of behavior in and of organizations they must do so in manners acceptable and intelligible to both the members of their broader societal culture as well as to those belonging to their academic subculture. The point of these analyses, including Merton's earlier theses, shows the relevance of the ultimate embeddedness of administrative and organizational science theories in the sociohistorical and sociocultural framework of a given society. Once we begin to recognize this explicitly, we may then prepare our field for practicing the Paradigm II view of proper science. In terms of the Paradigm II conception of science, scientific facts and truths are believed to be historically rooted and socioculturally sustained.

In Table 12.1 I present contrasting views of intellectual foundations and preferred styles of inquiry of Paradigm I- and Paradigm II-based administrative science. In this view, truth about organizational science is not something naturally occurring "out in the organizational world," but rather something that is generated and built through particularistic encounters among persons with divergent social ideologies in temporally fixed sociohistorical settings. It also appears that a time has arrived in the developmental history of the administrative and organizational sciences to recognize this Paradigm II conception. Mitroff's (1974) analysis of Apollo moon scientists essentially showed the existence of a Paradigm II view of science. Mitroff found that as opposed to a value-free conception of science (that is, a Paradigm I view), most renowned scientists are not objective, unbiased, and value-free analysts of scientific phenomena, but rather are committed to their subjective and value-laden viewpoint of empirical phenomena (Paradigm II view). Recognition of a Paradigm II conception would have a beneficial influence in improving the eventual intellectual performance and applicability of administrative and organizational science.

In Table 12.2 I present contrasting views of utilization for research outcomes based on Paradigm I and Paradigm II conceptions of administrative and organizational science.

CURRENT STATE OF THE DISCIPLINE

To continue this general philosophy of science assessment, I now pursue some observations of a more evaluative and concrete nature concerning the current intellectual performance of the field of administrative and organizational science. As a discipline, it seems better equipped methodologically to pursue its basic objectives now than it did 30 years ago. However, I agree with the conclusion reached by Roberts et al. (1978) that increased emphasis on studying narrower and narrower responses made by individuals in organizational contexts, or concentration of macrolevel variables to the exclusion of microlevel variables, will generate empirically precise knowledge about increasingly trivial matters. It is as though the general level of excitement results primarily from studying narrowly conceived, but well-structured (and thus easily amenable to a Paradigm I view) microlevel phenomena. A vast amount of experimentation has been conducted on the determinants and consequences of individual behavior within organizations. Our research has been greatly enhanced by the application of small-sample statistical decision theories, experimental design, and multivariate analysis. Perhaps as a result of the repeated application of these techniques, we now

TABLE 12.1. Contrasting Views of Paradigm I- and Paradigm II-Based Administrative and Organizational Science

Paradigm I	Paradigm II
Ontological Assumptions	
1. Scientific knowledge and truth are transcendent and hence independent of sociohistorical and sociocultural forces in organizational contexts.	1. Scientific knowledge and truth are sociohistorically generated and are said to be generated through particularistic and intrasubjective encounters in organizational contexts.
2. Organizational reality is a concrete and real phenomenon, and as one gains insight into the structural relationships between constituent parts, one gains significant insights into the nature of organizational functioning.	2. Organizational reality is, at best, an abstract social process that uniquely unfolds over time as participants themselves establish and reestablish the organizing rules of their loosely coupled interactions and behaviors (Pondy and Mitroff, 1979; Weick, 1979).
Assumptions about the Functioning of Human Mind in Organizational Contexts	
3. Human mind is assumed to abhor dissonance and so tries to cope with it through a variety of mental gymnastics (see Sampson [1981] for a detailed explanation of this perspective). In this view, both contradictions and their reconciliations are primarily inner events meaningful only to the person experiencing them. Objective contradictions and the process of real transformations of organizational and social reality are not deemed particularly important.	3. Humans can tolerate and, in fact, sometimes invite dissonance and inner contradictions that flow from the objective surrounds of the real life organizational world. Attempts at transforming the sociocultural nature of organizational functioning at an objective level are frequently made by organizational participants themselves.
Cultural Values as Espoused in Both Approaches	
4. Puritan Protestantism, male dominance, middle class, capitalistic, and liberal.	4. The value of awareness and cognizance of the scientist's unique sociocultural and sociohistorical position.

(Continued next page)

TABLE 12.1 *(contd.)*

Paradigm I	Paradigm II
Norms Governing Operationalization of Scientific Procedures	
5. a. Emotional neutrality of the scientist as the ideal condition for collection of information from organizational contexts.	5. a. Emotional commitment of the scientist as the ideal condition for maximizing the probability of obtaining relevant contextual information. The investigator is more inclined toward obtaining information based on free and informed choice on the part of the respondents.
b. Universalism: The acceptance or rejection of important scientific claims is independent of the social or personal attributes of their protagonists (Mitroff and Kilmann, 1978). Thus, race, sex, religion, and nationality are irrelevant considerations in the development of organizational science.	b. Particularism: The acceptance or rejection of important scientific claims is considerably influenced by the social and personal attributes of the scientist. The organizational scientist is made more aware of the sociohistoric, sociocultural, and temporal limits of his or her espoused theories.

have a dramatic expansion in the empirical basis of organization theory; but very little, as I alluded to earlier, in the way of generative theory.

The literature is rampant with empirical studies that seem to provide nothing more than information about the technical virtuosity of the investigator. Although innovative statistical techniques are continually emphasized in journal articles, there is a tendency to be obsessed with the technique or the method in sharp contrast to a lack of concern for richly articulated theoretical frameworks. A quote from Roberts, Hulin, and Rousseau (1978) will illustrate this trend:

> Every few years our attention moves from one new approach to a different new approach under a different (and new) label. All too frequently our newest development had been tried and abandoned several years before because promised results were honored more in the promise than in the keeping. Whatever approach is in vogue, it is normally fitted out with more elaborate statistical procedures than those proceeding it, and results are produced that initially appear to justify the use of the new methods. Unfortunately, the new wave of research frequently indicates that the clothing of the new emperor is just as transparent as that of the previous

TABLE 12.2. Contrasting Views of Utilization for Research Outcomes Based on Paradigm I and Paradigm II Conceptions of Administrative and Organizational Science

Paradigm I	Paradigm II
1. Research process is less sensitive to the discrepancy between the interventionist's and client's views on the nature and design of effective organizations.	1. Research process acknowledges the potential sources of discrepancies between the interventionist's and client's views on the nature and design of effective organizations.
2. Utilization of research outcomes do not necessarily involve organizational and subunit-based changes. Utilization process is generally static and short term in duration.	2. Utilization of research outcomes necessitates systemwide organizational changes. Utilization process is dynamic and long term in duration.
3. Interventionist expresses a preference for "self-contained individualism" in the guise of emotional neutrality, and is generally opposed to a collectivist or interdependent mode of orientation in proposing solutions. The interventionist is careful relating to the expression of personal values or ideology for generating and implementing knowledge in organizational contexts.	3. Interventionist acknowledges that despite traditional attempts to remain emotionally neutral, he or she is inevitably favoring certain forms of organized activity over others, certain participants in the organization over others, and certain values over their antitheses. The interventionist is not excessively concerned by the expression of personal values or ideology as motivational bases for generating and implementing knowledge. Thus, the research utilization process becomes fundamentally engaged in the struggle of competing values so essential to the dialectical view of the organization as a social system (Benson, 1977).
4. Organizations are not studied in terms of the historical, institutional, and political processes that created them. Also, any potential contradictions between the client organization and other organizing processes in the larger societal context are considered unimportant in the utilization process.	4. Organizations, like other social structures, are studied in terms of the historical, institutional, and political processes that created them. Also, potential contradictions between the client organization and organizing forces in the larger societal context are highlighted in the utilization process.
5. Organizations are treated as integral "actors" or "in action" in the abstraction (Thompson, 1967). The nature of organizations as active	5. Organizations are treated as specific constellations of groups and actors within organizational systems. The distinctive interests of these groups

(Continued next page)

TABLE 12.2 *(contd.)*

Paradigm I	Paradigm II
political systems is not an important element in the utilization process. The interventionist may be aware of both the political nature of the client system and the utilization process. But his or her mission is not to challenge the prevailing ideological bases of the organizations when called upon to utilize research outcomes (Nord, 1977).	and actors in terms of their political, economic, and social ethnic and class contradictions may serve as an important focal point in the utilization process. The interventionist is also keenly aware of the actors, forces, and interests on whose behalf utilization of knowledge is being implemented and the ideological dilemmas that accompany the utilization processes.
6. The interventionist assumes nonperishability of research findings, and in the final analysis is more concerned with theoretical and empirical verification of the recommendations from esteemed professional colleagues both within and outside the user system.	6. The interventionist assumes that research findings meant for eventual utilization may be perishable and that the legitimacy of the findings may be subject to special scrutiny and negotiation by those groups they affect. In the final analysis, the interventionist is concerned with being consistent with one's previously articulated ideological position, and this potential for perishability of his or her findings does not appear as a major threat to the effective utilization process.

one, and in fact, when we view him without our distorting prisms, we must conclude that he is just as naked as his predecessor was. (p. 118)

Following Cartwright (1979), I would like to suggest that this unfortunate state of affairs originates in the way the discipline of administrative and organizational science designs and distributes its rewards. Innovators of improved methodologies are rewarded, while those who would change the substantive content of the field are generally discouraged. The overall effect, as Dunnette has observed, often results in research emphasis being focused away from relevant and important scientific questions in favor of "subtle nuances of methodological manipulation" (1966, p. 344). As a result, research in some areas of administrative and organizational science has become instrumental in realizing the dream of some men and women of ambition and power (Gordon et al., 1978) rather than those of creative intellectual vision. Academic reputation and prestige are measured by some in terms of volumes of published papers regardless of their quality. Reward systems of universities sometimes reinforce this unfortunate practice by offering prestigious academic appointments to individuals who have been more "visible" and "active" (measured in terms of doing more) as opposed to those who might be less "visible" but pursue difficult and substantive research endeavors. Weick (1980) voiced similar concerns when he suggested that increased emphasis should be given to the "thoughts" of organizational scholars rather than to their published outputs alone (p. 185). These practices have resulted in unfortunate effects on the generation and application of usable organizational research.

One debilitating manifestation of this pressure to publish is exhibited in the act of publishing "little papers" (Sommer, 1959). A little paper or a short note is typically a five- to ten-page article dealing with one or two smaller and less significant aspects of a larger problem. Sommer noted that such little papers produce several undesirable effects on the development of a discipline. The nature of the investigation is unnaturally fragmented such that it becomes exceedingly difficult to assimilate information into more powerful explanatory models.

We must acknowledge that because of this pressure to "publish or perish" perhaps far too many are conducting research in the organizational sciences. Redfield (1948) argued that the intellectual faculties required for high-level research are "the perceptive understanding of human nature, the gift or skill in making significant generalizations . . . and a fresh viewpoint that questions previous views" (p. 186). Although the ability to conduct sound methodological research may well be present in these researchers, it is doubtful that all of them possess the "perceptive understanding" required to fashion a new conceptual trend in the discipline. Unless we attempt to modify the organizational reward structure of universities in ways that are consonant with the practice of innovative research, our efforts to build an integrative and applicable body of knowledge on organizations will not become a reality.

CONCLUDING OBSERVATIONS AND SUGGESTIONS

This analysis of the current intellectual performance of organizational behavior suggests that: the dominant research issues of the field emerged from pressures outside the discipline itself—especially from the world of industrial organizations; the field has developed a distinct reputation for its applied orientation, and many of the superior theories of the discipline predict primarily application-focused, pragmatic organizational criteria; the dominant paradigm of the field is essentially ahistorical and acontextual in nature, which is really the Paradigm I view of social sciences; this approach, by ruling out the contextual, temporal, and sociohistorical aspects of social science, provides an incomplete understanding of the nature of organizations; the unfortunate structure of reward systems in the universities and within the field has contributed to the present level of intellectual performance.

It is difficult to evaluate the performance of a field that is as dynamic and as multifaceted as the contemporary science of organizations. Many commentators in the field advocate even more rigorous adoption of multi-method research designs. Others (Roberts et al., 1978) have urged researchers to think in terms of well-articulated, nomologically sophisticated, and interdisciplinary concepts. This analysis refrains from presenting this kind of evaluative review. Instead, I have argued that our potential for moving beyond the present level of intellectual performance lies in our commitment to the continued exploration of ways to improve the quality of our theories. In order to move beyond the acontextual, ahistorical feature of Paradigm I view, I suggest the following steps:

First, a reexamination of the criteria used to evaluate the effectiveness of a research program is important. In the spirit of Paradigm II inquiry, it may be necessary to foster high degrees of accuracy in describing the phenomenon even though such an attempt may be accompanied by low levels of technical and methodological precision (that is, convergent and discriminant validities, and the like) from a conventional Paradigm I viewpoint (Argyris, 1980). Argyris noted that the practitioner is more likely to use conceptual models and findings that could indeed be characterized by high accuracy but low technical precision.

Second, relevance of the research program in terms of its usefulness for producing an effective understanding of the organizing processes should be emphasized along with the rigor of the methodological sophistication. The concept of relevance is to be understood and operationalized in terms of its situational, as opposed to universal, character. Emphasis should also be placed on acknowledging the fact that potential sources of discrepancies and conflicts may exist among the users of the research findings on the nature and design of effective organizations. (See Table 12.2.)

Finally, the reward structure of the discipline of organizational science and universities should encourage long-term commitment to a research program that is characterized by a Paradigm II mode of inquiry. In operational terms, it means that journal editors and deans of academic departments should place more emphasis on the quality of research information not only in terms of its rigor and methodological sophistication, but also in terms of its ultimate usefulness in describing an organizational world that is complex, context-dependent, and sociohistorically rooted.

With an emphasis on Paradigm II views of proper organizational science in light of the above suggestions, the intellectual performance and the utilization of the discipline of organizational science would improve. This is a view that is compatible with some philosophers of the science of psychology who advocate the bidirectional nature of human knowing and the twofold realms within which each mode may prove useful (Buss, 1975; Sampson, 1978; and others). Until there is an acceptance of a Paradigm II view, there will be little to motivate a synthetic understanding of the discipline. It is also argued that it is the theoretical interpretation of experience within organizations that has the capacity to transform radically the process of utilization of knowledge and not empirical evidence itself (that is, one based on a strict Paradigm I view of science). What seemed to Roberts et al. (1978) as "more precise knowledge about increasingly trivial matters" (p. 136) in the domain of organizational science could possibly be replaced by more synthetic, well-articulated, and context-dependent modes of organizational inquiry. It is hoped that such inquiries will be based on the ideas of generative theory (Gergen, 1978). Such inquiries will call for a reorientation in the present trend of organizational theorizing, but the overall effect on both the intellectual performance of the discipline, as well as the quality of utilization of the knowledge produced therein, will be significant. It seems clear that we need to work toward restructuring the dominant view of the Paradigm I-based science of organizations as a first step.

REFERENCES

Argyris, Chris
1976   "Problems and new directions for industrial psychology." In M. D. Dunnette (ed.) Handbook of Industrial and Organizational Psychology, pp. 160–171, Chicago: Rand McNally.
Argyris, Chris
1980   Inner Contradictions of Rigorous Research. New York: Academic Press.
Behling, Orlando
1980   "The case for the natural science model for research in organizational behavior and organization theory." The Academy of Management Review, 5:4:483–490.
Benson, J. Kenneth
1977   "Organizations: A dialectical view." Administrative Science Quarterly, 22:1:1–21.
Bhagat, R. S.
1980   "Effects of personal life stress upon individual performance effectiveness and work adjustment processes within organizational settings." James McKeen Cattell-invited address delivered to the Industrial and Organizational Psychology division of the American Psychological Association, Montreal, Canada.

Bougon, Michel, Karl E. Weick, and Din Binkhorst
1977   "Cognition in organizations: An analysis of Utrect Jazz Orchestra." Administrative Science Quarterly, 22:606–639.

Buss, Alan R.
1975   "The emerging field of the sociology of psychological knowledge." American Psychologist, 30:988–1002.

Cameron, Kim
1978   "Organizational effectiveness in institutions of higher education." Administrative Science Quarterly, 23:4:604–632.

Campbell, John P., and Marvin D. Dunnette
1968   "Effectiveness of t-group experiences in managerial training and development." Psychological Bulletin, 70:73–104.

Cartwright, Dorwin P.
1979   "Contemporary social psychology in historical perspective." Social Psychology Quarterly, 42:82–93.

Child, John
1981   "Culture, contingency and capitalism in the cross-national study of organizations." In Larry L. Cummings and Barry M. Staw (eds.), Research in Organizational Behavior, 3:303–356, Greenwich, Conn.: JAI Press.

Dachler, H. Peter
1979   "Constraints on current perspectives for the cross-cultural study of organizations." Paper presented at the Thirty-ninth Annual Meeting of the Academy of Management, Atlanta, Georgia.

Daft, Richard L., and John C. Wiginton
1979   "Language and organization." Academy of Management Review, 4:179–191.

Davis, M. S.
1971   "That's interesting! Towards a phenomenology of sociology and a sociology of phenomenology." Philosophy of the Social Sciences, 4:309–344.

Dubin, Robert
1976   "Theory building in applied areas." In M. D. Dunnette (ed.), Handbook of Industrial and Organizational Psychology, Chicago: Rand McNally.

Dunnette, Marvin D.
1966   "Fads, fashions and folderol in psychology." American Psychologist, 21:343–352.

Dunnette, Marvin D.
1976   "Mishmash, mush and milestones in organizational psychology." In H. Meltzer and F. R. Wickert (eds.), Humanizing Organizational Behavior, pp. 86–105. Springfield, Ill: Charles C. Thomas.

Frost, Peter
1980   "Toward a radical framework for practicing organization science." The Academy of Management Review, 4:4:501–508.

Galtung, J.
1970   "Diachronic correlation, process analysis and causal analysis." Quality and Quantity, 4:55–94.

Gergen, Kenneth J.
1973   "Social psychology as history." Journal of Personality and Social Psychology, 25:309–320.

Gergen, Kenneth J.
1976   "Social psychology, science and history." Personality and Social Psychology, 2:373–383.

Gergen, Kenneth J.
1977   "Stability, change and chance in understanding human development." In N. Datan and H. Reese (eds.), Life Span Development Psychology, New York: Academic Press.

Gergen, Kenneth J.
1978   "Toward generative theory." Journal of Personality and Social Psychology, 36:11:1344–1360.
Gergen, Kenneth J.
1980   "Towards intellectual audacity in social psychology." In R. Gilmour and S. Duck (eds.), The Development of Social Psychology, London: Auadim Press.
Gergen, Kenneth J.
1981   "Social psychology and the phoenix of unreality." In S. Koch (ed.), Psychology: A Century of Developing Science, New York: McGraw-Hill.
Goodman, Paul S., and Johannes M. Pennings, and Associates
1977   New Perspectives on Organizational Effectiveness. San Francisco: Jossey-Bass.
Gordon, Michael E., Lawrence S. Kleiman, and Charles A. Hanie
1978   "Industrial-organizational psychology: Open thy ears oh house of Israel." American Psychologist, 33:10:893–905.
Green, Stephen G., and Terrance R. Mitchell
1979   "Attributional processes of leaders in leader-member interactions." Organizational Behavior and Human Performance, 23:429–458.
Greiner, Larry E.
1979   "A recent history of organizational behavior." In S. Kerr (ed.), Organizational Behavior, Grid Publishing.
Hannan, Michael T., John H. Freeman, and Marshall W. Meyer
1976   "Specification of models for organizational effectiveness." American Sociological Review, 41:136–143.
Hulin, Charles L., and Milton R. Blood
1968   "Job enlargement, individual differences and worker responses." Psychological Bulletin, 69:1:41–55.
Israel, H.
1966   "Some religious factors in the emergence of industrial society in England." American Sociological Review, 31:589–599.
Kimberly, John R.
1976   "Issues in the design of longitudinal organizational research." Sociological Methods and Research, 4:3:321–347.
Kuhn, Thomas S.
1970   The Structure of Scientific Revolutions, Chicago: University of Chicago Press.
Lambright, W. Henry, and Albert H. Teich
1981   "The organizational context of scientific research." In P. C. Nystrom and W. H. Starbuck (eds.), Handbook of Organizational Design, pp. 305–319, New York: Oxford University Press.
Lewin, Kurt
1951   Field Theory in Social Science. New York: Harper & Row.
Lichtheim, G.
1967   The Concept of Ideology and Other Essays. New York: Vintage Books.
Locke, Edwin A.
1973   "Job satisfaction and job performance: A theoretical analysis." Organizational Behavior and Human Performance, 5:484–500.
Mackenzie, Kenneth D., and Robert House
1978   "Paradigm development in the social sciences: A proposed research strategy." Academy of Management Review, 3:7–23.
Mannheim, Karl
1936   Ideology and Utopia. New York: Harvest Books.

Mannheim, Karl
1971   From Karl Mannheim. In K. H. Wolff (ed.), New York: Oxford University Press (originally published 1927).
Merton, Robert K.
1957   Social Theory and Social Structure. Glencoe, Ill.: Free Press.
Mitchell, Terrance R., Stephen G. Green, and Robert Wood
1981   "An attributional model of leadership and the poor performing subordinate." In L. L. Cummings and B. M. Staw (eds.), Research in Organizational Behavior, pp. 197–234. Greenwich, Conn.: JAI Press.
Mitroff, Ian I.
1974   "Norms and counter-norms in a select group of apollo moon scientists: A case study of the ambivalence of scientists." American Sociological Review, 39:579–595.
Mitroff, Ian I., and Ralph H. Kilmann
1978   Methodological Approaches to Social Science. San Francisco: Jossey-Bass.
Morgan, Gareth, and Linda Smircich
1980   "The case for qualitative research." The Academy of Management Review, 5:5:491–500.
Mott, Paul E.
1972   The Characteristics of Effective Organizations. New York: Harper & Row.
Nord, Walter R.
1977   "Job satisfaction reconsidered." American Psychologist, 32:12:1026–1035.
Pfeffer, Jeffrey
1981   "Management as symbolic action: The creation and maintenance of organizational paradigms." In B. M. Staw and L. L. Cummings (eds.), Research in Organizational Behavior, 3:1–52. Greenwich, Conn.: JAI Press.
Pinder, Craig C., and Larry F. Moore
1979   "The resurrection of taxonomy to aid the development of middle range theories of organizational behavior." Administrative Science Quarterly, 24:1:99–118.
Pondy, L. R., and I. I. Mitroff ´
1979   "Beyond open system models of organization." In Barry M. Staw (ed.), Research in Organizational Behavior, 1:3–39. Greenwich, Conn: JAI Press.
Ratner, J.
1973   "Introduction to John Dewey's philosophy." In R. Handy and E. C. Harwood (eds.), Useful Procedures of Inquiry. Great Barrington, Mass.: Behavioral Research Council.
Redfield, R.
1948   "The art of social science." The American Journal of Sociology, 54:181–190.
Roberts, Karlene H.
1970   "On looking at an elephant: An evaluation of crosscultural research related to organizations." Psychological Bulletin, 74:327–350.
Roberts, Karlene H., Charles L. Hulin, and Denise M. Rousseau
1978   Developing an Interdisciplinary Science of Organizations. San Francisco: Jossey-Bass.
Roberts, Karlene H., and William Glick
1981   "The job characteristic approach to task design: A critical review." Journal of Applied Psychology, 66:2:193–217.
Rossides, D. W.
1978   The History and Nature of Sociological Theory. Boston: Houghton Mifflin.
Sampson, Edward E.
1977   "Psychology and the American ideal." Journal of Personality and Social Psychology, 35:767–782.

Sampson, Edward E.
1978   "Scientific paradigms and social values: Wanted—a scientific revolution." Journal of Personality and Social Psychology, 35:11:1332–1343.
Sampson, Edward E.
1979   What would a feminine social science be like? The path not taken in the knowledge game. Paper presented at the Eighth Annual Convention of the American Psychological Association.
Sampson, Edward E.
1981   "Cognitive psychology as ideology." American Psychologist, 36:7:730–743.
Schneider, Benjamin
1975   "Organizational climates: An essay." Personnel Psychology, 28:447–479.
Sommer, R.
1959   "On writing 'little papers.' " American Psychologist, 26:1010–1015.
Steers, Richard M.
1975   "Problems in the measurement of organizational effectiveness." Administrative Science Quarterly, 20:546–558.
Thompson, James D.
1956   "On building an administrative science." Administrative Science Quarterly, 1:102–111.
Thompson, J. D.
1967   Organizations in Action. New York: McGraw-Hill.
Urdang, L. (ed.)
1968   House Dictionary of the English Lanaguage. New York: Random House.
Weick, Karl E.
1979   "Cognitive processes in organizations." In Barry M. Staw (ed.), Research in Organizational Behavior, 1:41–74. Greenwich, Conn: JAI Press.
Weick, Karl E.
1980   "Blind spots in organizational theorizing." Group and Organizational Studies, 5:2:178–188.

13

THE ROLE OF FEEDBACK IN THE CREATION
OF USEFUL KNOWLEDGE

Mary Ann Von Glinow and Nirmal Sethia

INTRODUCTION

A theme of growing concern in recent years has been the seeming lack of relevance or usefulness characterizing much of the research produced in academic settings (Thomas and Tymon, 1982). Generally, the problem of relevance has been considered to be rooted in the guiding philosophy of current scientific research. Under the positivist assumptions that are the foundation of the natural science model of research, theoretical refinements and methodological rigor have been continually overemphasized while questions about real-world application have been frequently ignored (Susman and Evered, 1978; Mitroff and Pondy, 1978). More recently, efforts have been made to increase the usefulness of scientific research by understanding and improving the knowledge utilization process (Larsen, 1981; Kilmann, 1979). However, neither the "guiding philosophy" framework nor the "knowledge utilization" framework has addressed the issue of making research more useful by shaping the process of its generation by the researcher.

Our intention here is to examine carefully how usefulness or relevance can be integrated into the knowledge creation process. More specifically, we propose that feedback can be a valuable means of helping researchers make their work more useful to practitioners.

Defining Useful Knowledge

Before we can discuss the ways in which feedback can improve the usefulness of knowledge, it is necessary to define what constitutes "useful"

The research reported on here is supported by the Office of Naval Research, under ONR contrast number N00014-81-K0048.

knowledge. Within the organizational sciences, a recent operationalization of the usefulness concept by Thomas and Tymon (1982) seems most promising. After examining the major criticisms of the practical usefulness of academic research, they propose five criteria for assessing the usefulness or relevance of theories or findings for practitioners. These criteria are:

Descriptive Relevance: "refers to the accuracy of research findings in capturing phenomena encountered by the practitioner in his or her organizational setting" (p. 346). Academic research often concentrates on internal validity while ignoring the issue of external validity; it also tends to be oversimplified and unappreciative of phenomena that are less immediately observable. Research can be made more relevant if it demonstrates better external validity and better reflects the complexity and intricacies of organizational settings.

Goal Relevance: "refers to the correspondence of outcome (or dependent variables in a theory to the things the practitioner wishes to influence" (p. 347). If we note the basic/applied distinction, most academic researchers have concentrated on basic rather than applied problems.

Operational Validity: "concerns the ability of the practitioner to implement action implications of a theory by manipulating its causal or independent variables" (p. 348). For research to be relevant, variables addressed by it must be controllable by practitioners. Morever, these variables should represent concrete rather than abstract factors that can be changed or influenced in some way.

Nonobviousness: "refers to the degree to which a theory meets or exceeds the complexity of 'common sense' theory already used by the practitioners" (p. 349). Academic concern with demonstrating the truth of hypotheses often leads to oversimplified formulations that do not offer fresh insights for practitioners. To be useful, research should offer improvement over models being currently relied upon by the practitioner.

Timeliness: "concerns the requirement that a theory be available to practitioners in time to use it to deal with problems" (p. 349). Unlike scientists, practitioners cannot and will not wait for all the facts to be in before decision making occurs. In addition, situational determinants and behaviors can change dramatically over time.

Using these five dimensions as an operational definition of useful knowledge, the importance of feedback in creation of such knowledge can now be discussed.

Feedback as a Strategy for Creating Useful Knowledge

An obvious implication of the above criteria is that researchers must have a keen awareness of practitioner needs in order to produce useful knowledge. Thomas and Tymon (1982) themselves state that "the dimensions of relevance presented here are concerned with the *external* relationship between a study's findings and practitioners' needs" (p. 350).

An important means of heightening researcher awareness of practitioner needs and strengthening the relationship between research and practice is feedback to researchers on the practical relevance of their work. This feedback can come either directly from practitioners (or other potential users such as clients or beneficiaries) or indirectly from other researchers who have studied practitioner needs. This is in line with recommendations made by Thomas and Tymon, who suggest two complementary strategies for making organizational science research more useful:

> The first is to encourage studies that attempt to provide information about these aspects of the practitioner's situation to other researchers—in Argyris' (1980) words, to inform the field of the "ecological context" within which the practitioner operates. . . . The second strategy is to involve practitioners in *feedback* and *review processes*. (p. 350, emphasis added)

Feedback can be a very appropriate means of aiding the creation of useful knowledge. Although virtually no empirical studies are available at the present time to demonstrate the validity of this assertion, many well-established findings from the current literature do provide support for our suggestion that feedback can be used advantageously in this context.

Feedback provides information to individuals about their performance. In this capacity, its two basic functions are of *directing* and *motivating* performance (Annett, 1969; Ilgen, Fisher, and Taylor, 1979; Nadler, 1979; O'Reilly and Anderson, 1980; Lawler, 1976). In its directive function, feedback keeps goal-directed behavior on course. That is, it serves as an error-detection device and therefore as a stimulus to begin problem identification and solution (Nadler, 1979). Or, as Lawler (1976) observes, it gives the individual the information that is needed in order to correct behavior when it deviates from the standard or desired behavior. In its motivational function, feedback stimulates greater effort and makes it possible for the individual to exercise self-control (Lawler, 1976).

Thus, for those researchers who are concerned about the practical relevance of their work (though there are many, particularly in academe, for whom this is not the highest priority [Kilmann, 1979]), feedback can guide their work closer to user needs and also enhance their motivation and sense of self-control. This last point is noteworthy, for autonomy is always highly prized by professionals (Von Glinow, 1982) and even more so by academicians. Academicians need to know that they retain control over their actions so that their sense of professional freedom is not compromised.

EFFECTIVE FEEDBACK: A THREE-PHASE PROCESS MODEL

Effectiveness of feedback has usually been assessed and demonstrated in terms of the outcomes resulting from the way it is utilized by the recipient. Typical outcomes are increased recipient motivation, altered recipient actions, or tangible gains in the recipient's output. However, the impact of feedback occurs through a complex information-exchange process where a source communicates a message to a recipient about performance or task-related attitudes and behaviors, which in turn leads to certain outcomes. Thus, if we wish to understand the effectiveness characteristics of feedback as a process, we must concern ourselves not merely with a post facto evaluation of its outcomes, but also with factors that determine the likelihood that any impact, and therefore outcome, will occur.

The criteria that govern the likelihood of feedback having some impact fall into two broad categories: *acceptability* of feedback for the recipient and *usability* of the feedback for the recipient. Acceptability concerns factors that influence the recipient to pay attention to the feedback and regard it as a basis for future action. Usability deals with factors that make it easier or more difficult for the recipient to use the feedback or act in response to it (assuming the recipient has previously accepted the feedback). Once acceptability and usability factors have been taken into account, we can then analyze the outcomes of the feedback for their desirability. Thus, in practice, effectiveness of feedback is a broader question encompassing the acceptability, usability, and outcomes of feedback.

Based on the above, it may be helpful to consider the effectiveness of feedback as a three-phase process or impact. The first phase, which follows the feedback event most immediately, is the *acceptance* phase. Here, the recipient arrives at a basic judgment to either accept or reject the feedback information. This acceptance or rejection is greatly influenced by certain characteristics of the source, of the individual recipient, and of the feedback message. If the feedback is accepted by the recipient, then the next phase involves deciding on a plan of action, or *action planning*, in response to the feedback. During this second phase, usability of feedback is of primary concern. The final phase is of feedback *utilization*, where consequences or outcomes of the feedback take shape according to the way feedback information is utilized by the recipient. This basic model depicting the three phases of the feedback process is shown in Figure 13.1.

Acceptance Phase of the Feedback Process

Ilgen et al. (1979) suggest that "Acceptance refers to the recipient's belief that the feedback is an accurate portrayal of his performance. Whether or not this belief is correct is inconsequential to acceptance" (p. 356). To the

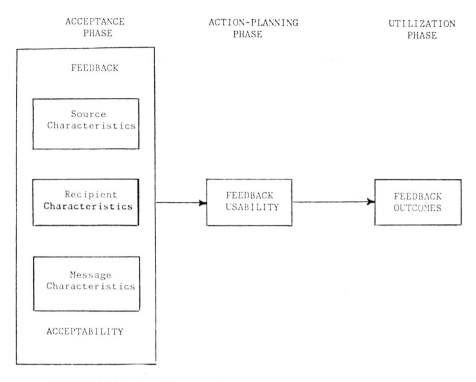

FIGURE 13.1. The Feedback Process: Outline of a Three-Phase Model

extent this definition relies solely on the recipient's belief regarding accuracy of feedback, it appears to be too narrow. In the model proposed here, acceptance signifies the recipient's inclination to pay attention to feedback and consider it as a basis for modifying a particular task-related behavior. As previously mentioned, acceptance of feedback is greatly influenced by characteristics of the source, of the recipient, and of the feedback message.

Characteristics of the Source

Sources of feedback can be classified into three categories: interpersonal, task, and self. Interpersonal sources are other individuals who have observed the recipient's performance and are in a position to evaluate it. This includes supervisors, coworkers, subordinates, and others such as clients or professional colleagues who may not actually be members of the recipient's organization. A task can be a source of feedback as it reaches a certain stage of completion or moves in certain directions. Finally, individuals may be able to judge their own performance and therefore serve as their own source of feedback. We deal here only with interpersonal sources of feedback as they represent the most complex source category and have maximum importance for professionals in organizational settings. Current research findings suggest credibility and power are the two most significant characteristics of interpersonal sources.

Source Credibility. Ilgen et. al(1979) have viewed credibility of source as a major factor influencing acceptance of the feedback and have identified two basic determinants of it: *expertise* and *trustworthiness* of the source. These authors suggest that expertise should include familiarity with the task itself as well as the recipient's task performance. As for trustworthiness, credibility of a source will be higher if the recipient finds the source nonthreatening and has trust in the source's motives. O'Really and Anderson (1980) have also emphasized the importance of trust in the feedback process. Giffin (1967) identified expertise and intentions toward the listener (what we have called trust) along with reliability, dynamism (boldness, energy), and personal attractiveness as dimensions of source credibility in the communication process. In our study (see Appendix), sources of useful feedback are characterized as knowledgeable, well-informed, respected, and so forth— suggesting the expertise qualities. Sources are also seen as concerned or well-meaning, understanding, honest, open, self-possessed, noncondescending— suggesting the trustworthiness dimension.

Source credibility may be influenced by two additional factors: *interdependence* between the source and the recipient, and *proximity* of the source to the recipient. Source-recipient interdependence suggests that the performance of either may affect the performance of and/or valued outcomes for the other, whereas usually the recipient only is dependent on the source. Ilgen, Mitchell, and Fredrickson (1981) have found that the supervisors whose own rewards are partially dependent upon the level of performance of their subordinates will respond in a more positive and helpful manner toward their subordinates when they fail to perform as well as the supervisor would like. Thus, if sources in interdependent situations are more likely to show helping and facilitating behaviors, then their own credibility, and consequently the acceptability of the feedback provided by them, is likely to be higher.

Source-recipient proximity can be physical, but of greater relevance is psychological proximity, or "psychological closeness" as discussed by Greller and Herold (1975). Their findings indicate a greater reliance on intrinsic sources—those psychologically "closer" to the individual—than on more external sources for feedback information. However, these authors also point out that "distance" may moderate the reliance on various "secondary" sources (such as coworkers), but not the reliance on a "primary" source like the supervisor.

Source Power. In addition to credibility, a basic source characteristic is power. Power based upon expertise is indirectly implied in the discussion of source credibility; however, power also derives from the actual or assumed authority to administer rewards and punishments. Such power can be unrelated to a source's credibility (that is, to expertise and trustworthiness). Ilgen et al. (1979) observe that "theoretically power is independent of credibility, although we should hope that in many settings they co-vary" (p. 351). These authors also suggest that "other things being equal, the higher the power of the source, the more likely the recipient is to attempt to respond in line with feedback" (p. 351). Kerr and Slocum (1981) note that feedback will have easier acceptance if the recipient perceives the source as a controller of important rewards and sanctions.

Characteristics of the Recipient

Acceptance of feedback is governed not only by characteristics of the source, but by the recipient's own characteristics as well. The most relevant categories of recipient characteristics are the individual's capability to respond to feedback and his or her receptivity to feedback.

Capability to Respond. Recipients are more likely to accept feedback if they find it possible to respond to the demands of the feedback. If the feedback recommends actions that recipients do not believe themselves capable of taking, or require skills they neither possess nor can hope to acquire easily, then it is unlikely that the feedback will be accepted. Expectancy theory (Vroom, 1964) makes it clear that beliefs about response capabilities are prerequisites to expenditure of effort in a performance situation. On this basis, Ilgen et al. (1979) have argued that recipients' belief in the effort-performance relationship should influence their desire to respond to the feedback. Heider (1958) has observed that ability and willingness to perform are not independent of one another; one's ability to perform a task often increases one's desire to do so. In our study (see Appendix), some of the respondents commented that useful feedback dealt with matters over which they had some degree of control.

Individual Receptivity. Different personality types have different needs and expectations in the performance context; hence, they would differ in their receptivity to any given feedback. Personality variables that have usually been studied in work settings include locus of control, self-esteem, and need for achievement (*n* Ach). On the basis of Rotter's (1966) research on internal-external locus of control, Baron et al. (1974) found that internals responded more to feedback from the task itself, while externals responded more to feedback from others. Weiss (1977) examined the influence of self-esteem in subordinates' tendency to model their own behavior after the behavior of their supervisors. He found that subordinates with high self-esteem modeled the behavior of their supervisors less, which suggests that individuals with high self-esteem might be less receptive to feedback from others. Individuals high on n Ach characteristically have a strong desire to know how well they are doing, and so they are likely to be more attentive to feedback. Since our focus here is on interpersonal (external) feedback, individuals with an external locus of control or high need for achievement might be expected to have a greater receptivity to and acceptance of this type of feedback, whereas those with high self-esteem might be expected to have a lower acceptance for it.

Characteristics of the Feedback Message

Characteristics of the feedback message can be discussed more meaningfully under the action planning phase of the model proposed here. However, the following two characteristics are more pertinent to feedback acceptance.

Importance of Message. Acceptance of a message will be higher if it is viewed by the recipient as important. If the feedback is largely trivial with no material consequence, it is unlikely that the recipient will consider it seriously for future action. Respondent comments in our study supported this reasoning about importance or relevance of the feedback message.

Information Value. Another message attribute that influences the acceptance of feedback is information value of the message. If the recipient is to take some specific action in response to the feedback, the information provided by the feedback should be more extensive than the information the individual currently possesses. Annett (1969) suggests that if the feedback is to augment the recipient's desire to respond, its informational content should not include information already known by the individual. Nadler et al. (1976) also state that an effective feedback system should increase information available to employees. We should note here that the recipient's own expertise and/or experience with respect to the task on hand can also determine the information value of feedback.

Action-Planning Phase of the Feedback Process

Once feedback has been accepted by the recipient, the next step is to decide upon a specific plan of action in response to the feedback. In this phase, the key issue is usability of the feedback for the recipient, which determines the likelihood as well as promptness of a response.

Usability of the Feedback

Usability refers to the factors that make it easier or more difficult for a recipient to use the feedback or act in response to it. From the available literature and our preliminary data, four factors emerge as the key determinants of feedback usability: validity, specificity, consistency, and timeliness of feedback information. Validity and specificity characterize the *content* of the feedback. Consistency and timeliness pertain to the *context* of the feedback.

Validity of the Feedback. Feedback about the recipient's actions or behaviors will be perceived as valid if the actions or behaviors referred to are considered relevant to task performance. Similarly, feedback about performance outcomes will be judged valid if it relates to legitimate performance criteria. Feedback, even if unfavorable or critical, can be seen as a proper basis for guiding future action to the extent it is perceived to be valid, accurate, and realistic.

Specificity of the Feedback. As Ilgen et al. (1979) have observed, feedback that is specific and detailed allows for setting specific goals; specific goals have consistently been found superior to general goals for bringing about improvement in performance. Kerr and Slocum (1981) also support this position.

Consistency of the Feedback. There is a considerable support in the literature for the importance of consistency of feedback (Ilgen et al., 1979; Kerr and Slocum, 1981). Consistency of feedback means that feedback from different sources, or from the same source at different points of time, has a coherent pattern with noncontradictory action implications. It is difficult for a recipient to use inconsistent or contradictory feedback information.

Timeliness of the Feedback. Timeliness has two distinct meanings. If the purpose of the feedback is to bring about corrective action, the feedback should be given while it is still possible to correct the error. If, however, the purpose of the feedback is to reinforce a desired behavior or discourage an undesired behavior, the feedback should be given while the behavior is still salient for the recipient. Ilgen et al. (1979), Kerr and Slocum (1981), Nadler, Mirvis, and Cammann (1976), and Nadler (1977) have all emphasized the importance of the timeliness element.

Utilization Phase of the Feedback Process

If feedback has been found to be acceptable and usable, the recipient is likely to utilize the feedback information to make appropriate changes in performance. The spheres within which changes occur and the extent of these changes are the outcomes of the feedback process. These outcomes serve as the final criteria of feedback effectiveness.

Outcomes of the Feedback

Changes in task performance (that is, quantity and/or quality of tangible output) constitute the outcomes of feedback that have been receiving maximum attention from researchers and practitioners alike. We may refer to such outcomes as the output or *performance* outcomes of feedback. Strong empirical support is available for the claim that feedback can improve performance outcomes (cf. O'Reilly and Anderson, 1980; Erez, 1977; Seligman and Darley, 1977; Becker, 1978).

There are other important areas too in which feedback leads to desirable changes. These changes contribute directly or indirectly to the recipient's tangible output or performance and therefore may be referred to as *instrumental* outcomes. Four key instrumental outcomes or functions of feedback are: direction, motivation, development, and attitude shaping.

Direction. In its directive or cue function, feedback can bring about error correction, role clarification, and goal adjustment (Annett, 1969; Ilgen et al., 1979; Nadler, 1979). For example, feedback may point out an error in the design of a piece of equipment and may call for components of different specifications to be used. Similarly, feedback may direct behavior by clarifying roles for organizational incumbents and offering prescriptions for future action. In addition, feedback may direct attention to adjusting goals subject to new constraints.

Motivation. Much has been written about motivation stemming from feedback in organizational settings (Locke, Cartledge, and Koeppel, 1968; Annett, 1969; Nadler, 1977; Ilgen et al., 1979; Kerr and Slocum, 1981). Similarly, effort has been studied within the expectancy framework (Vroom, 1964). Feedback aids intrinsic motivation by enabling recipients to judge their performance and feel a sense of competence on this basis (Hackman and Oldham, 1976).

Development. Feedback can be instrumental in bringing about new learning or new self-awareness to the recipient. This function as well as the attitude-shaping function have thus far received inadequate research attention. Research on the learning function however (cf. Annett, 1969; Nadler, 1979) covers many issues that are relevant to the development function.

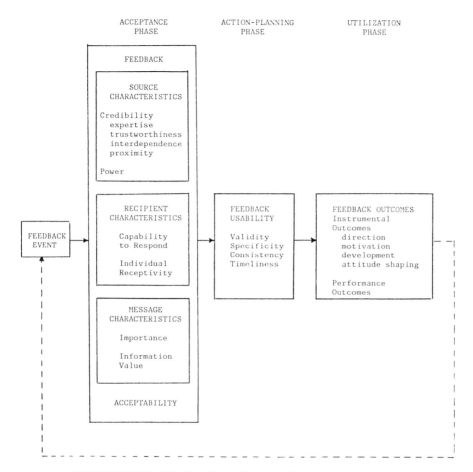

FIGURE 13.2. The Feedback Process: A Three-Phase Model

Attitude Shaping. Feedback has been shown to bring about positive changes in job attitudes. There is extensive literature relating feedback to job satisfaction (Ivancevich, 1972; Steers, 1976; Erez, 1977; Strang, Lawrence, and Fowler, 1978). Job involvement (Rabinowitz and Hall, 1977) and organizational commitment (Steers, 1977) are also favorably influenced by feedback.

Effective Feedback: A Three-Phase Process

Figure 13.2 depicts the three-phase feedback process in its entirety. We have argued that existing research has frequently concentrated on the outcomes of feedback without paying sufficient attention to the acceptability and usability dimensions. The utilization phase has been emphasized much more than the preceding phases of acceptance and action planning. Therefore, effectiveness of feedback can be rated solely on the basis of the outcomes, but it cannot be improved without fully taking acceptability and usability into account.

Having proposed a model for effective feedback, we can now examine the applicability and special significance of the various elements of this model in academic research settings.

APPLICATION OF THE FEEDBACK PROCESS MODEL

To establish the relevance of the three-phase process model of feedback for the creation of useful knowledge by an academic, we will examine each of the components of the model in the context of academic research.

Acceptance of Feedback in Academic Settings

Acceptance of feedback has been shown to be influenced by characteristics of the source, the recipient, and the feedback message. The significance of each of these characteristics in academic settings warrants discussion.

Source Characteristics

As previously mentioned, credibility and power have been identified as two basic source characteristics that affect the acceptability of feedback in our model. Of the two, power appears to be less important in academic settings because: first, values of academic freedom and professional responsibility substitute for hierarchical power as a means of control and influence; and second, under the peer-controlled reward system, power is somewhat diffuse—usually, no single individual has the authority to make a final judgment on the work of an academic professional.

Credibility, on the other hand, is inherently important in academic settings. Specialized knowledge and disinterestedness are highly valued by the academic community. Therefore, expertise and trustworthiness of the source of feedback are likely to be critical factors for academic researchers. Interdependence and proximity, two other factors in credibility, are also relevant for academics. These two factors should be primarily the result of collaboration or joint participation in various professional activities, which can provide a sound basis for making judgments about an individual's credibility. Importance of the credibility dimension for academics is confirmed by considerable literature on peer appraisals and their increased likelihood of acceptance by professionals (Von Glinow, 1983; Kerr, Von Glinow, and Schriesheim, 1977) over hierarchical appraisal systems.

Recipient Characteristics

While skills and abilities are basic determinants of one's capability to respond to performance feedback, the academic professional has been socialized to respect competence and expertise. Thus, an academic's capability to respond may be guided by professional norms and ethical standards.

Also relevant are the limitations of the theories and models used by the researcher. These limitations represent boundaries within which the researcher must operate and, as such, are role limitations that circumscribe one's capability to respond. For example, it may be relatively easy for a researcher to introduce additional variables in a model in response to practitioner needs, but it may be difficult for a researcher to obtain the high levels of certainty a practitioner might desire. Similarly, ethical and professional considerations may preclude certain types of research that might otherwise be easy to carry out (Von Glinow, 1982; Kerr, Von Glinow, and Schriesheim, 1977). Awareness of such factors is important in understanding a researcher's capability to respond to feedback and consequently the degree to which feedback is accepted.

Turning to individual receptivity as a predictor of feedback acceptance, it should be noted that there are considerable variations in the value and behavioral orientations characterizing scientific researchers (cf. Friedlander, 1971; Eiduson and Beckman, 1973; Sethia, 1980). Moreover, these orientations are susceptible to changes in professional career and personal life (Cotogrove and Box, 1970; Barnes, 1971). These value and behavioral orientations have substantial bearing on the type and scope of work that different researchers prefer, and this influences their receptivity to and acceptance of various types and sources of feedback.

Feedback Message Characteristics

As knowledge workers, academics are likely to be sensitive to the importance and the information value of the feedback. A feedback is unlikely to evoke their interest and gain their acceptance unless they find that it has bearing on some significant issues and it tells them something more than what they already know.

Usability of Feedback in Academic Settings

In the proposed mode, usability of feedback has generally been shown to be determined by its validity, specificity, consistency, and timeliness. These determinants of feedback usability are particularly relevant in academic settings. To be valid, feedback on a particular research project would pertain to variables, relationships, or problems that the research purports to deal with. Extraneous observations, even if appealing, cannot aid the validity. Similarly, feedback that points out specific strengths and weaknesses of the research is easier to act upon than indirect and general feedback. Further, if a researcher receives consistent feedback from different sources (various colleagues, practitioners, or users), or if successive feedbacks offered by the same source are consistent, then it may be easier for the researcher to respond appropriately. Inconsistent or contradictory feedback is difficult to respond to. Finally, timeliness of feedback also determines its usability. If colleagues or practitioners point out a weakness in the research design after the data collection is completed, the researcher will undoubtedly derive little immediate benefit from such information.

Outcomes of Feedback in Academic Settings

Acceptance and usability of feedback are important because they are expected to lead to desired outcomes. The ultimate outcome desired in the present context is knowledge that is useful to practitioners and other users or beneficiaries. Quantity and quality of useful knowledge produced is the "performance" facet of outcome in the proposed model. There is also the "instrumental" facet of outcomes, which is made up of factors that are not the ultimate desired outcomes, but directly or indirectly contribute to it. These factors include direction, motivation, development, and attitude shaping.

By its directing function, feedback should enable researchers to know where or how their work diverges from the course it needs to follow if it is to be useful for practitioners. Feedback for this purpose can provide information about specific variables and relationships that need to be explored. By its motivational function, feedback should result in increased effort to meet the usefulness criteria. This increased effort may be the result of a realistic assessment of the adequacy of the research effort and may also arise from a sense of competence. In its developmental function, feedback may be expected to bring about new learning by challenging a researcher to solve some pressing practical problem. Feedback can also directly cause new learning to occur by offering important new information to a researcher. Lastly, the attitude-shaping function of feedback, which can bring about more positive job attitudes such as job satisfaction, job involvement, and organizational commitment, should lead the researcher to a greater interest in useful research and greater identification with the institutional goals for such research.

Thus, the occurrence of instrumental outcomes implies:

The researcher getting necessary information on user situation and priorities (directive function);

The researcher being motivated to address user problems and to concentrate efforts on creating useful knowledge (motivational function);

The researcher being able to learn, change, and grow to meet the challenge of user problems in ways consistent with professional commitments (developmental function); and

The researcher feeling more favorably inclined to engage in useful research (attitude-shaping function).

If these instrumental outcomes occur, it would be reasonable to expect that the desired performance outcome of useful research will follow.

The above discussion has pointed out the significance of the various components of the feedback process model in aiding the creation of useful knowledge. However, the feedback process can promote the production of useful knowledge only if the institutional context permits its implementation. Therefore, it is necessary for us to examine the institutional implications of the proposed model.

INSTITUTIONAL MEASURES FOR EFFECTIVE FEEDBACK

By their very nature, academic institutions function as crucial mediators between users of knowledge and creators of knowledge. At the outset, there is usually an institutional screening of the type of users and their needs to be addressed. These users, more often than not, are institutionally steered to specific performers (this may not necessarily occur at the level of central administration, but at the level of deans, department chairs, or research center directors). Prior to and after research projects begin, their progress is materially affected by institutionally controlled resources. Upon completion, the researchers and research projects are evaluated in accordance with institutional guidelines. As a consequence, every facet of the feedback process, irrespective of any conscious choice, is shaped and circumscribed by the institutional context. Thus, institutional factors determine: who provides (source) what kind of feedback (message) to whom (recipient); how easy it will be for the recipient to use the feedback for planning future actions (usability); and to what extent the feedback can be utilized (outcomes). Under these circumstances, if initial steps can be taken at the institutional level to implement the feedback process model, its success can be reasonably guaranteed.

The discussion that follows is aimed at creating the desired institutional measures for effective feedback. Each of the three phases of the feedback process model—acceptance, action planning, and utilization—warrants specific actions or decisions at appropriate institutional levels. Because of the paucity of research on this topic, further investigation is needed to develop definitive guidelines. At present, we offer some general directions in which institutional efforts need to be directed.

Acceptance of Feedback

To ensure acceptance of feedback by the recipient (that is, academic researchers), institutional measures should be used selectively to match recipient needs and source strengths, and to influence the nature of the feedback messages.

Sources of Feedback

Sources of feedback should possess credibility and power. Credibility has been shown to be determined by expertise, trustworthiness, interdependence, and proximity. In considering expertise, institutions should encourage researcher evaluation and feedback by more experienced colleagues who have familiarity with practitioner needs, and by well-qualified users or practitioners. Moreover, in the interest of trustworthiness, individuals giving feedback should be user-friendly with a desire to nurture rather than control the researcher. Whenever possible, institutions should also support increased collaboration between more experienced and less experienced researchers, and between researchers and users (such as an executive-in-residence or an academic-practitioner exchange). The resulting increase in interdependence and proximity between the sources and the recipients of feedback should make for more acceptable feedback. However, it should be noted that closer ties between academics and outside users can be a sensitive area. Frequently, institutional forces mitigate against academics' involvement with external clients, for as Thomas and Tymon (1982) suggest, such involvement is viewed as less prestigious by institutions, and in some cases by the researchers as well. Thus institutions should consider the use of several promotional tracks, particularly for institutions with an applied emphasis. A "relevance track" might include working in an organization or taking over an organization to determine if one's theories really work. This also might include having an extended relationship with a company whereby research relevance is measured by the extent to which the researcher's ideas are judged useful and usable—in short, a reality test.

Power in academic settings rests mainly with the administrators, who typically make decisions on retention, promotion, and tenure. If the preferred sources of feedback, as suggested above, could be given a say in this power, their feedback could have even greater impact. One way of attaining this is to administer rewards or sanctions in closer consultation with those who are invited to carry out evaluation and feedback.

Recipients of Feedback

The likelihood of feedback being accepted will be greater to the extent that individuals are receptive to it and feel capable of responding to it. Since our concern is with feedback for the creation of useful knowledge, individuals receiving such feedback should be interested in "useful" research in the first place. Most institutions do have specialized subunits such as research centers or research programs for different interest groups. A greater clarity about the goals and purposes of such subunits, and about the terms of affiliation with them, can better insure that people will not be assessed on a criterion such as "usefulness of research" against their will.

Researchers will feel more confident of being able to respond to feedback if in their institutional environment occasional failures are tolerated, and willingness to change is not viewed as a sign of weakness or of lack of commitment. If researchers do not have the freedom to experiment and improve, they can become insular to any feedback and incapable of responding.

Feedback Messages

Certain steps are necessary to insure that feedback messages meet the criteria of importance and information value. If the individuals providing feedback are given adequate information about the goals and standards for the projects being assessed, and about the interests and capabilities of the researchers to whom they will be giving feedback, it will be easier for them to focus on important issues and offer more valuable comments.

Usability of Feedback

Institutional means need to be directed toward validity, specificity, consistency, and timeliness of feedback given to researchers if they are to benefit readily from feedback in planning their subsequent actions. Feedback is more likely to be valid and specific if the individuals giving feedback are fully familiar with the work being evaluated. Hence, institutions should select evaluators who either already possess knowledge of the projects to be reviewed or have the time and inclination to acquire detailed knowledge about the projects.

Consistency of feedback is a somewhat complex issue to deal with institutionally. If feedback is to come from more than one source, these sources should be advised to communicate with each other and be asked to provide the recipient with a rationale for their differences, if any exist. Besides, if an earlier phase of the same work has been previously evaluated, the current evaluators should be given those data. But it is also likely that in some cases evaluators may be unwilling or unable to integrate their differing perspectives. In such cases, institutional representatives associated with the evaluation process may have to reconcile the inconsistent or divergent feedback.

For feedback to be timely, evaluation should take place at appropriate stages of specific research work rather than at some preset, fixed time interval. In addition, evaluators should be accessible to the researchers so that they can request feedback when they feel it necessary. An obvious implication here is that the annual performance reviews and distinguished but hard-to-reach evaluators are not best suited for effective feedback.

In fact, researchers may find it necessary to retool, either for a specific research project or perhaps to each an unfamiliar topic. The institution should realize that with any new project or class there may be startup costs that will render any traditional productivity measures lower. In cases involving long-term, longitudinal studies, no clear-cut results may emerge to be evaluated for several years. The institution (perhaps in concert with the profession) should consider establishing work-in-process evaluations, and perhaps a WIP journal for those longer-term projects that many researchers are involved in.

Outcomes of Feedback

We have already noted that the progress of research work, and the performance outcomes of feedback, can be materially affected by institutionally controlled resources. Institutions are highly complex organizations in which human and material resources are strongly interdependent. Therefore, feedback can enhance performance only when it is accompanied by imaginative allocations of institutional resources.

Institutional support is critical for instrumental outcomes as well. Institutions should unambiguously convey to reviewers and evaluators that direction, motivation, growth, and attitude shaping are valued outcomes of feedback. Institutions should require effective feedback whenever the potential for the occurrence of such outcomes exists, such as when a academic may wish to: change a research design or strategy, or reorder priorities; enlarge the scope of the work and pursue it more vigorously; test new insights; or pursue career development. But if the institutional environment has too much bureaucratic inertia, such urges cannot flourish and the feedback will have little visible impact.

In this discussion we have demonstrated the importance of the institutional context for effective feedback and have offered suggestions regarding the needed institutional measures. If feedback is to be used successfully as a means of making academic research more useful, academic institutions should redesign their feedback structures in accordance with the model proposed here.

CONCLUSIONS

There is an urgent need for researchers to make their work more relevant to practitioners. We have suggested feedback as an important means for this purpose. A distinct advantage of feedback is that by bringing the knowledge creators (researchers) and users (practitioners) into close contact, and doing so at the very first step in the knowledge creation-diffusion-utilization chain, it greatly increases the likelihood as well as efficiency of practical utilization of research. Feedback also appears to have strategic value with reference to the criteria of "usefulness" offered by Thomas and Tymon (1982).

After establishing the importance of feedback in the creation of useful knowledge, we proposed a three-phase process model of effective feedback. We then demonstrated the applicability of this model in academic research settings. However, feedback cannot influence the character of academic research independent of its institutional context, which can either reinforce or nullify its impact. Therefore, we have also drawn attention to key institutional factors and their impact, and have offered suggestions as to how they can be made suitable for effective feedback. The criteria of effective feedback in the proposed model and the illustrative means of addressing these at the institutional level are summarized in Table 13.1.

We hope that our model of the feedback process and its institutional implications can serve as a starting point for research to understand further the determinants of feedback effectiveness in academic settings. We feel that in steering academic research toward greater usefulness and relevance, much attention also needs to be focused on understanding the complex interactive effects of feedback and the institutional forces.

APPENDIX

For the purpose of gaining a better understanding of the factors that govern the effectiveness of feedback to professional employees, an exploratory survey was conducted as part of a larger three-year study on performance appraisal and performance feedback (funded by the Office of Naval Research under Contract No. N00014-18-K0048).

The sample consisted of 136 high technology and/or professional employees from several departments of a large oil company headquartered in

TABLE 13.1. Criteria of Effective Feedback and Suggested Institutional Measures

Criteria for Effective Feedback	Suggested Institutional Measures
Acceptance of Feedback	
Source credibility	Select knowledgeable and trustworthy colleagues and practitioners as evaluators and sources of feedback. Encourage collaboration and other forms of professional interaction between sources and recipients.
Source power	Administer rewards in closer consultation with users and evaluators.
Recipient response capability	Give researchers freedom to experiment, retool, learn, and change; allow researchers periodic "time-outs" without enforcing traditional performance criteria.
Recipient receptivity	Allow researchers to pursue a particular type of research without fear of reprisals.
Message importance	Give evaluators detailed information about the work under review and about the interests and aims of the researchers.
Message information value	Familiarize evaluators with the expertise level of the researcher
Usability of Feedback	
Message validity	Give evaluators adequate information about research goals and theoretical and methodological concerns of the researcher.
Message specificity	Advise evaluators to avoid generalizations and to make their comments directly applicable to the work being reviewed.
Message consistency	Give evaluators information on the evaluations done at earlier stages of the work; evaluators should provide rationale for their differences.
Message timeliness	Rather than a preset schedule, arrange evaluation on the critical stages of the work; have evaluators who are accessible to the researchers.

(Continued next page)

TABLE 13.1 *(contd.)*

Criteria for Effective Feedback	*Suggested Institutional Measures*
Outcomes of Feedback	
Instrumental: Direction	Evaluators should comment on deviations from the research goals and what steps are required to get the research back on track.
Instrumental: Motivation	Evaluators should point out both strengths and weaknesses of the work, as well as encourage the researcher; on the annual performance review, institutions should as a matter of course reward dedication and extra effort.
Instrumental: Growth	Evaluators should descriptively point out the contributions of the researcher and offer encouragement; institutions should support researcher efforts with time and resources.
Instrumental: Attitude Shaping	Institution should commit its resources, not only in the short run, but to long-term projects as well, thus enabling researchers to make major commitments to certain research areas.
Performance: Output	Imaginative and flexible allocation of material and human resources at the institutional level.

the East. The respondents were asked to think of one instance of critical but useful/effective feedback, and one instance of critical and useless/ineffective feedback, and with respect to each instance describe: the setting in which feedback was given; the feedback giver's behavior and actions that made the critical feedback useful (or useless); and the outcomes or results of the feedback. In addition, they were asked to state the single most important reason that the critical feedback was useful in the first case and useless in the second. Content analysis of the lengthy replies surfaces several key issues in the feedback process, and these have guided the development of the feedback process model presented in this chapter.

REFERENCES

Annett, John
1969   *Feedback and Human Behavior.* Baltimore, Md.: Penguin Books.

Argyris, Chris
1980   *Inner Contradictions of Rigorous Research.* New York: Academic Press.
Barnes, S. Barry
1971   "Making Out in Industrial Research," *Science Studies*, 1:157–175.
Baron, Reuben M., Gloria Cowan, Richard L. Ganz, and Malcolm McDonald
1974   "Interaction of Locus on Control and Type of Performance Feedback," *Journal of Personality and Social Psychology*, 30:285–292.
Becker, Lawrence J.
1978   "Joint Effect of Feedback and Goal Setting on Performance: A Field Study of Residential Energy Conservation," *Journal of Applied Psychology*, 63:428–433.
Cotogrove, Stephen F., and Steven Box
1970   *Science, Industry and Society.* London: Allen and Unwin.
Eiduson, Bernice T., and Linda Beckman
1973   *Science as a Career Choice.* New York: Russell Sage Foundation.
Erez, Miriam
1977   "A Necessary Condition for Goal Setting—Performance Relationship," *Journal of Applied Psychology*, 62:624–627.
Friedlander, Frank
1971   "Performance and Orientation Structure of Research Scientists," *Organizational Behavior and Human Performance*, 6:169–183.
Giffin, Kim
1967   "The Contribution of Studies of Source Credibility to a Theory of Interpersonal Trust in the Communication Process," *Psychological Bulletin*, 68:104–120.
Greller, Martin M., and David M. Herold
1975   "Sources of Feedback: A Preliminary Investigation," *Organizational Behavior and Human Performance*, 13:244–256.
Hackman, J. Richard, and Greg. R. Oldham
1976   "Motivation Through the Design of Work: Test of a Theory," *Organizational Behavior and Human Performance*, 16:250–279.
Heider, Fritz
1958   *The Psychology of Interpersonal Relations.* New York: Wiley.
Ilgen, Daniel R., Cynthia D. Fisher, and M. Susan Taylor
1979   "Consequences of Individual Feedback on Behavior in Organizations," *Journal of Applied Psychology*, 64:349–371.
Ilgen, Daniel R., Charles R. Hobson, and Bernard C. Dugoni
1980   "Performance Feedback in Organizations: The Development of a Measure," Technical Report No. 2, Department of Psychological Sciences, Purdue University.
Ilgen, Daniel R., Terrence R. Mitchell, and James W. Frederickson
1981   "Poor Performers: Supervisors and Subordinates' Responses," *Organizational Behavior and Human Performance*, 27:386–140.
Ivancevich, John
1972   "A Longitudinal Assessment of Management by Objectives," *Administrative Science Quarterly*, 17:126–128.
Kerr, Steven
1975   "On the Folly of Rewarding A, While Hoping for B," *Academy of Management Journal*, 18:769–783.
Kerr, Steven, and John W. Slocum
1981   "Controlling the Performances of People in Organizations," in Paul Nystrom and William Starbuck (eds.), *Handbook of Organizational Design, 2*: 116–134. New York: Oxford University Press.
Kerr, Steven, Mary Von Glinow, and Janet Schriesheim

1977 "Issues in the Study of Professionals in Organizations: The Case of Scientists and Engineers," *Organizational Behavior and Human Performance*, 18:329–345.
Kilmann, Ralph
1979 "On Integrating Knowledge Utilization with Knowledge Development: The Philosophy Behind the MAPS Design Technology," *Academy of Management Review*, 4:417–426.
Larsen, Judith K.
1981 "Knowledge Utilization: Current Issues," in Robert Tich (ed.), *The Knowledge Cycle*, pp. 149–181. Beverly Hills: Sage.
Lawler, Edward E., III
1976 "Control Systems in Organizations," in Marvin Dunnette (ed.), *Handbook of Industrial and Organizational Psychology*, 1247–1291. Chicago: Rand McNally.
Locke, Edward, Norman Cartledge, and Jeffery Koeppel
1968 "Motivational Effects of Knowledge of Results: A Goal-Setting Phenomenon," *Psychological Bulletin*, 70:474–485.
Mitroff, Ian, and Louis Pondy
1978 "Afterthoughts on the Leadership Conference," in M. W. McCall, Jr. and M. M. Lombardo (eds.), *Leadership: Where Else Can We Go?*, 145–149. Durham, N.C.: Duke University Press.
Nadler, David
1977 *Feedback and Organizational Development*. Reading, Mass.: Addison-Wesley.
Nadler, David
1979 "The Effects of Feedback on Task Group Behavior: A Review of the Experimental Research," *Organizational Behavior and Human Performance*, 23:309–338.
Nadler, David, Philip Mirvis, and Corlandt Cammann
1976 "The Ongoing Feedback System," *Organizational Dynamics*, 4:63–80.
O'Reilly, Charles, and John Anderson
1980 "Trust and the Communication of Performance Appraisal Information: The Effect of Feedback on Performance and Job Satisfaction," *Human Communication Research*, 6:290–298.
Rabinowitz, Sam, and Douglas T. Hall
1977 "Organizational Research on Job Involvement." *Psychological Bulletin*, 84:265–288.
Rotter, Julian B.
1966 "Generalized Expectancies for Internal Versus External Control of Reinforcement," *Psychological Monographs*, Vol. 80 (Whole No. 609).
Seligman, Clive, and John M. Darley
1977 "Feedback as a Means of Decreasing Residential Energy Consumption," *Journal of Applied Psychology*, 62:363–368.
Sethia, Nirmal K.
1980 "Work-Value Orientations in Industrial R & D." Doctoral dissertation, Bombay: Indian Institute of Technology.
Steers, Richard
1976 "Factors Affecting Job Attitudes in a Goal-Setting Environment," *Academy of Management Journal*, 19:6–16.
Steers, Richard
1977 "Antecedents and Outcomes of Organizational Commitment," *Administrative Science Quarterly*, 22:46–56.
Strang, Harold R., Edith E. Lawrence, and Patrick C. Fowler
1978 "Effects of Assigned Goal Level and Knowledge of Results on Arithmetic Computation: A Laboratory Study," *Journal of Applied Psychology*, 63:446–450.

Susman, Gerald, and Roger Evered
1978   "An Assessment of the Scientific Merits of Action Research," *Administrative Science Quarterly*, 23:582–603.
Thomas, Kenneth, and Walter Tymon
1982   "Necessary Properties of Relevant Research: Lessons from Recent Criticisms of the Organizational Sciences," *Academy of Management Review*, 7:345–353.
Von Glinow, Mary Ann
1983   "Controlling the Performance of Professional Employees Through the Creation of Congruent Environments," *Journal of Business Research* (in press).
Von Glinow, Mary Ann, and Luke Novelli, Jr.
1982   "Ethical Standards within Organizational Behavior," *Academy of Management Journal*, 25:417–436.
Vroom, Victor H.
1964   *Work and Motivation*. New York: Wiley.
Weiss, Howard M.
1977   "Subordinate Imitation of Supervisor Behavior: The Role of Modeling in Organizational Socialization," *Organizational Behavior and Human Performance*, 19:80–105.

14

HIGH PRIESTS, DISCIPLES, AND DISBELIEVERS: A POLITICAL CONCEPTION OF KNOWLEDGE GENERATION AND UTILIZATION

V. K. Narayanan and Liam Fahey

The organizational studies field is undergoing a transition. There is increasing expression of dissatisfaction with the field and public debate in scholarly settings regarding the viability of the field as it is presently conceived. Some have questioned the underlying values propagated by the field (Argyris, 1970); the epistemological bases of inquiry within the field (such as Vaill, 1976; Sussman and Evered, 1979); the congruence between the espoused orientation of scientists and their orientation in use (Mitroff, 1974); even the appropriateness of the methods in vogue (MacKenzie and House, 1978). This questioning is an expression of the vitality of the field and a pointer to the immense challenges confronting it.

We seek to extend this discussion by examining: first, the influence of the organizational context within which "scientists" or researchers carry on their activities; second, the institutional milieu in which the organizations are embedded; and third, the broader sociocultural criteria that encompass all organizations and institutions. Our thesis is that much of the activity involved in "knowledge generation and utilization" is political in nature and serves to either enhance, maintain, or undermine the status quo. The spirit of the chapter is captured by the notion of "reflexivity" (Flanagan, 1981): the authors as active participants in knowledge generation and use are simultaneously the "objects" of this inquiry and the subjects carrying it out. As such, it is not our intent to present an exhaustive discussion of the politics of knowledge generation and use, but rather to highlight its critical dimensions.

We would like to thank John Tollefson for his comments on an earlier draft of the chapter.

A POLITICAL CONCEPTION OF KNOWLEDGE GENERATION AND UTILIZATION

Two sets of interactions and interrelationships are inherent in knowledge generation and utilization: one among scientists and researchers within knowledge-generating institutions; and the other between these individuals or groups and those outside knowledge-generating institutions who use this knowledge *or* those who provide the resources necessary for its generation. These interactions and interrelationships may be viewed as "social influence processes" that have long been acknowledged as a pervasive element in organizational life. Increasingly, such influence processes (and hence, organizations) are being depicted and investigated from an explicitly political perspective (Bacharach and Lawlor, 1980).

From a political perspective, an organization is viewed as a loose structure of coalitions and demands competing for organizational attention and resources, which results in conflicts that are never completely resolved (Tushman, 1977; Narayanan and Fahey, 1982). Organizational politics may be broadly defined as those activities and behaviors engaged in by organizational members to acquire, sustain, and exercise power and influence over others in order to have their preferred goals, options, or choices enacted (Pfeffer, 1981). Thus, a political conception of knowledge generation and utilization depicts scientists and researchers engaging in power/influence ploys and developing power/influence bases in order to achieve their own goals.

WORKING ASSUMPTIONS

The discussion that follows is anchored in a set of assumptions:

First, it is important to examine the sociopolitical and historical contexts in which knowledge is generated in order to consider the evolution of such evaluative criteria as usefulness and relevance. While the notion that the social sciences are neutral with respect to the phenomena they study has had a significant number of advocates, we concur with the position that what passes for knowledge in the social sciences is itself a product of the social processes investigated (Giddens, 1977; Berger and Luckman, 1966).

Second, those involved in the generation of knowledge are typically members of organized settings, such as academic institutions and professional organizations.

Third, the organized settings are embedded in an institutional milieu composed of a network of organizations. They are, therefore, open systems pervious to the influences of the institutional environment.

Fourth, these institutional networks are enmeshed in the sociopolitical and sociocultural structure and fabric of the broader society.

THREE SUBSYSTEMS IN KNOWLEDGE GENERATION AND UTILIZATION

Three interrelated subsystems are central in the process of producing useful knowledge: a knowledge generation subsystem, a knowledge utilization subsystem, and a resource-controlling subsystem. A knowledge generation subsystem is identified primarily by such activities as theory building and hypothesis testing; a utilization subsystem by such activities as translating knowledge into action and the adoption of innovations; a resource-controlling subsystem by the control and allocation of financial and other resources among competing claims, only one of which is knowledge generation (see Figure 14.1).

Many others have identified one or more of the subsystems noted above in their discussion of how useful knowledge is produced and disseminated. For example, Argyris (1970) notes the distinction between the interventionist and the client system, with the interventionist engaged in the generation of knowledge and the client system primarily in the application of such knowledge. The discussion of resources is attended to at various points of Argyris's exposition (for example, p. 32). Churchman (1971) similarly identifies the operations researcher/manager interface: the operations researcher belonging to the generation system, and the manager is viewed as a member of the utilization system. The distinction among the three subsystems is explicitly recognized in many treatments of innovation adoption; for example, Rich (1978) clearly distinguishes the roles of researcher, user, and sponsor.

Three observations are in order. First, in our conceptualization, we treat these subsystems from an organizational, rather than merely an individual, perspective. Thus, the interventionist in Argyris's case, the operations researcher in Churchman's case, and the researcher in Rich's case are members of a subsystem with its own organization: its own goals, structure, time horizon, and codes of conduct.

Second, distinguishing among the three subsystems enables us to focus sharply upon the social and psychological differences among them. Following Lawrence and Lorsch (1967), one could suggest that a functional differentiation of the kind offered here is associated with sociopolitical differences along the dimensions of goals, time horizons, and roles. These differences provide sources of conflict among the three subsystems.

Third, our criteria for distinguishing among subsystems is primarily a functional one—the kinds of activities carried on and processes inherent in

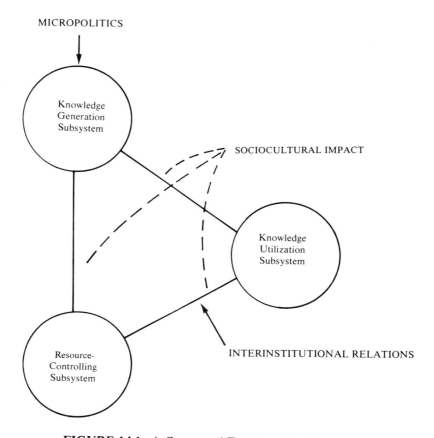

FIGURE 14.1. A Conceptual Framework for Discussion

each. Thus, there is no assumption that the activities of generation, utilization, and resource allocation should be located in different institutions. For expository purposes, our discussion depicts these activities as taking place in separate institutional settings.

Within a political framework, what is of interest are the interactions and relationships among individuals and groups within and across these three subsystems. These dynamics will be discussed at three levels.

KNOWLEDGE GENERATION: A MICROPOLITICAL VIEW

A micropolitical view of knowledge generation necessitates examination of the activities performed by researchers and scientists and the context within which they operate. Our basic premise is that the output—what is recognized as knowledge—emerges from a sequence of decisions made by the researcher. We draw upon MacKenzie and Barron (1970) to discuss this perspective and to highlight the distinction between the rational and political conceptions of knowledge generation. In doing so, we highlight the structural features of the context that lead to the role of power and influence as partial determinants of the output.

Knowledge as a Series of Decisions

A "rational" depiction of knowledge generation views the process as an orderly sequence of decisions (Coombs, 1964). These decisions involve selecting the problem, determining the type of phenomena to be observed, collecting and transforming data to test hypotheses, and interpreting the results. Each of these steps successively constitutes an additional transformation of the "real world." Within the rational framework, the activities within each decision are chosen prior to the investigation; these choices are guided by theory and consistent procedures are available for their implementation. These decisions are predominantly the result of "objective" deliberation; individuals' biases, prejudices, and opinions only minimally impact the inherent logic in the process. As MacKenzie and Barron (1970) note, under this research conception, the final report (except for the results) could be written before the beginning of the investigation.

MacKenzie and Barron (1970) point out that in the social sciences, this orderly progression does not accurately describe what takes place. Theories are not sufficiently detailed and tested and procedures are not usually precise enough: the aim of many experiments is to discover rather than test theories; the researcher has to rely on outside agencies to supply the data; the data are not always free of perceptual distortion, expecially if the researcher is emotionally involved in the results; and often a researcher's preferred experiment is compromised by ethical, financial, and replicability considerations. Thus, though the final report describing the results usually attempts to appear in conformity with the traditional model, "the real report which would describe mistakes, failures, deadends, shifts in procedure would in most cases differ significantly from the final report" (p. 231).

This description of the discrepancy between the idealized and actual version of the activities of the researcher points up two of the more important conditions confronting the social science research: low paradigm development (Kuhn, 1962), and dependence on others for financial resources, access to settings for investigation, and for information and data.

Structural Features Influencing Knowledge Generation

The observation that the field of organizational studies is characterized by low paradigm development relative to the physical sciences is shared by others (cf. Salancik, Staw, and Pondy, 1980). This implies a low degree of consensus among social scientists regarding the appropriate problems to be explored and the methods to be adopted in tackling them.

Low paradigm development and resource dependency suggest several critical implications for the field. First, the pressure to provide legitimacy to the field is higher relative to more widely accepted disciplines. Second, researchers are frequently strapped for resources (Lodahl and Gordon, 1973) and are thus compelled to legitimize ("sell") their own research endeavors. Third, especially in universities, the decision-making autonomy of researchers is becoming more circumscribed; they are under increasingly tighter control of some central administration. Thus, low paradigm development and scarce resources promote a context where scientists and researchers are compelled to employ power and influence over others to protect and advance their own interests. Two related questions must thus be broached: What bases of power/influence are available to scientists/researchers? How might they wield or exercise power/influence?

Bases of Power

Scientists and researchers in the organizational studies field can operate from a number of bases of power. First, there are status differentials. In considering the physical sciences, Capra (1980) noted a distinction between scientist and technician—analogous to the distinction drawn by Mitroff (1974) between theoretically oriented and experimentally oriented scientists—with the scientist having higher status than the technician. Second, there is differential access to resources. This is partly determined by the academic institution to which the individual belongs and partly by the individual's reputation. Resources include not merely financial support but access to "referees," other scholars working on similar problems, and so forth. Third, there are locational differences that influence access to streams of thought as well as to research sites, kinds of phenomena, or research questions that may be addressed. Fourth, there are differences in individuals' knowledge bases or reputations as reflected in their scholarly track record (publications). These bases of power are more often than not collinear; that is, typically individuals who are "known" have access to resources and are favorably located.

From a political perspective, these bases of power have a number of implications. Individuals often become identified with the viewpoints or paradigms they espouse. They then have a vested interest in ensuring the viability and acceptance of their ideas. Further, as representatives of their field, they feel the pressure to legitimize "their" paradigms, especially to outsiders. In this quest for legitimacy, they construct language schemes that are known to them and those in their sphere of influence; they recruit and convert the younger generation; they attempt to suppress those heretics who are threats to their favorite paradigms. Thus, we may capture the structure of organization of the field as a system of high priests and their disciples and a set of disbelievers who, at least in the short run, are often denied entry and lack the political finesse to break through.

Exercise of Power

Further understanding of how and why power/influence is wielded necessitates examination of some key features of the functioning of scientific communities. Professional associations and informal groupings are a dominant characteristic of most scientific communities. These serve to some degree to democratize the process by rendering access and information available to a wide population of aspiring scientists. However, they also reflect many of the characteristics of "organized anarchies" (March and Olsen, 1976): conflict among goals, ambiguity in tasks, fluid participation, and so forth. These organizational features suggest that an inner circle or elite is likely to develop (Thompson, 1967) and to control the structure and functioning of the organization. Such inner circles are similar to the "dominant coalition" observed by Cyert and March (1963) in business organizations. These are characterized by conflict among goals and minimal consensus. Professional associations often become arenas where individuals compete for attention and visibility. That the scientific community exhibits patterns of fierce competition is well documented in anecdotal literature (such as Watson, 1968). Conditions of competition create intense pressure on the members of the inner circle (and those outside it) to "win" (that is, gain acceptance of their preferred paradigms, beliefs, or opinions).

Given these pressures toward the acquisition and use of power/ influence, there are a number of ways in which individuals can exercise power/influence to achieve their goals. First, scientific communities typically legitimize their work through professional outlets such as journals and conferences. As noted earlier, the powerful act as gatekeepers in this process and serve in such roles as referees or editors. Despite the disclaimers of these gatekeepers regarding the rationality of the process and their portrayal of powerlessness (Pfeffer, 1981), they influence decisions regarding the acceptability of findings and conclusions. Beyer (1978), for example, found that decisions over what to publish are relatively easier in fields with more consensus. By implication, in fields like organizational studies where low paradigm development prevails, such decisions are relatively more difficult and are subject to vicissitudes of judgment (Thompson and Tuden, 1959).

Second, most researchers carry on their work in organized settings such as academic institutions. Researchers are not motivated only by the search for the elusive truth. Einstein (1934), for example, noted that both financial and power motivations were important to many physical scientists. Such motivations often find expression through and are shaped by institutional reward systems. Thus, MacKenzie and House (1978) and others have commented on the role of institutional rewards—and other barriers—in shaping "scholarly" output. Many academic institutions couple rewards with a notion of productivity; productivity is often expressed as exposure in scholarly journals. If the scholarly elites are predisposed toward their own preferred paradigms, the individual researcher will be strongly motivated to conform, in the expectation that this will bring exposure in professional outlets.

Third, educating the future generation of scholars assumes importance as it provides a mechanism by which the propagation of ideas can be accomplished. Since the academic community often cherishes such virtues as autonomy, decisions regarding the appropriateness of ideas for exposure are often initially left to the individual (faculty member) involved. Selective exposure to ideas, often inevitable, insures the longevity of the viewpoints espoused by the more entrenched proponents (Roszak, 1969).

Thus, one may visualize knowledge generation as taking place in various *conclaves* of high priests (elites) and their disciples. There is competition and conflict among elites regarding their preferred paradigms. Elites operate from different bases of power; we noted several ways in which the power is exercised. This is largely a political conception of knowledge generation.

Differences among Elites

Conflict and competition among elites imply differences among them. In terms of the subsystems previously discussed, of particular importance are differences among elites vis-à-vis their postures toward the knowledge utilization subsystem as it pertains to the issue of "usefulness" of knowledge. We focus on elites primarily because they serve as the gatekeepers of their respective conclaves and have dominant influence on the processes in each conclave.

At least three different views are available regarding the posture of elites toward the utilization subsystem. Each implies a different form of political behavior. These different views are portrayed in Table 14.1: the brokerage conclave, the collaborative conclave, and the scientific conclave. These models may be distinguished by the focus of inquiry, their relation to the utilization subsystem, the kind of methods adopted, and the criteria of usefulness apparent in each.

In the scientific conclave, the knowledge generation subsystem is dominant; the scientist as conceptualizer and knowledge generator dominates those whose function it is to accept, absorb, and apply knowledge. The essence of this dominance has been captured (perhaps unwittingly) by Weick (1969, p. 22) in discussing why the field of organization theory has been "stifled": "The only way in which understanding can be advanced is if the

TABLE 14.1. Critical Distinctions among the Three Conclaves

	Scientific Conclave	Collaborative Conclave	Brokerage Conclave
Relation to utilization subsystem	Dominant	Mixed degrees of dominance	Low dominance
Methods	Experimentation	"Action research," joint action with organizational elites and lower levels	Observation of organizational elites
Focus of inquiry	Scientifically valid knowledge	Valid knowledge and organizational effectiveness	Diffusion
Criteria of usefulness	Cumulative nature law-like postulates	Affirmation of "certain" (humanistic) values	Past success

symbols used by practitioners are removed, and the phenomena recast into language that has psychological or sociological meaning." This emphasis upon theoretical underpinnings has predictable implications for the criteria of knowledge usefulness: "The usefulness of a theory is not determined by its usability in the everyday business of running an organization or 'making out' in one. Theoretical usefulness is not defined in terms of 'pragmatics' " (pp. 19–20). From a political perspective, participants in the knowledge generation subsystem do not have to justify either their existence or their output to those in utilization subsystems. "Debate" with the utilization subsystem is unidirectional and one-sided. The expressive (that is, science for its own sake) rather than instrumental focus of the knowledge generation subsystem results in silence with regard to its impact on the utilization subsystem.

The collaborative conclave implies much less dominance; knowledge generation is a product of the combined efforts of representatives of the knowledge generation and utilization subsystems. Knowledge usefulness is thus predicated upon a strong pragmatic orientation: potential use or implementation becomes a critical consideration in knowledge generation. Thus, the knowledge generation and utilization subsystems are interdependent. Politically, a major implication for scientists in the knowledge generation subsystem is the necessity to cultivate and sustain coalitions with select members of the knowledge utilization subsystems.

The brokerage conclave defines its function as diffusion of knowledge: the function of the researcher is to understand and codify the practices of successful practitioners and to disseminate them to others. By definition, the brokerage conclave assumes a relationship of very limited dominance over the utilization subsystem. Typically, the researchers attempt to co-opt elites of utilization subsystems in order to examine their practices. The assumption is that successful elites are repositories of (practical) knowledge; the task of researchers is to unearth that knowledge.

In summary, differences among the three conclaves suggest that knowledge-generating institutions may be characterized by quite different political structures in terms of distributions of authority and influence (Bacharach and Lawlor, 1980) and different political processes.* A major implication of these differences, as noted in the above discussion, is the existence of varying conceptions of knowledge "usefulness." Before addressing a number of issues that emanate from the prevalence of conflicting notions of knowledge usefulness, we turn to a discussion of the politics of knowledge generation and utilization from the vantage points of the interinstitutional level and the sociocultural level.

INTERINSTITUTIONAL LEVEL

A sharper distinction between the rational and traditional conceptions of knowledge generation and utilization can be drawn by enlarging the discussion to include interinstitutional level dynamics. Traditional descriptions of scientific communities are anchored in the principle of insulating the academic institution from interference by outside forces. Probably the most graphic description of such a community has been presented by Hesse (1969) in his description of Castalia. Under this model, the scientific community is guided primarily by internal norms and pursues "academic" activity for its expressive value. That this is widely prevalent in the social sciences is noted by Simon (1979) in his assessment of the activities of economists. Elites in the academic community are free from interruptions from outside forces with regard to their ability to guide the scientific enterprise. As we noted, in relation to the field of organizational studies, the

---

*It is worth speculating if high priests in different conclaves are characterized by differences in patterns of exercising power over disciples. For example, the collaborative conclave may prefer power equalization and democratization in its internal decision-making practices, whereas the scientific conclave may be characterized by a higher degree of centralization of power. However, there is little systematic empirical evidence to support such speculation.

TABLE 14.2. Critical Distinctions among the Three Systems

	Knowledge Generation	Knowledge Utilization	Resource Allocation
Objectives of inquiry	Scientific validity	"Pragmatic" validity	"Optimal" allocation of resources
Time horizon	Limitless	Relatively time bound	Relatively intermediate
Dominant role	Researcher	User	Sponsor

academic community is dependent on outside agencies for resources and access to research settings. The traditional description becomes problematic as this dependence generates a context where the autonomy of elites is constrained by external agencies (Pfeffer and Salancik, 1978).

It was suggested earlier that in the generation and utilization of knowledge at least three entities may be distinguished: a resource-controlling subsystem, a utilization subsystem, and a generation subsystem. The generation subsystem is dependent on the resource-controlling subsystem for financial resources and access, and is dependent on the utilization subsystem for data and information. "Scientific" elites have to justify their activities by invoking criteria seen as legitimate by the other subsystems.

We have distinguished among the three subsystems primarily in terms of the functions and activities performed within them. In addition, the goals, time horizon, and roles associated with the three subsystems are also likely to be different (Table 14.2). Thus, the three subsystems reflect quite different points of view and are driven by different motives. In short, these subsystems serve different "interests." However, from a systems viewpoint, if knowledge is to be generated *and* utilized, these individual systems must be connected. Relationships among individual subsystem members across the subsystems constitute the primary connecting links. Thus, (academic) elites are embedded in a network of relationships characterized by dependency and divergence of interests. These relationships are inherently political. This structure of interinstitutional networks provides the context for the micro-politics.

The observation that resource access and information links influence knowledge generation is not new (see Galbraith, 1967; Bell, 1973). Resources may be channeled to particular areas of endeavor, access may be restricted, and information may be withheld, distorted, and disguised, thus detracting from the validity of results. The examination of the organization of cancer research (Epstein, 1979) exposed the role of interconnected pharmaceutical firms in determining the kinds of problems to be investigated in academic institutions. Cowan (1982) notes how he was denied access to study certain decisions, primarily because the organization felt they were too important to be brought under scrutiny. Distortion of information as a means of influencing the results of a study is not an unfamiliar experience to many field researchers (Glaser and Strauss, 1967).

Academic institutions and elites differ in their ability to influence interorganizational networks. March and Olsen (1976), for example, provide some evidence of four types of universities that differ in terms of reputation and sources and bases of finances. The relatively higher resource bases may enable richer universities to influence the networks, relative to poorer ones. This, however, does not detract from the suggestion that such networks influence the decision premises of the researcher.

The three conclaves of elites provide a convenient way of considering these networks. In the scientific model, the research is dominant (this often results in decoupling the subsystems and in the researcher pursuing his activity in an artificially created laboratory); in the brokerage model, the utilization system is dominant (and the brokerage conclave colludes with the utilization elites); the collaborative model lies somewhere in between. Despite these assumptions, the output of each model has been questioned as to such criteria as generalizability and validity. Thus, the scientific model is often critiqued for its lack of representativeness of organizational realities; the brokerage model for its sole reliance on elites of other subsystems; the collaborative model for its restriction to those settings that self-select themselves. The point here is not that these models are deficient, but that the outputs of the models are partly reflective of the interinstitutional networks that enmesh the researchers.

BEYOND THE INTERINSTITUTIONAL LEVEL

The interinstitutional systems of relationships (and their impact on knowledge generation and use) are themselves influenced by the larger sociopolitical or sociocultural context. Institutions and their interrelationships reflect patterns, trends, and values in the broader society. First, following Dumhoff (1970), Mills (1956), and Bell (1973), institutions exhibit forms of stratification somewhat parallel to the broader social and political milieu. Elites in the three subsystems, since they emanate from a common fountainhead in society, will share some orientations, values, and interests. This will ameliorate or soften the inherent conflict in the institutional roles across the subsystems. The larger sociocultural system, therefore, exerts an influence on the activities involved in knowledge generation and use through the value systems of elites.

Second, institutions are dependent on the broader sociocultural system for legitimacy. The rules of interaction among interinstitutional networks are partly governed by the dominant values within society (Baier and Rescher, 1969). Thus, the demands the subsystems place upon each other must ultimately be sanctioned by the larger society through its sociopolitical, market, or legislative mechanisms.

Third, all activities involved in knowledge generation and use are ultimately performed by individuals. As Berger and Luckmann (1966) have noted, individuals stand in a dialectical relationship to society; they therefore carry with them the heritage of the sociocultural system. Thus, all individuals (within and outside of elites) reflect broader cultural predispositions, values, and tendencies.

Fourth, the effects are dynamic in nature. Society and the institutions within it do not stand still; ideology, values, and morals are in a perpetual state of flux and change (Lodge, 1975). The persistent state of tension between change at the societal and institutional levels in the context of the scientific enterprise has been pointedly captured by Brooks (1973):

> The central problem of scientific organization is how to reconcile the scientific need for autonomy and integrity in its own internal processes of exploration and self-criticism with the demands of society that the fruits of science be guided into channels which society deems beneficial. This is a problem to which there is no single specifiable solution. Rather the situation is one of dynamic tension between science and society, a tension based on an equilibrium configuration that will change with time, resulting, perhaps, in somewhat different configurations in different political systems (p. 141).

A number of authors support this position. Pfeffer (1981) has argued that organizational studies are characterized by excessive fascination with rationality to the exclusion of power, primarily because rationality is a dominant cultural theme. Domhoff (1970) suggests that the sociocultural milieu is controlled by elites, showing in his discussion of the establishment of the American Economic Association that these societal elites control the premises of many social science fields. The example of Lysenko and the debunking of his theories is often regarded as the result of Stalinist ideology in the Soviet Union (Bernstein, 1978).

In contemporary organizational studies, the rise of humanistic technologies is often associated with a counterculture (Roszak, 1969), and their debunking is often traced to their being perceived as illegitimate in the social milieu (Golembiewski and Bloomfield, 1975). Traditional textbooks carry the idea that management thought is often a reflection of the temper of the times (see, for example, Dessler, 1976).

The critical implication of this observation is that the politics of knowledge generation is itself a reflection of larger sociocultural processes. As Peter Berger (1963) notes in his commentary on the sociology of sexual behavior:

> Cross cultural comparisons . . . bring home to us powerfully the near-infinite flexibility that men are capable of in organizing their lives. . . . What is normality and maturity in one culture is pathology and regression in another. [Such attributions] are constructed within the same precariousness that marks the entire social fabric. (p. 158).

KNOWLEDGE GENERATION AND THE NOTION OF USEFULNESS

The multilevel influences on knowledge generation discussed above suggest that political processes underpin attributions of "usefulness" and "validity" to knowledge (and scientific findings). These attributions are not easily explained within strictly "rational" models of the scientific process. From a political perspective, such attributions reflect the self-interests of the actors involved.

We noted that the micropolitical level may be characterized by the existence of different conclaves of elites (high priests), commoners (disciples), and heretics. Idealized versions of three differing conclaves—the scientific, collaborative, and brokerage—were presented. The three conclaves are in a constant state of tension, as the individuals belonging to each have strong vested interests in achieving dominance for their conclave and maintaining its legitimacy. The kinds of knowledge considered as "useful" will differ among the conclaves. From a political perspective, each conclave is likely to advocate selectively those criteria of usefulness that support its position and in turn deprecate the criteria espoused by others. The rhetoric of such advocacy in public forums is likely to assume a functional garb—wherein the criteria of usefulness are "objectified" and couched in rationalistic terms. One could, of course, cite differing degrees of polarization. At a minimum, advocacy may focus on differing emphases. For example, the notion that there is nothing as practical as a good theory (attributed to Lewin) may mean, "How can it be practical when it is *not* theoretical?" to the scientific conclave. At the same time, the collaborative conclave could claim that a theory is not theoretical *enough* since it is not practical. At an extreme, the scientific conclave may espouse the virtues of pursuing timeless science for its own sake and debunk the criteria and activities of the collaborative conclave as "narrow" or "pragmatic" or, as Mintzberg (1979) noted, useful only for "exploratory" purposes. The collaborative conclave may in turn focus on activities in "real" organizations and chastise the scientific conclave for never leaving the "ivory tower." The brokerage conclave may debunk both for not trusting the established wisdom of the practitioner.

From the political perspective, the espousal of criteria of usefulness (and defense of various kinds of knowledge generation activities as useful) reflects the self-interests of elites representing each conclave. Such self-interests include preservation and defense of a paradigm, advocacy of new paradigms, or a messianic zeal to advance certain (very often humanistic) values. Much of the debate that surrounded (and continues to surround) the Hawthorne experiment (Roethlisberger and Dickson, 1939) may be interpreted as an interplay of differing criteria of usefulness. To Mayo (1945), who was the "moral" force behind the researchers, the experiment was useful as it represented a medium for advancing and for humanizing the roles of management and supervisors. To others (such as Carey, 1967), the criteria centered on the validity of conclusions arrived at in the face of the available evidence; for these scholars, the conclusions and even the experiments are not very useful, as the scientific codes of knowledge generation were seriously compromised or violated.

An overriding implication is that political activity is not necessarily "good" or "bad," but that it is inevitable. A consensus around criteria of usefulness is unlikely given the politics involved. Consensus, when visible, should be interpreted as signalling the existence of both a relatively powerful conclave *and* incipient others who have not yet marshalled their power bases. As a corollary, the scientist qua scientist engages not only in "doing" science, but in the sociopolitical dynamics of the field. The scientist inevitably advocates certain points of view, attempts to persuade others, and sometimes even serves or acts out symbolic functions.

Decisions regarding knowledge generation and utilization are not restricted solely to the province of any single subsystem (cf. Gouldner, 1968). Power/dependence relations in the interinstitutional networks partly determine what knowledge outputs are generated and how they are utilized. A number of implications emanating from this perspective deserve mention.

First, dominance in interinstitutional networks depends on control of scarce resources. The resource-controlling subsystem has the potential to influence knowledge generation to a degree not fully acknowledged by any of the three conclaves. This is likely to happen when the central interests of this subsystem are at stake. When such interests are threatened, resource controllers can withhold and rechannel financial resources and access to settings; they could even marshall the bases of power to discredit the knowledge outputs. Further, in order to enhance their interests, they may attempt to seduce, co-opt, manipulate, or collaborate with the actors in the knowledge generation subsystem.

Second, knowledge can be put to use for purposes not intended by the knowledge generation subsystem; at best, it is modified to be congruent with the self-interests of the actors in the resource-controlling and utilization subsystems. Kilmann (1982) noted how as a real-time organization development consultant and thus as a representative of the collaborative conclave, he found himself compromising both the technical demands of the knowledge (in his case, organization design) and, perhaps more important, the values he wanted to espouse. Much of Argyris's (1970) critique of the scientific conclave hinges on how the theoretical schema and scientifically derived relations provide a convenient language and rhetoric, and thereby give legitimacy to the established power structures in other subsystems.

Of central significance is the notion that the usefulness of knowledge at interinstitutional levels may be viewed as an emergent concept—that is, what is useful emerges from the interaction of the three subsystems. Whereas at the micropolitical levels the three conclaves defend their preferred criteria of usefulness to themselves and to each other, the interinstitutional level dependencies create a context where what is generated, what is regarded as useful, and what is used are only partly controlled by the respective conclaves. A priori conceptions of usefulness may serve as starting points or as ideals for inquiry for each conclave, but these are invariably modified during the process. Thus, what is intended by a conclave is rarely realized; what is realized emerges from negotiations and bargaining among the conclaves on the one hand, and resource controllers and the utilization subsystem on the other. It is an output of a political process.

The sociocultural level dynamics point up the cultural relativism of the conception of usefulness. Scientists, as members of society, carry a cultural heritage into their work. Further, assessments of usefulness of knowledge outputs (both a priori and a posteriori) reflect interest groups and elites within society. As these change, so do conceptions of usefulness; the dynamic tensions in society impact knowledge generation and utilization. Dumhoff (1970), for example, noted how "young American academics" returning from Germany wanted to reshape the field of economics and thus formed the American Economic Association. "AEA was preparing to provide the economic expertise that was to be essential in the later efforts of big businessmen to rationalize the socio-economic system" (p. 160).

Cultural relativism implies that the question of what kinds of knowledge are useful cannot be completely separated from the question of for whom they are useful. Interest groups and elites within society influence the kinds of knowledge generated and regarded as useful. Resource allocation decisions are invariably a reflection of the interest groups in society. Such decisions revolve around questions of time (now versus later), relative priorities (organization studies versus engineering), and so forth. These decisions do not turn primarily on the intrinsic worth of knowledge, but are acts of judgment made by the society at large and the elites within them.

IMPLICATIONS AND CONCLUSIONS

The political conception of organizations underlying the discussion above has all too frequently received minimal attention in the literature on organizational design and effectiveness (Pfeffer, 1978). Our intent is to highlight some of the critical organizational design implications for the design and management of knowledge generation and utilization institutions.

At the micropolitical level, knowledge generation must be viewed as the outcome of the interactions of multiple individuals and groups who frequently manifest conflicting interests and goals and operate in an environment dominated by resource scarcity. The decision processes are not nearly as patterned, linear, and predictable as has often been suggested. The political conception of knowledge generation suggests a number of organizational design implications. First, designing the structure of knowledge-generating institutions is not simple and straightforward; it is not merely a matter of aligning clearly identifiable tasks with the appropriate individuals. Rather, it is a balancing act: we must take into account not only the fact that the tasks performed by the scientist qua scientist are often complex, ill-structured, and characterized by uncertain outcomes, but also that alliances and allegiances among the scientists themselves shift over time, and sometimes precipitously. Overly regimented and enforced structuring of any knowledge-generating institution that neglects its political dynamics will likely exacerbate underlying tensions and sustain rather than resolve conflict among organizational members.

Second, the design of knowledge-generating institutions must confront the need to circulate scientists and researchers both vertically and horizontally within these organizations. This is so for two reasons. Progress in science is an outgrowth of challenges to conventional wisdom. Thus, the structuring of knowledge-generating institutions needs to facilitate the continual emergence of a leadership and individuals who will publicly question and challenge existing assumptions. In other words, those in "authority" positions (the high priests) should not be allowed to maintain the status quo.

Third, while design must facilitate the free flow of ideas and individuals, it must simultaneously recognize that the conception of an organization as a *loose* structure of coalitions, interests, and demands implies a preference for autonomy and self-direction on the part of organizational subunits. These (political) desires are buttressed by well-established values within knowledge-generating institutions, for example, the importance attached to freedom of speech, truth and so forth. Thus, different elites and other subgroups must be accorded significant degrees of discretion to follow their own whims. The consequence here is one of fundamental importance to the advancement of knowledge: new paradigms or paradigmatic changes are much more likely to emerge in settings where individuals who develop and promote such ideas are given experimental or scientific protection from bureaucratic structures, systems, and regimes.

Fourth, major policy issues (such as what types of research are worthy of attention, how should research be conducted) are characterized by complexity in terms of the tasks involved and by uncertainty in terms of their outcomes. Given resource scarcity, we can thus hypothesize that major policy issues are likely to become battlegrounds that foster the emergence of clearly identifiable protagonists and antagonists. Such battles are fueled by the recognition that the outcome may be marked by clear "winners" and "losers." Should such an outcome transpire, policy implementation will certainly be problematical (Wildavsky, 1964; Allison, 1971). Thus, design needs to address the creation and maintenance of mechanisms or arenas within which both sides of an issue can be played out so that a middle ground or some modicum of consensus can be achieved. This avoids the dysfunctional consequences of prolonged conflict *after* policy "decisions" have been made.

At the interinstitutional level, a major focus of design efforts should be the development of strategies to marshall resources from the resource-controlling subsystem and to interface with the knowledge utilization subsystems. In other words, both of these tasks should be the consequence of design rather than dependent upon happenstance and the vagaries of interpersonal relationships.

To insure continual knowledge generation and utilization, interinstitutional relations need to be managed. From an organizational design perspective, the implication is that boundary-spanning roles or environment-scanning units may be needed to identify, monitor, and assess events and trends in the resource-controlling and knowledge-using systems. Political considerations emphasize that a core element in these activities is development and maintenance of coalitions with influential individuals or elites in other institutions. Thus, in the context of design, political skill and knowledge become pivotal criteria in choosing individuals to perform boundary-spanning and environment-scanning activities.

Finally, considerations of macrosocietal impacts on knowledge generation and use suggest some design implications. Organizational design must be responsive to the dynamic tensions that flow from the challenges that science and society continually throw at each other (Brooks, 1973; Bell, 1973). Knowledge-generating institutions, therefore, find themselves in an ongoing battle to establish and maintain both their legitimacy as institutions as well as the efficacy of specific enterprises upon which they have embarked. This is a role for which scientists and researchers are typically ill-equipped and poorly trained. Hence, organizational design may contribute something fundamental to the very survival of science-related institutions: the identification, development, and organization of individual scientists and researchers to fulfill science-related roles that involve interaction with nonscientists (and sometimes scientists) in their external environment.

REFERENCES

Allison, Graham T.
1971   *Essence of Decision: Explaining the Cuban Missile Crisis*. Boston: Little, Brown.
Argyris, Chris
1970   *Intervention Theory and Method: A Behavioral Science View*. Reading, MA: Addison-Wesley.
Bacharach, Samuel B., and Lawlor, Edward J.
1980   *Power and Politics in Organizations*. San Francisco: Jossey-Bass.
Baier, Kurt, and Rescher, Nicholas
1969   *Values and the Future: The Impact of Technological Change on American Values*. New York: Free Press.
Bell, Daniel
1973   *The Coming of Post-Industrial Society*. New York: Basic Books.
Berger, Peter L.
1963   *Invitation to Sociology: A Humanistic Perspective*. New York: Doubleday.
Berger, Peter L., and Luckmann, Thomas
1966   *The Social Construction of Reality*. New York: Doubleday.
Bernstein, Jeremy
1978   *Experiencing Science*. New York: Basic Books.
Beyer, Janice M.
1978   "Editorial Policies and Practices Among Leading Journals in Four Scientific Fields." *Sociological Quarterly*, 19:68–88.
Brooks, Harvey
1973   "Knowledge and Action: The Dilemma of Science Policy in the '70s," in The Search for Knowledge, *Daedalus*, Spring:125–144.
Capra, Fritjof
1980   *The Tao of Physics*. New York: Bantam.
Carey, A.
1967   "The Hawthorne Studies: A Radical Criticism." *American Sociological Review*, 32:403–416.
Churchman, C. W.
1971   *The Design of Inquiring Systems*. New York: Basic Books.
Coombs, C. H.
1964   *A Theory of Data*. New York: Wiley & Sons.
Cowan, David A.
1982   "Analysis of Four Organizational Decisions from Three Perspectives." Paper to be presented at the AIDS National Meetings, San Francisco.
Cyert, Richard M., and March, James G.
1963   *A Behavioral Theory of the Firm*. Englewood Cliffs, NJ: Prentice-Hall.
Dessler, Gary
1976   *Management: A Contingency Approach*. Englewood Cliffs, NJ: Prentice-Hall.
Dumhoff, G. William
1970   *The Higher Circles: The Governing Class in America*. New York: Vintage.

Einstein, Albert
1934   *The World as I See It.* New York: Covici, Friede.
Epstein, Samuel S.
1979   *The Politics of Cancer.* Garden City, NY: Anchor.
Flanagan, O. J., Jr.
1981   "Psychology, Progress, and the Problem of Reflexivity: A Study in the Epistemological Foundations of Psychology." *Journal of the History of the Behavioral Sciences,* 17:375–386.
Galbraith, John Kenneth
1967   *The New Industrial State.* Boston: Houghton Mifflin.
Giddens, Anthony
1977   *Studies in Social and Political Theory.* New York: Basic Books.
Glaser, Barney G., and Strauss, Anselm L.
1967   *The Discovery of Grounded Theory: Strategies for Qualitative Research.* Chicago: Aldine.
Golembiewski, Robert G., and Bloomfield, Paul B.
1975   *Learning and Change in Groups.* London: Penguin.
Gouldner, Alvin W.
1968   "Anti-Minotaur: The Myth of a Value-Free Sociology," in *The Planning of Change,* 2nd ed. Edited by Warren G. Bennis, Kenneth D. Benne, and Robert Chin. New York: Holt, Rinehart and Winston.
Hesse, Herman
1969   *Magister Ludi.* New York: Holt, Rinehart and Winston.
Kilmann, Ralph H.
1982   Review of *Organization Change and Development* by Michael Beer in *Academy of Management Review,* 7 (2):315–317.
Kuhn, Thomas S.
1962   *The Structure of Scientific Revolution.* Chicago: University of Chicago Press.
Lawrence, Paul R., and Lorsch, Jay W.
1967   *Organization and Environment.* Cambridge, MA: Harvard University Press.
Lodahl, Janice Beyer, and Gordon, Gerald
1973   "Funding the Sciences in University Departments." *Educational Record,* 54:74–82.
Lodge, George C.
1975   *The New American Ideology.* New York: Knopf.
MacKenzie, Kenneth D., and Barron, F. Hutton
1970   "Analysis of a Decision Making Investigation." *Management Science,* 17 (4):226–241.
MacKenzie, Kenneth D., and House, Robert
1978   "Paradigm Development in the Social Sciences: A Proposed Research Strategy." *Academy of Management Review,* 3 (1):7–23.
March, J. G., and Olsen, J. P.
1976   *Ambiguity and Choice in Organizations.* Bergan, Norway: Universitestorlaget.
Mayo, Elton
1945   *The Social Problems of an Industrial Civilization.* Cambridge, MA: Harvard University Press.
Mills, C. Wright
1956   *The Power Elite.* New York: Oxford University Press.
Mintzberg, Henry
1979   "An Emerging Strategy of 'Direct' Research." *Administrative Science Quarterly,* 24 (4):582–590.
Mitroff, Ian I.
1974   *The Subjective Side of Science.* New York: Elsevier.

Narayanan, V. K., and Fahey, Liam
1982   "The Micro-Politics of Strategy Formulation." *Academy of Management Review*, 7 (1):25–34.

Pfeffer, Jeffrey
1978   *Organization Design*. Arlington Heights, IL: AHM.

Pfeffer, Jeffrey
1981   *Power in Organizations*. Marshfield, MA: Pitman.

Pfeffer, Jeffrey, and Salancik, Gerald R.
1978   *The External Control of Organizations: A Resource Dependence Perspective*. New York: Harper & Row.

Rich, Robert F.
1978   "Innovation/Diffusion Research, Public Policy and Innovations," in *The Diffusion of Innovations: An Assessment*. Edited by Michael Radnor, Irwin Feller, and Everett Rogers. Northwestern University, Evanston, IL.

Roethlisberger, F. J., and Dickson, W.
1939   *Management and the Worker*. Cambridge, MA: Harvard University Press.

Roszak, Theodore
1969   *The Making of a Counter Culture*. New York: Doubleday.

Salancik, Gerald R., Staw, Barry M., and Pondy, Louis R.
1980   "Administrative Turnover as a Response to Unmanaged Organizational Inter-dependence." *Academy of Management Journal*, 23 (3):422–438.

Simon, Herbert A.
1979   "Rational Decision Making in Business Organizations." *American Economic Review*, 69 (4):493–513.

Sussman, Gerald I., and Evered, Roger D.
1979   "An Assessment of the Scientific Merits of Action Research." *Administrative Science Quarterly*, 23 (4):582–603.

Thompson, James D.
1967   *Organizations in Action*. New York: McGraw-Hill.

Thompson, James D., and Tuden, Arthur
1959   "Strategies, Structures and Processes of Organizational Decision," in *Comparative Studies in Administration*. Edited by James D. Thompson et al. Pittsburgh: University of Pittsburgh Press.

Tushman, Michael L.
1977   "A Political Approach to Organizations: A Review and Rationale." *Academy of Management Review*, 2:206–216.

Vaill, Peter B.
1976   "The Expository Model of Science in Organization Design," in *The Management of Organization Design: Strategies and Implementation*. Edited by Ralph H. Kilmann, Louis R. Pondy, and Dennis P. Slevin. New York: North Holland.

Watson, James D.
1968   *The Double Helix*. New York: Mentor.

Weick, Karl E.
1969   *The Social Psychology of Organizing*. Reading, MA: Addison-Wesley.

Wildavsky, Aaron
1964   *The Politics of the Budgetary Process*. Boston: Little, Brown.

15

INTELLECTUAL RESISTANCE TO USEFUL KNOWLEDGE: AN ARCHETYPAL SOCIAL ANALYSIS

Ian I. Mitroff and Ralph H. Kilmann

THE SETTING: MORAL OUTRAGE

That such a conference as this even needs to be held is in many, many ways an outrage. That the very concept, the very notion, of knowledge can apparently be defined, produced, and carried out independently of any criterion or concern with usefulness is more than just a telling commentary. It is one of the deepest insults that can be levied against the human spirit. How ironic it is that knowledge, one of the things that was supposed to liberate man, has now become one of the things from which man needs liberation. That knowledge and usefulness can even be construed in such a way that they have little to do with one another is an insult to one of the primary historical usages of the term "knowledge": knowledge as the employment of the most efficient means possible to serve socially desirable ends.

How then could a separation of knowledge and usefulness have come about? A complete response to this question would obviously involve a broader historical analysis of the roots of this phenomenon. Such an historical analysis, however valuable, is not the subject of this chapter. Instead, our topic is a psychosocial analysis of the kinds (archetypes) of people who are attracted to become academics or intellectuals in the first place. Our thesis is that those who are attracted to the academy have a deep resistance to usefulness as part of their basic psychological makeup. As a general rule, the university is resistant to useful knowledge because it has been designed precisely for that very purpose—both consciously and unconsciously—by those who are attracted to it.

We generally analyze the resistance of intellectuals to useful knowledge in terms of various characteristics: types of knowledge, types of academic or knowledge-producing organizations, types of intellectuals, and types of consumers or users of research. As among those who have contributed to this literature, we are obviously a part of the "problem." However, we no longer believe that our understanding of intellectual resistance goes to the heart of the issue. Both the depth and the degree of resistance that academics (and academic institutions) are capable of mounting toward useful knowledge call for a different kind of analysis, which we call "archetypal social analysis."

Archetypal social analysis posits the existence and functioning of a series of personality and social character types that are overlooked in most analyses. Following the pioneering leads of Jung and others, archetypes supposedly constitute the deepest layers of the human mind or psyche. They are the purest symbolic expressions of human experience of which we are capable of knowing. This chapter broadens the concept by postulating that archetypal social characters are the purest symbolic expressions of social forms, activities, and purposes of which we are capable of knowing. These characters get at the heart of intellectual resistance to useful knowledge.

THE CHARACTERS: SEVEN ARCHETYPES OF INTELLECTUALS

As part of a larger study on the influence of archetypes in social systems thinking and planning, Mitroff (1983) has made an extensive compilation of different collections of archetypes. One of the most interesting is presented by Carroll (1978). It is unquestionably the most pertinent to the present discussion.

Seven distinct types of intellectuals compose the system: the Mandarin, the Engineer, the Chess Player, the Chiliast, the Shaman, the Galahad, and the King's Fool. Since Carroll's descriptions are so well drawn, the depth of his analysis so penetrating and insightful, and because his work has not received the attention we believe it richly deserves, we have taken the liberty of quoting extensively from him. Although the relationship of Carroll's archetypes to our topic shall become apparent immediately, we shall relate them even more directly once we have gained some brief understanding of their nature.

The Mandarin

The scholar is an important figure in any society. He keeps the archives; his patience and diligence through long years of dwelling on the culture of conduct and its literary representations, of the deeds of the worthy forefathers, keeps alive the past, and makes possible a more sophisticated and self-conscious present. The mandarin is not principally interested in Truth: his passion is rather for the rules, the traditions of his vocation, and for confirming their strict maintenance as ritual. This zealous ritualism has its own social function: it demonstrates to the less ruly majority the virtues of self-discipline, that there are absorptions other than the sensual and immediate, ones that might bring a different and more enduring gratification. The mandarin, moreover, is an exemplar of public service, which is not, of course, to praise his motives. . . . the mandarin is a paradigm of resentment, as Nietzsche pointed out. He directs resentment against anyone who breaks the mandarin code, who crosses the boundaries between departments or disciplines, who dares to be both mandarin and creative writer in one (the great are bearable only at a distance, remote from extended comparison). The mandarin is typically paranoid, fearing loss of control, fearing the bottomless pit of uncertainty, guarding himself against an eruption of the forces in himself kept down by the halter of his ascetic calling. Mandarins do not fear philistines; they are threatened by their brothers who stretch the rules and thereby put in danger the entire order; the playfulness of these siblings is interpreted as a nihilistic aggression against their own family, fratricide on a mass scale.

At the same time, the mandarin's paranoia serves his calling. Out of exaggerated fears about the consequences of successful attack by critics, he works over his arguments, the weight of his evidence, his qualifications, with fanatical scrupulousness, and consequently produces work of extraordinary thoroughness. The scholarly virtue of rigor is dependent on the mandarin's paranoia-inflated fears of his peers, and his imagining of catastrophic consequences if he fails to keep his thesis intact. (Carroll, 1978, pp. 134–135)

The parallels between Carroll's Mandarin and other archetypes of anal compulsivity should be apparent, especially in their obsessive need for order and control—clear-cut, airtight compartments, strict separation of categories, feelings and emotions held strictly at bay.

The Engineer

The Mandarin, the Engineer, and the Chess Player are all versions of Jung's sensing-thinking (ST) type (Mitroff and Kilmann, 1978) although very different versions. This illustrates that STs are anything but alike, either in their personalities or in their professional callings. The Engineer is generally derided by intellectuals. His chief task is to make *things* work better, not to penetrate beneath the surface to unveil the mysteries of the universe. As such, he despises and is despised by idealists, those who are interested in conceptual ideas, revolutionary concepts, politics, philosophical systems, religious and spiritual symbols—all things that cannot be measured. Of this type it can be said that their greatest strength and their greatest weakness is their literalness. And yet, they are needed. They invent and oil the engines, the machines that make the world run. They are at their worst when they think they are being nothing but realistic. They fail to "see" that in their narrow insistence on realism, on evaluating everything by the strict dictum of "what works," they are being metaphysical in their own way. They are inputing a personal preference, their style to the whole of the universe. They are intolerant of other styles.

The Chess Player

Carroll lays bare the workings and the thinking of this type all too well:

> All intellectual activity serves as a means for gaining control, for drawing purpose out of chaos. The ultimate control is to will away death, the most real of all realities. There is in the withdrawal of the intellectual into the remote world of spirit an attempt to deny, to stave off this ultimate chaos. The chess game, as Ingmar Bergman perceived, is to spite death. And as much as death is separation from all warmth and nourishment, it stands as the final momentous reenactment of the child's early experiences of the loss of the mother. Chess is the form of social intercourse most therapeutic for the intellectual as paranoid. The competition is so strictly governed by rules that there is minimum danger of spasm of rage in a tense moment destroying the game, sending the opponent away hurt, the proceedings irretrievably sundered, as is likely to happen in real life. No, in chess, as in mediaeval warfare, the knight can move to only two places, and the consequences are accessible to thought. The game gradually tames fantasies of a shock violent attack from the opponent striking an unguarded spot; if he does strike home it is not as a monster, but as a civilized equal, bound by a camaraderie or rules. Such a successful sublimation of violence is the foundation of social harmony, and a rare achievement among that vain, unruly, headstrong breed, intellectuals.
>
> Moreover, the working within strictly defined rules to create perfect forms introduces another one of control's consolations. The real world is messy, and those who work in it, engineers, shamans, even mandarins (they test their arguments against the ultimate mess, that of reality's infinitude of facts), have to settle for small gains, minor clarifications. As long as one restricts onself to forms, to mathematics, perfection is possible. Individual life also is messy; the chess player in playing a peerless game takes his mind off his own imperfections, which he cannot much improve by practice, over which therefore he has little *control*. For a while he can identify with the sublimity of his play. The longing to create perfection is the phoenix longing to be reborn, without original sin, without infirmity, without blemish. (Carroll, 1978, pp. 136–137)

The Chiliast

If the first three types are varying versions of the rule-governed, rule-obsessed, compulsive order seeker, then among the latter are to be found the intuitive, idealist, and feeling types. They not only do not believe order is possible, but mock those who quest after it. In their own way they merely preach a different brand of order, a different future sense of things:

> But without hope our lot is no more than one of daily toil and drudgery. The chiliast reminds us that when Pandora opened the box and let evil into the world, hope too was freed. The chiliast lifts us out of our sluggish routines, enchants us with his visions, moves mountains that may be moved but usually are not. He seeks to make eternal the moment of self-transcendence, the moment of wonder, of rapture, of ecstasy, the idyllic moment of deep and direct communion with man or nature. If only we could loose ourselves from worldly pride, then one day:
>
> The wolf also shall dwell with the lamb, and the leopard shall lie down with the kid; and the calf and the young lion and the fatling together; and a little child shall lead them.
>
> The chiliast is of the idealist mold, attached to a vision of social revolution, of the transformation of the imperfect present into a utopian future. The future may come soon, or it may be the reward of an after-life. It may come as the result of human action, or divine determination. (Carroll, 1978, p. 139)

Like the others, his strength is his undoing. His visions carry him away. He believes them to be real, to be the very essence of reality:

> The chiliast intellectual, however, while he hankers to be relevant, is familiar solely with metaphysics; he takes the myth literally and as a result over-dramatizes things, seeking to quicken their pace, to precipitate crises, to cut Gordian knots, to crusade against evils, to declaim against "the strong and slow boring of hard boards" that forms the real politics of life. He is drawn to the imperial and the monolithic; he is excited by size, and favors centralization. He is better off left in the confines of the monastic university, where his heart is not carried away, and he can coolly reflect on the consequences of things. As La Rochefoucauld put it more cynically: "Philosophy triumphs with ease over past evils and evils to come; but current evils triumph over it." The intellectual should not seek to be very relevant, even very useful; his task is not to seduce the youth, but to prepare their minds for whatever challenges they wish to take up when they reenter the city. The monastery was an institution dedicated to the teaching of piety and humility. Our increasingly *relevant* universities, under the sway of chiliast fashion, are in danger of producing arrogant philistine revolutionaries. (Carroll, 1978, p. 142)

While we are in general agreement with Carroll, we would rather say, "*This* kind of intellectual—especially the pure extremes—should not seek to be relevant and should be confined to the universities where they are least likely to do real harm." Real harm (we note sarcastically) is the province of men of action, the doers.

The Shaman

The shaman, elected by spirits, descends into the underworld during his initiation. He is tortured by demons, his body is cut into pieces. Finally he is reborn with special powers of communication with the spirits. The initiate is under instruction from masters, but is welcomed as a fully-fledged shaman only if he manages to interpret his pathological crisis as a religious experience, and succeeds in curing himself. Then he is fit to cure others, which he does by using his own madness. Not that the shaman is himself mad; he is not actually possessed by demonic forces. Sickness is the condition in which the soul either wanders, or is captured by demons. When a patient suffers from sickness of the first type, the wandering soul, the shaman constructs a ritual of sympathetic ecstasy in which he dances and chants his diagnosis in a mythic form whose climax is the recapturing of the soul, and the replacing it in the body of the sick person. In the second case, of demonic interference, the shaman undertakes a highly dangerous ecstatic voyage into the underworld.

Like the engineer, the shaman works in the world, or rather enters it during the day from his retreat on its boundaries. Like the chiliast, his success depends on personal charisma, and his vocation is predicated on a belief in the transforming power of knowledge. But his patient is the sick individual, not the sick society.

The rise of science in the West had as one of its effects the standardization of the shaman figure in the form of the medical doctor. An exotic history or oracles, astrologers, Cassandras, Merlins, alchemists, mountebanks, potion and lotion tinkers, blood-letters, and hypnotists has been tamed. It is a commonplace, however, that the modern doctor depends no less than his ancestors on personal charisma: it is faith in him and his science that draws the patient to him. And his science, in spite of its pride in "objective research," is a maze of arcane lore, whose magical aura is intensified to an awesome level by its technology, its fantasia of chrome-decked machinery, flashing lights, pulsing cathode screens, and endless rubber tubes, pumps, bottles, multi-colored pills, microscopic gadgets, needles, operated by teams of surgeons, anaesthetists, nurses, physiotherapists, cardiographers, gynaecologists, who glide in white costumes along gleaming corridors. Indeed, the very objectivity of medical science has become magical. (Carroll, 1978, pp. 143–144)

Again, we see in the shaman many of the marks of the myth of the hero:

> The most charismatic of all our heroes, Jesus Christ, carried many of the marks of the shaman. He was born obscurely, elected by a long Judaic tradition preparing for the messiah, announced by portents, journeying seers, and John the Baptist; he underwent a pathological crisis in the wilderness, where he fasted for forty days and was tempted by the devil. On his return he began to preach, and to heal all those who had *faith*. (Carroll, 1978, p. 144)

The Galahad

In the Galahad is an archetype who is most often met under the name and guise of the Wanderer, he who is engaged in a quest, whether it be for perfection, Truth, or salvation.

> There is probably a trace of the Galahad in all men of literature, philosophy, and science. What characterizes the type is its life motif, that of the ascetic, passionate quest that is tyrannically absorbing. The precise nature of the Truth, not that there usually is any degree of precision, is of little importance. Indeed, about this Truth all that can be said is that it is an ideal, serving as the ultimate goal; and it promises some kind of comprehensive revelation. Everything is in the getting there. No day in the Galahad's life is futile, for each step is a move closer; even wrong turnings provide experience that is useful. There is no comprehension of either absurdity or scepticism.
>
> It is a mystical quest. The Galahad of twentieth-century philosophers, Martin Heidegger, calls his Grail "Being," the essence, the what-is of things. The knight's task is to think, or rather to theorize, in such a state of serenity that things lay bare their essences. Heidegger has in mind the Greek "theorea," which he interprets as "reverent observation of the disclosure of what is present." *Theorea*, a word of Orphic origin, does refer to a state of fervent contemplation, and participation in the sacred rites. There are countless other testimonials that the emotion that many great scientists and thinkers have experienced when deeply immersed in their work is one of awe, a cosmic wonder that carries them out of the constraining shell of their own egos. Belief in an unknown order has been for the scientist the equivalent to the mystic's belief in an unknown God. And he has often alluded to this order as preordained, the work of a divine mathematician, an infinitely complex yet perfectly conceived system underlying all things. In approaching his Grail, the scientist has had one ambition, that of Galahad, to look inside. Einstein wrote:
>
> > What a deep belief in the intelligence of creation and what longing for understanding, even if only of a meager reflection in

the revealed intelligence of this world, must have flourished in Kepler and Newton, enabling them as lonely men to unravel over years of work the mechanism of celestial mechanics.

Einstein also claimed that the serious research scholar was the only deeply religious human being left. (Carroll, 1978, p. 146)

The King's Fool

The fool exposes in mockery the vanities of man, his artifices, deceptions, and pretensions. He serves as a cultural counter-balance to pride: not the meek Christian alternative that preaches the antithetical virtue, humility, but the sceptical, nihilistic one that challenges man to know himself. . . .

The fools all pursue truth, not Truth. They are sceptics, doubting all ideals: goodness, beauty, progress, knowledge. . . .

The fool has a darker side. He is never far removed from the devil, the Mephistopheles, whose cynicism carries a mocking edge, who scorns, not out of benign sagacity or an urbane distance from men, but out of a rancorous need to disenchant, to poison the naive joys of those who are still able to play at living. Nevertheless, there is good sense to the words that Goethe put into the mouth of his Mephisto: "But one must not give one's brains too fierce a racking." (Carroll, 1978, pp. 147–148)

IMPLICATIONS REGARDING USEFULNESS AND THE UNIVERSITY

It should be clear by now that we are dealing with a fascinating and complex series of characters. Although the material thus far shows the bearing of these characters on the topic of usefulness, it is time to make the connection even more direct. One way to do this is to spell out the stance that each of our characters has toward usefulness and the informal norms or "rules of the game" that each seems to adopt, which kind of game each character plays. That is, it is not necessarily the case that each type is against useful knowledge per se. Rather, each archetype has a different concept of usefulness.

Finally, it behooves us to say something of the character type of the university and knowledge-producing institutions. Is there a prevailing distribution of types that tends to dominate our institutions? This is the only way we can get a deeper grasp on the enormity of the task in making universities more concerned with producing useful knowledge.

The Mandarin's Game

Like all the types, the Mandarin is not against usefulness per se but rather has a unique notion of usefulness, which is usefulness as self-service. The most useful knowledge is that which serves a very limited clientele, the Mandarin himself or his immediate (only to be trusted) family. By definition, usefulness is what furthers his career, his place in the official power structure. Knowledge per se or knowledge in general is neither of interest nor of use. The more confined, the more limited, the more direct, the more specific the knowledge, the better it is. Only such knowledge relates immediately to the Mandarin's chief concern: the securing and maintenance of power.

It is no random accident that the Mandarin tends to be elitist since he or she aspires to be at the very top. It is also no accident that the Mandarin tends to be an extreme (if not narrow) specialist, striving to maintain his uncontested toehold (expertise) in a complex, bewildering world.

Above all, the Mandarin is easily recognized in terms of the rules of the academic game he practices, preaches, and plays. These are:

Play the "right" game in town. Always know exactly who are in power and relate exclusively to them. Forget everybody else. They don't count—literally. If X is at a "leading university" and X says "Y is the most important problem of the year and Z is *the* way to approach," then by all means do as X says. Work on Y by prescribed means Z.

Publish in the "right" journals. This means of course the top journals in the field. Achieving disciplinary recognition is also part of the game. Do not do anything to raise suspicions that you are not exactly right in the heart of the mainstream. Avoid interdisciplinary journals. They not only make you suspect but also make you hard to peg and to identify. Never write for a broad audience.

Stay squarely in one discipline (see above). Become an expert in anything, the more obtuse and arcane the better. Explain away all potentially contaminating variables as "external to the field," unimportant, not relevant to consider. If pressed, be a reductionist. Do like the economists do. Say, "everything can really be explained in terms of costs versus benefits: love, war, marriage, death, you name it." Use lots of jargon and never, never write clearly.

Put down practitioners as an inherently inferior type of creature. Demean their humanity. Exalt theoretical, abstract knowledge because it is the only true end of the universe. Deny vehemently that by saying this that you just contradicted one of the earlier defining characteristics of the Mandarin—that is, that you really are not interested in abstract knowledge for its own sake, but only if it furthers your career. Ignore contradictions when convenient.

Speak only to those in the right schools, institutes, etc. Be arrogant, hostile, ready to attack every idea as unproven, trivial, unworthy of consideration. Derive pleasure in pouncing on those in inferior positions: graduate students, junior professors, those from "second-rate" schools. Perpetuate the myth that only those from first-rate schools can do first-rate work. Design a social support system that will confirm this myth.

And so on.

The Engineer's Game

At his best, the Engineer is a craftsman. He prefers to be left alone, to tinker in his shop, to produce the most skillfully crafted, perfected, and beautiful instruments the world has ever seen. He likes to make endless observations, to put his instruments to use.

The Engineer is of course the archetype of the professions, the professional schools, and institutions. Were he to be left alone, and were the world structured to suit him, he might indeed solve the problems of the world. The difficulty is that only just a small proportion of the world's problems are technical. On nontechnical problems, the Engineer is generally ineffective. Where the Mandarin excells in academic politics, the Engineer is clumsy, if not disdainful of them. He is insensitive of people's needs, even rude. He can not understand why people are not inherently curious like him and do not want to immediately adopt what is obviously better.

Because the Engineer is hard put to derive his inventions, often extremely ponderous and clumsy looking, from sound principles (i.e., from abstracted theory), he is extremely vulnerable to attack. A favorite ploy in the university is the put-down, "Quite inelegant you know; doesn't really understand it all; a bore; don't bother with him."

The Engineer is not exactly defenseless. He has his own power groups. But when all is said and done, he never really makes it in the academy. He has no well-worked out philosophy to counter the philosophy of the so-called pure types that prevail in the academy. He has never really understood the need to develop a philosophy and a theory of practice to counter the philosophy of "hands-off" that prevails in the university. Until he does so, he will remain on the outside.

Finally, the Engineer is predominantly male. There is very little of the feminine in him. Only very recently has he, and with great reluctance, admitted women into his fold. He still does not really understand why they are there and what they really have to contribute to the world outside.

The Chess Player's Game

The Chess Player is a solitary figure. He plays against himself or a mythical opponent such as Mother Nature. He is essentially a Hermit. The best game is one that he has invented and only he can understand. ("I can prove this theorem but you can't," one hears the great mathematicians saying.) He is a seeker after the perfect game, the one whose rules and structure are so elegant, so interesting, that were God Himself a mathematician, God would have created it. The sole reason for His existence is the game. It is perfection.

The Chess Player is removed from life. He has no desire to enter it. Only the perfect game matters. Indeed, the more removed a game is from all practical affairs, the better it is. The usefulness of a game should have no bearing whatsoever on it.

The Chess Player is an apt symbol for the modern university. With its extreme emphasis on individualism, the university essentially rewards those who play by themselves. Since game players are in turn taught by other game players (Chess Masters), each of whom plays his own game, there tends over time to be a proliferation of more and more solitary game players. We are bred for individualism. Unless others are exactly on our wavelength (that is, have been taught to play the same game), we can always take our marbles and go home (retreat to our own individual cells).

The university is a solitary place and has been created for that purpose. It neither rewards nor sets in motion the conditions that would promote team play; hence, it should not be surprised to find that team play has not occurred. Individual members within a particular department or discipline can spend years next to one another without ever having to talk. Some even take pride in this: "I'm micro; you're macro," or some such nonsense, is an all-too-common refrain. There is not much more discourse between departments.

Modern industrial corporations are certainly no paradigm of inter-organizational cooperation and communication. They are not perfect in any sense. But can one really imagine a firm where the marketing and the engineering departments never had to talk to one another? Yet, this is the design of the modern university. And we really wonder why there is such little connection between knowledge and usefulness?

The Chiliast's Game

The Chiliast is one who has sacrificed whatever practical side he once had to the future, the vision of what-is-yet-to-be. He is a full-time, if not professional, dreamer. He is a futurist, whether of the technologist or humanist persuasion. He is concerned neither with practicality nor with usefulness. Why solve today's problems when one can spend one's time dreaming of a world without problems? It is a nicer world, if only in the mind. Some of our best visionaries and planners are of this ilk. It is their first strength and first love. They are quick to accuse Mandarins and Engineers as being devoid of daring and imagination, of being afraid to dream big dreams.

The Shaman's Game

Of all our types, the Shaman is the one who most wants to heal the division between theory and practice. He agonizes over what the types before him and the types that will follow after him have made or will make of the university.

The Shaman is no longer just a healer of the individual soul. Modern Shamans have had considerable experience in healing organizations. He is concerned with the soul of organizations (at least those Shamans who live in modern departments of the organizational sciences).

The trouble is that more than ever before the Shaman doubts his own magic. He is near to totally losing his faith in his ability to heal. That is all he ever had. That is where his magic always lay, within himself. He fears that the sickness of man may have become so deep that man has become death, destruction, and sickness itself.

The Shaman is, as a result, the character who is always closest to falling into the clutches of the King's Fool, except that he will always be a cynic who cares. The Shaman will always like to be talked out of his despair. The King's Fool relishes it; he is only happy when he gloats over despair.

The Shaman's road is hard. His colleagues in the university do not respect him. He is never theoretical enough for them. In a way this is true, depending of course upon how one defines theoretical. The Shaman's concern is with spiritual theory, not mathematical or physical theory. He wants desperately to transform, to save the world through action. If his faith is strong enough, it will prevent him from leading a lonely life or dying a lonely death. He will at least heal himself.

The Galahad's Game

"I'm moving on; I've no time to stop and talk. Talk to the others."

The King's Fool's Game

"It doesn't matter; none of this is really worth talking about. Don't you see that it's all a sham? Don't you see that the others are more of a fool than I am? Who cares? So what?"

The Fate of the University

The error of the university has always been that of thinking itself a rational place. It has never been that. It is a haven for those who have sought refuge from the world. It is an institution designed to serve the hidden and repressed emotional needs of those who go there. It will thus not be changed by rational means. The overall design can not be defended rationally. What is the rationality of an organization composed primarily of and run essentially for Mandarins and Chess Players?

However, it does not follow that the university will be changed by irrational means. An academic may be defined as a Mandarin who thinks that if one is not rational, one is necessarily irrational. The nonrational—the great gray area inbetween—is our province.

The soul of the machine is not well. It needs healing as never before. The disease is fragmentation. Western university man is Fragmented Man. He splits himself up into disciplines and departments that make wholeness almost impossible. Who is the doctor that can heal the division that runs so deep within us? Where is the Shaman who can talk to all of the types that are perpetually within us all?

CONCLUSIONS

It might appear that we are overly pessimistic about the fate of the university, about whether any academics are likely to care about useful knowledge and to pursue it purposely. The deeper social analysis that results from the study of archetypes can even project a very gloomy side of life and human nature. Our belief is that we do not have to fear this shadow side, but rather that we will gain understanding by acknowledging the mood and insights that derive from an archetypal social analysis.

Furthermore, we do not mean to suggest that only academics and intellectuals have this gloomy side and that only academic institutions are fraught with deep resistances to pursuing the intended or rational purpose of the organization. Considering industrial firms and the practitioners who run them, Maccoby (1976) has provided an archetypal social analysis that also gets at the soul.

Specifically, Maccoby posits "four main psychological types in the corporate technostructure: the craftsman, the jungle fighter, the company man, and the gamesman" (p. 37).

The Craftsman

[He] holds the traditional values of the productive-hoarding character—the work ethic, respect for people, concern for quality and thrift. When he talks about his work, his interest is the *process* of making something; he enjoys building. He sees others, co-workers as well as superiors, in terms of whether they help or hinder him in doing a craftsmanlike job. . . . Although his virtues are admired by everyone, his self-containment and perfectionism do not allow him to lead a complex and changing organization. Rather than engaging and trying to master the system with the cooperation of others who share his values, he tends to do his own thing and go along, sometimes reluctantly, toward goals he does not share, enjoying whatever opportunities he finds for interesting work.

Some of the most creative and gifted scientists whom we have seen in the corporate world are included in this type, together with the most unhappy misfits, resentful failures whose gifts do not measure up to their ambition. What most distinguishes the "scientists" from the craftsman is their narcissism, their idolatry of their own knowledge, talents, and technology and their hunger for admiration. They are the corporate intellectuals and many are fascinated by esoteric issues (e.g., outer space or eternal life) only tangentially related to either corporate goals or social needs. . . . A grandiose scientist does not trust the public to understand him, and it doesn't occur to him that the reason may be that he does not create things that benefit the public. He invents what is demanded by those who pay him—the corporation and the state. Both at home and at work, the grandiose scientist seeks a protected nest. He wants an admiring mother-wife to meet his needs in return for a chance to share in his glory, and he seeks patrons at work who will agree to similar symbiotic relationships. (Maccoby, 1976, pp. 38–40)

The Jungle Fighter

[His] goal is power. He experiences life and work as a jungle (not a game), where it is eat or be eaten, and the winners destroy the losers. A major part of his psychic resources is budgeted for his internal department of defense. Jungle fighters tend to see their peers in terms of accomplices or enemies and their subordinates as objects to be utilized. There are two subtypes of jungle fights, lions and foxes. The lions are the conquerors who when successful may build an empire; the foxes make their nests in the corporate hierarchy and move ahead by stealth and politicking. (p. 40)

The Company Man

In the company man, we recognize the well-known organization man, or the functionary whose sense of identity is based on being part of the powerful, protected company. His strongest traits are his concern with the human side of the company, his interest in the feelings of the people around him and his commitment to maintain the organization's integrity. At his weakest, he is fearful and submissive, concerned with security even more than with success. The most creative company men sustain an atmosphere in their groups of cooperation, stimulation, and mutuality. The least creative find a little niche and satisfy themselves by feeling that somehow they share in the glory of the corporation. (p. 40)

The Gamesman

> [He] is the new man, and, really, the leading character in this study. His main interest is in challenge, competitive activity where he can prove himself a winner. Impatient with others who are slower and more cautious, he likes to take risks and to motivate others to push themselves beyond their normal pace. He responds to work and life as a game. The contest hypes him up and he communicates his enthusiasm, thus energizing others. He enjoys new ideas, new techniques, fresh approaches and shortcuts. His talk and his thinking are terse, dynamic, sometimes playful and come in quick flashes. His main goal is to be a winner, and talking about himself invariably leads to discussion of his tactics and strategy in the corporate contest. (pp. 40–41)

The hope for the academic institution is that the Shaman can keep his faith and mobilize the more productive sides of his other colleagues. The hope for the corporation is that the Gamesman will blend his talents and perspectives with the more desirable sides of his corporate fellows. The hope for the production and utilization of scientific knowledge to solve world problems is that the Shaman and the Gamesman will join forces, that the sparkling (rather than gloomy) soul of human nature will prevail.

Moreover, the social characters suggested for academics and for practitioners demonstrate the pervasive and underlying quality of archetypes. In a broader sense, the characters from either community are the same. The problems that the types create by their dynamics are the same. The awareness and social reform needed to heal the problems that have been created by these types are thus also the same. The "head" must be unified with the "heart."

REFERENCES

Carroll, J.
1978   "In Spite of Intellectuals." *Theory and Society*, Vol. 6, No. 1: 133–150.
Maccoby, M.
1976   *The Gamesman*. New York: Bantam.
Mitroff, I. I.
1983   *Stakeholders of the Mind: Towards a Nonfragmented Theory of Social Systems*. San Francisco: Jossey-Bass.
Mitroff, I. I., and R. H. Kilmann
1978   *Methodological Approaches to Social Science*. San Francisco: Jossey-Bass.

16

KNOWLEDGE FOR PRODUCING USEFUL KNOWLEDGE AND THE IMPORTANCE OF SYNTHESIS

Robert J. Waller

INTRODUCTION

Useful knowledge is defined here to mean the achievement of understanding in a given situation, such that courses of action can be developed and intelligent choices can be made in the context of the situation. One interpretation of the stated theme of this conference, producing useful knowledge *for* organizations, is that someone or something other than organizations produces knowledge for organizations. But, along with knowledge supplied by academic and similar institutions, organizational participants must create their own useful knowledge on a daily basis.

The production of such knowledge is a matter of both analysis and synthesis. While our educational systems spend a considerable amount of time developing analytic capabilities, virtually no effort is expended on improving the capabilities of people to synthesize (excluding such relatively frail attempts as word problems and case studies). Yet modern organizational participants are deluged with data and unassimilated bits of information on a continuing basis, with no provision as to how all of this might be manipulated to produce understanding. Hence, the concept of synthesis as one very important step in the production of useful knowledge will be defined and examined in this chapter.

CONFUSION, COMPLEXITY, AND ORGANIZATIONAL LIFE

Organizational participants are awash in reality. This reality is unstructured, formless, random, and scattered. Or at least reality appears this way to the participant, whose day-to-day world consists of a computer printout here, a meeting there, an article in a trade journal somewhere else. Days mount into weeks, weeks into months, while the bits of data and information keep coming. Somehow, people sense, all of this ought to fit together, but it does not. The cumulative effect is confusion.

When people attempt to bring order out of this confusion, they immediately confront complexity. There is a difference between confusion and complexity. Confusion is chaotic, a disordered state of affairs. Complexity emerges when an attempt is made to convert disorder to order. More precisely, complexity is composed of elements (people, objects, ideas, and data) that are related or are potentially related to one another in one or more relational dimensions. This definition will make increasing sense to the reader as the chapter progresses.

From a morass of confusion and then complexity, organizational participants are expected to produce a level of understanding sufficient to produce coherent plans, to make rational decisions, and generally to cope with the turbulence of modern organizational life. Furthermore, they are expected to do all of this within time horizons that are relatively short (compared to, for example, the rather luxurious horizons faced by academics purporting to produce useful knowledge for organizations). Except by accident or through trial and error, these expectations are not met for two reasons.

First, humans simply are not equipped cognitively to be successful in confrontations with complexity. When humans attempt to think and communicate about complexity, they confront a combinatorial richness overwhelming that part of the cognitive apparatus (the short-term memory) used for such thinking and communication. This has been amply demonstrated by Simon (1974) and has been more casually commented upon by others (Arbib, 1972; Forrester, 1971; Hammond and Brehmer, 1973; Langefors, 1970; Miller, 1956; Vaughan and Mavor, 1972). In addition, the present author (Waller, 1983) has combined Simon's work with aspects of behavioristic psychology to offer an explanation of why people do not even like to attempt confrontations with complexity.

A second reason why humans are not adept at dealing with complexity has to do with the nature of the educations provided them. In short, U.S. educational systems do not deal with the problem of making sense of complexity, let alone recognize the constraints imposed by human cognitive abilities.

Hence, propelled into organizational life with no way of dealing with complexity, people tend to exhibit one of two behaviors. The first is an avoidance of grappling with confusion and complexity (for example, an excessive focus on trivial problems that *can* be solved, or a consultant is hired). Alternatively, mired in a complexity thwarting clear thinking and communication, people, out of desperation or ignorance, press whatever feasible-looking policy lever or decision button that comes into view. The results are familiar: policies and decisions that ramify into dazzling configurations of unintended results.

SYNTHESIS: THE MYSTICAL FORM AND THE RATIONAL FORM

Synthesis Versus Analysis

The word *synthesis* is sometimes used to refer to a process and at other times to the result of the process. The process is the putting together of parts or elements so as to form a whole. The result is a whole made up of parts or elements put together. It is the process that is the focus in this chapter. Similarly, analysis can also refer to a process or a result. The process is a separating or breaking up of any whole into its parts so as to find out their nature, proportion, functions, relationship, and so on. Analysis is also used to refer to the results of this process. As with synthesis, it is the process that is of major concern here.

Synthesis as a Mystical Process

Poincare put his foot on the step of a bus. As he does, he suddenly understands a relationship between the Fuchsian functions he has been working on and transformations in non-Euclidean geometry (Ghiselin, 1952:37). Yeats (1956), at his desk, struggles with a phrase, refines it, and produces the flowing lyric, "I went out to the hazel wood, because a fire was in my head." What is occurring in these situations? No one really knows. Somehow, in some way, out of disorder have come knowledge and beauty, but the process is hidden from view. Yet when synthesis as a process is treated at all by educators, it is usually in exactly this fashion, under the rubric of something called "creativity." In this form synthesis is regarded as a result arising magically out of a vague process comprised of immersion in the problem, incubation, and a eureka event (along with some refinement) that produces wholes from parts. Unfortunately, the ability to carry out this process implicitly is attributed to the lucky few labeled "creative people."

Lest it appear the author is overly skeptical about the creative art, a caveat is in order. The histories of science and art are, of course, full of examples of just the kind of discoveries discussed in the previous two paragraphs. One must seriously question, however, whether such a view of synthesis has any utility for the day-to-day and month-to-month worlds of the organizational participant. This is not to rule out those grand, glorious moments when confusion dissolves and discovery emerges. Certainly, these moments can and do occur in organizational life, just as they occur in science and art. The point is whether or not such a mystical process can be relied upon to produce useful knowledge in a regular way for organizations. The answer, based on the author's experience, is a resounding no. This is true for several reasons:

The messiness surrounding people in organizations is quite different from the relatively well-structured problems faced by those searching for an elegant mathematical proof or just the right musical phrase.

The organizational time horizons mentioned earlier dictate the length of the incubation period. One simply does not, when asked for an opinion on a complex issue that must be resolved today, answer a superior's query by saying, "I am still incubating."

Organizational participants, even if immersion and incubation have produced results, generally are required to explain the process by which they arrived at a solution and to be able to defend and market the idea. Mysticism is usually not an acceptable explanation of one's approach (though perhaps it should be on occasion).

Most significant organizational problems, unlike mathematical proofs and the search for musical or literary phrases, do not stay solved. Not only are "solutions" imperfect, but the dynamics of organizational reality tend to make formerly good solutions obsolete as reality changes. There is, in other words, a fluidity involved that is just not present in those areas usually cited for creative endeavors.

Thus, while one hopes that creativity in all of its forms will be nurtured in organizations, the daily world of the organizational participant demands something more than just waiting for magic to occur.

Synthesis as a Rational Process

Humans and Complexity

Complexity is composed of elements and intricate relationships among these elements. When humans confront complexity, they must discover these relationships and (in organizational life)communicate them to one another in an intelligible form. Conscious manipulation of elements and relations, however, is a function of the short-term memory. As was noted earlier, this part of the human cognitive apparatus suffers from some severe limitations.

As the author has argued in greater detail elsewhere (Waller, 1983), this comes down to a design problem. On the one hand is complexity in all of its richness. On the other hand we see the human, restricted in terms of short-term memory, but with marvelous capabilities for long-term information retention, for judgment, for utilizing experience, for intuition, and, yes, for passion. Somehow, then, a way must be found that recognizes the central features of complexity and yet takes into account both the strengths and weaknesses of human cognition.

From a design point of view, this problem of helping the human to deal with complexity is similar to the problem of meshing form with content. But is the human the form that is to be designed to fit the context of complexity? Or is it the other way around? We must take both the human and complexity as given. Human cognitive abilities cannot be modified to fit the demands of complexity. But neither can complexity be changed. If a problem situation is simplified to bring it within range of human capacities, then we are no longer dealing with the original problem (in fact, this sort of "undermodeling" probably occurs all the time, since we are unable to grasp the relational abundance of complex situations with our cognitive abilities).

Since neither the human nor complexity can be changed, a way must be found to link the two without changing either. In engineering terminology, an interface device must be sought that will link humans and complexity, while preserving the original properties of each. Anyone who regularly deals with real problems in government and industry can testify that such a device has not yet been found and perfected. In fact, a dominant feature of organizations in both the public and private sectors is a continual shadow boxing with problems. Since humans have no way of handling the complexity before them, no way of dealing with what Woolsey and Swanson (1975:166) aptly have termed the "push-down, pop-up innate cussedness of Mother Nature," problems either go unsolved or the acts of desperation mentioned earlier are carried out.

We simply run around the edges of our problems, hoping for insight, looking for eureka solutions. What we need is an angle of entry, a way into the mess. The author has labeled this the *Archimedean Dilemma*. The reader may recall Archimedes' lamentation that if he only had a place to stand, he could construct a lever to move the world. Immersed in complexity, we cannot find a place to stand, a foothold for gaining purchase as a base from which to launch an assault on problems.

In order to overcome this dilemma, it is necessary to recognize that the central features of complexity—elements and relations—create problems that are, in their essence, structural. Once this is understood, a search for structural approaches to complex situations can be launched.

Complexity and Structure

Figure 16.1 is the centerpiece around which the author constructs his presentations in his management development practice. It has proved

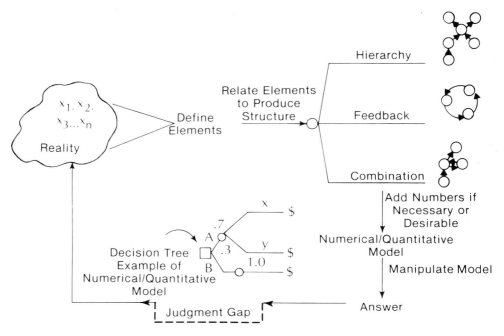

FIGURE 16.1. Diagram of Modeling Process

meaningful in that context to organizational participants from the level of first-line supervisors up. The purpose of using this figure is to locate in a precise way the locus of synthesis in the overall process of modeling complex reality. The idea of showing diagramatically a "judgment gap" between model output and reality is due originally to Raiffa (1968:297).

The discussion begins with the notion of reality, which is taken in a rather primitive way to mean everything in the physical, intellectual, and spiritual universe. For practical purposes, there is no need to define reality in a more precise fashion. At any given time, people are extracting from reality elements relevant to the task before them and are attempting to relate these elements to one another. When we prepare to cross a street, we build a model from those aspects of reality relevant to this act. We do the same thing when we drive a car or brush our teeth. But such mundane forms of modeling are not of interest here, where the focus is on synthesizing under conditions where no synthesis has been carried out before.

It can be seen from Figure 16.1 that the first two activities in modeling reality involve the central features of complexity discussed earlier. The first stage is analysis, which amounts to defining a universe of discourse by selecting from reality those elements that seem relevant to the problem at hand. It is the second stage of the process, relating the elements, that is the central thrust of this chapter, for this is where synthesis must occur.

It has been shown (Waller, 1976; Warfield, 1976) that a rational approach to synthesis can be viewed as follows:

Identify a set V of elements relevant to a problem situation, for example, factors in the energy problem, objectives for a public school system, types of information in an organization, and recipients of this information. (The reader will note again that this step is analytic; however, taken as a whole, the steps being described here constitute a process of synthesis.)

Define an appropriate contextual relation (Warfield, 1976) M, such as "impacts on," "contributes to the achievement of," "sends information to."

Form the Cartesian product $V \times V$. Use M to examine the ordered pairs of $V \times V$ to determine which, if any, of the (v_i, v_j) satisfy the condition of v_i M v_j (for example, v_i "impacts on" v_j). The set of pairs satisfying the condition is a binary relation M on V.

Connect all (v_i, v_j) satisfying the condition with one another using arcs (directed lines). Thus, if v_i M v_j, an arc is drawn *from* v_i *to* v_j. If the relation is transitive, the arcs implied by transitivity may be omitted, if it is so desired.

The outcome of this four-step process is a directed graph (digraph). When a real-world interpretation is given to the digraph (a fifth step), it is properly labeled as interpreted structural model (Warfield, 1976). A simple example of this process is shown in Figure 16.2. The reader should note that the matrix with ones and zeros is just a way of showing a Cartesian product and where the relation holds for various pairs of elements. As one reads across the rows of the matrix, the number one in a particular cell indicates that v_i M v_j. A zero indicates that v_i M' v_j (the relation does not hold).

Perhaps the reader harbors a tendency to dismiss what has just been done as rudimentary and obvious. This tendency should be resisted, for within this deceptively simple process is a host of subtle and profound ideas. Cast in the form of a methodology called Interpretive Structural Modeling (ISM) (Warfield, 1976), this process has been applied in more than 100 problem situations worldwide. Some examples of these applications may be found in Coke and Moore (1980), Fitz, Gier, and Troha (1977), Jedlicka and Meyer (1980), and Waller (1974, 1975). Furthermore, Warfield (1980) has identified some 200 books, articles, and monographs that deal directly or indirectly with the process described and the attendant subtleties and profundities noted above. Hence, these latter considerations will be given only tangential attention here. In addition, it is emphasized that although ISM will be used to exemplify other concepts in this chapter, the purpose

(a) Element Set. Factors in Corporate Success

= (Corporate Image, Good Labor Relations, Profits, Decreased Labor Unrest)

(b) Contextual Relation. M = "Contributes to the Achievement of."

(c) Filled-In Binary Matrix.

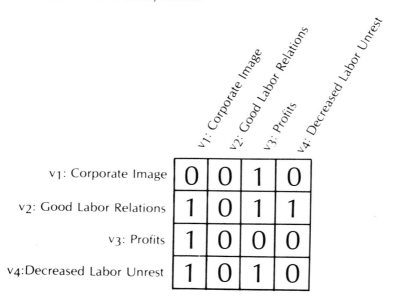

(d) Digraph And Interpreted Structural Model.

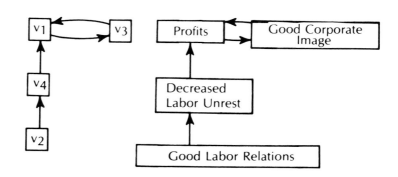

FIGURE 16.2. Illustration of Rational Synthesis Process

here is not to tout a particular methodology. Rather, the intent is to show that within methodologies such as ISM are the kernels for a powerful approach to synthesis and a language for dealing with complexity that can be of considerable value in generating useful knowledge for organizations.

When the synthesis stage has been carried out, a structural model portraying the interrelationships of the elements relevant to a given situation will be produced. Structural models, as we have seen, are digraphs, and many precise ways of classifying digraphs on the particular structure they exhibit have been developed. For examples the reader may consult Harary, Norman, and Cartwright (1965) and Busacker and Saaty (1965). But fundamentally, one of three types of structure will emerge: a hierarchy, a cycle, or a combination of these two structures. That is, the structure will be in the form of levels, with only one-way flows along the arcs; in the form of a cycle, where every element relates directly or indirectly to every other element; or in a form where both levels and cycles are present. The author finds the ramifications of this simple threefold classification staggering. In a universe filled with objects, ideas, and people, can it be possible that when structuring any subset of this infinity, only three general forms of structure are possible? It appears so.

Because people have not been formally educated to think in structural terms about complexity, the possibility of perceiving complexity in terms of levels and cycles goes unnoticed. Hence, complex situations often are not as complex as they seem at first glance. For example, Figure 16.3 shows the same structure in two different ways. The "bird's nest" in part (a) is the kind of result that emerges from the typical committee meeting or is what imperfectly floats around in the author's head when he tries mentally to conceptualize a complex issue. Part (b) of Figure 16.3 is the same structure, with two modifications: the structure has been organized according to levels, and arcs implied by transitivity have been omitted. Incidentally, this problem is derived from the author's involvement in assisting an environmental group concerned about the pollution of two branches of a creek. In Figure 16.3, elements 7 and 4 are the two branches of the creek, with the remaining elements being events in the pollution chain. In this case, a simple precedence relation was used. Part (a) of Figure 16.3 approximates very closely the convoluted nature of the group's thinking in the early stages of discussion. Part (b) is the result of applying ISM, which contains within it techniques for presenting structures in the clearest possible form based on levels and cycles.

It is important to note that thus far in the modeling process nothing has been said about numerical measurement at the level of interval and ratio scales. Essentially, the three types of structures shown in Figure 16.1 imply only ordinal or quasi-ordinal measurement. Numbers enter the process in two places. First, some recourse to data may be required to answer the

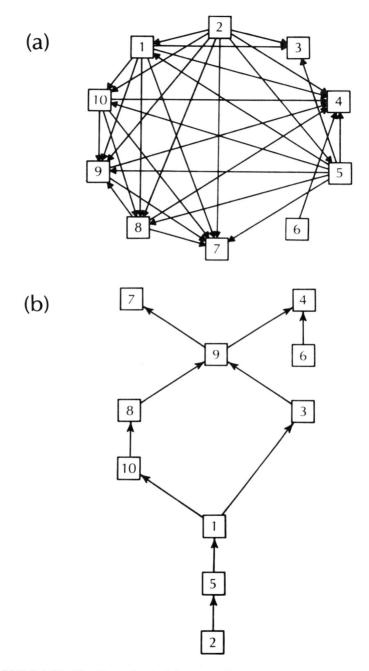

FIGURE 16.3. The Same Logical Structure Shown in Two Different Ways

relational queries involved in the process of synthesis. (It is emphasized, however, that the process as described earlier is amenable to the use of raw gut feel, or judgment based on experience, or numerical data, or values, or any combination of these.) Second, once a structure has been produced via the process of synthesis, along with refinements of the structure as deemed necessary, it becomes appropriate to ask whether the acquisition of data for converting the purely structural model to a quantitative model is desirable or necessary.

In both of these cases, though, it is the Socratic nature of the process that dictates the need for or desirability of numbers. That is, in synthesizing the structure, the inability to answer a binary query may suggest a search for appropriate numerical data. This is not a flaw in the process. On the contrary, it is one of its strengths: the process quietly points out that numerical data are needed and says something about the kind of data required by virtue of the query under consideration. Once synthesis of the structure has been completed, the Socratic nature of the process again emerges by forcing the question: Do I need numbers or do I feel that numbers are desirable? If the answer is yes, the structure provides detailed information about exactly what type of data is needed. For example, many complex situations involving decisions exhibit a hierarchical structure, or what is commonly called a "decision tree." When the tree has been constructed, its Socratic nature takes over and asks: What are the terminal values and are these values costs, revenues, or utilities; what are the probabilities and how may these be computed?

In other cases, the structure can implicitly represent a dynamic model. Hence, it may be necessary or desirable to know the quantitative impact of element v_i on v_j. This amounts to estimating via judgment or data analysis the time and weight coefficients that will be assigned to the arcs. From a structural point of view, this type of quantification involves a mapping or multiple mapping of the arcs into the set of real numbers, where the numbers represent weights denoting the strength of impact, or time, or both. In still other cases, probabilities or flow capacities may be relevant for the arcs. The Socratic nature of the model again emerges in all of these instances.

Whether numbers have or have not been used, one always must ask if the output of the model, the model's "answer," has any relevance to the real problem at hand. The need for this should be obvious, but the continual failure of operations research and management science to make much of a dent in organizational practice is due, at least in part, to the failure of those employing Buck Rogers management science techniques to remember that the relevance of a model's answer depends upon the extent to which the model represents the real problem. Finally, when all is said and done, the question of the model's relevance, whether to take the answer produced back to reality for implementation (and, if so, how) is always a matter of judgment.

Again, this is one of those things that should be obvious, but does not always seem to be.

It would be naive to suggest that modeling moves in the clear, linear fashion implied by Figure 16.1. Missing from the figure are the feedback loops from each stage of the process to all other stages of the process that are always present in modeling building. One advances and retreats, analyzes and synthesizes, adds and discards. This is the way of "logic-in use" (Kaplan, 1964:8) as opposed to the neat reconstructions of logic and discovery that characterize the view of science held by nonscientists.

Lands Of The Qualitative

Qualitative Solutions

Prior to the search for numbers with which to quantify models, one must pause to ask if numbers are really needed and, if numbers *are* needed, what numbers? This has been mentioned before, but the importance of the question cannot be emphasized too strongly. There is a decided tendency on the part of people to "run for the numbers" at the outset of a problem. Part of this tendency surely is due to the way our society and educational systems glorify the countable, a proclivity that perhaps is a legacy of nineteenth-century physics and the general awe with which people view the so-called hard sciences.

Let us next ask if there is a class of organizational problems that can successfully be assaulted qualitatively, where "qualitative" is taken to mean the use of structural modeling employing nothing more than ordinal and quasi-ordinal measurement scales. The answer is yes. For example, the setting of objectives, which is a very difficult problem, is inherently qualitative. Interval and ratio scale data may be used in discussing how objectives relate to one another, but the solution to the objectives-setting problem is an objectives *structure*. This qualitative nature of objectives becomes more apparent the higher one moves in an organization.

Another important set of problems within the class of qualitative problems concerns the matter of preference. Though preference structure are very sticky matters, a statement such as, "A is preferred to B," is qualitative. Similar kinds of problems emerge frequently in design and personnel questions.

What follows illustrates a qualitative approach to a problem. In 1979 the author was appointed dean of a college that had been established just one month earlier. The task was to take two departments, a large one and a smaller one, and meld them into a working academic college. Since this was the only new college established since the institution had been reconstituted into a university some years earlier, no guidelines were available for such an undertaking. Moreover, the subject matter areas of these two departments were just beginning to experience a period of growth in student enrollment that catapulted the new operation from a nonexistent college to the largest college in the university within three years. To say that confusion was present is to understate the case considerably. Compounding the problem was the fact that the author had no prior experience in academic management and controlled less than 5 percent of the university budget.

The preeminent problem was simply making sense of the confusion within which the author found himself. Hence, a structural model of the organization's problematique was constructed using ISM. A portion of this model is shown in Figure 16.4 (the signs on the arcs will be discussed later and should be ignored now). Only a portion is shown for two reasons: matters of privacy and the fact that the complete model is too large to present here. In addition, the dynamism of the organization dictates that additions to and subtractions from the model are constantly in progress.

A great deal can be said about the model. First of all, the process of synthesizing the structure raised many important questions and issues not previously apparent. This benefit is, of course, common to all good modeling procedures. Beyond that, however, the structure provided the author with an overview of his operation not possible in any other way. Early on in the process of constructing the new college, information systems had to be designed, authority structures needed to be established, and numerous other tasks had to be carried out within severe time and budget constraints. With a copy of the synthesized structure before him, the author was able to see immediately the ramifications of action taken in various parts of the overall system. Unless the reader actually has confronted such a situation, the value-added of the structure to the author's day-to-day management activities cannot be appreciated entirely.

In addition, the Socratic properties mentioned earlier are present. The structure sits there in quiet repose and asks questions such as:

What are the current teaching loads of the faculty?

Are these teaching loads appropriate in light of research and service requirements?

What is the college's share of the overall university budget? How may this share be increased?

What proportion of our students are transfers from community colleges? How well do these students perform relative to our "native" students?

How important is accreditation by the American Assembly of Collegiate Schools of Business? What are the costs of achieving accreditation?

Furthermore, and this point seems to be overlooked by all texts on decision making, decisions flow from problematiques. This can clearly be seen in Figure 16.4 and in the questions posed above. For example, one important decision involves faculty teaching loads. This immediately gives rise to alternatives such as: keep teaching loads the same overall; increase all teaching loads; decrease all teaching loads; and keep some teaching loads the same, while increasing and decreasing other faculty members' loads on a selective basis. As these alternatives are posed, the structure can then be used to trace the effects of various alternatives through the system (that is, assign terminal values to decision tree endpoints).

Even though synthesis, not the value of structural models, is the concern here, it most be pointed out that the visual importance of such models for comprehension and decision making is generally underestimated. For example, Harary, Norman, and Cartwright (1965:151) impute to Bertrand Russell the assertion that, "In the best books there are no figures." Zeleny (1982:xvii) writes disparagingly about what he calls "petrified snapshots of a dead 'tree'" in talking about decision trees. The present author obviously disagrees. In addition to the already mentioned advantages of structure, too little is yet known about the relationship between visualization and structural thinking to bury these notions prematurely.

Model Escalation

Whether knowledge is useful—in terms of its instrumentality for a given situation—cannot be determined independently of the organizational time horizon relevant for the situation. Methodology Z may be the most powerful idea around for attacking situation H. But if Z requires two weeks for its execution and H must be dealt with this afternoon, then Z is not useful in this situation.

This point is so obvious that it almost hurts to write it down. But academics, and often organizational staff people, simply do not seem to understand that useful knowledge is time dependent. The more enlightened among us can carp that good planning and foresight would have allowed the necessary two weeks for Z to be brought to bear. Those so blessed may be right. Nonetheless, Z is still not useful in this situation, and reminding people in the organization of their failure to think ahead is not likely to make them seek out our usefulness in the future.

Thus, any process purporting to deal with complexity and produce useful knowledge for organizations ought to be able to accommodate the time constraints common to organizational life. The modeling process just described does accommodate these constraints. If time permits only a rough-hewn structural synthesis, so be it. In this case the model can serve as a useful perspective on the problem rather than as a surrogate for the problem (Strauch, 1974).

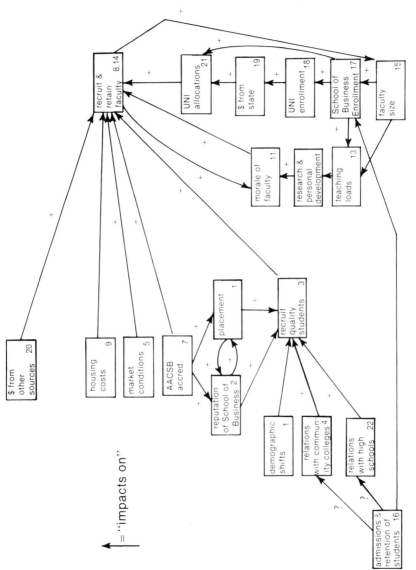

FIGURE 16.4. Example of Organizational Problematique

In addition, once a structure has been synthesized, it takes relatively little time to escalate the model to the level of a signed digraph, like that in Figure 16.4. Attaching signs to the arcs requires only that one be able to say whether the relationship between two elements, in the case of a causative model, is direct or inverse. Besides the general sense of causative movement through the system, which one gains from the use of signs, it is possible to derive other important insights more rigorously based in digraph theory. For example, an even number of minus signs in a given cycle indicates that the cycle incorporates positive feedback, causing it to move in a certain direction. On the other hand, an odd number of minus signs tells us that the system is self-equilibrating (negative feedback).

Aside from the frequent necessity to learn as much as possible about a situation in a short time, it may not be possible to do much more quantification even if time is available. Roberts (1974:3) has commented that "the signed digraph sometimes contains as much information as it is possible to gather accurately about the interrelationships among variables. This is true especially if some of the variables are hard to quantify, as for example, a variable like environmental quality." It should be clear, then, that an important feature of useful knowledge for both synthesis and analysis is its amenability to time constraints. As Warfield (1974:1–3) accurately observes, "The dichotomy of intuition versus formalism often is decided in favor of intuition, simply because there is no formalism that can produce results on a time scale that is realistic."

Language and Quality

Both the natural and mathematical languages possess strengths and weaknesses for dealing with complexity. The natural language is rich in opportunities for subtlety and coloration, and it is accessible to the nonmathematician. Mathematics, too, contains a subtlety of its own and is capable of a level of rigor and precision not found in the natural language.

The lack of precision and rigor in the natural language, coupled with human cognitive limits, prevents it from adequately conveying the essence of complex situations in an efficient and effective way. Words come from our mouths and from our typewriters in a straight line, so to speak. People with whom we are trying to communicate receive our words in a straight line as well. But, as we have seen, complexity is composed of levels and cycles layers in multiple dimensions. A great deal of confusion, in the sense that relationships are not clearly present or understood, occurs constantly because we try to explain complexity in a language not well suited for the task. But a major deficiency in mathematics is the inability to capture the meaningful vagueness desirable in certain situations; for example, it is difficult to say "I love you" in mathematics, while capturing all of the delicious properties attached to that phrase. Just as important, though mathematical sophistication draws back a curtain to disclose a world of power and clarity, the curtain remains closed for most people, including many who have much to contribute to problem solutions.

This question of language deficiency in the face of complexity is of vital importance not just to organizations, but to the practice of democracy. If democracy depends upon a knowledgeable citizenry intelligently debating the important issues of the time, then democracy does not have long to live. People are overwhelmed with the complexity they sense about them. Public discussion degenerates into simple generalization and argument, rather than enlightened debate. Anyone who has recently attended a public meeting on an important issue, such as where to locate an interstate highway within a city, can testify to the imminent demise of the democratic process, if the health of this process is judged by the quality of debate. People just do not have a language available to them designed to foster clarity of thought and debate.

Tucked away in the idea of synthesis via structural thinking is a hint of a language that combines both the natural language and mathematics. The author has emphasized this possibility in an earlier paper (Waller, 1983); only the essence of the idea will be mentioned here. In brief, if it is complexity we must think and communicate about, and neither the natural language nor mathematics is suitable for this task by itself, then we ought to design and use a language specifically intended for use under conditions of complexity. If complexity, composed of elements and relations among the elements, is structural in nature, then the language should account for this and be amenable to handling structural richness.

Basically, the language should allow people to talk in the natural language, but this communication should be bounded by the precision and rigor of mathematics. Consider the following: Take a nonempty finite set V of elements called vertices and a finite set A (possible empty) of elements called arcs, which are directed lines, and map A into $V \times V$. This set of instructions presented to a group of organizational participants will not be understood, except possibly by certain members of the operations research department. Yet, the author and his colleagues have done this many times in applying ISM in situations ranging from those involving high-level corporate executives to Mexican peasants. Exactly what occurs is beyond the scope of this chapter, but the idea is to construct a way of dealing with problems such that people can talk in the natural language, but yet be guided and constrained by the precision of mathematics.

In general, what might be the properties of such a language? It appears there are several (Waller, 1983):

1. It [the language] must come to terms with the central feature of complexity: the numerous and intricate relationships among many elements.

2. It must take into account the human cognitive limits discussed earlier.

3. It must accommodate values, experience, wisdom, and judgment, as well as objective data.

4. It must foster logical consistency and yet not constrain flights of intuitional creativity of the kind previously mentioned.

5. It must be amenable to computerization, in order that the machine may share our computational burdens.

6. For the enhancement of democratic processes and participatory assaults on problems, it must be both accessible to the ordinary citizen and usable in a group context.

7. In the process of discussing complex problems, it is often difficult to determine whether or not people really disagree. Hence, it is crucial that the new language also incorporate some process for comparing and combining ideas generated by different people and different groups or even the same person or group at different times. The foundations for such a process have already been constructed by the present author (Waller, 1979). The result of this recent development is that disagreements, agreements, and contradictions among various structural portrayals of complex problems can be readily discovered. This development also permits the construction of multidimensional systems using more than one relation with the same element set. These features of the technique appear to fit nicely with Mitroff and Kilmann's (1978) call for the presentation of alternative views of any problem.

Such a language also would enable one to draw a mathematically precise portrait of the person's or group's thinking at any place in the process of dealing with a complex situation. In addition to the quantification possibilities discussed earlier, the full power of 250 years of graph theory can be brought to bear on the structure. Yet such analysis of the synthesized structure can be translated into very simple terms, such as: What happens if we remove this arc or insert another element into the system?

Finally, this proposed language should be context-free, in the sense it can be transported from complex situation to complex situation regardless of the content of the situation. This property can be illustrated using Figure 16.5. As before, this structure portrays elements and relationships among the elements. The two columns above the structure show just a few of the many possible situations the structure might represent.

Within ISM (and perhaps other methodologies), then, exists the possibility of a language that will allow both organizational participants and people in general to find the needed angle of entry into complexity. Given the effects of the confusion and complexity within which we currently flounder, it is a possibility worth exploring with intense effort. If synthesis under

Elements	Relation
Countries	"is dependent upon for vital commodities"
Factors in the Energy Crisis	"impacts on"
Organizations	"supplies"
People	"pollutes the environment of"
Government Units	"sends information to"
Elements of a Complex Policy	"is a factor in the success of"

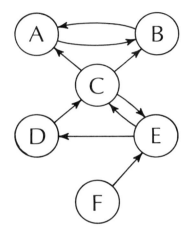

FIGURE 16.5. Illustration of Context-Free Structure

conditions of complexity is important, then it seems appropriate to examine the prospects for research and pedagogy in this domain.

Education and the Production of Useful Knowledge

There are two basic themes implicit in the previous portions of this chapter relating to the role of educational institutions in the production of useful knowledge for and in organizations. The first has to do with academic research and the prospects it has for making such contributions. The second theme involves educating young people to grapple with complexity effectively in the organizations most of them will enter. These two themes will be dealt with in turn, but the focus will be limited to the central thrust of this chapter: synthesis.

Measured against the large amount of ongoing research in universities, relatively little attention is paid to the art and science of synthesis. In fact, as Mitroff and Kilmann (1978) point out, synthesis as a special art is not even part of many disciplines. Although there are exceptions (Alexander, 1964; Koberg and Bagnall, 1974; Ackoff, 1974; Churchman, 1971), the count is meager.

A lack of interest in synthesis per se, however, should not be interpreted to imply a scarcity of attention paid to structural modeling. A fair-sized literature in the areas of graphs, digraphs, networks, and other approaches to structure does exist. But scant attention in these works is paid to the synthesis of structure; the focus instead is on the analysis of existing structures. Forrester's (1969) widely cited work on dynamic modeling exemplifies this focus.

There are probably several good reasons for the paucity of attention paid to synthesis; however, these are speculative and based solely on the author's own observations. First, academics do not seem to have much of a feel for the day-to-day pressures of nonacademic life. Time stretches like a vast carpet before the professional academic, particularly after tenure has been achieved. Furthermore, it is likely that a subtle self-selection process occurs that routes people into academic life. This process is such that reflective sorts, having little taste for decisions for which they might be praised or hanged, gravitate toward academic careers. If an academic plays it right, he or she may never, in the course of an entire career, have to make a really crucial decision, replete with moral implications, having large and pervasive effects for other people. Therefore, provided with the twin delights of time and no pressure to make important decisions, it is not surprising that academics see little need for better ways to synthesize useful knowledge efficiently and effectively.

Moreover, the need for synthesis is just not recognized. When we are young, we learn that we cannot jump very high or run very far. We learn this in the back yards of the world. In doing so, we understand and accept the need for technologies to overcome basic physiological deficiencies. Thus, elevators, stairs, automobiles, planes, and the like are embraced as a normal part of everyday existence. Similarly, we learn to put on more clothing when we are cold and take it off when we are warm. In other words, we take a commonsense approach to the use of technologies designed to help us overcome our salient physiological limitations.

On the other hand, we seem not to understand or accept the cognitive limits mentioned throughout this chapter. Yet, just as surely as we require elevators, clothing, and fire, we need technologies for dealing with complexity. At the risk of sounding too hardware-oriented, we need performance amplifiers that will allow us to make sense of complexity.

Beyond these matters just discussed is the important topic of academic specialization within narrowly defined disciplines, how this specialization is reflected in the academic structure, and the nature of the reward systems within universities that encourage ever more specialization. Though this topic is critical, in terms of the content of this chapter, it has been and is being addressed in a variety of literatures. Hence, coverage of the topic here is limited to the following observation: the study of synthesis under conditions of complexity requires that one move constantly back and forth across disciplines ranging from mathematics to psychology to the philosophy of science to semantics (incidentally, this is very similar to the kind of transdisciplinary passages one makes in working on real organizational problems). Given the narrow focus of most professional journals, this can be hazardous terrain for faculty members under pressure to produce publications in sizable quantities.

Finally, doing research in an attempt to produce useful knowledge requires that one go into the field and slam one's ideas up against reality. Not only does it require some entrepreneurship to obtain such opportunities, but the academic venturing into reality soon discovers a somewhat less pristine environment than that afforded by the scholar's desk and the laboratory filled with earnest graduate students. In fact, things can be downright brutish out there. Frequently, one is even required to say yes or no with not a single qualifier attached. Argyris (1980:7) echoes this when he points out that field research and intervention "require a rather high-degree of competence in dealing with stressful issues, on-line confrontations, and crisis requests."

All of this is not intended to imply that there is no hope for academic research in the domain of synthesis and complexity and, more generally, the whole area of producing useful knowledge for organizations. Rather, it just does not seem likely that this research soon will occur within the currently existing academic environment. As the recognition of complexity and the awareness of the need for different approaches to problems begin to emerge, however, it is possible that some redesign of academic institutions will take place.

In the meantime, what can and should arise is an "invisible college" engendered by conferences such as this one. These colleges will be composed of mature academics with a taste for reality and a bent for producing useful research with one another even though they may be located on different campuses, within different departments on the same campus, or in nonacademic organizations. Such invisible colleges already exist, though not necessarily oriented toward the topic of concern here. In addition, it may well be that nonacademic organizations, confronting the pressures imposed by complex reality, will decide to produce and transmit their own useful knowledge internally without waiting for academics to redesign disciplines and institutions. There is some evidence that this movement is already under way via the use of consultants and professional trainers.

Having said that much about academics and their research, let us turn to the question of how students might better be educated to deal with synthesis and complexity. Most academics conducting research base a fair amount of their teaching on their research. This is understandable. Thus, if it is true that little in the way of research on synthesis, complexity, languages for dealing with complexity, and so forth is being conducted, then it does not seem likely that a great deal of pedagogical effort will be devoted to these subjects. Time after time, in his university teaching and management development work, the author is met with the question: "This is useful stuff; how come nobody ever taught us this before?" The answer, based on what has been said above, is a lengthy one and is best discussed over drinks rather than in the management development classroom. The point is that some of us do teach synthesis and, more generally, how to deal with complex reality in a useful way. While the outline of an entire course or curriculum is beyond the scope of this chapter, there are certain fundamental attitudes and subject matters that can be discussed briefly here.

First, the students must understand the difference between synthesis and analysis. As part of this, the student must also see that real-world work involves moving back and forth between these two divergent ways of thinking. In terms of Figure 16.1, analysis produces an element set that is used in synthesis. The process of conducting synthesis will undoubtedly disclose imperfections in the original element set, at which time further analysis is needed. Or, suppose a tree structure has been developed describing a particular decision problem. Analysis of the problem likely will disclose imperfect alternatives, previously unrecognized states of nature, and so on. This leads to the synthesis of different alternatives or a restructuring of the tree to account for the new uncertainties recognized. Getting students to appreciate this movement back and forth between analysis and synthesis is not as simple as it might appear. This is particularly true after the student has spent years being inculcated with linear, analytic, reductionist modes of thought.

Moreover, a strange convention seems to have crept into our language. "Analysis" has become synonymous with "study." We have systems analysts, market analysts, and college courses labeled Elementary Analysis I. The author does not recall, though, of anyone being called a systems synthesist, or a market synthesist, or of any courses called Elementary Synthesis I. We seem bent on taking things apart rather than putting them together into wholes. Interestingly enough, it is the process of setting up the infamous "word problem," not the analysis of the structured problem, that bedevils students.

A second attitude has to do with the nature of data. Students think of data as numbers, but confrontations with complex reality demand that one learn to deal with numbers, facts, values, opinions, experience based on judgment, and the like. The student must recognize that all of these things are scraped together into the incredibly rich data structures found in real problems.

A third issue involves personality types. In general, people dislike ambiguity and like closure. Students are no different, and neither are managers. Though the author claims no expertise in the psychology of personality, it does seem that certain personality types are better suited to dealing with complexity than others. A key idea here is the notion of iteration. Real problems do not yield after a single run at them. One moves into the problem, learns, discards some things, adds other things, and keeps pounding. The basic notion is one of "bootstrapping," living with ambiguity, and putting off premature closure. The iterative personality can handle this attitude.

Related to the issue just discussed is the notion of problem amelioration versus problem solution. This was alluded to earlier in the chapter when mystical synthesis was evaluated. Most significant organizational problems do not really get solved with any sense of finality: they just get ameliorated. The axiom "poor is better than worse" is not a declaration of resignation, but an honest recognition of the way things are out there. Some personalities can handle iteration and amelioration; others cannot. People in the latter category lean toward careers in certain areas of accounting or computer programming where, even though ambiguity and lack of closure are ultimately present, the world seems circumscribed and problems appear solvable once and for all.

In terms of synthesis, specifically, students must be taught the key ideas and techniques involved in constructing structural portraits of complexity. These ideas and techniques require a thorough understanding of sets (and possibly fuzzy sets), relations, and other finite mathematics topics. The theory and application of relations, in particular, is a subject matter of great subtlety and is not understood by most scholars, let alone students (Waller, 1980). This latter assertion is especially true as regards the transitivity and symmetry properties of complex structures.

There are, of course, many other areas of mathematics that need to be covered in preparing the student for synthesis. Among these are graph and digraph theory and linear algebra, along with a reasonably thorough grounding in statistics and measurement theory. Probably the most over-emphasized area of mathematical study in a student's curriculum is calculus. The author is aware of the benefits often claimed by those advocating the study of calculus, but the organizational participant's world tends to be heavily slanted toward the finite rather than the continuous. Finally, is the importance of probability—when the subject is approached from the realistic perspective of its use as a language for talking about and estimating uncertainty, rather than as a mundane set of exercises involving balls and urns.

In general, the basic subject matters just discussed are found in any modest-sized university. What is harder to locate are the people who can teach these subjects with the proper philosophic outlook and relate them to complex reality. As an example of this, the author participated several years ago in the design of an entry-level mathematics course in a school of business. The basic theme of the course was using mathematics as a language for dealing with complexity and uncertainty. The course likely will be scrapped within the next year due to a chronic inability to recruit faculty who understand its philosophic thrust. In the main, though, it is possible to provide an interested student with the proper academic background for synthesis and complexity. It requires careful advising and the willingness to conduct several tutorial courses for purposes of inculcating the attitudes mentioned earlier and for integrating (synthesizing!) the diverse subject matter fields the student will explore.

No attempt has been made here to enumerate exhaustively and explore a complete curriculum for synthesizing complex structures. Important areas such as psychology (including exposure to "trapped behavior" in organizational contexts [Cross and Guyer, 1980]), literature, and the philosophy of science all have important roles to play in this training. In closing, it is noted that many of the attitudes and techniques mentioned can be taught even to very young children. This is particularly true of digraphs as a way of showing interrelationships, due to the highly visual aspect of the sketched digraph, which requires a very low level of abstraction to understand. Piaget (1973:50,102) recognized this when he said, "If logic itself is created rather than being inborn, it follows that the first task of education is to form reasoning." And: "a very clear-cut law of evolution: that all mathematical ideas begin by a qualitative construction before acquiring a metrical character." Piaget undoubtedly would applaud the modeling diagram in Figure 16.1.

The point not to be missed is that no massive redesign of academic institutions at the postsecondary level is necessary to begin educating a few students to deal with complexity. If this education produces bright, innovative students able to produce useful knowledge in the organizations where they work, as the author believes it will, the demand for such an education will increase and the process will achieve a momentum of its own. In the interim period, what is needed are a few key advisers, tutors, and integrative texts to serve as linchpins for students (the author currently is writing such a text).

THE PHYSICAL ENVIRONMENT OF SYNTHESIS

In addition to languages, research, and education for synthesis under complex conditions, attention must be paid to the physical environment within which synthesis, and more generally problem solving, is conducted. Obviously, many of the things talked about in this chapter can be done on the executive jet using the back of an envelope. But in many cases a full-scale assault on tough problems, particularly where groups are involved, requires a special kind of environment.

The lack of such environments and the use instead of bare rooms filled with tables and chairs stands as mute testimony to the dearth of knowledge about synthesis and what it requires. Most organizational environments for problem solving get no more sophisticated than an overhead projector and a lectern to facilitate the "talking head" approach to conveying information. Even worse are the motel/hotel meeting rooms used by organizations where one is likely to encounter red flocked wallpaper upon which the management of the facility will not allow the posting of so much as one flip-chart sheet. However, the grueling task of dealing with complex issues often demands access to computers via telephone lines, large video display screens for showing computer output, a copier, easy availability of word-processing capabilities, a drafting table for drawing large structures, audio recorders, multiple flip-chart easels, large blackboards, special wall surfaces for hanging and displaying materials, tables, and comfortable chairs.

Such environments, though not prohibitive in cost, are rare. Warfield (1981) has directed the construction of such a facility and now operates it under the rubric of the Center for Interactive Management. The present author brought his own facility on line in fall of 1982. It contains the capabilities just listed and is amenable to various arrangements depending upon the task at hand and the size of the group. A sketch of one configuration of the facility is shown in Figure 16.6. The cost of this facility, which originally was a well-worn classroom, was about $50,000, including remodeling and equipment. The majority of the money was contributed by local business firms that recognized the desirability of such an environment for tackling tough problems.

SUMMARY: SCIENCE AND SYNTHESIS

"Logic indeed sets the stage for measurement," says Beer (1966:162). That insight provided by Beer is one of the most important in the present author's intellectual development. Beer's statement is also a succinct summary of much of this chapter. In the preceding pages, an attempt was made to demonstrate that synthesis is a critical function in the production of useful knowledge. Although critical, synthesis is largely a neglected subject by those who try to produce useful knowledge.

The argument has been presented that synthesis, the putting together of elements via relations to form wholes, is necessary if organizational

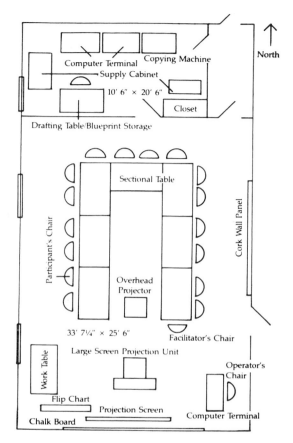

FIGURE 16.6. Example of Physical Environment for Problem Solving

participants are to make sense of William James's blooming, buzzing confusion surrounding them. It was contended that the mystical form of synthesis, the form most people are familiar with, is not reliable enough for the continual synthesis that must occur in organizations. Instead, though one hopes the mystical form will still be present on occasion, it has been suggested that synthesis can be viewed as a rational process that is best carried out by combining features of the natural language and mathematics. Several features of such a language were listed. A process based on modeling organizational reality in a decision-making context was described in order that the role of synthesis might be placed in perspective.

Following the discussion of synthesis and the need for a new language, the twin activities of research and teaching were held up for scrutiny to see what attention is being paid to synthesis in these activities. They were found wanting. On the bright side, it was proposed that most of the courses needed to educate students in the art and method of synthesis already are present in universities, and a rough-hewn sketch of some appropriate subject matters was presented. It was also recognized that mature academics with an understanding of reality will be required to provide students with the necessary guidance and integration of the somewhat diverse subject matters mentioned. In addition, a brief discussion of the proper physical environment for synthesis was presented and a layout of one such facility was provided. One possible conceptual overview of the chapter appears in interpreted structural model form in Figure 16.7.

There is still much to do. Those of us who have participated in the development of an important methodology for synthesis, ISM, are not experimental scientists. On the other hand, we are intensely interested in producing useful knowledge. ISM has developed by generating theory, testing this theory against reality in application after application, and then revising or augmenting the theory based on these experiences. In a sense, ISM has been developed "on the run" and hammered out in on-line confrontations with reality. This is not meant to imply that ISM is shallow either methodologically or philosophically. Portions of the basic theory are extremely elegant and rigorous. But, with all of their recognized drawbacks, carefully controlled laboratory studies are needed to elucidate some of the problems with ISM that hitherto have escaped notice. Furthermore, a serious study is needed to see just where ISM fits in terms of Churchman's (1971) concept of inquiring systems, for it seems that ISM embodies features of all of these systems.

It is fervently hoped that the reader does not view the content of this chapter as a proposal for a "technological fix." Quite the opposite is true. The author admits to frequent doubts about whether any technology is powerful enough to deal with the combinatorial richness of reality in any rational form. Perhaps it is the Tao that will prevail as an approach. Perhaps it is true that combinatorial richness is only the product of a disturbed mind (Ashvaghosha, 1900:78): "When the mind is disturbed, the multiplicity of things is produced, but when the mind is quieted, the multiplicity of things disappears."

For now, Eastern philosophies do not seem to have much of a chance for catching on in modern organizations. Thus, other sources of useful knowledge and how to produce it must be sought. The best possibility seems to be the development of an "action science." As Argyris (1980:177) states: "The purpose of basic research in action science is to produce knowledge that helps people in their face-to-face relationships to discover, invent, *and* produce actions under on-line conditions." It is believed that the approach to synthesis, via ISM and similar methodologies that might be developed,

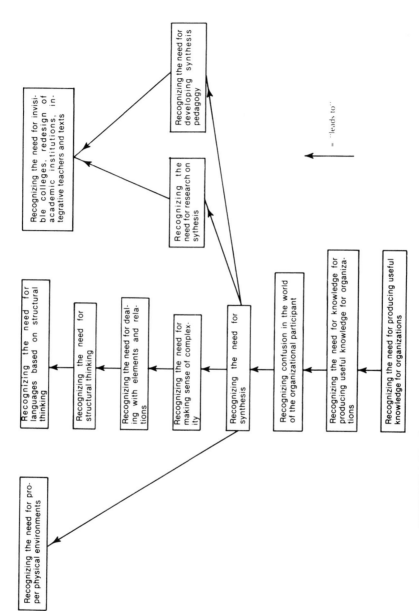

FIGURE 16.7. Conceptual Overview of Chapter in Interpreted Structural Model Form

described in this chapter meets Argyris's criteria. Furthermore, it is desirable that research in action science be motivated by a passion for ameliorating the pressing problems around us. The models produced by academics become more pure, while ghetto kids still fight off the rats at night. There is something inherently immoral about that state of affairs.

REFERENCES

Ackoff, R. L.
1974   Redesigning the Future: A Systems Approach to Societal Problems. New York: Wiley.

Arbib, M.
1972   "Complex Systems: The Case for a Marriage of Science and Intuition." American Scholar, 42, No. 1, Winter: 46–56.

Argyris, Chris
1980   Inner Contradictions of Rigorous Research. New York: Academic Press.

Ashvaghosha
1900   The Awakening of Faith. Translated by D. T. Suzuki. Chicago: Open Court.

Beer, Stafford
1966   Decision and Control. New York: Wiley.

Busacker, Robert G., and Thomas L. Saaty
1965   Finite Graphs and Networks: An Introduction with Applications. New York: McGraw-Hill.

Christopher, A.
1964   Notes on the Synthesis of Form. Cambridge, MA: Harvard University Press.

Churchman, C. West
1971   The Design of Inquiring Systems. New York: Basic Books.

Coke, J. G., and C. M. Moore
1980   "Group processes for making public expenditure reduction decisions." In H. C. Bryce (ed.), Managing Fiscal Retrenchment in Cities, Chapter 6. Columbus, OH: Academy for Contemporary Problems.

Cross, J., and M. Guyer
1980   Social Traps. Ann Arbor: University of Michigan Press.

Fitz, R. W., D. M. Gier, and J. Troha
1977   "A methodology for project planning using interpretive structural modeling." Proceedings of International Conference on Cybernetics and Society: 297–302. New York: IEEE.

Forrester, J. W.
1971   "Counterintuitive Behavior of Social Systems." Technology Review, January: 52–68.

Forrester, J. W.
1969   Urban Dynamics. Cambridge, MA: MIT Press.

Ghiselin, Brewster (ed.)
1952   The Creative Process. New York: Mentor.

Hammond, K. R., and B. Brehmer
1973   "Quasi-Rationality and Distrust: Implications for International Conflict." In L. Rappoport and D. A. Summers (eds.), Human Judgment and Social Interaction, 338–391. New York: Holt, Rinehart and Winston.

Harary, F., R. Z. Norman, and D. Cartwright
1965   Structural Models: An Introduction to the Theory of Directed Graphs. New York: Wiley.

Jedlicka, A., and R. Meyer
1980   "Interpretive Structural Modeling: Cross-Cultural Uses." IEEE Transactions on Systems, Man, and Cybernetics, January: 49–51.

Kaplan, Abraham
1964   The Conduct of Inquiry. San Francisco: Chandler.

Koberg, Don, and Jim Bagnall
1974   The Universal Traveler. Los Altos, CA: William Kaufmann.

Langefors, B.
1970   Theoretical Analysis of Information Systems. Lund, Sweden: Studentlitteratur.

Miller, G. A.
1956   "The Magical Number Seven, Plus or Minus Two: Some Limits on our Capacity for Processing Information." Psychological Review, 63:81–97.

Mitroff, Ian, and Ralph Kilmann
1978   "On Integrating Behavioral and Philosophical Systems: Toward a Unified Theory of Problem-Solving." Research in the Sociology of Knowledge, Sciences and Art, 1:207–236.

Piaget, J.
1973   To Understand Is to Invent. New York: Grossman.

Raiffa, Howard
1968   Decision Analysis. Reading, MA: Addison-Wesley.

Roberts, F. S.
1974   Weighted Digraph Models for Energy Use and Air Pollution in Transportation Systems. RAND Corporation Monograph R-1578-NSF. Santa Monica, CA: Rand Corporation.

Simon, H. A.
1974   "How Big Is a Chunk?" Science, 183, No. 4124, February 8: 482–488.

Strauch, Ralph E.
1974   "A Critical Assessment of Quantitative Methodology as a Policy Analysis Tool." RAND Paper Series. Santa Monica, CA: RAND Corporation.

Vaughan, W. S., Jr., and A. S. Mavor
1972   "Behavioral Characteristics of Men in the Performance of Some Decision-Making Task Components." Ergonomics, 15, No. 3:267–277.

Waller, R. J.
1974   "An Application of Interpretive Structural Modeling in the Field of Special Education." Proceedings of 1974 IEEE Conference on Decision and Control, 711–715. New York: IEEE.

Waller, R. J.
1975   "An Application of Interpretive Structural Modeling to Priority-Setting in Urban Systems Management." In M. Baldwin (ed.), Portraits of Complexity, 104–108. Columbus, Ohio: Battelle Memorial Institute.

Waller, R. J.
1976   "The synthesis of hierarchical structures: technique and applications." Decision Sciences, 7, No. 4, October: 659–674.

Waller, R. J.
1979   "Comparing and Combining Structural Models of Complex Systems." IEEE Transactions on Systems, Man, and Cybernetics, SMC-9, No. 9, September: 580–586. Reprinted in General Systems, 24, 1979: 103–109.

Waller, R. J.
1980   "Contextual Relations and Mathematical Relations in Interpretive Structural Model-

ing." IEEE Transactions on Systems, Man, and Cybernetics, SMC-10, No. 3, March: 143–145.

Waller, R. J.
1983   "Complexity and the Boundaries of Human Policy Making." International Journal of General Systems, 9, No. 1, January.

Warfield, John N.
1974   Structuring Complex Systems. Battelle Monograph No. 4, 1–3. Columbus, OH: Battelle Memorial Institute.

Warfield, J. N.
1976   Societal Systems: Planning, Policy, and Complexity. New York: Wiley.

Warfield, J. N.
1980   "Interpretive Structural Modeling and Related Work: An Annotated Bibliography." Charlottesville, VA: Department of Electrical Engineering, University of Virginia.

Warfield, J. N.
1981   The Center for Interactive Management (Brochure). Charlottesville, VA: School of Engineering and Applied Sciences.

Woolsey, Robert E. D., and Huntington S. Swanson
1975   Operations Research for Immediate Application. New York: Harper & Row.

Yeats, W. B.
1956   The Collected Poems of W. B. Yeats. New York: Macmillan.

Zeleny, Milan
1982   Multiple Criteria Decision Making. New York: McGraw-Hill.

17

THE USEFULNESS OF MACRO ORGANIZATIONAL BEHAVIOR: IN SEARCH OF "n" DIMENSIONAL CHESS PLAYERS

William D. Kane, Jr.

THE USEFULNESS OF MACRO O.B.

After reading the *Wall Street Journal* regularly for over four years, in an attempt to use one of the available maps to understand organizational territory, it is easy to conclude that if macro Organizational Behavior (O.B.) is useful it is not being practiced. Companies such as Chrysler, International Harvester, Braniff Airlines, Schlitz, Penn Square Bank, and Drysdale Government Securities, Inc. provide evidence that managers need assistance to tip the odds in favor of organizational survival. Industries such as automobiles, steel, banking, airlines, and education are facing stern tests of their ability to adapt and survive. If the assumption is made that one of the major uses of macro O.B. is to aid in the designing-organizing-adapting of organizations, and that the proper "doing" of macro O.B. contributes to these activities, a substantial amount of reportorial evidence indicates that the concepts of macro O.B. are either not useful or not utilized.*

One conclusion that can be drawn from the pages of the *Wall Street Journal* is that organizations conform to some approximate life-cycle model, and when organizations reach old age they naturally perish. Following this line of reasoning, it is in the natural order of things for organizations to fail. If we accept the natural order of things, when we can excuse management failure because by their nature organizations are unmanageable, they are going to perish regardless. The author rejects the determinism of life-cycle theory because of the proposition that organizations can be adaptive systems, but that rejection is not as strong as it once was.

---

*In the February 26, 1982 issue of the *Wall Street Journal*, Peter Drucker discusses innovative organizations and names three: Merck, Citibank, and 3M.

Another conclusion that can be drawn from the *Wall Street Journal* is that many organizations are poorly managed. Inept managers consistently get organizations into trouble because they do not know how to organize people, groups, resources, environments, interactions, and relationships to function as adaptive systems. With the turbulence of organizational environments in 1982, organizations that lack adaptability—and the resultant approximate fitness to the environment—are going to become increasingly dysfunctional. The primary purpose of the manager is to ensure the appropriate, approximate fit between the organization and the environment, and it may be that macro O.B. concepts can be useful in the manager's central task: adaptability.

WHY MACRO O.B. IS NOT USEFUL

Macro O.B. means the organizational level of analysis that typically includes such concepts as structure, goals versus effectiveness, communication, boundary spanning/environmental interaction, designing, power, leadership, and motivation. While some of the topics are treated at the individual and group levels of analysis, they are also treated at the organizational level of analysis, but differently. The emphasis at the organizational level of analysis has been on comparative research designed to uncover patterned relationships between organizations using large samples and multivariate statistics (Gerwin, 1979). As such, the question of the usefulness of macro O.B. is premature. While theorists have researched macro concepts, the research tends to be highly academic with little effort devoted to teaching managers or students how to "do" macro O.B. Teachers, researchers, and consultants have attempted for some time to teach practitioners how to do micro O.B. (individual level of analysis), but few similar efforts have been directed toward macro O.B. Macro O.B. has not been field tested. Workshops and courses are conducted on how to do motivation, leadership, conflict management, group dynamics, reward systems, stress management, and a variety of other concepts loosely labeled as human relations. But workshops on how to do size, technology, centralization, or formalization are rare. Not much effort has been devoted to operationalizing (theory testing), in an action-management sense, macro O.B. concepts. The closest attempts have probably been some organizational development efforts and, more recently, consultants' attempts to teach managers to "do" strategic management. However, it may be argued that there has been no concerted effort to teach managers, and therefore test, how to do macro O.B. Thus, the field knows little about the usefulness of macro concepts.

One of the reasons for the dearth of effort to make use of macro concepts is the frame of reference of comparative research. The entities that macro researchers compare are organizations. At that level of analysis the researcher is lured into thinking at that level of analysis—as an organization—and thereby gets trapped by the inherent abstraction. At the organizational level of analysis one cannot think about doing macro O.B. because there is no actor, only multiple levels of abstraction. For macro concepts to be useful there must be a focused point of action, and that point may be senior management rather than comparative researchers.

Senior managers are the enactors and integrators, by design or default, of all levels of organization, but research has yet to focus consistently on the manager as the enactor of the organization. Other than work like Mintzberg's (1973), McCall et al.'s (1978), Stewart's (1982), Kotter's (1982), and Boyatzis's (1982), there is little research on what managers do. Even less has been done on how managers integrate the researcher's multiple levels of analysis into an operable whole that approximately fits the current environment and has the ability to achieve an approximate fit to some set of future environments. The field of organizational behavior is fragmented into at least three levels of analysis: individual, group, and organization. Until all levels of analysis are simultaneously integrated at some focused point of action, macro concepts cannot be useful because there is no actor to enact them. If macro concepts are valid they are enacted by managers, but we have yet to focus on the concepts from the point of view of the enactor and they are therefore not useful. Neither do we know, conversely, if they are useless.

MACRO CONCEPTS AS SOCIAL PROCESS

Macro concepts such as structure, power, and communication are enacted through individual and group processes as they interact with environmental influences. As Weick (1979, p. 42) comments, "An organization is a body of thought by thinking thinkers." Organizational structure does not naturally occur; it is invented by some organization member for some purpose. Research at the organizational level of analysis has sought to identify patterned relationships without taking into consideration the origin of the phenomenon. There appears to be an assumption of an external, overriding rationality in that somehow structure occurs without human intervention, that structure is social fact rather than social definition (Blackburn, 1982). Pondy and Mitroff (1979, p. 28) comment that:

> Conceptually, the status of an organization shifts from that of an objective reality to one which is a socially constructed reality. Given such a concept of organization, to endow such concepts as technology with measurable and perceivable attributes is senseless. Instead we need to study how

participants themselves come to invoke categories such as "organization" and "technology" as a means of making sense of their experience.

If macro concepts, such as structure are socially defined, any usefulness must stem from the examination of the defining processes. Since that has yet to be accomplished, we may have useful information about process and we may have useful information about structure, but the linkage between the two has not been developed so we have no way to assess usefulness. To determine usefulness of macro concepts, some enacting point of reference is needed. That point of reference might be senior management.

N-DIMENSIONAL CHESS PLAYERS

In the "Star Trek" television series, First Officer Spock plays a three-dimensional chess game that is appropriate for Vulcan intelligence but too complicated for Earthlings. It is suggested that an appropriate metaphor for studying the enactment of macro concepts from the point of view of the manager is an N-dimensional chess game. A manager never knows for sure how many dimensions there are, what the exact parameters of those dimensions are, how many players are involved, what future moves an opponent might make, what the exact values of the pieces are, and is hindered by not being a firsthand observer of the game. A manager is seldom completely certain about the information the communication network provides about who moved where last, where various pieces are actually located, and whether or not the last instructions given were carried out as directed. Furthermore, there are few stated rules, the rules change constantly, other players intentionally distort the "truth," the location of the game shifts without notice, and the skills needed to play the game contradict the manager's training. Feedback may be infrequent, seldom accurate, and occasionally misleading. Decisions must be made using incomplete input information, often under time pressure, and without full knowledge of the decision's cost-benefit implications. An n-dimensional chess player is never sure whose turn it is, what the sequence of turns is, who moved last, what the last move was, and what impact his or her last move had or his or her next move will have.

If the above scenario appears unrealistic, consider the Bendix-Martin Marietta-United Technologies-Allied Corporation takeover battle played out in the pages of the *Wall Street Journal* in August and September 1982. According to the September 27, 1982 *Journal*, Bendix, the takeover originator, survives but only as a subordinate unit of Allied Corporation. Martin Marietta retained its independence but at the cost of $892 million in increased debt, which will cast a pall on its balance sheet for several years.

Allied, the apparent winner, emerged as the parent of the Allied-Bendix merger and also as a major stockholder in Martin Marietta, although it was the last player to enter the game. United Technologies Corporation appears to have been harmed the least, but was left on the sidelines and must content itself with looking for other prey. The point is our chess player lives in a turbulent environment and must cope with uncertainty, dishonesty, stupidity, misinformation, and other hard facts of organizational life. It is in this context that management enacts macro concepts. If the study of macro concepts ignores this context, the maps it draws will not be representative of the territory.

When this metaphor was suggested to Karl Weick he commented that things were already complicated enough—why make matters worse? While the metaphor may appear to violate the principle of parsimony, parsimony cannot be used as an excuse for drawing inaccurate maps of the territory. To study a complex problem it is necessary to break it down into its parts, but it is also necessary to develop some sense of what the complete picture looks like so that you are not misled by the relative simplicity of only studying components. If the idea of an n-dimensional chess player conveys the complexity of the organizational context, it is then possible to break n-dimensional chess playing into three major components: the game, the gaming, and the gamer. Some attention has been devoted to the game—management theory and strategic management. Some attention has been devoted to gaming—communication, control systems, leadership, motivation. Surprisingly, little attention has been paid to the gamer, who is responsible for the enacting, and no attention has been paid to the possible interactions among the game, the gaming, and the gamer.

There is an interesting parallel to the proposition of the existence of n-dimensional chess players. Zukav (1979, p. 33) writes about Wu Li Masters. One of the several interpretations of the term "Wu Li" is the "Chinese way of saying 'physics.' " A Wu Li Master is, therefore, a physics master. Zukav further discriminates between technicians and scientists:

> This brings us to a common misunderstanding. When most people say "scientist," they mean "technician." A technician is a highly trained person whose job is to apply known techniques and principles. He deals with the known. A scientist is a person who seeks to know the true nature of physical reality. He deals with the unknown.
>
> In short, scientists discover and technicians apply. However, it is no longer evident whether scientists really discover new things or whether they *create* them. Many people believe that "discovery" is actually an act of creation. If this is so, then the distinction between scientists, poets, painters and writers [also n-dimensional chess players] is not clear. In fact, it is possible that scientists, poets, painters, and writers [also n-dimensional chess players] are all members of the same family of people

whose gift it is by nature to take those things which we call commonplace and to *re-present* them to us in such ways that our self-imposed limitations are expanded. These people in whom this gift is especially pronounced, we call geniuses.

The fact is most "scientists" are technicians. They are not interested in the essentially new. Their field of vision is relatively narrow; their energies are directed toward applying what is already known. Because their noses often are buried in the bark of a particular tree, it is difficult to speak meaningfully of forests. (p. 36)

Zukav concludes by commenting, "we will use the word 'physicist' from now on to mean those physicists (people) who are not confined by the 'known'. From the little that we know about Wu Li Masters, it is evident that they come from this group" (p. 42).

The suggested n-dimensional chess player should parallel Zukav's notion of the Wu Li Master. Furthermore, the strength of the parallelism lends support to the proposition and also hints at where to search and for what one should search.

Task is Problematic Not Deterministic

It is quite possible that good n-dimensional chess players are rare. While it appears that educators have attempted to reduce the teaching of managing-organizing-adapting to the least common denominator, it is unlikely that the average manager possesses the skills, instincts, intelligence, toughness, and discipline necessary to become a master n-dimensional chess player. Also, the objectives of the n-dimensional chess player are misunderstood. Pondy and Mitroff (1979) argue that Thompson's view of organizations exemplifies the deterministic tradition of what managers should do. They comment that "Thompson's view of organizations suggests that administrators should be trained in the skills of 'co-aligning' environment, goals, technology, and structure in harmonious combination" (p. 29).

A good example of this deterministic thinking is Inland Steel Company. According to the July 6, 1982 *Wall Street Journal*:

Inland performed so well for so long that its executives became convinced it should remain in the steel business. So Inland has been nearly alone among U.S. steel companies in choosing not to diversify out of steel. And it has been all alone in spending about $1.2 billion since 1975 to modernize and expand its plant. [As a result] Inland has lost about $20 million in the last two quarters. It has cut its dividend by 60%. Bond analysts have lowered its credit rating. Its stock is trading near the 52-week low, which is a small fraction of book value. And its paltry 4.4% return on equity in 1981 was less than half the steel industry average.

By concluding that it could predict the future in a deterministic sense, Inland's management committed the company to a course of action that could only be successful in one, rather than several or many, future state of events.

Pondy and Mitroff (1979, p. 29) suggest that managers need to beware of "the boomerang quality of organizational rationality." It appears that n-dimensional chess players do not organize to achieve order or rationality; they organize to adapt. They know the consequences of the pursuit of organizational rationality and while they themselves may sometimes do so, they know that their main function is organizing a system that can rapidly adapt to whatever the environment dictates. Rather than living in a deterministic world that they are attempting to discover, they live in a probabilistic world that they invent as they go along. The secret to their master rating as an n-dimensional chess player is their ability to adapt to disorder, not create order.

Rationale for Existence

Given the dysfunctional aspects of organizational reward systems (for example, Kerr, 1975), why should anyone hypothesize the existence of n-dimensional chess players? Organizational rhetoric to the contrary, organizations seldom reward (probably more often punish) innovation, creativity, risk taking, high performing systems, and other eccentric behaviors. The education and training of managers discredits the skills, sensitivities, and intuitiveness likely to be appropriate for n-dimensional chess playing. There is not much of a support system within an organization for this kind of person either, since the organization's members probably do not understand him or her. There will be varying degrees of ability exhibited by players ranging from neophyte to master, but it is unlikely that many people could rank or even identify them, maybe only each other. There are not many master players in any one organization and some organizations will have none. If these master players exist, why has not organizational research discovered them already? In sum, why posit that master n-dimensional chess players exist?

The proposition is made that master n-dimensional chess players exist because it makes sense that they do. Organizational research has not discovered them because it has not looked for them at the right time, in the right place, with an appropriate methodology. Researchers have not asked the appropriate question. For example, leadership research is not the right question because that is only one of the many facets of master players that the players may or may not demonstrate.

If some number of people have mastered other phenomena of our world, why should there not be masters of this phenomenon (masters in a probabilistic sense, not a deterministic sense)? There is organization everywhere in nature, and organizations are supposedly social systems rather than natural systems, but is it unnatural to suggest that an "organizer" naturally exists?

In the particle physics world of quarks and charms and weak force and strong force, there is a notion of balance (Pagels, 1982). Physicists have posited the existence of as-yet-undiscovered particles because the phenomena known to date were out of balance, not necessarily in a quantitative sense but in a qualitative sense. Invariably, the *sense* of lack of balance led to the discovery of an additional particle that restored the balance but at the same time created a new imbalance that led to the discovery of another particle which. . . . In this sense the idea of complex organizations existing without n-dimensional chess players creates an imbalance, which equates with *non-sense*. To achieve at least a minimal sense of balance, it is necessary to posit the notion of an n-dimensional chess player in order to counter the phenomenon of organization.

People have aptitudes in various areas. Since organizations have been pervasive for a very long time, is it unreasonable to hypothesize the possibility that an organizing aptitude exists and that some individuals have well-developed organizing aptitudes along with well-developed skills of enacting organizations? With the apparent need so great and the intensity of the stimulus so high, despite lack of organizational reinforcement, the need and the skill may be socially learned. People may be attracted to the game by the excitement of playing. Individuals may believe the effort is worthwhile because they perceive it to be socially valuable. People may learn and play because it is ego satisfying. There are a number of reasons to hypothesize the existence of master players and, while the evidence they do not exist is strong, it is not overwhelming.

As most current research focuses on the game and the gaming, this discussion will focus on the gamer and possible interactions. The discussion begins with the assumption that master n-dimensional chess players exist. If they do not we need to invent them if we are to avoid the natural order of things, which by definition denies the long-term usefulness of management as a conscious act.

RESEARCH CONSIDERATIONS

The first order of business is to determine how to identify the phenomenon. How might you identify master n-dimensional chess players? What evidence might they leave? Where would be the best place to begin looking? What activities might these players be engaged in? How would they differ from other managers? What behaviors, different from average managers, might you predict? What methodologies might you employ? What observable skills might these players possess? Should you look for individuals or groups as Thomas (1974) might suggest? What kinds of maps would they have? What do they define as the territory? Do organizational members think the phenomenon exists? What might you predict that these players espoused theories and theories in use would be? The investigator might also use theory to suggest where the search should begin. As the search begins we must remember that while these players may be effective they are not magicians.

Theory in Use

The search should begin by using two already useful organizational theories: Hickson et al.'s (1971) strategic contingencies theory and Perrow's (1967) differentiation between machine technology and knowledge technology. Hickson et al. (1974) posited three variables of a subunit's task that would impact on intraorganizational power: coping with uncertainty, substitutability, and centrality. Power used here is in the action sense, not the structural sense (Kane, 1981). A subunit's power depends upon the task assigned to it, the amount of uncertainty associated with the task, the probability that some other subunit could provide a substitute for that task, and the degree to which the subunit's task is central to the purpose of the organization. The search for n-dimensional chess players should begin in places in organizations that strategic contingencies theory predicts have a high potential for power, for "doing" things. Like the astronomer predicting from theory an as-yet-unobserved celestial body and then searching to confirm or disconfirm its physical existence, so should the search begin for master n-dimensional chess players. Master players should be in strategically contingent spots because that is where the game is, that is where the action is. To do what master players do they will be attracted to strategically contingent locations because these have the highest potential for adapting the organization. If we can identify strategically contingent locations, we have the highest probability of observing the phenomenon.

Once this location is identified, what other clues might the searcher look for? Perrow (1967) provided a model of technology that differentiated subunits' technologies along two dimensions: few exceptions versus many exceptions and analyzable versus unanalyzable. In the many exceptions-unanalyzable region of Perrow's (1967) model is inherent the concept of knowledge technology (Hickson et al., 1969) (see Figure 17.1, quadrant 2). Knowledge technology includes the idea that there is a knowledge component, a cognitive component, that is a critical element of an organization's technology. This is generally associated with the materials technology of an organization. For example, in an electronics firm the materials technology

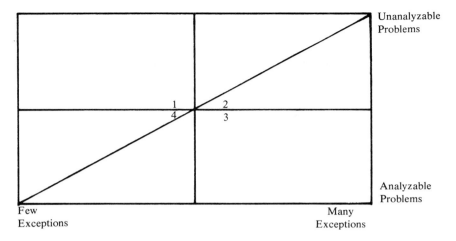

FIGURE 17.1. Technology Variable

Source: Perrow, 1967.

concerns the technology of electronics, and it may range in complexity from the routine to the nonroutine quadrants of Figure 17.1. There is a knowledge component of the materials technology that becomes increasingly critical as the number of unanalyzable problems and the number of exceptions increase, and that knowledge is about electronics. At the same time, there exists a separate task with a separate technology—management. While linkages between the two exist, they are separate and distinct tasks with separate and distinct technologies. Applying Perrow's (1967) model to management technology, it is possible to think about the knowledge component of management technology becoming increasingly important as the number of unanalyzable management problems and the number of management exceptions (increased complexity) increase. The knowledge component is about the technology of management, and it is distinctly different and separate from the technology of materials.

The n-dimensional chess player will understand and function in the many exceptions-unanalyzable problems region of the model (quadrant 2), particularly at the extreme of nonroutineness. This player will possess and use what diSessa (1979) calls knowledge-within-process. DiSessa (1979, p. 243) argues that "the structure of process itself can be a mode for knowledge representation," and defines knowledge-within-process as a form of knowledge representation "in which step-by-step analysis may not be appropriate (hence the use of the 'process' rather than 'procedure' in the name) in which the purpose of the knowledge is only evident in the control structure which evokes the process, or in the function it serves; indeed, the actual subject of the knowledge may be quite invisible." The n-dimensional chess player will have an awareness and capability of organizational process in the management task domain that will be substantially different from the average manager's. This awareness and capability should be evident in observable behaviors (of course this assumes an observer capable of awareness of behavior in this domain).

At the level of the individual manager it is proposed that n-dimensional chess players must possess some degree of selflessness, the opposite of selfishness (Levinson, 1980; Boyatzis, 1982).* Churchman (1982) relates ethics to organization good and comments that "Ethics means finding decisions that are good for the whole organization." Implicit in the comment is the manager making decisions based on organizational well-being as opposed to personal well-being. Within O.B. there is a myth about the congruence of personal goals and organizational goals. It remains to be demonstrated that effectiveness or efficiency results from individuals maximizing their personal goals. Much of the current criticism of MBAs can be interpreted as an expression of discontent with their selfishness, "What's in it for my career?" While it may be idealistic or naive, it is suggested that our master players will exhibit some degree of selflessness. They will put the well-being of the organization ahead of their personal goals, at least some of the time. It appears imperative that our master players have an organizational rather than personal well-being frame of reference. The real players will make decisions to adapt the organization, in favor of the organization, rather than themselves. In this idealistic sense the theory of congruence between individual goals and organizational goals could be useful, but only because the individual goal has been superseded by the organizational goal. One of the clues to look for in the search for master n-dimensional chess players would be manifestations of some degree of selflessness.

Another personal attribute that may be useful as a clue is the ability of a manager to view the organization from multiple perspectives (Levinson, 1980; Boyatzis, 1982). A phenomenologist would call this epoché or bracketing (Sanders, 1982). This does not imply indecisiveness but rather an openness to how others understand the world' so that the master player can come to understand the world in others' ways and in other ways. Neither does it imply that once a decision is made that the player lacks the toughness, the span of courage (Wertime, 1979), to carry out the decision against opposition. Rather, it does mean that the player can listen to a variety of

---

*Boyatzis's (1982, p. 161) concept is labeled self-control and "is a concept with which people inhibit personal needs or desires in service of organizational needs." However, the data did not support the relationship between the concept and managerial effectiveness: "It appears that the skill level of self-control as coded from the interviews is not related to managerial performance. The trait level of self-control is related to effective performance as a manager only at the entry level" (p. 164).

viewpoints relatively unfiltered by personal biases. That information is extracted from the communication before the listener's filters come into play and impose the player's frame of reference on the transmitter's communication. One of the strongest proofs of a nonplayer is a determined dogmatism whereby there is only one correct view: the nonplayer's. Determined dogmatism is different from persistently carrying out a decision in the face of opposition. The difference is the input to the decision process. In the dogmatic, the decision emanates from one perspective only; in the player, the decision originates from a number of inputs that provide an array of information, some of which may conflict. However, that information is distilled into a course of action that includes and excludes various amounts of the input information. The clue is the manager's genuine openness to a variety of information and viewpoints, and that variety is evident over time in the player's actions.

Kotter (1982, pp. 67–75) provides an additional clue for use in the search for n-dimensional chess players: the ability to network. Kotter observed his subject managers building and maintaining vast networks of peers, superiors, subordinates, competitors, suppliers, and complete outsiders. They built these networks, which sometimes numbered in the thousands of contacts, of people who could help them get things done. The managers accomplished their objectives through the relationships designed within these networks. They built these networks because they realized that the only way they could be effective was through the relationships. They carried out their work through the networks, which contained pieces of the formal organization, rather than exclusively through the formal system. The object of the search will probably be an excellent designer and user of networks.

One other point from Kotter deserves consideration. His subjects were general managers from a variety of enterprises, and it appears that their success might be associated with longevity in an industry or company as opposed to mobility. Kotter comments:

> On the average, 90 percent of the time in their careers was spent in the industry in which they were engaged at the time of the study. Only one person spent most of his career in a different, though related, industry. On the average, 81 percent of the time in their careers was spent with their present employers. Only three spent more than half of their careers with employers other than the current ones. In other words, despite all we hear about executive mobility from company to company, these GMs were not at all mobile in an interorganizational sense; they specialized in a particular industry and in a particular company. (p. 46)

What this longevity provides is the time to acquire massive amounts of detailed data about the industry, the company, and the people. An observant, thoughtful manager with longevity has the opportunity to build an enormously rich network and data base that could provide insights into both task and management knowledge technology. The manager who has been on the scene for a while could develop a powerful understanding of the organization's culture and context that should enhance the ability to manage culture and context. Based on Kotter's data, an additional clue to n-dimensional chess players might be time in the company or industry.

The last clue suggested is that of a manager's ability to theorize. Articulated or not, master players will have a coherent logic underlying their actions. They will have theories about cause-effect relationships so that when action one does not live up to expectations, the theory is reexamined, modified if necessary, and action two is tested. The first personality dimension of Levinson's (1980, p. 114) 20-point list for choosing executives is "capacity to abstract, to conceptualize, to organize, and to integrate data into a coherent frame of reference." One of the four underlying characteristics of Boyatzis's (1982, p. 111) leadership cluster he labeled conceptualization: "Conceptualization is a thought process in which the person identifies or recognizes patterns in an assortment of information; that is, the individual develops a concept that describes a pattern or structure perceived in a set of facts." In work with students over the last several years, it has been dismaying to observe their inability to establish a course of action-based theory. Action not based on theory is random or superstitious behavior. Tonn (1980, p. 13) comments, "Students seemed uneasy with the abstractness of theory and reported extreme difficulty moving from theory to their own experience and back again." Tonn (p. 13) also cites similar findings by Green and Taber (1978) and House (1979). A manager must have some coherent logic with which to generate, test, and modify ideas, or approximately fitted adaptiveness cannot occur on other than a chance basis. The work of Stewart (1982) and Mintzberg (1973) indicates that there are few, if any, theorist-managers; if we can identify them, perhaps we will have located an n-dimensional chess player.

ORGANIZATIONAL RESEARCH AND QUANTUM PHYSICS

In an attempt to understand better how to think about science, let us consider the thinking that initiated and developed quantum physics. The philosophy of science behind quantum physics is very revealing, and while this is somewhat tangential to the above discussion, it is apropos to the methodological issues. In retrospect, it is apparent that much organizational research is Newtonian in nature, deterministic, and seeks to discover the reality that exists. The science of organizations is purported to parallel the natural-physical science model. However, in physics, particularly quantum physics, the Newtonian view has been out of date since the turn of the century. Capra (1975, p. 61) writes:

> The first three decades of our century changed the whole situation in physics radically. Two separate developments—that of relativity theory and of atomic physics—shattered all the principal concepts of the Newtonian world view; the notion of absolute space and time, the elementary solid particles, and strictly causal nature of physical phenomena, and the ideal of an objective description of nature.

Einstein's theory of relativity provided the cornerstone for the massive upheaval in physics that was radically to alter the face of science. In the Newtonian view, a physical object has an absolute identity; in quantum physics, that is not so. For instance, light is either a particle or a wave depending upon how you measure it. Light is two things, not just one. In quantum physics you cannot accurately measure both the momentum and location of a particle at the same time. In quantum physics you cannot use statistical laws to predict the occurrence of individual events (Zukav, 1979, pp. 59–60); "it is the distribution of events that is specified by the quantum theory, not the individual event" (Pagels, 1982, p. 114). Pagels (p. 115) further comments that "The stability of an equilibrium is a consequence of the fact that the individual event is random and independent of similar events. Individual chaos implies collective determinism." Quantum physics denies the notion of gathering data and statistically predicting individual events, and this seems appropriate, at least at the organizational level of analysis. The prediction may be true for the distribution of organizations, but individual organization events might occur on a random basis. Ironically, the founder of modern physics, Einstein, refused to accept the idea of randomness in nature and spent the remainder of his career seeking to prove the harmony of nature. Pagels (p. 60) writes that when Einstein rejected the idea of randomness in nature he lost contact with the Old One, and he quotes Paul Ehrenfest as saying, "We have lost our leader" (p. 61).

As quantum physics pertains to atomic and subatomic particles, it is not suggested that it be applied realistically. However, it is suggested that it be applied metaphorically. Can organizational phenomena be two different things simultaneously? Could it be that theories appear to be weak because we attempt to predict individual events? Are we attempting to measure events simultaneously where it is not possible to do so? Is there a reality in organizations just as shockingly different as quantum physics is from Newtonian physics? Are there ways of engaging in science that we are forbidding ourselves to see? A mythology has been built up about how science is conducted, and organizational research bought into that mythology in search of respectability. It is, however, a myth. Goodfield (1981), a philosophy-of-science writer, writing about her observations of a scientist doing breakthrough cancer research, comments that:

> It is the same with the contemporary journals; they provide no help either. I realized this in September, 1965, when Sir Peter Medawar gave a talk on the BBC Third Programme entitled "Is the Scientific Paper a Fraud?" and thus inadvertently provided the impetus for the project of which this book is the result. He was not asking, do most scientists cheat?, though some indeed have been known to do so. He was asking whether the writings of scientists, as published in such prestigious journals as *Nature* or *Science*, in any way reflect the human endeavors that underlie scientific invention. To this there is only one answer: a resounding no! For as Medawar reminds us the scientific paper not only conceals but actually misrepresents the individual human creativity which is its source. (p. 217)

Quantum physics, as a metaphor, may be one way of thinking about initiating the search for n-dimensional chess players. If we search with tried-and-true methodologies we will continue to come up empty-handed. You cannot discover a quark using Newtonian physics.

CONCLUSION

Macro concepts do not exist in the void as realities awaiting discovery. They are phenomena enacted by managers as they go about adapting their organizations. Unfortunately, many of them do it poorly. As Kennedy (1981, p. 10) comments, "Organization structures have no meaning except as related to enabling human beings to get things done." Structure is another term for relationships, not necessarily patterned, put into place to accomplish some purpose. Rearranging the relationships, whether between person-person, person-resources, or resources-resources, produces different structure and possibly different outcomes. Schwartz and Davis (1981, p. 31) label the ongoing relationships organizational culture and suggest that "These mundane routines buried deep in companies' cultures (and subcultures) may be the most accurate reflections of why things work the way they do, and of why some firms succeed with their strategies where others fail." The n-dimensional chess player will understand an organization's culture and will know that changing outcomes is dependent upon enacting a cultural change, modifying relationships. The master player understands Davis's (1982) notion of context and why it is imperative for organizations occasionally to change their context and how to go about doing that. Macro O.B. research has yet to provide useful information about these issues because researchers have not been concerned with practical usefulness.

This chapter suggests a metaphor for initiating the search for useful information with the point of focus being the enactor of the organization. It is assumed that if we can find an n-dimensional chess player and investigate macro concepts from that player's point of view then we will have identified significantly different concepts. If macro concepts are teachable they must be different than they are now because their current abstractness renders them practically useless. It must also be remembered that researchers have artificially divided the organization into multiple levels of analysis. Yet, managers perform at all levels and if they can do micro O.B. they should be able to do, and in fact do, macro O.B. The academic is not likely to be able to tell us how to perform macro O.B. because, as Pagels (1982, p. 143) tells us, "You cannot talk about events in the world without actually observing them." Until academics locate and study an n-dimensional chess player, they are unlikely to provide useful information. As Thomas and Tymon (1982, p. 390) note, "Without this interaction, Caplan et al. argue that knowledge producers and knowledge users become two separate communities, rather than integrated parts of a single knowledge production/utilization system."

White	*Black*
Pawn to King 4	Pawn to King Bishop 3 . . .

REFERENCES

Blackburn, Richard S.
1982 "Dimensions of Structure: A Review and Reappraisal." Academy of Management Review, 7:59–66.
Boyatzis, Richard E.
1982 The Competent Manager. New York: John Wiley & Sons.
Capra, Fritjof
1975 The Tao of Physics. Berkeley, California: Shambhala.
Churchman, C. West
1982 "Epistemology of Organization Information." Verbal presentation to the Producing Useful Knowledge for Organizations Conference, Pittsburgh, Pennsylvania.
Davis, Stanley M.
1982 "Transforming Organizations: The Key to Strategy Is Context." Organizational Dynamics, Winter.
diSessa, Andrea A.
1979 "On 'Learnable' Representations of Knowledge: A Meaning for the Computational Metaphor." In Jack Lochhead and John Clements (eds.), Cognitive Process Instruction. Philadelphia: Franklin Institute Press, 239–266.
Drucker, Peter
1982 "The Innovative Company." Wall Street Journal, February 26.
Gerwin, Donald
1979 "The Comparative Analysis of Structure and Technology: A Critical Appraisal." Academy of Management Review, 4:41–51.

Gigot, Paul
1982 "Inland, a Longtime Star of Steel Industry, Is Getting Hurt by Its Failure to Diversify." Wall Street Journal, July 6.

Goodfield, June
1981 An Imagined World. New York: Harper & Row.

Hickson, David, Derek Pugh, and Diana Phesey
1969 "Operations Technology and Organizational Structure: An Empirical Reappraisal." Administrative Science Quarterly, 14:378–397.

Hughey, Ann, and Frank Allen
1982 "Allied Takes 'Quantum Leap' in Bid to Become High Technology Firm." Wall Street Journal, September 27.

Kane, William D., Jr.
1981 "Power: An Action Oriented Organizational Perspective." Working paper, Western Carolina University.

Kennedy, Allan A.
1981 "Ruminations on Change: The Incredible Value of Human Beings in Getting Things Done." EXCHANGE: The Organizational Behavior Teaching Journal, 6:4–11.

Kerr, Steven
1975 "On the Folly of Rewarding A, While Hoping for B." Academy of Management Journal, 18:769–783.

Kotter, John
1982 The General Managers. New York: Free Press.

Levinson, Harry
1980 "Criteria for Choosing Chief Executives." Harvard Business Review, 58 (4):113–120.

McCall, Morgan, Ann M. Morrison, and Robert L. Hannen
1978 Studies of Managerial Work: Results and Methods. Technical Report Number 9. Greensboro, North Carolina: Center for Creative Leadership.

Mintzberg, Henry
1973 The Nature of Managerial Work. New York: Harper & Row.

Pagels, Heinz R.
1982 The Cosmic Code: Quantum Physics as the Language of Nature. New York: Simon and Schuster.

Perrow, Charles
1967 "A Framework for the Comparative Analysis of Organizations." American Sociological Review, 32:194–208.

Pondy, Louis R., and Ian I. Mitroff
1979 "Beyond Open System Models of Organization." In Research in Organizational Behavior, Barry M. Staw (ed.). Greenwich, Connecticut: JAI Press, 1:3–39.

Sacks, Sheldon (ed.)
1978 On Metaphor. Chicago: University of Chicago Press.

Sanders, Patricia
1982 "Phenomenology: A New Way of Viewing Organizational Research." Academy of Management Review, 7:353–360.

Schwartz, Howard, and Stanley M. Davis
1981 "Matching Corporate Culture and Business Strategy." Organizational Dynamics, Summer.

Stewart, Rosemary
1982 Choices for the Manager. Englewood Cliffs, New Jersey: Prentice-Hall.

Thomas, Kenneth W., and Walter G. Tymon, Jr.
1982 "Necessary Properties of Relevant Research: Lessons from Recent Criticisms of the Organizational Sciences." Academy of Management Review, 7:345–352.

Thomas, Lewis
1974   The Lives of a Cell. New York: Bantam.
Tonn, Joan C.
1980   "Learning to Use Theory Through the Development of Critical Thinking Skills."
        EXCHANGE: The Organizational Behavior Teaching Journal, 5:13–18.
Toulmin, Stephen
1982   "The Construal of Reality: Criticism in Modern and Postmodern Science." Critical
        Inquiry, 9-1:93–111.
Weick, Karl
1979   "Cognitive Processes in Organizations." In Research in Organizational Behavior,
        Barry M. Staw (ed.). Greenwich, Connecticut: JAI Press, 141–174.
Wertime, Richard
1979   "Students Problems and 'Courage Spans.' " In Cognitive Process Instruction, Jack
        Lochhead and John Clements (eds.). Philadelphia: Franklin Institute Press,
        191–198.
Zukav, Gary
1979   The Dancing Wu Li Masters. New York: Morrow.

18

PROVIDING USEFUL POLICY KNOWLEDGE FOR ALTERNATIVE ARGUMENT STYLES IN PUBLIC ORGANIZATIONS

David J. Webber

INTRODUCTION

The rapidly developing knowledge utilization literature has reached a consensus on several points. Among these are the important distinction between conceptual usefulness and instrumental usefulness of knowledge, the importance of the two-communities theory in explaining the underutilization of social research, and the necessity of providing information and knowledge in a form that is useful to policy makers. For the most part, however, this literature has ignored the decision-making environment in which policy decisions are made. Consequently, little attention has been focused on either organizational design to foster policy knowledge use or the characteristics of useful policy knowledge from a public organization perspective. The unstated conclusion of the knowledge utilization literature is a pessimistic one: as long as both policy makers and policy researchers go about their jobs according to standard operating procedures, little communication exchanging policy knowledge is likely to occur.

While the relationship between knowledge and action has been a matter of continuing controversy, the attention directed at "policy analysis," "policy research," and "knowledge utilization" implicitly assumes that the output of policy researchers—policy knowledge—is intended to be "used" by policy makers. Sound public policy requires a blend of information relating to the "internal logic of the policy issue" and the "external logic of the policy issue." The former refers to information describing or explaining how the policy under consideration will actually operate. The latter pertains to ideological, ethical, and political considerations that are important in selecting an alternative policy, but not in understanding the mechanics of a policy (Caplan et al., 1975). Information relating to the internal logic of the policy issue, which may be more objective or scientific information than that relating to the external logic, is policy knowledge. Information relating to the external logic of the policy issue is political knowledge.

While public and private policy makers are similar in individual characteristics and motivations, public and private organizational environments differ in the incentives and restraints facing policy makers. A major difference between public and private organizations is the relative openness of the public policy-making process in terms of the breadth and volume of inputs and influences. Public policy makers solve problems in a complex political environment that includes numerous and varied participants. These participants are largely responsible for how, and when, a policy issue is defined as a policy problem. Policy makers seek to formulate, adopt, and implement a solution to the policy problem in a way that is satisfactory to other participants in the political environment. A basic tenet of this chapter is that policy knowledge is useful in public policy-making organizations to the extent that it contributes to the definition and solution of policy problems.

By understanding how policy makers reason (or argue) about problems and how they are motivated to search for knowledge, the use of policy knowledge can be furthered. There are two aspects that need to be addressed in discussing ways to provide more useful policy knowledge to organizations. First, attention must be focused on designing public organizations that are more likely to provide useful policy knowledge to policy makers. Second, characteristics of useful policy knowledge must be identified so that researchers can provide knowledge that is more readily useful to policy makers.

PURPOSIVE MODEL OF PUBLIC DECISION MAKERS' USE OF POLICY KNOWLEDGE

A decision maker can use policy information to understand the mechanics of a policy proposal in order to improve the probability that a policy will perform according to the decision maker's design and expectations. Assuming only that decision makers are rational actors attempting to minimize the effort necessary to achieve a specific goal, a grand proposition can be stated: decision makers will search for policy information only if the related costs are compatible with the contribution that the obtained information makes to increasing the probability of attaining their goal. While this proposition is too general to be more than trivially useful, it identifies two topics that need to be examined in understanding policy information search strategies: First, what are the individual objectives of policy makers and how do they motivate policy information use? Second, since decision makers must make the search decision prior to knowing the value of the information desired, how do they decide to search?

While a discussion of the extent to which policy information is used in decision making might suggest an examination of the rational-comprehensive and incremental conceptualization of the policy-making process, such a study is not required here. Although there has been considerable debate about the accuracy and usefulness of the rational-comprehensive description of the policy-making process (see Steinbrunner, 1974), the concern here is with the search behavior of an individual decision maker and not the behavior of the policy-making process in toto. At this level of analysis the distinction between the two paradigms narrows considerably if rational actors are conceived of as satisficing instead of maximizing (Simon, 1959:262–264). Satisficing entails that a decision maker select a particular course of action, without examining all possible alternatives, if that alternative satisfies a predetermined standard. Satisficing decision makers act efficiently given the complexity of the decision-making environment, their limited capabilities, the cost of policy information searches, and the competing demands on their time.

Policy makers are formally responsible for proposing, enacting, or evaluating public policy and therefore engage in a variety of policy-formulating activities intended to meet those responsibilities. A policy maker will not, of course, undertake a policy information search while considering all issues, but instead selects a small number of issues to study. A policy maker must be motivated to undertake an information search by the circumstances of a policy problem. Because of the lack of time, attention, staff, and interest, a policy maker will not seek information for all decisions that must be made. Instead, policy makers only conduct a "problemistic search" for information when there is a problem or difficulty related to a specific policy decision at hand.

Downs presents a model of information search that rests on a combination of maximizing elements and satisficing elements, and posits how a decision maker searches. Downs outlines this model in seven steps:

1. All decision-makers continuously scan their immediate environment to some degree through a combination "unprogrammed free information streams" and "habitually programmed scans";

2. Each decision-maker develops a level of satisfactory performance for his/her behavior and that of other parts of the organization relevant to him/her;

3. A "performance gap," defined as the perceived difference in utility between the actual and the satisfactory level of performance of an official or organization, motivates the decision-maker to undertake a search. The larger the gap the greater is the motivation to undertake searches directed at the identification of alternatives that will reduce dissatisfaction;

4. If a completed intensive search fails to reveal any ways that will result in a return to the satisfactory level of performance, the decision-maker will lower his/her conception of the satisfactory level;

5. If the constant, automatic search process reveals the possibility that a new course of action might yield more utility than the present satisfactory level of performance, an intensive search is undertaken to evaluate new alternatives:

6. Once a new course of action has been adopted, the new performance level becomes the satisfactory level; and

7. After the decision-maker has moved to a new higher level of performance (which then becomes the new satisfactory level) or has discovered that the prior performance level cannot be improved (so that lower level becomes the new satisfactory level), the search effort is reduced back to the normal "automatic" search. (Downs, 1967: 168–171)

This model does not stipulate that an intensive search takes place on each policy issue, nor does it ignore the importance of the continual search that a policy maker might reasonably be expected to undertake. Instead, it outlines a process that identifies when a decision maker will go beyond the ordinary automatic search.

A decision maker's automatic search, that combination of "unprogrammed free information streams" and "habitually programmed scans," includes a wide variety of information sources. Examples of habitual scans include the popular news media, professional journals or magazines, and, perhaps, newsletters of interested organizations. Unprogrammed information streams vary widely among policy makers and fluctuate frequently depending upon the point in the policy-making cycle. These information sources include interest groups, other policy makers, staff, and those affected by the issue. Although periodic and sometimes random information sources, these unprogrammed sources are part of an automatic search because they are familiar, routine sources that have an established record with the policy maker.

Following Downs's formulation of an information search, decision makers will rely exclusively on their automatic search sources as long as they are satisfied with their own behavior and the policy's performance. When they are not satisfied with the performance of the policy process in general, they will be motivated by this dissatisfaction to conduct an intensive search to improve the consideration of a specific policy.

Even when policy makers recognize their lack of knowledge and desire information, there are at least two factors that limit the inclination to conduct an intensive information search. First, in a collective decision-making body or a bureaucratic organization, single decision makers may not receive the rewards necessary to motivate policy information searches. Second, before policy makers undertake a broad information search, they must have a reasonable basis to expect the information to be helpful. As the policy information searched for becomes more specialized and complex, it is increasingly likely that the policy maker will have difficulty interpreting it in a useful, applicable way. This limitation has been considered in the research utilization literature and is discussed below as one of several obstacles to policy information use.

ALTERNATIVE ARGUMENT STYLES AND THE USE OF POLICY KNOWLEDGE

As problem solvers, public policy makers gather and process information found in the environment in selecting a proposal for solving a problem. Policy makers process available information in different ways. Dunn identifies six ways of processing policy information in reasoning from policy information to conclusions about the most appropriate action to undertake. These six argument styles can be compared in terms of styles of evaluating and processing policy information:

> 1. Authoritative—based on arguments from authority: information is selected based on assumptions about the status of its producers. Examples include the testimony of scientific experts;
> 2. Intuitive—based on arguments from insight. For example, the insight, judgement, or tacit knowledge of policy makers might be used as an argument to accept a particular policy alternative;
> 3. Analycentric—based on argument from method: information is used based on assumptions about the validity of methods used by the policy researcher;
> 4. Explanatory—based on arguments from cause and effect. For example, an argument for selecting a particular policy alternative might be based on general propositions or laws within theories about organizational behavior;
> 5. Pragmatic—based on arguments from motivation, parallel case, or analogy to other policy issues; and,
> 6. Value-critical—based on ethics; justification for a specific policy is stated in terms of rightness or goodness of policies and their consequences. (Dunn, 1981:67–68)

Argument styles are the underlying processes policy makers and researchers use in formulating and considering a problem. In addition to defining the problem in a particular way, they contribute to shaping information filtering and alternative posing. The way that policy makers interpret and process policy information determines the extent of policy information used as well as the type of policy information most likely to be used. For example, policy makers who routinely use the pragmatic argument style will ignore information stated in the analycentric or explanatory style.

Of the six argument styles, the value-critical style is not relevant here because policy knowledge pertains to knowledge about how a policy works. While the value-critical style may be one of the more frequently used argument styles among political decision makers, it is not helpful in discussing how to provide more useful policy knowledge to decision makers except to remember the prevalence of value-critical reasoning in policy making.

Although not often stated, policy researchers usually implicitly assume that their effort to develop knowledge through various type of studies and research reports will contribute to the betterment of public policy. There are, however, several alternative ways that policy knowledge can be used in the policy process in addition to this direct application. Among these alternative uses are to: postpone making a decision; reduce dependence on other policy makers; convince colleagues and other policy makers of the correctness of one's views; and justify adopted policy action to other participants in the policy-making process.

The policy research utilization literature is a useful starting point in conceptualizing the notion of knowledge use. For the most part, "use" is understood to mean "consider" and has been measured by interview questions such as "Would you find this type of research helpful?" or "Have you considered this type of research when making a specific decision?" The exact process of use has been given various interpretations. Weiss identifies several meanings of "research utilization" commonly appearing in the knowledge utilization and policy analysis literature. Of these seven models, summarized in Table 18.1, the knowledge-driven, problem-solving, and enlightenment models are of immediate relevance for a discussion of providing more useful policy knowledge to public organizations. (Weiss, 1977, 1979).

The first two are the most popular "ideal types" of research use employed in the social sciences, and the enlightenment model has received the most empirical support. The knowledge-driven model asserts that:

> [B]asic research discloses some opportunity that may have relevance for public policy; applied research is conducted to define and test the findings of basic research for practical action; if all goes well, appropriate technologies are developed to implement the findings, whereupon application occurs. (Weiss, 1979:427)

This model most closely approximates the process of utilization of the physical sciences, where the research itself is compelling enough to force

TABLE 18.1. Characteristics of Seven Models of Policy Information Use

Model of Use	Description	Initiator of Use	Potential for Alternative Use on Policy Information
Knowledge-driven	Application of basic research	Policy maker	Low
Problem-solving	Agreement on problem, communication for solution	Both policy maker and information provider, policy maker more active	Low
Enlightenment	Education of policy maker	Policy maker, indirect use	Low
Political	Rationalization for previous decisions	Policy maker	High
Tactical	Undertake research to delay action	Policy maker	High
Interactive	Many competing information sources	Policy information provider	Moderate
Intellectual	Research is just one of many intellectual pursuits	Both policy maker and information provider, policy information provider more active	Moderate

Note: The seven models of use are based on Weiss' models of research utilization (1977, 1979).

implementation. Social science-based policy research is less compelling according to Weiss, who states:

> [U]nless a social condition has been consensually defined as a pressing problem and unless the condition has become fully politicized and debated, and the parameters of potential action agreed upon, there is little likelihood that policy-making bodies will be receptive to the results of social science research. (Weiss, 1979:427).

The problem-solving model is the scientific method at work in the policy-making process. The major responsibility of policy researchers is the identification and analysis of the appropriate means to achieve the agreed upon goal.

Weiss argues that policy research can enter the policy process in one of two ways. First, policy makers can search the preexisting research for assistance in formulating and considering the problem. This research can be brought to their attention by "aides, staff, analysts, colleagues, consultants, or social science researchers," or they may be exposed to it through "professional journals, agency newsletters, or at conferences." Second, policy researchers can be directly commissioned to "provide the data, analytic generalizations, and possibly the interpretation of these generalizations to the case at hand by way of recommendations." Weiss formulates this process sequentially: (1) definition of pending decision, (2) identification of missing knowledge, (3) acquisition of social science research, (4) interpretation of the research for the decision context, and (5) policy choices (Weiss, 1979:427).

Several recent empirical studies of government officials have suggested a less demanding enlightenment model of policy research use. In this model policy research is not utilized in the sense of an analytical comparison of the policy researcher's findings, but rather as a contributor to the gradual modification of the way the policy maker sees social problems (Weiss, 1979:427). Caplan et al. use the terms "instrumental utilization" and "conceptual utilization" to differentiate between the textbook model of applying specific research to a specific problem in an isolated decision and the "consciousness-raising" effect of the use of policy research (Caplan et al., 1975; Knorr, 1977).

The process underlying the enlightenment model is less formal and rigid than either of the two more popular notions of research use. Here policy research is diffused widely through professional journals, mass media, personal communications, and lobbyists, and it slowly alters the way the policy maker sees the world. Weiss acknowledges the difficulty of tracing the source of information through the policy-maker information network:

> Rarely will policy-makers be able to cite the findings of a specific study that influenced their decisions, but they have a sense that social science research has given them a backdrop of ideas and orientations that has had important consequences. Research sensitizes decision-makers to new issues and helps them turn what were non-problems into policy problems (Weiss, 1979:429–430).

In addition to these three decision-oriented models of policy information use that posit that the decision maker relies on policy information in the making of a decision in order to "improve" the soundness of that decision, there are alternative uses of policy information. These are provided for in the remaining four models identified by Weiss. The tactical model expects that policy information is requested in order to postpone making a decision and to delay policy action. Additionally, the tactical model anticipates that policy makers may generate their own sources of information in order to remain independent of other policy makers. The political model sees policy makers' use of information as a rationalization for previous decisions and as an explanation of decisions to critics without the direct, decision-oriented use of such information. Both the tactical and political models expect that alternative use of information will exceed decision-oriented use of information.

The interactive model, on the other hand, expects a blend of alternative use with direct use. It also allows for the competition of different types and sources of policy information among policy makers in attempting to convince each other of their positions. These attempts at convincing other policy makers are more similar to rationalization than to the sharing of information that might occur in the decision-oriented models. Likewise, the intellectual enterprise model expects policy makers to use multiple sources and types of policy information for a variety of purposes that include decision-oriented use as well as alternative uses.

While argument styles pertain to how individual policy makers interpret and evaluate policy information, and the models of policy information use describe the process an organization or decision-making structure uses in applying information to decisions, argument styles and models of use are interrelated. Table 18.2 relates the individual-based argument styles with the process models of policy information use in terms of the demand for knowledge that is provided by researchers.

As presented in Table 18.2, the knowledge-driven model of use requires that policy makers rely on the intuitive, analytical, and explanatory argument styles. Since the policy knowledge provided by researchers is expressed either in disciplinary language or an interpretation of disciplinary language, the knowledge-driven model places a heavy burden on both policy makers and researchers.

The problem-solving model of use provides for all five argument styles to be used by policy makers. The route of obtaining the information will vary, however, depending on the argument style used by the policy maker. The importance of organizational design in providing routes of entry for various types of policy information will be discussed below.

The enlightenment model of use depends heavily on the intuitive argument style as the most frequently used style and, to a lesser extent, on the explanatory and pragmatic styles. The political and tactical models of policy information use both are compatible with the authoritative, explanatory, and pragmatic argument styles, although it is most likely that the authoritative style will be most frequently used in both models.

TABLE 18.2. Argument Styles Compatible with Models of Research Use

Model of Use	Argument Styles				
	Authoritative	Intuitive	Analycentric	Explanatory	Pragmatic
Knowledge-driven	—	Interpretation of disciplinary language	Disciplinary language	Disciplinary and common language	—
Problem-solving	Reputation of policy researcher	Interpretation	Disciplinary language	Disciplinary language	Common language
Enlightenment	—	Interpretation of disciplinary language	—	Interpretation of disciplinary language	Common language
Political	Reputation of policy researcher	—	—	—	—
Tactical	Reputation of policy researcher	—	—	—	—
Interactive	Reputation of policy researcher	—	Policy researchers are one of several actors; provide interpretation of this analysis	Interpretation of disciplinary language	Common language
Intellectual enterprise	—	Interpretation	—	Interpretation of disciplinary language	Common language

As shown in Table 18.2, the last two models place a slightly different demand on policy researchers. Since the interaction model views researchers as just one of several actors interacting in the policy process, researchers will be required to present their analysis, and policy makers relying on the analycentric argument style will evaluate the policy research. Additionally, the authoritative and, to a lesser extent, the explanatory and pragmatic styles are provided for in the interactive model. Finally, the intellectual enterprise model incorporates three argument styles: intuitive, explanatory, and pragmatic. Here the policy maker evaluates research as being an important component of making sound public policy, but as only one of several factors to consider.

ARGUMENT STYLES AND THE DEVELOPMENT OF MORE USEFUL POLICY KNOWLEDGE

In addition to positing alternative reasoning styles, the alternative argument styles are useful in considering the various types of research offered to policy makers. Policy information, as defined above, is information relating to the "internal logic of the policy issue" in that it describes how a policy actually works, or might work if it were adopted. Fact gathering, an essential component of policy information, is the most primitive form since no effort is explicitly made to delineate the workings of a policy. Likewise, most managerial reports investigating reorganization alternatives and recommending specific allocation of staff and resources are policy information, but a primitive form given that the analysis of the organizational aspects of the policy are often not clearly linked to policy outcomes. Budgetary analysis, "sunset" reports, and managerial audits often take the form of an inventory of facts and expenditures.

More systematic types of policy information link various aspects of a policy and explain how a modification in one aspect will affect another. Systematic policy information includes any causally linked information that a policy maker relies on when considering a policy alternative. The complexity and completeness of the various types of information are, in the final analysis, determined by the policy maker, but generally increase according to the following ordering:

Common sense—popular accounts that explain how a policy would work;

Popular journalism—reports widely available that investigate and help explain a policy issue;

Practitioners reports—comprehensive accounts by those involved about how a policy actually works;

Policy research—specific studies that attempt to form general conclusions about a specific policy;

Policy-oriented research—academic or research organization-sponsored work that was not undertaken to study a specific problem but that has immediate application for explaining how a policy works; and

Academic research—academic books or articles that are helpful in understanding the general background of a policy issue.

Common sense as a policy information type is similar to the general meaning of ideology: a set of beliefs about society and the political system. Ideology usually pertains to a grand set of beliefs, while common sense as policy information relates to more mundane popular accounts that "everybody knows" that link an expected policy consequence to a specific policy action. The notion of conceptual usefulness developed in the research utilization literature reflects how policy research can be transformed into common sense. When this occurs the decision maker cannot recall the source or specific content of the policy research.

Popular journalism presents a wide variety of approaches to describe and explain a policy issue. While journalistic explanations may not be general and complete, they are useful because they are the most readily available types of policy information. Additionally, they are often broad in coverage and familiar in outlook, giving a policy maker a long-term perspective about the trustworthiness of various journalistic approaches and explanations.

Practitioners' reports are often made by administrators to policy makers explaining how a policy works. The most prevalent instances of such reports are related to the oversight function and take the form of specific requests for an explanation of how a policy works. Additionally, policy makers often request, from those individuals whom a policy will affect, judgments about how the policy will work.

Policy research may originate within the public policy organization or be provided from outside sources. Externally provided research includes that provided by academic or research organizations that studies a specific policy, or research provided by trade associations and interest groups that examines a specific issue in a general and comprehensive way.

Policy-oriented research is prepared outside the organization and made available through consultants, contacts with researchers, and libraries. Most of the analysis undertaken by social scientists is policy-oriented research; it is applied research, but is not undertaken to study a specific instance of a policy problem. Policy-oriented research is generally intended for other researchers, but is often directly usable by policy makers if communicated in a timely and effective fashion.

Academic research is the final type of policy information. While the most general of these information types, it is usually incomplete and may not

TABLE 18.3. Prevalent Argument Styles for Six Types of Policy Information

Types of Policy Information	Prevalent Argument Style
Common sense	Intuitive
Popular journalism	Intuitive, occasionally pragmatic
Practitioners' reports	Authoritative, intuitive, pragmatic
Policy research	Explanatory, pragmatic
Policy-oriented research	Analycentric, explanatory, pragmatic
Academic research	Analycentric, explanatory

be directly applicable to a policy maker's decision. Academic research is limited by both its jargon and generality, as well as the lack of a distribution system flowing into the policy-making environment.

While all six types of policy information, as well as factual information, are potentially useful to a policy maker, the last three are more specialized and less widely distributed. These three types of information—policy research, policy-oriented research, and academic research—are, however, the more systematic type of information and are the types most often provided by researchers.

Table 18.3 presents the more prevalent argument style associated with the six types of policy information. Common sense, by definition, depends solely on the intuitive style. Analysis of issues presented in popular journalism usually are intuitive and occasionally pragmatic. Practitioners' reports rely on the intuitive and pragmatic styles when they attempt to explain how a policy works, and on the authoritative style when their interpretation of how a policy works is accepted because of their position. Thus, the three less systematic types of information rely heavily on the intuitive argument style and occasionally the pragmatic style.

The three more systematic types of policy information rely mainly on the explanatory and analycentric styles and occasionally the pragmatic styles. Policy research, while often relying on the analytic style in the development of the research, attempts to present the findings of the analysis in the explanatory and pragmatic styles. Policy-oriented and academic research both rely more heavily on the analycentric argument style.

Based on the purposive model of decision makers' use of policy knowledge discussed above, decision makers will mainly rely on their habitual information scans, expanding their search only if there is a performance gap in a policy area. This implies that the frequency of use of the six types of information by policy makers varies with the complexity of the information. There are two reasons that the more systematic types of information are less useful than the simpler types. First, policy makers often do not have the incentive to go beyond their habitual search for information. Second, the more systematic types of policy information are not expressed in the argument styles most familiar to policy makers. The former reason is a problem of institutional and organizational design (and is addressed below), while the latter is a problem of the form of policy research.

For policy research to be useful in public organizations, it must be provided in the intended user's argument style. Traditionally, researchers have provided analysis, usually through disciplinary publications, with the dim hope that it would be of assistance in formulating public policy. From a researcher's perspective, there are several pathways for providing more useful knowledge to policy makers in public organizations. In addition to the general prescription that policy researchers should provide knowledge in the language and argument style of the intended users, more specific recommendations are outlined in Table 18.4. For each argument style, Table 18.4 presents the requirements for increasing policy knowledge use, a proposal involving policy researcher action for furthering policy knowledge use, and the appropriate type of information to focus on in increasing policy knowledge use for each style.

Decision makers relying heavily on the authoritative argument style will increase their use of policy knowledge only as researchers' prestige and political influence increase. It should be emphasized that policy makers who "use" information in this way are doing so in a political or tactical sense and not as conceptual or instumental use. The authoritative argument style does not require that policy makers fully comprehend and evaluate the knowledge, but that they rely on policy researchers who have sufficient prestige and influence to persuade other participants in the policy process to adopt the desired alternative.

For knowledge to receive wider use according to the authoritative style, researchers must become more active in the policy process. Establishing policy research clearinghouses, engaging in professional lobbying efforts, and becoming politically involved through existing nonactive professional organizations will contribute to increasing the prestige and influence of policy researchers.

Attempting to further policy knowledge use in a way that is compatible with the authoritative argument style can be costly for policy researchers. First, researchers may be forced to operate in a fashion for which their professional training did not prepare them. Second, active involvement in the policy process requires that factors other than the soundness of an argument be considered. Thus, a researcher must engage in nonanalytical discussions and decisions. Finally, active participants in the policy process must be willing to accept the abuses of defeat as well as the spoils of victory. Academic freedom notwithstanding, active participation by university-related researchers can be a costly undertaking.

TABLE 18.4. Recommendations to Increase Policy Knowledge Use for Alternative Argument Styles

Argument Style	Requirements for Increased Policy Knowledge Use	Required Policy Researcher Action	Appropriate Policy Information Type
Authoritative	Increased prestige and political influence	More active in policy process; establish clearinghouse, professional lobbying efforts or politically involved professional organization; "go public" with press conferences, etc.	All, mostly policy
Intuitive	More meaningful expression of policy analysis for policy makers	More personal involvement with policy makers, as staff member or advisor. Must reinforce each other's perception of policy problem	Less systematic types
Analycentric	Educate policy makers to importance of methodology	Hold seminars, serve on study commissions	Policy-oriented and academic research
Explanatory	Examine causal relationships at the level of analysis that is controlled by policy maker	Engage in contract research to allow policy makers to pose the research question; serve as a policy researcher within the organization	More use of combined practitioner reports and policy research
Pragmatic	Must emphasize familiar parallels in policy and policy-oriented research	Gain experience in the organization as staff or policy researcher to be able to select parallel cases; provide policy research through a task force or study committee	Policy and policy-oriented research; try to upgrade popular journalism

Increasing policy knowledge use among decision makers using the intuitive argument style also requires a heavy involvement by researchers but in a more personal, ongoing way. The major requirement here is that knowledge must be more meaningfully expressed to policy makers. Researchers' involvement as staff aides and advisors may be required to achieve the level of trust and ease of communication necessary for the intuitive exchange of policy knowledge. In addition to the heavy demands placed on policy researchers in these capacities, it is doubtful that researchers can continue to function as analytical researchers while maintaining such a close personal relationship with individual policy makers.

Increasing policy knowledge use according to the remaining three argument styles does not require direct involvement of researchers in the policy process as do the authoritative and intuitive styles. While the analycentric, explanatory, and pragmatic argument styles are most familiar to researchers, these styles are infrequently used by policy makers. Therefore, researchers must refocus their research and its presentation to further its use by policy makers. For decision makers who use, or are open to, the analycentric style, researchers can clarify the importance of research methodology in limiting the usefulness of research. Researchers can provide knowledge through seminars addressing issues from a policy research perspective and serve on study committees or task forces as policy researchers. Both of these activities allow the policy researcher to function as a policy researcher in communicating knowledge in a way consistent with the professional training and expertise of a researcher.

Decision makers using the explanatory and pragmatic styles can be assisted in increasing their use of research by the way that the information is presented. Reliance on the explanatory style requires that researchers examine causal relationships that focus on the factors that are controlled by the policy makers who will receive the analysis. Researchers can better identify these policy-controllable variables through research that is contracted with public agencies or by serving as a researcher in that public organization.

Knowledge will be more useful among decision makers relying on the pragmatic style when research relies on familair parallels or case studies in presenting the analysis. Service on task forces or study committees will assist the researcher in selecting meaningful parallel cases. Policy research relying on the explanatory and pragmatic argument styles of its users will be more useful if it allows policy makers to identify and state the research question.

By considering the compatibility of research with the argument styles of policy makers, the form and content of research can be examined and efforts to further the use of policy knowledge can be considered. Researchers interested in providing more useful knowledge have two alternatives at their disposal. First, they can increase their direct participation in the policy process providing the more systematic types of policy information in a way that is useful to policy makers. Second, researchers can alter the presentation style of analysis, making it more similar to the less systematic types of policy information so that it is compatible with policy makers' argument style. Both of these alternatives place a heavy demand on researchers to alter the traditional practice of policy research.

ORGANIZATIONAL DESIGN ENCOURAGING USEFUL POLICY KNOWLEDGE

Many notable works in the loosely defined field of organization theory concur on the low likelihood that organizations will routinely use new information, knowledge, or evaluation about the organization's performance. Wildavsky (1972), for example, argues that policy evaluation and organizations are to some extent contradictory, since evaluation implies change and organization implies a structured rigidity and adherence to the status quo. At the same time, Thompson (1967) asserts that consensus among constituents or clients of an organization contributes to determining the organization's objectives and behavior. A public organization's legitimacy is rooted in the political environment and is subject to the demands other participants in the policy process make for rationality and analysis in developing public policy. For example, there is an entire research and consulting industry that has been stimulated by legislative and executive requirements for evaluation of many organizational policies. Thus, the questions of both legitimacy and policy information availability appear to be at least superficially satisfied.

As the purposive model of policy maker behavior discussed above posited, individual decision makers in organizations undertake limited searches for new information. Landau (1973:535) asserts a similar point, but one that focuses on the organization rather than the individual decision maker:

> I am afraid, however, that the picture of an agency asserting its claims on the foundation of a demonstrable knowledge is a rather rare phenomenon. It is more likely the case that agencies do not conceive of themselves as *knowledge producing organizations*. We need to emphasize that the language of public administration and public management prompts us to forget that the management or administrative function is fundamentally *analytic*. When we speak of control, supervision, planning, coordinating, integrating as management tasks, this phraseology—all too often— obscures the fact that these are *cognitive* behaviors which require both

analytical skill and knowledge, much of which is not immediately proximate to the matters at hand. [Emphases in original.]

While the largest obstacle to additional policy knowledge use by public decision makers is the lack of organizational incentives to motivate policy makers to search for and use research, there are two issues that must be addressed from an organizational design perspective. First, since most public organizations are not knowledge producers, entry points for information must be built into the organization so that the latest knowledge is available. Second, mindful of the prevalent argument styles of policy makers, information providers must be a part of the organizational structure.

The prevalent argument styles of policy makers identify several criteria an organization that satisfactorily provides useful knowledge will likely meet. First, as identified by the authoritative style, research providers must be of high stature and influence if their efforts are to be received by policy makers. This suggests that interns or specialized assistants may not, by themselves, contribute to providing useful information to decision makers. On the other hand, the intuitive argument style requires that meaningful communication and trust exist to further policy knowledge use. Providing a setting compatible with the intuitive style in a large, complex organization is a difficult task. The analycentric, explanatory, and pragmatic argument styles appear consistent with an organization characterized by specialization of tasks. In such organizations, providers of policy research can be departmentalized and asked to prepare analyses for the organization's decision makers. To the extent that specialization and departmentalization construct barriers to meaningful communication of policy research, this approach is inconsistent with the intuitive argument style.

Table 18.5 describes five organizational alternatives intended to provide knowledge to decision makers in public organizations. Each of these alternatives is compared in terms of organizational accountability, compatibility with alternative argument styles, and its principal weakness in providing useful knowledge. Attempting to provide policy information through the creation of a staff position is usually the initial effort made by an organization to improve information use. While a research-trained staffer, or policy specialist, may be able to satisfy the communication requirements of the intuitive argument style, the close involvement with specific decision makers may reduce the staffer's effectiveness in providing policy research. This is especially problematic if there also exists an age or education difference between the staff and policy makers.

A technical or research department, independently placed in an organization, can preserve the specialist identity of its members, but at the risk of being isolated from the rest of the organization. A rather successful example of this organizational structure is the legal counsel or solicitor staff

TABLE 18.5. Organizational Alternatives in Providing Policy Knowledge

Alternative	Accountable To	Argument Style Compatibility	Principal Weakness
Staff	A specific decision maker	Intuitive	Staff person may not function as policy researcher
Technical/research department	Organization head	Authoritative (if successful); provider of explanatory and pragmatic type information	Poor communication; policy maker might require formal approval to motivate use
Task force	Not really accountable; reports to a specific decision maker	Pragmatic	Little authority; can easily be used for political and tactical purposes
Outside consultant	A specific decision maker	Analycentric, explanatory, and pragmatic	Lacks authority, poor communicator, little organization commitment
Policy research facilitator	Organization head	Potentially compatible with each style	Not an active participant; requires a decision maker to actually carry the policy issue

that exists in many organizations. It is, perhaps, because legal considerations are generally recognized that the approval of a policy action by the legal staff is an acceptable procedure to most policy makers. There is, then, a driving force behind the acceptance of independent legal departments in public organizations. Unless a similar driving force, requiring the involvement of other technical or research departments, can be institutionalized, it is unlikely that this organizational alternative will be widely successful in providing more useful policy knowledge to decision makers.

Task forces and outside consultants are alternatives that enlarge an organization's formal boundaries. Besides having the limitations of temporary, issue-specific responsibilities, these two alternatives can easily be used for political and tactical purposes rather than providing policy information for conceptual or instrumental use. Also, both task forces and outside consultants require a liaison between them and the policy maker. This additional element in the organization structure reduces the contact of the policy maker with the research, sacrificing the opportunity for more intense interest of the policy maker.

An organization alternative that appears to be most attractive is the policy research facilitator who is responsible for translating and transferring policy research from researchers to policy makers. The best example of a policy research facilitator is the Congressional Research Service, which provides background research and summaries of policy research for members of Congress. By being independent and permanent, it has developed a sound reputation similar to that required by policy makers relying on the authoritative argument style. Additionally, being under the general direction of the Congress, and responding principally to individual legislator's requests for information, the Congressional Research Service is compatible with the intuitive argument style. Finally, the staff of specialists is qualified to provide policy research consistent with the analycentric, explanatory, and pragmatic styles that are tailored for members of Congress—a specific group of policy makers.

To be successful in other public organizations, the policy research facilitator must not be viewed as a clearinghouse of policy information, which requires little organizational commitment, but rather as a part of the organization's design and structure. When viewed this way, the policy research facilitator is potentially compatible with each argument style because of its integration with other components of the organization, its independence, and its flexibility in providing different types of policy research reports. The difficulty in designing an organization that can receive and more readily use policy information is a large one. An alternative that incorporates policy makers' motivations and behaviors and is compatible with how policy makers consider and evaluate information in deciding a policy issue will have the highest likelihood of succeeding.

REFERENCES

Caplan, Nathan, et al. *The Use of Social Science Knowledge in Policy Decisions at the National Level.* Ann Arbor: Institute for Social Research, 1975.

Downs, Anthony. *Inside Bureaucracy.* Boston: Little, Brown, 1967.

Dunn, William E. *Public Policy Analysis.* Englewood Cliffs, N.J.: Prentice-Hall, 1981.

Knorr, Karin D. "Policy Makers' Use of Social Science Knowledge: Symbolic or Instrumental?," pp. 165–182 in Carl H. Weiss (ed.), *Using Social Science Research in Public Policy-Making.* Lexington, Mass.: D. C. Heath, 1977.

Landau, Martin. "On the Concept of Self-Correcting Organizations," *Public Administration Review,* 33(1973):533–542.

Simon, Herbert A. "Theories of Decision-Making in Economics and Behavioral Science," *American Economic Review,* 49(1959):253–283.

Steinbrunner, John D. *The Cybernetic Theory of Decisions.* Princeton: Princeton University Press, 1974.

Thompson, James D. *Organizations in Action.* New York: McGraw-Hill, 1967.

Weiss, Carl H. "The Many Meanings of Research Utilization," *Public Administration Review,* 39(1979):426–431.

Weiss, Carl H. Introduction, pp. 1–22 in Carol H. Weiss (ed.), *Using Social Science Research in Public Policy-Making,* Lexington, Mass.: D. C. Heath, 1977.

Wildavsky, Aaron. "The Self-Evaluating Organization," *Public Administration Review,* 32(1972):509–520.

19

USEFULNESS AS A RESEARCH CRITERION: REFLECTIONS OF A CRITICAL ADVOCATE

Mary Elizabeth Beres

The suggestion that usefulness be made a criterion for selecting and designing research is an important development in organization science. Concern about relevance reflects a growing realization that social science research is only one part of a knowledge production/utilization system (Caplan, Morrison, and Stambaugh, 1975; Beyer, 1982a). The attention the issue is receiving indicates an increasing awareness of academic researchers' responsibilities to practitioners.

Recent discussions of usefulness, however, show early signs of the bandwagon cycle that has so often characterized the brief history of organization science. Advocates are focusing entirely on the merits of a usefulness criterion (Helmreich, 1975; Susman and Evered, 1978; Frost, 1980; Thomas and Tymon, 1982). Even Behling's (1980) defense of natural science criteria fails to offer substantive criticisms of a revelance standard. Such an uncritical advocacy usually leads to unrealistic expectations. Then, as problems arise, initial excitement is replaced by disillusionment; the idea is set aside for some new alternative.

The effects of uncritical advocacy are already appearing. For example, articles in *Administrative Science Quarterly*'s special issue on utilization (Beyer, 1982b; 1983) either evaluate the usefulness of existing theory or offer recommendations for improving the utilization process. Both types of papers assume that the meaning of usefulness is clear. As will be seen, however, recent literature gives usefulness several different meanings. Thus, the usefulness criterion being employed to assess research and develop norms for the conduct of science is an ambiguous standard.

I would like to acknowledge the constructive criticisms given an earlier draft of this chapter by Richard Koenig, Walter Tymon, Jr., Gerald Zeitz, and the blind reviewers for the conference. Their comments and the conference itself have helped clarify my thinking.

As managers know well, evaluations based on vague criteria are problematic. Ratings vary with interpretations of the standard. As a result, instead of guiding performance, an ambiguous criterion becomes a focal point for political conflict. For many scientists, the ambiguity of a concept is sufficient justification for its abandonment. In an effort to forestall the premature death of an important advance, this chapter offers a critical examination of usefulness as a criterion for organization science research.

THE MEANING OF USEFULNESS

Recent literature treats usefulness or relevance as a simple, self-evident concept. Upon examination, however, proponents of a usefulness criterion tend to take two different approaches. The pragmatically oriented associate relevance with application. They define usefulness in such terms as: the practical relevance of research (Rapoport, 1970; Thomas and Tymon, 1982), research's ability to influence social action (Lewin, 1946), show how new ideas can be used (Haire, 1964), solve practical problems (Susman and Evered, 1978), or create a better world (Frost, 1980). The common property of this approach is an emphasis on practitioners and action. Useful knowledge is knowledge that explains how to make organizations work properly.

Epistemologically oriented advocates relate usefulness to validity. Research is relevant when its assumptions about social reality and its methods fit the phenomena studied (Motamedi, 1978; Morgan and Smircich, 1980). This approach is part of the current philosophical debate about the nature of organizations. Proponents of a relevance criterion argue that organizations are subjective and/or holistic phenomena (Pondy and Boje, 1975; Susman and Evered, 1978; Cummings, 1981). Useful knowledge is knowledge that explains the functioning of organizations in terms of these characteristics.

Both approaches to usefulness appear in the conference proceedings. For example, Molhrman, Cummings, and Lawler; Bowers; Serpa; MacKenzie; and Bray (Chapters 33, 26, 7, 6, 22) equate usefulness with application. Others, such as Churchman, Bhagat, and Davis (Chapters 11, 12, 25), are concerned with the fit of research to the reality studied.

The bond uniting the two approaches to usefulness is dissatisfaction with the logical positivism that has dominated organization behavior research. Epistemological proponents of a more relevant science have described several alternatives (Morgan and Smircich, 1980). The implications of adopting other philosophical perspectives, however, have not been critically explored. In particular, different philosophical approaches imply quite different types of usefulness standards.

A purely applications-oriented perspective constitutes a shift from positivism to pragmatism. Such a change alters the role of scientists without affecting assumptions about the nature of organizations. Instead of being disinterested observers, researchers become practical problem solvers. Because problems continue to be viewed as objective events, standards for solutions are universal. In this type of pragmatic context, usefulness is a practitioner-oriented, universal standard.

Phenomenology is one of the most actively supported epistemological alternatives to positivism (see Churchman, Chapter 11, for an exception). This philosophical shift affects assumptions about organizations without altering the researcher's responsibility to practitioners. Instead of being viewed as objective entities with universal characteristics, organizations are seen as subjectively relative phenomena (Pondy and Boje, 1975; Cummings, 1981). Researchers become interpreters of this phenomena, rather than problem solvers. In such a phenomenological context, usefulness continues to be a researcher-oriented standard concerned with the epistemological validity of a study's assumptions and methodology.

Combining the applications and epistemological arguments for change produces a shift from positivism to pragmatic phenomenology or a phenomenological pragmatism. In either case, scientists become concerned with practical problems that are viewed in subjectively relative terms. This change leads to a practitioner-oriented, relative standard of usefulness. Figure 19.1 illustrates these three philosophical alternatives to positivism and their implications for a usefulness criterion.

Because the concept of usefulness has not been rigorously defined, it is difficult to determine which type of standard is actually being advocated. On the surface, arguments address either pragmatic or epistemological issues. Most pragmatic rationales treat practitioners as a global, undifferentiated group (Rapoport, 1970; Susman and Evered, 1978), which implies a universal, practitioner-oriented standard. Epistemological arguments have concentrated on validity, a researcher-oriented standard. An analysis of unidimensional arguments suggests, however, that in many cases the underlying philosophical perspectives combine elements of pragmatism and phenomenology.

With regard to pragmatic approaches, the proposed criterion is not usefulness per se, but usefulness to practitioners. Research, after all, has always had to demonstrate some type of usefulness to a scientific community. If there are differences between the interests of practitioners and scientists, however, then usefulness is, by definition, a relative standard. Usefulness is a function of the user, a phenomenological assertion.

Pragmatic arguments for useful research actually incorporate phenomenological assumptions in several different ways. For example, Haire (1964) suggests that managers and scientists may evaluate organizational

CHANGE
DIMENSIONS

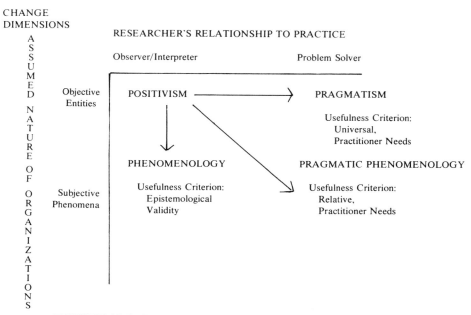

FIGURE 19.1. Philosophical Shifts and Resulting Usefulness Criteria

changes differently. After describing five pragmatic relevance criteria, Thomas and Tymon (1982) mention that specific users must be identified before the criteria can be applied. Susman and Evered (1978) define usefulness in strictly pragmatic terms and then proceed to develop a phenomenological justification for the validity of action research methods. Thus, it appears that there are at least implicit links between pragmatic concerns about usefulness and phenomenological assumptions about social reality.

Epistemological arguments for useful research focus on the validity of alternative assumptions about organizations. In most of the discussions, relevance is considered a function of validity, and applications are expected as a natural consequence of relevance. This line of reasoning seems to imply that useful research can be produced without consulting practitioner concerns.

From a phenomenological perspective, however, validity is a necessary but insufficient condition for usefulness. Relevance depends, in addition, on perceptions; and perceptions depend on subjective interests. Since the experiences and goals of scientists and practitioners are different, their subjective interests will be different. Hence, if research is to be useful to practitioners, researchers will have to consider explicitly practitioner needs. Although it has not yet been addressed in epistemological arguments for usefulness, this pragmatic dimension is a logical consequence of phenomenological assumptions.

Since they contain elements of both pragmatism and phenomenology, most recent arguments for useful organization research logically imply a practitioner-oriented, relative standard of relevance. However, the emphasis that has been placed on one or the other dimension of philosophical change has tended to obscure the complexity of the proposed criterion. Usefulness, therefore, has often appeared to be a simple, universal standard.

PROBLEMS INHERENT IN A USEFULNESS CRITERION

Organization scientists have been accustomed to universal research standards that, while difficult to meet, are clear and independent of the user. To add a criterion that is practitioner-oriented and relative is, therefore, a radical departure. With a relative standard, the value of research becomes a function of the evaluator and the context. If user interests conflict, value can also become a function of power. The proposed usefulness standard has all three of these characteristics. Specifically, usefulness is a function of the user; it is a function of time; and it may easily become a function of power.

These types of relativity introduce new problems in a science that has assumed knowledge is value-free. Unless the problems are identified and addressed, establishment of a usefulness criterion could create more difficulties for organization science than it resolves. Hence, the following discussion examines some major complications associated with each dimension of a usefulness criterion's relativity.

Usefulness Is a Function of the User

A relevance criterion explicitly distinguishes between scientific and practitioner research objectives. This distinction implies that at least the application of knowledge, if not knowledge itself, depends on user interests. Usefulness is in the eye of the beholder.

If all user interests are compatible, then a relative usefulness criterion merely reflects the limited domain perspectives of differentiated groups. In this case, complications are minimal. They include added complexity and the corresponding need for integration across diverse domains.

On the other hand, a relative, practitioner-oriented standard becomes a new type of problem under either of two conditions: incompatibility between practitioner interests and the basic purpose of science (that is, the production of knowledge); or incompatibilities of interest among diverse practitioners. If either of these conditions is present, conflicts will arise over the conduct or operational meaning of useful research. Organization science could then be put in the position of deciding whose special interests to serve. The experiences of action researchers and phenomenological analyses of organizations indicate that both types of incompatibilities exist.

The evidence of action researchers comes from their direct experience conducting practitioner-oriented research (Lewin, 1946; Rapoport, 1970; Helmreich, 1975; Susman and Evered, 1978). They have found that, where scientists seek generalizable knowledge (Webb, 1961), practitioners want solutions to their own specific problems. Reflecting on Tavistock studies, Rapoport (1970) concluded that a relevance requirement places constant pressure on science to become a relatively inexpensive consulting service solving (sometimes trivial) problems for top management. Even when practitioner and scientific objectives converge, conflict can arise between a researcher's need to publicize findings and a manager's desire to maintain the competitive advantage of secrecy. Thus, action research experience indicates that a dialectic tension exists between the practitioner's need for competitively advantageous solutions and the scientist's responsibility to develop generalizable solutions and make them publicly available.

As Webb (1961) and McGuire (1973) have noted, practical relevance alone does not assure value. An exclusively practitioner orientation could merely change the nature of scientific irrelevance. Instead of being too impractical and abstract, organization research could become too situation-specific and nontransferable.

Whereas action research sheds light on incompatibilities between scientific and practical uses of research, phenomenological or subjectivist analyses of organizations point to incompatibilities among practitioner interests. The logical implications of subjective assumptions have been developed in action theories of organization (Silverman, 1971). According to such approaches, structural differentiation leads to divergent subjective orientations. March and Simon (1958) label the process goal displacement. Benson (1977) and Brown (1978) refer to contradictions arising from the social processes that produce organizations.

Action theories of organization also indicate some of the boundaries across which conflicting subjective orientations may develop. The goal displacement concept identifies role differentiation as a source of incompatibilities (March and Simon, 1958). Hence, research goals of an organization's customers, suppliers, employees, owners, and neighbors may conflict. Within an organization, practical concerns may diverge along functional lines and between hierarchical levels. Thomas's (1982) comparison of manager and mediator goals in conflict management illustrates some of the differences than can occur.

Max Weber (1968) relates subjective orientation to forms of dominance. His analysis suggests that practitioner interests will depend on the type of compliance in an organization (Etzioni, 1975) and the systems used for coordination and control (Mintzberg, 1979). Sociocultural models, in turn, relate types of organization to cultural differences in subjective orientation (Beres and Portwood, 1979, 1981). Thus, incompatible practitioner interests may arise in different cultures, different types of organization, and different organizational roles.

The existence of incompatible orientations is already evident in organization research. For example, Thomas and Tymon's (1982) concern about efficiency, effectiveness, output, and performance measures reflects a top management, decision-making perspective. For these scientists, useful research would improve the operation of organizations. On the other hand, Frost's (1980) concern about injustice and alienation is oriented toward lower participants. For him, useful research would radically change organizations. Some empirical differences between these perspectives are evidenced in Tichy's (1974) study of change agents and Haire's (1964:6) observation that:

> in most changes considered by management, management decides that someone else should change; [whereas] in general, the social scientific concepts suggest that management change.

Thus, action theories of organization imply one of the most serious problems with a usefulness criterion. Conflicting subjective orientations are an inherent consequence of structural and cultural differentiation. Given conflicting orientations, what one group sees as useful another group will see as threatening. If a usefulness criterion is too narrowly operationalized, then organization science will intentionally serve the interests of some at the expense of others.

Usefulness Is a Function of Time

Two arguments for a more relevant organization science focus on time. In the epistemological debate, critics charge that positivism ignores historical influences. A more relevant science, they argue, would view action in a temporal context (McGuire, 1973; Smith; 1976; Susman and Evered, 1978; Frost, 1980). Applications-oriented critics contend that positivist science works too slowly in a rapidly changing environment (Cummings, 1978;

Thomas and Tymon, 1982). They suggest that relevant research would concentrate on present problems of organizations.

Of these rationales, the practical argument, in particular, links usefulness to time. According to pragmatists, change often makes yesterday's knowledge irrelevant in today's environment. By the same token, however, today's knowledge may well be useless tomorrow. Thus, because of change, the temporal usefulness of research is problematic.

The problem with a practical relevance criterion is that it could focus research efforts on issues in one time horizon to the exclusion of others. Current advocates, for example, emphasize the need for applied research on today's problems (Susman and Evered, 1978; Thomas and Tymon, 1982). By their own arguments, this research will eventually become irrelevant. If organization science focuses only on the present, then it will always lag behind, rather than anticipate, change.

All research along the basic-to-applied continuum makes a potential contribution in some time horizon. Applied research, of course, has the shortest time frame. It applies established knowledge to the solution of contemporary problems. Because of its short time perspective, applied research operates within the existing social framework.

Developmental studies have an intermediate time horizon. This research develops the practical implications of new ideas. Such studies identify viable directions for change and generate knowledge about how to implement new social systems.

Basic research has long-range usefulness. It uncovers hidden properties of action. As dissatisfactions arise, the discoveries of basic science provide seeds for developing new alternatives. Max Weber's (1968) work illustrates the value of basic research. When organization science needed concepts for understanding formally ordered behavior, it found his description of bureaucracy. Now, in the search for an alternative to positivism, Weber's analysis of the subjective meaning of action is useful. In both cases, the availability of the ideas has saved discovery and development time.

Paradoxically, basic and developmental research are more important in a dynamic, uncertain environment. In this case, change has a momentum of its own that demands new ideas. In a stable environment, there is little pressure for alternatives.

It might be argued that responsibility for basic and applied research could be differentiated among various social sciences. Primary disciplines, such as sociology and psychology, could focus on basic research, while organization science concentrates on applied research. There are four difficulties with this alternative.

First, the basic disciplines themselves, most notably social psychology (Helmreich, 1975; Smith, 1976), are debating the issue of practical relevance. They too feel pressure from practitioners who supply resources for research (McGuire, 1973). In addition, Helmreich (1975) concluded that the separation of experimental and applied research results in unproductive competition and a lack of communication between scientists.

Second, if basic and applied research were separated, developmental studies would be neglected. Since it has properties of both perspectives, developmental research would belong in neither area. The serious consequences of ignoring developmental research have been discussed by Haire (1964) and Abernathy (1982) among others.

Third, an exclusively applied orientation would focus organization science on a very short time horizon. Such a move seems unwise in an environment that attributes declining performance to the absence of a long-term perspective (Abernathy, 1982).

Finally, as an interdisciplinary field, organization science has direct exposure to behavioral interdependencies that are of only marginal interest in specialized disciplines. This experience provides an important opportunity for basic discoveries about action. Hence, overemphasis on applied issues could seriously limit organization science's contribution to knowledge. Cummings (1978) has similarly concluded that the boundaries of organization science should be based on unit of analysis.

In summary, from a time perspective, any relevance criterion that emphasizes the present at the expense of the future becomes a problem. In a rapidly changing environment, practitioners need long-range as much as short-range research. Organization science is uniquely qualified to address practical organizational problems along the entire continuum of basic to applied research.

Usefulness Is Potentially a Function of Power

One of the major justifications for a usefulness criterion is that it would focus attention on the interdependence between science and action. Critics of positivism argue that an emphasis on objective data and internal validity makes social science artificially independent from the phenomena it studies. The result is unrealistic, useless research (Cummings, 1978; Motamedi, 1978; Kilmann, 1979; Thomas and Tymon, 1982).

A practitioner orientation, however, could swing the research pendulum in the opposite direction. Instead of being at least philosophically independent, organization science could become a staff function implementing management directives. Science could be co-opted by an organizational elite.

The potential for co-optation lies in power relations within the scientific system. To conduct empirical research, scientists need money and access. These resources are primarily under the control of top management, whether of the private sector, government agencies, or the military. Quite naturally, managers are most likely to support studies they view as useful. Thus, control of critical resources gives top management a strong advantage in determining the direction of research.

If managerial, organizational, and societal interests were always consistent, managerial control would be beneficial, not problematic. As the analysis of user orientations indicated, however, this is not the case. Managers, at least sometimes, prefer to do what is comfortable for themselves rather than what is more useful for the organization (Haire, 1964). Recent events demonstrate that what is "good for General Motors' executives" is not always "good for General Motors."

It is also questionable whether the interests of organizations are always consistent with the interests of society. The potential for conflict appears most starkly in the military-industrial complex. For economic survival, arms producers need military conflicts. But for its survival, society needs to eliminate military conflict. Thus, one problem with a usefulness criterion is that it could promote research beneficial to managers at the expense of organizations and society.

There is evidence that organization science already is biased in the direction of management interests. Rapoport (1970) has reported pressures from management on the orientation of action research. Tichy's (1974) study indicated co-optation of change agents who work for an organization through top management. Benson (1977) and Brown (1978) have demonstrated how organization theories rationalize and justify management interests. Motamedi (1978) has detected a significant top-down orientation in organization behavior theories.

The subtlety of co-optation can be illustrated in the case of motivation theory. Psychologists working in this area are interested in the sources of individual behavior. Their theories are concerned with the value or meaning of behavior to the actor. When organization science uses these theories, "motivation" becomes "motivation to work" (Lawrence and Lorsch, 1969) and behavior becomes performance. Thus, in organization science, motivation theories are concerned with the value or meaning of behavior to management. Through this shift in perspective, theories become (often unintentionally) vehicles of manipulation and alienation.

The gross distortions that can occur are evidenced in the use made of Maslow's concept of self-actualization. As he explains in *Toward a Psychology of Being* (1968), this concept refers to a transcendent mode of relationship in which a person becomes totally at one with the environment. Self-actualization can occur for any person in any environment. In organization behavior, self-actualization is interpreted as a need for self-development or personal growth. This need is then translated into a description of the type of environment or job an organization should provide for employees. Not surprisingly, managers and professionals are assumed to have the strongest self-actualization needs. In the process of co-optation, Maslow's concept loses the dimension of integration and becomes associated with status. In addition, organization behavior assumes for management a responsibility to fulfill a need that is actually dependent on an individual's own psychological relationship to reality.

Co-optation of organization science by top management would affect not only the selection and definition of concepts, but also the time orientation of research. As the dominant coalition, management has a vested interest in preserving and enhancing its power. This power is a function of the existing social system. The managerial elite, therefore, would be most interested in applied research that increases the effectiveness and efficiency of its control.

As indicated earlier, applied research focuses on the present. Developmental and basic research are more relevant for the future and change. Most change, however, poses potential threats to an elite's power. For this reason, management can be expected to have less concern about, or even resistance to, developmental and basic research. These types of studies, however, are important to the long-run interests of organizations and society. In his analysis of the U.S. consumer electronics and automobile industries, for example, Abernathy (1982) has attributed productivity problems to the dominance of one such single-minded, short-term management orientation.

Thus, co-optation by a managerial elite would produce a conservative research program. Organization science would find itself defending existing social structures with their advantages and flaws. Leadership for change would have to come from some other source.

Summary

The preceding analysis has identified four problems inherent in a practitioner-oriented, relative usefulness criterion. These problems arise from the relativity of usefulness with respect to user, time, and power. First there is a dialectic tension between practitioner needs and the purpose of science. Second, there are conflicts among diverse practitioner's interests. Third, in a rapidly environment, an exclusive emphasis on applied research jeopardizes the usefulness of science in the future. Fourth, because of unequal distributions of power, organization science could be co-opted to serve conservative interests of an organizational elite.

Given the difficulties, it might be tempting to abandon usefulness as a criterion for research. Past evidence suggests, however, that the problems of relativity affect research even in the absence of an explicit concern about relevance (see also Van de Ven and Astley, 1981). Hence, a more constructive solution would be to address potential difficulties through the operational definition of a usefulness criterion.

OPERATIONAL CRITERIA FOR A ROBUST
USEFULNESS STANDARD

The major danger in establishing a usefulness criteria is that relevance will be defined too narrowly. Because of relativity, a narrowly operationalized criterion would focus on some user needs or a particular time frame to the exclusion of others. The result would be a subjectively biased organization science.

A biased approach serves the interests of neither science nor practitioners. If practical studies are based on a limited view of the issues involved, results will give incomplete information about forces contributing to a problem. Such research would produce distorted theories of organization and inadequate advice for practitioners. Because biased theories are only partial explanations, their applications produce unintended consequences. March and Simon's (1958) analysis of classical administrative theories illustrates the dysfunctional consequences of inadequate theory.

When phenomena are subjectively relative, one way to develop an unbiased science is to use a multilectic form of analysis. This type of approach recognizes and counterbalances the multiple interests of all parties. By focusing attention on relationships among all users and time frames, a robustly defined usefulness criterion would provide a foundation for unbiased, multilectic analysis.

A robust criterion can be developed by identifying scientific objectives that address problems inherent in a subjectively relative research standard. These objectives can then be translated into criteria for operationally defining usefulness. The following discussion identifies such criteria corresponding with the four problems examined in the preceding analysis.

The first problem is that there is a dialectic tension between practitioners' need for specific, competitively advantageous solutions and science's responsibility to learn general properties of action and make this knowledge available to all. A dialectic is a composition of opposites in which both parts are essential to each other. The difficulty with positivist research criteria is that they ignore practice. A pragmatic criterion could lead to the opposite problem, ignoring science. To maintain an appropriate balance, a useful organization science should continue to have as an objective the production of generally relevant knowledge. In order to meet this objective, a usefulness criterion should be operationally defined in such a way that it recognizes the separate, legitimate objectives of both science and practice.

The second problem is that different groups of practitioners have conflicting interests. If usefulness is defined in terms of a subset of users, then research will be shaped by their specific interests, rather than by the nature of the phenomena studied. The result would be a very limited relevance. To avoid a partisan orientation, organization science should openly pursue knowledge. This means that a usefulness criterion should be defined so that it explicitly recognizes competing practitioner orientations.

The third problem was identified by Haire in 1964. The omission of any step in the research cycle jeopardizes the usefulness of organization science. If researchers focus exclusively on basic, developmental, or applied studies, then relevance is limited to the time frame of that type of research. A truly useful science should be continuously viable over short-, intermediate-, and long-range time horizons. To meet this objective, a usefulness criterion should promote an integrated cycle of basic, developmental, and applied research.

The fourth problem is that power relationships could lead to the co-optation of science by organizational elites. This problem sharply focuses one of the serious questions before organization science: What is its role? Does it serve a dominant coalition, organizations as a whole, or society? Clearly, there are many situations in which all of these interests converge. But there are also areas of conflict. Where conflict exists, the dominant coalition has a natural advantage.

The problem of co-optation is a special case of serving a limited set of users. Asymmetric distributions of power increase the probability that science will serve the special interests of the powerful. Control of science by powerholders is actually not even in their best interests. Research that is dominated by specific biases usually produces self-confirming results rather than valid knowledge about organizational realities.

To be useful, science must be free from manipulation. To maintain this freedom, a usefulness criterion should promote constructive criticism of existing practice. A critical attitude is especially important when science enters directly into the world of action.

Table 19.1 summarizes the scientific objectives and operational criteria that address four of the problems inherent in a usefulness research standard. These objectives and criteria identify some of the requirements for a robust

TABLE 19.1. Requirements for a Robust Usefulness Criterion

Scientific Objectives	Operational Criteria
Generalizable relevance	Recognize separate, legitimate objectives of science and practice
Open pursuit of knowledge	Recognize competing practitioner orientations
Continuous viability	Promote an integrated cycle of basic, developmental, and applied research
Freedom from manipulation	Promote constructive criticism of existing practice

usefulness criterion. By meeting these requirements, research systems should be able to avoid potential negative consequences of a relative research standard.

INSTITUTIONALIZING A ROBUST USEFULNESS CRITERION

Using the operational criteria for a robust standard as a basic, the concluding section of this chapter offers five suggestions for institutionalizing usefulness as a research criterion. Each suggestion builds upon previous recommendations. The areas addressed are: editorial policy; dialogue between scientists and practitioners; coordination of research; academic reward systems; and training of organization scientists. The first four suggestions redirect the efforts of current researchers; the fifth focuses on the next generation of scientists. In every case, the objective is to promote an environment in which scientists meet diverse practitioners as peers and people of action are seen as neither ignorant nor all-knowing.

The design suggestions are specifically concerned with the academic research environment. In-house research activities already serve an important function in fulfilling the needs of practitioners. The latter research, however, is usually limited to the concerns of the sponsoring organization. It is assumed in this chapter that academic research has the unique responsibility of serving the general interests of all parties. Hence, the following suggestions are designed not only to promote an interdependent relationship between science and practice, but also to preserve the freedom of academics to study controversial issues.

Editorial Policy

Establishment of a usefulness criterion for research, at the very least, means that publications should be required to meet some standard of relevance. Since usefulness is relative, however, any attempt to define relevance in terms of specific properties will favor some interests over others. To maintain an open intellectual environment, relevance should be viewed in terms of continuous dimensions rather than yes or no categories (Rosenzweig, 1980). Hence, the first suggestion is that editors require researchers to report how their studies are relevant along a series of dimensions.

To facilitate reporting, components of relevance need to be identified. This chapter suggests that user and time are central dimensions. Thomas and Tymon (1982) identify five components. Instead of using the components to select research projects—a process that favors particular interests—they could be used to describe types of relevance. Thus, a researcher would report the nature of a study's relevance in terms of: degree of external validity; user goals to which research relates; position of the research on the basic, developmental, applied continuum; extent to which the study tests common practice versus generates unexpected knowledge; and present versus future time orientation. Requiring scientists to report relevance within an open framework of continuous dimensions should sensitize them to the practical significance of research without limiting studies to the interests of some special group or one particular time frame.

Dialogue among Scientists and Practitioners

As Susman and Evered (1978) and Kilmann (1979) have noted, organization research has become increasingly distant from the problems and needs of organizations. To identify more relevant research topics, Thomas and Tymon (1982) suggest that scientists dialogue directly with practitioners. In light of the requirements for a robust usefulness criterion, two qualifications are added to their recommendation. First, to be representative of diverse practitioner interests, discussions should include people from: different roles within and interacting with organizations, different types of organizations, and different cultures. Second, to provide an opportunity for critical reflection, written synopses of the dialogues should be regularly and broadly disseminated to scientists and practitioners. Both of these qualifications generate a need for ongoing coordination. Therefore, establishment of a Center for Dialogue on Research Usefulness is suggested.

Creation of a center offers several advantages. With regard to dialogue, a center could provide the management needed to balance effective discussion with broad representation. More specifically, a center could create representative dialogue through an orchestrated sequence of sessions. Individual meetings would consist of small, unrepresentative groups. The cumulative series of meetings would cover a full range of user orientations. Dissemination of summaries would offer each participant an exposure to all perspectives.

With regard to critical reflection, a center could promote research on the issue of usefulness. Already several topics have been identified. These include: exploration of the dimensions of usefulness (Thomas and Tymon, 1982); identification of alternative user orientations (Frost, 1980; Thomas and Tymon, 1982); and analysis of relationships between actors' roles and their subjective orientations (Benson, 1977; Brown, 1978). The center's dialogues between scientists and practitioners would generate, no doubt, a continuing series of questions. Then, in addition to being a repository for this research, the center could circulate findings in an annual series on the usefulness of organization science.

Through both dialogue and research, a center could become the focal place for debate on relationships between science and action. Scientists could gather with fellow scientists, as well as practitioners. This would provide opportunities for continuing examination of the role, responsibility, and performance of organization science. By means of such activities, a center would contribute to the balancing of scientific and practitioner initiatives in research (Rapoport, 1970).

Thus, a Center for Dialogue on Research Usefulness would help scientists: become familiar with the diverse views of practitioners, maintain a critical awareness of current practice, and review relationships between science and practice. In addition, a center would provide the continuity needed to carry a good idea through implementation. In the spirit of a robust usefulness criterion, such a center should function as an open clearinghouse and coordination point, rather than a centralized mechanism of control.

Coordination of Research

A problem in the present research environment is that studies are often isolated, independent projects. On the one hand, useful new ideas are left undeveloped (Haire, 1964). On the other hand, action researchers find it difficult to pursue general research questions that arise in client-sponsored projects. (Rapoport, 1970). To maintain a balance between scientific and practitioner interests, Rapoport (1970) recommended the establishment of coordinated research programs.

Research programs are larger than any one study. They provide researchers a measure of independence from a specific client's interests. With the program as a context, a scientist is better able to distinguish between knowledge-generating applied research and situation-specific consulting. In addition, a research program provides continuity in the study of an issue. Results from one project influence the design of the next (Rapoport, 1970). In this respect, programs help integrate basic, developmental, and applied studies. Thus, research programs provide a scientific context for the selection of clients and research questions.

As Rapoport (1970) also indicated, however, development of a research program is difficult in the relatively unorganized world of social science. Tavistock Institute research is one of the exceptions that illustrates the problem. Maintenance of a program requires coordination of efforts. The proposed Center for Dialogue would be, of course, an excellent vehicle for fostering research programs. At the very least, the center could function as a clearinghouse for the analysis and integration of disparate studies; at most, it could directly manage research programs.

Academic Reward Systems

The preceding recommendations advocate changes in the behavior of organization scientists. To a significant extent, these changes run counter to the criteria used in academic tenure, promotion, and merit systems. As long as reward systems value internal over external validity, basic over developmental and applied research (Kilmann, 1979), and independent objectivity over involvement with practitioners, it will be difficult to redirect the efforts of researchers. Thus, the fourth recommendation is that academic reward systems be differentiated to correspond with the diverse needs of a useful organization science.

In light of requirements for a robust usefulness criteria, two types of reward differentiation are needed. First, developmental and applied research should be valued equally with basic studies. Under present conditions, potentially useful ideas are generated, but studies that operationalize the ideas are neglected (Haire, 1964; Van de Vall, Bolas, and Kang, 1976). Equal recognition for all three types of research could encourage more developmental and applied study without swinging the pendulum entirely to a short-range perspective.

Second, rewards should be differentiated to encourage collaboration. Specifically, diverse contributions to study teams should be recognized equally. Research requires a variety of skills and scientists vary in their relative abilities. By encouraging a pooling of talents, this change would increase the efficiency of organization science. In particular, collaborative research could draw upon different scientists for client-oriented and theory-oriented skills. Then, client relations specialists could focus on operational validity, and theorists could concentrate on epistemological validity (Van de Vall, Bolas, and Kang, 1976). According to Rapoport (1970), teamwork like this provides both the distance needed for a critical perspective and the involvement needed to obtain valid information. As a result, he recommends research teams as a way of balancing and integrating scientific and practical research objectives.

One of the obstacles to differentiation of academic rewards is the similarity between applied research and consulting. Academic systems do not have the resources to recompensate researchers for paid services to outside clients. Thus, an ability to distinguish knowledge-generating research from routine consulting is a precondition for either type of change in rewards.

Implementation of the first three suggestions would help identify valid applied research. Development of relevance dimensions would provide a framework for describing the research contributions of an activity. Dialogue and research on usefulness would help identify scientific objectives for applied studies. As already indicated, coordinated research programs would specify the knowledge-generating function of an applied study. Taken together, the four suggestions become a reinforcing system of changes that could redirect the efforts of current organizational scientists.

Training of Organizational Scientists

The final suggestion concerns the preparation of the next generation of researchers. As future participants in an interdependent research system, students need two types of experiences. To become familiar with the realities of organizations, they need contact with practitioners. To develop independent insights, they need to develop critical skills (Webb, 1961; McGuire, 1973; Frost, 1980). In order to meet these objectives, doctoral programs should include supervised interaction with practitioners and comparative study of social philosophies.

Through interaction with practitioners, students would be exposed to the complexities of organizational action. They would have an opportunity to learn the problems of practitioners and the language of practice. This experience should improve future scientists' ability to understand users' concerns and communicate with them about research. Through supervision, these interactions should be made an integral part of a student's total development as a scientist.

To foster a student's unbiased development, the supervision of practitioner contacts should have three objectives. First, faculty should be sure students learn to translate between the languages of practice and theory. Second, students should have direct exposure to diverse and competing practitioner perspectives. Third, faculty should assist students in analyzing the effects of roles on practitioner orientations. By meeting these objectives, faculty can help students understand the significance of their interactions and develop a balance between empathy for practitioners and criticism of practice.

Critical skills are as important for a scientist as an understanding of practical problems (Webb, 1961; McGuire, 1973). It is through analysis and interpretation of phenomena that science generates knowledge for solutions. A study of social philosophies should help students develop the necessary critical perspective.

Comparative analysis of philosophies would expose students to different views of reality. In the process, they should gain an appreciation of how subjective perspectives affect the definition of problems. Comparisons should also lead students to reflection on their own philosophical orientation, its effect on their attitudes, and its relationships to other philosophies. Through an exposure to alternatives, future scientists should develop an ability to articulate and critically assess their own subjective perspective and that of others. Development of a critical perspective among researchers is the single most important guarantee of a creative (McGuire, 1973) and unbiased (Benson, 1977; Brown, 1978) organization science.

Socialization of the next generation of academics is one of the more effective ways of institutionalizing a change in research criteria. If future scientists have a critical yet sympathetic appreciation of practitioner concerns, they are more likely to view research in terms of its practical relevance, support a differentiated academic reward system, and participate in coordinated research programs. Having learned the language of practitioners, they will find it easier to engage in dialogue. On the other hand, any changes in current academic processes would facilitate changes in the training of doctoral students. A Center for Dialogue would provide a forum for exposing students to practitioners, much like the student colloquia sponsored by the Academy of Management. A change in editorial policies and reward systems would reinforce faculty efforts to involve students with practitioners. Coordinated research programs would not only provide students an opportunity to develop research skills, but also a context in which to learn relationships between scientific and practical research goals. Thus, there are mutual feedback relationships between suggestions addressed to current research processes and suggested changes in the training of future researchers.

Summary

Taking the perspective of a critical advocate, this chapter has identified four problems inherent in the relativity of usefulness with respect to user, time, and power. To address these problems, four operational criteria for a robust usefulness standard have been identified. These criteria have led, in turn, to five suggestions for the redesign of academic systems. Table 19.2 summarizes the relationships between operational criteria and design suggestions. Implementation of any one suggestion, by itself, can increase the relevance of organization science. As the previous discussion indicated, however, the design changes reinforce each other. A change in editorial policy, establishment of a Center for Dialogue, and coordination of research would make it easier to differentiate academic reward systems. On the other hand, a change in academic rewards would make it easier to implement a new editorial policy, maintain a Center, and coordinate research. A Center for Dialogue could help develop a new editorial policy and coordinate research programs. The four changes above would support changes in doctoral education, and a change in doctoral education would socialize new standards in the next generation of scientists. Figure 19.2 illustrates the reinforcing relationships among the five suggestions. If these changes were implemented as a system, they would have a powerful impact on the efforts of current and future researchers.

TABLE 19.2. Contributions of Design Suggestions to the Usefulness of Organization Science

Suggestions	Operational Criteria for Usefulness			
	Recognize separate, legitimate objectives of science and practice	*Recognize competing practitioner orientations*	*Promote an integrated cycle of basic, developmental, and applied research*	*Promote constructive criticism of existing practice*
Editorial Policy: Report relevance in terms of continuous dimensions		X	X	
Scientist/Practitioner Dialogue: Establish a Center	X	X		X
Coordination of Research: Develop research programs	X		X	
Academic Reward Systems: Give equal weight to diverse research contributions	X		X	X
Student Training: Include interaction with practitioners and a study of comparative social philosophy	X	X		X

Having identified desirable changes, the next problem is mobilization of resources for change. This issue is left for future consideration. Assuming the resource problem can be solved, institutionalization of the five suggestions would promote development of an organization science that is relevant to the complex forces operating in today's dynamic environment.

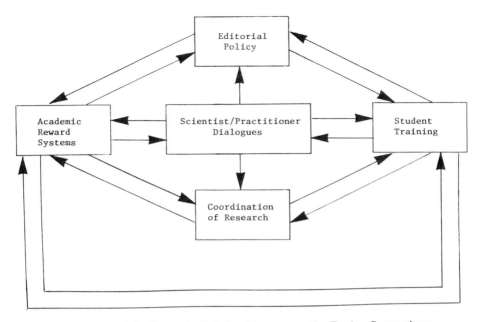

FIGURE 19.2. Systemic Relationships among the Design Suggestions

REFERENCES

Abernathy, William J.
1982   "Competitive Decline in U.S. Innovation: The Management Factor." Research Management, 25:5, 34–41.
Behling, Orlando
1980   "The Case for the Natural Science Model for Research in Organizational Behavior and Organization Theory." Academy of Management Review, 5:4, 483–490.
Benson, J. Kenneth
1977   "Organizations: A Dialectical View." Administrative Science Quarterly, 22:1, 1–21.
Beres, Mary Elizabeth, and James D. Portwood
1979   "Explaining Cultural Differences in the Perceived Role of Work: An Intranational, Cross-cultural Study." In G. W. England, A. R. Negandhi, and B. Wilpert (eds.), Organizational Functioning in a Cross-cultural Perspective, 139–173. Kent, Ohio: Kent State University Press.
1981   "Sociocultural Influences on Organizations: An Analysis of Recent Research." In G. W. England, A. R. Negandhi, and B. Wilpert (eds.), The Functioning of Complex Organizations, 303–336. Cambridge, Mass.: Oelgeschlager, Gunn and Hain.
Beyer, Janice M.
1982a   "Introduction." Administrative Science Quarterly, 27:4, 588–590.

Beyer, Janice M. (ed.)
1982b "Special Issue, Part 1: The Utilization of Organizational Research." Administrative Science Quarterly, 27:4, 587–685.
1983 "Special Issue, Part 2: The Utilization of Organizational Research." Administrative Science Quarterly, 28:1, in press.
Brown, Richard Harvey
1978 "Bureaucracy as Praxis: Toward a Political Phenomenology of Formal Organizations." Administrative Science Quarterly, 23:3, 365–382.
Caplan, N., A. Morrison, and R. J. Stambaugh
1975 The Use of Social Science Knowledge in Policy Decisions at the National Level. Center for Research on Utilization of Scientific Knowledge, Institute for Social Research. Ann Arbor, Mich.: University of Michigan.
Cummings, Larry L.
1978 "Toward Organizational Behavior." Academy of Management Review, 3:1, 90–98.
1981 "State of the Art: Organizational Behavior in the 1980's." Decision Sciences, 12:365–377.
Etzioni, Amatai
1975 A Comparative Analysis of Complex Organizations, 2d ed. New York: Free Press.
Frost, Peter
1980 "Toward a Radical Framework for Practicing Organization Science." Academy of Management Review, 5:4, 501–507.
Haire, Mason
1964 "The Social Sciences and Management Practices." California Management Review, 6:4, 3–10.
Helmreich, Robert
1975 "Applied Social Psychology: The Unfulfilled Promise." Personality and Social Psychology Bulletin, 1:4, 548–560.
Kilmann, Ralph H.
1979 "On Integrating Knowlege Utilization with Knowledge Development: The Philosophy Behind the MAPS Design Technology." Academy of Management Review, 4:3, 417–426.
Lawrence, Paul R., and Jay W. Lorsch
1969 Developing Organizations: Diagnosis and Action. Reading, Mass.: Addison-Wesley.
Lewin, Kurt
1946 "Action Research and Minority Problems." Journal of Social Issues, 2:34–46.
March, James, and Herbert Simon
1958 Organizations. New York: Wiley.
Maslow, Abraham H.
1968 Toward a Psychology of Being, 2d ed. Princeton, N.J.: Van Nostrand.
McGuire, William J.
1973 "The Yin and Yang of Progress in Social Psychology," Journal of Personality and Social Psychology, 26:3, 446–456.
Mintzberg, Henry
1979 The Structuring of Organizations. Englewood Cliffs, N.J.: Prentice-Hall.
Morgan, Gareth, and Linda Smircich
1980 "The Case for Qualitative Research." Academy of Management Review, 5:4, 491–500.
Motamedi, Kurt Kourosh
1978 "Toward Explicating Philosophical Orientations in Organizational Behavior (OB)." Academy of Management Review, 3:2, 354–360.
Pondy, L. R., and D. M. Boje

1975   "Bringing Mind Back In: Paradigm Development as a Frontier Problem in Organization Theory." American Sociological Association Meetings, San Francisco.

Rapoport, Robert N.
1970   "Three Dilemmas in Action Research." Human Relations, 23:6, 499–513.

Rosenzweig, James E.
1980   "Editorial Comment." Academy of Management Review, 5:4.

Silverman, David
1971   The Theory of Organizations. New York: Basic Books.

Smith, M. Brewster
1976   "Social Psychology, Science, and History: So What?" Personality and Social Psychology Bulletin, 2:438–444.

Susman, Gerald I., and Roger D. Evered
1978   "An Assessment of the Scientific Merits of Action Research." Administrative Science Quarterly, 23:4, 582–603.

Thomas, Kenneth W.
1982   "Manager and Mediator: A Comparison of Third-Party Roles Based upon Conflict-Management Goals." In Gerard B. J. Bomers and Richard B. Peterson (eds.), Conflict Management and Industrial Relations, 141–157. Boston: Kluwer Nijhoff.

Thomas, Kenneth W., and Walter G. Tymon, Jr.
1982   "Necessary Properties of Relevant Research: Lessons from Recent Criticisms of the Organizational Sciences." Academy of Management Review, 7:3, 345–352.

Tichy, Noel M.
1974   "Agents of Planned Social Change: Congruence of Values, Cognitions and Actions." Administrative Science Quarterly, 19:2, 164–182.

Van de Vall, Mark, Cheryl Bolas, and Tai S. Kang
1976   "Applied Social Research in Industrial Organizations: An Evaluation of Functions, Theory and Methods." Journal of Applied Behavioral Science, 12:2, 158–177.

Van de Ven, Andrew H., and W. Graham Astley
1981   "A Commentary on Organizational Behavior in the 1980's." Decision Sciences, 12:388–398.

Webb, Wilse B.
1961   "The Choice of the Problem." American Psychologist, 16:5, 223–227.

Weber, Max
1968   Economy and Society, 3 vols. New York: Bedminster Press.

PART III

RESEARCH STRATEGIES

20

USABLE KNOWLEDGE FOR
DOUBLE-LOOP PROBLEMS

Chris Argyris

Put simply, implementation means to carry out or to execute some action. This, in turn, means that there is a design or an intention that is to be implemented. The notion that it involves the *discovery* of a problem, then a *design* of a solution, and the taking action to *produce* the solution is not a novel one. The idea of such a process dates back at least to writers such as Dewey.

We have been uncovering some complex and not so obvious features in this process when it is applied to solving double-loop problems. Double-loop problems are those that cannot be solved by simply changing behavior. The solution of a double-loop problem requires the reexamination and changing of underlying values and policies that govern the behavior (see Figure 20.1) (Argyris and Schön, 1974).

The first not so obvious finding developed as we watched individuals attempt to solve double-loop problems. They succeeded at the first phase of double-loop problem solving, namely, discovering the problem. They could design a correct solution. Yet when it came to the third phase—implementing that solution—individuals were unable to produce their designed solutions even if they had enough control over the situation to do so, even if the others involved cooperated, and even if they believed that they had the skills to do so. The second not so obvious feature was that individuals who were exhibiting these discontinuities were unaware of them while they were producing them.

Such findings have important implications for producing usable knowledge to deal with double-loop problems because they occur with a wide

I should like to thank Dianne Argyris, Robert Putnam, and Diana Smith for their helpful comments.

377

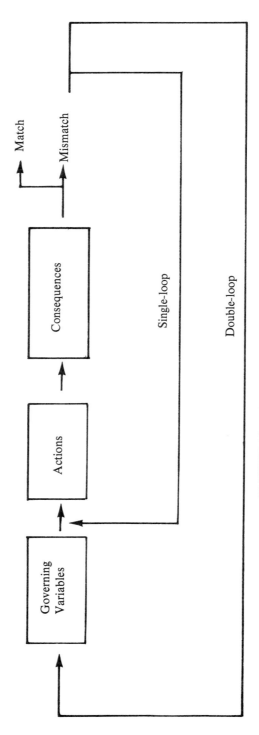

FIGURE 20.1. Single- and Double-Loop Learning

variety of problems, ages, education, organizations, and political contexts. The problem of producing usable information to solve double-loop problems is systematic and widespread. Thus, we can no longer expect to solve such problems without always encountering these difficulties.

The relevant concepts and findings upon which these assertions are based have been published elsewhere (Argyris and Schön, 1974, and 1978; Argyris, 1976b, 1980, 1982b). I will summarize six major conclusions below.

REASONING FOR DISCOVERY AND FOR DESIGN

All human beings reason when they strive to discover problems, to invent solutions or designs, and to take action. The reasoning processes for discovery and design are often different from and inconsistent with the reasoning processes embedded in the action taken.

For example, individuals are given a case where a superior Y attempts to help subordinate X "shape up or ship out." Most individuals consistently diagnose (discover) Y as being blunt and insensitive in trying to help X become a more effective performer. Next, they often design a solution, which is to advise Y to behave with more sensitivity and less bluntly with X in order to minimize X's defensiveness. But when the same individuals attempt to implement their advice with Y (by role playing or in real life example), they act toward Y in precisely the same ways for which they have criticized Y. They do this in two ways: either they behave bluntly and insensitively toward Y or, more likely, in ways that ease-in. The easing-in process may be described as asking questions and being nondirective to help Y discover his ineffectiveness. The difficulty is that the recipients sense that the easing-in covers up negative judgments already made of them. Hence, they feel covertly judged and that these feelings are undiscussable because the other has covered up his or her judgments. The end result is a state of defensiveness and misunderstanding between the players that is precisely what was not advised or designed in the first place (Argyris, 1982a).

The reasoning used during the phases of discovery and design may be described in the form of a microcausal theory.

If Y behaves bluntly and insensitively toward X:

> *then* X will feel defensive,
> *then* there will be little constructive learning.

A heuristic for action that follows is: Y should not behave bluntly and insensitively. He should ease-in in order to minimize X's defensiveness.

However, when we examine the reasoning process embedded in the actual production of the easing-in behavior, we identify two more heuristics. They are:

> Ask questions that, if the other (in this case Y) answered correctly, he would figure out what information is being hidden from him.

> Ask the questions in a way that covers up that negative evaluations of Y are being hidden and cover up the fact that there is a coverup.

Note what happened. The heuristics embedded in the reasoning processes during the discovery and design phases were aimed at reducing defensiveness. The heuristics embedded in the action enhanced defensiveness and made it less likely that it would be discussable.

PROGRAMMED UNAWARENESS COUPLED WITH UNAWARENESS OF THE PROGRAM

Individuals tend to be unaware of these inconsistencies while they are producing them. Our research suggests that they are unaware because: they rarely receive overt feedback on their true impact since most people follow the above heuristics; they hold espoused values such as to be sensitive and supportive so strongly that they tend unrealizingly to distance themselves from their responsibility for violating them; and they have a theory of coping that instructs them to win not lose, to remain in unilateral control which, in turn, leads them to unilaterally blame the other for any misunderstanding and escalating errors that may arise.

Thus, their unawareness is programmed by the basic values they hold and by the coping mechanisms they use to protect themselves.

This means that unawareness does not result from a hole in our knowledge; rather, it results from a program in our heads designed to keep us unaware. These programs have a peculiar feature. If the actors focus on their content, they will be unaware of their function to keep the actors unaware. Thus, if I focus only on how I am trying to be supportive, sensitive, and "in control," then it is unlikely that I will see these features as either counterproductive or keeping me unaware. Indeed, from this perspective if anyone is to be blamed, it should be the other person. After all, it is human nature to be "in control" and how can anyone be against sensitivity?

ESPOUSED THEORIES AND THEORIES-IN-USE

Individuals may be said to hold two kinds of theories of action. First are the theories that they actually use when they act (theories-in-use). Second are the theories that they espouse (espoused theories). When individuals deal with double-loop problems, they appear to be unaware of their theories-in-use and almost always aware of their espoused theories: indeed, they are often invoked when trying to explain why one did what one did. For example, when conversing with Y, individuals often state in one form or another, "It is important to be sensitive to X's feelings and to be supportive," yet individuals do not state, "It is important to withhold my evaluation and ask questions that will lead them to it."

There appears to be a wide variance in the espoused theories that individuals hold and in the behavior that they produce in any given situation. However, when we examined the meanings embedded in their actions, we found very little variance. They are always consistent with theory-in-use that we have called Model I (see Figure 20.2).

REASONING AND CONSTRUCTION OF REALITY

The reasoning individuals use to discover and to design their actions can be described as generating premises and then deriving conclusions from these premises (Popper, 1969). The premises become the world as they construe it (Lewin, 1951; Schutz, 1968). The act of constructing premises and deriving conclusions is quite complex, but often is completed in milliseconds. It appears almost automatic because it has been learned (probably through socialization); hence, it is highly skilled. As such it tends to achieve the intended consequence, it often appears effortless, the actors rarely pay conscious attention to it, and consequently the reasoning that informs it is often tacit.

THE LADDER OF INFERENCE

The reasoning processes individuals use to diagnose and design appear to be ordered along the following ladder of inference (see Figure 20.3). The first rung is the relatively directly observable behavior that individuals have observed or taken into account. The second rung represents the meanings they infer are embedded in the behaviors. These meanings are those that are culturally understood. No special or technical theory is needed to infer these meanings. The third rung is the meanings that the individuals superimpose on the second-level meanings. The theories-in-use begin to take hold here. For example, Y's statement to X that, "Your performance is not up to our standards and unless it is changed, corrective action will have to be taken," is the relatively directly observable datum (rung 1). The culturally acceptable meaning (rung 2) would be, "X, your performance is unacceptable." The

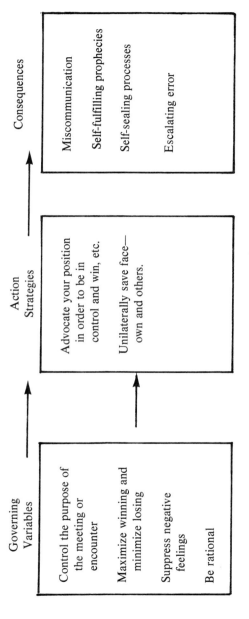

FIGURE 20.2. Model I Theory-in-use

4	Researcher's imposed meanings
3	Respondent's imposed meanings
2	Culturally understood meanings of data
1	Relatively directly observable data

FIGURE 20.3. Ladder of Inference

meaning imposed by the individual trying to help Y, "Y behaved bluntly and insensitively toward X," is rung 3. The fourth rung contains the meanings imposed by the researcher, in our case, Model I theory-in-use meanings.

If our research is correct, all rung 3 meanings should be consistent with Model I (rung 4) and not with some other model.

O-I LEARNING SYSTEMS

To the extent that individuals hold Model I theories-in-use, then they will tend to create conditions that inhibit double-loop learning in any context or organization in which they are embedded. The primary feature of these conditions can be predicted and organized into a pattern of interrelated variables called organizational Model I (O-I) learning system (see Figure 20.4). The consequences of O-I learning systems are to reinforce Model I theories-in-use and the defensive actions associated with them.

RESEARCH METHODS TO PRODUCE IMPLEMENTABLE KNOWLEDGE FOR DOUBLE-LOOP ISSUES

Since practitioners as well as researchers are predisposed to distort and make errors, the propositions should be in a form that practitioners can test publicly what they are doing. In a Model I and O-I world described above, the predisposition for distortion and error is very high. Hence, the normal science requirement for empirical disconfirmability is crucial if we wish to reduce this predisposition to error, thus creating propositions that are usable by human beings in everyday life. Moreover, the propositions should be in the form that practitioners can publicly test what they are doing and the consequences that they are having. Empirical disconfirmability is not only important for the researcher, it is equally important for the practitioner.

The second feature of the knowledge is that it should be organized in ways that make it easy to store and retrieve under on-line conditions. If the knowledge cannot be stored economically and retrieved quickly, it is unlikely that it can be used. This probably means that the knowledge should be

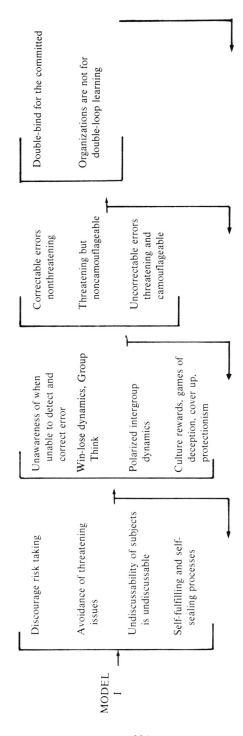

FIGURE 20.4. O–I Learning System

384

packaged in the form of logically interrelated propositions or theories. Other features being equal, the theory that is more comprehensive in coverage yet requires fewer untested assumptions and axioms is the more useful theory.

Readers will no doubt recognize that these are two fundamental requirements for most of normal science. Hence, the basic features of usable knowledge for double-loop issues and those of normal science are the same.

The differences arise in the methodologies that can be used to produce disconfirmable and elegant theories about double-loop issues. The basis for the difference lies in the fact that although normal science espouses valid information, the theory-in-use of rigorous research is consistent with Model I, and hence counterproductive to producing it when dealing with double-loop problems. The researchers are in unilateral control; they strive to win, not lose; they focus on rationality; they deceive whenever they believe it is necessary to do so and act as if they are not doing so (Argyris, 1980).

This means that the research methodology of normal science will not tend to produce results that are different from Model I. If the world is primarily Models I and O-I, and if normal science focuses on describing the world as is, then its results will remain within Models I and O-I. In a review of the literature related to such topics as effective human relationships, leadership, and organization effectiveness, it was found that all the advice derived from rigorous research by social scientists remained within Model I even though the researchers often espoused a model of a world that had liberating features (Argyris, 1970, 1980).

What is needed is a methodology whose governing variables are consistent with empirical disconfirmability and theoretical elegance, yet minimizes some of the counterproductive features of Model I. Illustrations of this methodology have been described in some detail (Argyris, 1980, 1982a).

Stated briefly, the research conditions under which the propositions are obtained include:

First, there should be no requirement that the action scientists have unilateral control over the context of inquiry and the context of applications. The theory developed should be powerful enough that the hypotheses can be disconfirmed with high internal validity, even though the researcher does not have unilateral control. This means the theory should contain variables that are relevant and difficult to fudge openly or covertly.

Second, the research methodology should not require that the context for falsification be benign or supportive of the hypothesis. Internal validity should not be easily threatened because the researcher has little control over the context.

Third, the research methodology should not require that the hypotheses be kept secret from the subjects in order to be rigorously tested. Internal validity should not depend upon secrecy.

For example, on the basis of a simple case format in the X and Y case alluded to above, it is possible to ascertain the degree of Model I-ness of the subjects. It is possible to predict that to the extent the individuals hold a Model I theory-in-use: all the scenarios they write to help Y will be consistent with Model I; all the role playing they do will also be consistent with Model I; and any occasions where they try to solve similar problems in real life, the actions will also be Model I.

Whenever these hypotheses have been put to a test they have not, to date, been disconfirmed. Moreover, this has been true even when the subjects were told the hypotheses ahead of time *and* they insisted that they would not behave as predicted by the researchers (Argyris, 1982).

There are two reasons why the researcher should not require Model I conditions in order to obtain relatively high degrees of internal and external validity. First, Model I research methodologies in a Models I and O-I universe will necessarily produce propositions that cannot be utilized for double-loop learning. Second, all social science propositions intended to be used for action necessarily imply the theory-in-use of the normal science methodology used by the researcher. For example, the proposition "such and such a reinforcement schedule should lead to the following consequences" should include the conditions, "if the relationship between the creator of the schedule on the one hand and the recipient on the other is similar to the relationship of the experimenter who is in unilateral control over the subject."

In short, in order to produce implementable knowledge, the user will necessarily apply the model of whatever substantive theory is involved as well as the model of research methodology with which the knowledge was produced (Argyris, 1968, 1975, 1980). It is necessary therefore that both of these models be consistent with theories-in-use that encourage double-loop learning. One such candidate is Model II (Figure 20.5). It can be used as model for interpersonal, group, and intergroup relationships; for organizational learning systems; and as a research methodology.

It is also necessary to conduct research where the intent is to intervene in ongoing situations to produce double-loop learning. Two categories of such situations are: solving difficult problems within organizations that require reexamination of governing variables as well as actions of the players; and learning environments created within or outside of organizations in order to help individuals learn Model II and create O-II learning systems. An example of the former would be an organization reflecting on why it did not recognize that it had been producing important errors. An example of the

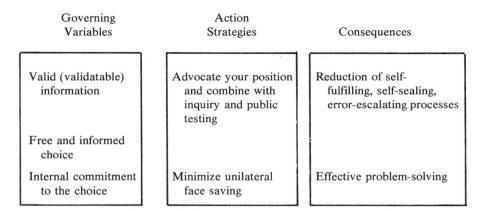

Governing Variables	Action Strategies	Consequences
Valid (validatable) information	Advocate your position and combine with inquiry and public testing	Reduction of self-fulfilling, self-sealing, error-escalating processes
Free and informed choice		
Internal commitment to the choice	Minimize unilateral face saving	Effective problem-solving

FIGURE 20.5. Model II Theory-in-use

latter would be a learning environment to help the players to correct the factors that produced the errors as well as the organization's inability to realize that errors were being produced.

One consequence of such research is that subjects now become clients. They will see themselves in a relationship where the researcher is trying to help them. Could not such a relationship influence the kind of data obtained? Our research suggests that there are no neutral research situations. Normal science or the action science that I am recommending each produces its unique set of dangers to distortion. The resolution is to create conditions where the subjects and the researchers will actively seek to identify intended or unintended distortions (Argyris, 1980, 1982a). When subjects are clients who hope to learn from the data they are generating, they will have an interest in correcting distortions.

IMPLICATIONS FOR USER-FRIENDLY PROPOSITIONS

Since human beings reason when they discover, design, and act by using tacit, causal microtheories, user-friendly propositions should be in the form of causal statements such as, "Under these conditions, if one acts in the following way(s), the following specified consequences should occur. . . . "

Since the purpose of human action is to bring about intended consequences, then a basic question with which they are continuously involved is: How well did they accomplish their intended consequences? This means that the causal propositions described above should be about effectiveness. Effectiveness is defined as creating a match or discovering and correcting a mismatch in such a way that it is possible to continue doing so.

The actions embedded in the propostions should be producible under on-line conditions without the actor requiring a disproportionate control over the natural flow of events. Recalling our ladder of inference, if the propositions are stated in theoretical terms at rung 3 or 4, it should be possible to translate them into relatively directly observable data such as conversation (rung 1). Propositions that cannot be transformed into actual conversations are not applicable.

Propositions such as x and some functions of y are rarely producible by actors under on-line conditions. These propositions are information rich and arrived at only after careful distillation and analyses by researchers. The difficulty is that in order to be used in real life, the actor will probably be faced with an equally complex situation in which distillations and analyses will also be required. But such activities take much time. They require that life's ongoing activities be slowed down or even stopped until the analysis is generated.

Propositions should be storeable and retrievable under everyday life constraints. Elsewhere I have suggested that one of the important values of Lewin's topological drawings is that they may be examples of the kind of maps that are valid for action (Argyris, 1980).

For example, Lewin, Lippitt, and White (1939) describe a topological map (see Figure 20.6) of an authoritarian leader as one who is a gatekeeper. The four subordinates cannot reach their goal without going through the gate. The leader controls the gate and who goes through it. The authors are then able to show that under these conditions the subordinates will tend to become competitive with each other, dependent upon the leader, submissive to the leader's desires, and so forth. Many of the dynamics identified with authoritarian leadership can be coordinated to Figure 20.6. It is easy for the user to store this "dog-bone theory of leadership" and retrieve it quickly. Democratic leadership can be shown graphically by placing the four subordinates at the gate where they now jointly control who goes through and under what conditions.

The correct and overt use of the proposition should make it unlikely that the causal consequences embedded in the propositions should *not* tend to occur.

It is possible to derive action propositions from a series of famous social-psychological experiments in communication that if used correctly and overtly will led to unintended consequences. For example, if the audience is friendly, present one side of the argument. If the audience is

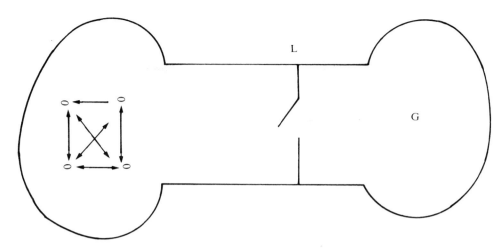

FIGURE 20.6. Lewin's Gatekeeper Concept

composed of individuals who are not very smart, present one side of the argument. If the listeners are smart, present both sides of the argument (Argyris, 1980). It is unlikely that the predictions of effectiveness will occur if those using them were to make these rules public. For example, if they tell the listeners that they will be given one side of the argument because they have been judged as not being very smart, it is unlikely that communication would be effective. It was effective in the experiments because the rules were kept secret.

RESEARCH INSTRUMENTS TO PRODUCE KNOWLEDGE ABOUT DOUBLE-LOOP ISSUES

The first requirement for empirical research is that it must differentiate among actions, espoused theories, and theories-in-use. The questionnaires and interviews most frequently used in research may be valid for espoused theories. Conversations (taped, observed, or recollected) are the basis for inferring theories-in-use.

The X-Y case is an example of a simple instrument that can be used for studying and producing double-loop changes (Argyris, 1982a).

The respondents are able to identify a problem in everyday life that, in their view, is important to their effectiveness, one that requires knowledge and skills they wish to improve.

The respondents are asked to describe the strategy they intend to use to solve the problem, and the reasons behind that strategy. This provides insight into their espoused theories of action.

The respondents then write a scenario of what they said (or would say) when dealing with the problem. On the left-hand side of the page they write any thoughts or feelings they had but did not communicate to the other person. This gives data to infer any discrepancies between espoused theory and action. In our case, it also makes it possible to infer their theory-in-use.

When participants are asked to generate cases from their own experience using the X-Y format, the cases give insight into the issues they presently consider important. Such cases also identify the knowledge and skills they seek to improve and, by implication, those they do not: their espoused theories of action; their theories-in-use; discrepancies among espoused theory, behavior, and theory-in-use; their awareness of such discrepancies; their criteria for effective performance; the way they deal with others; their self-censoring mechanisms; and the second order consequences such as self-fulfilling prophecies, self-sealing processes, and escalating error.

When such cases are generated in a group of people from the same organization, the cases produce rich data about the organizational learning conditions—to what degree they facilitate or inhibit the identification and correction of error. The cases also produce a great deal of data on group conformity, group competitiveness, intergroup rivalries, interorganizational rivalries, and the games people play to protect themselves and survive in the organization.

The second requirement of empirical research is that more attention should be paid to producing models of alternative worlds, including the intervention that could actually enact the new models in the "real" world. Basic research about genuine alternatives must combine description of the world as it is with models of the world as it might be, and should include information about how to get from here to there. This combination cannot be decomposed into the sequence: first explain the world as it is, then design an alternative, then figure out how to get from here to there. For instance, developing the X-Y case required a theory about what was dysfunctional about Models I and O-I. Confronting clients with their inconsistencies effectively requires reasoning and skills that are not derivable from Model I.

Embedded in the first two requirements for empirical research is a third, namely, that basic research in this field must be concerned about effectiveness. Valid propositions about effectiveness, in turn, require normative criteria; hence, we are back to the requirement of normative models of what the world might be.

A fourth requirement of research designed to produce usable knowledge for double-loop learning is to realize that most rigorous quantitative models not only distance the actor from the world of action, but often may disconnect that actor. For example, the early Lewin, Lippitt, and White research (1939) on leadership may have produced more usable heuristics than the more rigorous empirical research that Lewin's colleagues conducted in subsequent years (Argyris, 1980).

It is difficult for many of us to believe that rigor might well be achieved by combining sloppiness with iterative learning in order to produce accurately the consequences we intend. Often we generate explanatory maps that are rigorous and complete, that we admit may not be usable by individuals, and we degrade the maps that they do use.

For example, let us review Naylor, Pritchard, and Ilgen's (1980) recent treatise of human behavior in organizations. Examining the systematic, schematic presentation of their theory, one is impressed by their attempt to produce an ideal map of the relevant variables and their interrelationships, and also by the complexity of this map. The authors are aware of this, and periodically they pause to give comments such as:

> Unfortunately there is an increasing body of evidence indicating that people do not utilize the cognitive system in its pure, or theoretically most effective sense. They tend instead, for one reason or another, to use degraded versions of the system. These degraded judgmental strategies are often simpler ways of dealing with the making of judgments, and are based upon rules, or principles, of simplification that may be intuitively appealing or "logical" to the individual but which may or may not be effective substitution strategies for the entire "pure" process. (p. 110)

What is the evidence that this is a degraded decision tactic? Can it not be an elevating one? I believe their answer would be that the process is degraded because people do not behave according to the authors' ideal descriptive model.

Note the reasoning. Scholars who develop a rigorous, descriptive model, one that probably has not been empirically tested, assert that their model is the correct one to use in the real world; that people would act consistently with it if only they were truly rational (a tacit normative position). The increasing evidence that people do not act consistently with such scholarly models they explain by asserting people degrade their reasoning.

I would like to suggest an alternative hypothesis. People upgrade their reasoning by using heuristics because they have developed vague rules of use that produce accuracy. As Von Neumann (1958) noted years ago, the human mind's effectiveness may be the result of being able to tolerate noise, whereas computers require a more precise calculus and conditions of minimal noise. Under action constraints, it may be most rational to couple vagueness and sloppiness with accuracy through the medium of iterative learning.

DISCONFIRMABILITY OF PROPOSITIONS

We have stated above that all individuals appear to use Model I action strategies such as unillustrated attributions and evaluations or advocacy with neither inquiry nor testing. This suggests that social scientists should focus on predicting the theory-in-use meanings people produce (rung 4) and not on predicting to rungs 1, 2, and 3. The predictions would not be about the actual words but the theory-in-use meanings of these words. The empirical research would have to focus on all the rungs of the ladder, but the predictions would be about the theory-in-use meanings.

For example, a theory of action perspective predicts that if the respondents are programmed with Model I theories-in-use, then what they will write in their diagnoses, say to each other during their discussion, and say in any setting where they are dealing with threatening double-loop issues, will be consistent with Models I and O-I and not with other theories-in-use.

Such a perspective will permit the testing of propositions with anecdotal or conversational data. Now a single sentence or a single case can be shown to be an illustration of predictable features of theory. The test is rigorous in the sense that an a priori prediction can be made as to what meanings will and will not be imposed by the respondents.

We are suggesting that the creation of one sentence, of several sentences, or a thousand sentences is a complicated design act that is informed by a theory-in-use; that there is nothing random about the meanings individuals impose. If we are trying to predict what meanings individuals will or will not include, we must begin with relatively directly observable data (rung 1) and work up to the predicted imposed meanings (rungs 3 and 4). We are then able to state propositions such as the following:

If individuals (ascertained at time T to hold Model I theory-in-use) are faced with a threatening double-loop problem, they will act consistently with Model I theory-in-use, which means:

(a)They will communicate the threatening issues either directly, or by easing in, or in a combination of both approaches.

(b)They will produce the above with Model I behavior strategies (for example, unillustrated evaluations and attributions, advocacy with no inquiry).

This will lead to second-order consequences such as misunderstandings, self-fulfilling prophecies, and self-sealing processes.

Those descriptive propositions can also be formulated in terms of the rules the actors use in their respective theories-in-use. For example:

Whenever I believe what I have to say will make the other person defensive, I should ask those questions through which, if he answers them correctly, he will realize what I am hiding (easing-in).

Whenever the other person reacts defensively, interpret that as evidence that my diagnosis is correct and continue the easing-in approach. Do not test publicly the attribution that the other person is reacting defensively—act as if I do not hold such an attribution.

These findings, whether stated as descriptive propositions or rules for action, are hypothesized to hold whether individuals are reacting to an experiment or to a real-life situation; whether the issues are substantive or interpersonal or whether they gain insight into their impact or not. The only condition is that they have to be double-loop or threatening.

Similar predictions can be made for the organizational context. For example, a group of officers experienced a one-day seminar with the X-Y case. At the end of the day, they identified an area in their business where their learning was directly applicable, namely, the periodic evaluations of top professionals. We predicted that even though they and their subordinates had been exposed to new concepts, they had not learned to translate the new ideas of performance evaluation from espoused theory to theory-in-use. Since the officers and subordinates wanted to continue to learn, all agreed to have the sessions taped, and invited me to attend as an observer. All the sessions began with Model I interactions. I was asked to help them reflect on their actions with the intent of changing them. After several sessions, the clients began to act more competently. Those who did learn to produce Model II behavior have continued to use it over a four-year period, not only in performance evaluations but whenever threatening messages are being communicated (Argyris, 1982a).

Another situation involved top management and the issue of whether to spend time and effort to learn to reason differently—that is, to learn Model II or to put that same effort into the establishment of a new financial system. Management opted for the latter. Later interviews with the officers confirmed that all those who had pushed for the financial change agreed that the Model I competitive, self-protective games continued and that the Model I system did not help to uncover more threatening errors. Indeed, some feared that it would now be even more difficult to overcome such elements because they were so intertwined with the management information system being used.

SUMMARY

We have described a research methodology that combines inquiry and learning; one where the respondents are subjects *and* clients. It is a methodology that can be used to study not only features of the universe as it is, but also to study and to create alternative universes. The propositions are directly usable. They make it possible to go beyond the status quo to create alternative universes. The research setting includes a learning environment for teaching navigation from the present to the alternative universe. The propositions are publicly testable and disconfirmable in real life settings as well as in the learning environment. Indeed, the tests are tougher than those accepted by normal science because people are acting in real situations where they are vulnerable. The propositions can be integrated into elegant theories; that is, theories that require a minimum number of axioms and concepts for maximum comprehension.

REFERENCES

Argyris, Chris, *Reasoning, Learning, and Action: Individual and Organizational*, Jossey-Bass, San Francisco, 1982a.

Argyris, Chris, "Why Individuals and Organizations Have Difficulty Double-loop Learning," in Paul S. Goodman (Ed.), *Organizational Change*, Jossey-Bass, San Francisco, 1982b.

Argyris, Chris, *Inner Contradictions of Rigorous Research*, Academic Press, New York, 1980.

Argyris, Chris, *Increasing Leadership Effectiveness*, Wiley-Interscience. New York, 1976a.

Argyris, Chris, "Single- and Double-loop Models in Research on Decision-making," *Administrative Science Quarterly*, v. 21, 1976b.

Argyris, Chris, *The Applicability of Organizational Sociology*, Cambridge University Press, Cambridge, England, 1970.

Argyris, Chris, "Some Unintended Consequences of Rigorous Research," *Psychological Bulletin*, v. 70, 1968:185–197.

Argyris, Chris, "Dangers in Applying Results from Experimental Social Psychology," *American Psychologist*, v. 30, 1975:469–485.

Argyris, Chris, and Donald Schön, *Organizational Learning*. Addison-Wesley, Reading MA, 1978.

Argyris, Chris, and Donald Schön, *Theory in Practice*, Jossey-Bass, San Francisco, 1974.

Lewin, Kurt, *Field Theory in Social Science*, Harper & Row, New York, 1951.

Lewin, K, R. Lippitt, and R. K. White, "Patterns of Aggressive Behavior in Experimentally Created Social Climates," *Journal of Social Psychology*, v. 10, 1939:271–301.

Naylor, James C., Robert D. Pritchard, and Daniel R. Ilgen, *A Theory of Behavior in Organizations*, Academic Press, New York, 1980.

Popper, Karl R., *Conjectures and Reputations: The Growth to Scientific Knowledge*, Routledge and Kegan Paul, London, 1969.

Schutz, A., *The Phenomenology of the Social World*, Northwestern University Press, Evanston, IL, 1968.

Von Neumann, J., *The Computer and the Brain*, Yale University Press, New Haven, 1958.

21

INSTITUTIONAL DYNAMICS OF ACTION RESEARCH

Noel M. Tichy and Stewart D. Friedman

We are interested in keeping action research alive and well. We adhere to the Lewinian notions that the best way to understand a social phenomenon is to try and change it and that the best theories are useful ones. It is through the collaborative efforts of academicians and practitioners in organizations that an advance in scientific knowledge about organizations can be and should be made. But, for maturation of our still young science of organizational studies to continue, we must take heed of the forces that foster and those that inhibit action research endeavors.

THE CASE FOR ACTION RESEARCH

Action research involves the creation and refinement of theory based on the application of theoretical principles of organizational science in an effort to alter a social system. More specifically, an action research endeavor, according to French and Bell (1973),

> is the process of systematically collecting research data about an ongoing system relative to some objective, goal, or need of that system; feeding these data back into the system; taking actions by altering selected variables within the system based both on the data and on hypotheses; and evaluating the results of actions by collecting more data. (pp. 84–85)

There are two primary reasons why this type of research is a necessity for our field. First, tests of utility of methods and theories about organiza-

We are indebted to Stanley E. Seashore for his enlightening remarks on an earlier draft of this chapter, yet we retain responsibility for the material presented herein.

tional behavior must occur in organizations. Ideas that germinate in nonorganizational contexts may appear useful but may prove to be otherwise. The use of T-groups, for example, as a means to develop greater self-awareness in organization members was not as successful in effecting organizational change as its early proponents had hoped. T-groups were known to have desirable outcomes for most participants. However, the theory and practice of T-groups were based on experiences with unstructured groups having no ongoing organizational affiliations. For members of work organizations, the beneficial effects of T-group experiences did not last long after the laboratory training was over. The cultures of most organizations, immersed as they were in the culture of the greater society and subject to the overriding exigencies of the day-to-day business world, were generally unsupportive of the behavior learned in the T-group. As a result, T-groups were ultimately considered by most to be inappropriate for organizational applications. The conclusion that T-groups have limited utility is itself an instance of learning that obtains from useful action research: Knowledge about T-groups and about organizations was gained by evaluation of efforts to effect change. The usefulness of theories and methods pertaining to organizations must be tested inside these realms. Unfortunately, because of the paucity of well-supported and well-done action research, there is not much that is currently useful to work organizations from the field of organizational science.

The second reason bears on the need for researchers to observe organizational phenomena as nonmembers in order to create and refine their theories about organizations. Nonmember status grants the required objectivity for dispassionate analysis; being in and around organizations stimulates theorizing and refinement of theory. Perhaps the most successful example of this kind of discovery of theory in organizational reality was Trist and Bamforth's (1951) experience in the British coal mines in the late 1940s. Sociotechnical systems theory, which has enjoyed successful applications in many spheres, arose from their work in a live organizational setting. Freud's pioneering work in psychoanalysis, a kindred field wherein a theory of human behavior is applied to human problems, evolved continuously because of new insights gained from his clinical practice. Freud was foremost a scientist; he saw patients primarily because it was only by applying his theory that he could derive corrections and reformulations to it.

In addition to these two arguments—that utility must be tested in organizations and that observation is critical in generating and refining theory—we refer here to Susman and Evered (1978), who show how the philosophical underpinnings of action research differ from those of "positivist science." The positivist model, they suggest, is useful for the physical and biological sciences but not for organizational science. As a basis for the generation of useful knowledge for organizations, positivist science is not appropriate because it:

Assumes its methods are value neutral;

Treats persons as "objects of inquiry even though they are subjects or initiators of action in their own right";

Does not include historical forces in its analyses;

Considers intuition, hunches, interpretations, and so forth, as beyond its legitimate domain; and

Assumes that knowledge about the scientists and their world view is not pertinent to an understanding of how knowledge is generated.

Action research takes the opposite view. Susman and Evered view it as a corrective to the positivist approach. Action research, they say, is appropriate for generating useful knowledge because it:

Is future oriented—people are seen as goal-directed, purposive;

Is collaborative—the researcher is not a distanced observer; rather the researcher is viewed as a person whose own ethics and values ought to be clear and explicit;

Implies system development (see Bowers, this volume)—it encourages the client organization to become an independent, problem-solving entity in its own right;

Generates theory grounded in action; and

Is situational—definition by the actors of the context in which action occurs is a prerequisite to the successful link between plans and intended outcomes.

This contraposition of positivist science and action research is similar to the distinction between two conceptions of valid and useful data described by Seashore (1976). The two conceptions, exemplified in the works of Argyris and of Campbell, are viewed by Seashore as contrasting yet complementary. "Each of the opposites," he says, "can contribute in ways that the other cannot to scientific enterprise" (p. 115). There are tradeoffs with either approach. In any particular case, the strengths and weaknesses of each ought to be weighed in light of the overall fit of the research design. There is variety in types of scientific contribution, in client demands, and in the kinds of data needed to achieve the ends of science and of social action. Awareness of the varieties augments the likelihood of optimal choices being made in each case of action research.

To advance organizational science, Runkel and McGrath's (1972) suggestion for a "balanced" research strategy ought to be followed. In this approach, more than one research method is used—including laboratory experiment, sample survey, simulation, observation, and action research—with the choice of method made to exploit the strengths and weaknesses of each (for example, degrees of objectivity attainable by the researcher). An action research effort may best contribute knowledge in the context of a larger, programmatic set of research projects. McGrath's (1964) advice on the "logical path for programmatic research" is an idealized course to follow; nevertheless, we ought to select research methods and settings on the basis of their applicability to the stage of theoretical advance at which we find ourselves. Therefore, the action research mode should be an integral part of a balanced research strategy for developing knowledge about organizations.

TECHNICAL, POLITICAL, AND CULTURAL FACTORS IN ACTION RESEARCH

We will present the forces for and against action research using a tripartite framework of organizations. For analytical purposes, we trisect organizations according to their technical, political, and cultural subsystems; these are concerned with three core dilemmas, respectively (Tichy, 1982, 1983).

The first dilemma is the *technical design problem*. Here, the organization faces a production problem; social and technical resources must be arranged so that the organization produces some desired output. Second is the *political allocation problem*, the problem of allocating power and resources. The uses to which the organization will be put, as well as who will reap the benefits from the organization, must be determined. The third is the *ideological and cultural mix problem*. As social tools, organizations are, in part, held together by normative glue, by the sharing of certain important beliefs by its members. Awareness of these beliefs—how they form, develop, and affect behavior—is an essential ingredient in the design and control of organizations.

All three dilemmas are ongoing problems because organizations are always experiencing shifts and change. These three problems are viewed as systems of interrelated sets of components, each organized around a coherent logic. The technical system includes the interrelationship of all those elements required to deal with the production problem. The political system includes all the practices, activities, and elements used to work on the allocation problem. The cultural system involves the symbols, values, and elements organized to address the dominant ideology problem. In the remainder of this chapter, technical, political, and cultural will refer to factors related to these three systems in both work organizations and academic institutions.

Technical, political, and cultural forces impinge on the conduct of action research from the point of view of the host organization and of the academic/research institution in which the researcher is based. We examine these forces in turn.

TABLE 21.1. Forces for and against Action Research in the Host Organization

Force	For	Against
Technical	• Change efforts can add value to the bottom line. • Evaluation of change leads to greater awareness of best ways to manage.	• Control groups difficult to employ. • Measurement difficulties. • Development needed in staff skills.
Political	• Information is power; can be used by coalitions to advance positions. • Allocation of resources based on research, not politics.	• Costs may be high. • Rewards are for profit and for short term. • Action researcher loses objectivity; overadvocacy.
Cultural	• Japanese influence toward greater experimentation. • Contribution to society; good citizenship.	• Macho image of home run hitter. • Quick fix mentality.

The Host Organization's Perspective

In the technical sphere, the major force in favor of action research is that change efforts can add value to the bottom line (see Table 21.1). The introduction of quality circles, for example, may lead to modifications in operating procedure that reduce cost. By examining such projects with action research methodology, the extent of the value can be assessed with some accuracy. The organization can obtain knowledge about itself and about how to improve itself via the evaluation of planned change. However, there are difficulties in the measurement of change; ethical and pragmatic obstacles to using control groups; and a lack of research skills in most organizations. These forces deter the conduct of useful action research.

Politically, the information obtained in action research projects can be a very powerful leverage point. Any information that implies a shift in an organization's priorities will have political consequences for stakeholders. For some, the dissemination of such information may mean an opportunity to enlarge their domain of control; for others, it may indicate the opposite. To the extent that action research brings to light the need for reallocation of resources based on a valid assessment of the current state relative to some objective, and not only on political considerations, it serves well the interests of the organizations. The political forces operating in the host organization against the conduct of valid research are: the costs may be high; the reward system in most organizations is for short-term profits—results from many action research projects are long-term and difficult to quantify; and the action researcher, because he or she may be paid by the client, is in danger of overadvocating his or her position, thus biasing the conclusions drawn from the research. Biased research may be worse than none at all for the client to use in guiding policy decisions.*

The cultural factors supporting action research in client organizations are: the influence of Japanese management is forcing a reevaluation of our traditionally nonresearch-oriented approach to change—the notion of the "experimenting organization" (Staw, 1977) may be the norm for U.S. managers in the coming years; if action research can serve the interests of society as well as the company in which it is conducted, then the company is seen as making a contribution to the greater good. For many firms, this meets their stated philosophy of being "good citizens." The primary cultural factor acting against action research is the typical U.S. corporate image of the "macho man" who takes the ball and runs with it. This attitude is contrary to one in which the measurement and assessment of incremental changes guides future action. The mentality of the "quick fix" pervades corporate culture. Impatience for results—fast solutions—tends to be the American style. The aspects of organizations in which action researchers intervene often demand a long-term perspective. Organizational cultures, the subject of many action research change efforts, take a long time to evolve and a long time to modify. In product development the stages of research and evaluation can be mapped out in a relatively clear manner since the criteria for success are "hard" (such as sales volume). Not so for elements of organizational life such as leadership, communication, or commitment. These are phenomena with "soft," fuzzy definitions and comparatively weak operational grounding. Some aspects of U.S. industry may be conducive to research, but when the focal subject is human behavior and the time perspective is long, the interest of policy leaders in controlled research is difficult to retain.

The Academic/Research Institution's Perspective

In the technical sphere, the primary force that encourages action research is that it provides opportunities to study theoretical propositions about organizations (see Table 21.2). Experience in field settings is a

---

*The political implications of an action research project ought to be recognized explicitly by the researcher and by the organization. The action researcher is faced with an intense and complex set of ethical problems because complete knowledge of who is at risk and of the forces at play cannot be gained (see Mirvis and Seashore, 1976 for a discussion of these dilemmas).

TABLE 21.2. Forces for and against Action Research in the Academic/Research Institution

Force	For	Against
Technical	<ul><li>Opportunities to test hypotheses, to generate theory.</li><li>Applied fields require immersion in "real life" settings.</li></ul>	<ul><li>Field skills not taught well in graduate schools.</li><li>Methods of research ingrained.</li></ul>
Political	<ul><li>Sponsors more sophisticated, wider market.</li><li>Field-tested theories more useful, applicable.</li></ul>	<ul><li>Rewards are for short term.</li><li>Organization's control of results may introduce bias.</li></ul>
Cultural	<ul><li>Contribution to society.</li><li>Heritage of action research growing.</li></ul>	<ul><li>Applied work is "selling out."</li><li>Academes and corporate executives have different styles representing different cultures.</li></ul>

precondition for the generation of ideas about how organizations function. In applied fields such as ours, immersion in the phenomena in "real life" settings is required, at least for some of us. However, since field skills are generally not well taught in our graduate programs, where instead the emphasis is on different academic concerns, the cadre of well-trained action researchers remains relatively small. Another problem is that particular methods of research tend to be ingrained in certain schools of thought; action research calls for a versatility and range of capabilities on the part of the researcher. Flexibility is needed because the researcher does not always know what demands or opportunities will emerge during the action. Also, in collaborating with practitioners the researcher forfeits to others some control over the methods he or she wishes to employ.

Among the political forces encouraging action research are: first, sponsors in the private sector now have more sophistication about action research. For many, this sophistication brings with it knowledge of the value of action research. Hence a wider, more receptive market exists for action researchers. Second, the field of organizational studies has achieved some theoretical advances. Action research can bring us closer to more useful applications as well as refine our theories. The more useful and clear the potential applications, the greater the likelihood of continued support for action research. Political forces against action research are: first, rewards for academics tend to be short-term oriented (for example, promotion decisions must be made within a short time span; "publish or perish" inhibits longitudinal research reporting); and second, if private industry is paying for the research, then they own the results. As we noted above, ownership of the data by anyone but the researcher may introduce a bias in drawing conclusions from the research. For the academic institution this is clearly an obstacle to the accumulation of knowledge.

The cultural factors supporting action research are: first, it meets the needs of some social scientists to produce knowledge that enhances the life quality of the community-at-large; and second, some academics have developed the entrepreneurial style necessary to garner support for action research projects. The legitimacy of consultative relationships between researchers and organization members has gained wider acceptance throughout academe. Thus, there is a heritage of action research that can be nurtured within the academic community. On the other hand, there are those who feel that to be associated with applications of science is to be impure. Basic research, unconfounded by the vagaries of "real life," is extolled in many academic circles; selling out is not. Also, academicians in many cases have a different style in their work lives than do most corporate executives; the respective cultures of business and academe often clash.

TYPES OF INSTITUTIONAL ARRANGEMENTS FOR ACTION RESEARCH

For organizations and for academic/research institutions there is variation in the arrangements made for the conduct of action research. We examine the differences in approach below.

Host Organizations

Organizations can assume one of five orientations vis-à-vis the evaluation and monitoring of change. Each one has a set of technical, political, and cultural tradeoffs associated with it. These are summarized in Table 21.3.

Informal Anecdotal Orientation

This is probably the most frequently found approach in U.S. corporations. There is little technical sophistication required on the part of those collecting information. Information is picked up via members' observations—anecdotes told in very informal meetings are how data are trans-

TABLE 21.3. Generic Orientations to Evaluating and Monitoring Organizational Change

Type of Orientation	Trade-Offs		
	Cultural	*Political*	*Technical*
	Depth of Commitment to Systematic Evaluation	*Risk and Commitment of Resources*	*Sophistication and Capability*
	High	*High*	*High*
Basic Research and Development	↑	↑	↑
Experimenting Intervention Orientation			
Guidance System Orientation			
Managerial Audit Orientation			
Informal Anecdotal Orientation	↓	↓	↓
	Low	Low	Low

mitted. There are minimal political risks and the commitment to evaluation is low since nothing formal is going on. Obviously, this orientation is associated with a cultural value that does not place high value upon systematic evaluation and monitoring.

Managerial Audit Orientation

The audit approach is one that is fairly common to organizations. Management makes some effort to stand back and assess what is going on; it audits its own activities. An example of such a process might be periodic review meetings where managers are asked to summarize what they are doing in a particular area and then evaluate the plusses and minuses. One company has been using this approach in its quality of work life (QWL) effort. The company has over 500 quality circles, gainsharing experiments, new training and development activities, and the like. Periodic review meetings are held by senior management at which business managers present what they are doing in the QWL area. An attempt is then made to critique what is going on. This differs from the guidance system approach (see below), which includes systematic measurement and evaluation. Technically, the audit approach requires a different kind of sophistication. Political risks and commitments are not critical because the managers themselves control what they bring to the review sessions. They can, and usually do, color their reports to support what the power figures want. The depth of cultural commitment to evaluation is low because there is a great deal of distortion and the information is quite informal under these conditions.

Guidance System Approach

The guidance system approach differs from the following one in that systematic data are used to guide an overall change strategy, but it does not include experimental variations to learn how different things might work under different conditions. For example, a company decides to undergo a major QWL effort. Instead of experimenting in some of its plants first, it may launch the program in all its plants, starting with a survey and some other data-collection techniques, and then using the information over time to guide the change effort to see what changes have occurred or have not occurred, making adjustments based on the data. But there would not be an effort made to vary the types of interventions, thereby employing a quasi-experimental design. The guidance system approach calls for a moderate degree of technical sophistication; the use of tools like surveys and other systematic data-collection techniques is often used. Politically, there is a moderate number of risks and commitment of resources needed. By making the measurement of change somewhat systematic, it is easier for people to become visible and to be held accountable. Culturally, it must be an organization that values having systematic data put on the table to examine as the change process unfolds.

In many ways the guidance system approach has similarities to other control systems found in organizations in the production and the financial area. There is one major cultural difference: many of these systems are set up to catch or forestall mistakes; the guidance system approach is only viable where the predominant reason is *not* to catch mistakes, and then punish them, but to assess errors in judgment and then to problem-solve and learn from them. Punitive control systems may be appropriate in some highly structured, routinized contexts. In an organizational change activity, however, it is inevitable that there will be conditions and actions that appear harmful; the issue is how to learn from them. Thus, there must be a cultural value that supports evaluation of action in the absence of fear. This is like the learning and adjustment identified by Pascale and Athos (1981) in Japanese organizations that allow them to make strategic accommodations. For example, Toyota introduced a car model in its early days in the United States, and the product was unsuccessful. But the organization had the capability for learning. The prevailing norms were not to punish those responsible; rather, the norms supported fact-finding, learning, and replanning.

Experimenting Intervention Orientation

The experimenting intervention orientation and the basic R&D approach (following) are the two preferred types of action research. These two differ in degree rather than substance. They both require a fairly high technical sophistication, a fairly high political risk and commitment of resources from the organization, and a fairly high cultural value commitment to systematic evaluation and monitoring. The major difference is that the basic R&D orientation requires the organization to put aside separate resources and protected environments to experiment and examine phenomena related to organization and management change, whereas the experimenting intervention orientation requires that measurement be done around naturally occurring change in the organization.

The history of Volvo's efforts in the quality of work life (QWL) area is an example of a company that had an experimenting intervention orientation to change. In the late 1960s there was a number of experiments done on job rotation and job enrichment, and a limited amount on teamwork. Each of these experiments was extensively measured and there was a commitment to evaluate and assess what had been learned. Furthermore, different interventions were tried in different groups so that they were done as quasi-experiments, with explicit attention given to having some control groups. By the early 1970s the QWL effort at Volvo had been expanded. There was even a new assembly plant designed from the ground floor up at Kalmar, where workers, union, management, and staff people participated in an innovative design of the production system. Throughout this effort there was an experimenting mode of work. Measurements were taken on both the people-side and the productivity-side as the plant was opened and the innovations were implemented. Some things were tried one way, and then another way with systematic measurement to help determine what were the best ways of proceeding. Ultimately, this line of activity, including the transformation of plants like the Skovda Engine plant, moved Volvo toward the model of semi-autonomous work groups and the sociotechnical system as a way of life. The evolution of this approach, however, took a ten-year period in which the basic orientation of Volvo could be described as an experimenting intervention orientation.

Basic Research and Development Orientation

This approach is one in which the organization is committed to approaching organizational change in the same way one approaches good research and development on a product: that is, there is systematic testing and evaluation of the change as it unfolds. This includes doing experiments to determine different ways of accomplishing change goals. It could involve setting up special laboratory-like conditions to test out new concepts and ideas. An example of this might be the General Foods' Topeka plant, which was set up as a prototype or model. The Topeka plant ended up being a very successful experiment in the short run, showing how innovative, socio-technical design of new plants could lead to high productivity and high satisfaction among the employees. It succeeded technically but failed due to political and cultural dynamics. As an R&D activity, it did not contribute to strategic, long-term change at General Foods (Walton, 1975).

In looking at this failure, we can better understand the conditions needed to create a basic R&D orientation in a company. From a traditional point of view, the General Foods' Topeka example did work. They had the necessary technical expertise to treat the plant as an experiment from which they could learn and derive principles for dissemination to other parts of the organization. Where it ran into trouble—where it was counter to the General Foods organization—was in the cultural and political area. Politically, problems were created because other plants and other plant managers became jealous. A disproportionate amount of attention and resources went to this plant, which made the other plants resentful and competitive. There was pressure to either do things better than Topeka or to isolate it and make it into an aberration. The latter course was taken, thus politically preventing dissemination in other plants. The others did not have to copy the change. Furthermore, there was not the political support at high levels of management for treating this as an experiment. Therefore, the plant became isolated and seen as a nontraditional, alien appendage.

The political problems were clearly linked to cultural ones. The culture did not value treating organizational change as an R&D activity; rather, you either made a policy to do something one way or you did not. The result was that those who supported the Topeka plant had to overadvocate it as a panacea, thus threatening the more traditional plants. There was not a culture that enabled them to problem-solve and sort out what worked and what did not, and how to apply lessons to other parts of the company. As a result of these political and cultural forces, they lost the opportunity to conduct meaningful R&D on approaches to managing plants that are in the General Foods network.

The ideal basic R&D orientation will occur in an organization where: there is the technical sophistication represented in the General Foods example; there is a deep cultural commitment to conducting R&D on organizational innovations and changes; and there is an alignment of the political structures that allows people to take risks, fail, learn from mistakes, and ultimately develop new orientations. Such political and cultural orientations are very difficult to create. To our knowledge, there is no company we would currently categorize as having a basic R&D orientation to organization and management.

Even though the set of organizations having or willing to have an action research orientation toward evaluating and monitoring organizational change activities is small, we predict that as we move through the turbulent 1980s, where increasingly organizations face major transformations, the set will enlarge. The extent to which this occurs will depend, in part, on the role academics take in encouraging more collaborative action research.

Academic/Research Institutions

Action research calls on the academician to be a researcher and a practitioner. These two roles demand different skills for their successful fulfillment. The skills of the researcher and those of the practitioner are rarely found in the same person at the same level of excellence. Hence, an often useful approach is to conduct action research collaboratively, in teams, with members who have complementary skills. Academic/research institutes that allow for project teams to be formed of one or more members at any point in time will facilitate action research.

A MODEL AND SOME GUIDELINES FOR AN INSTITUTIONAL BASE FOR ACTION RESEARCH

We have tried to clarify some of the technical, political, and cultural forces that make it difficult to conduct action research in academic settings. In spite of these forces, there are some research institutes that have been able to sustain a long-term commitment to action research. In England, the Tavistock Institute has more than 30 years of experience in action research that has resulted in many contributions to organization theory. The Tavistock Institute is not part of a university system and thus is more akin to what has occurred in the United States in other social science fields, namely, a Brookings Institute or a Center for Policy Research. These provide one type of model, but one that does not have as much viability as a university-based one.

One university-based model that may be better suited to U.S. settings is that of the Institute for Social Research (ISR) at the University of Michigan. It too has over 30 years of experience in research on organizations, much of this being action research. Through the works of such ISR staff as David Bowers, Cortlandt Cammann, Basil Georgopoulis, Robert Kahn, Daniel Katz, Edward Lawler, Rensis Likert, Stanley Seashore, and Arnold Tannenbaum, and the scores of Ph.D students trained under their auspices, ISR has been a major force in shaping the field of organizations studies.

Before continuing with ISR as a model, some background is required. We are not proposing that ISR as a total entity is replicable, nor is it necessary to contemplate such an undertaking to accomplish action research aspirations. ISR is a large social and behavioral science research center within the University of Michigan. It has an annual research volume of over

$12 million and a senior research staff of between 80 and 100, with an additional support staff and research assistant staff of around 200. There are multiple centers within the institute focusing on different problems and disciplines including behavioral economics, political studies, organization behavior, group dynamics and others. ISR generates its own research funding with slight aid from a university subsidy. This provides a great deal of autonomy, but at the cost of giving up security.

The part of ISR we will focus on is the organization behavior group, made up of between eight and twelve principal researchers. The number varies from year to year depending on projects and commitments of faculty to their various academic departments. Most ISR staff hold joint appointments in academic departments ranging from 20 percent to 80 percent of their time. Because ISR is a separate entity at the University of Michigan, its members wear two hats. The chairs or deans of academic departments or professional schools are parallel to the director of ISR. As we shall point out, this is an important element in why action research is able to thrive at ISR.

At ISR the persistent attempts to conduct research using a variety of approaches—including action research—have been largely, but not completely, successful. The technical, political, and cultural conditions that encourage these efforts at ISR and the potential lessons for other academic settings desiring to foster this type of research arrangement are presented below.

Technical Factors. Because ISR's mission, strategy, and structure are all focused on research, it has an infrastructure in place with state-of-the-art capabilities in field interviewing, sampling, data management, accounting for complex research funding arrangements, publication facilities, as well as a cadre of graduate research assistants from the business school, oranizational psychology, social psychology, and sociology. The freestanding nature of ISR within the University of Michigan reduces conflicting goals for the institute in terms of teaching versus research. However, while ISR does not offer courses or degrees, and in that sense has no students, it still lives with a strain between optimizing research effectiveness and aiding the production of competent scholars and researchers.

Another significant technical factor is physical space. ISR has its own six-story building, which houses all of its staff. It provides a self-contained unit that fosters interaction, integration, and a sense of permanence. This sense of physical and technical permanence provides an important momentum to research.

Technical implications for other academic institutions desiring to foster action research include the importance of: creating a self-contained unit with a clear research mission and nonconflicted goals; permanent research support staff committed to the mission of the unit; and physical space to house the activities of the unit.

Political Factors. The ISR-based action researcher must acquire funding by way of grants and contracts with external agencies (public or private). Financial security is affected not by the decisions of department chairpersons as it is by the researcher's own ability to acquire research grants. As a result, the researcher, buffered from many internal academic pressures, has a great deal of autonomy and hence power. The link to the academy is not in terms of funding, but in terms of collegial interaction. This reward system encourages entrepreneurship, yet it comes with a political cost: security. ISR tenure, as to salary, is limited to whatever operating reserves ISR is able to accumulate and maintain. One can survive for a time without "covering" oneself, but not for too long. On the other hand, once a research scientist has acquired funding at ISR, there is greater time to do research as it does not conflict with teaching, which is not done at ISR. As to the researcher's academic freedom that comes with tenure, political intrusions have been successfully fought.

With this as the political backdrop, let us focus on a few of the specific political factors that make ISR function effectively. First, there is reduced conflict between opposing goals such as those of teaching versus research found in most departments. This conflict is especially relevant to business schools that derive their revenues from large numbers of MBAs who require a great deal of faculty attention. Second, resource allocation conflicts are moderated. In teaching academic departments there is often a crunch around secretarial, duplicating, and support services with teaching taking priority. At both the Columbia Business School and the Michigan Business School, secretarial resources are given first priority to teaching needs; research is second place. Not only is the support staff not expert in research activities, they are given conflicting priorities adding to the hassle level of researchers. Third, ISR is self-contained politically. It has its own funding base and buys the time of the faculty from academic departments or, as is the case for the majority of the ISR senior staff, the academic departments buy time from the staff whose primary base is IRS. The other side of this coin is security. All ISR support and faculty research time is carried on soft money. The researcher must be sufficiently entrepreneurial to operate in this environment.

Political implications for other settings include creating a unit that: has research as its primary goal, allowing the allocation of scarce resources to reflect unambiguously this priority; and is politically self-contained so that researchers' time can be protected to do research. The explicit accounting of researchers' time necessary to operate such a unit also puts pressure on the individual researcher to be productive. Teaching demands are not a legitimate excuse for not delivering on one's research commitments, as the research unit does not have teaching goals. One can visibly and explicitly succeed or fail in two separate arenas, research and teaching. The price to be paid for such a system is loss of security on the part of faculty. This is tempered some by appointments in which the faculty's home base is in an academic department where the individual may have subsidized, "hard money" tenure even though a major fraction of their annual time is allocated to ISR work.

Cultural Factors. The culture of ISR reflects its historically bound tradition of producing useful knowledge. The founding fathers of ISR were of one mind in acknowledging the ethical imperative incumbent on social scientists to work for the betterment of humankind. Since action research is often a collaborative venture, among researchers as well as with clients, the norms that encourage joint endeavors at ISR fit with the needs of the organization behavior field. Rensis Likert was well known to foster "supportive relationships" among colleagues. This attitude prevails at ISR today and is deeply embedded in the culture. To conduct research of the highest quality, to be able to work cooperatively or alone, to do problem-centered research in a way that advances science, and to serve society are the values that dominate the ISR culture. They are fully congruent with the values underlying action research in its various modalities.

Cultural implications for other settings include having: a value position regarding the role of social science research in contributing to the solution of real world problems; and a set of norms supportive of collegial cooperation and collaboration. This culture needs to be enacted via the leadership of several key individuals who can act as role models.

In sum, the technical, political, and cultural factors at play at ISR mutually reinforce each other to provide an environment that fosters action research. The implications for other settings are not to try and replicate ISR, but to set up structures that create the technical, political, and cultural conditions suited to their own setting. One example of such an endeavor is the Center for Effective Organizations at the University of Southern California, which former ISR member Edward Lawler has established. It is a good example of a small-scale ISR that meets most of the technical, political, and cultural conditions identified above (see Lawler in this volume). Such units provide the environment for action research. An example of a typical action research project is presented below. It is the type of project easily carried out at ISR, but one that would be extremely difficult to contemplate in a traditional academic department.

A Case Example

The following is a description of an action research project that, from the client organization's perspective, can be considered as an instance of the experimenting intervention orientation. From the academic/research institution's viewpoint, it is a collaborative effort that is confronting both theoretical and "real life" organizational problems.

In a study currently under way at ISR, three senior research scientists, along with three graduate students, are studying a quality of work life program. In three plants of a multiplant paper products corporation, a survey of attitudes (a version of the Michigan Organizational Assessment [MOA] created at ISR) was administered in fall 1981 for two reasons: to use as a baseline indicator against which to measure change, and to inform the efforts of the consultants (non-ISR staff) who were to guide the action. Following the survey administration and feedback, which was conducted by a pair of ISR team members at each site (one senior person, one graduate student research assistant), the change agents employed by the firm entered and began their work. There were three change agents: one worked one site; the other two collaborated on the other two sites. The survey data guided the change effort, but to varying degrees at the different locations.

Throughout the past year ISR has been monitoring events at each site by way of weekly telephone interviews with key people in the plants. We have also been receiving archival data (such as presentation handouts, attendance records) from the sites. In fall 1982 a second survey, as well as personal interviews and observations, were carried out by ISR to assess the changes and attitudes resulting from the program and to guide its future development. These data will be part of the information base that a corporate steering committee will draw on to decide whether or not the pilot program at the three locations ought to be expanded to include other plants. In addition to the surveys, the corporate group will have the reports of the ISR evaluation and monitoring team, documentation provided by the plants and by the change agents, as well as their own impressions formed during site visits and through informal contacts with key players.

Here then is a classic case of a data-based change program. It is an instance of experimenting intervention. Results of the pilot study in the three plants will play a large part in determining how best to employ change techniques in the other 37 plants of the company. Yet the data from the ISR surveys and interviews will serve not only the interests of the client; they are the stuff from which scientific contributions to organization theory are currently being generated. At the time of the first survey, the ISR team developed a set of approximately 20 research questions for use as a framework for coding and analyzing the data. For each question or topic (such as role of the plant manager, effects of external forces, and outcomes of the program) we consider its technical, political, and cultural aspects separately. The change effort will be evaluated in terms of these three factors. It is hoped that our analysis will provide some insight into the dynamics of organizational change.

The above case is offered as an illustration of how the ISR structure supports action research endeavors. The first contact with the client was initiated by the client. A representative of the organization, aware of ISR's work in the QWL area, expressed an interest in pursuing such a program. This occurred in 1978. An ISR research scientist, after a brief, initial diagnosis, told the client that the organization was not yet ready to engage in a QWL activity, not until it had dealt with significant problems in its pay system. The client agreed and requested a reevaluation of the organization's readiness for a project about two years later. Negotiations with senior ISR staff took place, and a contract was agreed on.

For ISR, the responsibilities were: to suggest potential change agents, who would be cleared by the corporation; to collect and feed back survey data at T_1, T_2, and T_3; to monitor progress at each site; to meet regularly with the corporate steering committee as advisors to the project; and to report findings and to make recommendations regarding the dissemination of QWL activities throughout the corporation. To accomplish these tasks, the ISR research scientists formed a team that consisted of two faculty from the Graduate School of Business Administration (one of whom has a joint appointment at ISR and the Graduate School of Business Administration) and one research scientist at ISR. In addition, three students from the doctoral program in organizational psychology were hired as assistants. Administrative support staff, including clericals, accountants, and data managers, were signed on to the project as well. The structure of ISR made it a relatively easy task to form this team and to assure its continuity over a projected three- to five-year study. By contracting with change agents external to ISR, the research effort assumed a relatively objective stance. Some of the studies in the QWL series at ISR have followed this model: research team, change agent, and client remain autonomous though interdependent entities.

The research instruments (T_1 and T_2 surveys) were designed with the participation of the client organization, which also signed off on the research topics that were decided on after T_1. Many of the survey items (drawn from the MOA) have been used in similar projects conducted by ISR. The data from this project thus build on an ever-expanding data set that has become a most valuable resource for researchers in our field. Numerous and varied theories of organizational life can be, and have been, brought under empirical scrutiny with these data.

The project will affect the client organization and its technical system by the introduction of a program that may well lead to productivity gains and improved worker satisfaction. If the opposite result obtains, the organization will have learned that such a program may not be a wise investment for the future. In either case, learning will occur. Politically, the project may become a platform on which certain key players can argue for more control in directing the corporation's future. On the contrary, some may lose power if the project they backed is deemed a failure. Culturally, the very initiation of a QWL project indicates at least a sense that the company's values may need examination if not alteration. The implied move toward a more participative style of management is encouraged by the project's methods and aims.

From ISR's viewpoint, the opportunity to examine in depth a change effort at three separate sites, with two distinct change agent approaches, using refined research tools comparable to other studies, is quite a boon. In addition to enriching the data bank, this project provides a training experience for students with some background in the area. Politically, the ability to draw support from the private sector is crucial in these hard economic times. As the theory and practice of organizational behavior matures, the likelihood of attracting further support increases: proven theories and their methods are more attractive to clients than new, untested ideas about organizational change. Culturally, the project reinforces the norm of doing service to society. But the service component to the project stands in conflict with the research component. Still, the effort to foster more participative management styles with ISR's historical concern for improving the effectiveness of and the quality of life in organizations.

To illustrate the variety of methods employed by action researchers at ISR, a brief summary of a second case is presented. A cultural audit of a 2,100 person petrochemical plant was undertaken. As in the first case, the results of the audit served the client in primarily two ways: first, as an indicator of the current state of the plant—a benchmark—prior to an organization development initiative; and second, as a way to target the particular strengths and weaknesses of the plant's culture in order to guide the imminent changes.

Methods of assessing an organization's culture are not yet as sophisticated as those used to tap specific features of organizational life (such as pay satisfaction). In this audit we did not use a questionnaire composed of close-ended items. Instead, we asked organization members to describe their first day at the plant; to relate stories often told; to describe an extraordinary event (good or bad); to list the things it takes to survive; and so forth. After conducting group and individual interviews with representatives of all levels and departments in the plant, and after two trips to the site during which we attempted to capture our anthropological observations in copious field notes, we were able to feed back a description of the culture that was enlivened by an appendix of stories and suggestions for improving life in the plant. In particular, the suggestions concerned a set of problems in the management of human resources: staffing, appraisal, rewards, and training and development. These problem areas are presumed to effect and to be effected by the culture in important ways. For the action researchers, then, this project afforded an opportunity to expand on the domain of available methods for assessing organizations. Content analyses of the stories and of other qualitative data (that is, observations and archival data) yielded a different sort of picture than one derived from analyses of close-ended questionnaires only.

IMPLICATIONS AND SUMMARY

In this chapter we have stated a case for the importance of action research vis-à-vis the growth of our field. The technical, political, and cultural dynamics of host organizations and academic/research institutions were considered as they affect action research endeavors. Alternative arrangements for action research in these two kinds of entities were reviewed. ISR's structure was presented as one model for action researchers. Finally, an example of a recent action research project was described to illustrate the utility of the ISR model and to point to the technical, political, and cultural gains that may accrue to host organizations and to academic/research institutions engaging in. action research. Another example was offered to show the variety of methods used in action research projects at ISR.

The field of organization studies has shown some signs of division, or polarization, on issues of theory and method. Some investigators even contend that action research is the one and only "good" method and the rest are useless, or vice versa. We are most likely to advance the field through the use of several alternative and complementary modes of theory construction and of empirical study; in some cases this might occur in one study. The action research approach is to be championed not above all others, but above others only when the situation is ripe for it.

The challenge before our field is to remain vital in a climate of constricting research resources and a concurrent demand for our services in helping organizations cope with change. As scientists we need to be able to generate knowledge; as participants in society we need to contribute. Action research is a bridge that can provide the integration.

REFERENCES

Bowers, D. G. Scientific Knowledge Utilization as an Organizational Systems Development Problem. In R. H. Kilmann et al. (Eds.), *Producing Useful Knowledge for Organizations.* Chapter 26.

French, W. L., and Bell, C. H., Jr. *Organization Development.* Englewood Cliffs, N.J.: Prentice-Hall, 1973.

Lawler, E. E., III. Creating Practical Knowledge: Structure, Process, and Content Issues. In R. H. Kilmann et al. (Eds.), *Producing Useful Knowledge for Organizations.* Chapter 33.

McGrath, J. E. Toward a "Theory of Method" for Research on Organizations. In W. W. Cooper, H. L. Leavitt, and M. W. Shelley (Eds.), *New Perspectives in Organizational Research*. New York: Wiley, 1964, pp. 533–537.

Mirvis, P. H., and Seashore, S. E. Being Ethical in Organization Research. *American Psychologist*, 1979, *34*, pp. 766–780.

Pascale, R. T., and Athos, A. G. *The Art of Japanese Management: Applications for American Executives*. New York: Simon and Schuster, 1981.

Runkel, P. J., and McGrath, J. E. Planning a Study: Settings and Strategies for Research. In P. J. Runkel and J. E. McGrath (Eds.), *Research on Human Behavior*. New York: Holt, Rinehart and Winston, 1972.

Seashore, Stanley E. The Design of Action Research. In A. W. Clark (Ed.), *Experimenting with Organizational Life*. New York: Plenum Press, 1976, pp. 103–118.

Staw, B. M. The Experimenting Organization: Problems and Prospects. In B. M. Staw, *Psychological Foundations of Organizational Behavior*. Santa Monica, Calif.: Goodyear, 1977, pp. 466–486.

Susman, G. I., and Evered, R. D. An Assessment of the Scientific Merits of Action Research. *Administrative Science Quarterly*, 1978, *23*, pp. 582–603.

Tichy, N. M. Managing Change Strategically. *Organizational Dynamics*, Fall 1982.

Tichy, N. M. *Managing Strategic Change: Technical Political and Cultural Dynamics*. New York: John Wiley & Sons, 1983.

Trist, E. L., and Bamforth, K. W. Some Special and Psychological Consequences of the Long-Wall Method of Coal-Getting. *Human Relations*, 1951, *4*, pp. 3–38.

Walton, R. E. The Diffusion of New Work Structures: Explaining Why Success Didn't Take. *Organizational Dynamics*, Winter 1975, pp. 3–21.

22

PSYCHOLOGY AND ORGANIZATIONS: ARE SCIENCE AND UTILITY COMPATIBLE?

Douglas W. Bray

Some 27 years ago I was handed, on a silver platter, the opportunity to produce useful knowledge for an organization. AT & T, the parent company of the Bell System, had decided to initiate a longitudinal study of managerial careers and invited me to join them as the designer and principal researcher of such an investigation. That research, titled the Management Progress Study, and the personnel actions and additional research undertakings it spawned is the reason, I take it, for my inclusion in this conference. I am happy to observe that both within and outside the Bell System there is a conviction that much useful knowledge has indeed been generated.

In using the words "useful knowledge" and reflecting on the Management Progress Study, one is constrained to consider the words "knowledge" and "useful." To consider the latter first, it is certainly possible that some useful knowledge has not as yet been used. This is, indeed, a frequent lament of behavioral scientists. On the other hand, it may be that some knowledge, or purported knowledge, is used but is not useful. Furthermore, merely conducting research may produce organizational results even before research findings have come anywhere near close to the status of scientific facts. With these considerations in mind, caution suggests the simple declaration that the Management Progress Study and auxiliary research produced much organizational change in the Bell System and elsewhere. The balance of this chapter will clarify how and why this happened.

In order to do this, it is necessary to present a summary description of the study and some of its results to date. The great volume of data available and the many analyses completed and in process preclude any complete overview of the findings.

BEGINNINGS OF THE STUDY

The original concept of the research at the time I was employed was that a representative group of beginning Bell System managers would be followed longitudinally for the first part of their managerial careers (Bray and Howard, 1982a in press). A definite period of time was not settled upon, but no more than eight years was contemplated. It was believed that by that time it would be possible to discern which of the participants were doing well, moving up rapidly, and therefore destined for high places, and which were those whose careers would be more pedestrian or even less. No methodology for evaluating the participants or monitoring their careers had been decided upon.

A major decision, one that was to have profound effects, was to evaluate each of the participants in the study by means of an assessment center. I had been extremely attracted to the assessment center method ever since reading the *Assessment of Men* (OSS, 1948) some seven or eight years earlier and was delighted to discover that my boss, although not a psychologist, was aware of the method and sympathetic to its use. The decision to use an assessment center was not lightly made because of its complexity and expense. In this case it involved assembling a staff of nine psychologists who would assess only twelve participants per week, putting them through a variety of interviews, tests, and simulations. Since it was anticipated that a fairly large number of new managers would be included in the study (it turned out to be 422), the use of an elaborate assessment center was ambitious indeed. It contrasted sharply with the alternative possibility of merely conducting an interview supplemented by paper-and-pencil tests and questionnaires.

The first assessment center staff was put together from several sources. Some were recent Ph.D.s from various universities. Others were from the Educational Testing Service. Still others were newly employed Bell System psychologists who had worked as consultants with the Bell System. With such diverse backgrounds it was only to be expected that their views of how to do research and what methods to use would vary considerably. The majority, however, were heavily steeped in quantitative approaches, and at least one was a militant spokesman for dust bowl empiricism. Happily, such viewpoints prevented no one from making substantial contributions of time and effort to the assessment work, up to perhaps twice the normal work week, but it did produce some lively arguments that revealed the conviction that I, as the director of this enterprise, was out of my mind. To the amazement of nearly all the staff, I was hell-bent for the judgmental organismic approach heralded by the authors of the *Assessment of Men* and disdainful of elementalists. Fortunately for the smooth running of that first management assessment center, no utter diehards were present, and it was possible to cajole or coerce my colleagues into doing things my way.

This first assessment center was conducted in Michigan with the participants being recent college graduates just hired by Michigan Bell as probably future middle and upper managers. Since not all Bell System Telephone Companies would be expected to participate in the research, it had been decided to sample from a different company each summer for five years until the total sample was accumulated. (This plan was followed except for the last summer of the study, during which the participants came from two neighboring telephone companies.) The second summer found another assessment staff, about half of whom were repeats from the previous year, at work in Washington assessing new college hires from the Chesapeake and Potomac (C&P) Telephone Companies. By the end of that summer a total of approximately 140 participants had been assessed in the Michigan and C&P companies combined.

Shortly thereafter my boss, the same one who had known about assessment centers, thought that it was time for me to present some early results to the annual conference of Bell System Personnel Vice-Presidents, who represented all 23 operating telephone companies. Whether he would have done this in any case I am not sure, but I certainly had made no secret of my conviction that no more than half of the young men we had been assessing had the level of management potential that the college recruiters had intended to procure. I proceeded to present this conviction to the assembled vice-presidents, undeterred by the fact that none of us making the judgment had more than a few months of Bell System experience, including several who had never worked in any large organization. Nobody was unkind enough to mention this.

My report was made more plausible by at least one objective fact. College recruiters were supposed to place heavy emphasis upon rank in college graduating class because of older Bell System research that had demonstrated the predictive power of this index (Bridgman, 1930). Yet in the two companies we had visited, more than half of the rank in class data recorded on employment forms were substantially in error, biased, as one might expect, upward. The recruiters had relied mainly on information from the interviewee himself. These college seniors did not know their exact rank in class and were inclined to overestimate it. In any case, the assembled vice-presidents received the bad news gracefully enough so that the groundwork was laid for a thoroughgoing refurbishing of Bell System management employment methods.

One of the tests given at the assessment center in the C & P company was the newly available School and College Ability Test (SCAT) published by Educational Testing Service. The concern voiced at the vice-presidents' conference about a significant number of subpar college graduates led to an auxiliary piece of research. It was decided to administer the SCAT to all college graduates hired into the telephone companies on the College Employment Program during the 1958 recruiting year. This was the program designed to provide a pool of candidates for future middle and upper management. The test was administered nationwide on an anonymous basis with all answer sheets being sent directly to AT & T for scoring, with no report on individuals available to the telephone companies.

When the results were tabulated, wide differences among the 23 telephone companies appeared. My boss was able to bring these results to the attention of the president of AT & T, who straightaway took them to an upcoming conference of telephone company presidents. This led rather speedily to the adoption of the SCAT as an addition to the methods used for the selection of college graduates for employment as beginning managers.

Once the participants in the Management Progress Study were assessed, there was the necessity of follow-up to find out was was happening in their early careers. Once again an ambitious, although not novel, method was decided upon. Each participant would be interviewed annually at an off-the-job location, usually within commuting distance of the participant's work place, by a psychologist retained by AT & T. In addition, someone in the participant's telephone company in a position to observe him and his performance (in later years his boss) would be interviewed by another interviewer. Because of the geographical dispersion of the participants and the fact that there were eventually more than 400 of them, this was a relatively expensive operation. Fortunately, we did not have to rely on mail questionnaires.

The follow-up interviews conducted in 1957 and 1958 with the first two groups of participants revealed that about half felt that their experience on the College Employment Program was not challenging and was, in fact, rather boring. This program was essentially a job rotation program through a variety of low-level jobs in several departments rather than a real opportunity to manage. From the company point of view this lack of managerial responsibility also had its drawbacks. It afforded little basis for judging the potential of the newcomers.

These unsettling findings about both the selection and development of college recruits led to the creation of a replacement for the College Employment Program called the Initial Management Development Program. This new program encompassed both selection and development aspects. On the selection side, strict emphasis was placed upon rank in college graduating class (top half required), performance on the SCAT (top half required), and demonstrated extracurricular leadership during the college years. As far as development was concerned, hand-picked managers were selected to be the supervisors of new management recruits. These managers were third- rather than second-level managers, and they were given special training for their responsibilities. There was a strong emphasis upon providing challenging assignments for the recruits in a high-risk, high-reward mode. That is, if they demonstrated a high degree of managerial potential they would be moved along much faster than usual. If they did not, they would be asked to leave.

Thus, within three years of the start of the Management Progress Study, sweeping changes were made in one aspect of organizational functioning: the selection and early experiences of future management. Such quick effects were not anticipated from research with an eight-year design. More cautious investigators would have waited the eight years and then related individual and environmental variables to criteria, such as management level, available at year eight. Allowing some time for data analysis and remembering that the original assessments occupied five summers, it would have been 1969 instead of 1958 that Bell System executives would have been alerted to any need for change.

At about the same time that management employment practices were being revised, a completely different type of development was taking place. During the first assessment center in Michigan Bell in the summer of 1956, the top managers of that company had been briefed on the assessment center method in order that they would be knowledgeable about the experiences their young managers were having. Among these executives were the senior managers of the Plant Department, that portion of the company responsible for the telephone lines, switching gear, and other equipment needed for the transmission of telephone messages. They saw the assessment center method as a possible valuable addition to existing procedures, mostly informal appraisal, used in the selection of nonmanagement employees to be promoted into the first level of management. The title for most of those jobs in those days was "foreman." They proposed that the method be adapted to this purpose and, more important, adapted so that the process could be carried out by telephone managers, few of whom would have any background in behavioral science. Such an adaptation was made, and the first operational use of the management assessment center took place in 1958. This effort was soon judged to be highly worthwhile by Michigan Bell, and the assessment center began to diffuse throughout the Bell System. This was not because any official at AT & T headquarters pushed the idea; that did not happen until several years later. Michigan Bell managers, as well as the author, became crusaders for the method, and the existence of the center in Michigan that others could visit and observe served as an ongoing demonstration. The management assessment center has flourished in the Bell System in a variety of applications since that time. Between 30,000 and 40,000 persons go through AT & T assessment centers annually.

It was not long before the assessment center method began to spread to other organizations. The first non-Bell application was in Standard Oil of

Ohio in 1961. Shortly thereafter, other companies including IBM, Sears, and General Electric began to experiment with the approach. Since then many hundreds of other organizations have adopted one version or another of the assessment center, and a Tenth Annual International Congress on the Assessment Center Method was held in Pittsburgh earlier in the year.

Once again it must be pointed out that the start of the assessment center movement took place considerably before any direct evidence was available that assessment results were related to managerial performance. The effort was based on the conviction of both professionals and managers with firsthand experience with the method that performance at the assessment center must surely be significantly relevant to performance on the job. Some might call this "face validity." I would describe it as an informed, if unproven, judgment that content and construct validity were apparent in the approach.

LATER RESEARCH

The early 1960s saw the Bell System telephone companies devoting much activity to the Initial Management Development Program and operational assessment centers. In consequence, there was a general belief that the investment in basic research represented by the Management Progress Study had been worthwhile. In the meantime, my colleagues and I had become convinced that it would be invaluable to reassess the participants in the study. The original design would have allowed predictive research (that is, the correlation of initial characteristics with later criterion information), but would not have yielded information about how important components of managerial ability and motivation change over time. We proposed, therefore, that instead of terminating the study at eight years, we put the participants through another three-day assessment center paralleling or duplicating the original procedure. We had little difficulty having our proposal accepted, which might not have been the case had the study not stimulated change during earlier years.

At approximately the same time, data analysis on the materials already collected began in earnest, and findings appeared on a fairly regular basis. Some of these findings and their organizational effects will be touched on later. For now, however, it is sufficient to report that this continuous activity paved the way for still another assessment of the study participants at the 20-year mark! Perhaps equally remarkable was the acceptance of an expansion of the scope of the study to include the challenges and changes of middle life as represented by such assessment dimensions as adjustment and happiness. It had become apparent that AT & T was engaged in a major study of lives and not merely some research on how to pick better managers. We are now fantasying that 1991 will see the beginning of still another round of assessment, at which time the participants will average 60 years of age and half of whom will probably be retired.

A weakness of most longitudinal research is the confounding of age changes with societal changes. Since the participants represent one period of time, it is difficult to say whether changes observed are due to age and life experiences or to a general cultural shift. The Management Progress Study was subject to this weakness. It did not seem reasonable, however, to expect AT & T to support the study of another cohort. The investment in the original research was already considerable. Yet such support did miraculously materialize and arose from telephone company personnel executives themselves. They believed that the Management Progress Study had been a firm basis for management selection and development, but they were aware of the general belief that young people of the late 1970s were different from those of the 1950s. If this were so, then new research was needed. Thus my colleague, Ann Howard, and I were empowered in 1977 to start the Management Continuity Study, in parallel to the older research (Bray and Howard, 1982a in press).

SELECTED RESEARCH RESULTS

The first major analysis of Management Progress Study data was conducted in the mid-1960s. Donald L. Grant, one of my colleagues at AT & T, suggested that the time had arrived to dig into the Management Progress Study data. The result was the first extensive report on the managerial assessment center and the first major publication deriving from the Management Progress Study (Bray and Grant, 1966). One most important finding was that those participants who had done well at the assessment center had in fact progressed much more rapidly than the others. The adoption of the assessment center on the basis of its inherent logic and attractiveness had apparently been well advised. The bottom line figure was that by 1965, 42 percent of the men who had been well rated by the assessment staffs had reached third-level management or higher, as compared to only 7 percent of the remainder. (The reader is reminded that assessment results were not available to any one other than the researchers and played no part in promotion decisions. Not even the participants had been given a feedback.)

Another aspect of the analyses in this first publication was an attempt to get at the underlying factors in management potential. It was reasoned that if the assessors were making accurate predictions on the basis of some 26 dimensions, many of them interrelated, then an analysis of the ratings on those dimensions might reveal the nature of management potential. A factor analysis of the dimension ratings was performed, and a number of factors emerged. The two most important factors underlying assessor judgments were administrative skills and interpersonal skills. Of lesser importance, but still of considerable significance, were general mental ability, work involvement, advancement motivation, and stability of performance. (Several of these factors have recently been renamed.) Of least importance, but statistically significant, was independence of others.

The analysis of the study data following the eighth year reassessment, in preparation for *Formative Years in Business* (Bray, Campbell, and Grant, 1974), showed that the participants were rated no higher at the assessment center at year eight than they had been originally on such managerial characteristics as administrative and interpersonal skills. Because of the importance of this finding, a special review of all the reports and judgments in the two assessment centers was undertaken. This review, conducted by two psychologists with many years of experience in assessment center work, substantiated the conclusion that these two critical management skills had not improved in the period between the two assessment centers, essentially the first eight years of business experience. This result, although startling, was consistent with the data showing that initial assessment ratings predicted management level at year eight quite well.

One of the noteworthy findings that emerged when the participants in the study were assessed 20 years after their original assessment was that the now middle-aged managers were, on the average, far less motivated for advancement than they had been at the outset. Scores on an inventory of upward mobility aspirations had dropped from the fiftieth to the fifteenth percentile. This decline was substantiated by other assessment techniques, notably the personal interview and the projective tests. Only 29 percent of the college graduate participants were now rated high in advancement motivation by the assessment staff, as compared to 42 percent originally and 40 percent at the eight-year mark. The noncollege participants, who already had about nine years of service when they were originally assessed, had declined earlier from an original 34 percent rated high on need advancement to 18 percent at the eight-year reassessment and 16 percent at year 20. These changes had not occurred, of course, because everyone had reached the top. The modal college graduate participant was at the third level of management in a hierarchy in which the top level was seven, while the average noncollege participant had reached only second level (Bray, 1982a).

These declines were doubtless due to a number of factors. Some participants had reached the level to which they originally aspired. Others had adjusted to the inevitable over the years as it gradually became apparent that their ceiling was limited. Failure to advance further was not a source of grave dissatisfaction by year 20. The correlation between the overall happiness rating and management level was essentially zero, .06 (Bray and Howard, 1980).

As contrasted to the decline in advancement desires, the 20-year data showed a sharply heightened interest in motivation for achievement, the satisfaction in doing a difficult job well, as measured by the Edwards Personal Preference Schedule. At original assessment the college participants had scored at the sixty-second percentile and the noncollege participants at the fifty-fourth percentile on Bell System college recruit norms. At 20 years they scored at the eighty-second percentile and seventy-fourth percentile, respectively. That the participants were still concerned about maintaining good performance in spite of their lesser desire for advancement is further attested to by their assessment ratings on the dimension of Inner Work Standards. Here there was no significant change over the period of two decades (Bray and Howard, 1982a in press).

Although many of the changes observed over the first 20 years of the study were general and not related to success in management, others were significantly related to level attained (Bray and Howard, 1982a in press). Although an analysis of the interviews at the beginning of the study showed no difference in involvement in the occupational sphere of life, the 11 interviews conducted between then and year 19 revealed considerable differences. Those who were to attain the higher levels of management rapidly became involved in their work right from the outset, while those who were to find themselves eventually at the lower levels of management showed an early and continued decline. Other differences included a sharp decline in motivation for affiliation among the more successful; in contrast, they became much less authoritarian in their social attitudes.

The opportunity to assess a new generation of college graduates in the Management Continuity Study led to the discovery of some important differences between this group and the older managers as they had been 20 years previously. Although they were no less capable or less interested in job challenge, they were much less motivated to rise in the corporate hierarchy and had a far less optimistic view of what life would be like as a Bell System manager. They had, furthermore, markedly less desire to play a leadership role even in a nonhierarchical setting. On the other hand, their needs for succorance and nurturance, to give and receive help and sympathy from peers, were much higher than those of their counterparts 20 years previously (Howard and Bray, 1980).

Mention has already been made of two sets of important organizational actions that resulted from the Management Progress Study long before any research results were available. These were the modifications toward much greater rigor in the selection of and early experience provided to new college recruits into management, and the use of assessment centers as an aid in promotion decisions. The research findings of the 1960s indicated that this emphasis on selection was justified. Success in management was, in fact, quite predictable, and one could not trust to mere experience in lower-level management jobs to produce general management skills. Thus, the research results solidified the practices already well under way. The intrinsic appeal of the assessment center plus compelling longitudinal research data have resulted in the continuation and intensification of its use some 24 years after its operational introduction.

Surprisingly enough in an organization with many personnel practices well standardized, the Bell System had no systemwide method of appraising potential for advancing in management. In the 1970s, however, such a plan was developed and successfully introduced. Its nucleus was found in the factor analysis of the Management Progress Study assessment dimensions, referred to above, and in the assessment center method. Eight dimensions were used, including communication skills, planning and organizing, decision making, inner work standards, and so forth. It was planned that training in the new approach would be similar to that given to an assessment center staff member, since bosses would be rating these dimensions on the basis of observed behavior on the job. Such training was provided, although unfortunately it proved impossible to secure more than one day of managerial time for this purpose. (This, however, is one day more than many appraisal plans are given.)

Later research results have attracted great interest both inside the Bell System and elsewhere (Howard and Bray, 1982) and seem of great potential utility, but direct methods for quickly taking advantage of them have not been apparent. Some, however, suggest that inaction is appropriate, and this itself is useful knowledge. The findings that most middle-aged managers have maintained their work standards while no longer strongly upward motivated and that failure to advance does not often spoil one's happiness in life mean that business can stop worrying about an imaginary problem. What they should be worrying about is the other side of the coin: how to provide continued job challenge and achievement satisfaction to the many managers who have plateaued. They also have to be concerned about the perhaps one-fifth of middle-aged managers who do have the motivation and potential for further advancement (Howard and Bray, 1980).

More perplexing are the action implications of the motivational characteristics of today's young college graduate recruits into entry-level management jobs. A generation ago it was possible to take a sink-or-swim approach toward those in the very early years of management careers. Some would sink, but there would be enough of them with leadership and advancement drives sufficient to survive mediocre early experiences. Now that seems not to be the case. Some of the problems confronting remedial action will be touched upon later.

THE SEARCH FOR USEFUL KNOWLEDGE AND UTILITY

Having been engaged for the past 26 years in trying to produce useful knowledge in a large organization and having seen substantial changes in that organization result from these efforts, with perhaps more in the wings, and having been invited to do so by the sponsors of this conference, I will now propose some principles relevant to producing useful knowledge for organizations. These principles should, of course, be viewed as hypotheses.

Merely conducting research may induce organization change. A quick change in employment methods for new management recruits was certainly not an initial goal of the Management Progress Study. Yet the observation that many of the current recruits did not seem to have a high degree of management potential, supplemented by the systemwide administration of the School and College Ability Test, had that result. The information on which this change was based can hardly be called "knowledge" in the sense of the discovery of some new principle or generalization. The activity could better be described as "fact finding." One way that research intended to produce useful knowledge causes things to happen organizationally is that some incidental fact finding is likely to occur at many stages of the research. One reason that the Management Progress Study measured abilities at the outset of managerial careers was because of its interest in what would happen to such abilities over the course of managerial lives. Such a question would be of much more interest to behavioral researchers than the mere factual question of how a particular cohort of management recruits shaped up. The management of an organization may be expected to have the opposite emphasis, and probably quite rightly so.

The other way in which carrying out research may stimulate organizational change, possibly entirely aside from the researcher's goal in respect to knowledge, is the display of a method. The assessment center was used in the Management Progress Study to collect baseline data concerning the abilities and motivations of the participants. The method itself, as reported above, proved attractive enough to a sufficient number of senior managers to result in its wide use. This use necessarily predated by a number of years any demonstration that the judgments made at the original study assessment centers were predictive of managerial success. Thus, the Management Progress Study would have produced significant organizational results even had it been summarily discontinued. It was, in fact, some of the findings uncovered by the study and its introduction of a method that management found attractive and useful that guaranteed the study's continuation.

Organizations should not request particular products in terms of programs or procedures from the knowledge producer. They should not, for example, ask the researcher to develop a program to reduce management turnover. They might rather ask the researcher whether the organization should be concerned about management turnover and, if so, what the causes of such turnover might be. Such a formulation would give the researcher much more scope in investigating abilities, career motivation, and the organizational environment than the request for a product. Research might demonstrate the the product is not really needed and would almost certainly, as a by-product, produce much incidental useful knowledge. The more general the question, the more the investigator is free to conduct basic research, which in the long run is the most useful kind of research.

Knowledge producers must mount research efforts ambitious enough to attack the problem under investigation. Recent commentaries on the utility of research have emphasized that producing useful knowledge usually requires a major effort. "To do really good research in psychology, research that really breaks new ground or gives definitive answers to important questions [as opposed to research that simply makes it into journals], is exceedingly difficult . . . to conduct really adequate studies requires enormous resources of time and money" (Wachtel, 1980, p. 402). In the Management Progress Study, the participants have undergone nine days of assessment over the first 20 years of the research, plus 11 interviews lasting two hours or more. In addition, their supervisors have been interviewed 11 times. One staff member of my section at AT & T, Kerry Bunker, has been conducting research into managerial stress. Another, Manuel London, has recently been studying career motivation. In both cases we have developed a two-day assessment center, and in the former research we have for the first time brought spouses into a part of the assessment situation. An AT & T human resources executive recently commented concerning such ambitious methods that this is the kind of substantial evidence you must have if you are going to stand up and say that you think you know something.

In discussing the contributions of social science, Tornatzky and Solomon (1982) tend to place the blame for poor research on policy makers. They state that "some of the worst and most embarrassing usage of social science knowledge have occurred when researchers have been forced by impatient decision makers to conduct quick studies and shallow analyses" (p. 745). (Incidentally, in lamenting the failure of social technologies to achieve widespread utilization and adoption, this article is strangely silent on the subject of assessment centers, which are now used in hundreds of organizations.) Others would add failure to provide appropriate resources of money and staff as a reason for research whose methods are inadequate to the problems addressed. No doubt all of this is true, but researchers themselves should not be held completely blameless. Over the years I have been appalled at the methods used by many in my field who work with organizations either internally or as consultants. Thirty-minute questionnaires are expected to generate the knowledge required to reduce turnover, increase productivity, eliminate managerial stress, improve morale, or almost any desirable organizational goal. Not only do such methods not produce useful knowledge, they are unlikely to impel action on the part of the policy makers. Such researchers reveal a limited view of the complexity of the psyche and the multiple determinants of behavior.

Knowledge producers should avoid current bandwagons. The knowledge producer should not worry about being current, that is, to do research in the area that is "hot" in the journals or in the Sunday supplements. Many such fads, fashions, and folderol, as Marvin Dunnette (1966) has labelled them, rest more on catchy phrasing than on sound theorizing or hard data. Researchers might better start with the skeptical stance that no one really knows anything about what they are about to study than to believe that a lot is known and they are simply contributing a minor refinement to established truth.

Knowledge producers should work at the organismic rather than the elementalistic level. A key distinction in the study of human beings in organizations was emphasized by the authors of the *Assessment of Men*, the book devoted to the OSS Assessment Center during World War II (OSS Assessment Staff, 1948). The elementalistic approach, they noted, calls for the accurate quantitative measurement of isolated processes, as narrow and specific as possible. The hope is that in the long run, probably the very long run, someone will be able to put all these pieces together again back into useful knowledge. The organismic approach, on the other hand, starts with the whole person or, perhaps more accurately, with major aspects of the whole person. Once such significant aspects have been defined and studied, some breakdown of these aspects may follow.

An example is the dimension of need advancement, the motivation to be advanced faster and further than one's peers, used in both the Management Progress Study and the Management Continuity Study. This complex dimension has turned out to be a most important predictor of eventual management level (Bray and Howard, 1982b in press). This finding, in itself, has action implications for organizations, since any sophisticated way of evaluating advancement motivation at the time of employment is extremely rare. When this motivation is looked at longitudinally over time in the Management Progress Study, it is found that by middle age such motivation has declined sharply for the vast majority of managers. Such knowledge can cause quite a change in management's thinking about incentives and rewards for the older manager. When this motive is looked at between generations in the Management Continuity Study participants compared to those in the Management Progress Study, significantly lower motivation for advancement is observed in today's management recruits. This may also require a rethinking of incentives and rewards for young managers.

Since it is obvious that need advancement is not just one unitary motive, some analysis of it is necessary to make action implications clearer. Among the likely components of this motivation are the desires for money, recognition, dominance, and achievement. Once it is established that need advancement is an important dimension in hierarchical organizations, then the importance of the desire for recognition, for example, as compared to economic motivation, becomes important in the management of managerial resources. Note, however, that such subdimensions are still quite organismic.

The evaluation of such complex dimensions can, it appears, be accomplished only by rating methods. Such methods go against the grain of many who have been taught to seek more precise quantification by means of psychometric devices. The fact is that psychometric instruments do not exist for many managerial dimensions, and as Livson points out, "only ratings seem capable of quantifying naturalistic samplings of behavior over a wide range of situations" (1973, p. 102).

Producing useful knowledge differs from building a science. In their book *Usable Knowledge*, Lindblom and Cohen (1979) describe the typical organizational researcher as aiming to produce "authoritative knowledge." By this they mean knowledge so thoroughly researched that no administrator could fail to use it. They go on to present a number of convincing reasons why such knowledge is not likely to be produced. Researchers attempting to be useful to organizations therefore must seek to have their findings utilized even when they are not judged airtight by their more academic colleagues. After all, their still possibly fallible knowledge is probably more than the organization now has. In this connection it must be remembered that organizations do not run on science but, rather, on informed judgment. When top managers decide between selling stock and issuing bonds as a method of raising capital, they may have much data and the predictions of economists, but there can be no complete certainty that they have made the right decision.

Tomkins (1981) has recently commented on the high degree of conservatism in research. Describing scientists who appear more interested in combating error than stimulated by the possibilities of discovery, he declares that they "enjoin us to let many exciting possibilities go lest we contaminate the house of science with one lie" (p. 316). However one feels about such a stance in building a science, it is inappropriate for those who seek to benefit organizations. This does not, of course, excuse sloppy methods, the use of inappropriate statistical techniques, or other methodological lapses.

Not all useful knowledge will be used. Ambitious research programs may be expected to produce more knowledge than organizations can act upon. Data from the Management Continuity Study indicate significant motivational problems in today's college recruits into management. When such results are presented publicly, an immediate question is "What are you doing about it?" This is a perfectly reasonable question, but often the questioner is not fully aware of the difficulties of implementing appropriate action. The Bell System, where these results were obtained, takes on between 4,000 and 6,000 college graduates a year, and most of these report to different bosses. No simple dispersal of findings about the average motivation of all these college recruits to these thousands of supervisors could be expected to produce appropriate behavior on their part even if they were to "read, mark, and inwardly digest," as the Anglican collect suggests. Yet some way of impinging on the supervisory behavior of all these bosses toward their new subordinates appears to be needed, as well as some way of communicating directly with the recruits themselves. It is not, however, advisable for researchers actually to carry out implementation. This will seriously reduce, and possibly end, their knowledge-producing efforts. Yet nonprofessional administrators are often unable to devise the kinds of programs and practices suggested by research findings. Possibly some intermediate staff is needed to bridge the gap between research and application.

Knowledge producers should have, or cultivate, managerial skills. Among these managerial skills are those relating to administering research efforts and to representing the results of those efforts to the organization. If the researcher has a team, he or she should assure that the efforts of each member of the team contribute to the team's particular thrust. Several major research groups have had less impact than they might have had because staff members have followed their own particular interests, which have carried them off in various unrelated directions. In respect to dealing with the organization, communication skills, both written and oral, are of prime importance. Managers do not usually take action because they have read a complete technical report nor on the basis of a simple statement of the conclusions. It may be a bit mundane after flying high in the realms of science, but a well-conceptualized condensation of the research accompanied by legible visual aids can do wonders.

In dealing with the managers of the organization, researchers must be like other good managers: assertive but deferential, persistent but flexible, respectful but sociable. In short, they must be able to flourish in a complex culture. My experience has been that the majority of managers are supportive of and receptive to research once they understand what you are doing and why you are doing it. On the other hand, there are two types of managers who represent the Scylla and Charybdis between which the research may sometimes have to navigate. One of these is the completely close-minded manager who has no sympathy for research no matter what its methods or results. Such managers want things run by the knowledge and experience they believe all good managers have accumulated even as they have. At the other extreme is the eager consumer of behavioral knowledge and its counterfeits who chases every new fad that has crept into the business press or been presented by consultants at business conventions. To the first type the researcher is likely to be an impractical dreamer, to the other a conservative stick-in-the-mud.

Are the science of psychology and organizational utility compatible? If one has the usual model in mind, the answer is no. This model is one that imagines researchers conducting studies in which the elements are precisely measured, all extraneous variables controlled, and findings not communicated until a high degree of statistical reliability is reached and until they are, or would be, accepted by the most careful guardians of truth. At that point the organization is informed of the results. They are so compelling that the managers of the organization take immediate steps to devise, modify, or eliminate an organizational practice. If they do not, they are clearly uncomprehending and unsympathetic victims of organizational inertia.

A more realistic picture is that the contribution of research to organizational practice is complex. Merely conducting research can lead to changes in practice, and such changes may turn out to be lasting and beneficial even if the research is never completed. Such changes, seen as deriving from the research, might mobilize support for continuing the research efforts. As they continue, results will begin to appear, results that may not yet be completely certain. If the researcher is willing to chance it and communicate the findings, and do so effectively, additional changes in organizational practice may ensue. Some may say this is not science. Maybe it is not, but I have found that this is what happens on the way to science.

As research continues, findings that may qualify as scientific will, it is hoped, appear. Some of these will bring about additional changes in the organization, but it is highly unrealistic to expect that all such knowledge will be used by a particular organization. If the research has been well done, however, all knowledge produced will contribute to the science and profession of psychology.

REFERENCES

Bray, D. W.
1982   The assessment center and the study of lives. *American Psychologist, 37* (2), 180–189.
Bray, D. W., Campbell, R. J., and Grant, D. L.
1974   *Formative years in business: A long-term AT & T study of managerial lives.* New York: Wiley.

Bray, D. W., and Grant, D. L.
1966   The assessment center in the measurement of potential for business management. *Psychological Monographs, 80* (17, Whole No. 625).

Bray, D. W., and Howard, A.
1980   Career success and life satisfactions of middle-aged managers. In L. A. Bond and J. C. Rosen (Eds.) *Coping and competence during adulthood.* Hanover, New Hampshire: University Press of New England.

1982a   The AT & T longitudinal studies of managers. Chapter for book in press, K. W. Schaie (Ed.).

1982b   Personality and the assessment center method. Chapter for book in press, C. D. Spielberger and J. N. Butcher (Eds.).

Bridgman, D. S.
1930   Success in college and business. *Personnel Journal, 9* (1), 1–19.

Dunnette, M. D.
1966   Fads, fashions, and folderol in psychology. *American Psychologist,* 343–352.

Howard, A., and Bray, D. W.
1980   Continuities and discontinuities between two generations of managers. Paper presented for the symposium: Today's college recruits, managerial timber or deadwood? American Psychological Association, Montreal, Canada

1982   AT & T: The hopes of middle managers. *New York Times,* March 21, 1982.

Lindblom, C. D., and Cohen, D. K.
1979   *Usable knowledge: Social science and social problem solving.* New Haven: Yale University Press.

Livson, N.
1973   Developmental dimensions of personality: A life-span formulation. In P. B. Baltes and K. W. Schaie (Eds.), *Life-span developmental psychology: Personality and socialization.* New York: Academic Press.

OSS Assessment Staff
1948   *Assessment of Men.* New York: Rinehart.

Tomkins, S. S.
1981   The quest for primary motives: Biography and autobiography of an idea. *Journal of Personality and Social Psychology, 41* (2), 306–329.

Tornatzky, L. G., and Solomon, T.
1982   Contributions of social science to innovation and productivity. *American Psychologist, 37* (7), 737–746.

Wachtel, P. L.
1980   Investigation and its discontents: Some constraints on progress in psychological research. *American Psychologist, 35* (5), 399–408.

23

THE PRODUCTION OF USEFUL KNOWLEDGE: REVISITING TRADITIONAL ORGANIZATIONAL AND BUREAUCRATIC THEORY

Robert F. Rich

The organizational investment for research and development in advanced industrial societies—in the public and private sectors—is considerable. In 1981 the United States spent $34 billion on applied research "aimed at practical application of knowledge" (*NY Times*, 1982).

Decision makers and administrators need to access information because of the nature of the requirements of their work. The job requires actions that are goal-oriented (Simon, 1976). "Purposiveness" characterizes and distinguishes the job requirements of decision makers and administrators from others in society. The need to act dictates that administrators will, by necessity, be concerned with means/ends relationships. The emphasis on instrumental actions that are designed to lead toward specific objectives leads to the reliance of decision makers on information:

> The function of knowledge in the decision making process is to determine which consequences follow upon which of the alternative strategies. It is the task of knowledge to select from the whole class of possible consequences a more limited sub-class, or even (ideally) a single set of consequences correlated with each strategy. (Simon, 1976, p. 69)

Decision makers require broad-based, comprehensive knowledge. Unlike the scientist, the practitioner (that is, the decision maker as the "practitioner" of policymaking) finds it difficult to assign certain areas of inquiry to the category of being completely inapplicable, "inappropriate," or "irrelevant."

I am grateful for the suggestions and help provided by Neal M. Goldsmith.

It is a valid scientific problem to deduce the empirical law that would hold under certain simplified hypothetical conditions, even though these conditions do not prevail in practice—the theoretical scientist can talk about "rigid bodies," "perfect vacuums," "frictionless fluids," etc. But the practitioner must allow for the effects of elasticity, air pressure, or friction, if they are present and substantial, no matter how much this complicates his problem of selecting the corrective alternative. . . . The scientist can choose only those consequences of the system that he wishes to be concerned with, and ignore the others. It is a valid scientific problem to ask: "What effect upon the total weight of this airplane will specified changes in design have?" The problem of practical decision, however, is to balance a possible weight-saving against an increase in cost, or a loss of maneuverability, or other qualities. The practitioner can never choose to disregard conditioning facts or consequences simply because they fall outside the scope of his theory. (Simon, 1976, p. 70)

The practitioner (decision maker) should, therefore, be concerned with developing a systematic foundation of knowledge that can be applied on an "as-needed basis."

This phenomenon has been labeled by social scientists and others as the 'bias" toward rationality. In fact, it is at the foundation of most nineteenth- and twentieth-century theories of bureaucracy, organizations, and administration. It extends beyond a system for organizing economic actions/decisions (that is, the economy is organized around coordination through voluntary exchange; this relationship "rests on the elementary—yet frequently denied—proposition that both parties to an economic transaction benefit from it provided that the transaction is by-laterally voluntary and informed" [Friedman, 1962, p. 13]) to a system of "substantive rationality" in which "action is based on 'goal oriented' rational calculation with the technically most adequate available methods" (Weber, 1968, p. 85). Purely formal rationality in the sense of organizing the economy is considered to be of "quite secondary importance or even as fundamentally inimical" to the process of reaching specific ends (Weber, 1968, p. 86).

The administrator requires knowledge to perform his official duties:

Bureaucratic administration means fundamentally domination through knowledge. This is the feature of it which makes it specifically rational. This consists on the one hand in technical knowledge which, by itself, is sufficient to ensure it a position of extraordinary power. But in addition to this, bureaucratic organizations . . . have the tendency to increase their power still further by the knowledge growing out of experience in the service. For they acquire through the conduct of office a special knowledge of facts and have available a store of documentary material peculiar to themselves. (Weber, 1968, p. 225)

Bureaucracy, thus, is in the business of creating an information base that it draws on for a variety of purposes: securing the position of the organization, serving decision makers, and ensuring for organizational survival (Halperin, 1974, pp. 158–172). As Weber points out, "bureaucracy is the means of transforming social action into rationally organized action" (Weber, 1968, p. 987).

The knowledge base of bureaucratic organizations is developed through the "expertise" of individuals recruited to them as well as the ability of officials within the organization to access state-of-the-art knowledge.

> Two characteristics are especially valuable in enhancing the influence of any body of experts within a bureaucracy. The first is the possession of a highly technical body of knowledge that the laymen cannot readily master, and the second is the capacity to produce tangible achievements that the average man can easily recognize. This combination of obscurity and clarity of results seems an irresistible formula for success. (Rourke, 1978, p. 227)

Since it is in the interest of the bureaucratic organization to develop a comparative advantage over other corporate actors in society (Weber, 1968; Rourke, 1978; Halperin, 1974), there is a tendency to develop very specialized fields of expertise: "The more complicated and specialized modern culture becomes, the more its external supporting apparatus demands the personally detached and strictly objective expert" (Weber, 1968, p. 975). With demands for specialized knowledge and true expertise,

> bureaucratization offers above all the optimum possibility for carrying through the principle of specializing administrative functions according to purely objective considerations. Individual performances are allocated to functionaries who have specialized training and who by constant practice increase their expertise. "Objective" discharge of business primarily means the discharge of business according to *calculable rules* without regard for persons. (Weber, 1968, p. 975)

An individual's expertise is acquired through formal training in educational institutions (universities):

> Educational institutions on the European continent, especially the institutions of higher learning—the universities, as well as technical academies, business colleges, gymnasia, and other secondary schools—are dominated and influenced by the need for the kind of "education" which is bred by the system of specialized examinations or tests of expertise increasingly indispensable for modern bureaucracies. (Weber, 1968, p. 999)

There is little doubt that government has attempted to attract very well trained officials into the public service. Of all officials in government, 21.2 percent are considered to be "professional and technical personnel"; the percentage in the private sector is only half that amount, 11.6 percent (Mosher, 1982, p. 113). In some advanced industrial states, the ratio is probably even higher. Leaving aside political appointees,

> Public leadership as such is an administrative profession [that] consists of a very wide variety of professions and professionals in diverse fields, most of them related to the missions of the organizations in which they lead. (Mosher, 1982, p. 113)

In most Western societies, a civil service developed that was meant to epitomize the notion that administration represents a profession that is a highly desired and valued career. It is fair to conclude that the development of a professional civil service embodies a "faith in knowledge, rationality, and applied research to solve the problems of society" (Mosher, 1982, p. 48).

The faith is reflected in the reliance placed on universities and institutions of higher learning to train those who will ultimately serve in government. This is consistent with the influential German university system—the Humboldt model—which places a strong emphasis on supporting science and research in the service of the state. The laws that served as the foundation for the development of the U.S. civil service system emphasized the need for formal training and the production of applied research.[1] The need to train civil servants can be seen as an opportunity to support "scientific development and a nexus between the sciences and professional occupations" (Mosher, 1982, p. 48).

At the turn of the century, there was a growing acceptance of the role of the university in preparing students for professional careers:

> The development of specialism and professionalism in university curricula was accompanied by a growing recognition of broadening social goals of universities in contributing to progress and in solving social problems. In the latter part of the 19th century, a handful of university presidents became acknowledged civic leaders and shaped some of the university programs to confront such problems—a far cry from the earlier emphasis upon the classics. (Mosher, 1982, p. 51)[2]

Professions, in general, have relied upon the university to arm individuals with skills as well as theoretical and practical knowledge that will be required in solving the problems assigned to them. (This is even more true in medicine, law, and in engineering than it is on a formal basis for the public service.) In the last half century, students have become increasingly oriented toward specialized training for a concrete objective: the specific job leading to a successful career.[3] University degrees certify that students have been subject to specific educational programs.[4]

Education that emphasizes the evolution of skills and knowledge may be at the foundation of developing a relationship between production of information and its application in organizational decision making. (Although the tendency has been clearly in the direction of specialization and fragmentation, there is also some recognition of the need to train generalists with broad based knowledge and expertise [Snow, 1959, 1960].)[5] Bureaucracy is, then, served by the individuals who are subjected to the formal educational system. Their expertise is grounded in specific professional training:

> Through the educational system and the requirements for expertise in the job . . . bureaucracy promotes a "rationalist" way of life, but the concept of rationalism allows for widely differing contents. Quite generally, one can . . . say that . . . bureaucratization . . . very strongly furthers the development of "rational matter-of-factness" and the personality type of the professional expert. (Weber, 1968, p. 998)

The "rationalist way of life" within an organizational environment operationally means an emphasis on substantive rationality: goal-oriented action/behavior that is controlled by the ultimate ends that are desired. The ultimate ends may be the function of ethical, political, utilitarian, hedonistic, futile, and egalitarian considerations (Weber, 1968, p. 85). The bureaucrat may not always be in the position to implement the most direct, efficient means toward a specific objective; the ultimate ends may alter the plans for implementation. Thus, the bureaucrat needs access to an information base that allows him to address the question: "If Y is my long-term objective, which actions $(X_1, X_2 \ldots X_n)$ will lead to Y under Z conditions?" At any given point in time, the bureaucrat, his superiors, or his clients may want to assess a dimension of the overall problem: that is, how to achieve specific objectives within specified constraints.

The "rationalist way of life" promoted by bureaucracy is strictly tied to the requirements of the occupation. Unlike the scientist, the bureaucrat is not in the business of hypothesis testing. He cannot make the ceteris paribus assumption; he cannot control in an experimental or quasi-experimental sense for variation in the conditions affecting the outcome being measured. For most political and administrative problems, "other things" are usually not equal and it is next to impossible to control for variations in the environment. Indeed, one needs to be cognizant of the variations and how they affect the problem-solving process.

The need to know and to be confident of the organization's ability to martial the information sources required for a broad set of problem-solving activities is at the foundation of the rationalistic/bureaucratic state. The problem of rationality is, therefore, not primarily one of producing or applying scientific research. It is one of building capacity within the constraints of organization goals, "ultimate ends," and constraints. This form of rationality, which emphasizes the organizational level of analysis, is oriented toward recruitment and design of organizations and has little to do with the application of science and scientific findings to public sector decision making. It would be misleading to equate this with "optimizing" and "suboptimizing" strategies. Optimal behavior, from an organizational perspective, is not expressed in terms of the ability to access all information sources for a given, discrete problem. Instead, organizational activities are much more fluid. Decisions often do not have specific points at which they are initiated and terminated (Weiss, 1982). Consequently, the notion of developing organizational capacity and inventory is far more realistic. Rationality is expressed in terms of the ability to reach organizational objectives, and not in terms of the ability to access all potentially relevant sources of information. Irrationality is not a function of whether or not organizations incorporate the most up-to-date research (usually university-based research) into the decision-making process.

The focus of organizational behavior is not on the communications network developed by individual decision makers and by the collectivity. The extent to which scientific research is integrated into the decision-making process is relatively uninteresting. Instead, the focus is on recruitment, training, and the development of expertise. The expert has highly developed information skills that are expressed in terms of: the knowledge he brings to the job; the ability to gather new information; and the ability to synthesize information that can be readily accessed. Expertise implies that the most up-to-date information will be accessed, if it is relevant and needed. Indeed, it is probably available as part of the organizational inventory.

Capacity building in the area of knowledge development reached its peak during and after World War II. During World War II, university professors from all branches of the sciences served in the OSS and in the Bureau of the Budget. The contributions made by these experts were as important as the dramatic technological advances of the West (for example, the product of the famous Manhattan project). There is little doubt that the World War II period represents a watershed in terms of institutionalizing channels of outside expertise into government. University professors became regular advisors and sources of information for the bureaucracy. They also became permanent members of the bureaucracy. Their expertise was incorporated into the organization and became part of the regular organizational capacity/inventory.

As part of the commitment to expertise after World War II, government definitely tried to create the capacity to produce potentially relevant information "on demand." As part of this series of developments, bureaucracies were formally assigned the responsibility for creating and disseminating knowledge on many policy problems: through the National Center for Health Statistics, through the National Center for Educational Statistics, through the Congressional Research Service and the Congressional Office of Technology Assessment, through the General Accounting Office, and through the Office of Management and Budget. These offices and agencies all represent examples of providing the capacity to produce relevant information that could be stored for a time when it would be needed. They are responsible for collecting information, doing research, and reviewing state-of-the-art research findings.

Another example of the influence of substantive rationality on the development of government agencies can be found in the area of program evaluation. During the 1960s, programmatic funds authorized by Congress included a requirement to conduct program evaluations. Indeed, in some areas (such as Community Mental Health Centers) Congress required that a certain percentage of the program's operating budget be allocated for program-evaluation research (Cook and Shadish, 1982; Goldsmith, 1982).

Moreover, government has invested heavily in routinized/institutionalized official channels for receiving expert advice and information from individuals or groups of individuals: the Council of Economic Advisors, the National Security Council, and the Office of Science and Technology Policy in the White House. The executive branch of government, with the support of Congress, has encouraged the development of systematic sources of information that can be accessed and used by bureaucrats, elected officials, and citizens as a whole: the unemployment index, strategic planning, environmental impact statements, and social indicators. Computer technology has also made it quite easy to provide the relevant information almost instantaneously to the potential user (Rich, 1982).

In this context, it is worth noting that the "rationalist way of life" and the commitment to development of institutionalized information resources (for example, research, access to expert advice within government) are not tied to a particular set of assumptions about ultimate use and applications. This may be because organizations and organizational theorists do not conceptualize the information problem as one of gaining access to the most up-to-date information, or as one of building bridges between scientists outside of government and relevant decision makers (the so-called two communities or two cultures problem). The emphasis has not been on how best to utilize the research being conducted by scholars within universities, corporations, and research laboratories or within the government itself. The emphasis is on developing an inventory of information resources that can be accessed by government officials (Feldman, 1982). As Arrow points out:

> Once the investment has been made in information and an information channel acquired, it will be cheaper to keep on using it than to invest

in new channels, especially since the scarcity of individuals and input . . . implies that the use of new channels will diminish the product of old ones. (Arrow, 1974, pp. 39, 41).

The focus is on the investment and the capacity that follows from it rather than on the utilization process per se. A limited set of assumptions concerning applications are being made: information that is needed will be available, easily accessed, and used for particular problems facing the administrator; the available information base—including the presence of experts and routinized channels of expertise—will be used frequently because of its relevance to the problems facing the organization; and little attention needs to be paid to the process of utilization because it naturally follows from efforts oriented toward achieving a state of "substantive rationality." In other words, effective utilization of information resources, in the sense of translating information into decisions on setting the organizational agenda, the policy options being considered, and the policies ultimately implemented, is assumed to be built into the organizational capacity-building efforts.

This summary of the role of information resources in shaping organizational decisions/actions is helpful only if it reflects the ways in which information is accessed and used within public organizations. Given the emphasis on capacity building and access to an inventory of information resources, as well as the minimal attention devoted to utilization as a separate phenomenon, one would expect to find: frequent attempts to use relevant information resources; a reliance upon one's own staff and other government agencies as the primary source for providing information; little differentiation or sophistication with respect to understanding the utilization phenomenon; and an emphasis on organizational factors in assessing the desirability of using information resources.

EMPIRICAL RESULTS

Frequency of Utilization

In the winter and spring of 1980, 479 officials (policy makers and administrators within public sector mental health policy-making organizations at the federal, state, and local levels were interviewed.[6] They were asked about their information-seeking and utilization behavior. Moreover, they were asked to identify factors that affect individual and organizational attitudes and beliefs concerning knowledge production and knowledge utilization.[7]

TABLE 23.1. The Number of Types of Research and Analysis Used by Mental Health Policy Makers (percent)

Number of Information Types Used	Information Use (%)	Cumulative Use (%)
0	3.8	3.8
1	2.9	6.7
2	5.6	12.3
3	8.9	21.3
4	15.2	36.5
5	15.4	51.9
6	13.9	65.8
7	15.9	81.7
8	11.4	93.1
9	6.9	100.0

Mean: 5.271
Standard Deviation: 2.298
Valid Cases: 447

The study was designed to measure the use of relevant, policy-related information in the process of making and implementing mental health policy. Two key substantive areas of decision-making activity in this field include: policy with respect to the delivery of mental health services and policy with respect to the financing of mental health services. A review of the literature in these areas reveals that there are key types of information that relate to these decision-making areas: statistical information, evaluation information, demonstration projects and models, policy analysis generally, and expert advice.[8]

Given the review of the literature on organizational theory, the first question is: How often are the relevant sources of information used by a variety of mental health policy makers? Table 23.1 shows the results of an analysis of frequency of use for all nine types of information. On average, the decision makers interviewed in this study used more than five types of information to inform their decision making process. Approximately 34 percent of the respondents used seven or more sources of information on a regular basis.[9]

Table 23.2 illustrates the extent of utilization for each type of information. It is not surprising to find that statistical data, expert advice, and policy analyses are the information resources used most often within mental health policy-making organizations. These are the resources represented within typical organizational inventories. Studies that ordinarily are thought of as having to be conducted by individuals or organizations outside of

TABLE 23.2. Utilization of the Policy Information

Information Type	Utilization Score*	Overall Rank	Rank Within Policy Area
A. *Service oriented*			
1. Program Evaluations	.59	5	4
2. Demonstration projects	.48	7	5
3. Policy analyses	.65	3	3
4. Statistical data	.71	2	2
5. Expert advice	.75	1	1
Averaged subtotal	.64		
B. *Finance oriented*			
1. Cost-efficiency studies	.45	8	3
2. Financing models or patterns	.40	9	4
3. Statistical data	.64	4	1
4. Expert advice	.55	6	2
Averaged subtotal	.51		
Average grand total (N = 457)	.58		

*Utilization scores range from 0 to 1; where 0 equals "Information not used," and 1 equals "Information used." (This score, therefore, may be interpreted as the percentage of valid respondents using the information.)

government are less frequently used (for example, the production of financing models, cost efficiency studies).[10]

Sources of Information

Given these general patterns of utilization, it was important to examine the channels through which information is transmitted to mental health decision makers and administrators. Given the emphasis on capacity building and inventory, one would expect that the information that is frequently used is most often transmitted from individuals within one's own organization or from other closely related government agencies (that is, those with similar organizational missions).[11] The results show that officials do rely upon their own agencies and other government agencies to provide them with information resources (see Table 23.3). In the case of policy analysis and statistics, less than 20 percent of the information used is provided by sources outside the respondent's agency or another government agency. In the case of the other information resources, with the exception of "expert advice," less than a third of the information is provided by outside or external

TABLE 23.3. Who Provides Information for Mental Health Policy Makers? (percent)

Type of Information	Respondent's Agency	Other Government Agency	Other	Respondent's Agency	Other Government Agency	Other
Program evaluation	52.6	24.6	32.8			
Demonstration projects	36.3	30.2	33.5			
Policy analysis	55.4	25.8	18.8	65.6	23.1	11.1
Statistics	58.9	30.6	11.5	17.3	35.8	46.9
Expert advice	13.3	31.6	55.1			
Cost-efficiency study				58.3	18.1	23.6
Financing models				13.6	54.4	32

sources. These results dramatically underscore the point that officials rely upon the organizational capacity that they have developed within their own agencies and within related government agencies to meet their information needs.[12]

Sophistication with Respect to Knowledge Utilization

The third dimension on which it is possible to test the suitability of the synthesis of organizational theory provided is in the area of conceptualization of the utilization phenomenon itself. Do officials have a sophisticated conception of knowledge utilization? Do they understand the phenomenon itself?

During the course of interviews with mental health policy makers (and those who are important in influencing policy), we were interested in the extent to which there are unique patterns of utilization. Are certain types of information consistently used in conjunction with each other? Moreover, do decision makers differentiate the purpose for which they are using information, and are certain types of information more likely to be used in the formulation of policy and others used in the implementation of it? Alternatively, one could assume that there is an inventory of information available, and it is drawn upon on an as-needed basis. In this case, there would be little differentiation made on the part of the user concerning the purpose for which information is being used. He is making the assumption: utilization is utilization is utilization.

Table 23.4 presents the analysis of clusters or patterns of information use. Cluster analysis reveals some interesting results.[13] There are 512 possible combinations of use of the nine research types (from nonuse through any combination of use of one through eight different types of information, to the use of all nine types). Out of the 512 possible combinations that could have emerged, 187 actual clusters of information were shown. Ultimately, what was found was that 43.2 percent of the respondents could be categorized as having used research in a manner represented by only 5.1 percent of all possible clusters (26 out of 512 clusters of information) (Goldsmith, 1982).

On the face of it, this result points to the fact that a large proportion of the respondents do use information in distinct patterns; it is not simply a matter of random use of one type of information with another type. However, upon closer examination, the data reveal that the clustering is occurring in relation to organizational mission. As pointed out earlier, expert advice, policy analysis, and statistics are closely related to the central organizational mission within mental health policy-making agencies. Out of the 26 most often used clusters of information, either service-oriented or finance-oriented statistical data or expert advice was included in 24 of the 26 clusters.

It is interesting to note that the largest single cluster of information used was the cluster that showed all types of information were being used by the same individuals. This indicates that the inventory of available policy research resources is being drawn upon on a regular basis.

Along the other dimension of "sophistication," with respect to utilization it was found that users did not tend to distinguish the purpose for which the information was being used. (See Tables 23.5, 23.6, and 23.7.)

In designing the questionnaire administered to mental health policy makers and administrators, it was hypothesized that there are different stages of the policy-making process: defining issues, defining options, defining programs, justifying decisions, and defining solutions.[14] To the extent that these stages accurately describe phases of the policy-making process, one would expect that if officials were at all cognizant of or concerned with the utilization process, they would not utilize information in the same manner or frequency for all stages. Presumably, some types of mental health officials focus on one stage more than on other stages of policy making; if this is accurate, there should be different patterns of utilization across the five categories.

One might very well expect that the patterns of utilization obtained for adjacent steps on this policy-making continuum (such as between "defining the issues" and "defining options") would be more similar than patterns observed among steps at the extremes of this continuum (such as between "defining the issues" and "defining solutions"). This is the expected pattern because of the hypothesized progression in the policy-making process from problem definition to identification of solutions. However, as shown in Tables 23.5, 23.6, and 23.7, the hypothesized behavior was not confirmed. The correlational analysis employed depicts no clear relationship that is stronger between adjacent stages than between distant stages in the policy-making process. In fact, there is no clear progression of levels of correlation at all. Both the service provision and financing policy areas, research and analysis are used to similar degrees over the range of policy-making tasks and requirements (stages).[15]

Decision makers apparently use information to help solve whatever problems are on the organizational agenda at a given point in time. Information is accessed to work with particular issues, and little attention is paid to particular stages or phases of policy making. Differentiation among these stages or phases is not a conscious part of the organizational members' cognitive processing style. It is assumed that information will be available for whatever problem arises. To the extent that the organizational inventory or capacity is being relied upon, then the finding that stipulates that frequency of utilization does not vary significantly from stage to stage in the policy-making process is logical and consistent. The official is responsible for a broad range of issues/problems across the entire policy-making process. Information is

TABLE 23.4. Most Often Used Clusters of Information

INFORMATION

Service-Oriented

Cluster	Evaluation Research	Demonstration Projects	Policy Analyses	Statistical Data	Expert Advice
1 (none used)					
2					X*
3					
4					X
5				X	
6	X	X	X		X
7	X	X	X	X	X
8	X			X	
9	X	X	X	X	X
10	X	X	X	X	
11	X		X	X	X
12		X		X	X
13	X		X	X	X
14	X			X	X
15		X	X	X	X
16	X		X	X	X
17	X		X	X	X
18		X	X	X	X
19		X	X	X	X
20			X	X	X
21	X	X	X	X	X
22	X	X	X	X	X
23	X	X	X	X	X
24	X	X		X	X
25	X		X	X	X
26 (All types used)	X	X	X	X	X

*X = Information was used by respondent

TYPE

	Finance-Oriented			Percent of Respondents in each Cluster	Percent of 26 Clusters
Cost Effectiveness Studies	Financing Models	Statistical Data	Expert Advice		
				4.0	9.3
				1.4	3.2
		X		0.9	2.1
			X	0.9	2.1
X		X		0.9	2.1
				1.2	2.8
				0.9	2.1
X		X		0.9	2.1
				1.2	2.8
		X		1.2	2.8
		X		1.2	2.8
		X	X	0.9	2.1
		X	X	1.2	2.8
X		X	X	0.9	2.1
		X	X	0.9	2.1
X		X	X	2.3	5.3
	X	X	X	1.2	2.8
X		X	X	0.9	2.1
	X	X	X	1.6	3.7
X	X	X	X	0.9	2.1
X	X	X		0.9	2.1
X		X	X	3.0	6.9
	X	X	X	2.8	6.5
X	X	X	X	0.9	2.1
X	X	X	X	2.8	6.5
X	X	X	X	7.3	16.9
		Cumulative %:		43.2%	100.0%
		(N = 182)			

TABLE 23.5. Information Utilization at Stages in the Policy-making Process (percent)

First, *overall* to what extent has existing analysis and research about *the provision* of mental health services been helpful in . . .

	To a Great Extent	To Some Extent	Slightly	Not at All
(1) defining the issues surrounding service delivery?	21.7	53.6	19.5	5.3
(2) defining specific policy options?	19.1	42.1	30.3	8.6
(3) designing programs?	21.0	42.3	24.4	12.2
(4) justifying policy or program decisions?	26.0	44.1	21.8	8.1
(5) Defining solutions?	13.4	42.4	32.1	12.1

Next, *overall* to what extent has existing analysis and research about *financing* mental health services been helpful in . . .

	To a Great Extent	To Some Extent	Slightly	Not at All
(1) defining the issues?	21.3	40.0	26.6	12.0
(2) defining specific policy options?	20.8	41.6	26.5	11.2
(3) designing programs?	15.9	41.9	25.5	16.6
(4) justifying policy or program decisions?	24.1	40.0	20.3	10.6
(5) defining solutions?	12.5	40.6	32.7	14.2

TABLE 23.6. Intercorrelations Between the Use of Services-Oriented Policy Information at Stages of the Policy-making Process*

	Defining Issues	Defining Options	Defining Programs	Justifying Decisions	Defining Solutions
Defining issues		.47	.35	.35	.41
Defining options			.32	.39	.38
Defining programs				.30	.45
Justifying decisions					.40
Defining solutions					

*All correlations are Kendall's τ at the $\alpha \leq .001$ level

TABLE 23.7. Intercorrelations Between the Use of Finance-Oriented Policy Information at Stages of the Policy-Making Process*

Policy-making Stage	Defining Issues	Defining Options	Defining Programs	Justifying Decisions	Defining Solutions
Defining Issues		.59	.40	.43	.45
Defining Options			.46	.52	.51
Defining Programs				.47	.46
Justifying Decisions					.53
Defining Solutions					

*All correlations are Kendall's τ at the $\alpha \leq .001$ level.

needed (or not needed) at all stages; the need does not vary in a systematic or predictable fashion. Hence, the correlational analysis does not document a particular pattern or set of patterns.[16]

Factors Affecting Utilization

Our interviews also focused on factors that affect utilization: the assessment of the extent to which a series of factors will decrease or increase the likelihood that policy-related information will be used. Generally, the factors are variables that were addressed following the three categories: those related to maximizing rationality of the individual decision maker, those related to how organizations and bureaucracies operate, and those related to improving communications.[17] As Table 23.8 reveals, bureaucratic/organizational factors are the only ones that are significantly and positively associated with utilization.[18]

Within the category of organizational factors, several specific findings are important:

43.5 percent of the respondents said that "findings which challenge existing institutional arrangements" decrease the chance of utilization;

67 percent of the respondents said that "findings which should not agree with potential user's intuition" decrease the likelihood of utilization;

41 percent of the respondents said that information "which casts doubt on a policy position already taken" decreases the likelihood of utilization; and

TABLE 23.8. Factors that Affect Utilization of Research-Based Information by Mental Health Officials (Chi Square Measures)

Categories of Factors Affecting Utilization	Utilization Measure
Rationality	nonsignificant
Bureaucratic	< 0297
Community	nonsignificant

68.9 percent of the respondents agreed with the statement "government agencies tend to ignore research findings that are not in line with agency assumptions and philosophies."

These findings stress the importance of understanding organizational procedures and constraints as they relate to information-seeking and utilization behavior. These appear to be the factors that shape how information is used in organizations.

CONCLUSION

Organizational and bureaucratic theory provides a framework for a systematic understanding of information-seeking and utilization behavior. It is in the interest of the organization (that is, it is a critical part of the organizational mission) to invest heavily in developing information resources. In building an information base within an organization, a broad set of resources is required: expertise represented by individual experts, statistics, policy analysis, program evaluation, models/forecasting, and other policy-relevant sources of information.

An emphasis on organizational capacity and the development of an information inventory is consistent with: frequent use of many potentially relevant sources of information; reliance upon one's own staff and other government agencies as the primary source for providing information resources; and very little concern with processes or utilization. Utilization of bureaucratically "acceptable" information follows from the development of inventories of organizational information.

NOTES

1. This tendency is reflected in the Morrill Act (Civil War period) and the Smith-Hughes Act of 1917.

2. Mosher cites as important examples the president of Johns Hopkins University and the president of the University of Chicago.

3. Mosher points out that more than three-fifths of all bachelors and higher degrees granted in 1977–78 were in professional fields: "About one-quarter were in the sciences—physical, biological, social, and mathematical . . . one-tenth were in the humanities" (Mosher, 1982, p. 53).

4. Increasingly, in an attempt to protect themselves, professions have also instituted licensing and certification procedures (e.g., for psychiatrists, psychiatric nurses, social workers). Education is important, but the licensing exam is a critical litmus test for knowledge and expertise.

5. C. P. Snow and others have been particularly concerned with educating individuals in the humanities and the sciences.

6. Individuals from five different types of organizations were interviewed: the official state mental health entity, Community Mental Health Centers and other service agencies, advocacy groups, the umbrella health and social service agency, and legislators and their staff.

7. The utilization measure employed in this study was a composite variable that combined the objective, yes-or-no use of nine types of information with responses concerning the rating of four degrees of "importance" of information that was used. The resulting measure of degrees of utilization was found to be more sensitive to nuances in use than the standard all-or-nothing use measures typically employed in the utilization literature. This composite variable was aggregated to the level of the two policy-making areas included in the study: the provision of services and the financing of mental health services. (That is, weighted averages were taken for the five types of information related to mental health service delivery and a separate weighted average for the four types of information related to finance-oriented information, to form measures of information utilization generally in the policy areas studied.) These two measures were found to be more useful than either nine different measures of use of each type of information or one overall, global use measure.

8. We try to tailor our questionnaires/interviews to tap into each of these generic categories of information for both policy-making areas. The pretest showed that decision maker's concern with financing did not identify "policy analysis generally" as being a salient resource. Consequently, the five generic areas were asked about in the area of mental health service delivery, and four were asked about in the area of financing.

9. The specific question asked was "In the past year, have you/has your office used (a particular type of information) in making decisions concerning (financing or mental health services)?"

10. In general, Table 23.2 reveals that information related in the policy area concerned with the delivery of mental health services is used more often than information related to policies concerning financing. The delivery of mental health services is closely related to the "essence" of mental health policy-making organizations. They are the heart of legislative mandates and day-to-day operations.

11. Respondents were asked: "Thinking of the last time that you used 'X' type of information, could you tell me the type of organization that did the research: respondent's agency organization, other government agency, service organization, research consulting firm—profit, research consulting firm—non-profit, university-research institute, university-independent faculty, community/advocacy group, professional society, other."

12. When controlling for organizational affiliation (that is, whether the respondent is a member of a community mental health center, official mental health entity, an advocacy group, a health bureaucracy, or a legislature), there is no change in the overall relationship. In other words, no matter what organization one belongs to, the same pattern of reliance upon internal sources of information persists.

13. This is not cluster analysis in the formal, statistical sense of the term.

14. Using this scale (to a great extent, to some extent, slightly, not at all), *overall* to what

extent has existing analysis in research about the provision of mental health services/financing of mental health services been helpful in: (1) defining the issues surrounding service delivery; (2) defining specific policy options; (3) designing programs; (4) justifying policy or program decisions; and (5) defining solutions." A rating was obtained for each of these five categories from every respondent.

15. The relationship observed is not altered through the use of any intervening variables: age, length of tenure in office, organizational affiliation, education, and training. This is apparently a robust relationship that is upheld across both policy-making areas.

16. Alternatively, one may want to argue that levels of sophistication are at stake. Mental health decision-makers and administrators view utilization as a unidimensional phenomenon: utilization is utilization is utilization. •

17. In light of the limited ability of computer generated factor analysis, another approach was taken to factor analyses. The study questionnaire was designed to include a wide variety of items intended to represent sources of influence on information use. These variables were drawn from each of the three broad approaches to explaining utilization which were identified through a review of the research literature.

Variables from each of the Rational Actor, Communications and Bureaucratic Politics approaches were standardized and then combined to create a set of three individual variables, scaled from zero to one, and intended to reflect the overall ratings of all variables associated with each approach.

18. This is true in the area of mental health services policy but not in the area of policy with respect to mental health financing.

BIBLIOGRAPHY

Arrow, Kenneth. *The Limits of Organization.* New York: Norton, 1974.

Cook, T. D. and Shadish, W. R., Jr. In G. Stahler, and W. R. Tash (eds.), *Innovative Approaches to Mental Health Evaluation.* New York: Academic Press, 1982.

Feldman, Martha S. "Producing Policy Papers," paper presented for symposium on information processing in organizations, Carnegie-Mellon University, October 1982.

Friedman, Milton. *Capitalism and Freedom.* Chicago: University of Chicago Press 1962.

Goldsmith, Neal M. *The Study of Knowledge Utilization in Mental Health Policy-making.* Doctoral Dissertation, Claremont Graduate School, 1982.

Halperin, Morton, H. *Bureaucratic Politics and Foreign Policy.* Washington, D.C.: Brookings Institution, 1974.

Mosher, Frederick C. *Democracy and the Public Service.* New York: Oxford University Press [Second Edition], 1982.

New York Times. "Federal Spending for Research and Development," New York Times, February 16, p. C5, 1982.

Rich, Robert F. "Knowledge Utilization and the Rationalistic State: Revisiting C. P. Snow's Two Cultures," paper prepared for Conference on Knowledge Utilization: Theory and Methodology, Communications Institute, East-West Center, Honolulu, Hawaii, April 1982.

Rourke, Francis E. "Variations in Agency Power," in Francis E. Rourke (editor), *Bureaucratic Power in National Politics.* Boston: Little Brown [Third Edition], 1978.

Simon, Herbert A. *Administrative Behavior.* New York: Free Press [Third Edition], 1976.

Snow, C. P. *The Two Cultures and the Scientific Revolution.* New York: Cambridge University Press, 1959.

Snow, C. P. *The Godkin Lectures*, Cambridge, MA.: Harvard University Press, 1960.

Weber, Max. *Economy and Society* (edited by Guenther Roth and Claus Wittich). New York: Bedminister Press, Vols. 1 and 3, 1968.

Weiss, Carol, "Policy Research in the Context of Diffused Decision-making," in Ray C. Rist, ed., *Policy Studies Review Annual*, Vol 6. Beverly Hills, CA. Sage, 1982.

24

DESIGN AS A SETTING FOR USEFUL RESEARCH

Joseph A. Litterer and Mariann Jelinek

The search for "useful research" immediately raises the question, "Useful for what?" Research on organizations, like research in general, has seen the generation of knowledge as an important end in itself, assuming that all knowledge would ultimately serve in some utilitarian way. This premise has increasingly come under attack. Thomas and Tymon (1982), who offer a recent summary of a large body of criticism, make three particularly telling points. First, much research has been conducted to maximize internal validity, downplaying external validity to such an extent that findings have scarcely any discernible relation to reality. Second, the outcomes or dependent variables often have not reflected the things managers and designers want to influence as organizational outcomes; that is, they are low on goal relevance. Third, the variables examined were often not subject to control by managers: they lacked operational validity because there is no way to use them in an organization.

Pressures toward knowledge research are perhaps generated by the requirement that research be generalizable, rather than being directed to understanding one event, person, entity, or problem. The basic intent is to uncover general laws of nature or behavior. Researchers are constantly beset by the need to prove the validity of their findings and come up with a formulation general enough to cover a large body of cases. The more generalizable, the more "pure" the research. Research undertaken solely in pursuit of knowledge can be called "knowledge research." At the extreme, such research is a long way from the organizational world of payrolls, problems, products, and profits.

Organizational sciences have also undertaken action research, directed to a client's unique problems. Action research is the opposite of knowledge research in that it claims little generalizability, if any, and is defined and initiated by the client, not by the scientist. The core of this research is a methodology and a set of skills, not a body of knowledge. Not only is there no need for the findings to be general, but the investigator may actually be enjoined by the client from revealing the results outside the client firm. While some scientists do both types of research, most seem to restrict their efforts to one or the other. Different values and requirements for knowledge research and action research often impede communications between the two schools, resulting in considerable loss to both. Luthans and Davis (1982) are only the most recent authors to suggest that some combination of perspectives might be fruitful.

Organization design, the practical application of general knowledge to a specific client organization's unique problems, shares properties of both action research and knowledge research. Like action research, its ultimate objective is to help solve an individual client's organization problem. Like knowledge research, it is concerned with general relationships and concepts that can be broadly applied. The scientist concerned with organization design is concerned with knowledge that is general in the sense of applying to more than one or a few situations, but which at the same time is reducible to specific application. Design knowledge needs to include a great deal more information about contingencies, limits, and contexts than much knowledge research findings. The design scientist needs not only the economy of bringing together already developed bodies of knowledge, but also guidance on what further client-specific knowledge needs to be developed through action research.

Organization design has often been mentioned as a topic in the literature of organizations, but it has received little serious research attention until quite recently. Given its special position between "pure" knowledge research and highly applied action research, design presents an unusual opportunity to bridge the gap between pure and applied by offering guidance for the sort of knowledge research most needed, as well as guidance from pure research on focuses for action. In the remainder of this chapter we will explicate this opportunity, showing how design can offer a fruitful guide for research that avoids failures of goal validity, external validity, and operational validity on the one hand, and those of missing generalizability on the other.

DESIGN AND RESEARCH CONTRASTED

While some writers clearly recognize that design is a process different from research, a surprisingly large number treat design as merely an extension or application of research, requiring no special perspective.* This blurring of distinctions has very likely played an important role in perpetuating or even encouraging the problems identified earlier. We will examine the differences between research and design not only to demonstrate their existence, but more important, to lay the foundation for understanding how design can provide a context to frame and develop useful organizational research.

The predominant mode of research in the field of organization studies identifies a research question, states a hypothesis, gathers data to answer the question or test the hypothesis, and then draws conclusions or interprets the data. Such research is analytical, breaking large issues or questions into smaller, more tractable ones. Two, or occasionally three, variables are examined in search of correlations or causality (We might add, as others have, that by far the majority of such research uses cross-sectional data and statistical methodologies incapable of supporting causal inferences.) The objective of most organizational research is verified information, generalizable to significant portions of the relevant environment. Reasoning is objectivist, rational, and largely deductive (Lundberg, 1976; Susman and Evered, 1978; Burrell and Morgan, 1979). Judgment is important in selecting researchable topics, appropriate research methodologies, and research settings (see Table 24.1).

In contrast, design begins with the identification of a problem with or opportunity for specific collective action. It proceeds through the examination of alternate arrangements for organizational elements, combining or modifying these to meet specific needs or constraints. Design is synthetic, taking smaller elements and combining them into a larger whole. While the designer may begin with a few variables (say coordinating several activities to facilitate a technology), the finished organization design must eventually achieve the regulation of throughput flows into and out of the environment, the commitment of organization members, and the integration of the collective effort around organization goals, among many other aims.

Design deals with the many interdependent elements of a complex system. Designers must approach their task with awareness of this com-

---

*While some writers explicitly state that design is not a type of research, most write about design as if it were an activity using essentially the same methods as research, or as if the findings of research were the materials of design, requiring only to be used. Typically, no explanation of how research findings might be utilized is provided. Still others make both assumptions, that design is both itself research and a simple extension of existing organizational research. As illustration see: Triandis, H. C., "Notes on the Design of Organizations", in Thompson, J. D. (ed.), *Approaches to Organizational Design*, 1966, University of Pittsburgh Press, Pittsburgh; Lorsch, J. W. and Lawrence, P. R., *Studies in Organizational Design*, 1970, Irwin-Dorsey, Homewood IL.; Galbraith, J., *Organization Design*, 1977, Addison-Wesley, Reading, MA; Ullrich, R. A. and Wieland, G. F., *Organization Theory and Design*, 1980, Irwin-Dorsey, Homewood IL.

	Research	Design
Process	1. Identify question	1. Identify problem with, or opportunity for, collective action
	2. State hypothesis	2. Examine alternate arrangements generic model archetypes
	3. Gather data	3. Combine or modify to fit constraints
	4. Draw conclusions	4. Test and revise
Method of proceeding	Analytical—breaks large issues into smaller	Synthetic—takes smaller, combines into whole
	Uses 2–3 variables	Many variables, deals with interrelationships, limits, and constraints
	Often correlational (doubtful causality)	Multiple interrelationships, integration of complete system
Aim	Verified information, wide generalizability	Specific, workable solution, plan for an actual organization
Judgment	Selecting topic, method, and setting	Choosing tradeoffs between alternatives
Ideal sought	At the "cutting edge" of the field, test of hypothesis	Effectiveness then efficiency Adaptability
Summary	Rational Deductive Objectivist	Intuitive Inductive Incremental

TABLE 24.1. Characteristics of Research and Design

plexity and interdependence. Thinking is inductive, incremental, and intuitive. The output is a plan for organization, a solution to the unique problems of a specific organization. In design, emphasis falls first on effectiveness, next on efficiency. More recently, adaptability to environmental change and organization learning have been added as design criteria.

Design links general knowledge with specific, unique solutions. If the cutting edge of research is the test of the hypothesis, the cutting edge of design is the tradeoff decision between alternative designs and modifications. Judgment is needed for recognizing when design is necessary and what elements have to be included in the design, as well as for establishing the order of priorities to be used in tradeoff decisions and for weighing the impact of elements whose effects are poorly understood or unknown.

The characteristics of research and design are sharply different—so different, in fact, that we may question whether a person good at one task could also be good at the other. At minimum, the differences cast serious doubt on the notion that design is essentially the same as research or a simple extension of it. At the same time, it is clear that design draws upon research, or more accurately, that design could and should be drawing upon and interrelated closely with research. The reasons lie in the characteristics of the organization design process.

The Process of Design

The process of organization design is less well understood than that of research, and it lacks the clearly articulated values and criteria of research. Direct observation of organization design, interviews with organization designers, and a survey of accounts of design in the literature reveal considerable agreement on the basic outline of a process quite reminiscent of the problem-solving, program-innovating process described by March and Simon (1958). The process generally goes through the following steps.

Identification of a Need for Organization Design

To begin with, most organization design is redesign. It starts with a problem—performance difficulties, strain on key organization members, inadequate resources, or the opportunity to expand or add new products, functions, or technology. Recognizing these conditions in advance, or even at their inception, is the exception rather than the rule. Typically, a problem becomes a crisis before it is seen as the occasion for organization (re)design. In fact, even after recognition, the option of design is often ignored, perhaps reflecting an awareness of "sunk costs"* in the existing organization form. Some attempt may be made to treat the problem by less drastic means, such as transferring personnel, working over time, and so forth. Only after it becomes apparent that the costs of not reorganizing exceed the sunk costs, and that other means will not adequately handle the problem, is the need for organization design acknowledged.

---

*Costs here is used to include financial, emotional, time, or other costs.

Identifying Criteria and Constraints

The second step in the practice of design is the identification of factors to be taken into account. Initially, this may take the form of a simple, general statement such as, "We want to get a better control over sales activities," or a more extensive review of the unit's mission, present and preferred conditions, and operating modes. Ultimately, criteria to be satisfied will include constraints such as resources available, political constraints, environmental conditions, and forecast changes, among others. Typically, the criteria list expands as the process of design continues, in an incremental, intuitive fashion. Typically, too, judgment of an almost aesthetic sort, going well beyond the purely rational, is required in identifying and appropriately weighting the criteria to be satisfied.

Examining Alternatives: Finding Organizational Archetypes and Using Generic Models

The search for possible design solutions involves examination of organization archetypes (such as functional or departmental structure, product or geographic divisions, or matrix forms) that can be used to guide design. If the designer's personal repertoire of archetypes seems insufficient, the search may be extended to exploit other pools of information—for example, by visiting other organizations or using consultants. Such archetypes or patterns constitute the raw material of design.

Preparing an Organization Plan

The examination of alternatives usually reveals that no one archetype design is fully adequate, but that several are possibilities. Now comes a stage in which archetype designs are adapted and combined into a prototype plan for the organization. Characteristics of one archetype may meet one criterion of design, while alternative patterns better satisfy other criteria. The prototype design is tested by modeling in some way its anticipated performance and the conditions it will create both internally and externally. Most frequently, some form of scenario analysis is used, as managers seek to understand the "what-ifs" of the prototype. This information is compared against the desired outcomes and key constraints, including members of the future organization, their abilities, preferences, and responses, and anticipated conditions in the external environment.

Since some of these conditions will be new, additional information is often necessary to determine whether these outcomes will be acceptable, or what additional efforts might be necessary to make them acceptable. For example, a union might not go along with redesigning many workers' jobs without additional negotiations; breaking up existing work groups could cause resistance; laws may inhibit plant closings, making alternative approaches more desirable. Initial prototypes often require considerable adjustment, so the process of preparing an organization plan may be repeated several times before a satisfactory design is achieved.

The designer's creative task of examining, adapting, and combining archetypal organization forms is guided by a generic organizational model that identifies the components and functioning of any organization. Such models may be relatively simple and concrete, such as a pyramidal form where positions are differentiated hierarchically (by authority and responsibility) and horizontally (by function such as manufacturing, personnel, or finance). Complex, elaborate models like Barnard's are also used. Generic models guide the designer both in examining archetypes and in planning the actual organization, in part by highlighting the essential elements to be taken into consideration, or the key relationships to be maintained.

Developing Plans to be Used

The final design necessarily involves making difficult tradeoffs. Choosing any one design achieves or facilitates some desired outcomes while it excludes or diminishes others. Any design incurs certain costs, but avoids others. The final choice is necessarily complex, since the tradeoffs involve benefits and costs in technical, social, and administrative systems simultaneously. Specialists may be able to evaluate costs and benefits within any one subsystem, but the crucial assessment concerns tradeoffs among systems, for the organization as a whole. This is the unique and lonely task of the designer. Much that needs to be known isn't, leaving intuition, creativity, and judgment to bridge the gaps.

Types of Research Encouraged by Design

This examination of the design process reveals several different types of information the designer needs that research could provide. Research directed toward these information gaps would be highly useful and, as we shall see, of significant scientific merit as well. Needed research could be so structured to meet multiple needs, and certainly a variety of approaches seems appropriate.

Archetypes of Organization Forms

Central to the design process is examination of alternative designs. The richer in variety and detail the designer's store of basic, ideal, or archetype organization forms, the better prepared the designer will be to create the final design. To fill out the catalog of organizational archetypes, research needs to answer such questions as: What basic archetype forms of organization have been used, or could be used? What are the component elements of these archetype forms? What performance characteristics do these forms have? What conditions must be met for various archetypes to operate? Are some conditions more conducive to effective operation of some forms than other conditions? Which conditions, and which forms? What is the basic logic of each form's operation?

Ideal archetypes are widely used in other research and design areas. Engineers use ideal heat engine cycles such as the diesel or carnot cycles, which outline the basic options for engine design and the ideal performance of that engine. Designing, for the engineer, involves selecting the ideal form best suited for current purposes (the model) and then making an actual design that comes as close as possible to the characteristics of the chosen model, given constraints of size, materials, and so on. Ideal models in organization science would include Weber's model of bureaucracy, and Burns and Stalker's organic and mechanistic forms. Surely, there are others as well. At the moment, appropriate methodologies for this basic or pure research in organization design is not well developed. Indeed, we have primarily rules of thumb and anecdotal accounts of various organization forms' characteristics. Substantial opportunity exists here for research aimed at systematically uncovering organizational archetypes.

Closely allied is the need for typologies to help order and arrange organizational archetypes. To be useful, typologies need to differentiate among organization types, using organizationally relevant dimensions. Burns and Stalker differentiate between organic and mechanistic organizations by means of the repetitive nature of the work, the predictability of the environment, and the role of rules in the organization. Woodward and Thompson distinguish different archetypes by the technology employed. Others use more problematic dimensions to differentiate, such as ownership. There may well be other dimensions, especially since many typologies are old and most are based exclusively on manufacturing firms. In an increasingly service-oriented economy, surely service-oriented typologies would be of use.

The Generic Organization

The generic organization, more general and more basic even than the ideal archetype, is a template of what has to be included in any organization design. In designing a house, the architect may not at first know what the final house will look like, but the concept of the generic house stipulates that it must have properties like space, its layout or arrangement, and isolation from the environment (by doors, walls, and roof). The generic house concept also notes the house's response to environmental change (through heat or air conditioning) and functional properties like security. All these can be specified by reference to the generic type. The designer uses elements like concrete, brick, steel, and glass; processes like heat loss through walls or air flows; and conditions that must be faced, like snow load and the shearing effect of wind. All are part of preliminary design. Such generic conceptions offer considerable guidance by laying out parameters or boundaries for design. We need a similar generic organization to guide the organization designer. The generic model must identify the essential elements and processes of any organization, their basic functions and relationships. Many practicing designers seem to use the simple pyramidal organization form as their generic type. Increasingly, however, others are using a systems form that includes inputs, throughputs, outputs, and feedback loops. However, neither of these, at least at the moment, adequately includes things we know need to be addressed from the very beginning of organization design. Responsiveness to versus isolation from the environment, requisite buffering of the core technologies, integration, interrelating structure with strategy and size are among some of the more obvious considerations not well included.

Properties of Organizational Elements

The principal elements in organizations are of course human elements, both individuals and groups. More research is needed into the impact of variations in organization properties such as job content, centralization or decentralization of authority, work flow arrangements, and information density (among others) on individuals and groups. We know, for example, of the general importance of autonomy and participation. We need to know considerably more about the contingencies, limits, and tradeoffs involved. Some people seem not to value autonomy and participation highly. Which persons? Under what conditions? The impact of variations in the characteristics of individuals and groups on organization properties and outcomes is also of interest. There is great need for research that will continue to explore connections between elements typically covered in organization behavior studies (such as communication patterns and motivation) and the more applied, organizationally relevant, and managerially applicable concepts, looking at links between motivation and leadership, or locus of control and control systems, for instance. A number of traditional OB research topics acquire new significance if linked to the design characteristics that affect them.

Characteristics of Organization Properties and Processes

Given the scope of the effort in studying organizations, the number of properties or variables that have been identified is thus far limited. Span of control, organization slack, specialization, formalization, technical core, and uncertainty absorption are among the more commonly mentioned members of this small set. More work is needed to expand our knowledge of the properties and processes that make up organizations. Work could proceed empirically—by noting things that happen to which we have not paid attention—and theoretically—by noting where the existence of some element or process is necessary to explain things we do know to go on. We would scarcely be original in suggesting that practicing managers' and organization designers' insights into elements missing from the researchers' notebooks could provide significant guidance.

Once properties and processes have been identified, we need to know more about them. As Simon noted, one of the troubles with "principles" or "proverbs" of administration is that they are often contradictory. Moreover, we do not know when one proverb applies and another does not.

One research question that a design perspective makes painfully obvious concerns specialization. Adam Smith and a long list of others have pointed to the advantages of more finely subdivided work, while numerous recent studies have shown the cost in both human and economic terms of highly specialized, repetitious work. To our knowledge, there has been no work to determine the range over which specialization has positive results. The proposition that, "If a little is good, a lot is better," is inadequate as a guide for organization design; more sophisticated appreciation of limits is required. Span of control is one of the few organizational constructs that have been studied in this way at all, and the results indicate some of the complexities of this field of investigation.

Methodological Issues of Organizational Research

For decades the literature of organizational studies has proclaimed that systems models were appropriate for organization research. Regrettably, research has seldom recognized this condition, much less achieved it. The gap between exhortation and practice in part reflects an absence of methodological and analytical tools, rather than indolence or ignorance. We have few or no tools to address the complex interrelationships of the systems perspective: we must develop them. New nonparametric and graphic analytical techniques offer some promise. There is a serious, even desperate, need to develop research methods that address the reality of the phenomenon studied, rather than distorting that world to serve existing methods, as is so often the case.

Action Research

If the process of design described here is to proceed usefully, investigation is needed about every step along the way. Here action research opens rich opportunities. Specific instances of problems or incidents that start the process must be studied. Research should be carried out on the "sunk costs" of existing organization forms and the deferred costs of not changing, to build a repertoire of examples from which more general inferences might be drawn. Investigation is needed also into conditions, such as structure or decision-making programs that exist at the time the redesign is considered; and into the future conditions the changed organization will have to interact with and the possible outcomes of that interaction.

Action research on instances of organization design can significantly contribute to our understanding of the design process. Action research, while not generalizable from any single instance, might well be generalizable if care is taken to document many single instances. At minimum, richly documented action research accounts can provide preliminary case data for other researchers carrying out more knowledge-oriented research.

Reporting Research

Research that could be valuable for design often cannot be used because not enough information is provided about the situation in which the study was conducted. Micro and macro research perspectives rarely interact, although interaction between these perspectives is crucial for good organization design. Studies on structure often tell us nothing about the technology employed or the environment faced; studies of work design usually leave us in the dark about the communication networks, the strategy of the firm, or the overall control system that exists. The systems view has been accepted as conventional wisdom for several decades, yet most research is reported as if the phenomenon examined stood in splendid isolation from the rest of the organization. Such interconnections themselves also offer a significant opportunity for research.

DESIGN AS A CONTEXT FOR RESEARCH

The context of design generates broad areas of organizational research topics. Equally important, design provides a perspective on what should be studied about those topics. In addressing topics concerned with the design of actual organizations, investigators will be designing research to identify and measure organizational properties, processes, and outcomes of interest to designers. Research utility is built into the perspective, and the context provides a tug toward external validity and goal relevance. Since the research audience will include the designer (rather than solely other researchers, for instance), the investigator will continually have to ask how the designer might handle or control the elements under investigation. This provides another big tug toward operational validity. Hence, the design context exerts strong pressures on organization research to correct the unfortunate biases that

Thomas and Tymon (1982) identify as impeding usefulness of so much existing research.

Placing organizational research in a design context will doubtless affect organizational scientists in several ways. We will examine two of these.

To begin with, investigations undertaken with an eye toward design usefulness will set new priorities for what is important, in some cases reversing present trends. External validity rather than internal validity will be paramount; output and controllable variables will be utilized. Research methodologies more easily explicable to nonspecialist practitioners may come into vogue. Design-oriented values, such as effectiveness in preference to efficiency, will become more important. The real impact of research findings in an organization will also be a criterion. Researchers carrying out such investigations are likely to be much in demand as consultants and popular with practitioners. However, until values shift among academic peers, the rewards of regard, prestige, promotion, and pay may be slower in coming or even perhaps be endangered, since such design-oriented studies will not look as "rigorous" or as elegant to those who treasure internal validity with limited variables and tight controls.

There is a long-standing, quiet myth that applied research—or for that matter any research that has direct usefulness—is not as significant, important, or prestigious as basic research in pursuit of knowledge or "truth." As a result, scientists are supposed to eschew practicality and embrace pure research. However, as Pelz and Andrews (1966) found, scientists who formerly did pure research (on topics that were chosen for their importance to their discipline, rather than because their findings would have any application) willingly undertook research of commercial importance when brought into the planning process of product development. Scientists have many interesting questions they could explore. When some of those could also lead to results deemed useful and important not only to other researchers but also to nonscientists like marketing executives, they willingly choose useful topics. In a similar fashion, using design as a context for organizational research may help both in defining interesting and challenging research questions and in giving them the added attractions of utility and practical importance.

Given factors like these that could make design an attractive, fruitful, workable context for research, will this shift in the research paradigm occur? Perhaps; however, to give future events a nudge in this direction, we might do a number of things:

> Sponsor general conferences where designers in organizations, line executives, consultants, and organizational scientists can meet to describe their current work, the prospects and problems they see, and their needs. The intent of such show-and-tell conferences would be to

make the members of these groups better informed about what others are doing and to encourage interchange. A recent conference on Strategic Management in Montreal, organized on this model, produced much valuable interaction—and many new ideas for research.

Sponsor conferences such as this one on Useful Research, where a relatively small group of organization designers and scientists will work on the needs identified earlier, where they will have an opportunity to develop "wish lists," elaborate on their needs, communicate them to one another, and also articulate the limits on what they can provide for others.

Encourage professional journals to invite practitioners to write review articles in which they would examine the articles appearing in the journal during the past year and comment on their usefulness for organization design.

Seek the establishment of "Scientist in Residence" or "Visiting Manager" positions in business, government, and service organizations for a week, month, semester, or year in which organization scientists would be invited to "tag along" with operating managers and internal consultants as they design organizations.

Include a section on organization design, akin to existing chapters on research methods, in Organization Behavior texts to help students understand how the knowledge they are acquiring might be used.

CONCLUSION

If we draw back from the specific issue of design, this chapter is proposing a new, or rather an additional, perspective for research. The typical stance of the scientist is to look at the latest findings of research and ask, "Now that we know this, what is the next thing we should find out?" An "interesting" research question is not just a dramatic or unusual question. It is a question that will add new information along the moving frontier of knowledge and, it is hoped, connect several other previously known things into a new and larger meaning. It is also something that the scientist can examine with available tools and methods. Hence it is a selection among a constrained set of options.

In addition to this view, we are proposing that the scientist also look at new knowledge to ask, "In light of this knowledge, how will, could, or should people apply it in organizations? How will, could, or should they use it in making decisions?" We are suggesting that when organization scientists look ahead to frame the next research project, they not only examine the next blank space of knowledge and the tools of investigation, but that they also consider what nonscientists need to know to make better decisions and create a better organizational world.

REFERENCES

Argyris, Chris
1980   Inner Contridictions of Rigorous Research. New York: Academic Press.

Barnard, Chester I.
1938   The Functions of The Executive. Cambridge: Harvard University Press.

Burrell, Gibson and Morgan, Gareth
1979   Sociological Paradigms and Organizational Analysis. London: Heinemann.

Clark, Peter A.
1972   Organizational Design. London: Tavistock.

Cummings, Larry L.
1978   "Toward Organizational Behavior." Academy of Management Review, 3:90–98.

Kilmann, Ralph, Pondy, Louis R., and Slevin, Dennis P.
1976   The Mangement of Organization Design. New York: North-Holland.

Lundberg, Craig
1976   "Hypothesis Creation in Organizational Behavior Research." Academy of Management Review, 1:5–12.

Luthans, Fred and Davis, T. M. R.
1982   "An Idiographic Approach to Organizational Behavior Research: The Use of Single Case Experimental Designs and Direct Measures." Academy of Management Review, 7:380–91.

March, James G. and Simon, Herbert A.
1958   Organizations. New York: Wiley, 178–82.

Pelz, Donald C. and Andrews, F. M.
1966   Scientists in Organizations. New York: Wiley.

Pinder, Craig
1977   "Concerning the Application of Human Motivation Theories in Organizational Settings." Academy of Management Review, 2:384–97.

Simon, Herbert A.
1947   Administrative Behavior. New York: Macmillan.

Smith, Adam
1776   The Wealth of Nations. London: Strahan and Candell.

Sussman, Gerald I. and Evered, Roger D.
1978   "An Assessment of the Scientific Merits of Action Research." Administrative Science Quarterly, 23:582–603.

Thomas, Kenneth W. and Tymon, Walter G., Jr.
1982   "Necessary Properties of Relevant Research: Lessons from Recent Criticisms of the Organizational Sciences." Academy of Management Review, 7:345–52.

25

MANAGERIAL COGNITION AND BEHAVIOR: MODELING THESE PROCESSES MORE ACCURATELY

Tim R. V. Davis

The theme of this conference suggests two things: that much organizational research is not useful, and that it is time we began to look at research from the point of view of those who attempt to use it. While this is a sad comment on our research, few would disagree with either of these points. A great deal of research can be viewed as useful only in the narrow sense of perpetuating research in the academic community. Practitioners, who should be the beneficiaries of most organizational research, rarely read these studies let alone make any attempt to use them.

This chapter approaches the problem of generating useful knowledge from the perspective of the practicing manager. Managerial research can and should contribute to the practice of management. This is unlikely to happen, however, unless we start to develop theories and models that are more consistent with how managers think and act on the job. Many existing concepts and theories of organizational behavior and management build in assumptions about the nature of managerial work that are not supported by empirical studies of managers in action. This chapter points out what some of these assumptions are and proposes a process model that attempts to provide a more realistic view of managerial behavior.

ASSUMPTIONS ABOUT THE NATURE OF MANAGERIAL BEHAVIOR

In an earlier article (Davis and Luthans, 1980), managerial behavior was classified on a continuum distinguishing three modes of behaving: proactive, reactive, and adaptive (see Figure 25.1). *Proactive* or instrumental behavior was described as behavior following a goal-oriented course.

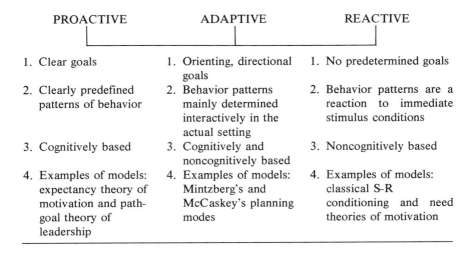

PROACTIVE	ADAPTIVE	REACTIVE
1. Clear goals	1. Orienting, directional goals	1. No predetermined goals
2. Clearly predefined patterns of behavior	2. Behavior patterns mainly determined interactively in the actual setting	2. Behavior patterns are a reaction to immediate stimulus conditions
3. Cognitively based	3. Cognitively and noncognitively based	3. Noncognitively based
4. Examples of models: expectancy theory of motivation and path-goal theory of leadership	4. Examples of models: Mintzberg's and McCaskey's planning modes	4. Examples of models: classical S-R conditioning and need theories of motivation

FIGURE 25.1. A Continuum of Managerial Behavior Types (Davis and Luthans, 1980).

This is rational-cognitive behavior and refers to those occasions when the manager acts with a clear idea of the behavior required and the results to be achieved. Most of the recognized management and organizational behavior models tend to build in proactive-instrumental assumptions of managerial behavior. For instance, the management-by-objectives approach to planning and control (Odiorne, 1965), the cognitively based expectancy model of motivation (Lawler and Suttle, 1973), the goal theory of motivation (Locke, 1968), the path-goal theory of leadership (House, 1971), and the economic and exchange theories of decision making, all assume that managers act in a proactive-instrumental manner.

Reactive or expressive behavior lies at the opposite extreme from proactive-instrumental behavior and refers to noncognitively mediated responses to external or internal stimuli. These would include habitual, overlearned responses that the manager engages in with no awareness. As with proactive behavior, models of reactive behavior tend to build in self-supporting assumptions about the nature of managerial behavior. For instance, the classical S-R (stimulus-response) approach assumes that behavior is a mechanical reaction to external stimuli. Similarly, the popular motivation theories of Maslow (1954), McClelland (1961), and Herzberg (1966) assume that behavior is a reaction to internal needs.

Adaptive or directional behavior is a hybrid of these two extreme forms of managerial behavior. With this type of behavior, the manager has a general orientation or direction rather than a precise view of the behavior and desired end results. This behavior is partly a reactive response to the stimulus conditions in the setting and partly a proactive response based on the manager's cognitive orientation to the situation. Here the manager adapts behavior to the interactive stimulus environment as the situation unfolds. With the exception of the approaches to planning advocated by Lindblom (1959), Mintzberg (1973a), and McCaskey (1977), there are virtually no models that subsume or integrate adaptive assumptions of managerial behavior.

Models dealing with the various popular concepts used to represent managerial behavior (planning, organizing, controlling, motivating, leading) have not generally taken into consideration these different modes or ways of behaving. The majority of theories tend to build in the assumption that managerial behavior is proactive. Very few models exist that view managerial behavior as either reactive or adaptive. What evidence exists for accepting this view?

Findings from Studies of Managerial Behavior

The findings from observational studies do not support the view of managers as proactive planners who carefully organize and control their work and motivate and lead subordinates toward goal attainment. A consistent finding from studies of managerial work and behavior (Dubin, 1962; McCall, Morrison, and Hannan, 1978) is that the manager's day is broken up with frequent interruptions and unplanned interactions with others. This consists of unexpected visits from coworkers, urgent phone calls, inflowing paperwork, unscheduled conferences, and chance meetings with colleagues in hallways. Managers typically spend two-thirds to three-fourths of their time communicating with others. Much of this time is spent in short face-to-face conversations of ten minutes or less. Managers have to keep on top of a lot of issues and must maintain relations with a large number of people. It is an emotional world marked by pressure and stress. Mintzberg (1973b) concludes from his observational studies that managers are "adaptive information manipulators" in an "environment of stimulus-response." Much of a manager's time is spent persuading, justifying, and legitimating past, present, and future courses of action as different situations arise.

Kotter's (1982) recent study of 17 general managers also confirms that managers spend a great deal of their time responding to the flow of people and events going on around them. Most of the managers made no attempt to lay out an elaborate set of rational, goal-oriented activities; instead they worked from a changing mental agenda of what had to be done. The more successful managers were effective in developing and maintaining an informal network of organizational relationships that they used to obtain needed information and prompt required action. The following incident taken from one of Kotter's studies provides an example of how managers adapt to environmental opportunities in order to get their job done.

> Jack Martin, on his way to a meeting, bumped into a staff member (who did not report to him) near the elevator. Using this opportunity, in a two minute conversation he: (a) asked two questions and received the information needed in return; (b) helped reinforce their good relationship by sincerely complimenting the manager on something he had recently done; and (c) got the manager to agree to do something that Jack needed done (Kotter, 1982: 88).

As Kotter notes, the lack of precise plans and specific agenda setting that seems inefficient may really be very efficient given the unpredictable, opportunistic nature of the manager's world. This does not mean that no events are formally planned in advance; it does mean that, like a basketball game, many of the moves cannot be planned. Managers must frequently adapt and make their plays while interacting in the situation. Many of the responses may be reactive, habitual responses of which the manager has little awareness; others may be adaptive and calculative in which a manager actively shapes and uses a situation as it occurs. The distinction between reactive and adaptive behavior needs to be recognized. Kotter (1982) and Stewart (1979) distinguish proactive and reactive "agendas" in their discussion of managerial work, but they do not define these concepts or discuss them in behavioral terms. A more complete model of managerial behavior must not only recognize all three modes of behavior (proactive, adaptive, and reactive), but must also examine these ways of acting in considerably more depth than has previously been the case.

A PROCESS MODEL OF MANAGERIAL BEHAVIOR

Given the amount of research dealing with aspects of management and managerial performance, it is surprising that so little work has been devoted to observing managers' actual behavior (Campbell, Dunnette, Lawler, and Weick, 1970; McCall, Morrison and Hannan, 1978). Mintzberg's (1973b) ten roles of managerial behavior (figurehead, disseminator, disturbance handler, and so forth) currently comprise the most accepted model of managerial behavior. Mintzberg's roles are cited in over 40 contemporary management and organizational behavior texts. A weakness with Mintzberg's is that the roles refer to the content of managerial work; they do not shed much light on the processes of managers in action. Stewart (1982: 94) has commented that too much attention is being given "to trying to measure and assess his [Mintzberg's] general and abstract roles, rather than using his insights to further develop our conceptual understanding." The most urgent requirement is for conceptual understanding of the interactive aspects of managerial behavior. A proactive-adaptive-reactive approach to examining managerial behavior can improve our understanding of these processes.

The Limits of Proactive Behavior

If managers do not appear to plan, organize, and control their work and behavior in the manner of rational, linear, goal-oriented models, it is important for both the practitioner and the researcher to understand why this does not occur and what factors inhibit proactive behavior. The answer may be found in the manager's information-processing limits, the cognitive programs managers use to accomplish their tasks, and the stimulus influences that constantly disrupt their behavior.

In his studies of managerial work, Mintzberg emphasized information processing as a critical skill and stressed the importance of the cognitive programs or strategies managers use to do their jobs. Proactive behavior may be looked upon as the manager's ability to process information into coherent programs that describe what needs to be done. In effect, the manager has to plan and anticipate the consequences of a sequence of behavioral events before they happen. What Mintzberg, Kotter, Stewart, and others found was that managers carry around a general idea of what needs to be done in their heads and rely on information provided in each particular situation to decide on the program of action that needs to be taken. In other words, most managerial behavior involves very limited *prospective rationality* or *prospective cognition*.

Information theorists (Newell, Shaw, and Simon, 1958; March and Olsen, 1976; Ungson, Braunstein, and Hall, 1981) provide a host of reasons why managers may be unable to set clear goals and program actions both for themselves and others. Among them, the managerial task may be ambiguous and difficult to predict; managers vary in their ability to create and organize information; language and symbols tend to be inexact guides to events in the empirical world; people's perceptions of problems frequently go through a process of redefinition, they do not remain constant.

When these considerations are combined with the stimulus demands confronting the manager in the situation, it is not surprising that managers are not able to predict or program actions very far into the future. Proactive behavior may be possible in managing highly structured repetitive tasks where knowledge is gained through repeated rehearsals. It may also be possible to manage proactively certain subtasks of a major task. However, as March and Simon (1958: 136–171) note in their discussion of the cognitive limits of rationality, the consequences of many actions are discovered only after acting them out in the situation.

Forms of Adaptive Behavior

Adaptive behavior has sometimes been referred to as disjointed incrementalism (Lindblom, 1959) or directional planning (McCaskey, 1977). Here the manager has an agenda (Kotter and Lawrence, 1974; Kotter, 1982; Stewart, 1979), or a broad set of orienting priorities, but the manager must, for the most part, rely on others to clarify what needs to be done and how it is to be done.

Adaptive behavior frequently takes two forms: either managers decide what to do next as the situation arises—what may be termed *concurrent rationality or cognition*—or managers decide what they have done after they have done it—termed *retrospective rationality or cognition* (Weick, 1969, 1979; Staw, 1981). Concurrent rationality can be expected, for example, when the managerial task is difficult to predict, when the next move has to be decided by consensus, or when the manager prefers to wait and see what sort of job a subordinate does before deciding on the next move. In other words, the manager handles situations incrementally as they arise. Concurrent rationality also gives recognition to the fact that rationality is embedded in the words and language managers use to describe their situations. A great deal of a manager's behavior is verbal behavior. Concurrent rationality derives from spontaneous verbal behavior as managers and organization members interact in the setting and decide what needs to be done.

Retrospective rationality may not seem like managing at all unless it is recognized that managers frequently act or talk before thinking and then have to justify and rationalize what they do and say both to themselves and others. The manager's ability to manage others' interpretations of what he or she did and said after the event is an important task. Managers who ignore retrospective rationality are neglecting an important political aspect of their jobs. Developing skill in retrospective rationality may be as important an accomplishment as developing skill in prospective rationality. The perception of virtually every organizational event is subject to some level of negotiation and change (Silverman, 1971; Culbert and McDonough, 1980).

Ubiquitous Reactive Behavior

Reactive behaviors refer to managers' responses to stimulus cues that take place with no conscious awareness. These are acognitive reactions mainly to the stream of people and events in the manager's immediate environment. These habitual responses comprise what Mintzberg (1973b) has described as the most concrete aspects of managerial work: walk-in visitors, incoming phone calls, incoming paperwork. These seemingly insignificant events can, and often do, take up the better part of a manager's day. To some extent, many of these habitual behaviors can be an efficient and adjusted way of responding. If every action had to be thought through afresh each day, managers would probably not accomplish anything new. However, many of these behaviors may be dysfunctional for managers and their staff, such as allowing constant interruptions while delegating work to subordinates, disorganized systems for handling paperwork, half-hour telephone conversations that could have been completed in five minutes.

One explanation of why these behaviors are so persistent is because of the controlling influence of immediate stimuli in the environment and the powerful reinforcing consequences of responses that minister to these stimuli (Luthans and Davis, 1979). For instance, answering a ringing phone, seeing walk-in visitors, reading papers placed on the desk, all take care of immediate stimuli in the environment. The short-term effect is satisfying but the long-term effect of these constant disruptive responses may be dysfunctional because they displace proactive or adaptive goal-oriented behaviors.

Because of the daily incidence of these behaviors, these actions can constitute an important part of managerial work. The way to bring these acognitive responses under greater control is by managing those aspects of the stimulus environment that are responsible for eliciting them. Strategies for managing the stimulus environment have been discussed at length elsewhere (Luthans and Davis, 1979; Andrasik and Heimberg, 1982).

Summary

Proactive behavior describes managers' efforts to *operate on* their environment; adaptive behavior concerns managers' attempts to *adjust with* their environment; and reactive behavior deals with managerial behavior in which managers merely *respond to* the environment. These different behavior modes and the accompanying cognitive states are outlined in Figure 25.2A. Extreme proactive behavior assumes that the manager has full or complete knowledge of how to behave (or what to do) in a situation prior to the event. In other words, the manager has prospective cognition. Adaptive behavior assumes that what a manager does in a situation is partly derived from prior thoughts or cognitions of how to behave (prospective cognition), partly derived from spontaneous cognitions or verbal utterances in the situation (concurrent cognition), and partly derived from reactions of interpretations of these reactions (retrospective cognition) in the setting. Extreme reactive behaviors are acognitive, managerial responses to stimuli in the setting. These may be spontaneous reactions that have never occurred before or overlearned habitual responses that the person engages in continually.

Thus far, these modes of behaving have been discussed separately in order to distinguish their characteristics. At different times, managers may be described as being more proactive, adaptive, or reactive—depending upon

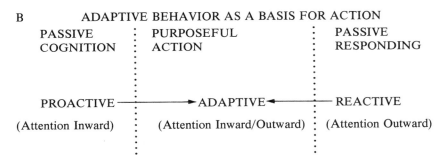

A   MANAGERIAL BEHAVIOR MODES AND COGNITIVE STATES

Behavior Mode: PROACTIVE———ADAPTIVE———REACTIVE

Level of Cognitive Understanding:	Full	Partial Emerging	None
Cognitive Type:	Prospective Cognition	Prospective Cognition	Acognitive Habits
		Concurrent Cognition	
		Retrospective Cognition	

B   ADAPTIVE BEHAVIOR AS A BASIS FOR ACTION

PASSIVE COGNITION	:	PURPOSEFUL ACTION		:	PASSIVE RESPONDING

PROACTIVE ———————→ADAPTIVE◄——————— REACTIVE

(Attention Inward) : (Attention Inward/Outward) : (Attention Outward)

FIGURE 25.2. Proactive-Adaptive-Reactive Model of Managerial Behavior

where they are perceived to be behaving on the continuum—but most purposeful managerial behavior is adaptive.

Adaptive behavior is a hybrid of proactive and reactive (see Figure 25.2B). Here managers have a general idea of what they want to do but adjust their behavior to the evolving demands of the situation. In practice, this is the only way the manager can act purposefully. Extreme proactive or reactive behaviors are passive states. With extreme proactive behavior, attention is turned inward in full cognition. Here the manager is totally immersed in reflective thought; no attention is focused outward on the demands of the changing environment. With extreme reactive behavior, attention is turned outward to the environment. Here the manager has no internal awareness and passively responds to the stimuli in the environment. Adaptive behavior involves successively turning the attention outward to observe the effects of one's behavior on the environment and turning the attention inward to evaluate these effects on one's cognitive agenda. Adaptive behavior occurs in the middle region (within the broken vertical lines of Figure 25.2B) between the two extremes of proactive and reactive behavior.

ADAPTIVE BEHAVIOR IN ACTION

Adaptive behavior is required from managers in the numerous conversations they have each day. In order to manager their behavior effectively in these situations, managers must be able to focus and refocus attention on: what they know about the topic being discussed; what the other person is saying and doing; and where the conversation is going. In doing this, the manager switches attention inward and outward and uses prospective, concurrent, and retrospective rationality to guide, sustain, and evaluate the conversation (see Figure 25.3).

Concurrent cognition is the rationality and cognition rooted in the present dialog and topic. It is indispensable to the ongoing conversation and is cued by the verbal inputs and responses of the other person. Here attention alternates between the manager's inner images, ideas, and feelings, and the manager's outer awareness of what the other person is saying and doing. A second set of cognitions involves both prospective rationality and retrospective rationality. These are before (prospective) and after (retrospective) metacognitions (cognitions about cognitions, Watzlawick, Beavin, and Jackson, 1967) that respectively guide and evaluate the dialog and where the dialog is going. They are not essential to sustaining the ongoing conversation and are not cued by the verbal inputs or responses of the other person.

For a conversation to produce satisfactory outcomes, both types of cognitions are necessary: concurrent as well as prospective and retrospective cognition. In addition to maintaining the overt conversation with the other person, managers must be able to introduce their own inner subvocal cues that ask "Where do I want this conversation to go?" (prospective) and "How am I doing?" (retrospective). Frequently, managers' subvocal agendas of planning and evaluating cues break down and the conversation blunders on without direction, mired in concurrent rationality.

In order to gain more control over this adaptive behavior, the manager must learn to balance inward and outward attention-switching and overt and covert communication. Too much attention to one's subvocal messages detracts from watching and listening to what the other person is saying and doing. Conversely, too much concentration on the other person with too little attention to one's own thoughts, feelings, and subvocal agenda is likely to be equally maladaptive.

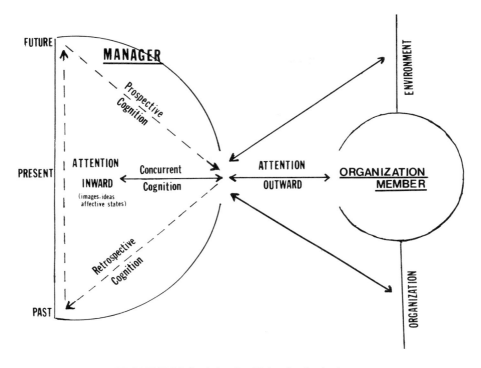

FIGURE 25.3. Adaptive Behavior in Action

The difficulty for managers is that most conversations are unplanned encounters. Meaning is created spontaneously in the situation by the participants as they talk. Managers frequently do not know what they will say before saying it and do not know what the other person will say in reply. With the exception of conversations that consist of overlearned verbal responses that are run off by the participants with little thought and awareness, other more critical conversations may involve managers switching their attention between a large number of different sources of information. These may include:

1. What managers hear themselves saying overtly to the other;
2. What the other person says in return;
3. The other person's nonverbal facial expressions and actions;
4. Managers' awareness of their own nonverbal behavior;
5. Managers' subvocalizations dealing with ideas and information pertinent to the dialog;
6. Managers' covert rehearsals of what to say next;

7. Managers' covert self-statements about where they think the conversation should be going;

8. Managers' subvocalizations of what they think the other person is trying to get out of the conversation;

9. Managers' awareness of their own feelings in the situation;

10. Managers' subvocal interpretations of their own feelings; and

11. Other stimuli in the environment that draw the manager's attention.

What the manager and the other person say aloud is only a small component of the internal and external stimulus environment that the manager is interpreting and reacting to. Some of these responses are concurrent responses consisting of thoughts, feelings, and overt reactions to the present dialog; others are retrospective responses qualifying and interpreting what is taking place. Note the distinction between 9.—managers' awareness of their own feelings in the situation—and 10.—managers' subvocal interpretations of their own feelings. The former is a concurrent response, the latter is a retrospective response. Affective responses such as fear, panic, and anger can often be highly disruptive. Stress of this sort tends to inhibit cognitive functioning and the ability to process information (Folkman Schaefer, and Lazarus, 1979). With stress, frequently the key is not the stressful nature of the situation per se but how the manager cognitively interprets the situation. Managers need to possess skill in cognitively interpreting the situation in positive terms so as to avoid paralyzing their ability to think and act effectively.

Bear in mind that the manager's covert self-statements about where the conversation should be going usually can be arrived at only as the conversation proceeds and the situation unfolds. The manager must weigh information provided by the other person, decide what needs to be done, and negotiate with the other person what can be accomplished. The manager is dependent on the information and cooperation of others in order to keep current and stay in charge of what is happening. The manager must therefore get used to collecting and interpreting information and constantly changing priorities based on this information (Kotter, 1982). The challenge for the manager is getting used to this adaptive mode of operating and being able to exploit it advantageously:

> The fragments that compose the executive's working day can be used as a succession of opportunities to tackle bits of the issue stream. It is precisely the fragmented nature of their activity that permits top managers to fine tune, test, and retest the general strategic direction they are trying to impart. . . . fragmentation of time, properly exploited, can yield a rich

variety of information. Within reason, the more views and visits in the top executive's schedule and the more numerous the interruptions and unscheduled encounters, the better informed he is likely to be. (Peters, 1979: 166)

As Peters (1979: 172) notes, the task of the manager "is not to impose an abstract order on an inherently disorderly process, but to become adept at the sort of intervention by which he can nudge it in the desired direction and to some degree control its course."

Adaptive behavior of this sort does not mean that managers cannot plan conversations or have a purpose in mind before talking to someone. The point is that the nature of these interactions makes them very difficult to plan. A conversation is frequently disorderly and haphazard even when the participants have given some thought to what they wish to achieve. If managers must accomplish their goals, or whatever momentary purposes they have in mind, through these interactions, the conversation needs to become a key unit of analysis in managerial and organizational research. Virtually every behavioral process—including leadership, motivation, decision making, performance appraisal, and delegation—is accomplished through conversations with others. We need to develop greatly improved understanding of how this behavior can be managed more effectively.

CONCLUSION

The main intent in developing this proactive-adaptive-reactive model of managers in action has been to point out that some of the prevailing assumptions about managerial behavior may be at fault and that new conceptual models are needed to guide our understanding. Neat, rational, contemplative models of planning, controlling, leading, and motivating appear to be discrepant with what actually takes place in organizations.

If managerial research is going to become more useful, an important first step is to provide an improved representation of managers' behavior in action. A second step is to find out what managerial behavior is in most need of improvement. The suggestions provided here are a tentative step in this direction. Other steps in this process that go beyond the scope of this chapter include discovering what models managers are prepared to use and coming up with methods or procedures to ensure that managers actually use them.

At this stage, it is difficult to disagree with Mintzberg (1973b) and Stewart (1982) that the most important research requirement is for improved conceptual understanding of managerial behavior. The proactive-adaptive-reaction model begins the process of replacing some of the terms and assumptions with which we approach the study of managerial cognition and behavior. It is hoped that further models will follow that either improve the approach outlined here or propose better ways of viewing managers in action.

REFERENCES

Andrasik, Frank, and Judy S. Heimberg
1982   "Self-management procedures." In Lee W. Frederiksen (Eds.) Handbook of Organizational Behavior Management. New York: Wiley.
Campbell, John P., Marvin D. Dunnette, Edward E. Lawler, III, and Karl E. Weick
1970   Managerial Behavior, Performance and Effectiveness. New York: McGraw-Hill.
Culbert, Samuel A., and John J. McDonough
1980   The Invisible Wall: Pursuing Self-Interests at Work. New York: Wiley.
Daft, Richard A., and John C. Wiginton
1979   "Language and organization." Academy of Management Review, 4:179–191.
Davis, Tim R. V., and Fred Luthans
1980   "Managers in action: a new look at their behavior and operating modes." Organizational Dynamics, 9:64–80.
Dubin, Robert
1962   "Business behaviorally viewed." In Chris Argyris, Robert Dubin, Mason Haire, R. Duncan Luce, W. Lloyd Warner, William Foote Whyte and George B. Strother (Eds.), Social Science Approaches to Business Behavior: 11–55. Homewood, Ill.: Irwin.
Folkman, Susan, Catherine Schaefer,and Richard Lazarus
1979   "Cognitive processes as mediators of stress and coping." In V. Hamilton and D. Warburton (Eds.) Human Stress and Cognition: 265–298 New York: Wiley.
Herzberg, Frederick
1966   Work and the Nature of Man. Cleveland: World.
House, Robert J.
1971   "A path-goal theory of leader effectiveness." Administrative Science Quarterly, 2:321–339.
Kotter, John P., and Paul R. Lawrence
1974   Mayors in Action. New York: Wiley.
Kotter, John P.
1982   The General Managers. New York: Free Press.
Lawler, Edward E., and John L. Suttle
1973   "Expectancy theory and job behavior." Organizational Behavior and Human Performance, 9:482–503.
Lindblom, Charles E.
1959   "The science of muddling through." Public Administration Review, 19:79–88.
Locke, Edward A.
1968   "Toward a theory of task motivation and incentives. Organizational Behavior and Human Performance, 3:157–189.
Luthans, F., and Tim R. V. Davis
1979   "Behavioral self-management—the missing link in managerial effectiveness." Organizational Dynamics, 8:42–60.
March, James G., and Herbert A. Simon
1958   Organizations. New York: Wiley.
March, James G., and Johan P. Olsen
1976   Ambiguity and Choice in Organization. Bergen, Norway: Universitetsforlaget.

Maslow, Abraham H.
1954   Motivation and Human Personality. New York: Harper.
McCall, Morgan W., Jr., Ann M. Morrison, and Robert L. Hannan
1978   Studies of Managerial Work: Results and Methods. Greensboro, NC: Center for Creative Leadership.
McCaskey, Michael B.
1977   "Goals and direction in personal planning." Academy of Management Review, 2:454–462.
McClelland, David C.
1961   The Achieving Society. Princeton, NJ: Van Nostrand.
Mintzberg, Henry
1973a   "Strategy making in three modes." California Management Review, 16:44–53.
1973b   The Nature of Managerial Work. New York: Harper & Row.
Newell, Allen, J. C. Shaw, and Herbert A. Simon
1958   "Elements of a theory of human problem solving." Psychological Review, 65:151–166.
Odiorne, George S.
1965   Management by Objectives. New York: Pittman.
Peters, Thomas J.
1979   "Leadership: sad facts and silver linings." Harvard Business Review, 5:164–172.
Silverman, David
1971   The Theory of Organizations. New York: Basic Books.
Staw, Barry M.
1981   "The escalation of commitment to a course of action." Academy of Management Review, 6:577–587.
Stewart, Rosemary
1979   "Managerial agendas—reactive or proactive." Organizational Dynamics, 8:34–47.
1982   Choices for the Manager. Englewood Cliffs, N.J.: Prentice-Hall.
Ungson, Gerardo Rivera, Daniel N. Braunstein, and Phillip D. Hall
1981   "Managerial information processing: a research review." Administrative Science Quarterly, 26:116–134.
Watzlawick, Paul, Janet H. Beavin, and Don D. Jackson
1967   Pragmatics of Human Communication. New York: Norton.
Weick, Karl E.
1969   The Social Psychology of Organizing. Reading, Mass.: Addison Wesley.
1979   Cognitive processes in organizations." In Barry M. Staw (Ed.) Research in Organizational Behavior. Greenwich, Conn.: JAI Press.

26

SCIENTIFIC KNOWLEDGE UTILIZATION AS AN ORGANIZATIONAL SYSTEMS DEVELOPMENT PROBLEM

David G. Bowers

Knowledge about organizational processes—the methods by which one directs, leads, and motivates human beings in collective settings—has accumulated for centuries. For five decades, more or less, the canons of scientific inquiry have been applied to the accumulation process. The result is that there exists today a very large body of scientific knowledge about organizations and their management. As is the case with other bodies of scientific knowledge, the gap between what is known and what is utilized is enormous. A small proportion of what is known is widely applied. Much that is known is either ignored totally or applied in an ineffective, piecemeal fashion. In most instances, the time lag between generation of the knowledge and any significant implementation is quite long.

THE NATURE OF THE SKU (SCIENTIFIC KNOWLEDGE UTILIZATION) PROBLEM IN ORGANIZATIONAL SCIENCE

To understand the form that the problem takes in organizational science, let us consider the particular way in which the utilization question might be posed in the organizational behavior field. Unfortunately, it is difficult to state it simply, but an approximation of it would be: How can user systems be influenced to function in ways that research findings indicate would be beneficial to their outcomes?

Unlike other formulations of the more general question, in this one the scientific knowledge is not inherently distinct from the user system and its behavior. In fact, it is concerned with that very functioning, not with an external something that is acquired or issued. In systems theory terms, it is the throughput process itself, not inputs nor outputs nor artifacts that it employs, that is the focus.

The knowledge consists, in integrated form, of a body of theory extracted from a large number of research studies on organizational functioning and development. It is a theoretical statement, based upon empirical research, of how things work in organizations and how to get them to work better. It is a model of behavioral movement in organizations.

If this is scientific knowledge in the organizational field, what is *utilization*? It consists of *inducing behavior patterns and processes that replicate those of the model.*

OBSTACLES TO THE RESEARCH-UTILIZATION LINK

Three points relevant to this induction process may be cited from the literature. Morrison (1974), in a study of social science knowledge utilization by federal policy makers, tested three widely offered sets of theories concerning nonutilization. She found that only one of these—the Two Communities theory—accounted for any substantial amount of variance in utilization. According to this, scientific knowledge tends not to be utilized because researchers and users live in separate communities, with different values, rewards, thought processes, and languages. The other two categories of theories examined, Knowledge Specific theories and Situational Constraint theories, apparently had little real impact.

This is quite consistent with the integrative statement by Havelock and Havelock (1973) that, for utilization to occur, a form of linkage must exist by which researchers and users become able to simulate one another's thought processes.

Finally, there are the observations by Steele (1975). Discussing innovation in big business, he notes that a transmission process directly from researchers in a generating organization to users in an adopting organization is among the least likely to work. The Two Communities concept is implicit in his thinking, for he recommends that the route be either from researchers to applied persons in the generating organization and from the latter to their applied counterparts in the adopting organization, or from researchers to researchers across the organizational boundary and from the latter to users in the adopting organization.

These three issues—the Two Communities problem, the thought process linkage problem, and the over-the-border problem—have, it would seem, been serious obstacles to utilization in the organizational science area. Those of us who have conducted the research that has generated the body of scientific knowledge in this field have for the most part been academics. In the understandable effort to succeed in our institutions and disciplines, we have designed the research, conceptualized the problems, and written the findings in a way most likely to impress each other. We have, for the most part, published them in scholarly journals read only by ourselves. However, these knowledge-specific aspects may have been in themselves less damaging to the utilization process than has been the distance they have placed between ourselves and potential users. So to the problem that, in the organizational area, utilization amounts to inducing changes in the very being of the potential user, we add the problem of having distance ourselves and the knowledge from those very users whose being we must impact.

Stated in a highly general form, the problem appears to be that of spanning or bridging from basic researchers to applied researchers to users, three distinct groups. Basic researchers are issue-oriented, their values are scholarly, and their rewards presumably proportional to scholarly creativity. Their thought processes focus upon questions intrinsically critical to the knowledge base itself, and their language reflects that.

Applied researchers are problem-oriented. While they value rigor often as much as do basic researchers, it is valued as it is instrumental to solving an applied problem that has been posed to them from those who presumably face it. Their rewards are supposedly proportional to the efficient, effective solving of such applied research problems, rather than to scholarly creativity per se.

Finally, users are tactic-oriented. They place value upon tools or procedures that can be readily implemented by them in handling problems and challenges. They are rewarded for action, not for insight or creativity, and for success in pursuit of whatever outcomes their organization has established concerning them.

The three groups live in different communities, therefore, and the first and the third in this often-expected flow sequence (basic researchers and users live in *very* different communities. Compartmentalized as they ordinarily are, these three groups have at best a limited ability to simulate each other's thought processes, and border crossings are (for the knowledge involved) haphazard, perilous, or even nonexistent.

In contrast to this, the usual knowledge flow assumes conditions that are unlikely. It assumes, for example, that basic researchers will address fundamental issues in the knowledge base and publish their findings. Once they have done so, it assumes that basic researchers will pick up on these and use these breakthroughs to address the more applied questions posed to them. Then, in turn, users will take these applied solutions and implement them. The barriers, however, make it highly likely that basic researchers will be off target in the issues that they address, at least as far as their downstream counterparts are concerned. Applied researchers, in their turn, will address applied problems with less than the implementability of the solutions in mind. Finally, users will cope as best they can, taking advantage of an only occasional nugget of knowledge that appears.

TWO METHODS OF STIMULATING UTILIZATION

In the author's experience, two methods of solving these compounded spanning or bridging problems have been reasonably successful. They may be termed the *Interinstitutional Massed Resources* approach and the *Downstream* approach. The first follows somewhat the recommendation of Steele, but is more coincident than sequential. The second involves researchers themselves following their findings downstream to implementation. In the examples that follow, each effort resulted in both new scientific knowledge and utilization of that and existing knowledge by the user organization. They represent, therefore, instances of successful linkage.

An example of the Interinstitutional Massed Resources approach is that of the General Motors/Institute for Social Research (ISR) project of 1969 to 1972. The project was originally conceived in a series of discussions between ISR research staff members and top corporate officials. It stemmed from a developing hunch by those officials that the body of scientific knowledge and practice in the organizational area, developed by researchers over the years, might contribute to the constructive solution of several problems of great concern to that company and its industry. These problems were: absenteeism, which was an increasingly disruptive factor; grievances, which were occurring in alarming proportions in some parts of the company; and product quality, an issue of concern to a cost-conscious company, as well as to consumer groups, which were becoming increasingly visible and vocal.

Four locations were selected by corporate officials as most appropriate for the pilot effort that was envisioned. Several criteria affected the selection: comparability of location and labor market; comparability of technology; contrasting patterns of operating effectiveness; and multidivision representation

As selected, the four appear to have met these criteria reasonably well. In each of two cities, two locations with nearly identical technical operations were selected. The choice of cities permitted each of the two sets of intracity locations to differ markedly in operating effectiveness as assessed by management at the outset of the study. The four locations consisted of: two large foundries differing slightly in technology but located in a single labor market and differing in effectiveness; two large assembly-line manufacturing plants, almost identical in technology, located in a single labor market, and also differing from one another rather widely in effectiveness.*

Manning the change teams for each of the four locations called, in the original planning, for resources from General Motors Institute and from the Institute for Social Research, as well as from the separate plants. Accordingly, two change agents from the ISR staff were assigned full-time to the project (one per city, splitting his time in some proportion between the two locations in each city), with a third, more experienced change agent supplementing their efforts and serving a coordinating, planning, training-of-change-agents function. General Motors Institute provided one full-time resident change agent per location (a total of four), plus a full-time, more experienced change agent counterpart to the third ISR person. The plants themselves provided, at the outset, in-plant change agents. The assembly plant at Location L had two and the plant at Location D had one; the foundry at Location M supplied two and there were three at Location C.

Although a considerable amount of consultation with corporate, GMI, and ISR change team members occurred, selection of in-plant change agents was largely the responsibility of the local management in each location. Several criteria were provided to local key management persons by the project staff to aid them in the selection process: the persons selected should be system-credible—that is, they should be persons whose background and ability (and experience) would provide recognized competence in that facility's operations; they should be reasonably young (not approaching imminent retirement) and preferably be seen as rising young managers; they should have some degree of recognized interpersonal competence (that is, some degree of sensitivity to, and appreciation for, the feelings and views of others); and they should be reasonably flexible and adaptable.

When the selection process ended, the criteria appeared to have been at least adequately met. In-plant change team members were, on the whole, young, flexible, system-credible persons. By background, two had been drawn from the industrial relations function, one from fiscal-accounting, and the remaining five from line management and/or industrial engineering.

A staff of 14 on-line change agents, intertwined with approximately 16 researchers, plus clerical and support staff, all from three institutions, is an elaborate apparatus. However, the plant populations, indicated in Table 26.1, provide some measure of perspective. Figure 26.1 presents in diagrammatic form what eventually became the interinstitutional structure employed by the project.

---

*One of the foundries consisted of two distinct plants adjacent to one another; thus the study really occurred in five plants in four locations. In most instances, this chapter will treat the two as one and refer to four plants.

TABLE 26.1. Plant Populations, Salaried and Hourly

Plant	Salaried	Hourly	Total
L	746	4,260	5,006
D	575	2,265	2,840
M	651	2,124	2,775
C	837	6,300	7,137
Total	2,809	14,949	17,758

In the early months and prior to the actual launch, the general design for the project was developed by a group made up of nearly all persons in the central and first-removed levels. Meetings were held weekly or biweekly in each of the three locations in rotation. Functional subgroups were formed on a temporary basis to complete some element of the overall design, for presentation at the next meeting of the overall group. The product of this planning phrase was a document presenting the design. It was subsequently approved by all three institutions, and the launch step was undertaken.

With the designation in each institution of those persons who would occupy positions at the second- and third-removed levels, the cast of participants quickly grew. By the second or third meeting, following approval of the design, it became apparent that the mechanism was unwieldy. Accordingly, a differentiated, yet integrated, structure was developed.

Linkage Group—The ISR Project Manager, GMI Senior Administrator, and Senior Corporate Manager were formed into a group whose function was to keep the project effectively linked to top GM Corporate and Divisional Management. In the succeeding months it met roughly monthly, and it periodically held briefings for top managers. It served as well to keep a flow of relevant information going back into the project itself.

Research and Measurement Group—Research persons from the first- and second-removed levels of all three organizations were formed into a group whose function was to collect, analyze, and disseminate data necessary for both survey feedback O.D. activities and formative evaluation. For the remainder of the project, the group met approximately biweekly. It was linked to the Linkage Group by the presence of the Corporate Senior Staff Manager, also a researcher.

Change Agentry Group—Consultants from the first- and second-removed coordinate, amplify, and make mid-course corrections in the overall implementation. It met approximately monthly, more often in the early months and somewhat less frequently in the later months of the project.

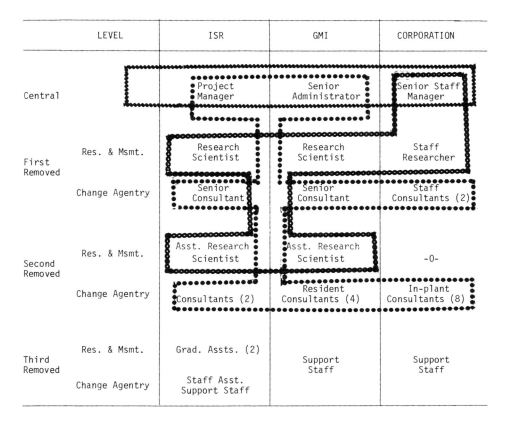

LEVEL		ISR	GMI	CORPORATION
Central		Project Manager	Senior Administrator	Senior Staff Manager
First Removed	Res. & Msmt.	Research Scientist	Research Scientist	Staff Researcher
	Change Agentry	Senior Consultant	Senior Consultant	Staff Consultants (2)
Second Removed	Res. & Msmt.	Asst. Research Scientist	Asst. Research Scientist	-0-
	Change Agentry	Consultants (2)	Resident Consultants (4)	In-plant Consultants (8)
Third Removed	Res. & Msmt.	Grad. Assts. (2)	Support Staff	Support Staff
	Change Agentry	Staff Asst. Support Staff		

********* Linkage Group (L)

ooooooo Research and Measurement Group (RAM)

•••••• Change Agentry Group (CAG)

FIGURE 26.1. Interinstitutional Mass Resources Approach: The GM-ISR Project

Additional linkage came, of course, through intra-institutional linkages within each of the three institutions.

It is worth noting that, because of common professional interests and the sheer proportion of time spent in the interinstitutional groups, the bonds of identification within these three functional groupings became quite strong. They were, in fact, at least as strong as the ties members had to their colleagues from the same institution.

Perhaps the most significant contribution this structure made lay in its transducer effects. As the term is used in physics, a transducer is a device that transfers energy or information from one system to another, in the process ordinarily converting it to a form in which it may circulate in the receiving system. In systems theory, it is used to refer to subsystems that transfer and convert information at the input, throughput, and output stages.

In this instance, the structure brought researchers from the knowledge-generating system into close working contact with researchers from the user system. Whereas the former brought general concepts and methods and conveyed them to their counterparts, the latter helped remold, rephrase, and adapt those concepts and methods to the real world of the client system. In the change agentry function, a similar process occurred among consultants from the three institutions.

No doubt throughput transducer effects were important as well, as researchers and consultants within and across institutions shared information and adopted concepts and procedures. Finally, output transducer effects also occurred, as the information was transferred to the ultimate users: managers, supervisors, and employees in the four plants.

Beyond transducer effects, two other important contributions came from the structure. For one thing, it promoted a more collaborative stance, in the process reducing to manageable levels the natural rivalry among institutions, a rivalry that could only have increased resistance to change. For another, it provided a shield, in part through the linkage group, which kept the support of top management visible and the organizational antibodies at bay.

The project was a success, as published accounts have indicated. Positive change did occur, particularly in one of the two less effective plants. More important, that change was sufficiently persuasive that it led, in succeeding years, to widespread extensions of similar kinds of efforts throughout the corporation.

An interesting sidelight concerns the persons themselves. In the years following the project, eight of the ten most central persons in the project structure changed functions, institutions, or both. An additional five persons whose careers are known also changed functions, institutions, or both. Of these fifteen, 100 percent of the changes for research persons involved a movement away from research and toward application or consulting. None of the changes involving consultants was toward research; rather, the changes were in institutional affiliation. It is, of course, not at all clear that participation in this structure caused these changes. What is clear is that there was an associated drift toward application and away from knowledge generation.

An example of the Downstream approach can be found in the work our program has undertaken with the U.S. Navy. In this instance, we began in

1966 what was called the Michigan InterCompany Longitudinal Study (ICLS). It was designed to be a five-year, multicompany research effort on time-lag effects in organizations and organization development. While the participating firms were expected to fund the measurement and consulting activities in their own firms, other funding had to be sought to support the cross-organizational research component. The Office of Naval Research was approached and agreed, in 1968, to fund a modest three-year contract for such analyses. In the three years of that contract, the program did indeed conduct substantial research with the funds provided. Thirteen technical reports were written, submitted, and distributed to a large number of Navy commands and offices.

In 1972 the potential relevance of much of the program's findings to the Navy itself as a human organization became apparent to in-house research administrators. A proposal was accordingly submitted to the Navy's Manpower Research and Development Program, focusing at that time upon all-volunteer force issues. It was funded, and work began. Data similar to those from the original studies of private-sector organizations were collected from a representative unit sample of Navy personnel and, for comparison purposes, from a representative national cross-section of civilians. This effort went on for an additional three years. The final report was a book-length summary of Navy manpower and human resource requirements, plus values and practices. It was supported by another 20 major technical reports.

During the course of this second, more applied research phase, program staff members were asked periodically to brief key Navy role occupants in the Personnel area about progress and emerging findings. As it became increasingly apparent that the civilian findings were replicated in Navy settings, interest began to build among persons then developing the Navy's new Human Goals effort, to have them converted into the concepts, procedures, data systems, and manuals necessary for implementation in Navy settings. Accordingly, another two years of effort were funded in which program staff members worked actively with the new formalized Human Resources Management (HRM) system. Serving now as outside resources of a consulting kind, we helped them construct, test, and refine a survey instrument; construct the beginnings of a normative data bank; work through the important issues of confidentiality and access; train an incoming cadre of HRM consultants; and build the necessary linkages among centers, detachments, and support agencies.

Since 1977 we have maintained an active contact with the HRM program, assisting them in minor ways, providing periodic refresher training, transmitting innovative procedures and findings, and occasionally helping them think through issues of development strategy.

The important feature of this experience was that it involved program members following their results down the "R&D Stream," from basic research through applied research to advanced systems development to ultimate implementation. They moved gradually from other in-house basic researchers and research-oriented persons, to in-house applied researchers, to those concerned more with the advanced development of an on-line human resources system, and finally to the on-line users themselves.

At each transition point, the original researchers necessarily, gradually, and almost unconsciously began the process of immersion in the next segment of the user system. We learned their ways, their structures, and their environmental constraints. We learned their acronym system, their role structure, and their interaction-influence system. They learned ours as well, particularly as these related to the scientific knowledge in question. We learned something of each other's languages and thought processes.

Some of these effects were simple, even plain. We learned to say "command climate" instead of "organizational climate," "billets" instead of "positions." Other effects were more subtle; for example we became aware of seashore rotation, detailing, "brown shoes" and "black shoes," all of them relevant facets of Navy life. Most important of all, we began, not just to toss the words around, but actually to *think* in those terms. In many ways, it was analogous to the experience many of us have had in learning a foreign language, as we went from conscious construction of sentences, to second-nature use of words, to suddenly finding ourselves thinking in the foreign language.

Over the years, this process led users to become more aware of the relevance of the knowledge to their own immediate, real-world situations. It led them as well to recognize the potential that our efforts had for further such generation. It led us, the researchers, to recast portions of our research into forms, designs, and questions which, still accomplishing our research purposes, were more likely to have currency for their situations.

As with the first approach, an interesting sidelight concerns persons involved. Of the five principal researchers who were a part of this effort through all stages, two have moved toward application; three have not; and all but one have continued academic or research careers. On the other hand, many of the internal persons have moved upstream to some degree, and two have joined the author's application organization!

IMPLICATIONS OF THE TWO APPROACHES FOR THE RESEARCH PROCESS

Neither of these two approaches seems likely to be a comfortable fit to research as we have known it. The Interinstitutional Massed Resources approach requires that basic researchers immerse themselves for large portions of their time and for protracted periods in organizations and situations not their own. The expectations, norms, and commitments that very certainly emerge are not the same as those of their home (normally academic) institutions, and they are very, very real. There is also some risk that the identifications involved in close, collaborative work with a constant cast of characters will change the researcher's identity away from research.

The Downstream approach lacks this last dynamic, since the persons with whom the researcher is involved change much more frequently and are more varied. However, it contains other features perhaps equally distasteful to many researchers. For one thing, it requires that the researcher not close the books once a piece of basic research has been completed and simply go on to another. Instead, for some substantial time period the researcher must abandon the world of basic research and transport the knowledge into the user system. For another, it makes the researcher accountable for the form, adequacy, and translation of the scientific knowledge *in the user's eyes*.

Finally, neither of these systems bodes well for the classic, academic research orientation. Traditional criteria of academic excellence—scholarly pieces in refereed journals—are at best irrelevant to what these approaches would consider to indicate success. Furthermore, whatever is disseminated in printed form is likely frequently to be jointly authored, or even unauthored. Heavy involvement in academic affairs would be limited, by time alone, if nothing else. Academic norms would lose some of their force, and academic role structures would change.

The costs and benefits of these approaches are difficult to assess. In the author's experience, they have shown themselves to be successful methods of getting scientific knowledge utilized in the organizational area.

Whether they are limited in their applicability to large-scale efforts is uncertain. The Interinstitutional Massed Resources approach requires resources, human and financial, in a scale clearly beyond those available to small or single researcher efforts. However, it might be conceivable that much more limited versions could be developed—for example, the linking of a basic researcher, an applied researcher, and a user in some form of task force or team over a period of time.

The Downstream approach requires opportunities and shifts that might be difficult to obtain or manage for those in small settings. Here again, however, it might be possible for an individual researcher to move, along with his or her own findings, down the utilization stream. There are, no doubt, other approaches with perhaps greater benefit and lower cost. To the extent there are, they deserve to be explored.

REFERENCES

Havelock, R. G. and Havelock, M. C.
1973   Training for Change Agents: A Guide to the Design of Training Programs in Education and Other Fields. Ann Arbor, Michigan: Institute for Social Research.

Morrison, Andrea
1974   Policy Makers' Views on Three Categories of Non-Utilization Theories. Paper presented at VIII World Congress of Sociology, Toronto, Ontario.

Steele, L. W.
1975   Innovation in Big Business. New York: American Elsevier.

27

UTILIZATION AS REVERSE SIMULATION: MAKING THE WORLD MORE LIKE THE LABORATORY

Karl E. Weick

INTRODUCTION

Traditionally, the laboratory experiment has made only an indirect contribution to utilization, usually through the mechanism of theory development. When experimental findings support a theory the theory, not the findings, is generalized to the world outside the laboratory and people predict what will happen in that world based on the theory. This chapter argues that laboratory experiments can be used more directly and more fully if their technology is also generalized.

To illustrate the generalization of technology, we examine the procedures experimenters use to explore a determinant of memory called the environmental reinstatement effect.

The Environmental Reinstatement Effect

When subjects learn new material, it has been demonstrated that they remember more of this material when they are tested in the original environment where they learned the material than when they are tested in a different environment. Smith (1979) made the important discovery that environmental reinstatement need not be physical; it can also be mnemonic or pictorial and memory is still improved relative to recall that is undertaken in a strange setting.

To demonstrate mnemonic reinstatement, people were exposed to 80 individual words presented at three-second intervals on slides in Room A. Then they were given a recognition test involving 20 words, 10 of which were old ones they had already seen and 10 of which were new. Their task was to rate whether each of the 20 words was new or old. Then the subjects were dismissed for the day and seemingly their testing was over.

On the second day, some subjects were brought back to Room A where they had studied the 80 words the day before and were told to write as many words as they could remember in 10 minutes. All other subjects were brought to Room B (a room in which they had *not* learned the syllables) and were given a variety of instructions. Some were given the identical instructions given to people in Room A. Some were asked first to remember features of Room A and then to use that memory to help recall words. Some were shown slides of Room A before they tried to recall the words. A final group was asked to spend an equivalent amount of time visualizing a room at home, an activity that was portrayed as good "mental warmup for remembering."

The mean number of words recalled for each of these five conditions was:

Sit in Room A = 18.8
Sit in Room B, see slides of Room A = 18.8
Sit in Room B, visualize Room A = 17.2
Sit in Room B, no mention of Room A = 11.0
Sit in Room B, recall room at home = 9.6

The first three groups did not differ significantly from one another; people recalled significantly more words than they did when there was no reinstatement of the input room. It was concluded that contextual associations made at the time of original learning can be accessed either perceptually or mnemonically; the physical presence of the context is not necessarily needed for the reinstatement to occur.

Generalizing the Technology of Environmental Reinstatement

Based on these data, we could conclude that context affects recall and settle for that generalization as the primary value of the experiment. We then apply the generalization by predicting that as differences between environments for learning and recall increase, the accuracy of recall decreases.

But the experiment could be used more directly and more fully by building more of the laboratory technology into the world. Specifically, whenever people have to reproduce something such as a conversation that was learned in a different setting, they would be instructed to do several things before attempting the recall task. Specifically, the person would be instructed to,

List any 10 things they can remember seeing in the room where the original learning took place;

Then take two additional minutes to think about that original room, what it looked like, what sounds and smells were there, where it was, and the way it made them feel

Then they should try explicitly to use their memory of this original room to help them recall the items they learned earlier;

As a supplement, the person could examine photographs of the original setting, although the Smith data suggest there is no special advantage to this additio 1. However, it clearly did not hurt performance either.

Having done these activities that simulate the laboratory in the field, people should now exhibit more accurate recall than if they had remembered some irrelevant setting prior to performance or remembered no setting at all.

Environmental Reinstatement as Reverse Simulation

The preceding discussion suggests that the environmental reinstatement effect can be used more fully than it has been in the past if more of the conditions that were present when the effect is demonstrated are exported into the world. In effect, the experimental procedures are simulated in the world, which reverses the more common practice of simulating the world's procedures in the laboratory.

The phrase "reverse simulation" is used to portray this approach to utilization because the word "simulation" preserves the key elements of the tactic. A simulation is a representation, an analogue, an idealization of a generally more complex system, the essential properties of which are retained in the analogue. In constructing a replica of a complex system, there is always selective incorporation and simplification of processes found in the reference system. Simulation is *not* an attempt to get a perfect reproduction. As James Coleman has described it, a simulation is a "caricature of social life." There is selective enlargement and shrinkage of events that usually occur.

Given this standard description of simulation, the nonstandard twist implied by the phrase reverse simulation is that the referent reality being simulated, abstracted, caricatured is events in the laboratory, not events outside the laboratory. My interest is in those occasions when we try to imitate in everyday life a reference system that consists of a standard laboratory experiment.

Simulation normally consists of attempts to reconstruct real world phenomena such as the economic system, World War I, the human brain, or international negotiations under more controlled conditions. My interest is in simulating laboratory events—such as communication networks (Shaw, 1964), generational transmission of culture (Zucker, 1977), the next-in-line effect (Brenner, 1973), self-fulfilling prophecies (Snyder, Tanke, & Berscheid, 1977), means-interdependent triads (Raven & Eachus, 1963), or surveillance and trust (Strickland, Barefoot, & Hockenstein, 1976)—in the real world in such a way that predictions that worked in the lab still work in the field because analogous systems have been constructed.

THE ROLE OF PREDICTION AND CONTROL IN UTILIZATION

People are often hesitant to use social science because they make the wrong assumptions about application. They assume that before people can control phenomena using social science ideas, the ideas themselves must first generate accurate predictions. First, we try to predict who will get cancer, shoplift, take risks, or follow the fast track, then we create settings and interventions that bring these behaviors under control. Since social scientists can not predict behavior very well, it is unlikely they will do any better at the more pragmatic task of controlling what they can not even predict.

The basic error in that vignette is that prediction does not precede control, it follows control. Control makes prediction possible, but prediction does nothing for control. Or at least that is what happens in fields like chemistry and physics. Chemists and physicists know that futures can not be predicted, but they also know that futures can be invented.

Prediction Within Constructed Systems

The reason physicists and chemists have a better hit rate than psychologists is that they predict the reactions of systems that are constucted strictly according to their requirements. Chemists make their predictions within closed constructed systems, not within open, natural systems. Social scientists seldom create a system anew and *then* predict how events will go together in that system.

From this perspective, physical science has won its great prestige in prediction on systems it has itself created. Social science keeps playing to mixed reviews because it

> is expected to predict "undisturbed" phenomena and to do so in areas that are either beyond human control or are controlled by non-scientific personnel (for instance, to produce "reformed" criminals in an institu-tional framework created by nonscientists, with aims other than reforma-tion in mind, and run by nonscientific personnel, against with aims other than reformation). As Homans once remarked, many of the problems the social sciences try to solve a respectable physical scientist would just give up on. Physical science does try to predict in "natural" systems (for

example the weather in meteorology, earthquakes and oil deposits in geology), but it is worth noting that, with the important exception of "near space", it has been less frequently satisfactory here and usually less dramatically successful. (Henshel, 1971, p. 215).

Social scientists try to control behavior on the basis cf fallible predictions they apply to natural systems. Physical scientists try to predict behavior on the basis of less fallible controls they embed in systems of their own construction. Given this disparity, it is not surprising that physical science comes off better than social science.

Experiments as a Source of Constructed Systems

If we assume that one way to improve utilization is to make predictions within constructed systems, the question becomes: What is the source of these constructions? In the natural sciences, one source of constructed systems is laboratory procedures. That occurs less often in social science.

For example, many organizational scholars are interested in organizational design (Kilmann, Pondy, & Slevin, 1976). If we ask where their designs come from, we would find that they originate in such sources as intuition (I think people have too much information to cope with), in what other people are doing (if it works for the Japanese it ought to work for us), in idealized views of organizations (we need to make our organization more like the military, not less like it), or in values (we need to give people more of a say in what affects them because this is the right and humane thing to do). This assortment of sources varies greatly in the generality, accuracy, and simplicity of the data from which the designs are extracted. More important, the fine-grain detail of precisely how the designs are to be implanted and run is left unspecified.

None of these shortcomings is quite as serious when the source of the design is an intact bench experiment—the source of design used in the physical sciences. We should make greater usage of intact experiments as our sources for designs when we try to utilize social science. I take my inspiration for this suggestion from Richard Henshel's recent (1980) description of an alternative way to think about generalizing between the real world and artificial laboratory experiments. The text from Henshel that I will be working with and glossing (Weick, 1981) in the remainder of this chapter, is as follows:

> Instead of asking whether an interesting phenomenon produced in a social laboratory can be found at present outside laboratory walls, so that the laboratory finding can be generalized, one might ask: Does the investigation uncover a desirable result (for example, high morale) that can be lawfully described in the confines of the experiment, even though

the regularity may be otherwise nonexistent? If so—if (a) the result was a desirable effect and (b) the conditions were "unnatural"—then perhaps the theory guiding the experiment can be used to create that result beyond the laboratory walls by deliberately reproducing the strange, hitherto nonexistent conditions in the outer world.

Many of the laws of the natural sciences apply only under artificial conditions. That the concepts of physics have become embedded in the theoretical language of pure science should not obscure the fact that many physical laws have no empirical referent outside of those artificial, specially designed man-made systems that are ordinarily considered the domain of engineering. Electronic laws in particular appear to be of this sort; many deal exclusively with transformed phenomena inside engineered systems.

To use a single natural science example, Goodrich's discovery of the vulcanization process, from heating rubber on a hot stove, is of little consequence in the understanding of natural physical systems. Although it might peripherally be used to explain what happens to rubber trees in a forest fire, it really has very little generalizability to the naturally occuring world outside of the laboratory. However, it has profound consequences for the prediction, control, and understanding of certain constructed physical systems (Henshel, 1971). Similarly, experiments in social communications networks may have little worth in explaining and predicting existing social phenomena. However, if it seems desirable, such networks can be created outside of a laboratory precisely to produce the effects detected in the laboratory. Whenever a potentially beneficial effect is observed in the laboratory, the objective might be to make the external world match the laboratory, not to make the laboratory match the external world. (Henshel, 1980, pp. 474–475)

THE REVERSE SIMULATION OF BIOFEEDBACK EXPERIMENTS

There are several examples of reverse simulation from which lessons for the utilization of laboratory work could be inferred: McClelland's (1965; McClelland and Winter 1969) exporting of laboratory procedures to assess motive acquisition into training programs for entrepreneurs; Blake and Mouton's (1964) rewording of basic research on consideration and initiating structure as grid managerial styles; the exporting of operant learning technology into organizational behavior modification (Duncan, 1982); the exporting of the nominal group manipulation in classical studies of group problem solving into a repackaged Nominal Group Technique (Delbecq & Van de Ven, 1975); and the exporting of basic survey instruments into survey-feedback interventions (Bowers, 1980).

Instead of reviewing these examples, we have chosen to study biofeedback because of current widespread interest in the phenomenon, the fact that the validity of the research is still under review (Qualls & Sheehan, 1981; Holmes, 1981), because it contains both psychological and physiological components (which is probably true for most other examples of reverse simulation, though both components are less visible), and because physically, the technology used to practice biofeedback is almost identical to the technology used originally to demonstrate the phenomenon. Part of the attractiveness of biofeedback lies in the fact that the observer literally can see that the field looks just like the lab. The purest case of reverse simulation is one in which all the laboratory technology is moved intact into the world. With the example of biofeedback as an ideal case, we can then explore gradations that approximate this case.

We have also chosen to examine biofeedback because it shows, with vividness and economy, the way in which experimental procedures can assist both discovery and application. In few other experiments is this dual contribution quite so obvious.

The Nature of Biofeedback

"Biofeedback may be conceptualized as a procedure in which data regarding an individual's biological activity are collected, processed, and conveyed back to him, so that ultimately he can modify the activity" (Everly & Rosenfeld, 1981, p. 143). Three operations, most of which are performed electronically, are involved: first, the detection and amplification of the biological response (detection of brain waves, skin temperature, heart rate, electrical activity in muscles); second, the conversion of the amplified signal to an easily understood or easily processible form (raw electrical signals from the heart are converted to an electrical signal proportionate to rate, which is then converted to a digital readout or a variable pitch); and third, the feeding back to the person, on a relatively immediate basis, the signals from the second step.

The important property of biofeedback is that it helps people discriminate externally subtle internal sensations, a discrimination that is necessary for learning.

> Biofeedback can enhance discrimination of subtle physiological functioning because it produces an external "effect" whereas previously the effect was so subtle as to be below awareness. As Sheffield (1965) has noted, an inherent feature of Thorndike's (1911) law of effect is that the *effect* of a response determines what is learned. Therefore, the effect of a response must in some way be detected by the organism or recorded in its nervous system. If a physiological response has little or no sensory feedback, it is difficult to understand how the nervous system can take

account of the fact that the response has occurred. The "effect", the making of the internal external, is the biofeedback. This electronic means of enhancing discrimination of subtle internal sensations not only provides precise, easy-to-assimilate information about the response but, in most instances, provides accurate quantification of the response as well. (Budzynski & Peffer, 1980 pp. 419–420).

Biofeedback in the Context of Discovery

The basic argument of this chapter is that a greater proportion of what happens in a laboratory experiment can now be used to improve everyday life. Experiments are useful in more ways than simply as vehicles that generate findings. Before examining how the technology of laboratory biofeedback demonstrations has been simulated in the world, it is instructive to see a slightly less direct way in which experimental procedures are useful.

Laboratory experiments are important for discovery as well as verification. Traditionally, this fact has been regarded as more important for scientists than practitioners. The example of biofeedback shows that experimentation is just as important for practitioners as it is for researchers.

Practitioners usually view experiments as artificial and therefore of little value for everyday problems. The implied prescription in this evaluation is that experiments will become more useful if they resemble more closely the settings with which practitioners work.

The crucial point about biofeedback is that experimentation that faithfully reproduced external world conditions would never have detected it:

> Neither humans nor other organisms are capable of monitoring their own brain waves in the slightest extent without special, artificial arrangements. It required experimenters who wondered what *would* happen *if* humans could see their own brain wave output. Not only could people not monitor such things for themselves, but the bodily conditions they learn to control were, under older knowledge, supposed to be totally involuntary. Through conscious attempts at experimentation under artificial conditions we have a clear case of new phenomena being observed, new relationships being discovered, and old truths overthrown. (Henshel, 1980, p. 473).

One reason social science has not been used more often may be that it has not been artifical enough. This paradox arises from the fact that genuine discovery often comes from putting elements together that do not routinely occur together in nature. Experimentation goes beyond common sense precisely when it does things that common sense does not, when it juxtaposes events that common sense and common action do not join together, when it enables people to observe combinations of events that are concealed in other settings.

From this standpoint, experimentation should be faulted because it has been too conservative, too concerned with simulation and mundane realism, too concerned with reproducing the props of everyday life that blind people to novel explanations. Deliberate artificiality is vital for utilization— artificiality is not the culprit people claim it is.

Biofeedback in the Context of Utilization

Biofeedback research can be generalized and used only if the outside nonlaboratory world is constructed to resemble the laboratory in which the phenomenon was first discovered. If you examine pictures of biofeedback setups, you cannot tell whether those pictures were taken in a laboratory or in a clinician's office.

Biofeedback generalized because the laboratory was simulated in the outside world. The exact nature of this reverse simulation provides some important clues concerning factors that may facilitate implanting other technologies in the world. There seem to be several reasons why biofeedback was moved from the laboratory to the field so successfully. If other technologies meet these same criteria, they too might be used more fully than they are now.

Biofeedback Has a Technology

The principle suggested is that it is easier to do reverse simulation when there is technology than where there is not. Technology, however, can include such things as scripts, instructions, formats, and sequences, so this is not as limiting a condition as it might appear. If the rise of computers has done nothing else, it has taught us that software, not hardware is power.

Biofeedback Gives People Useful Information

If someone provides information you did not have before *and* shows that it is crucial to your functioning, then you are likely to use it, depend on it, monitor it, and accommodate it. Examples of people incorporating laboratory procedures into their daily routines are found in people who self-monitor their time management, eating, feelings, and thoughts in the interest of change (Mahoney & Mahoney, 1976). Both the activity of monitoring and the content of the monitoring are direct exports of measuring procedures formerly used in the laboratory. (See Mountjoy & Sundberg, 1981, for a description of Ben Franklin's experiments with self-management and self-monitoring.)

Biofeedback is Counterintuitive

The finding that people can control supposedly involuntary functions was so implausible, so counterintuitive (I can change my heart rate? Are you crazy?), so open to skepticism, yet so intriguing, that people remained attentive to the phenomenon and wanted to see for themselves if the claims were warranted. Interesting phenomena attract attention, remain salient, and generate their own audience, which frequently assists the transition from the lab to the field.

Biofeedback is Individualized

Biofeedback has an immediacy and individuality not found with many other procedures. Just as soon as people are attached to the apparatus, they can see and hear their own physiological functioning and no interpretation is necessary. Furthermore, people are usually able to change feedback only by thoughts, images, or devices that are unique to them. The specific suggestions one makes to oneself to reduce heart rate are not specified in advance. What works for some people does not work for others. Individuals are left to experiment and find their own fantasies and images that produce the physiological outcomes.

For example, while autogenic phrases such as "I am calm," "My right arm is heavy and warm," "My arm is warm and relaxed" work with many people, Budzynski and Peffer (1980) report an experience where one of their clients, "having failed with autogenic phrases, achieved hand warmth control by means of silent recitation of a short prayer featuring God's grace converted into a warming substance which entered her hands and feet" (p. 425). The search for something that works can be frustrating until it is successful, but the point is that personally meaningful images are what usually produce success. People are reinforced for activating what is most meaningful to them.

Biofeedback Gives People Added Control Over Their Functioning

Recent work (Perlmutter & Monty, 1979) on perceived control shows that as the sense of control over a situation increases, symptoms of stress decline. It is conceivable that merely attaching people to a biofeedback apparatus and giving them the *prospect* of heightened control is sufficient to reduce stress without exposing them to the full biofeedback protocol. The parallel here would be the case of sham operations. It was found that the trauma associated with being prepared for lobotomy surgery was sufficiently intense by itself that people exposed to the preparation, but *not* the surgery, showed just as much reduction in psychotic behavior as did the people who went ahead with the surgery (Underwood, 1957)

While the presumed underlying processes (excess trauma versus prospect of control) are quite different between biofeedback and lobotomies, the fact that the crucial dynamics occur very early in the process could be shared.

Biofeedback Involves an Overdetermined Phenomenon

It is almost impossible to administer biofeedback without other things such as relaxation, visualization, imagery, social support, reassurance, listening, care, interest, and warmth also being given. While it is true that biofeedback has been exported intact and put in a closed, constructed system, it is also true that when that system was closed, several things in addition to pure feedback of biology were sealed in with it. Any of these things taken by themselves could cause some improvement in perceived well-being (simply being able to get away from the hassles of everyday life for a quiet hour might have its own soothing effects quite apart from whether one is hooked up to any apparatus). People who are concerned with utilization welcome, rather than cringe at, the reality of overdetermination (McClelland, 1965; Varela, 1971).

Blanchard and Epstein (1978) note that when biofeedback training is compared with some form of relaxation training, both procedures lead to clinical improvement but neither has an advantage over the other. They conclude that biofeedback appears to be one of many ways of teaching people to relax. Relaxation seems to be the final common pathway to the clinical benefits that occur when people lower their arousal. Whether biofeedback is the best or most efficient or only the most publicized means to secure the clinical benefits of relaxation remains to be demonstrated.

People working with biofeedback have not intentionally tried to overload their procedure with every possible prompt that will improve their chances of success. However, something approximating overdetermination seems to have occurred. Thus, the apparent success rate for biofeedback may be higher than it actually would be with a pure treatment, although this is probably not unique to biofeedback. Reverse simulation in general may be most successful when it too is similarly overdetermined.

Biofeedback Presumes More Understanding than Actually Exists

A fascinating thing about biofeedback is that no one knows for sure precisely how or why it works. That obviously has not deterred its use. The point is, people did not wait for researchers to settle their disagreements, tidy up the loose ends, or understand the phenomenon fully before they simulated it in the real world.

"Premature" utilization may be important for several reasons. It could allow for more reciprocal interaction between the lab and the field. Each learns things that are new and useful to the other. It is also possible that, because there are so many loose ends, unknowns, and requirements for improvisation, people are forced to fit the apparatus and the procedures to their own requirements and experience and this customizing improves the usefulness. In the design sense, this is a perfect example of an underdesigned system that needs to be specified further by the user. In finishing what was left unfinished, the user adapts the procedure to local idiosyncrasies, thereby improving its chances of being beneficial.

Biofeedback Mixes Biology and Psychology and Straddles the Mind-Body Split

Earlier we mentioned that natural science works with constructed systems while social science works with natural systems. Biofeedback involves an interesting mixed case. It is partially a constructed system (physiological indicators are artificially coupled with themselves through human volition that is inserted in the self-correcting feedback loop) and partially a natural system (the content of the volitional addition to the feedback is left unspecified and no experimenter could predict precisely which suggestions would work for which people). The problem of predicting which suggestions would work for which people is akin to predicting earthquakes or the weather. In both of these situations, natural scientists have no clear advantage over social scientists in the accuracy of their predictions.

Conceivably, mixed systems are best suited for reverse simulation with humans because they allow for voluntary inputs from unique human beings within a structured setting. Even though no one knows for sure just what the mind-body linkage is, it may be the virtue of biofeedback that no answer is necessary. Biofeedback "incorporates" the answer even as people are not sure what the details of that answer are.

Biofeedback's Usefulness is Open-ended

Blanchard and Epstein (1978) make the sobering statement that

It is thus theoretically possible to treat an ever widening range of disorders: for any problem for which there are neural connections between the CNS and the response effector, it may be possible to design a biofeedback treatment. It may be that any response which can be classically conditioned including such things as presence of clotting factor in the blood, can also be brought under biofeedback control. The limiting conditions appear to be (1) the ability to measure moment to moment changes in the response system and (2) some sort of neural connections between the response system and the CNS. Within the limits imposed by these two conditions the range of biofeedback effects may be very great and the extent of "mind-body" interactions profound. (pp. 186, 189).

A more detailed glimpse of just what this expanded world of biofeedback might look like is found in Dossey's (1982) stunning description titled "Myocardial Infarction: 2000 AD." Sam Platte, a man in his fifties is fishing alone in a remote location when he has a heart attack. Through a series of volitional acts (all of which have some plausability given research conducted through 1981), he constricts blood vessels in the periphery of his body, which raises blood pressure; he controls his terror so heart rhythm irregularities decrease; he consciously produces a release of pain-relieving chemicals; he reverses the pathological clotting process in the coronary artery by use of mental imagery; and then he falls asleep. A few hours later he wakes up and walks back to camp.

Whether one chooses to label such an account as hyperbole, science fiction, or mere extrapolation, the fact remains that applications of biofeedback have not been exhausted—the prospects are even more intriguing than current practice (for example, it may be used to reduce space sickness among astronauts [Waldrop, 1982]). There is no solid ground on which one can say that the extrapolations are wrong. One effect of this open-ended quality is that everyman becomes experimenter as well as consumer.

Biofeedback Meets a Current Need

Burnout, stress, and pain are all syndromes to which people's attention has been drawn and from which they now seek relief. Refined technology may have alerted people to stress problems they did not know they had before, or people may have sensed these problems first and then technology was developed to solve them. Whatever the case, interventions said to aid stress management are taken more seriously than are interventions that make no such claim. The technology of biofeedback and the diagnosis of stress mutually reinforce one another in such a way that people have used a more artificial set of procedures, developed less fully, earlier, than might have been preferred by more conservative experimenters. Reverse simulation is more likely when it meets important needs (for example, India had strong needs for entrepreneurs when McClelland's achievement training started).

Biofeedback is a Noninvasive Procedure with no Side Effects

This point is self-explanatory. People do not incur either immediate or long-range costs when they use biofeedback, yet it can have a significant positive effect on their well-being.

Biofeedback Capitalizes on a Widely Accepted Principle: Feedback is Good

Whether people try to improve their marriages, children, jobs, or athletic performance, they know that feedback is instrumental to improvement. The groundwork for biofeedback has already been created by the everyday associations built up between feedback and better outcomes. Suppose that instead of being called biofeedback, the procedure had been called biophrenology or biohypnotics. The associated imagery could well have wasted the procedure before it ever had a chance to take hold.

Biofeedback is Profitable

People can make lots of money selling biofeedback equipment. The basic technology is simple and the basics can be dressed up with lots of high-margin options such as wood cases, special sensors, high-grade wiring, refined meters, and so forth. Given the combination of a simple apparatus that lends itself to cosmetic touches and a mechanism that is mysterious but works, it is predictable that firms will try to convince people that biofeedback is the route to health and happiness. Also attractive from a commercial standpoint is the fact that basic information can be displayed in a variety of ways (visual, auditory), information can be secured from a variety of physiological activities either singly or in combination, and the basics can be made portable.

Biofeedback Originated in Good Science done by Credible Researchers

The famous psychologist Neal Miller did some of the earliest reputable work that eventuated in the biofeedback technology. Miller's reputation undoubtedly did a great deal to mark this topic as serious, well-grounded, and worthy of attention. The fact that early reports of this work were featured in *Science* (1969), a tightly refereed journal read by scientists of various specialties, undoubtedly contributed to its respectability. In the beginning, biofeedback was hard science, done on rats.

Extension of Utilization Criteria to Other Laboratory Studies

Biofeedback is an example of reverse simulation in which the world is made to resemble the laboratory. Characteristics of biofeedback that may have facilitated the ease with which it was moved from the laboratory to the field include the facts that it:

1. has a technology;
2. gives people useful information;

3. is counterintuitive;
4. is individualized;
5. gives people added control over their own functioning;
6. is overdetermined;
7. presumes more understanding than actually exists;
8. mixes biology and psychology;
9. has open-ended usefulness;
10. meets a current need;
11. is a noninvasive procedure with no side effects;
12. capitalizes on a widely accepted principle: feedback is good;
13. is profitable; and
14. originated in credible science.

The other five examples mentioned earlier also exhibit most of these 14 properties:

McClelland's program of motive acquisition contains all of the properties except 8 (there is no obvious biological grounding of nAch in theory or in practice).

Blake and Mouton's grid theory contains all of the properties except 3 (importance of attention to people and tasks is not counterintuitive) and 8 (no obvious biology).

Organizational behavior modification contains all the properties except 3 (it is not counterintuitive that people repeat actions that are rewarded) and 11 (behavior mod does have side effects).

The Nominal Group Technique contains all the properties except 3 (it is not counterintuitive that private opinions differ from public statements), 7 (the phenomenon is understood), and 8 (no biological component).

Survey feedback interventions contain all the properties except 3 (it is not counterintuitive that people respond to information about themselves), 4 (aggregate rather than individualized feedback is common), 7 (phenomenon seems to be understood), and 8 (biological component not obvious).

The hypothesis implicit in the preceding tally is that laboratory research that has been less successfully simulated outside the laboratory—research on topics such as the prisoner's dilemma, interpersonal attraction, expectation state theory, bargaining, coalition formation, equity, turn-taking, or concept formation—should fall short on more of these 14 grounds than is true for laboratory research where reverse simulation is more successful.

To take just one example, the case of the prisoner's dilemma, while there is a technology (the matrix representation), people are not given useful information about themselves, the work is not counterintuitive (apply the rule of win stay, lose change), the inputs are individualized, no added control over functioning is gained, the outcome is overdetermined, the phenomenon is understood more fully than is true for many other topics in social science, there is no biological component, the usefulness is not open-ended because there seem to be no uses yet identified, the work meets no current need (it may be a metaphor for disarmament, but we don't need mere metaphors), the procedure is noninvasive, feedback can occur but is not inevitable (knowledge about partner choices and preferences can affect decisions but is not always available), there is no money to be made from prisoner's dilemma, and the phenomenon did originate in prestigeful science. Thus, at least eight of the properties associated with biofeedback are missing from the case of prisoner's dilemma, more than for any other procedure we have reviewed so far. We would expect that other studies, which have not been successful when taken outside the laboratory, would show the same pattern as prisoner's dilemma.

We would also predict that experiments that have not yet been simulated outside the laboratory but that share many properties with biofeedback, would be judged useful applications when moved outside the laboratory. For example, to return to the experiment with which we started—the environmental reinstatement effect—we would expect it to be simulated successfully outside the laboratory because the only two things that it lacks are 8 (it has no biological core) and 12 (the place of feedback is not clear). Working in favor of its reverse simulation are such features as: a tangible technology in the form of the actions to be taken before recall is attempted; provision of useful information in the form of more accurate descriptions of prior events that can be used more fully in current decisions; counterintuitive grounding in the nonobvious finding that mnemonic recall of the original learning situation facilitates recall; people invoke customized representations of their original learning settings to improve recall; people gain added control over their ability to remember; mnemonically assisted recall is overdetermined; mnemonically assisted recall is used even though scientists do not fully understand how environmental reinstatement works (for example, it seems to work for recall but not recognition [Baddeley, 1982]); usefulness is open-ended in the sense that newer applications to training settings are still being identified; it meets a current need to have better data available for decisions; it is noninvasive although there could be side effects (the facilitation of recall for some items could lead to poorer recall for related items); it could be profitable (audiovisual equipment could be packaged as a method to retain, in sound and picture and with diagrams and checklists, the original learning setting, which is then replayed just before recall is attempted); and the work originated in credible science.

REFINEMENTS OF REVERSE SIMULATION

Several problems with the basic argument have been dormant up to this point and it is important to acknowledge their existence.

First, there is the implication that laboratory experiments are moved directly from the laboratory to the field without intervening steps. This apparent abrupt transition needs to be reexamined because chemists seldom move directly from the laboratory bench to full-scale plant production. Instead, they make use of scaleups and pilot plants. Social scientists may not have that option.

Second, the preceding examples of successful reverse simulation involve mostly micro, individual phenomena, which raises the question of the extent to which reverse simulation is relevant to more macro phenomena.

Third, since reverse simulation is a representation, there is the crucial question of what should be selected for exporting and what should be ignored. To conduct reverse simulation is to be concerned with the fine-grain detail of what actually happens in experiments.

These three issues do not exhaust the connotations of reverse simulation, but they do establish an agenda for further discussion of this approach to utilization.

Reverse Simulation and Scaleups

Chemists seldom enlarge their laboratory equipment directly into a full-scale production facility such as a refinery. Instead, they insert intermediate steps in the form of scaleups and pilot plants to detect problems of mixing, flow, and accumulation that appear when the scale is changed.

An example of the differences between laboratory studies and commercial plant operation is the case of impurities:

> Impurities literally get lost in small-scale experimentation. They may be lost due to long standing of feed stock samples which allow settling. Soluble impurities may disappear, because of adsorption or reaction with metal equipment surfaces. The ratio of equipment surface to process materials is usually much greater in small-scale equipment than in commercial equipment. Impurities may not be found in laboratory work because of lack of analytical tools or difficulties with the small samples available. Further, short runs are typical on experimental equipment. Under this condition, an impurity in the feed stock or process stream frequently may not reach a concentration at which its effect on the process is noticeable. However, in commercial operation with long operating periods, these impurities may well reach concentrations which are significant and sometimes very costly. (Kopf, 1958, pp. 74–75).

Unexpected factors such as the existence of trace concentrations that become consequential are discovered only by process simulation in pilot plants. Relative to the less codified world of social scientists, the problems of chemical scaleup are more straightforward. The key issues to which scientists must remain sensitive include: dimensional factors (does the total quantity of change per hour depend on the length, surface, or volume of the vessel within which the reaction takes place); time factors (does the process proceed at a constant rate or does the rate vary over time); operating variables (these are variable under the operator's control and include temperature, pressure, concentration, rate of flow, and residence times); and physical properties (conventional laboratory data concerning chemical properties). Each of these classes of quantity represents a possible source of error when it is introduced into a rate equation without experiment (Johnstone & Thring, 1957).

It is not clear how human experiments would be "gradually enlarged" since the relevant dimensions are not that obvious. A common dimension noted in human studies is time. Lab studies are relatively short-lived; life outside the lab covers considerably longer spans of time. Thus, to scaleup an experiment is to allow people longer periods of time to recall previous learning, monitor biological feedback, reflect upon their achievement motivation scores, and so forth. Scaleup also might involve inserting competing sources of attention, since people in everyday life seldom focus on one thing for a sustained period the way they do in the laboratory. While more items could be added to this speculative list, the point is that when laboratory technologies are generalized, they will have to be altered to fit local regularities. It is not obvious that intermediate steps in the transfer reduce this necessity or provide any special insight into what will have to be altered.

Social scientists may not have the luxury of scaleups because they do not have the luxury of developed theory that tells them what is changing systematically as they move from the lab to the field. If that is plausible, then the time spent working with a scaleup might better be spent either doing another experiment to test the reliability and durability of the technology that will be generalized, or directly implanting the technology in an ongoing organization to see what happens, after which an experiment might then be designed to verify hunches concerning why things happen the way they did.

Social scientists do run pilot programs (the Hawthorne studies were a pilot program). The thrust of the present analysis is that such programs may be less informative than people realize because the identity of crucial variables is not known, the form and extent of interactions among the relevant variables is unknown, and external variables not contained within the pilot programs will appear when the technology is disseminated. It may make most sense in doing reverse simulation simply to plunge in, insert the technology, design swift, trustworthy feedback into the system, and monitor the effects continuously and at sites relatively far removed from the intervention.

The sequence associated with chemistry—lab experiment to pilot plant to commercial operation—may need to be modified when applied to humans because the theory is less well developed. The more plausible sequence with humans may be lab experiment to commercial operation to pilot plant. In this latter sequence, the lab phenomenon might fail completely when it is put directly into the world where there is more competition for attention and energy. There is no way to guarantee that will not happen.

But that high level of risk is not unique to reverse simulation. The guarantees are not any better when people implant technologies that derive from other sources, such as their past consulting experience, folklore, or fads. Risk remains high in any of these cases because so little is known about human behavior. The risk lies with application of flawed knowledge and is not confined to the generalization of laboratory technology.

The assumption in this chapter is that exporting an intact lab technology that coheres and has had demonstrable effects when scrutinized closely is an improvement on the applications that are usually urged on people. Applications that originate in other sources commonly contain components from a variety of theories, experiments, and concepts, and can be internally inconsistent, contradictory, and subject to unexpected interactions.

In summary, chemists do have a body of knowledge that bears directly on reverse simulation. That knowledge concerns scaleups and pilot plants. These gradual scaleups are meaningful and cumulative because they are theory driven and theory interpreted. Equations that will guide the final process can be continually tuned because of the advanced state of understanding.

Scaleups involving reverse simulation of human experiments contain many more unknowns than a chemist's scaleup. Thus, the return on scaleups is likely to be less for social scientists than it is for natural scientists. Given this possibility, social scientists may have to adopt the riskier practice of directly implanting lab technology in everyday life, remaining attentive to what happens as technology unfolds, and fine tune and modify the unfolding process as it runs into problems. On the basis of what actually happens in the world, the social scientist might go back to the lab quite late in the process of utilization to see more clearly why unexpected outcomes have occurred in the outside world. The "pilot" study, therefore, comes late in the sequence of utilization, not early.

The Reverse Simulation of Macro Phenomena

Most examples of reverse simulation discussed so far have been individual phenomena similar to those studied by psychologists rather than sociologists. Since organizations typically involve groups of individuals and groups of groups, the question arises of whether reverse simulation is of much value for issues that are inherently larger in scale than a mere laboratory experiment with a few actors.

A case can be made that macro phenomena are not a serious problem for reverse simulation. Several lines of argument converge on this point.

First, there is a concerted move toward integration of micro and macro perspectives (Knorr-Cetina & Cicourel, 1981) such that the distinction itself is beginning to blur. Furthermore, integration seems to be moving in the direction of smaller size entities (such as concrete communicative interaction between two or more people) and toward cognitive rather than normative integration devices. The net result of this movement is that the crucial processes necessary to explain so-called large-scale phenomena may turn out to be phenomena that exist on the scale of standard laboratory experiments. That outcome would mean that the generalization of laboratory technology would be relevant to a substantial portion of organized life.

Second, a key property of macro phenomena is that interaction among people is mediated rather than face to face. Laboratory settings such as communication networks also do not involve direct interaction, so they are not likely to be modified when exported into a world where such contact is rare. To the extent that people in experiments are guided by imagined reactions of imagined others, they are not acting much differently than they would in an ongoing organization.

Third, there is evidence that small changes can amplify, especially when variables are connected in deviation amplifying feedback loops. Macro effects need not originate in macro-sized antecedents (Hardin & Baden, 1977). The Tragedy of the Commons makes this point as well as any demonstration currently available. The basic dynamic behind the Commons problem is demonstrable in the laboratory, and the means by which the tragedy might be averted can also be exported rather than directly from the laboratory.

Fourth, relatively large-scale organizations have already been built in the laboratory (McCall & Lombardo, 1978). Ironically, these technologies seldom are themselves exported back into the world as designs. For example, the Looking Glass simulation is an edited version of an actual ongoing organization. What has yet to happen is for that edited version to be exported back to the original organization and used as the structure inside of which the firm now conducts its business.

When simulations are built in the laboratory, editing is inevitable. The simulations never duplicate all the complications in an actual organization, which may be their biggest advantage. Simulations prune away features of ongoing organizations that those organizations themselves might well also prune away in the interest of improved functioning. Simulating the laboratory version of the organization back in the organization that originally inspired the simulation would exemplify exactly the kind of utilization being described in this chapter.

The Choice of What to Simulate

To do reverse simulation is to be attentive to fine-grained detail in experiments. It is striking how often the exact procedures used in experiments are ignored and replaced by rough approximations that fail.

Brainstorming, for example, fails almost every time the laboratory setting in which it was first refined is imperfectly reproduced. In the original brainstorming procedure, people took turns making suggestions, the leader went around the group systematically and asked each member for a single suggestion, and then repeated the process. If a person did not have a suggestion, that person would say "pass" and on the next round the person who passed would again be asked for a suggestion. If a person dropped out for one round, that person was not ignored for the remainder of the time during which additional solutions were gathered. In the field, however, once a person seems to have run out of contributions, that person is often not called on again. The leader's failure to call on the person again assumes that subsequent suggestions have had no effect on the associations or ideas of the person who had momentarily drawn a blank. That assumption usually is inaccurate. When people employ brainstorming without systematic turn-taking, they are not constructing the system within which the original predictions worked.

Obviously, the question of which fine-grained details need to be exported and which are superfluous is a judgment call. Environmental reinstatement, for example, should occur when people recall something other than five-letter words and we do not view that as a detail that needs to be reproduced. Even then, a surprising amount of what people seem to recall when they summarize a presentation, conversation, or diagnosis, consists of specific adjectives or nouns—warm, cold, suspicious—rather than connected discourse.

The issue of detail can be considered in the context of Milgram's obedience experiments (1974). First, it is not clear precisely what would be reproduced in the field to simulate Milgram. One thing people repeatedly miss when they discuss Milgram's work is that obedience dropped sharply when the experimenter was physically removed from the laboratory. Only 20 percent of the subjects were willing to administer the maximum voltage when the experimenter left. This suggests that obedience is dependent on surveillance and face-to-face contact and that if this experiment is to be simulated, this quality must be preserved.

> If we are to draw an analogue from the Milgram experiment to obedience in the modern state, the face-to-face character of obedience in the laboratory seems closest to that of the policemen and the traffic offender. If this is the appropriate analogue, it narrows Milgram's findings quite dramatically (Helm and Morelli, 1979, p. 336).

Authority that rests on face-to-face contact would seriously limit the options available to a modern state.

To simulate Milgram requires not only that the experimenter maintain face-to-face contact, but also that he or she systematically prod the person giving shock when that person hesitates to increase the voltage that is administered. If you look closely at the interaction that took place between subjects and experimenters when subjects hesitated to increase the voltage (such as, the Fred Prozi exchange), it consists largely of coaxing, reassurance, and suggestions uttered in a matter-of-fact tone rather than blunt commands. The language of obedience is simply not what experimenters were using here:

> Rather than obedience to authority, the interaction between subject and experimenter has the flavor of a parent (figure of authority) trying to convince a child (subject) with all the "tools" available that he should at least try to swim a bit. With a mixture of coddling, nonthreatening support, recounting of his own childhood experiences, and taunting of his "manliness" the first tentative strokes are taken. (Helm & Morelli, 1979, p. 338).

Experimenters in these studies actually said they would take full responsibility and that the experiment had to continue. When that failed, subjects were told that the experiment was not dangerous and that it must go on once begun. What is actually operating is a mixture of obedience, compliance, acquiescence, acceptance, resignation, and persuasion, but not just simple, pure obedience.

There are no firm rules concerning the selection of what should and should not be exported when the simulation is moved from the lab to the field. The safest rule of thumb would be the rule of reverse parsimony— generalize the largest amount of the experiment. When reverse simulation is not guided by theory, more is better. Since the experimenter knows that the effect occurs when the procedure is intact, the more of the procedure that is generalized, the higher the probability that the effect will be replicated.

When procedures must be edited, experimenters should delete those features that are farthest removed from the cause-and-effect interpretations that were tested. The last things that should be deleted are the operationalizations of the independent and dependent variables. The first things to go should be the features of the study that have an indirect relation to these variables.

Under the assumption that action is guided by perception, determinants of perception should be retained longer than determinants of action or feeling. If the perceptions are reconstructed in the field, then it is probable that the appropriate actions will then flow from these perceptions (O'Reilly and Caldwell, 1979).

Furthermore, content is usually less crucial than process. If the experiment can be partitioned into content (for example, the exact five-letter words used by Smith when he tests for environmental reinstatement) and process (spending two minutes recalling the original room where learning occurred), content will usually be more dispensable than process. When people are exposed to learning situations, they typically engage in deutero-learning as well as first-order learning. That is, they learn how to learn at the same time that they learn specific words. First-order learning tends to be more short-lived than second-order learning. To be concerned with process rather than content when choosing what should be simulated is to take that finding seriously.

If an experimenter simply asks the question, "What do I consider most interesting in this experiment?", and then exports whatever is contained in the answer, reverse simulation is apt to be successful. That assumes that whatever attracts the experimenter's attention will also attract attention from people in the organization and dominate their actions (Taylor & Fiske, 1978). Furthermore, interesting phenomena are probably less common in organizations than are minor departures from ordinary routines. Said differently, interesting aspects of experimental procedures are likely to be true innovations that have not yet been seen or tried within the organization. Therefore, they may have the highest likelihood of being solutions that do not duplicate something that has already been tried. The innovations may not work either—but at least they are not redundant. If the problem has been that people in the organization keep making the same old mistakes, then importing an interesting procedure may break the set with which they have been perceiving problems.

Those portions of an experiment should be exported that practitioners regard as more plausible, more sensible, and more rational. This criterion does not contradict the concern with interest. Instead, it simply acknowledges that people resist changes they cannot comprehend. Less plausible properties of a simulation should be deleted before more plausible properties. If that rule threatens the essence of the experimental procedures, then special efforts should be made to dress the procedures in a cover story that sounds reasonable (in the environmental reinstatement experiment, the strange request to think about a room at home was rationalized as an activity that helped to warm up memory processes).

Other criteria could be listed and readers are encouraged to add their own. Whenever someone generalizes anything, whether it be an assertion, an experiment, or an experience, some editing has occurred. Self-conscious attention to the nature of successful editing should suggest ways to prune experimental procedures in the interest of assisting the ease with which they are incorporated into the outside world.

CONCLUSION

It may seem ludicrous to discuss the laboratory—which is a place set aside from the flow of everyday life, containing events that are staged in the interest of understanding rather than improvement—in a book about utilization. My decision to focus on the laboratory was informed both by a sense of disappointment at the imaginativeness and plausability of ideas and techniques people now use in managerial practice, and by a sense that things that happen in the laboratory are often self-contained, valid technologies that are improvements on what people now do.

There is no escaping the fact that the laboratory *is* a different world:

> In all the previous laboratory research I've conducted there was little latitude for the subjects to improvise. They were placed in a contrived stage setting where they were patiently led step by step to notice "this" or to think "that" was insignificant, to listen intently to the prepared script of the experimenter and assorted confederates before being asked to deliver their part. Their part was the only element which was allowed to vary— like a brief jazz solo in a musical composition for classical orchestra and jazz soloist. But the limits of variation were narrowly prescribed: "I will wait alone or with others"; "I believe Johnny Rocco was responsible or it is the fault of his environment"; "I will eat a fried grasshopper or I will refuse"; "I will accept more electric shocks or I will not"; etc.
>
> Viewed this way the experimental hypothesis is just a bet that the "House" can successfully predict which of the limited alternatives each subject will select when the occasion for responding is presented. Nothing else matters except that single verbal statement, check mark on a scale, button pressed, action made or withheld. If the staging of the experimental situation has been meticulously attended to according to the prescriptions of the theory being tested and the intuitions of the experimenter, the subject will perceive that the limited alternatives available are "rational" and "appropriate." If so, the experiment is a success. If, in addition, the response is the one predicted, the researchers gamble is also a proven "success." (Zimbardo, 1975, p. 36).

The setting Zimbardo describes is not all that different from settings commonly found in many ongoing organizations. Most important, Zimbardo has also described exactly the kind of *constructed* system that social scientists work with. What Zimbardo describes is the psychologist's equivalent of a table full of flasks, bunsen burners, and tubing that a chemist works with, and then exports in the form of a refinery, which is nothing more than an enlarged version of those same tubes, burners, and flasks. Departures from the chemist's lab setup produce unexpected refined products (Porter &

Rollinson, 1957), just as departures from the psychologist's lab setup produce unexpected reactions. The predictions of each work best when applied within constructed systems of their own design.

People may assume either that it is impossible to create constructed systems for social science findings or they may think it is possible but distasteful. In either case they will probably work with natural systems. If they make this choice, they should realize that predictions probably won't work in natural worlds and that utilization will fail more often that it will be successful.

The analysis I have constructed involves four assumptions and, with a quick review of these, I will conclude:

Control improves prediction, and prediction neither precedes nor improves control.

Control requires closed, constructed systems rather than open, natural systems.

Theories are not the only things that can be generalized from laboratory studies (Webster & Kervin, 1971). People can also generalize procedures, settings, scripts, tasks, and technologies used in the laboratory. Phrased in terms of an imagery common among experimenters (Carlsmith, Ellsworth, & Aronson, 1976), if experimenters maximize *experimental* realism they can still generalize something other than theories. They can also generalize the vivid procedures that produced the effect.

Laboratory procedures are themselves a theory just as any organizational structure is a theory. The theory implicit in an experimental procedure simply says, if you do these things, to these people, in these settings, they react by doing these things. That is a regularity. People may dismiss it, but it is a regularity. In answer to the question, how do you get this regularity to happen again, the answer is, do the experiment again. This is largely what happens when you simulate the essential properties of the experiment in some other setting.

REFERENCES

Baddeley, A. D. Domains of recollection. *Psychological Review*, 1982, *89*, 708–729.

Blake, R. R., & Mouton, J. S. *The managerial grid.* Houston: Gulf, 1964.

Blanchard, E. B., & Epstein, L. H. *A biofeedback primer.* Reading, Mass.: Addison-Wesley, 1978.

Bowers, D. G. OD techniques and their results in twenty-three organizations: the Michigan ICL study. In D. Katz, R. L. Kahn, & J. S. Adams (Eds.), *The study of organizations.* San Francisco: Jossey-Bass, 1980. Pp. 506–52.

Brenner, M. The next-in-line effect. *Journal of Verbal Learning and Verbal Behavior*, 1973, *12*, 320–323.

Budzynski, T. H., & Peffer, K. W. Biofeedback training. In I. L. Kutash & L. B. Schlesinger (Eds.), *Handbook on stress and anxiety*. San Francisco. Jossey-Bass, 1980. Pp. 413–427.

Carlsmith, J. M., Ellsworth, P. C., & Aronson, E. *Methods of research in social psychology*. Reading, Mass.: Addison-Wesley, 1976.

Delbecq, A. L., Van de Ven, A. H., & Gustafson, D. H. Group techniques for program planning. Glenview, Ill.: Scott, Foresman, 1975.

Dossey, L. *Space, time, & medicine*. Boulder: Shambhala, 1982.

Duncan, P. K. (Ed.). *Current topics in organizational behavior management*. New York: Haworth, 1982.

Everly, G. S. Jr., & Rosenfeld, R. *The nature and treatment of the stress response*. New York: Plenum, 1981.

Hardin, G., & Baden, J. *Managing the Commons*. San Francisco: W. H. Freeman, 1977.

Helm, C., & Morelli, M. Stanley Milgram and the obedience experiment: authority, legitimacy, and human action. *Political Theory*, 1979, *7*, 321–345.

Henshel, R. L. Sociology and prediction. *American Sociologist*, 1971, *6*, 213–220.

Henshel, R. L. The purposes of laboratory experimentation and the virtues of deliberate artificiality. *Journal of Experimental Social Psychology*, 1980, *16*, 466–478.

Holmes, D. S. The use of biofeedback for treating patients with migraine headaches, Raynand's disease, and hypertension: a critical evaluation. In C. K. Prokop & L. A. Bradley (Eds.), *Medical psychology*. New York: Academic, 1981. Pp. 423–437.

Johnstone, R. E., & Thring, M. W. *Pilot plants, models and scale-up methods in chemical engineering*. New York: McGraw-Hill, 1957.

Kilmann, R. H., Pondy, L. R., & Slevin, D. P. *The management of organization design*. Vols. I & II. New York: North-Holland, 1976.

Knorr-Cetina, K., & Cicourel, A. V. *Advances in social theory and methodology: toward an integration of micro- and macro-sociologies*. Boston: Routledge & Kegan Paul, 1981.

Kopf, F. W. Pitfalls in scale-up. In R. Fleming (Ed.), *Scale-up in practice*. New York: Reinhold, 1958. Pp. 69–85.

Mahoney, M. J., & Mahoney, K. *Permanent weight control*. New York: Norton, 1976.

McCall, M. W., Jr., & Lombardo, M. *Looking Glass, Inc.: An organizational simulation*. (Tech. Rep. 12). Greensboro, N.C.: Center for Creative Leadership, 1978.

McClelland, D. C. Toward a theory of motive acquisition. *American Psychologist*, 1965, *20*, 321–333.

McClelland, D. C., & Winter, D. G. *Motivating economic achievement*. New York: Free Press, 1969.

Milgram, S. *Obedience to authority: an experimental view*. New York: Harper & Row, 1974.

Mountjoy, R. T., & Sundberg, M. L. Ben Franklin the protobehaviorist I: self-management of behavior. *Psychological Record*, 1981, *31*, 13–24.

O'Reilly, C. A., III, & Caldwell, D. F. Informational influence as a determinant of perceived task characteristics and job satisfaction. *Journal of Applied Psychology*, 1979, *64*, 157–165.

Perlmuter, L. C., & Monty, R. A. (Eds.). *Choice and perceived control*. Hillsdale, N.J.: Erlbaum, 1979.

Porter, F. W. B., & Rollinson, C. V. The development of a new process (Autofining) for the catalytic desulphurisation of petroleum distillates. *Joint symposium on scaling up: 1957*. London: Institution of Chemical Engineers, 1957. Pp. S109–S119.

Qualls, P. J., & Sheehan, P. W. Electromyograph biofeedback as a relaxation technique: a critical appraisal and reassessment. *Psychological Bulletin*, 1981, *90*, 21–42.

Raven, B. H., & Eachus, H. T. Cooperation and competition in means-interdependent triads. *Journal of Abnormal and Social Psychology*, 1963, *67*, 307–316.

Shaw, M. W. Communication networks. In L. Berkowitz (Ed.), *Advances in experimental social psychology*. Vol. I. New York: Academic, 1964. Pp. 111–149.

Sheffield, F. D. Relation between classical conditioning and instrumental learning. In W. F. Prokasy (Ed.), *Classical conditioning*. New York: Appleton-Century, 1965.

Smith, S. M. Remembering in and out of context. *Journal of Experimental Psychology: Human Learning and Memory*, 1979, 5, 460–47.

Snyder, M., Tanke, E. D., & Berscheid, E. Social perception and interpersoanl behavior: on the self-fulfilling nature of social stereotypes. *Journal of Personality and Social Psychology*, 1977, 35, 656–666.

Strickland, L. H., Barefoot, J. C., & Hockenstein, P. Monitoring behavior in the surveillance and trust paradigm. *Representative Research in Social Psychology*, 1976, 7, 51–57.

Taylor, S. W., & Fiske, S. T. Salience, attention, and attribution: top of the head phenomena. In L. Berkowitz (Ed.), *Advances in experimental social psychology*. Vol II. New York: Academic, 1978. Pp. 249–288.

Thorndike, E. L. *Animal intelligence*. New York: Macmillan, 1911.

Underwood, B. J. *Psychological research*. New York: Appleton-Century, 1957.

Varela, J. A. *Psychological solutions to social problems*. New York: Academic, 1971.

Waldrop, M. M. Astronauts can't stomach zero gravity. *Science*, 1982, 218, 1106.

Webster, M., & Kervin, J. B. Artificiality in experimental sociology. *Canadian Review of Sociology and Anthropology*, 1971, 8, 263–272.

Weick, K. E. Psychology as gloss. In R. Kasschau & C. N. Cofer (Eds.), *Psychology's second century*. New York: Praeger, 1981. Pp. 110–132.

Zimbardo, P. G. Transforming experimental research into advocacy for social change. In M. Deutsch & H. A. Hornstein (Ed.), *Applying social psychology*. Hillsdale, N.J.: Erlbaum, 1975. Pp. 33–66.

Zucker, L. G. The role of institutionalization in cultural persistence. *American Sociological Review*, 1977, 42, 726–743.

28

COPING WITH INSTITUTIONAL RACISM: A MODEL FOR SOCIAL PROBLEM-SOLVING

Raymond G. Hunt

In a book he wrote in 1969 called *Cure for Chaos*, a scientist-founder of the TRW Corporation, Simon Ramo, envisioned a "golden age" when enough trained professionals would exist to allow a "full application of logic, objectivity, and all the facets of science and technology" to solving social problems (Ramo, 1969:16). About a decade, he thought, would be enough time for us to start seeing the happy results of this development. During the 1970s, from federal expenditures alone, social problem solving did become a $2 billion industry (Study Project on Social Research and Development, 1978). But, in substantive terms, Ramo's estimate was plainly and extravagantly optimistic, even for the limited domain of organizational life. System analysts, organizational scientists, and applied social researchers have so far proven rather less than magical as practical problem solvers. Their institutional impact has been modest at most; the "knowledge" they produce commonly goes unused, and their relations with decision makers are sometimes "recriminatory" (see, for example, Weiss & Weiss, 1981; Guba & Lincoln, 1981; Levitan & Hughes, 1981; for a lively as well as somewhat skeptical reflection on the utilization "problem," see Knott & Wildavsky, 1981).

A very early version of this chapter was presented to a faculty seminar in social science at Buffalo. My colleagues in the seminar would probably fail to see much similarity between this essay and that presentation. For that I thank them, as I do my colleagues in the School of Management, especially Brian Becker, Richard Butler, Cynthia Fukami, and Frank Krzystofiak, for their comments on more recent drafts and my discussion of it at a kind of "brown-bag" challenge match. I am particularly grateful to Paul Diesing for his careful reading and tolerant critique of my ideas, and for his generosity with his own. These parties and others at the Pittsburgh Conference are not to blame, of course, for what I made of their help—then again, maybe they are.

Granting the problem, one wonders what is wrong. Is there something peculiar about the human or social sciences? Other scientists, after all, seem to have done well enough with problems in the "real world"—putting a man on the moon and all. Why not social scientists? Have they just plain overrated their special potential as practical problem solvers? Or have they badly misconceived what social problem solving entails and what science has to do with it? One way or another, the answer to all of these questions is yes. A growing number of scholars and practitioners would agree with this, as many have initiated thoughtful criticism of customary forms and strategies of problem-oriented social research and development (R&D) directed to discovering where we are going wrong.

This chapter concentrates on two central difficulties in the applied social/organizational research enterprise: first, an absence of conceptual closure on a generally satisfying construction of the role of research and researchers in social and organizational decision and policy making; and second, a related problem of uncertainty about which operational strategies and tactics are appropriate for social R&D.

The treatment of these two difficulties will range over three methodological topics. One is the concept or theory of knowledge, the epistemology of problem solving, as it were. This will be a modest treatment, however, which will highlight certain more or less recent tendencies in the philosophy of science that are especially instructive to a critical project like this.

The second topic is closely linked to the first: the matter of research methods or knowledge-development strategies. Consideration of this subject will bring us into contact with questions about explanation, understanding, warranting assertion, compelling belief, and "old" versus "new" paradigms for research.

The third topic is a procedural one: how to organize and manage the knowledge-development process. This topic is closely related to the other two and will get a large share of our attention. The emphasis is on the role of the researcher in multiparty problem-solving efforts whether in an intra-organizational context, such as that of a staff specialist providing information to a decision maker, or in an interorganizational one where one organization (such as a consultant) provides information for another (a client). The problem will be cast within a framework of organizational/managerial formats apparently conducive to innovation and the development of new technology.

One thing this chapter will not do is argue the essential feasibility of rationalist projects for social betterment through knowledge acquisition and application. This matter and such cognate notions as the "experimenting society" (Campbell, 1969) and the enervating institutional role of organizations in society (Scott & Hart, 1979) are both eminently debatable and tempting topics; but, for the present, our limited text is Drucker's pronouncement that "a primary task of management in the developed countries in the decades ahead will be to make knowledge productive" (1974:32). This is a sufficiently demanding exegetical theme, and one that in any case warrants development whether in or out of context with "bigger" institutional analyses.

The theme will be tied to a concrete social problem-solving project that was undertaken in hopes of assisting some police organizations with problems of institutional racial discrimination. This project was initiated several years ago by the Institute for the Study of Contemporary Social Problems in Seattle, Washington. Part of a long-term program of action research under the title "Police, Institutional Racism, and Change," it was the object of this program to identify and remedy race-related inequalities in a specimen set of five U.S. police agencies.[1]

DEALING WITH INSTITUTIONAL RACISM

A focus on institutional racism signifies a fundamental concern not with the attitudes and beliefs of individuals, but with ways that race is used "even if unconsciously, as a criterion for determining the distribution of social benefits" (Bromley & Longino, 1972:183; see also Jones, 1972; Bowser & Hunt, 1981; U.S. Commision on Civil Rights, 1981). Thus, institutional racism may be taken to name a social situation where

> basic racial controls have become so well institutionalized that prejudicial attitudes or discriminatory actions by individuals occupying positions within an organizational structure generally are not necessary to perpetuate the racial consequences. The rules and procedures of organizations already have pre-structured the office holder's choices and their consequences. Conformity to the organizational norms and implementation of established policy, regulations, and procedures are all that is required for continued discrimination. Conscious racism on the part of individuals in organizations need not be present at all. (Bromley & Longino, 1972:187)

Strategies for eradicating institutional racism or ameliorating its effects must necessarily orient to social structure reform and not to individual attitude change, although the latter might be a welcome, even hoped-for, by-product of the former.

For reasons both of tactics and practical economics, the Institute's program for institutional reform in police agencies was divided into two separate projects. The first one occupied three years of effort spread over some four-and-one-half calendar years. It focused on "internal racism," which is to say that it concentrated on manifestations of institutional racism within the police agencies themselves. At issue in this project were mainly departmental personnel policies and practices ranging from recruitment through training to discipline and firing, plus some broader matters of organizational climate. (Fuller descriptions of this project have been published by Locke and Walker, 1980, and by Hunt, 1981).[2]

The internal racism project dealt with the intraorganizational use and management of human resources. Its auspices were, however, interorganizational: a collaboration of the Institute, the police departments, and albeit not actively, the NIMH. We set out to exploit research and other analytic techniques in order to develop information about the "state of the intraorganizational system" and, in later stages, about the effects of "interventions." Our plan involved using various research techniques (opinion surveys, field interviewing, content analysis of documents) to generate information that would be enlightening on the subject of institutional discrimination in the participating police departments and helpful to local decision makers in coming to grips with it. Our general strategy for doing this comprised five basic elements:

Establishment of liaison with each participating department, jointly via the chief of police and a minority representative, and construction of an organizational/operational base in the form of a task force of department members—a project organization, in effect, in each participating agency;

A multimethod "fact-finding" or "enlightenment" effort focused on departmental manifestations of institutional racism;

The preparation of diagnostic reports and recommendations to the departments based on fact-finding;

Review and critique of these reports by and with the departments; and

Development by the departments, in concert with Institute staff, of "need assessments," action plans, and concrete programs to ameliorate institutional racism in the departments, and its consequences for their members.

Thus, the "Police, Institutional Racism, and Change" project accepted as a basic premise that racism was a social problem solvable in some sense by rational (which is to say purposive), knowledge-based means. It furthermore oriented solution seeking at the level of the organization and thereby decomposed the social problem-solving process into a program of organizational change projects. My immediate concern then and now was and is with how constructively to conceive such projects and then execute and manage them.

Some Methodological Issues

It has been the frequent fate of action research efforts such as ours to prove disappointing. Indeed, as Sarason said, "most scientists who entered the arena of social action have left it bloodied, disillusioned, and cynical" (1978:379). In a small but important recent book, Lindblom and Cohen (1979) also remark on the common mutual dissatisfaction of the suppliers and users of social research, the first because no one listens to them, the other because they do not hear anything worth listening to.

In hopes of forestalling these discouraging eventualities, our internal racism project was structured as an exercise in collaborative problem solving as between the police department ("clients") and the Institute ("contractor-consultant"), the problem being, of course, that of how to eliminate institutional racism. The project was conceived in the form of what Whitaker (1980) has called a "coproduction" and Patton (1978) has referred to as "utilization-focused evaluation." Its methods were chosen with an eye to increasing the chances that decision makers would "hear" something from social research that was worth listening to—worth listening to in the sense that it would help them interpret and "cope" better with their situations and get things done, affirmative action things in particular. As the project went on, we endeavored jointly with the departmental task forces to stimulate a dialogue within which to define and indicate, in locally meaningful terms, manifestations of the global problem of institutional racism and then to decompose them into manageable pieces that could be fixed by the departments one-by-one or a few at a time. It became clear in the course of events, as it was not at the outset, that the Institute's most important role in the project would not be as a provider of solutions, but rather as a facilitator of some long-range process and mechanism of change in the separate organizations. If in any meaningful sense institutional racism was to be eradicated in those organizations, it was essential that the departments develop their own contextually appropriate means of coping effectively with it beyond the period of the project and independently of any special purpose "third parties."

A difficulty with this pragmatic collaborative approach to action research is that, in addition to often being undramatic, it necessitates sacrifices of apparent methodological purity to practical relevance. Consequently, it is hard to evaluate on customary science-based standards. This of course is not so much a difficulty for the consumer of social research as it is for the providers of it, or rather for the professional research communities where aesthetic formality is at least as important in research designs as utility.

In their provocative book, Lindblom and Cohen (1979) voice some especially well-formed thoughts on this subject of appropriate methodologies for social research and problem solving. Their ideas are worth reviewing in detail. Important in themselves, Lindblom and Cohen's ideas serve as well to generalize the methodological crux of our own antiracism change efforts with police departments and to link them up with some wider methodological themes.

ON THE NATURE OF SOCIAL PROBLEM-SOLVING

Lindblom and Cohen define social problem solving quite freely as "[any] processes that are thought to eventuate in outcomes that by some standard are an improvement on the previously existing situation" (1979:4).[3] They go on to point out that social problem solving can take different forms, at least two of which contrast sharply.

Social Problem Solving as Definitive Research

First, social problem solving can be construed as a quest for definitive answers to particular social questions or issues. Rigorous and comprehensive analysis by disinterested professional specialists is a featured methodology of this detached enterprise. Analysis, suffice it to say, is a cognitive strategy for problem solving. It aims to solve a problem by understanding it, and it seeks to understand it by decomposing it into its elements. Scientific analysis simply features a systematic, disciplined use of formal symbolic and empirical tools for this purpose. Its goal, a la Campbell and Stanley (1966), is an authoritative, value-free knowledge base on which to found technically optimal solutions to particular social and organizational problems. Lindblom and Cohen call this species of rational problem solving Professional Social Inquiry (PSI). Its expert practitioners they call pPSI—practitioners of Professional Social Inquiry. PSI includes a range of scientific policy-oriented, program planning, and evaluation disciplines. The products of PSI tend to be relatively expensive and often come more or less elegantly packaged as definitive answers to policy and program questions, or, more frequently, elegantly packaged apologies for why definitive answers are unavailable.

Traditionally, research and writing on policy making, program planning, and evaluation has emphasized finding definitive solutions to problems, institutional discrimination included (cf. Churchman et al., 1957). It has commonly addressed itself (at least as if) to engineering well-crafted major shifts of policy or program design and to their subsequent unambiguous assessment (cf. Nagel & Neef, 1979). Yet, as Lindblom warns, "neither revolution nor drastic policy change, nor even carefully planned big steps are ordinarily possible" (1979:517). Moreover, the usual vagueness of criteria for measuring the success, failure, or usefulness of policies and programs renders authoritative evaluation a special rather than a general case of PSI. Big-change-oriented hopes for knowledge-driven social reform, as in Etzioni's (1968) wishful vision of the "active society," have mostly been disappointed. "Directed" social R&D, in the fashion say of the National Science Foundation's now-defunct program of Research Applied to National Needs, remains an unvindicated aspiration. Small wonder then that, more and more, suppliers and users of social research are dissatisfied.

PSI has so far failed as a universal means of social problem solving. Having said this, however, I hasten to add agreement with Lindblom and Cohen who, while enlarging at length on PSI's inadequacies, note that their judgment does not "add up to a rejection of PSI . . . but to a proposal that pPSI study, think about, and reconsider some of their most venerable beliefs and practices about how PSI is made useful to social problem-solving" (1979:93).

Major among these questionable beliefs is the faith in PSI as a definitive, conclusively authoritative, value-free means of conquering the complexities of nature. Prominent among its dubious practices is the requirement that PSI be disinterestedly "scientific" and not only conclusive but synoptic as well in a search for all-encompassing "final" solutions to social problems.

The meaning of "solution," of course, is vague; but, whether in lay usage or in science, a problem may be thought of as "solved":

> (a) when it does not have to be solved again because the operations that lead to the solution can be demonstrated to be independent of who performs them, (b) when the solution is *an* answer to a question or set of related questions, and (c) when there is no longer any doubt that the answer is the correct one. If there are competing answers, the problem has not yet been solved. (Sarason, 1978:374)

These are hard criteria to satisfy; certainly as regards social problems, they often cannot be. Some problems—possibly most social-organizational problems—on such categorical standards are surely unsolvable or, as Sarason says, intractable. A nondeterminative and meliorative concept of "solution," therefore, seems preferable in general to any consummate alternative.

"Overestimating PSI's conclusiveness accounts for serious failures and flaws in the practice of PSI and points toward desirable new practices" (Lindblom and Cohen, 1979:41). These are practices in which interaction and ordinary knowledge have major roles. Because the knowledge derived from PSI is almost never conclusive, it is therefore best conceived as a supplement to other knowledge—ordinary knowledge and the outcomes of interactions. The usual (and quite useful, one might add) effect of PSI,

Lindblom and Cohen suggest, "is to raise new issues, stimulate new debates, and multiply the complexities of the social problem at hand" (1979:48). The usual effect, in short, is not definitive solution of the social problem at hand, but perhaps an increment to understanding and, in any event, some new questions (see also Kaplan, 1964).

Analysis and interaction complement each other, of course. In fact, that is the essential thesis of this essay. As a basis of knowledge each contributes something the other does not (and, for that matter, cannot). Together they provide a hermeneutic strategy of social problem solving or technology development that promises to be more helpful than either one alone. Ordinary and interaction-based knowledge underwrite the usefulness of PSI.

Social Problem Solving as Coping

Contrasting with PSI is an orientation to social problem solving known as "coping." In Lindblom's lexicon, coping is an incrementalist (or meliorative) strategy. It may not always get things done, but when it does it gets them done a little at a time; and sometimes what gets done is an improvement.

Like definitive problem solving, coping employs knowledge as an implement of decision making. Unlike definitive problem solving, however, it treats PSI not as the sole dependable source of knowledge, but as a complement to ordinary knowledge. Ordinary knowledge is something anybody may have, which is why it is ordinary. It derives from common sense, casual empiricism, or thoughtful speculation and analysis. Highly fallible, ordinary knowledge is nonetheless indispensable to decision makers.

The usual distinction between ordinary and extraordinary or scientific knowledge is a qualitative one based on the presumption of a fundamental difference between the methods of knowledge generation in the two cases. Because of its breeding, scientific knowledge is typically thought of as inherently superior to ordinary nonscientific varieties. Indeed, ordinary "knowledge," in the conventional view, is hardly knowledge at all; rather, it is mere belief or prejudice. The privileged status of scientific knowledge is based on its ostensible freedom from bias, on its "objectivity." Ordinary knowledge, on the other hand, is "subjective," or, as Morton (1980) so nicely puts it, "susceptible to desire," and therefore untrustworthy (see also Nisbett & Ross, 1980, for another recent expression of this normative viewpoint). But is it so certain that scientific and ordinary knowledge are fundamentally different?

Distinctions about forms of knowledge have been regular subjects of argument among philosophers of science since Plato. Their epistemological debates have gained relatively wide notice in the past decade or so, mainly because of spreading discontentment with positivist definitions of the scientific project,[4] especially among social scientists, and because of the particular influence of Thomas Kuhn's widely noted book *The Structure of Scientific Revolutions* (1970).

Kuhn's imagery of science as puzzle solving dominated in its routine practice by derivations from past intellectual achievements in the immediate form of "paradigms"—that is, stipulations of those problems of fact, theory, and method that are taken as "solved," together with criteria for choosing new problems—is a skeptical account of both scientific objectivity and the priviliged quality of scientific solutions to the puzzles upon which it attends. Demystified, "normal science" appears in Kuhn's account as a cultural practice, like any other, subject to the pulls and shoves of value, ideology, and prejudice, and hence not so unlike what Lindblom and Cohen call ordinary knowledge and Rorty (1979) has spoken of as "ordinary discourse." Kuhn's revisionist thesis that science is a cultural practice inherently subject to and expressive of the beliefs and values of its time and place has been powerfully developed in Rorty's critique of epistemology. Pivoting on linguistic metaphors of "culture as conversation" and inquiry as discourse, the principal target of Rorty's argument is

> The conviction that science differed from softer discourse in having "objective reference" to things "out there" . . . the thought that even if there were no such things as Aristotelian essences that could become immaterially present in the intellect, there certainly were points of contact with the world in the presentations of sense. This contact, plus the ability to characterize the essence of the referent in terms of the presentations to be expected from it, seemed to give science what was lacking in religion and politics—the ability to use contact with the real as the touchstone of truth. The horror which greeted Quine's overthrow of the dogmas, and Kuhn's and Feyerabend's examples of the "theory-ladenness" of observation, was a result of the fear that there might be no such touchstone. For if we once admitted that Newton was better than Aristotle not because his words better corresponded to reality but simply because Newton made us better able to cope, there would be nothing to distinguish science from religion or politics. It was as if the ability to tell the analytic from the synthetic, and the observational from the theoretical, was all that stood between us and "irrationalism." (1979:268–69).

Rorty's essential message is that we must renounce the unhelpful partition between "objective" fact or data and "subjective" interpretation. Data, observations, "fact," are not and cannot be privileged "mirrors of nature," independent of their subject. They are necessarily theory-dependent, method-dependent, observer-dependent, and they change as theory (belief) does. Indeed, to identify data or fact as something "real" and invariant "behind" the human interpretations that may be made of them is worse than useless for, as Ricoeur (1981) has said, it misdirects scientific attention to a quest for unattainable truth instead of the modest but achievable aim of education, understanding, or, as Rorty prefers to call it, "edification": "this project of finding new, better, more fruitful ways of speaking" (1979:360). Moreover, posing scientists (or pPSI) as privileged possessors of truth (or the unique means to it) misconceives their relation to knowledge and at the same time attenuates their potential for helpful engagement with others in practical problem solving.

To quickly summarize Rorty's pragmatic philosophy, it maintains that knowledge is interpretation—the adduction of meaning. The development of knowledge is a social affair: "a conversation between persons, rather than a matter of interaction with non-human reality" (Rorty, 1979:157). Language is the instrument of knowledge and action its point. The principal danger to knowledge comes from tendencies to block the flow of conversation by insisting upon some fictive "canonical vocabulary for discussion of a given topic" (Rorty, 1979:386–87). The distinction between knowledge and belief is a weak one at most; "grounding" belief and warranting assertion is a matter of persuasion—the only usable conception of "factual" or "objective" being a social one of agreement and consensus about what is "true." The goal of inquiry is "edification," the "test" of which is the practical or existential one of how it enables one to cope; and the "method" of edification is hermeneutics (see Bleicher, 1980; Ricoeur, 1981; Reason & Rowan, 1981; as well as Rorty for informative discussion of hermeneutic philosophy).

Hermeneutic Inquiry

Hermeneutics is fundamentally a "critical" enterprise. Commonly called a study of the methodological principles of interpretation, hermeneutics is an alternative attitude to the positivist one still prominent in contemporary PSI. As Rorty insists, it is not another way of knowing. Most especially, hermeneutics is not "the name for a discipline, nor for a method of achieving the sort of results which epistemology failed to achieve, nor for a program of research" (Rorty, 1979:315). Rather, it is a "struggle" against the notion that there is some definitive set of rules for determining "how rational agreement can be reached on what would settle [an] issue on every point where statements seem to conflict" (Rorty, 1979:316). Hermeneutics, in other words, is a liberal perspective on the game of science and, more generally, on the tasks and processes of knowledge acquisition and utilization. It is a strategy of inquiry disposed to settling claims to knowledge by social means and hospitable to a variety of procedures.

The focus of hermeneutics has been the so-called human sciences, anthropology in particular. Certainly the hermeneutic stress on understanding the meaningfulness of phenomena strikes a resonant chord in these disciplines where such ideas are historically familiar themes. It has also been suggested that in the human sciences criteria of scientificity may be different from those appropriate to other sciences. Silverman (1971), for example, proposes that neither the phenomena nor the forms of explanation are alike in the natural and social sciences. For the latter, the centrality of meaning results in a uniquely "subjective" basis of human action and necessitates indeterminate explanations of it. Consequently, the two sciences "share only a [broad] commitment to a systematic and rigorous analysis of their material" (Silverman, 1971:128; see also Mitroff & Kilmann, 1978; Reason & Rowan, 1981). Both Rorty (1979) and Ricoeur (1981) are skeptical about such arguments as these, however. Each denies an antinomy of ways of knowing as between, say, social and physical sciences; and Reason and Rowan (1981) have, in fact, insisted that *all* knowledge is hermeneutical—culturally rooted and history bound.

Still, a special affinity between the human sciences and hermeneutical concerns with meaning, social action, imagination, and its opposition to subjective-objective distinctions and positivist posturing seems clear enough. The important point is that hermeneutics does not turn on what Ricoeur calls a "disastrous" distinction between rigorous scientific "explanation" and casual pro- or nonscientific (hermeneutic) "understanding." In practice, hermeneutic analyses of issues frequently appear more casual than insistently rigorous, but those who like to talk about hermeneutics do not propose some new kind of method ("a suspiciously 'soft' kind") as a substitute for the "scientific method." Most research practices are, in any case, rather less formal than either their ex post facto description or textbook idealization often suggests. Consequently, Kaplan, for example, has felt obliged to distinguish between what he calls "logic-in-use" and "reconstructed logic," the former being "what scientists do when they are doing well as scientists" (1964:8) and the latter either an idealization or hypothesis about it. Any correspondence between the two logics may be very loose indeed. Hence, as Scriven has remarked, "it is dull to hear people preach operationism [for instance] when nobody has practiced it—ever" (1964:180). What hermeneutics proposes is a distinctly tolerant, or, more accurately, radical naturalistic attitude toward methodology. In harmony with Polanyi's (1951) understanding of science as a rebellion against stultifying authority, it intends a liberating influence on processes of inquiry and encouragement of "new paradigms" for social research.[5]

NEW PARADIGMS FOR SOCIAL RESEARCH

In a recent volume, Reason and Rowan (1981) have presented a collection of papers that they describe as a "sourcebook of new paradigm research," one that goes beyond critique to a description of alternative methods of proceeding. The general plan of their approach is to give a bigger play to "naive inquiry" (ordinary knowledge), and to devise alternative approaches to research that will do greater justice than "orthodox" varieties do to the "humanness of all those involved in research endeavor" (Reason & Rowan, 1981:xi). However, whereas Reason and Rowan provide a detailed characterization of the "old paradigm" they are against, they give no real definition of the new one they favor. The features of the new paradigm are mostly left to one's inference by noting the targets of Reason and Rowan's opposition. But this is typically hermeneutic. As Rorty comments:

> In our time, Dewey, Wittgenstein, and Heidegger are the great edifying, peripheral thinkers. All three make it as difficult as possible to take their thought as expressing views on traditional philosophical problems, or as making constructive proposals for philosophy as a cooperative and progressive discipline. They make fun of the classic picture of man. . . . Great edifying philosophers are reactive and offer satires, parodies, aphorisms. They know their work loses its point when the period they were reacting against is over. (1979:366)

One must not be dismayed or deceived then by the relative ambiguity of "new paradigms. In the first place, "new paradigm" is revolutionary sloganeering; but it is not, therefore, without further point nor altogether lacking substance. Those who advocate new paradigm research in the human sciences generally emphasize realist, humanist, nonpositivist imagery set over and against old paradigm normative, mechanistic varieties. The paradigm shift for which they hope has two basic aspects: first, a shift of methodological orientation from a normative one of how science *ought* to be used, to a descriptive or naturalistic one of which methods actually *are* used (see Diesing, 1971); and second, a shift with regard to the "entities" being studied, from a mechanistic to an "anthropomorphic" model of man (Etzioni, 1968; Harré & Secord, 1972; Harré, 1981).[6]

Respect for qualitative research and case analyses is much more a part of the "new" human science than of the "old" (although even Campbell, 1975, has shifted ground here). This is due partly to the former's emphasis on people as "conscious social actors capable of controlling their performances and commenting upon them" (Harré & Second, 1972:*v*), and partly to a complementary emphasis on hermeneutical, context-relative, holistic interpretation of human action.

Diesing, who has been uncommonly articulate on the disciplines of case study and qualitative research technique, argues the holistic hermeneutic thesis (which in 1971 he termed a systems logic) that "a theme and also a relation is explained by specifying its place in [a] pattern . . . [if new themes and relations] prove puzzling, one explains them by tracing out more and more of the pattern" (Diesing, 1971:158). In his own version of the hermeneutic circle,[7] Diesing notes that in the holistic viewpoint there can be no sharp distinction between "explanans and explanandum," for both are at the same level of generality. Both are system-particular, standing in relations of part-to-whole, and hence, are context-dependent. The point Diesing stresses in his discussion of system relations is the infeasibility of holistic analysis based exclusively on statistical survey or other context-free data, for "data" have no "meaning" alone. Their function is as grist for an interpretive mill the model for which, regardless of the particular techniques employed, is qualitative analysis. For this, context is crucial.

Typically, the evidence supporting holistic models is not highly reliable by itself. Any particular interpretation is questionable as plausible alternatives exist. The larger the network of relations embraced by a model, however, and the more varied the evidence for it, the more compelling it is (a general idea that is also the basis of so-called triangulation strategies for field research [Webb et al., 1966]). Developing and extending patterns is the means of compelling belief in a model's veracity; hence, the holistic emphasis on extended in-depth analysis of the complex patterns discernible only in particular cases. As Diesing says, "to the holist, generalizations and general laws do not explain, only specific circumstances do" (1971:160).

The key, then, both to breaking the "model-building circle" and to the society veracity "explanations" is their application to practical problems. "Theory is of practice, and must stand or fall with its practicality" (Kaplan, 1964:296), where "practicality" refers either (and both) to what a theory can do for intrascientific interests, or, as in the present case, for extrinsic problems. Utility for coping with problems serves then—both as generator and test of models (theories)—in science and in the world of affairs.

Quite like the administrative style Lindblom (1959) 20 years ago christened "muddling through," coping is a generally applicable problem-solving (or problem management) strategy. In a specifically organizational context, it treats administration as a continuous heuristic process of dealing with organizational situations characterized by sociotechnical complexity and ambiguity (March & Olsen, 1976). In such an environment social change is typically "organic" (Hunt, 1974; 1981). It occurs, when it does, mostly in the form of modest stepwise departures from a still easily recognized status quo.[8]

Interactionist Methodology for Social Research

Together with some currently popular organization theorists, such as Weick (1980), Lindblom and Cohen note that social problems sometimes are solved by interaction—mutual adjustments as between persons or groups and the like—without the intermediating agency of either planning or even comprehension. "Understanding a problem," Lindblom has proposed, "is not always necessary for its amelioration" (1979:525). Action may be substituted for thought. Indeed, good reasons exist for suspecting that much organizational "choice" results from the adventitious "nonrational" coincidences suggested by the "garbage can" metaphors of Cohen, March, and Olsen (1972), and that in human behavior generally "action precedes thought" (Weick, 1979:194).

There are two related principles here. One is methodological and the other epistemological or theoretical. The epistemological/theoretical principle holds that thought, or more exactly, conceptualization, is essentially retrospective sense making that derives from transactions between a person and an environment which, in some respects at least, is equivocal.[9] In Weick's view, for instance, situations are "decision-interpreted" rather than "decision-guided." Posited is a process of cognitive reconstruction by an actor-observer of noncognitive behavior—a process, incidentally, that exactly parallels the operations of scientific observation and theory building. Weick refers to this hermeneutic enterprise as an "enactment" of experience, with the implication that one has no experience until one does something in a situation (see also Einhorn, 1980). Via interaction one, in effect, "discovers" not things but ways of thinking about things—of modeling them, making sense of them, and of coping with a situation.

Both Patton and Lindblom (to name two) have made of this interactionist idea a methodological principle. Lindblom and Cohen, for example, distinguish between analytical and (noncognitive) interactive problem solving, pointing out that problems "can be attacked by understanding, thought, or analysis . . . or by various forms of interaction among people" (1979:20). As an illustration of direct interactive problem solving, they offer the example of voting, pointing out that the matter of naming a president of the United States is one that might be settled (indirectly) by PSI, but instead is handled by an "elaborate ceremony of action" (1979:21).

Decision by flipping a coin is another simple interactional stratagem, and a much more complex one is the phenomenon of markets. In markets, "the problem of determining the goods and services to which the nation's resources should be allocated . . . is 'solved' as a by-product of countless acts of buying and selling" (Lindblom & Cohen, 1979:22). Significantly, when market interactions yield unacceptable solutions, Lindblom and Cohen point out that recourse commonly is had not to "direct frontal analysis," but to other forms of interaction, such as bargaining and negotiation (as for wages).

> Practitioners of PSI know that some kinds of issues have to be settled by the interactions called "politics" rather than by analysis. But how much that simple fact reveals about the limitations of PSI they have not fully

explored. Nor are the many forms of interactive problem solving outside the political arena familiar or yet explored. (Lindblom & Cohen, 1979:24–25).

Patton has similarly remarked on a case of the hermeneutic circle that he calls "the paradox of decision making," observing that

> effective action is born of reaction. Only when organizations as open systems take in information from the environment and react to changing conditions can they act on that same environment to reduce uncertainty and increase discretionary flexibility. . . . Action emerges through reaction and leads to adaptation. (1978:127–128)

Furthermore, Patton says, much in organizational decision making that passes for action really is nondecisional buying of time (Bacharach & Baratz, 1963) or making the best of things until circumstances allow a more positive sort of activism.

One may take this "making the best of things" to be an existential or political process, in Lindblom and Cohen's interactional meaning. It has at least two intriguing if awkward consequences:

> What often obscures our appreciation of interaction as a method of problem-solving is that interaction often—perhaps typically—produces both outcome and implementation together. . . . The problem-solving capacity of interactions is also obscured because the interactions often do not result in a decision by an official or collective authority explicitly resolving a recognized problem. (Lindblom & Cohen, 1979:25–26)

These are awkward circumstances, which Diesing (1971), too, has cited in commenting on the inchoate nature of case studies; but they are awkward only because they correspond poorly with certain conventional rationalist presumptions about such things as: the roles of decision makers in organizations; received opinion about the orderliness of policy making and program operation; and assumptions about the rigor with which problems can ordinarily be analyzed to produce a conclusive judgment on their effects. Most especially they are awkward, however, because they correspond poorly with PSI's somewhat naive imagery of a world generally hospitable to customary canons of research design that derive largely from contrived laboratory environments (cf. Sarason, 1978; Smith, 1981) and evaluation research protocols that presume a clear segregation of process and outcome, of "experimenter" and "subject," and that overrate the unilateral authority of researchers in matters of applied research design (cf. Glaser & Taylor, 1973; Torbert, 1981). In an interactionist strategy, such as Patton's utilization-focused approach to evaluation, however, the burdens at least of tactical choice are shared among researchers, decision makers, and information users. The result, when suitably organized and conducted, is a "politically rational" approach to inquiry.

Politically Rational Inquiry

In his treatment of *Reason in Society*, Diesing (1962) distinguished among several varieties of rationality: technical/economic, social, legal, and political. The last of these, political rationality, he nominated as a fundamental kind of reason because it deals with the preservation and improvement of the decision "structures" that are sources of all operational decisions. Indications are that these structures will need to vary in form as a function of the tasks an individual or an organization is called upon to perform. They are, in short, contingent structures.[10] Political decision making is a way of referring to processes of planning and forming decision structures in relation to action settings. Negotiation and Lindblomian mutual adjustment are basic to these processes, although their prominence may be greater in some organizations and circumstances than in others.

Diesing identifies political decision making chiefly with actors in central organizational positions, that is, with leaders. But even when no clear-cut leader exists and there are only partisans of different interests—which, on a general view of organizations as mixed-interest coalitions (cf. Hickson et al., 1978), I would argue is most of the time—"discussion relations" for joint decision making naturally tend to form (except perhaps, as Diesing says, when ideological impediments to them exist).

As a matter of practice, ideas such as these suggest a need for (politically) rational ways of organizing multiparty social problem solving. I have called such an organizational paradigm a Joint Management Model (J-model) for applied research (Hunt, 1980a).

A JOINT MANAGEMENT MODEL FOR
SOCIAL PROBLEM SOLVING

The J-model was first described in an earlier article (Hunt & Rubin, 1973) as a "shared leadership" model. That article was about ways of organizing customer-supplier relations in federal government-sponsored research and development. The model is generalizable, however, to other forms of contracting for services and, still more generally, to multiparty social problem solving of the sort exemplified by the internal racism project.[11] I have elected now to call it a joint management rather than a shared leadership model simply because I prefer the connotations of the former to those of the latter. Whatever its name, the essential idea is the same.

It is easiest to appreciate the J-model by contrasting it with a more customary one I shall call a formal (F) model. An F-model conceives the working relations between clients or users of social research, on the one side, and applied researchers (or consultants), on the other, as an impersonal, transitory, task-relative linkage of structurally and operationally independent parties. The separate rights, obligations, and functions of the parties are agreed to more or less explicitly at the inception of their relationship or project.[12] Subsequently, each party acts largely autonomously. Though complementary in particular respects, their actions are independently determined and controlled by essentially private *intra*-organizational management decisions.

In an F-model of applied social research, a supplier provides research and a user consumes or applies it. After their initial agreement, how and when the supplier does that research, and how it is reported to the user, are the supplier's unilateral choices. The user may influence the supplier's inputs and even veto outputs, but ostensibly at least does not determine "through-put" processes. Those are governed by universalistic professional standards originating outside the project and "enforced" by a research community to which the *supplier* belongs.

Why I call this a "formal" model must be plain. The Weberian rational-legal aura of formal contract is its essence. One might, therefore, properly call it a "bureaucratic" model of the knowledge-making enterprise. It is a model that has been (implicitly) popular in both pure and applied science, where it comports with Price's (1977) idea of science as a producer of "consumption goods" and a Cartesian model of scientific roles in which "the search for Truth takes precedence over all other considerations [and] therefore science is inevitably . . . neutral . . . [and the] public [or client] has only one role, that of patron" (Bevan, 1980:780).

The central problem with an F-model for multiparty social problem solving is that it cannot cope well with uncertainty. To the extent that problems and their solutions for whatever reasons are vague or changeable, the inflexible F-model is disabled. Strains from uncertainty and change call for procedural flexibility, coordination, and mutual adjustment of activities by and among the parties to such a program. High rates of communication are vital for rapid and appropriate adjustment to changing and unanticipated situations, and to the reconceptualizations of problems and potential solutions that come with experience in exploring them. An F-model is not up to these organizational challenges. No "restricted interaction between autonomous parties" model of multiactor social problem solving can prove anything but a disappointment in social problem solving; hence, the J-model alternative.

The Joint Management Model

The fundamental feature of the J-model is a more or less even, although perhaps periodically fluctuating, distribution of power between the supplier and the user of social research.[13] A division of labor may exist in a J-model project, but it is likely to be rather fuzzy with individual project participants or teams conferring extensively and trying to decide on mutually acceptable courses of action. Instead of unilateral decision making, the process of "choosing" alternatives is one of discussion, negotiation, accommodation, and possibly compromise.

The essence of J-model problem solving is hands-on activity and informal communication. Forms and procedures, "decision structures," are needed for any responsible project, obviously, but effective multiparty problem solving, as Churchman (1979) stresses, must operate in such a way that the parties to it can make known their changing interpretations of what they are about and adapt their problem-solving procedures to those evolving ideas. A J-model for applied research has, then, these three principal objectives:

> Formation of a project organization adapted to the requirements for problem solving, that is, one open to information and procedurally flexible from start to finish;
>
> Maintenance of a project organization in which the user of social research is an influential participant, where everybody's hands get dirty, so to speak, and which provides a forum where the user can continuously clarify (changing) wishes and interests to the supplier in a way that assures their consideration in the planning and implementation of the project; and
>
> The production of more useful research, including PSI, or at least construction of an applied research-technology enterprise where the supplier is no more to blame than the user if its results are useless.

On one level the J-model is an application of hermeneutic ideas about knowledge and inquiry to a problem of organized action. It conceives of inquiry after a Baconian model, that is, as a "social enterprise, a cooperative activity within a professional community marked by a . . . division of labor but bound by a simple shared altruistic commitment to the promotion of human welfare" (Bevan, 1980:781). Knowledge, in this view, is an "investment good" without intrinsic social value, but gaining value as it gives rise to beneficial application (Price, 1977).

On another level, the J-model is a generalization of familiar thinking about project management viewed as an alternative to classical functional-scalar organization (cf. Nelson & Yates, 1978; Herbst, 1976; Hill & White, 1979). Project and especially matrix organizations featuring a functional axis focused on managing "the man and his knowledge" and another "project" axis focused on work and tasks are what Drucker (1974) has called "knowledge organizations." Their fundamental virtue is their capacity to facilitate innovation, invention, and creativity (see Davis & Lawrence, 1977; Hansen, 1979; Agassi, 1978; Harrison, 1981; the latter with particular reference to ideas about integrating all contributing organizations into a unitary, panorganizational project structure).

Just as the F-model is "idealized" so, of course, is the J-model. Real-world situations are unlikely ever to correspond completely with the implementation assumptions of either model. For one thing, the prescribed informal quality of J-model project organization means that it will work best when the parties to it are in relatively close physical proximity. That is not always possible. But be that as it may, the essential point is that, whatever the technical problems of organizing are, the usual circumstances of social problem solving are better imagined by a J-model formulation than by those in F-forms. Useful social research and effective social problem solving are apt to result from F-form organizations only by accident. As Klein (1977) points out, the interactive stimulus of demand for and supply of ideas is a potent impetus to innovation and a powerful argument for J-model practices for problem solving. Yet we counterproductively persist in F-model forms because of strong institutional and cultural constraints and incentives that favor "normal" customary practice, even in the face of frequent failure (cf. Kuhn, 1970).

ON THE SOCIOLOGY AND POLITICS OF DOING USEFUL SOCIAL RESEARCH

Useful PSI has been a primary objective of the Institute's J-model plans for reforming institutionally racist police agencies. We have sought to generate helpful information for decision makers coping with difficult social problems, often in volatile political contexts where they are major stakeholders. Our approach to planning and change, in addition to treating PSI as a complement to other sources of knowledge, has grown increasingly interactionist with experience—indeed, as the J-model suggests, interactionist is the same operational sense that Patton uses this term to describe the continuing sequences of mutual adjustments by which evaluators and clients learn (or interpret) one another's interests and capacities and accommodate them.

Small Change and Causal Ambiguity

One difficulty with operating in this mode is that while it is relatively easy to say what was done in a social research program, it is not at all easy to evaluate its consequences in conventional terms. The interactionist nature of things makes it well-nigh impossible to link project operations unambiguously with either concurrent or subsequent organizational developments. Furthermore, long-term effects may not be well indicated by short-term effects, even when the latter can be identified. If the outcomes of coping are incremental, which is likely, they are, by definition, small.

We have here two methodological issues that have important "political" implications: social changes are more apt to be nickel-and-dime than impressively large, and, in any event, they will tend to be causally ambiguous. From the standpoint of policy and program evaluation, each of these issues is problematic. Quite aside from its unexciting nature, nickel-and-dime incremental social and organizational change may be hard to detect. Useful programs may consequently be aborted, abandoned prematurely, or at least discredited by evaluation when the problem is not that the program has not "worked," but that too much was expected of it or that measurements sufficiently sensitive to detect its effects were lacking.

The causal ambiguity of social change is, if anything, even more of a conundrum that its incremental nature. In the case of engineered change efforts, it means that programs may receive credit for effects they had little to do with, or conversely, be denied credits they in some sense much deserve. In the real world (as distinct from textbooks on research methods or planning and evaluation), the assessment of program impact and of responsibility for social change, is a matter of interpretation—an exercise in hermeneutics. A "holistic" task, it requires one to work in all directions, so to speak, in order to do it. Thus, as Rorty says in a version of the hermeneutic circle:

> we cannot understand the parts of a strange culture, practices, theory, language, or whatever, unless we know something about how the whole thing works, whereas we cannot get a grasp on how the whole things works until we have some understanding of its parts. This notion of interpretation suggests that coming to understand is more like getting acquainted with a person than like following a demonstration. In both cases we play back and forth between guesses about how to characterize particular statements or other events, and guesses about the point of the whole situation, until gradually we feel at ease with what was hitherto strange. (1979:319)

Consider from this interpretive perspective some of the developments that occurred during the span of our work with the five police departments in the institutional racism in law enforcement project. In one or another department these included:

> Formation of a standing affirmative action committee (including minority and women) to plan programs and review grievances about hiring, promotion, assignment, discipline, and service to citizens;

Development of a performance-based personnel evaluation system designed to enhance equity department-wide, but also to make supervisory sergeants and training officers more accountable in their fate-controlling judgments of probationary officers;

Design and implementation by minority officers (using departmental resources) of minority-oriented recruiting and recruit-support methods;

Reform and reorientation of a police cadet program to serve as a more effective means of minority entry to police work;

Development of a minority police officer organization to support the interests of minority personnel and act as a semi-official bargaining agent vis-à-vis departmental authority with respect to usual terms and conditions of employment, but also general departmental policy and community relations;

Institution of department-wide small group discussion programs, partly as a consciousness-raising stratagem, but also as a sounding-board for stimulating and facilitating structural and procedural innovations to advance affirmative action goals—a process that was accompanied by transfer of this department's one black command-level officer to line command from the traditionally "innocuous" community relations assignment of minorities;

Elementary, but critical, command-based changes in General Orders to effectuate affirmative action philosophy and concepts of racial (and sexual) equality;

A requirement that oral examinations for the rank of captain and above include questions that ask the candidate to discuss the problem of institutional racism in policing and suggest ways of dealing with it as an organizational phenomenon; and

Formation of project-department coalitions to seek change in crucial policies and practices outside direct departmental control (such as county/city personnel policies and practices, union representation rules).

These developments probably seem basic enough, like small change even. Yet where they were instituted they were "innovative," to the point sometimes of seeming almost radical. They regularly stimulated tension and sometimes open conflict in the departments and their communities. Much time was spent in the project "negotiating" about them and about the sociopolitical power relations they touched. The long-term results of the negotiations, and of the antiracism changes (or anticipations of change) that occasioned need for them, we cannot now divine. We can only say that we sought to help install durable structures and programs to encourage the changes, sustain them as they appeared, cope with reactions to them, and generally increase minority influence in departmental affairs.

How well these tactics succeeded in eradicating institutional racism in the five police departments we cannot truly say. But more to the point of this chapter anyway is the inherent causal ambiguity of social problem-solving outcomes. Would the developments cited above have occurred without the project? As soon? In the same forms? And who or what was responsible for which developments, or of particular features of them? There are no conclusive answers to these questions.

We believe that the project was effective, albeit not so much so as we would have liked. There is no way of extricating the definitive contributions of specifically Institute or project operations from the unspecified contributions of the departments or even of their environments. In the first place, design and implementation of project operations was collaborative with departmental agents.[14] Hence, the contributions of the several parties were entwined and confounded. Change plans and efforts emerged from steady J-model interaction of project with departmental staff. Some changes may well have been unplanned by-products of these interactions rather than deliberate outcomes. The point in statistical language is this: as among project operations and departmental efforts, in J-model social problem solving there are no independent main effects, only interactions. Take as an illustration of this our procedure for working out intervention strategies. It was divided into three basic steps:

> A review with participating departments of project staff findings about institutional racism and its recommendations on the subject;[15]
> Preparation of a consensus-based departmental "needs assessment" as a basis for planning remediation; and
> Coproduction of an action plan for the final phase of the project.

The particular procedures followed in taking these steps were these:

> In preparation for a preliminary verbal report by the Institute's project director to each department's task force, an outline and summary was presented to the department's chief for comment, suggestions, and discussion.[16]
> The task force then assembled to hear the project director's preliminary report. No recommendations were offered at this session. The meeting's purpose was to test, clarify, and reformulate a "factual" information base—a common belief system—on which later recommendations could be founded. The project director's essential focus in the preliminary report was on the question, "Do we understand?" The meeting sought to: evaluate the substance of findings about institutional racism in the department; review and critique the documentation of those findings; and generate recommendations for revision of the report

of findings or development of additional documentation. Its point was to decide upon whether or not we have arrived at a reasonable, "consensually valid" understanding of the "world" of each police agency.[17]

Subsequent to these meetings, a formal written draft report of findings went from the project director to the chief of each department from transmittal to the task force. This report included provisional recommendations for action.

The task forces then prepared and forwarded to the Institute project director a formal written response to his draft report. This response included: a point-by-point evaluation of the validity of the stated findings (with the reasons for any suspected invalidity); a detailed evaluation of the documentation offered by the project staff for each finding, considering both the essential validity of the points and whether they seemed likely to prove persuasive to significant outsiders as well as insiders; and an evaluation of the project director's recommendations together with a statement of the task force's agreement with them and an indication of any likely barriers to their wider acceptance or achievement.[18]

Following receipt of the task forces' critiques of the project director's draft report, an Institute staff position paper was prepared as a response. This paper, when possible, undertook to suggest consensus positions rather than simply argue the merits of staff viewpoints.

The project director then met with each task force (and chief) to try to build consensus positions with respect to departmental needs and remediation goals.

The task forces then were left with the task of preparing, with technical assistance from project staff, a formal "needs assessment" to serve as a basis for action planning.

Finally, the task forces, again with project staff support, produced "action plans," consisting of specific procedures by which needs and goals for change would be met, and their effectiveness evaluated.

This outline naturally leaves out many details of J-model coproduction; and it does not capture at all the density of informal exchange that accompanied each of its steps. It does reveal, however, the Patton-like active-reactive-adaptative interactionist nature of the program, as well as its nondoctrinaire incrementalist attitude to evaluation-based change. It also depicts the project's emphasis on problem solving by successive approximation (Lindblom & Cohen, 1979), a strategy of choice in dynamic political environments such as those of policing. The institutional racism in law enforcement project treated social research and social change explicitly as political processes, as species of what Lindblom (1979) has referred to as "incremental politics." Whether Lindblom is right when he reacts to criticism that incrementalism "enforces inertia and agitates against innovation" (Etzioni, 1968:299) by arguing that "incrementalism in politics is not, in principle, slow moving" (certainly it seems commonly to be so), he is surely correct in maintaining that it is not necessarily "a tactic of conservatism" (1979:520). Save in special circumstances,

> incremental politics ordinarily offers the best chance of introducing into the political system those changes and those change-producing intermediate changes that a discontented citizen might desire. (Lindblom, 1979:521).

Ideas such as Lindblom and Cohen's about problem solving as coping and Patton's about focusing evaluation on managerially useful subjects undoubtedly encourage practitioners to violate some precepts of nominally rational science and rigorous, disinterested outcome evaluation. As if this were not bad enough, their incrementalist posture bucks the tides of professional aspiration and of the politics of social science and social programming. After all, professional reputations are built on big accomplishments. Federal bureaucracies need to defend and justify their programs and budgets in a competitive intragovernmental market. In these circumstances, incrementalism is not an altogether appealing prescriptive prospect.

A major reason for the dissatisfaction with PSI highlighted by Lindblom and Cohen is the frequent disparity between the promises of pPSI and their fulfillment. The politics of grantsmanship conspire with instrumentally rationalistic intellectual traditions to constrain toward maximization strategies. The dispositions of pPSI run toward proposing much—toward promising a big bang for the bucks. What sponsor, after all, thinks small or, as a matter of policy, takes the long view? In the face of keen competition for ever more-limited funds, what proposer can risk suggesting it? By the same token, what proposer in a customary contractualist F-model environment can risk proposing social problem solving in realistic interactionist modes? (See Fineman, 1981, for a discussion of funding problems with some U.K. illustrations.) And, even if they do so, by what standards are their proposals to be judged? Because of these imponderables, impracticably rigorous applied research designs are presented only to be abandoned subsequently as infeasible (with suitable apology) or, what is worse, ritually implemented at the price of irrelevance.

For these and other similar reasons, it can hardly be surprising to learn that as a strategy for action research and problem solving, interactionist incrementalism, virtuous as it may be, is an idea that has not yet caught on or been taken very seriously (except occasionally in the abstract). This is so despite the considerable personal prestige of such advocates as Charles Lindblom and the wide citation of his works. Quite simply, the institutional infrastructure of social research is uncongenial to it in the main, and PSI belief systems remain essentially hostile to it. Yet if organizational and applied social research is to become more consistently useful to its consumers, its methodology is a topic that needs basic attention in both the policy and research communities. In common with Lindblom and Cohen, it has been the thesis of this chapter

> that PSI is to a degree incapacitated in contributing to social problem solving because of its own metaphysics, fashions, traditions, and taboos. These incapacities need to be examined, not as amusing peripheral phenomena in PSI, but as important constraints on it. (Lindblom & Cohen, 1979:95)

The question I am promoting is one posed by Lindblom and Cohen:

> Could PSI institutions and traditions be so changed as to promote greater wisdom in project choice [and method] without placing the entire burden on the uncoordinated efforts of isolated individuals? Are there ways of reorganizing the social system of PSI as opposed to reforming individual pPSI so that interaction would share with analysis some of the burden of solving the problem of what pPSI should study as research [and how]? (Lindblom & Cohen, 1979:98)

This chapter has presented a way of organizing applied social research programs and projects, the J-model, that is responsive to Lindblom and Cohen's queries, at least with respect to strategy. It is a framework intended expressly to foster interactionist and more hermeneutic approaches to social problem solving in which PSI has an important part to play, but is neither paradigmatic nor liturgical.

NOTES

1. Beginning in 1976, funding for the project was provided by the Center for Minority Group Mental Health Programs of the National Institute of Mental Health. Hubert G. Locke of the University of Washington was principal investigator and for most of the project's life I was project director.

2. A second project was envisaged to complement the first by dealing with "external" racism. It, too, was planned as a multimethod action research project continuous with the internal racism project but concentrating on subcommunity distributions in both the quantity and quality of police services. For a number of reasons, this second project has not been initiated.

3. My own preference, described more completely in a recent paper (Hunt, 1982), is to treat social problem solving as a psychological process of interpreting or modeling a situation while interacting with it. "Solutions" to problems are technologies. They may be expressed in physical or social ways, but they are basically cognitive. Like Simon (1977), therefore, I regard technology as knowledge, not as things.

4. Briefly, positivism is a normative-realist philosophy bottomed on an empiricist assumption of the reducibility of the language of science to sense data. From the positivist standpoint, logic and epistemology are occupied with establishing rules (syntactical propositions) for eliminating bias from observations and for certifying claims to knowledge. Central to the positivist plan for the scientific project is development of an "objective" observation language with which to describe "reality." The terms of this language must be, then, not "mere" constructs—i.e., convenient inventions—but genuine representations of nature. The idea of eliminating surplus meaning from scientific concepts by equating their definition to specific mechanics of observation is a methodological extension of the positivist theme known as operationism (Feigel & Brodbeck's [1953] anthology is an excellent source on these subjects; see also, Hempel, 1952).

5. *New paradigms* is a somewhat ostentatious term that I mistrust. For one thing, they often are not all that new. But the term has become popular and it does make the point of a breaking with traditional intellectual harnesses, so I shall stick with it here even though the word perspective—or even concept—might actually be better.

6. By an anthropomorphic model I mean a view of man as socius, as thinker, as purposive sense-maker, man as active controller as well as reactor to a milieu, that is, man as self-conscious planner and learner—all these human attributions plus passionate, committed man.

7. Well-described by Kockelman (cited by Reason & Rowan, 1981),the hermeneutic circle defines a general dialectical model of all human knowledge development. It asserts that there can be no knowledge without foreknowledge. The meaning of "parts" or components" is determined by foreknowledge ("prejudice," as Ricoeur, 1981, calls it) of a "whole," whereas knowledge of the "whole" is corrected and deepened by incremental knowledge of components. Knowledge, thus, is a continuous circular spiral of whole-part, phenomenon-context, knower-known accretions.

8. Liberal thinkers incline to a rather more optimistic attitude toward the possibilities of social reform than this one must seem to be. Etzioni (1968), for example, has hoped to retain for praxis under his "theory of societal and political processes" a rational prospect of transformational as well as incremental societal changes. Accordingly, his critique of Lindblomian incrementalism includes a distinction between "fundamental" and "incremental" decisions. The latter he conceives of as tactical or "bit" decisions made incrementally, as Lindblom suggests, but within the constraints of other "larger" context-setting fundamental or strategic decisions. "Bit" decision making, it will be noted, sounds very much like what Kuhn speaks of as meliorative puzzle solving—i.e., "normal science"—done within contextuating paradigmatic frames. Etzioni's sanguine thesis, which otherwise has much in common with the ideas set out here, simply envisages a higher density of fundamental decision making (i.e., paradigm or Gestalt shifts) than does either Lindblom's or mine—or, for that matter, Kuhn's. At the very least it imagines that structural knowledge-driven arrangements can be made and decision strategies followed ("mixed scanning")—given the will to do it—that will regularly accomplish major yet orderly social change.

9. This postulate is in fact an implicit cornerstone of strategies that seek, as our internal racism project did, to accomplish the eradication of racism chiefly via social organizational (structural) changes rather than via individual attitude change (see Bowser & Hunt, 1981; U.S. Commission on Civil Rights, 1981). It is epistemological in the sense that it signifies a theory of knowledge; it is at the same time theoretical in that it is a statement about human behavior.

10. I shall discuss this relativist idea shortly in more detail, but for now will simply say that I take as evidence for it the organizational literature on the apparent dependence of organizational structures on putatively exogenous variables such as technology (see, e.g. Jelinek, 1977). Mitroff and Kilmann (1978) have also argued in support of contingent styles of inquiry, although from quite a different point of vantage.

11. My regular use of the word "multiparty" can be read to mean interorganizational, as in the relation between the Institute for the Study of Contemporary Social Problems and a police department. The reader will keep in mind, however, that it applies equally well to the intra-

organizational case, as when one department of an organization provides research for another to use in making policy, products, or what have you. In fact, it applies to any case where the producer and the user of research are not the same unit.

12. The agreement may be formally contractual, or it may be a more quasicontractual professional "understanding," or it may be altogether implicit as it is in intra-organizational role relations. In any event, the model is at least tacitly contractual.

13. Many others have discussed or proposed joint decision structures of one sort or another for one reason or another. I have already mentioned Diesing, Patton, and Whitaker. Guba and Lincoln (1981), in their effort to improve the usefulness of evaluation research, in addition to advocating nonpositivist, "naturalistic" methods, also stress the need for "responsive" program organizations oriented politically to "stakeholders." Reason and Rowan (1981) similarly describe research (in their case, all research) as a collaboration between the "researcher" and his or her "subjects" in a hermeneutic sense-making project. On the subject of collaborative inquiry, Torbert lists a series of distinctions "between the kind of knowledge it seeks and the kind of knowledge sought under the current paradigm of social science" (1981:145). The twelfth, last, and most developed item in his list has to do with development of "the relationship between the initiating actor-researcher and any other person invited to engage in collaborative inquiry" (1981:149).

Etzioni, however, while much concerned with organizing the production and utilization of knowledge, perceives virtue as well as vice in separating the user from the producer of knowledge (1968:Ch 8). Fearful (like Kaplan, 1964) of the stifling effects of narrow "communities of assumptions," he is attracted to pluralistic control of knowledge and its structures, although mainly with regard to basic research. Applied research he considers less vulnerable to contextuating corruption and hence profitably organized as a producer-user collaboration. (See also Hunt, 1980b, on organizational issues in doing basic and applied research and segregating the one from the other.)

14. If anything, it was less so than we might have wished. A more thoroughly integrated interorganizational project structure of a kind familiar in many cases of military-contracted R&D might well have produced superior outcomes.

15. This occurred some 18 months after the start of the project and was based largely on information provided by the department, including an employee survey (see Hunt & McCadden, 1980), supplemented by information from extradepartmental sources.

16. An axiom of the project was that the chief deserved to be saved from surprises.

17. This is a plain example of interactive problem solving, of which Lindblom and Cohen (1979) identify two forms. In one form, PSI (in our case, for example, in the results of analysis of a formal employee survey) is used to provide background information and analysis helpful to participants in playing their interactive roles. In the other, PSI is employed to ground action programs designed to restructure patterns of interaction. Lindblom and Cohen point out that the first form is readily distinguished "from PSI that makes a direct frontal attack on a problem on the supposition that it is to be solved wholly analytically and not interactively" (p. 60). The second form, however, is easily confused with a frontal attack on a problem. This was a confusion to which we occasionally fell prey when working with departmental task forces. The role of the task force as problem solver sometimes receded from view in favor of a hope for solution "from the doctor," i.e., via exogenous pPSI analysis. Asymmetries of expertise and cultural traditions about the role of consultants make it hard sometimes to maintain an interactionist collaboration; but it is especially hard when one is dealing with emotion-charged subjects like racism. It is easier to allocate responsibility (and possible blame) for solution to expert pPSI, who, for their part, must beware of this subversive trap.

18. The procedures here have much in common with Harré and Secord's (1972) dramaturgical model for analyzing "episodes" of social action based on reconstructed "scripts." With the researcher cast in the role of an "audience," his or her construction must agree somehow with those of actors in the episode. When an episode is equivocal or "enigmatic," such concordance can only be negotiated.

REFERENCES

Agassi, J.
1978   "Shifting from physical to social technology." In P. T. Durbin (ed.), Research in Philosophy and Technology: An Annual Compilation of Research, Vol. I: 199–212. Greenwich, CT: JAI Press.
Bacharach, P. and M. S. Baratz
1963   "Decisions and nondecisions: an analytic framework." American Political Science Review, 57:632–642.
Bevan, William
1980   "On getting in bed with a lion." American Psychologist, 35:779–790.
Bleicher, J.
1980   Contemporary Hermeneutics: Hermeneutics and Method Philosophy and Critique. London: Routledge and Kegan Paul.
Bowser, Benjamin P. and Raymond G. Hunt
1981   Impacts of Racism on White Americans. Beverly Hills, CA: Sage.
Bromley, D. G. and C. F. Longino, Jr.
1972   White Racism and Black Americans. New York: Schenkman.
Campbell, Donald T.
1969   "Reforms as experiments." American Psychologist, 4:409–429.
Campbell, Donald T.
1975   " 'Degrees of freedom' and the case study." Comparative Political Studies, 8:178–193.
Campbell, Donald T. and Julian C. Stanley
1966   Experimental and Quasi-Experimental Designs for Research. Chicago: Rand-McNally.
Churchman, C. W.
1957   The Systems Approach and Its Enemies. New York: Basic Books.
Churchman, C. W., R. L. Ackoff, E. L. Arnoff
1957   Introduction to Operations Research. New York: Wiley.
Cohen, Michael D., James G. March, and Johan P. Olsen
1972   "A garbage can model of organizational choice." Administrative Science Quarterly, 17:1–25.
Davis, Stanley M. and Paul R. Lawrence
1977   Matrix. Reading, MA: Addison-Wesley.
Diesing, Paul
1962   Reason in Society: Five Types of Decisions and Their Social Conditions. Urbana, IL: University of Illinois Press.
Diesing, Paul
1971   Patterns of Discovery in the Social Sciences. Chicago: Aldine.
Drucker, Paul
1974   Management: Tasks, Responsibilities, Practices. New York: Harper and Row.
Einhorn, H. J.
1980   "Learning from experience and suboptimal rules in decision-making." In T. S. Wallsten (ed.), Cognitive Processes in Choice and Decision Behavior: 1–20. Hillsdale, NJ: Erlbaum.
Etzioni, A.
1968   The Activity Society: A Theory of Societal and Political Processes. New York: Free Press.
Feigl, Herbert and May Brodbeck (eds.)
1953   Readings in the Philosophy of Science. New York: Appleton-Century-Crofts.

Fineman, Stephen
1981   "Funding Research: Practice and Politics," in Peter Reason and John Rowan (eds.), Human Inquiry: A Source Book of New Paradigm Research. New York: Wiley. 1981 p. 473–484.

Glaser, E. M. and S. H. Taylor
1973   "Factors influencing the success of applied research." American Psychologist, 28:140–147.

Guba, E. G. and Y. S. Lincoln (eds.)
1981   Effective Evaluation. San Francisco: Jossey-Bass.

Hansen, Grant L.
1979   "Eight basic tasks for successful program management." In J. Stanley Baumgartner (ed.), Systems Management: 9–13. Washington: Bureau of National Affairs.

Harré, Rom
1981   "The positivist-empiricist approach and its alternative." In Peter Reason and John Rowan (eds.), Human Inquiry: 3–17. New York: Wiley.

Harré, Rom and Paul F. Secord
1972   The Explanation of Social Behavior. Totowa, NJ: Rowman and Littlefield.

Harrison, F. L.
1981   Advanced Project Management. Aldershot, Hants, Eng.: Gower Publishing.

Hempel, Carl G.
1952   Fundamentals of Concept Formation in Empirical Science. International Encyclopedia of Unified Science, Vol. I, no. 7. Chicago: University of Chicago Press.

Herbst, Ph. G
1976   Alternatives to Hierarchies. Leiden, Neth.: Martinus Nijhoff.

Hickson, D. J., R. J. Butler, R. Axelson, and D. Wilson
1978   "Decisive coalitions." In B. King, S. Streufert, and F. E. Fiedler (eds.), Managerial Control and Organizational Democracy: 31–42. New York: Wiley.

Hill, Raymond E. and Bernard J. White (eds.)
1979   Matrix Organization and Project Management. Ann Arbor, MI: Graduate School of Business Administration.

Hunt, Raymond G.
1974   Interpersonal Strategies for System Management. Monterey, CA: Brooks/Cole.

Hunt, Raymond G.
1980a   "Use of the award fee in Air Force system and subsystem acquisition." Final Report to Air Force Business Research Management Center, Wright-Patterson Air Force Base, Ohio. Buffalo, NY: School of Management, State University of New York.

Hunt, Raymond G.
1980b   "The university social research center: its role in the knowledge-making process." Knowledge, 2:77–92.

Hunt, Raymond G.
1981   "Combatting institutional racism in police departments: applications of a problem-remedy strategy." Consultations of the Affirmative Action Statement of the U.S. Commission on Civil Rights, Vol. I: Papers Presented: 132–147.

Hunt, Raymond G.
1982   "Technology and organization: a psychological interpretation." Proceedings, 19th Annual Meeting, Eastern Academy of Management: 97–101.

Hunt, Raymond G. and Karen S. McCadden
1980   "Race-related attitudes and beliefs of police personnel." Social Development Issues, 4:31–49.

Hunt, Raymond G. and Ira S. Rubin
1973   "Approaches to managerial journal in interpenetrating systems." Academy of Management Journal, 16:296–311.

Jelinek, Maryann
1977   "Technology, organization and contingency." Academy of Management Review, 2:17–26.
Jones, James M.
1972   Prejudice and Racism. Reading, MA: Addison-Wesley.
Kaplan, A.
1964   The Conduct of Inquiry: Methodology for Behavioral Science. Scranton, PA: Chandler.
Klein, Burton H.
1977   Dynamic Economics. Cambridge, MA: Harvard University Press.
Knott, J. and A. Wildavsky
1981   "If dissemination is the solution, what is the problem?" In R. F. Rich (ed.), The Knowledge Cycle: 96–146. Beverly Hills, CA: Sage.
Kuhn, Thomas S.
1970   The Structure of Scientific Revolutions, 2d ed. Chicago: University of Chicago Press.
Levitan, Laura C. and Edward F. X. Hughes
1981   "Research on the utilization of evaluations: a review and synthesis." Evaluation Review, 5:525–548.
Lindblom, Charles E.
1959   "The science of 'muddling through'." Public Administration Review, 19:79–88.
Lindblom, Charles E.
1979   "Still muddling, not yet through." Public Administration Review, 39:517–527.
Lindblom, Charles E. and David K. Cohen
1979   Usable Knowledge: Social Science and Social Problem Solving. New Haven, CT: Yale University Press.
Locke, Hubert G. and E. E. Walker
1980   "Institutional racism and American policing." Social Development Issues, 4: whole no. 1.
March, James G. and Johan P. Olsen
1976   Ambiguity and Choice in Organizations. Bergen, Norway: Universitetsforlaget.
Mitroff, Ian I. and Ralph H. Kilmann
1978   Methodological Approaches to Social Sciences. San Francisco: Jossey-Bass.
Morton, Adam
1980   Frame of Mind: Constraints on the Common-Sense Conception of the Mental. Oxford, Eng.: Oxford University Press.
Nagel, S. S. and M. Neef
1979   Policy Analysis in Social Science Research. Beverly Hills, CA: Sage.
Nelson, R. R. and D. Yates (eds.)
1978   Innovation and Implementation in Public Organizations. Lexington, MA: Heath.
Nisbett, R. and L. Ross
1980   Human inference: strategies and shortcomings of social judgment. Englewood Cliffs, NJ: Prentice-Hall.
Patton, Michael Q.
1978   Utilization-Focused Evaluation. Beverly Hills, CA: Sage.
Polanyi, Michael
1951   The Logic of Liberty. London: Routledge and Kegan Paul.
Price, D. de S.
1977   "An intrinsic value theory for basic and 'applied' research." In J. Haberer (ed.), Science and Technology Policy. Lexington, MA: Lexington Books.
Ramo, Simon
1969   Cure for Chaos: Fresh Solutions to Social Problems Through the Systems Approach. New York: David Mackay.

Reason, Peter and John Rowan (eds.)
1981   Human Inquiry: A Sourcebook of New Paradigm Research. New York: Wiley.
Rich, Robert F. (ed.)
1981   The Knowledge Cycle. Beverly Hills, CA: Sage.
Ricoeur, Paul
1981   Hermeneutics and the Social Sciences. Cambridge, Eng.: Cambridge University Press.
Rorty, Richard
1979   Philosophy and the Mirror of Nature. Princeton, NJ: Princeton University Press.
Sarason, Seymour B.
1978   "The nature of problem solving in social action." American Psychologist, 33:305–314.
Scott, William, G. and David K. Hart
1979   Organizational America. Boston: Houghton Mifflin.
Scriven, Michael
1964   "Views of Human Nature," in T. W. Wann (ed.), Behaviorism and Phenomenology. Chicago: University of Chicago Press. p. 163–183.
Silverman, David
1971   The Theory of Organizations: A Sociological Framework. New York: Basic Books.
Simon, Herbert A.
1977   The New Science of Management, rev. ed. Englewood Cliffs, NJ: Prentice-Hall.
Smith, N. L. (ed.)
1981   Metaphors for Evaluation: Sources of New Methods. Beverly Hills, CA: Sage.
Study Project on Social Research and Development
1978   The Federal Investment in Knowledge of Social Problems. Washington: National Academy of Sciences.
Torbert, William R.
1981   "Why educational research has been so uneducational: the case for a new model of social science based on collaborative inquiry." In Peter Reason and John Rowan (eds.), Human Inquiry: 141–153. New York: Wiley.
United States Commission on Civil Rights
1981   Affirmative Action in the 1980's: Dismantling the Process of Discrimination. Washington: United States Commission on Civil Rights, Clearinghouse Publication 65.
Webb, E. J., D. T. Campbell, R. D. Schwartz, & L. Sechrest
1966   Unobtrusive Measures: Nonreactive Research in the Social Sciences. Chicago: Rand McNally.
Weick, Karl E.
1979   The Social Psychology of Organizing, 2d ed. Reading, MA: Addison-Wesley.
Weiss, Janet A. & Carol H. Weiss
1981   "Social scientists and decision makers look at the usefulness of mental health research." American Psychologist, 36:837–847.
Whitaker, G. P.
1980   "Co-production: citizen participation in service delivery." Public Administration Review, 40:240–247.

29

TOWARD NEW PARADIGMS FOR USEFUL KNOWLEDGE ABOUT CORPORATE FINANCE

William H. Weekes

The usefulness of conventional finance theory paradigms in corporate planning has been criticized recently in several quarters. This chapter will describe a research program that originated in a large Australian company and has subsequently been refined in a classroom laboratory. The next stage in the program is to implement in organizations the processes that have been developed so far, and to evaluate their potential for producing useful knowledge for the planning procedures in those organizations.

BACKGROUND

Criticism of the usefulness of normative finance paradigms has been made in particular by Hayes and Abernathy (1980), Hayes and Garvin (1982), and McInnes and Carleton (1982). These writers have identified anomalies in the normative paradigms when applied in organizations. Normative theory is still described in terms of a paradigm that is borrowed from mechanistic engineering systems (Jantsch 1980a). Planning in such a framework focuses on a structure-oriented approach that deals with a system as if it were a machine to be engineered and controlled from the outside. Most planning models also tend to take a "bottom up" approach that tends to emphasize cybernetic (negative) feedback processes. A deeper knowledge of the evolutionary processes of natural systems—in contrast to the operation of engineered systems—would recognize that positive feedback processes are characteristic of the way in which many natural systems manage to live and evolve. These systems could be described as self-transcendent open learning systems, exchanging energy with their environments.

In a further development of the evolutionary view, Prigogine (1976) has shown that partially open systems—so-called dissipative structures in a state of sufficient nonequilibrium—try to maintain their capability for energy exchange with the environment through the principle of "order through fluctuation," by switching to a new dynamic regime whenever entropy production becomes stifled in the old regime (Jantsch 1980b).

The research program considered whether knowledge of the evolutionary paradigm—in particular knowledge about dissipative structures and the interactions between variables in open or partially open systems—could be usefully applied in the design of corporate-planning processes that may help to resolve some of the anomalies perceived in the application of normative finance theory to planning processes in organizations.

ANOMALIES IN NORMATIVE FINANCE PARADIGMS

Hayes and Abernathy believe there is a preponderance of techniques that emphasize mathematical elegance and analytical detachment. This has resulted in a tendency for the present generation of managers to concentrate on decisions that maximize return on investment in the short term at the expense of investments in product and process development that may have low short-term profitability, but could provide substantial benefits in the long term (in particular, portfolio analysis, which emphasizes short-term cash flows and return on investment).

More specifically, Hayes and Garvin have said that discounting techniques favor those projects that have a high return in the early stages of their lives and lower initial outlays. Moreover, a narrow use of the present value criterion could argue for expanding facilities already in use rather than investing in new, smaller, more modern, and better focused plants.

From a study of the conventional models of financial theory compared with the corporate modelling processes that were used by a group of companies in the Boston area, McInnes and Carleton concluded that a wide gap existed between finance theory models and what the better managed companies are actually doing. They said that normative finance theory provides a design framework, in a rational cognitive mode, for approaching the definition of a decision structure and its related information requirements, but that it is predominantly static in the way that it represents the problem. It treats decision making as a discrete activity that is largely dissociated both from the dynamics of the resolution of uncertainty and the measurement of performance through time. It is also somewhat divorced from the organizational context and the motives of managers within which information is developed, communicated, and used in the decision-making process. On the other hand, organization theory is beginning to provide some insight into this process. Coupled with advances in data-processing technology, this could provide the potential to link the structural perspective of finance theory with the process perspective of organization theory.

POTENTIAL FOR USEFUL LINKAGES

The potential for useful linkages may exist in the application of evolutionary paradigms to managerial decision processes. One of Einstein's (1960) basic contributions to physics was his view that the relationships between the parts of a system are different relative to the vantage point of the observer. Relationships between the elements in a system would be perceived differently by an observer situated outside of the system than they would be perceived by a person who is situated within the system and who is himself a part of that system.

In physics, Planck's notion was that energy is not transmitted in continuous waves but rather in quantum jumps, or "quantor" of indivisible units of energy. This led to the Heisenberg effect, which recognized that the position and the velocity of an individual electron are interrelated in that they both cannot be determined at the same time; hence, the behavior of the electron cannot be precisely calculated. The same effect is also apparent in the relationship between investment and finance decisions (Baumol & Quandt, 1965).

The concept of autopoiesis (Nicolis & Prigogine, 1977) is also a critical area of knowledge for our purposes. It describes the evolutionary characteristic of living systems to renew themselves continuously and to regulate this process in such a way that the integrity of their structures is maintained. Whereas a machine is geared to the output of a particular product, a cell is concerned with renewing itself. This paradigm of self-organization and evolution is thus a unifying paradigm. If a business organization can be conceptualized as an open system, it can be visualized as possessing two sets of regulatory processes: primary and secondary regulatory processes (Miller, 1976). According to Miller, primary regulatory processes are concerned with the design of the structures of the system—slow processes of long duration—which maintain the energy conversion processes of the system in interaction with the environment through positive feedback. Secondary regulatory processes are concerned with negative feedback functions—quick processes of short duration—where the regulation is based on pre-established energy conversion mechanisms and pathways arranged in an input/transformation/output configuration. The causal chains within this feedback system are linear and unidirectional, and the feedback structures are open with respect to incoming information but closed with respect to matter and energy.

Knowledge of the self-organizing evolutionary paradigm, if applied to organizations, could provide a useful metaphor to link the structural perspective of normative finance theory with the process perspective of organization theory. It emphasizes the interconnectedness of natural dynamics at all levels of evolving macro (primary) and micro (secondary) systems. It could also serve to unify both the organization and the environment of which it is part. Both the organization and the environment evolve and adapt in what is a co-evolution. This is achieved by creatively reaching out beyond the boundaries of the organization's existence in the immediate here and now. It provides an ecosystem of new scientific concepts that support a unified, nonreductionist view of self-organizing evolution.

In many branches of science, the scope of space and time accessible to observation has widened immensely. Interconnections and patterns have emerged in the expanded space-time continuum that are primarily of a dynamic nature and have given for the first time a scientific base to the idea of an overall, open, evolution that is interconnected at many irreducible levels. The idea of an organization itself should no longer be tied to a specific spatiotemporal structure, nor to a changing configuration of particular components, nor to sets of internal or external relations. An organization should be perceived from a vantage point within the system as a set of coherent, evolving, interactive processes that are temporarily manifest in globally stable structures that have nothing to do with the equilibrium or the solidity of technological structures.

APPLICATIONS OF THE EVOLUTIONARY PARADIGM IN CORPORATE PLANNING

Corporate planners should be able to recognize that the corporate planning process represents the positive feedback evolutionary process in organizations, conceptually perceived as a combination of the characteristics of dissipative structures plus symbiosis. This knowledge may also be useful to conceptualize the different vantage points from which an organization may be viewed, as well as the different kinds of regulatory processes that exist in organizations. A knowledge of these differences may prove useful in distinguishing how the various paradigms of normative finance theory and management control could be related in an overall conceptualization of organizations. These relationships are depicted in Figure 29.1.

The dimensions in the Figure 29.1 matrix are not meant to be rigid. They simply delineate the distinctions between both the more mechanistic paradigms of the secondary regulatory processes (and some of the primary regulatory processes when viewed from outside the system), and the more

Regulatory processes/ feedback *Vantage point of observer*	*Primary Regulatory Processes* *Positive Feedback (Structures)*	*Secondary Regulatory Processes* *Negative Feedback (Functions)*
Inside System	*Corporate Planning* *Stimulation* *Autopoiesis*	*Management Accounting* *Operations Management*
Outside System	*Normative Finance Theory*	*Financial Accounting*

FIGURE 29.1. Relationships between Regulatory Processes and Observer's Vantage Point.

evolutionary paradigms that are characteristic of the primary regulatory process inside the organization. Rather than being discrete and conflicting, the concepts should be seen as complementary.

The evolutionary processes of corporate planning could be envisaged as a decision tree with a free decision to be made at each branching point. The individual minds of the managers coordinate the space-time structure of the transformation process in organizations. The typical cycles of growth in autopoietic systems are exponential and could even be hyperbolic. But the type of autocatalytic reactions in self-organizing systems are circular. The combinations of these reactions, and their interconnectedness, mean that considered from whatever angle of view, evolution is always a spiral (Jantsch, 1980c). The usefulness of these ideas is that they provide a metaphor that would reinforce images of the organization as an evolving, self-organizing, multidimensional exponential spiral that is continuously renewing itself, instead of as something more akin to a mechanistic engineered system.

COMPARISON WITH NORMATIVE PARADIGMS

Normative finance theory for capital expenditure analysis in corporate planning evolved from engineering economy studies, which compared different options for executing a specific project, assuming they would be financed by a redeemable debenture (Grant & Ireson, 1970; Weekes, 1979). Each project was considered in isolation and from the vantage point of an observer situated outside the system.

Portfolio analysis and such concepts as the capital asset pricing model and the cost of capital in capital budgeting also reflect a view of the system from the same vantage point. Normative finance theorists would seem, therefore, to need to acquire a knowledge of the kinds of interconnectedness that appear in the relationships between the elements of a system when viewed from a vantage point within the system, where the managers and planners themselves form part of the system. The image of an organization that is held in the head of an investor is quite different from the image of that same organization, and the knowledge of its processes, that is held in the head of managers and planners who form part of that system. In other words, the paradigms of normative finance theory have been developed independently of the organizational paradigms that are acceptable to managers.

Moreover, a kind of economic counterpoint (Chamberlain 1968) exists in business decision making in terms of a continual conflict between short-term and long-term objectives. Even this, however, should not be considered in dialectic terms (tension fields between opposites) as if seen from the outside, but rather in complementary terms (as opposites containing each other) as seen from the inside (Jantsch 1980d).

A dialectic view could be associated with finance theory as espoused for investors, which is essentially aimed at maximizing profits in the short term and ignores the important longer-term aspects necessary for the organization's survival. This should form part of a manager's cognitive set, as Hayes and Abernathy have pointed out.

The individual components of an investment portfolio generally are able to be sold more or less instantaneously—to this extent it is a liquid portfolio. On the other hand, capital expenditure made within a firm is often a sunk cost and cannot be sold or converted to cash very readily. Certainly, divestments of some parts of a business are sometimes possible, but generally this would not be envisaged when an investment is initially made—unless the business is functioning more as a merchant banker, which is the approach that Hayes and Abernathy criticize. The concept of vantage points has also been recognized by Amey (1973), who said that the cost of capital could be viewed as a discount rate or as a cost of investment, depending on whether you are inside or outside the organization.

There is a good reason for this. Investment decisions made within an organization are initially self-funding; that is, the funding model of a public company is one where the earnings of past and present investments provide the funding base for future investments, aided by external funds to augment retained earnings and depreciation (savings) at appropriate intervals. On the other hand, a purely investment company, although it may rely upon the earnings of its various investments for income and for funding the purchase of other investments, can always obtain funds almost immediately—by selling investments—in a way that other self-funding (self-renewing) organizations cannot do. To this extent, its investments are more like bank deposits earning interest than the self-renewing investments of, say, a manufacturing concern. In a manufacturing organization, problems of technological obsolescence and self-renewal through a depreciation-funded savings base occur, which do not exist for an investor. The relationship between capital investments and finance mixes in a manufacturer are both symbiotic and simultaneous.

TOWARD THE APPLICATION OF NEW KNOWLEDGE IN ORGANIZATIONS

The usefulness of the new knowledge that has been outlined in this chapter for organizations is that a new kind of image could be retained in the heads of management and planners. The image of the organization for capital budgeting purposes should consist of a series of forecast future balance sheets that would represent the multidimensional exponential spiral of growth referred to earlier. This assumes that the organization produces some kind of product or service. On the other hand, a purely investment company could still rely on the normative paradigms. It would be easier for investment managers to carry mathematical images in their heads, as the simultaneous and symbiotic relationships between investment and finance mixes are less complex. The purely investment organization is more closed than open as a system, and is thus more likely to be described in terms of unidimensional linear models. In producing organizations, however, because the investment and finance decisions are interactive, a Heisenberg effect exists.

A more suitable methodology would be a simulation process where the most satisfactory combination of variables can be arrived at over the duration of the planning horizon that would at least sustain survival through growth. It would also maintain the value of shareholders' equity in the market by matching planned earnings growth with the growth in earnings anticipated by the market when valuing shares.

TOWARD AN EVALUATION OF USEFULNESS

The normative finance models used in corporate planning that this chapter is concerned with involve the investment decision—in which mathematical models for capital budgeting and the cost of capital using discounting techniques are employed; the financing decision—in which mathematical models are used to determine the best finance mix or capital structure for the firm; and the dividend decision—which is related to the financing decision.

In general, the models of normative finance theory treat each investment decision in isolation from the others. Moreover, we stated earlier that the investment decision is interrelated with the financing decision and that a Heisenberg effect exists. Yet normative finance theory tends to treat the financing decision separately from the investment decision. Also, in treating each investment decision in isolation, and in using discounting techniques, the normative models tend to favor those investments with high returns in the early stages of their lives and with lower initial outlays, as Hayes and Garvin have stated.

These anomalies seem to have arisen because normative finance theory treats decision making as a discrete activity rather than as part of a continuous, self-organizing, evolutionary renewal process. A new evolutionary paradigm can be developed for corporate planning purposes from within which new and more useful conceptualizations of organizations may emerge. If an organization is visualized as a dissipative structure in a state of evolutionary growth, this could be more useful than the existing normative paradigms.

The primary regulatory processes in organisations that comprise corporate planning can be structured in terms of the evolutionary spiral of self renewing growth. The first question planners should ask is: What spiral pattern of evolutionary growth should we aim for?

Instead of the mathematical models of normative finance—which treat each investment decision in isolation from the others—simulation processes can be designed to arrive at that combination of finance mix, return on investment, and planned rates of growth in incremental new investment that will provide answers to this question as the first stage in corporate planning. An interactive computer program has been designed that simulates ten-year balance sheet forecasts on a VDU. Combinations of input variables are altered by trial and error until the most satisfactory projection of the planned evolution of the organization is arrived at. The input variables are symbiotic and react simultaneously. As such, the model cannot be easily solved mathematically for optimal values of all the variables.

When a suitable combination of variables has been determined, this can then be printed out in the form of a ten-year balance sheet forecast that discloses:

Growth in earnings per share
Imputed market value of shares
Shareholders' net income
Imputed value of shareholders' income
Rate of growth in new investment
Average return on new investment

This is the first step in the overall corporate planning process, which does not seem to have been adequately described in the literature. (It could well be that the normative finance models represent but a step along the pathway of knowledge about organizations, and that the rapid advances in computer technology have provided the impetus for a new step along that path).

The next stage involves the determination, by management, of investment programs for specific projects that will meet the organization's objectives after allowing for the inputs of product and process technology that are necessary for survival and growth. Individual investment opportunities can then be searched for with long-term objectives in mind, as the long-term evolution of the business can be visualized in the form of the multidimensional exponential spiral delineated in the printout of the ten-year balance sheet forecast.

The discounting techniques of normative finance theory are used, but in a complementary way to the initial evolutionary processes. Discounting is employed as a technique to rank different competing options for a specific project.

In this new sequence of decision processes, investment projects are not looked at in isolation from each other, nor in isolation from financing decisions. The corporate planning process is viewed holistically and investment projects would be considered in terms of their contributions to overall organizational objectives. The usefulness of this approach lies in the fact that it more closely matches the organizational context and the motives of managers within which information is developed, communicated, and used in the decision-making process. The develolpment of such programs would draw heavily on the insight of managers that has been gleaned from the learning processes of experience. Elements of normative finance theory would then be employed where appropriate, but to support, rather than supplant, the primary processes of corporate planning.

So far, the new processes have not yet been formally installed in a productive organization; consequently, their usefulness to organizational participants has not been formally evaluated. However, the processes have been tested by students of corporate planning at Deakin University. These students studied the normative models of capital budgeting employing discounting techniques, and also the portfolio analysis techniques of the PIMS and BCG models. The students developed a simulation model for a public company of their own choice. Based upon the work of Byrne and Wolfe (1979), students completed a questionnaire (see appendix) asking them to evaluate the usefulness of the interactive simulation model compared with the normative models that they had studied. This was done in terms of 25 learning descriptors using a Likert-type scale rating. While it is acknowledged that students may not have the same criteria as managers and that it is possible that some students may have responded to the "demand characteristics" of the situation, the findings still are interesting. The results confirmed the usefulness of the simulation processes for students in all areas where a positive response was anticipated.

CONCLUSION

The next step in this research program would be to install the new procedures in an ongoing productive organization and then to undertake tests that would evaluate the usefulness of the simulation processes for management in that organization. It is believed that the new approach, based upon a knowledge of the evolutionary paradigm, would be a useful tool in corporate planning and provide the link that seems to be missing between the complementary aspects of both the evolutionary paradigm and the more engineering-based paradigms of normative finance theory.

Further research could also be undertaken into how the evolutionary paradigm could result in more generic models in other business discipline areas where at present the more engineered kinds of mathematical models are applied. Organizational areas such as marketing and human resources, which involve the kinds of symbiotic, positive feedback relationships that occur in the primary regulatory processes of evolutionary systems, could provide fertile areas for research.

In investigating these issues, it would be necessary to discover the organizational paradigm that is appropriate to each particular decision setting, and then to determine whether the mathematical models being employed are suitable, and whether anomalies are present because of the failure of the model to match the organizational paradigm. If the decision setting is situated in the primary evolutionary processes of the organization, then it would be expected that simultaneous and symbiotic relationships would exist between the variables in the decision model. In such settings, it could be envisaged that an interactive simulation model, appropriately designed to match the requirements of the situation, would be more useful than some of the more formal mathematical models that may be employed.

What is needed are processes that perceive the organization from a vantage point within the system and see decisions as a set of evolving interactive processes linking the structural perspective of normative models with the process perspective of organization theory. Moreover, such decision processes could be designed so as to incorporate a greater input of managerial insight and experience that would recognize the complementarity (and also the conflict) between long-term and short-term objectives that may be missing from decision processes that rely too heavily upon formalized mathematical models alone. Organizations could be seen to develop as open learning systems only temporarily manifest as globally stable structures, rather than as solid technological structures seeking static equilibrium.

REFERENCES

Amey, L. R.
1973 Management Accounting: A Conceptual Approach. London: Longmans.
Baumol, William J. and Richard E. Quandt
1965 "Investment and Discount Rates Under Capital Rationing—A Programming Approach." Economic Journal, 75 (June), 317–329.
Byrne, Eugene T. and Douglas E. Wolfe (eds.)
1979 Experiential Learning in Professional Education. Dallas: Edwin L. Cox School of Business, 245–262.
Chamberlain, Neil, W.
1968 Enterprise and Environment: The Firm in Time and Space. New York: McGraw-Hill.
Einstein, Albert
1960 The Meaning of Relativity. London: Methuen.
Grant, Eugene L. and W. G. Ireson
1970 Principles of Engineering Economy. 5th ed. New York: Ronald Press.
Hayes, Robert H. and W. J. Abernathy
1980 "Managing Our Way to Economic Decline." Harvard Business Review, July-Aug., 67–77.
Hayes, Robert H. and D. A. Garvin
1982 "Managing as if Tomorrow Mattered." Harvard Business Review, May-June, 70–79.
Jantsch, Eric
1980 The Self Organizing Universe. Oxford: Pergamon. a. 37, b. 38–39, c. 227, d. 59.
McInnes, J. Morris and Willard J. Carleton
1982 "Theory Models and Implementation in Financial Management." Interfaces, in publication.
Miller, James Grier
1976 "Second Annual Von Bertalanffy Memorial Lecture." Behavioural Science, 21, 219–227.
Nicholis, G. and I. Prigogine
1977 Self Organisation in Non Equilibrium Systems: From Dissipative Structures to Order Through Fluctuation. New York: Wiley Interscience.
Prigogine, I.
1976 "Order through Fluctuation: Self Organisation and Social Systems" in E. Jantsch & C. Waddington (eds.). Evolution and Consciousness: Human Systems in Transition. New York: Addison Wesley.
Weekes, William H.
1979 "Applications of General Systems Theory to Corporate Planning." Proceedings of Silver Anniversary International Meeting of the Society for General Systems Research, London, England, August, 484–492.

APPENDIX

Usefulness of Corporate Planning Stimulation Model Compared with Normative Models of Finance Theory

	Responses	
A. Anticipated Positive Responses	*Positive*	*Negative*
1. Gained knowledge of top-level organizational complexities.	26	1
2. Helped experience implementing own ideas.	20	7
3. Provided meaningful feedback about own ideas.	18	9
4. Helped to experiment with new behavioral patterns.	24	3
5. Helped assume more responsibility for self-development.	19	8
6. Improved judgment.	23	4
7. Helped ability to plan and organize.	26	1
8. Improved problem analysis potential.	22	5
9. Improved ability to learn.	21	6
10. Increased motivation to managerial learning.	24	3
11. Improved knowledge of management control.	26	1
12. Enhanced sensitivity to management issues.	25	2
13. Developed decisiveness.	19	8
14. Improved financial analytical ability.	26	1
15. Developed flexibility.	17	10
16. Improved intuition.	23	4
17. Improved tolerance for stress.	16	11
18. Improved risk-taking potential.	21	6
19. Improved organizational sensitivity.	23	4
B. Anticipated Negative Responses		
1. Improved oral communication skills.	8	19
2. Improved oral presentation skills.	10	17
3. Improved written communication skills.	12	15
4. Improved listening skills.	9	18
5. Improved sales ability/persuasion skills.	6	21
6. Developed leadership attributes.	10	17

30

MAKING KNOWLEDGE MORE USEFUL THROUGH THE PROPER DEVELOPMENT AND USE OF THEORY

Harry J. Martin

GENERAL ORIENTATION

The model used by the natural sciences to acquire knowledge is the best framework from which to build a cumulative understanding of organizations. Numerous arguments have been made both for and against this view, especially as it pertains to the behavioral sciences (Argyris, 1979; Behling, 1980; Gergen, 1973; Manis, 1976; McCall & Lombardo, 1978; Mintzberg, 1982; Schlenker, 1974). Researchers have been criticized for: being preoccupied with hypothesis testing instead of hypothesis generation (Bass, 1974; Lundberg, 1976); emphasizing internal validity at the expense of external validity (Kilmann, 1979); overemphasizing statistical analysis (Tosi, 1979); investigating issues that are too commonsensical (Gordon, Kleiman, & Hanie, 1978); and generally ignoring the concerns of practitioners (Cummings, 1978; Susman & Evered, 1978). While these criticisms are valid, they do not indicate a flaw in the natural science model but rather its misapplication.

If the main purpose of scientific investigation is the building of a cumulative body of knowledge, then the typical research study is as irrelevant to the purpose of science as it is to the needs of the practitioner. Much of the blame for irrelevance of existing work has centered on the pseudoscientific overemphasis on method and the trappings of science. While this criticism is warranted, it unfortunately has led to skepticism regarding the usefulness of the scientific model in general as a method of understanding organizations (Mitroff & Pondy, 1978). The problem is one of separating the essence of scientific inquiry from the "scientism" of existing work. The lack of accumulation and pointlessness of present research is due more to the inadequate formulation of concepts than the method of investigation. In other words, the problem of usefulness stems from inadequate theory with an overemphasis on the trappings of science surfacing as a symptom of this malaise. This is not to say that there is no room for improvement in the use of research methods. Many techniques of organizational inquiry exist other than those currently favored and their use should be encouraged. However, this chapter focuses on the origin and development of theories that these methods are designed to evaluate. If in the past the organizational sciences had followed more closely the recommendations of the natural science model regarding theory construction, then many of the present difficulties with cumulation and usefulness could have been minimized.

WHAT SCIENTIFIC KNOWLEDGE SHOULD LOOK LIKE

Before elaborating on the role of theory in promoting usefulness, there must be some definition of what a theory should do and what it should look like. To provide such a definition, the uses of scientific knowledge, characteristics of a good theory, and basic research strategies will be discussed. Much of the following has been derived from more comprehensive treatments of the subject by Freese (1980), Kaplan (1964), Kuhn (1970), Nagel (1961), Reynolds (1971), Wallace (1971), and others.

Uses of Scientific Knowledge

While users of knowledge concerning organizations undoubtedly have numerous reasons for wanting such information, the following represents a basic list of what scientific knowledge should provide. First, it should provide a means of classifying objects and events that are of interest. To be maximally useful, such a typology should be exhaustive, unambiguous, and have nonoverlapping categories. Second, scientific knowledge should provide a description of past events that may also serve as a basis from which future predictions can be made. Third, scientific knowledge should provide the user with a sense of understanding about the event of interest. This is provided only when the causal mechanisms that link various concepts together have been fully described. Finally, scientific knowledge should suggest to the user potential ways of controlling events. In this manner available knowledge may be used to change variables and their interrelationships to produce desired results.

For example, suppose a manager wants to acquire power to influence the behavior of others. The manager would be interested in scientific knowledge that provides: a clear and comprehensive listing of types of power; a description of how power has been used previously to gain compliance and how it presently could be used to obtain similar results; an understanding of why certain types of power are effective in gaining compliance and under what circumstances; and suggestions as to how the manager may alter either the situation or his or her behavior in order to acquire greater power and influence. While on the surface this process seems simple and straight-forward, it actually involves the careful development and systematic evaluation of a theory.

Characteristics of a Good Theory

For scientific knowledge to be maximally useful, it must be abstract. Consumers of organizational knowledge are not generally interested in John Doe's use of power at Company A, even though it may make a good story. They are interested in those abstract concepts that describe and explain John's use of power and why he was (or was not) successful in gaining compliance. The issue is one of generalization.

For knowledge to be generalizable it must be abstract. Abstraction frees empirical observations from the bonds of time, space, and culture. Once a concept is placed in an abstract form, a manger can use it today as well as tomorrow, at Company A or Company B, in New York or in Tokyo. Knowledge based solely on the observation of events and not stated in an abstract form is not easily generalized. The situation is much like that of a long-distance telephone call. In order to travel great distances, one's voice first must be transformed into electrical impulses, transmitted, then decoded at the other end of the line. Similarly, to bridge the gaps of space, time, and culture, empirical data and experience must first be put into abstract terms, communicated, and then converted back into observable events. One could avoid the process of abstraction and try shouting but this procedure would not get the user very far. This process of abstraction is called *theory construction*.

Perhaps Kurt Lewin said it best with the phrase "There is nothing quite as practical as a good theory." A theory can be defined as a set of statements that, when taken together, describe a particular phenomenon in abstract terms and explain the various states that an object or event has taken in the past and is likely to take in the future. All managers have their own prejudices, biases, and pet "theories" that they use daily to explain events and make decisions. However, these vague conceptualizations and descriptions are not the things to which the present term "theory" refers. Present usage implies the following set of formal characteristics.

First, a theory must be *abstract*. As mentioned above, for a concept to be useful across variations in time and location it must be free of terms and descriptions unique to any particular time or setting. Even though specific historical events are frequently used to generate the ideas from which theories are made, they must be avoided when actually stating the theory. For example, suppose a PERT network was used to build an appliance-manufacturing plant in North Carolina. It is not the location or the type of plant that makes this planning technique useful. It is the complexity, sequential pattern, and nonrecurring nature of the project that makes PERT useful. If North Carolina and appliance manufacturing are used to describe the "theory" of PERT networks, it will not generalize very far. On the other hand, if the concepts of complexity, sequential processes, and nonrecurring events are used to define the concept, then the theory is free of time and location and can be transmitted easily.

Second, a theory must have *exact definitions*. Even though a theory should be abstract it should not be ambiguous. Care must be exercised when defining new concepts and using existing terminology to ensure agreement among relevant scientists and users. While language is imprecise, concern for shared agreement when formulating a theory can greatly reduce its ambiguity.

Third, a theory should have *scope conditions*. It is unlikely that a hypothesized relationship will exist between variables irrespective of other important factors. Therefore, one needs to define precisely those conditions under which relationships explained in the theory are expected to hold.

Fourth, a good theory should also have *precise statements*. These statements can be grouped according to whether they claim the existence of a concept (existence statements) or whether they describe relationships between concepts (relational statements). Relational statements can be subdivided further into statements of association and causality. Associational statements merely state that two concepts covary in a particular fashion. Causal statements, on the other hand, specify the mechanisms through which changes in one concept determine changes in another. Existence statements provide a classification system or typology for the phenomenon of interest, while explanations, predictions, and a sense of understanding depend on relational statements.

Fifth, theories must be *logically consistent*. Theories usually contain a number of statements, and it is important that these statements be combined to form a unified explanation of the phenomenon of interest. If the statements can be combined in ways that lead to multiple explanations of the phenomenon, then the theory does not possess "logical rigor." This development of a logical system of explanation is a major undertaking. Fortunately, other systems such as mathematics and symbolic logic can be employed by the organizational scientist to assist in this endeavor.

Sixth, theories should be *parsimonious*. Kaplan (1964) suggested that an important criterion for evaluating the usefulness of a theory is its aesthetic quality. In addition to the other criteria for a good theory, one's conceptualization of a particular phenomenon should possess a certain beauty and elegance. More often than not, this quality is achieved through a logical system that is simple and direct. It is unlikely that awkward and cumbersome theories will have much utility. While most organizational phenomena are exceedingly complex, theorists should always avoid adding unnecessarily to this complexity.

Finally, a theory must have *empirical relevance*. To evaluate a theory and put it to work solving problems, one must be able to convert its abstract concepts into concrete observable events. If a theory cannot be compared with objective research, then it cannot be validated by the scientific community and will be of little use to practitioners. Empirical relevance is achieved by providing an operational definition for key statements. This involves a set of procedures that one should perform to obtain information indicating the existence of a theoretical concept. Just as a telephone receiver converts electrical impulses into sound, an operational definition converts theoretical concepts into observable events. For example, the concept of power may be assessed by using various methods such as trained observers, rankings, or questionnaires. Issues concerning the reliability and validity of measuring instruments and procedures are relevent here.

Research Strategies

An important part of the development of a scientific body of knowledge is the gathering and use of empirical data. The relationship of research data to the construction of theories can take one of two forms: research-then-theory (inductive approach) or theory-then-research (deductive approach).

The research-then-theory model involves observation of the phenomenon of interest from which explanations and predictions are made. This approach can help to provide a useful typology and description of events and may be quite accurate in making predictions. However, it does not answer the important question "why" and gives the user little indication as to how to control events or what action to take if predictions fail.

With the theory-then-research approach, the researcher first develops a theory that explains the phenomenon of interest and reasons behind certain events, then evaluates the theory using empirical data. This strategy requires that the researcher: develop an explicit theory conforming to the characteristics discussed previously; select key statements generated by the theory for comparison with the findings of empirical data; design an appropriate research project to "test" the degree of correspondence between the selected statements and the data; make appropriate changes in the theory or research design if the statements tested do not correspond to the results and continue with the research; and if the statements tested do correspond to the research findings, enhance the confirmation status of the theory by selecting additional statements for testing or by extending the applicability of the theory to include other events (that is, widen the scope conditions). This deductive approach not only provides the user with a typology, description of events, and predictions, it is also the only framework that provides a sense of understanding regarding the phenomenon.

In practice, both approaches to theory development are employed to take advantage of the strengths of each. At the outset, important events and outcomes are observed and described using an inductive research approach. From these observations, a series of empirical generalizations are formed that serve as a basis for the creation of a deductive explanatory framework. Propositions derived from such a theoretical framework can then be evaluated against observable events. This combined approach can preserve the descriptive richness often associated with inductive analysis while simultaneously providing a sense of understanding of the phenomenon of interest and suggestions for its potential control.

Middle-Range Theory

One may get the impression that this model favors the development of grandiose theories that attempt to explain a wide range of organizational phenomena with a single set of propositions. Arguments have been made that question the viability of such full-fledged theories in the behavioral sciences. For example, Merton (1968) has advocated development of "middle-range theories" that are narrower in scope and less developed than "grand" theories, but that provide a causal framework for explaining events absent in empirical generalizations. Given the nature of the discipline, middle-range theories appear quite attractive. However, regardless of whether the researcher's purpose is the development of grand theory or more modest middle-range theory, the principles of clarity, parsimony, empirical relevance, and so forth outlined above are applicable and efforts should be made to implement these concepts.

THE REALITIES OF ORGANIZATIONAL KNOWLEDGE

Now that a model of what scientific knowledge should look like has been presented, a comparison may be made with what actually exists in the organizational sciences. When one makes this comparison it can be said that what knowledge exists differs greatly from what it should look like. This has prompted some to suggest that the model described is not applicable to the behavioral sciences and should be discarded. While criticisms of research in the field are justified, this chapter vigorously opposes the suggestion that the natural science model should be scrapped in favor of some other system of knowledge accumulation. The poor marks that have been given to the organizational sciences thus far (Bass, 1981; Campbell, 1979; Miner, 1975; Mintzberg, 1982; Sayles, 1979) are due to the fact that researchers have generally failed to follow the abovementioned recommendations. This is especially true when current "theories" are considered. Most "theories" are not theories at all. Much of what has been written is as distinct and precise as an astrology prediction. Definitions are incomplete and vague, scope conditions are frequently nonexistent, ambiguity is substituted for abstraction in theoretical statements, logical consistency is rare, and models are so convoluted they can only be referred to as "ugly." Under these conditions, empirical relevance is difficult to attain. Present organizational theory generally assumes the form of a series of vague assumptions, loosely tied together, which seem to lead to certain hypotheses. Statements and hypotheses are so vague that they can never be proven wrong and, as such, are "puncture proof and self-sealing" (Nisbet, 1968, p. 989). Trait theories of leadership (Bass, 1981) immediately come to mind as an example.

This state of affairs is not due to the complexity of the phenomena encountered in the study of organizations (even though events are exceedingly complex). A number of scholars have attempted to develop theories that contain the elements of good theory with some measure of success. Examples include Emerson's treatment of social exchange (1981), the treatment of status characteristics and expectation states by Berger and his associates (Berger, Rosenholtz, & Zelditch, 1980), and House's work on leadership (House, 1971; House & Mitchell, 1974). There exists ample evidence that the elements of a good theory are attainable by researchers in the behavioral sciences. The inability to achieve these standards appears to be due, in part, to ignorance of what scientific knowledge should look like and how it is created, and the unwillingness of researchers to invest the time and energy necessary to construct theories.

A central theme of this chapter is that knowledge of organizations is most useful when it is abstract and theoretical. However, while the terms "abstract" and "ambiguous" are not synonymous in this context, they are often substituted for one another in practice. This occurs, in part, because most researchers have not received adequate training in theory construction. While most doctoral programs in management and business administration have rigorous courses in research methods, statistics, and computer programming, few have required courses in theory construction. Thus, while doctoral candidates are well versed in how to *answer* questions, there is a general lack of understanding of how properly to *ask* questions. It can be said that such training is unnecessary and that acquisition of this ability is a natural by-product of obtaining an advanced degree. However, this is equivalent to saying that simply because a manager occupies a particular position in an organization's hierarchy that he or she automatically has the administrative ability required to do the job effectively.

Given the emphasis on methodology in the training of researchers, it is no wonder that writers in the field are preoccupied with hypothesis testing rather than hypothesis generation (Lundberg, 1976). However, as Freese (1980) has stated, "What does it profit an investigator to produce unambiguous, elegant data to evaluate an ambiguous, inelegant theory?" (p. 56). It does not take a Ph.D. or DBA to collect sophisticated data. Technicians, pollsters, journalists, and others are equally good at it. Doctoral candidates should spend more time learning how to generate ideas before graduation and formulating ideas following graduation.

Even though researchers may be able to formulate theories, why should they? What is the payoff? As evidenced by the rigorous criteria used to evaluate a "good theory," this activity is likely to be very time-consuming. This, in turn, leads to fewer publications. While the material published probably would be of much greater value than current works, it runs counter to the publish-or-perish criteria against which younger scholars are judged.

Thus, it is suggested that the problems associated with the accumulation of knowledge in the organizational sciences can be traced to a lack of training in theory construction, ignorance of what scientific knowledge should look like and how it is created, and performance evaluations that are tied primarily to the quantity of output, not its quality.

THE GAP BETWEEN RESEARCHERS AND PRACTITIONERS

Another criticism is that current knowledge lacks relevance to practitioners and their needs. Once again, fault for this situation has been attributed to the natural science model of investigation. It is proposed, however, that this problem stems primarily from the exclusion of practitioners by researchers when they construct theories and decide what aspects of organizations should be studied. Pointlessness can originate from inadequate theory as well as from the selection of topics that are irrelevant to the needs of the practitioner. Thus far the discussion has dealt with the issue of inadequate theory. However, theories can be valid but unimportant. The cumulation of knowledge through proper development of theory is a key element in the usefulness question. The other key element is the relevance of this knowledge. It can be argued that a good theoretical treatment of a topic is a necessary but not sufficient condition for usefulness.

The sense of understanding of some organizational phenomenon provided by a theoretical treatment of the subject is perhaps the most valuable tool reseachers can provide practitioners. A good theory will be of service to managers throughout their careers regardless of which company they are associated with and where they are located. "Canned" solutions to organizational problems rarely exist and most likely will not fit the specific situation without some adaptation (cf. Lorsch, 1979). In contrast, a properly constructed and validated theory not only will inform the practitioner when the concept is applicable, what the important variables are, why certain events occur, and how one can adapt to meet specific needs, it will also be useful at different times and across various situations because it is abstract.

However, a major reason a gap exists between practitioners and researchers is because the topics that have been of interest to academicians generally are not relevant to the problems encountered by managers. In the quest for precision and methodological rigor, researchers frequently have lost sight of more important issues pertaining to the significance of the questions asked. This is understandable given the absence of a firm theoretical basis with which to guide research. But this problem is also due, in large measure, to the lack of interaction and dialogue between practitioners and academicians. If scholars spend most of their time talking to other academics and rarely venture out into the world to interact with practicing managers, then it is not surprizing that they have a distorted view of organizations and their members (Susman & Evered, 1978). However, it is proposed that this is primarily a function of the infrequency and poor quality of interaction between these groups, not of the demands of the scientific model of inquiry. For theory to be relevant it must incorporate the practitioner's point of view (Dubin, 1976; Thomas & Tymon, 1982). To accomplish this there must be a dialogue established between the academic and practitioner communities.

MAKING ORGANIZATIONAL KNOWLEDGE MORE USEFUL

The proposed causes behind the apparent lack of accumulation and utility of organizational knowledge suggest several courses of action that may be taken to correct the current situation. The proposed solutions have direct relevance to academic institutions, how they train and reward new scholars, and how their members relate to practitioners. These suggestions fall into the categories of training, interaction, and reward systems.

Training

It has been suggested that a likely cause of current difficulties is a lack of education on the part of academicians in the art of theory construction. The solution to this problem is straightforward. Why not require doctoral students to take courses in theory construction and development much like they are required to take courses in research methods and statistics? Detailed works on the nature and characteristics of good theories as outlined here are widely available. Information on theory construction is readily available, and the academic community should demonstrate to their students their high regard for theory by requiring students to become familiar with the art of its construction. This suggestion does not require major changes in educational institutions nor does its implementation require a substantial amount of money. However, it does promise to return handsome dividends in terms of more effective accumulation and increased utilization of knowledge.

Interaction

The apparent trivialization of organizational research is partially due to the researcher's lack of understanding of how to ask questions and partially due to a lack of input on the part of practitioners. The training recommendations discussed above should help to eliminate the first problem. Greater involvement on the part of practicing managers in formulating theories and research questions should help to eliminate the second problem.

Earlier it was recommended that the theory-then-research strategy of knowledge development should be used by organizational scientists because of its ability to provide a sense of understanding. However, this leads to the question, "Where do the ideas originate from which theories are created?" In practice, knowledge development is often a combination of both inductive and deductive processes. Events are observed, problems encountered, and questions asked about particular phenomena. From these observations and discussions, preliminary theories are formulated and tested. However, a problem arises when academicians choose empirical events for study without consultation with organizational participants who may have better first-hand knowledge of the subject. It has been suggested that such interaction between academicians and practitioners is vital to producing useful knowledge (Mintzberg, 1982). On the other hand, some have suggested that making such interaction a requirement may take the "fun" out of scientific inquiry (Schriesheim, Hunt, & Sekaran, 1982). It is proposed that such interaction is vital, especially in the early stages of concept development, and that this interaction need not take the fun out of conducting research. The increase in the researcher's intuitive understanding of organizational phenomena that is potentially available through such interaction far outweighs the small risk that one's freedom of inquiry will be restricted. In addition, making inductive use of the practitioner's understanding and experience will help reduce the problems of descriptive relevance, goal relevance, operational validity, and nonobviousness identified by Thomas and Tymon (1982). This combined inductive-deductive approach also encompasses the need to research organizations from both idiographic and nomothetic perspectives (Luthans & Davis, 1982).

Therefore, a model of scientific inquiry for the organizational sciences is proposed that incorporates both deductive and inductive approaches to knowledge development and includes the active participation of practitioners in the formulation and evaluation of theories. This model is outlined in Figure 30.1. The process starts with interaction between researcher and practitioner regarding problems and questions of mutual interest. Together the two parties systematically observe and discuss events believed to be related to the problem or process under consideration. When researchers believe they possess an adequate intuitive understanding of the problem, a theory is constructed using the guidelines contained in this report. If practitioners have not been actively involved in formulating the theory, they should be invited to comment on it, especially with regard to its elegance and potential usefulness. Once researchers and practitioners are reasonably satisfied with the product and when it contains all the elements of a "good theory" then researchers can begin generating and systematically testing hypotheses. Based on empirical results, certain revisions and modifications may be necessary. Over time, the confirmation status of the theory may improve to the point where its dissemination to both academicians and practitioners is warranted. However, the process should not end here. Users should be encouraged, once again, to participate in the theory's ongoing development by having researchers periodically contact practitioners regarding their success and failures when using the theory. From these data, the scope conditions may be expanded to apply in a wider variety of situations and the theory's statements made more precise.

As with training, this model could be easily implemented without great expense or a restructuring of present institutions. It is suggested that schools and colleges of business institute an "Organization-In-Residence" program. Through negotiations with local business firms, governmental agencies, and nonprofit organizations, each school could arrange for the faculty's access to the organization's managerial staff. Retreats or meetings could be arranged where faculty could present seminars on topics of interest and managers could elect to work informally with researchers in exploring these issues further. Managers could also assist by allowing the researcher access to their employees for observation and pilot testing. This would give the academician an opportunity to gain valuable insights into specific organizational phenomenon and the manager could receive feedback and information concerning the relevant problem in return. It is understood that many researchers already implement a similar procedure on their own; however, it is felt that greater interaction needs to be encouraged and such a residency program would greatly facilitate such interactions.

Beyond improving the relevance of theory and research (Thomas & Tymon, 1982), such a program would have a number of advantages. It would serve as a mechanism for improving understanding and communication between practitioners and academics. The problems of a lack of trust/confidence, language barriers, differing conceptual frameworks, low credibility, misunderstanding of cultures, lack of insight, improper operationali-

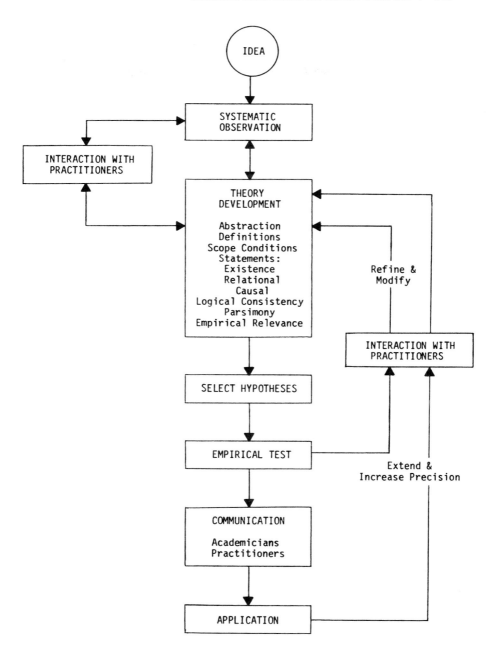

FIGURE 30.1. A Model of Knowledge Development for the Organizational Sciences

zation of constructs, and low external validity could be ameliorated to a large extent by such a linkage mechanism. In addition, it would provide researchers with a mentor who could guide them around and help them get their foot in the door. The interaction process would also encourage research *with* organizations instead of merely *on* organizations. In short, practitioners will be more receptive if they know what the researcher is doing, why, and has some input or stake in the process.

However, such a program is not without its limitations. Both the participating organization and faculty members should first be surveyed regarding their readiness to interact and cooperate in such a program. If projects are not viewed as a joint enterprise, then the participants are not likely to benefit greatly from the experience. The issue of time constraints presents other difficulties. The practitioner has little time to devote to such an endeavor. This can be compensated for to a degree by the researcher's handling of most of the activities associated with theory construction and evaluation. However, the problem of timeliness is more difficult to overcome. The manager's need for action on specific problems typically does not lend itself to the time investment required by the careful development of theory proposed by this model. This inherent discrepancy between the time frame of the practitioner and researcher is not insurmountable, but its resolution is likely to be quite challenging. In addition, there is a need to provide incentives for the manager's involvement in the program. Some individuals are likely to participate simply out of curiosity or their desire for advice on a particular problem. However, the long-term investment in feedback and refinement often required in theory development, while borne by the researcher to a large extent, may be difficult to sustain. Top management support for the program and encouragement of practitioner contributions to the literature may be helpful in this regard.

Reward Systems

Finally, there needs to be some payoff for the researcher to justify the time and energy necessary to develop and construct theories. The present system appears to reward the generation of a large volume of empirical studies regardless of their theoretical or practical significance. To counter this trend, it is proposed that colleges and schools of business create standards for promotion and tenure that require young scholars to produce X number of publications of a "theoretical nature" in order to qualify. This procedure is flexible enough not to restrict academic freedom, while at the same time being specific enough to encourage a balance of hypothesis generation and hypothesis testing. It may be argued that not enough publication outlets exist that handle strictly theoretical treatments of a subject. While this is probably true, agreement among journal editors and colleges and schools of business to encourage theoretical analyses will create enough demand that publishers of new journals will be likely to emerge.

CONCLUDING COMMENTS

The natural science model of knowledge development has been criticized unfairly in assessing the causes for the failure of organizational knowledge to be cumulative and relevant. The academic community's failure to properly implement this model and its lack of interaction with practitioners lie at the root of these problems. A renewed commitment to the development of sound theoretical treatments of organizational phenomena is necessary to help the field grow and prosper. However, those who create knowledge cannot afford to ignore those who will use this knowledge. By encouraging the training of scholars in the nature and purpose of theory, creating channels of communication that will facilitate interaction between researchers and practitioners, and placing some emphasis on theory development in the reward systems of academic institutions, it is anticipated that current problems with the lack of accumulation and utility of organizational knowledge will be greatly reduced. While other approaches to the study of organizations should be explored and their development encouraged, the scientific model is a faithful employee of the discipline who is salvageable and should not be terminated.

REFERENCES

Argyris, Chris
1979   "How normal science methodology makes leadership research less additive and less applicable." In J. G. Hunt & L. L. Larson (eds.), *Crosscurrents in Leadership*: 47–63. Carbondale, IL: Southern Illinois University Press.
Bass, Bernard M.
1974   "The substance and the shallow." *American Psychologist*, 29:870–886.
1981   *Stogdill's Handbook of Leadership*. New York: Free Press.
Behling, Orlando
1980   "The case for the natural science model for research in organizational behavior and organization theory." *Academy of Management Review*, 5:483–490.
Berger, Joseph, S. J. Rosenholtz, & M. Zelditch, Jr.
1980   "Status organizing processes." *Annual Review of Sociology*, 6:479–508.
Boehm, Virginia R.
1980   "Research in the 'real world'—A conceptual model." *Personnel Psychology*, 33:495–503.
Campbell, David
1979   "The cutting edge is dull." *Contemporary Psychology*, 24:248–249.
Cummings, L. L.
1978   "Toward organizational behavior." *Academy of Management Review*, 3:90–98.

Dubin, R.
1976   "Theory building in applied areas." In M. Dunnett (ed.), *Handbook of Industrial and Organizational Psychology*: 17–39. Chicago: Rand-McNally.

Emerson, Richard M.
1981   "Social exchange theory." In M. Rosenberg & R. H. Turner (eds.), *Social Psychology: Sociological Perspectives*: 30–65. New York: Basic Books.

Freese, Lee
1980   *Theoretical Methods in Sociology*. Pittsburgh: University of Pittsburgh Press.

Gergen, Kenneth J.
1973   "Social psychology as history." *Journal of Personality and Social Psychology*, 26:309–320.

Gordon, M. E., L. S. Kleiman, & C. A. Hanie
1978   "Industrial-organizational psychology: Open thy ears O house of Israel." *American Psychologist*, 33:893–905.

House, Robert J.
1971   "A path-goal theory of leadership effectiveness." *Administrative Science Quarterly*, 16:321–339.

House, Robert J., & Terence R. Mitchell
1974   "Path-goal theory of leadership." *Journal of Contemporary Business*, 3(4):81–97.

Kaplan, Abraham
1964   *The Conduct of Inquiry*. San Francisco: Chandler.

Kilmann, Ralph H.
1979   "On integrating knowledge utilization with knowledge development: The philosophy behind the MAPS design technology." *Academy of Management Review*, 4:417–426.

Kuhn, Thomas S.
1970   *The Structure of Scientific Revolutions* (rev. ed.). Chicago: University of Chicago Press.

Lorsch, Jay W.
1979   "Making behavioral science more useful." *Harvard Business Review*, 57(March–April):171–180.

Lundberg, Craig C.
1976   "Hypothesis creation in organizational behavior research." *Academy of Management Review*, 1(2):5–12.

Luthans, Fred, & Tim R. V. Davis
1982   "An idiographic approach to organizational behavior research: The use of single case experimental designs and direct measures." *Academy of Management Review*, 7:380–391.

Manis, Melvin
1976   "Is social psychology really different?" *Personality and Social Psychology Bulletin*, 2:428–437.

McCall, Morgan W., & Michael M. Lombardo
1978   *Leadership: Where Else Can We Go?* Durham, NC: Duke University Press.

Merton, Robert K.
1968   *Social Theory and Social Structure*. New York: Free Press.

Miner, John B.
1975   *The Challenge of Managing*. Philadelphia: Saunders.

Mintzberg, Henry
1982   "If you're not serving Bill and Barbara, then you're not serving leadership." In J. G. Hunt, U. Sekaran, & C. A. Schriesheim (eds.), *Leadership: Beyond Establishment Views*: 239–259. Carbondale, IL: Southern Illinois University Press.

Mitroff, I. I., & L. R. Pondy
1978   "Afterthoughts on the leadership conference." In M. W. McCall & M. M. Lombardo (eds.), *Leadership: Where Else Can We Go?*: 145–149. Durham, NC: Duke University Press.

Morgan, G., & L. Smircich
1980   "The case for qualitative research." *Academy of Management Review*, 5:491–500.

Nagel, Ernest
1961   *The Structure of Science*. New York: Harcourt, Brace, & World.

Nisbet, Robert
1968   "Review of Amitai Etzioni 'The Active Society'." *American Sociological Review*, 33:988–991.

Reynolds, Paul D.
1971   *A Primer in Theory Construction*. Indianapolis: Bobbs-Merrill.

Sayles, Leonard R.
1979   *Leadership: What Effective Managers Really Do . . . and How They Do It*. New York: McGraw-Hill.

Schlenker, Barry R.
1974   "Social psychology and science." *Journal of Personality and Social Psychology*, 29:1–15.

Schriesheim, Chester A., James G. Hunt, & Uma Sekaran
1982   "Conclusion: The leadership-management controversy revisited." In J. G. Hunt, U. Sekaran, & C. A. Schriesheim (eds.), *Leadership: Beyond Establishment Views*: 290–298. Carbondale, IL: Southern Illinois University Press.

Susman, G. I., & R. D. Evered
1978   "An assessment of the scientific merits of action research." *Administrative Science Quarterly*, 23:582–603.

Thomas, Kenneth W., & Walter G. Tymon
1982   "Necessary properties of relevant research: Lessons from recent criticisms of the organizational sciences." *Academy of Management Review*, 7:345–352.

Tosi, Henry
1979   "The need for theoretical development in organizational behavior: Or, if the past is a prologue in organizational behavior, economics will be replaced as the dismal science." *Exchange: The Organizational Behavior Teaching Journal*, 4:5–7.

Wallace, Walter L.
1971   *The Logic of Science in Sociology*. Chicago: Aldine.

PART IV

REDESIGN OF
ACADEMIC INSTITUTIONS

31

FUNCTIONS AND ORGANIZATIONS OF UNIVERSITY BUSINESS SCHOOLS

Tom Lupton

INTRODUCTION

Once again, management education is under critical review. This time the question is not whether university management schools are, or ought to be, academically respectable; rather, it is whether they can, or should be, both academically rigorous *and* relevant to business and to the pressing concerns of managers, MBA programs are under scrutiny because they are said to neglect development of managerial competencies. The experience of the leading British schools may be of some relevance to the discussion. They were required by their charter to be both rigorous and relevant and this has influenced their development.

In 1965 the British business community, acting through the Foundation for Management Education, and the British (Labour) government jointly, equally, and generously funded the establishment of two postgraduate centers of excellence in management education: one attached to the University of Manchester and the other to the University of London. A number of special requirements distinguished these schools from other university-attached graduate schools, and have strongly influenced their subsequent development. First, they were to be financially independent of the universities to which they were attached. A government subsidy was to be granted annually directly to both schools so as to leave them free to develop independently, outside the budgeting constraints of their own universities. Second, the government budget (which was channeled like all university finance through the University Grants Commission) was to be initially only half of the total running expenses of the schools; enough to sustain the masters and doctoral programs. Third, there were generous government scholarships and bursaries to support candidates for those programs, and some sponsorship from business firms. Fourth, and very significantly for their subsequent development, the schools were required to earn the other half of their income by charging economic fees for such Executive Development Programs as they could find a market for and to break even year by year. With the passage of time and the reduction of government budgets for university education, the schools have had to raise more and more from fees to compensate for the falling off of government funding for capital and recurrent expenditure, and for scholarship income. Manchester Business School in 1982 is funded one-third from government sources and two-thirds from its own earnings, and the government share is still falling fairly rapidly.

This is mentioned partly by way of background for those who are unfamiliar with management education and the funding arrangements for university education in the United Kingdom, but mainly to emphasize the point that continuing education for business managers has been from the beginning a very large part of what Manchester and London Business Schools have done. The same can also be said of the other university-attached schools in the United Kingdom.

Manchester and London provide a variety of residential short programs ranging from one day to ten weeks, and from the very general to the very specific. They cater to managers at every level in organizations, both public and privately owned, and from the very small to the very large. These courses take place in the same buildings and residential facilities and at the same time as the graduate and doctoral work of the school; they also are taught by the same faculty members. In any week of the year of these year-round schools, a member of the faculty could have been engaged with the first-year MBS class, the second-year MBA class, a middle management group on a ten-week general program, a group of very senior executives on the three-week updating seminar, a supervision of a doctoral student, and so on. In other weeks, on other days, the faculty member could be engaged with managers on a program specially designed for a particular company.

This has meant, and still means, that there is continuing and persistent pressure on the schools and their faculty to be relevant in all they do to the development needs of managers and the problems of their organizations. The criteria of relevance are applied to program design, to the material presented, and to the method and style of presentation. Because fee income is closely connected to success in all those things, no one who wants job security is foolish enough to ignore relevance. The funding of research and the provision of facilities for management learning, such as computers and audiovisual services, depend also on fee income, as indeed does financial support for MBA students as government finance diminishes.

However, the schools also have a requirement to be rigorous. As university institutions they must promote the scholarly virtues. The research and publications of the faculty must stand up to the established canons of judgment in fields of academic knowledge and their teaching must reach high levels of technical competence and objectivity. Like all university teachers, their careers depend to a large extent on how well they shape up to these requirements.

THE ORGANIZATIONAL REQUIREMENT

Given a mission to become more deeply involved in continuing education on a larger scale, how can (should) graduate business schools organize themselves to combine rigor and relevance fruitfully, economically, and flexibly? What kind of people does one need to do it effectively? These are not rhetorical questions. In Manchester we have been seeking an answer to them for 16 years, and we are still changing in response to changes in markets. Although my analysis of the problem will be general, my references, naturally enough, will refer to my own school. That is as it should be. Manchester has been notably more adventurous and innovative than most European schools in tackling the problem.

Let me put three questions and propose an answer to them:

What is (should be) the job(s) of a postgraduate, postexperience, university-based business school?

How could (should) business schools be organized to do the job effectively?

How shall their effectiveness be measured?

The short answer to the first question is that the job of a business school is to link, reciprocally and fruitfully, fields of action with fields of knowledge. This means that the activities that go on in the schools and those that faculty get involved in outside the schools (such as research and consulting) should all be directed to that end, and that the schools should be so organized that the job is done effectively.

Fields of Action

Fields of action are the settings in which managers do their work (organizations large and small, public and private, industrial and commercial) and what goes on in those fields (what managers do, why they do it, and with what outcomes). How many business schools see it as their job to be involved in fields of action? How many business school faculty could give a convincing answer to the naive critic who says "Why don't business schools teach about what managers do, rather than what management professionals do (as professionals not managers) and what academics prefer to teach"?

There is a pat response, namely, that it is not and should not be the job of a university school to be as practical as all that. From such a perspective, the job of a university is to train young minds to think straight and to provide a protected setting where the young can experiment with values and ideas, generally position themselves in society, and prepare themselves for responsible citizenship and professional work. When one thinks, however, of mature graduate students in their mid-twenties already committed to a career in management, such a perspective is surely difficult to justify. In the case of a divisional managing director aged 45, attending a senior executive program, it sounds a bit ludicrous. There are still some who would say that university business schools ought not to get themselves involved with such people. I cannot see how they can escape involvement. Indeed, I believe that they should actively seek it. This implies that the schools should address themselves to such questions as what managers do, what they ought to be doing, and what skills and competencies they need so as to carry out their tasks effectively. As it happens, there is some systematic general knowledge about those questions.

Henry Mintzberg (1973) collated the published results of all the systematic observations he could find of managers at work, and added some of his own. He concluded that there are ten managerial roles, all of which can be found in any manager's job (weighted and proportioned differently from job to job). Most managers recognize these easily. I was one of the authorities cited by Mintzberg (Horne and Lupton, 1965), and the middle managers I studied in Birmingham, England, in the early sixties were involved in all the roles. I can recognize the roles myself in the work I do as director of a business school. The curious thing is that when one compares the curriculum of MBA programs and the design of executive development programs with the work managers actually do, the problems they encounter, and their needs for skill and competence to resolve them, one always feels a certain unease at not seeing as many connections as one might reasonably expect.

Recent work by Boyatzis (1982) identifies the competencies associated with successful management. Few of these are deliberately developed in business schools either at MBS level or in continuing education for managers.

In Mintzberg's list of ten roles there are three interpersonal roles, three informational roles, and four decisional roles.

Interpersonal	Informational	Decisional
Figurehead	Monitor	Entrepreneur
Leader	Disseminator	Disturbance handler
Liaison	Spokesman	Resource allocator
		Negotiator

These are, of course, abstract general ideas derived from empirical observations of activity. Some of the characteristics of these activities are that they are made up of episodes of relatively short duration, have great variety, and exhibit no obvious regularity and continuity.

> Managers must shift moods frequently and quickly, fragmentation and interruptions are commonplace—especially for those managers closest to the action. (Mintzberg, 1973)

No MBA or executive development program I know of gives instruction on how best to perform the ten Mintzberg roles, how to acquire the competencies identified by Boyatzis, or how best to cope with managerial job characteristics such as variety, fragmentation, and brevity. The design of our programs and projects at Manchester gives some opportunities for learning to cope, but these are mostly by-products. One thing is sure: managers in their jobs do not usually require a skill of listening to lectures, making notes, and analyzing cases. Most programs are overweighted with these activities, with the resource allocation role, and to some extent the informational roles. Sometimes practice in management skills is included; for example, in Manchester we use "live" real-time consulting projects. However, it is invariably the economics, the behavioral sciences, the finance, the accounting, the marketing, and the business policy—in short, the fields of knowledge—that are the building blocks of classroom-bound curricula, and not the learning of managerial competencies.

Fields of Knowledge

University business schools are commonly peopled by specialists: economists, sociologists, psychologists, accountants, financial analysts, operational researchers, marketing, personnel, and production specialists. They usually are marked off from each other by the boundaries of discipline departments representing distinct fields of knowledge, each with its journals and jargon and its own canons of judgment of published work; on the quantity and quality of which preferment so largely depends. When in the late 1950s the U.S. business schools were somewhat concerned about their image, they were advised to make sure that their research outputs were as good as (or better than) those coming out of single discipline departments in universities (Gordon and Howells, 1959). Some would say, "And rightly so!" The charter of my own University says, for example: "the object of the University shall be to advance learning and knowledge by teaching and research." There is nothing there about fields of action. There are many fine scholars at Manchester to whom the idea that what they are doing in research and teaching might or should be of fairly short-term relevance to anyone is unacceptable. It was in a Manchester laboratory that the atom was first split by Rutherford and his team. He was asked in the first flush of his triumph, or so the story goes, whether he could think of any practical uses to which his discovery might be put in the future. He looked astonished and said that nothing came immediately to his mind.

The model that many academics work with is one in which fields of research are deliberately insulated from fields of action because of the possibilities of value contamination. The problems for research are therefore derived from the fields of knowledge and the findings are put back there to be criticized and improved upon. If others wish to turn the findings to practical use then so be it, but it is not the researcher's job. I do not see how medical schools and business schools can be like that. They must for the most part derive the questions for research from the fields of action, and the results of research should be used and tested in fields of action so as to define more problems for research. If we look at it like that, then our problem of business school organization is defined. They must be organized not just to respond flexibly to shifts in the fields of action, but to influence them—via teaching, action research/consultancy, and in other ways to be described below. We should also be sensitive to what is going on in fields of knowledge and influence them too. Our faculty should, however, be oriented to task and problem rather than to discipline.

BUSINESS SCHOOLS AND THE CHANGING ENVIRONMENT

Consider the business school in a changing environment as illustrated in Figure 31.1. The organizations (box c) responding to (and influencing) those changes via arrows c and d, are themselves systems where managers learn by their experience of managing (arrow f), supplemented by in-house training (arrows h and i), which will also be available for the potential managers (box b) recruited from the labor market (arrow p), from university courses in nonmanagement subjects (arrow n), and from undergraduate or postgraduate courses (arrows m and l). Universities and university management schools must also respond directly to the changes taking place in the general environment (arrows a and b), and indirectly and very significantly via the effects on the environment of the organizations that are their clients or potential clients and the employers or potential employers of their graduates (arrows m and l). To the extent that the response of business schools is inadequate to the needs for manager development—that is to say, if their postgraduate and undergraduate course designs are not relevant to the competencies now required by potential managers, and their executive development offerings are not relevant to the new challenges of managers in-post—so will organizations do the job of manager development themselves.

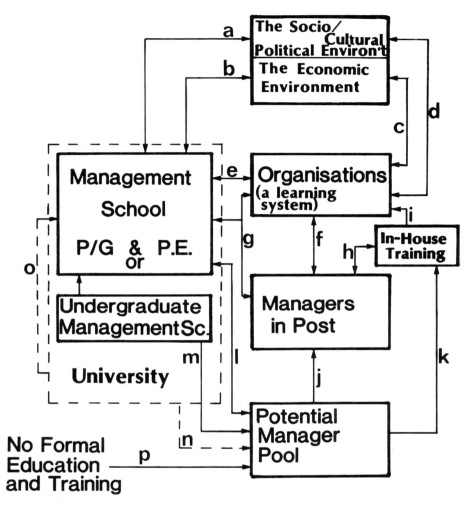

FIGURE 31.1. The Environment of Management Schools.
Source: Lupton, 1981.

This would tend to isolate organizations from direct access to fields of knowledge, and business school faculty from fields of action. Large organizations will find it much easier, however, to get access to fields of knowledge than business schools to fields of action, which will complete the isolation of the schools.

It is noticeable already that many large European and U.S. companies are moving in this direction, or have already created their own business schools to serve their own management development needs. As Figure 31.2 indicates, there is a stern logic behind such decisions that links manager development to the wider corporate aims. From this standpoint, the business school can be and mostly is seen as a peripheral resource, a place where occasionally a company-trained manager can meet briefly with managers from other companies to broaden his perspective. Some companies regard the schools as sources of possible faculty for company programs designed by company trainers. This can be a profitable sideline for faculty of business schools. This is not a healthy development; what is needed instead is a partnership that will join the strengths of company management with the strengths of business school faculty. In this way both enhance their competence via joint diagnosis and resolution of company problems. In Manchester we have developed a flexible vehicle for accomplishing this, which we describe as the "joint development activity." This, and other modes of joint work, will now be briefly described and exemplified.

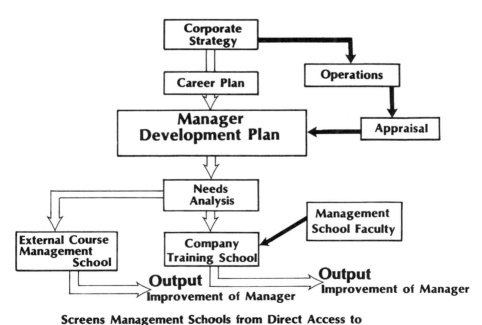

FIGURE 31.2. Schematic Showing Logic of In-Company Management Development

Modes of Joint Work

Work that links fields of knowledge and fields of action can range from action learning to individual faculty consultancy, via joint program and curriculum design. This includes: action learning, action research, organizational development (in its various forms), joint development activities, "live" student projects, joint program design, and consulting work. Some of these, particularly action research and organizational development, have resulted in scholarly publication, so that as well as being joint ventures, they satisfy traditional academic purposes.

Action Learning

It is hardly surprising that innovation in the development of useful knowledge for managers, and of assistance putting it to use, has not been in general part of the institutional role of business schools. This is due to the organization structures and reward systems of university business schools. Take, for example, action learning as developed by Revans (1980). Action learning rests on the proposition that managers learn best by the experience of doing things, but do not usually have the time, the habit, or the inclination to extract all the learning that is possible; nor have they normally the diagnostic tools to accomplish explicit learning. Action learning claims to inculcate in managers the skill of learning how to learn while they are making a useful practical contribution.

The process of action learning detaches individual managers (or small groups) from their own organization to work on a problem in some other organization or some other part of their own after having been instructed by academic specialists in the investigative and diagnostic skills needed. The "host" will expect the problem to be solved. The participant will expect to be of practical help in that way, as well as developing personally from the experience.

In the 1960s Revans found business schools unreceptive and left his university job. Some large British companies in recent years have adopted his method, for example, General Electric Company (Casey & Pearce, 1977). Only a handful of business school faculty (as individuals) have ever been involved fully in action research. One very good reason why is that when confronted with a choice of helping managers to use received knowledge to solve problems and improve on it in the process, where there are no obvious career rewards, or publishing papers that will accumulate career points, the academics will make the obvious choice.

Action Research

Action researchers identify themselves with the practical problems of a client (Clarke, 1972). Their investigations are designed to help the client to work toward a sharper focus on the problem and an understanding of the setting in which it has arisen. Participants from the "client system" are usually involved in the processes of fact-finding and diagnosis, and in the discovery, monitoring, and implementation of solutions.

The discovery and development of action research was not due directly to any business school faculty. It happened independently, mainly in the Tavistock Institute where it was derived from clinical psychology and social anthropology (Lewin, 1951; Trist et al., 1963; Jaques, 1957; Rice, 1963). Although action research has been fruitful in developing the open socio-technical systems approach to organization diagnosis and prognosis, serious action research followed by published results is still rare in business schools, although there are good examples (Lupton and Tanner, 1980). One explanation for the unpopularity of this kind of work among academics is that it does not respect discipline boundaries. It also places the researcher in a context that is not easily amenable to control, requires the skills to manage social process, and limits the possibilities for the quasiscientific experimental work so beloved of the referees and editors of academic journals. Empirical work leading eventually to practical procedures for problem solving, a milder form of action research, is a little more common (CS. Lupton and Gowler, 1969; Lupton and Tanner, 1981).

Organizational Development

When organizational development is defined as a deliberate, designed process that will radically change organizational structures and cultures in pursuit of some desired end (such as efficiency of resource use, employee satisfaction, or flexibility), experience shows the need for some intervention from outside. Indeed, there is a literature that shows this is exactly what has happened (Lupton et al., 1974; Argyris, 1970; Warmington et al., 1977). Even more than action research, organizational development is usually a very lengthy process, full of uncertainties, where the links between the process and the outcomes are difficult to establish—not exactly the best form of academic research when time is short and the rewards unpredictable. However, some business school faculty have become involved as consultants in these processes of organizational change. They have not been adopted, to my knowledge, as a rewardable institutional activity in business schools.

Joint Development Activity

The joint development activity (JDA), which is in some ways akin to the action learning developed by John Morris of the Manchester Business School and is much used there as a pedagogical method, combines individual management development with organizational development in four stages:

Stage 1. *In Company*. Company senior management, working closely with senior business school faculty, define a list of salient company problems. The company selects a group of younger managers to join the JDA.

Stage 2. *At Business School* (four or five days). Senior managers discuss the problems they have selected with the younger managers chosen for the program. The company managers then explore the resources available in the business school. The problems are then shaped into projects that small groups can work on. Business school resources are identified and attached to the groups. Project plans are drawn up.

Stage 3. *At the Company* (three to six months). Young managers return to the company. They meet to work on their projects perhaps one day a week during company time, and they are given access to the data they need. They also know that they can telephone the business school for help and can use its facilities as they reasonably wish. (During Stage 3 there may be short project review sessions of one or two days at the business school or in the company.)

Stage 4. *At Company* (one day). Project findings and recommendations are presented to the senior management of the company, during which the contributions of business school and its faculty are frankly assessed.

JDAs result in internal company reports that are often analytically rigorous as well as of practical utility. They are hardly ever of general scholarly interest or located in a single discipline field. It is notorious that academics in the search for generality weave increasingly abstract and complex thought patterns of dubious utility—and are rewarded for it. Managers in the search for problem solutions work with real complexity at very low levels of abstraction. They seek the simplest solution that makes purposive and responsible action possible. The only published work on JDAs describes and comments on the process (not the outcomes) as observed by the participants, and lacks the objectivity that comes of being a relaxed observer and not a beleaguered participant (Lupton et al., 1977).

Live Projects

At the Manchester Business School, the MBA programs and the taught part of the doctoral program are project based and not based on a course of lectures or cases; most projects in the second year of the MBA program are "live" projects. The typical Manchester project has three stages.

First, students learn ideas and skills to use on the project. Second, they carry out the project. In a live project they do it for a client, on the client's premises, on a problem of real interest to the client. Third, reports are prepared for the faculty for grading, in which the use of theoretical ideas and research methods is under test. The client is given practical solutions to his problem, usually in a separate presentation.

The setting up, administration, supervision, and evaluation of projects is extremely time-consuming business—and has no pay off in publications and erodes time that could be used for the conventional research that produces quick and frequent publication in refereed journals.

Joint Program Designs

Like JDAs and student projects, joining faculty with client organizations to produce program designs that are appropriate to the development needs of particular populations of managers and management specialists is a fascinating pursuit. It offers intense mental and social stimulation and intrinsic job satisfaction, but no publications and no career rewards.

FIELD OF KNOWLEDGE RESEARCH

It does not follow from my argument that there is no place for field of knowledge research. In business schools we ought not to be concerned only with the practical use of received knowledge, but also with the development of new knowledge. My plea is only that we should seek more opportunities to derive field of knowledge research problems from the study of practical questions.

Research and development activities appropriate to the mission of business schools to balance effectively the claims of rigor and relevance fall into three overlapping categories: professionally relevant activities; contributions to fields of knowledge derived from relevant activities; and field of knowledge research on problems derived from fields of knowledge. It goes without saying that they all ought to be carried out equally rigorously.

The criterion of relevance is well satisfied by the first category, many examples of which have already been given. The overlap with the second category arises when, for example, action research leads not only to practical prescriptions for improvement but also to the publication of ideas that enrich fields of knowledge. A beautiful example of this is the study of technical innovation in British coal mines (Trist and Bamforth, 1951). In the field of organization design, one thinks particularly of the work of Argyris (1967).

The second category includes examples where the initial reason for investigating an organization is a practical difficulty, where the work is financed by the client with the problem, but the outcome is a model to explain the causes of the difficulty and to predict the consequences of remedial action, which appears to have wide generality and to be testable in other settings. One example is Gowler's work, which began as an investigation of a specific case of high labor turnover and produced much multidisciplinary scholarly work, a theory of the regressive spiral in labor markets, and a contribution to occupational role theory (Gowler, 1969; Gowler and Legge, 1971–72; Tainio, 1977a and 1977b). Tom Burns's work, which contributed significantly to organization theory, began as an investigation of the possibilities of siting high technology plants in areas of declining traditional heavy industry in the United Kingdom (Burns & Stalker, 1961).

The third category describes what is usually done in academe generally and in university business schools. It is hardly necessary to cite many examples. The internationally known work of the Aston group in organization theory (Pugh & Hickson 1976) did not originate with a desire to resolve a particular practical difficulty for a client. The object was rather to take the emerging contingency theory of organization beyond vague assertions that "it all depends" and to discover ways of characterizing and measuring accurately the differences between organizations, and of examining the significance of these differences for organization performance. The work of Lawrence and Lorsch (1967) had a similar objective, a different methodology, and equally interesting outcomes. Of course, work such as this could be utilized when trying to resolve practical difficulties, but it was not designed explicitly to do so. Woodward's work, which really launched the contingent approach to the relation of organization design and organization performance, is on the overlap between categories 2 and 3. It arose out of dissatisfaction with the classical prescriptive writers such as Fayol (1949) and Urwick (1943), and with a practical concern with the design of organizations for high performance (Woodward 1965).

THE ORGANIZATION STRUCTURE OF BUSINESS SCHOOLS

Business schools that are organized in traditional ways find it difficult to conceive, set up, and carry out research and development work of the first two categories. This is one reason why in Manchester we have continually experimented with new organizational forms designed to facilitate interchanges across the boundaries of business schools and other organizations, which makes us very different from the traditional university school. Figure 31.3 shows (in only slight caricature) the traditional business school organization. The significant interfaces are those between departments of specialists and the fields of knowledge that those specialists cultivate and harvest. Courses of lectures and cases are made up of building blocks from single disciplines, and in the teaching programs the building blocks are the disciplines themselves. Students come in directly from other schools and

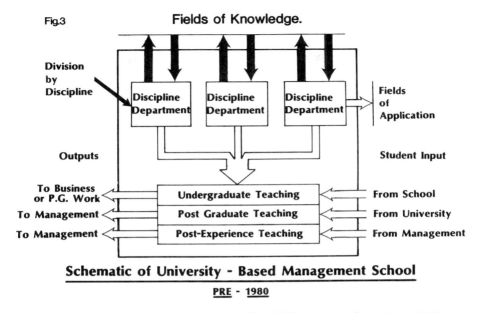

FIGURE 31.3. Schematic of University-Based Management School, Pre-1980.

universities where this form of activity is familiar, and graduate later into fields of action. The modes of learning in fields of action are very different indeed, and in carryover the ex-student has to find practical ways of joining the rigor with the relevance fruitfully, a task for which his previous training gives him few skills. Some say that the case study performs this function. I believe it to be, on the contrary, a brilliant device for isolating the classroom from problems in real life and real time, and for distancing the teacher from the students.

In the traditional structure, the links with fields of action can only be through the individual consulting work of faculty, or by using organizations as sources of data for cases or for field of knowledge research. Sometimes practitioners are invited into the classroom, where for the most part they are not very much at home nor very effective because the rules of the game are written by and for the scholars.

Our solution at Manchester to the organization structure problem evolved and is still evolving from our innovative style of discovering and organizing processes for learning, such as the live project and the JDA. Sixteen years ago we set our faces firmly against establishing discipline departments as the main organizing principle of the school. We organized by task instead, and we derived the tasks in the process of relating to fields of

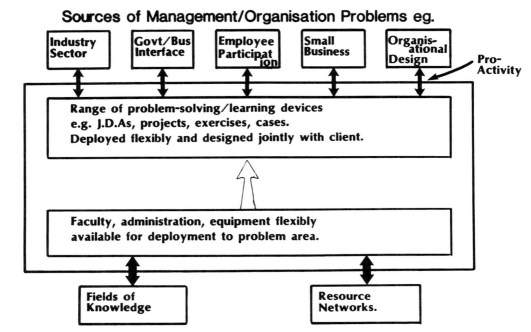

FIGURE 31.4. Schematic of any Management School, Post-1980.

action. The faculty and other resources to pursue the tasks are enlisted by personal negotiation between program directors (who are faculty on job rotation) and individual faculty members. All faculty members are encouraged to start and to direct new programs. With a lively faculty, all this is a recipe for generating variety and that is what has happened. To handle the variety we started to group activities of similar kinds into centers, each relating to its own fields of action and each with its own director with a high degree of autonomy. At that point it occurred to us that if what we were doing were further developed, it could be a general answer to the problem of linking rigor and relevance. These general ideas are illustrated in Figure 31.4.

At the top of Figure 31.4 are some possible types of interface with the fields of action. The units of organization (our centers) are shown as proactively relating each to its own part of the field of action, and, as the double-headed arrows show, developing its own materials and methods for doing that job effectively. The materials and methods are also derived from fields of knowledge as faculty are deployed flexibly to the changing tasks deriving from fields of action, and as resources for the tasks are enlisted from outside the school through "knowledge networks," wherever they may be.

Since 1980 we have moved rapidly to consolidate an organization pattern based on that general idea. We have six centers now. Our international banking center is related to a particular industry and companies in it. Our small business center deploys expertise about new enterprises and small ones. Our executive development center meets a particular need for residential courses for managers drawn from many sectors. The language learning center at MBS was set up to meet an urgent current demand in international operations. The graduate center is devoted to the task of preparing young people for managerial careers via master and doctoral programs. Finally, our new development consortium is devoted to experimentation with ways of linking fields of knowledge and fields of action, and is headed by John Morris, who introduced the JDA idea in the United Kingdom.

The teaching faculty are all located in the graduate center, and are a cost to that center. Other centers negotiate faculty into their programs at a transfer price, and all faculty are available to all centers. All centers are cost centers, and are normally expected to earn a surplus year upon year, which is transferred to a central fund to finance the general facilities that service them all: audiovisual, computer, printing, library, and so forth. The central fund also supports field of knowledge research, research of a fundamental kind. Research specifically directed to particular fields of action is funded from the earnings of the relevant center.

The variety that such a system generates demands an open, democratic, and flexible set of coordinating procedures and styles, a culture, and participative ways of defining acceptable strategic and tactical directions. Like most organizations, we are better at dividing things up than getting them together. However, we are aware of the need for organization "glue," and we are busy manufacturing it for our special purposes.

THE EFFECTIVENESS OF BUSINESS SCHOOLS

The answer to our third question—How is effectiveness to be measured?—is by now fairly obvious. If the efforts of schools and their faculty are directed to fields of action, then the criterion of success must be how those efforts contribute to the resolution of the problems that have been jointly defined and tackled in those fields of action, as in the JDA and the live project—where outcomes are known. The test must also be how well the research in fields of knowledge can be deployed in problem definition and resolution, for example, in action research, where the researcher is concerned with solving his client's problems and adding to scholarly output at the same time. In a business school, the sole criterion can never be the volume of papers published in refereed journals, although that can be one measure among many.

There are many problems about careers and rewards involved in the organizational "tilt" toward fields of action that we have made in Manchester. We are still trying to solve them. To describe what they are, however, and how they might be resolved would take me beyond the limited scope of this chapter.

REFERENCES

Argyris, Chris
1967 "Todays problems with tomorrow's organisations" *Journal of Management Studies* 4, pp. 31–55.
1970 *Intervention Theory and Method, A Behavioural Science View.* New York: Addison-Wesley.
Boyatzis, S.
1982 *Competent Manager.* New York: John.
Burns, Tom & Stalker, G. M.
1961 *The Management of Innovation.* London: Tavistock.
Casey, D., and Pearce, D.
1977 *More than Management Development: Action Learning at GEC.* London: Gower Press.
Clarke, P. A.
1972 *Action Learning: New Techniques for Management.* London: Blond and Briggs.
Fayol, Henri
1916 *Administration industielle et generales.* Paris: Dunod.
1949 Translated as *General and Industrial Management.* London: Pitman.
Gordon, R. A., and Howells, J. E.
1959 *Higher Education for Business.* New York: Columbia U.P.
Gowler, Dan
1969 "The determinants of the supply of labour to the firm." *Journal of Management Studies* 6, pp. 73–95.
Gowler, Dan., and Legge, Karen
1971– *Occupational Role Development* I & II *Personal Review*, Vol. I. pp. 12, 58.
  72
Horne, J. H., and Lupton, T.
1965 "The work activities of 'middle' managers: an exploratory study." *Journal of Management Studies* Vol. 2, pp. 14–33.
Jaques, E.
1957 *The Changing Culture of a Factory.* London: Tavistock.
Lawrence, Paul R., and Lorsch, Jay W.
1967 *Organisation and Environment.* Harvard Business School, Division of Research.
Lewin, Kurt
1951 *Field Theory in Social Science.* London: Tavistock.
Lupton, T., Berry, A. J., and Warmington, A.
1977 The Contribution of a Business School to a Joint Development Activity. *Management Education and Development 7.*

Lupton, T., and Gowler, D.
1969   *Selecting a Wage Payment System.* Engineering Employers Federation. Research Paper 3.

Lupton, T., and Tanner, I.
1980   "A self-regulating structure at plant level." *Personnel Review* 9, 21–26.

Lupton, T., and Tanner, I.
1981   "Organisational change for productivity improvement." *Proc. Int Conference. European Federation of Productivity Services. Zurich.*

Lupton, T., Warmington, A., and Clayton, T.
1974   "Organisational development at pilkingtons." *Personnel Review* 3, pp. 4–7.

Mintzberg, Henry
1973   *The Nature of Managerial Work.* New York: Harper and Row.

Pugh, D. S., and Hickson, D. J.
1976   *Organisational Structure in its Context.* London: Saxon House.

Revans, R. W.
1980   *Action Learning: New Techniques for Management.* London: Blond and Briggs.

Rice, A. K.
1963   *The Enterprise and its Environment.* London: Tavistock.

Tainio, Risto
1977a   *Determinants of Labour Turnover in a Firm.* Helsinki: Helsinki School of Economics.
1977b   *Research on the Factors Associated with the Propensity to Stay in an Organisation.* Helsinki School of Economics.

Trist, E. L., Higgin, G. W., Murray, H., and Pollock, A. B.
1963   *Organisational Choice.* London: Tavistock.

Trist, E. L., and Bamforth, K. W.
1951   "Some social and psychological consequences of the Longwell method of goal getting." *Human Relations* 4, p. 38.

Urwick, Lyndall, F.
1943   *Elements of Administration.* London: Pitman.

Warmington, A., Lupton, T., and Gribbin, G.
1977   *Organisational behaviour and performance.* London: Macmillan.

Woodward, Joan
1965   *Industrial Organisation.* Oxford University Press.

32

MATRIX ORGANIZATION DESIGNS TO PRODUCE USEFUL KNOWLEDGE

Harvey F. Kolodny

The late Fritz Roethlisberger used to advocate the involvement of faculty members in teaching, research, and consulting. He believed that all three were necessary to the task of becoming an effective academic. Rather than engage in a lengthy discussion of how one defines "effective" or what constitutes "relevant knowledge," I will confine myself to the term "useful knowledge," and state how I plan to use the term.

I would like to identify two classes of knowledge that might be generated within organization behavior, applied sociology, or similar university units that I will hereinafter refer to as "organization studies" groups. Both classes are essential to the advancement of the organization studies field. One class has immediate applicability to organizational problems, and I will refer to it as "useful" knowledge. The other class contributes to the development of a body of knowledge in the organization studies field, and I will refer to it as "developmental" knowledge. It may also have immediate applicability, but does not need to.

They are both necessary to the advancement of the field. On the one hand, the developmental knowledge class needs direction from the useful knowledge class to orient its activity (that is, to stay within the bounds of "organizational studies" and not wander too far afield into other areas such as psychology, sociology, anthropology, and so forth). On the other hand, the useful knowledge class needs new knowledge both to apply to current problem areas and to stimulate creative problem search, and it depends on the developmental knowledge class for this.

This chapter will discuss structural arrangements designed to change the balance that currently exists in the generation of useful knowledge versus developmental knowledge. However, a priori, it is necessary to emphasize that these two classes of knowledge are not contestants in an either-or

600

situation. The structural arrangements to be discussed here will foster an increase in the amount of useful knowledge, but these same arrangements will also maintain a high level of generation of developmental knowledge.

Like the matrix organization arrangements that will be advocated to foster advancing the two, the balance between the two is not seen as static. The balance must shift as the environment demands that it does. It is currently demanding more useful knowledge than we have had in the past. The matrix structures advocated here allow such shifts to take place within an ongoing organizational setting.

INDIVIDUAL OR ACTOR-LEVEL MODELS FOR GENERATING USEFUL KNOWLEDGE

Organizational studies groups have always produced individuals who have excelled in generating useful knowledge. For the most part, they seem to be academics who fit Professor Roethlisberger's model: they do research, they teach, and they consult. The assumption in this model is that the consulting experience keeps them close to organizational problems so that the direction of their research is, accordingly, more useful than developmental. There is some evidence, for example, that academics in teaching hospitals tend to have a perspective that is balanced between their multiple tasks of teaching, research, and practice (Charns, Lawrence, and Weisbord, 1977). Carrying out multiple tasks with very different orientations is, however, difficult. As a model, it has been satisfactory for some, but clearly not for enough, or else the field would not be striving for more of the outcomes that come from these few.

An alternative individual model is based on rotation. Medical students use it in their required internship program as well as in a system of being constantly exposed to more experienced practitioners through medical rounds. Rotation seems to be an effective training strategy because, of late, cooperative programs have become increasingly popular with employers (both cooperative programs in engineering degree programs and, to a lesser extent, the few that exist in commerce and MBA programs).

Rotation can also be achieved by having academics take a turn or spend a sabbatical year in industry, with industrial people doing the reverse. This occurs infrequently. A diluted form of this occurs more often when people change careers, as when people with an industrial background seek out new careers in academe and vice versa. The latter have no incentive to produce new knowledge, useful or developmental. The former should be able to make significant contributions, but too often come under the influence of a reward system that devalues their previous experience and credits developmental knowledge only.

It would be desirable to implement a kind of rotation or internship program into doctoral students' programs of organizational studies to foster more useful knowledge generation. However, this would extend an already too lengthy study program. Given current economic conditions with limited doctoral student funding, this appears to be an unlikely development.

STRUCTURAL ARRANGEMENTS TO GENERATE USEFUL KNOWLEDGE

Are there structural arrangements that can achieve the integrative effects that occur in academic "superstars" who generate useful research as a result of their simultaneous exposure to teaching, research, and consulting orientations? If we examine our current concepts about academic organizations as loosely coupled enterprises (Weick, 1976), they do not appear well adapted to the task of producing useful knowledge, except through the individual superstar route. In maintaining their independence through loose coupling, many academic units are also decoupled from their application areas. It is not surprising that so many practitioners consider the professional faculties where their field is studied to be "ivory-towered" (Overing, 1973).

More useful knowledge has to mean tighter coupling between the problem domains or application areas and the academic institutions. But tighter coupling may destroy the valued and valuable independence that has allowed developmental knowledge to flourish. Can you have tighter coupling, increase useful knowledge as a result, and not harm developmental knowledge generation? If you can, what are the resulting problems?

More formal matrix designs than the loose matrix structures that now prevail in many business schools are proposed here as a structural solution. Some of the inevitable dysfunctions associated with this formalization will also be identified. However, it would be desirable to precede this discussion with a brief overview of the environmental conditions that have set the stage for making this proposal reasonable. They are conditions similar to the ones that have driven many other organizational sectors to begin wholesale adoption of matrix designs (Davis and Lawrence, 1977).

THE CONDITIONS FOR MATRIX ORGANIZATION

The amount of new knowledge in the behavioral sciences has increased enormously in the last few years. Teachers in the field find themselves harder pressed every year to contain within a course the minimally required introductory knowledge needed even to introduce the field to students. There always seems to be too many good new concepts and theories that just have to be included. Some of the new knowledge is in application areas or within the useful knowledge domain (such as Japanese management, new human resources management programs, job and organization design experiences) and some lies in the developmental knowledge classification (social learning theories, population ecology models, resource dependence explanations, and attributions theory).

Both classes of knowledge seem to be important to the advancement of the field. Both vie for places in the curricula of courses and programs. Faculty are torn between whether to add more applied courses (such as human resources management) to attract large numbers of business students away from finance and marketing electives, or whether to add more seminar-type electives that will introduce new concepts in the field (such as the effects of decision-making theories of organization on the behavior of middle managers) to particularly interested organizational studies students who wish to explore these more deeply. They worry that should they choose one orientation, they will have to pay heavily in the other in the longer run.

In effect, two of the conditions for matrix organization design are described above (Lawrence, Kolodny, and Davis, 1977): two orientations are simultaneously important (useful and developmental knowledge) and there are high information-processing requirements (as faculty cope with the number of new content areas, the rate at which knowledge in them is changing and the impact new knowledge has on existing content areas).

The third condition for matrix organizations refers to the need to share resources—a need particularly important in times when academic budgets are being cut or, at best, maintained constant while faculties are expected to deliver the same services or even increase the services offered. This can be accomplished only by more extensive sharing of faculty resources: across disciplinary areas (the purer disciplines and the professional schools); across concentration areas (being asked to teach both micro and macro courses or both skills-training workshops and personnel administration techniques); and across teaching areas (day and evening classes; undergraduate classes through to Ph.D. seminars).

If these are the conditions for matrix, they would appear to exist in the current situations in academic institutions—particularly in business schools. It is not surprising that many business schools already believe themselves somewhat structured in matrix format. The practical experience of matrix organizations suggests that the form will work best in those settings where some of it already exists; this is because the particular environments have been demanding it for some time and shaping these organizations accordingly.

How would more formal matrix designs in business schools help produce more useful knowledge? How would they shift the balance between useful and developmental knowledge to put more emphasis on the former? How would they ensure that both orientations would be maintained? What would such structures look like?

MATRIX STRUCTURES IN BUSINESS SCHOOLS

The last question is the hardest to answer because there is not too much well-documented experience. I can speculate from my own experience with matrix organizations in other sectors and attempt to translate that experience to business school settings. Figures 32.1, 32.3, and 32.4 will help with this explanation of what a formal matrix in a business school might look like. Figures 32.1, 32.2, and 32.3 describe the operating structure of a typical business school faculty. Figure 32.4 outlines the governance structure.

Figure 32.1 illustrates the teaching operations. Faculty in the various disciplinary areas are usually assigned to several programs, simultaneously offering their functional competence to particular courses taught within the curricula of the different programs.

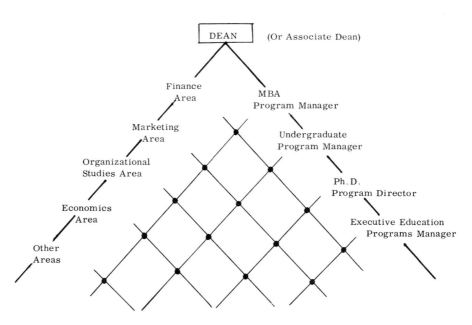

FIGURE 32.1. Teaching Structure

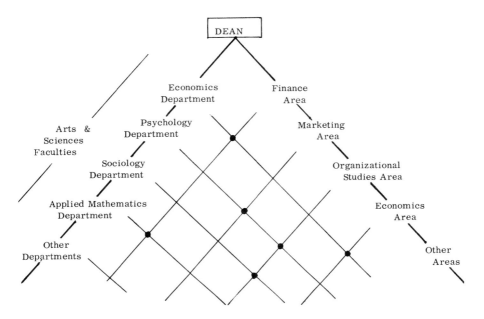

FIGURE 32.2. Developmental Knowledge Diagram

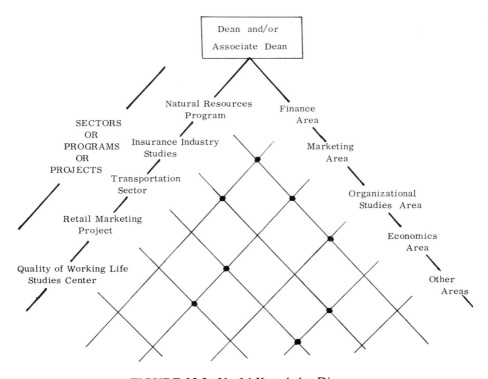

FIGURE 32.3. Useful Knowledge Diagram

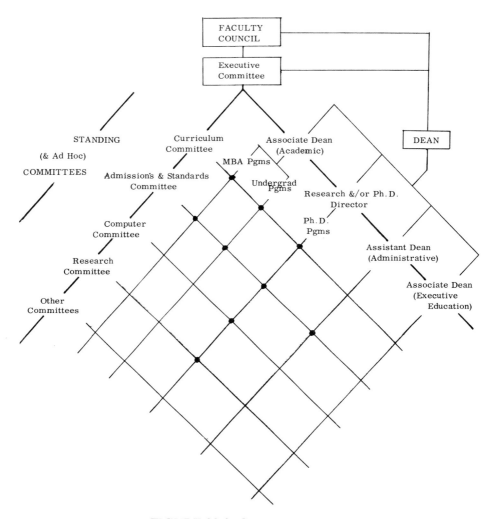

FIGURE 32.4. Governance Structure

Formalizing this aspect of the matrix probably means making the program management roles more formal than they may have been in the past (if they existed at all). Not only are program managers given credit for carrying out the program management task (such as via teaching course releases), but they should be held accountable for performance within the program. This can mean minimizing hassles (reducing student complaints, handling grievances over scheduling, assignments, room allocations, and so forth) and improving performance (more contact with potential employers to improve employment prospects, better utilization of faculty).

Holding program managers accountable for performance probably means long-term assignments as well as subjective, but previously agreed upon, criteria in addition to the objective ones that can be identified. It is a necessary thing to do, because only by holding program managers accountable will they, in turn, make demands for higher performance from the disciplinary areas (such as re-assigning a poor teacher). It is a tough role because the program manager is also, usually, a full-time member of one of the disciplinary areas.

Figures 32.2 and 32.3 are illustrated as matrix operations but are only partially so. Figure 32.2 represents the developmental knowledge operations. The cross-disciplinary ties tend to be few. For example, only marketing and organizational studies would likely interact with the psychology faculty. As such, the matrix representation tends to be both very informal and, to a large extent, overstated.

Figure 32.3 represents the useful knowledge operations. This diagram is the one most directed at the problem of increasing useful knowledge. By focusing on one or several specific sectors (or "majors" or "concentrations") or problem areas, the issue of directing disciplinary areas toward producing useful knowledge is confronted directly. The faculty must decide on the criteria it wishes to establish to allow a sector or problem area to become relevant. Table 32.1 lists some possible criteria. The choice will depend on the institution, its location with respect to industries and institutions that might hire its graduates or support its research, the availability of state, municipal, or federal funds that might be committed to a particular problem, the interests of the faculty, and so forth.

The choice of problem areas or sectors is crucial for a faculty. Each choice probably constitutes a long-term commitment. Each will affect the faculty's reputation over time, so the thinking about problem areas must take into account how the faculty's work in these areas will be desseminated, what it will mean for the recruitment of new faculty, new students, and, possibly, attendance at executive training programs. Furthermore, each faculty is resource limited and cannot assume more than a few problem areas or sectors. By choosing some and not choosing others, the faculty runs the risk of alienating both external resources and existing resources (for example, faculty who have their own unique interest that can not be applied to any of the chosen problem areas).

The strength of the design for fostering increased useful knowledge is related to several things: first, the ability to find enough interested faculty, preferably from different disciplinary areas, to want to commit to a problem area—because the objective is to accumulate considerable knowledge about the problem area so that, over time, the faculty earns the right to consider

TABLE 32.1. Some Criteria for a Sector or Problem Area or Program

1. The "useful knowledge" area(s) selected should be able to attract a reasonably long-term commitment (at least five years) from a "core" of faculty (preferably one or several with high status in the institution). The greater the number of faculty areas involved the better. Broad involvement can also be achieved by allowing some people to commit to a "network" of interest (that is, a kind of secondary interest that comprises a lower level of commitment than the core people promise).
2. The sector or problem area or program should probably have considerable local environment or regional interest if it is to be attractive to students as well as to resources. This does not discount selecting an interest area that is also national or international in scope. To attract a reasonable cross-section of faculty it may be necessary to compromise on some local interests (but this can have important long-term implications, for example, for developing local issue management-training programs or local issue-oriented pedagogical materials). It also depends on the institution's location with respect to local industry or business or government departments or institutions or even local problems (such as, unemployment or underdevelopment).
3. The useful knowledge sector or problem area or program selected will almost certainly have to be, or have the potential to be, self-financing. More significant, it should be selected to have the capacity to grow and spin off funds for use in the developmental knowledge areas. This is one of the areas that local versus national or international issues come in conflict with because larger resource pools tend to address more national than local issues.
4. The "useful knowledge" area(s) selected should be areas with which the faculty would like to be identified over the next decade (including those faculty who may not wish a particularly active role in a sector).
5. Sectors or problem areas or programs selected should provide future employment for the institution's graduates.
6. The areas chosen should be potentially attractive to faculty from other departments in the university (although this depends on how much value the institution places on cross-disciplinary faculty relations within the university or, possibly, between universities).
7. The sector or problem area should violate no university of faculty standards or ethics or guidelines (for example, some industries might only financially support activities that would give course credit to their managers, many of whom might not otherwise meet graduate school entry standards).

Note: This list is a sample list. Each faculty must develop its own criteria. More significant, "buying in" to the concept is a critical process and total faculty involvement is an important way to either buy in or to establish the constraints on what is acceptable to the institution as a whole.

itself expert in the problem area (for only then will resources become more easily available); second, the ability to pick a problem area where the need for the kinds of resources the faculty possesses is strong and where the faculty actually has relevant knowledge (in its developmental knowledge classification) that can be brought to bear; third, meaningfulness and challenge in the problem area that both students and faculty will find of high interest, so that the capacity to develop teams of researchers, case writers, interviewers, and so on is maintained.

Figure 32.3 is a matrix configuration. It suggests that a manager for each problem area or sector will be needed to oversee the "team" activity. It is likely that the activities within the team will often be more individual than team oriented, in keeping with academic work habits. But the conditions for occasional joint activity will still exist, and cooperative endeavors are more likely in this model than in more traditional models.

Some illustrations might help clarify Figure 32.3. My own faculty in Toronto has had a natural resources program for several years. Several natural resources companies, particularly oil companies, have funded this program with medium-sized grants renewed at three-year intervals. The money is used for several purposes. It contributes toward the salaries of two faculty members who research the finance and economic aspects of the petroleum industry. They have conducted studies, written reports, and supervised the writing of cases in these areas. Many of these materials find their way back into the courses taught by these faculty and, as the better material has become known, into courses taught in other universities. The material is timely and of local relevance, so it is of high interest to the students.

The money in the program has also been used to provide part-time and summer work for MBA and Ph.D. students as case writers. It has also been used to fund some studies in other natural resource areas, for example, a study of mechanical harvesting work groups in the woodlands area of the forest products industry.

Over time, there has been enough interest and material stimulated and developed that the faculty now offers a course in the marketing of natural resources. It also devotes a substantial portion of some of the finance course to natural resources projects financing.

Another example illustrates how a new sector is developed in the faculty. One faculty member, working with a government department, learned of an interest the government had in studying small business success and failure. The dean found several faculty members with an interest in the subject and organized them into a legally constituted "consulting organization," with shares owned by all interested faculty members (at a one dollar nominal subscription), to bid on a $250,000 contract to carry out such a study. They won the contract, conducted the study, and they and the client are pleased with the result.

Small business is beginning to be a concentration area in the faculty. The contract spun off a pool of new research dollars for the faculty and promised some nice paid research time for quite a few of the faculty and some of the students. The "consortium" (with some different members, as appropriate) has now bid on another similar study. It has been one of the more successful cooperative faculty endeavors. Perhaps because it was successful, the faculty member who served as project leader has won some overdue recognition from colleagues that serves as reward on the "useful knowledge" side. He won that for several reasons: by managing the project well; by providing resources (research money) to the developmental knowledge side; and by developing a good relationship for the faculty with an important external organization. Many of these skills tend to go unrecognized in most traditionally oriented faculties.

Figure 32.4 illustrates the governance structure of the business school depicted in Figures 32.1, 32.2, and 32.3. It is likely that the governance structure will want an active voice in the choice of problem areas or sectors since the long-term impact on the faculty is so significant.

SUPPORT SYSTEMS

The structural arrangements are simple to draw. The support systems are more difficult to establish. Traditional academic reward systems will work against those who want to spend much of their time in the problem areas. Their outputs are more likely to be reports and case studies than traditional academic articles. If the reward system is to be modified to recognize their activity, what should it consider? The quality of the reports and case studies clearly should be considered, but the judging is bound to be more subjective than conventional academic refereeing. Will the system allow that? The client's (problem area's?) satisfaction is also an indicator of accomplishment. However, an important indicator must be the attitudes of the developmental knowledge side of the organization. The purpose of the exercise is to integrate developmental and useful knowledge, to apply developmental knowledge, to offer useful knowledge problems for developmental knowledge resolution, and direction for further study. The reward system will be a difficult one to implement.

So will the role structure. It is too easy in academe to create two classes of citizens, with those in the useful knowledge class categorized as second class. It demands that some people with high profiles in the developmental knowledge areas take active roles, as role models, in some problem areas if equal role status is to be maintained in the two knowledge classes.

In industrial settings that have matrix designs, the matrix is made to work primarily by having functional managers become proactive and go to project managers to help them carry out their tasks (Kolodny, 1981). It is no less an issue here. The useful/developmental knowledge matrix in a business school will work best if key faculty with reputations in the developmental side of the discipline take at least occasional, but active, roles in useful knowledge activities.

SOME POTENTIAL PROBLEMS

This proposal presents some difficulties for people accustomed to a more independent, more individualistic way of working. It requires more interaction between people—but not so much as to make it unrealistic. It still allows people to carry on relatively independently within their discipline, but does demand their occasional willingness to cooperate with, if not others on the faculty, at least other members of their own discipline who have chosen to work in the more applied useful knowledge area.

The proposal also makes it clear that people will be rewarded for more than one kind of research and publication. That, too, may be unacceptable to some. Because it can shift the balance of emphasis in the faculty, an overzealous dean who uses the desire to shift the balance in a heavy-handed way can make the atmosphere unacceptable to those who wish to maintain a strong developmental knowledge orientation. As with all matrix organizations, the person at the top must understand the operation of the matrix system intimately and know exactly how to balance power.

There is only limited experience with formal matrix designs in academic settings. It is not known, as yet, whether a person who chooses to spend some time in the useful knowledge domain can return comfortably to the developmental knowledge domain. It depends a lot on the person's particular field of expertise and the rate at which that knowledge in that field is changing.

CONCLUSION

The useful knowledge matrix model proposed here is not novel. Many schools utilize some aspect(s) of it, but few recognize the structure openly. As such, they often forego opportunities to improve its functioning because they understand it only a little.

The model can foster more useful knowledge generation because: it concentrates faculty resources on a particular problem area or sector; it brings diverse resources to bear on the problem (and diversity is often held to be a condition for creative problem solving [Maier, 1970]); it singles out an individual to manage the activity in the area; it maintains existing orientations and allows strengths in developmental areas to carry on; it attempts to integrate new activities with existing ones rather than create separate activities that might divide the faculty.

Matrix organizations have always been difficult to manage and there is no reason to believe they would be less difficult to manage in academic settings. Academic institutions, including business schools, are not known for their abilities to manage and administer. If business schools have been slow to formalize their informal matrix arrangements, it may be because they could not do any better.

There is some preliminary evidence that matrix designs and high rates of new product and process innovation go hand-in-hand (Kolodny, 1980). If the obstacles to implementing more formal matrix structures in business schools can be overcome, the area that might benefit most from the new innovation might be the useful knowledge generation area.

REFERENCES

1977   Charns, Martin P., Lawrence, Paul R., and Weisbord, Marwin. Organizing Multiple-Function Professionals in Academic Medical Centers. In Paul C. Nystrom and William H. Starbuck (eds). Prescriptive Models of Organizations. TIMS Studies in Management Sciences. Amsterdam.

1977   Davis, Stanley M. and Lawrence, Paul R. *Matrix*. Reading, Mass.: Addison-Wesley.

1980   Kolodny, Harvey F. Matrix Organization Designs and New Product Success. *Research Management*, 23(5), 29–33.

1981   Kolodny, Harvey F. Managing in a Matrix. *Business Horizons*. 24(2), 17–24.

1977   Lawrence, Paul R., Kolodny, Harvey F., and Davis, Stanley M. The Human Side of the Matrix. *Organizational Dynamics*, 6(1), 43–61.

1970   Maier, N. R. F. Problem Solving and Creativity in Individuals and Groups. Belmont, Calif.: Brooks/Cole.

1973   Overing, Robert. Toward a Redefinition of Teacher Education. *Interchange*. 4(2/3): 19–27.

1976   Weick, Karl Educational Organizations as Loosely Coupled Systems, *Administrative Science Quarterly*, 21:1–18.

33

CREATING USEFUL RESEARCH WITH ORGANIZATIONS: RELATIONSHIP AND PROCESS ISSUES

Susan Albers Mohrman, Thomas G. Cummings, and Edward E. Lawler, III

WHAT IS USEFUL INFORMATION?

Useful information can be defined as knowledge that serves an actor's purpose, such as contributing to decision making, guiding behaviors, and solving problems. This implies that usability of information can only be determined relative to particular users and their purposes. Consequently, two key questions must be clarified in addressing the usability issue: Useful for whom? Useful for what?

Useful for Whom?

Research endeavors generally have multiple stakeholders—individuals, groups, and other social aggregates who have a potential interest in the findings and the use to which they are put. Generally, one set of stakeholders resides in the research community and consists of researchers, research institutions, and academic disciplines. Another set comprises the user community and includes a myriad of people and groups who have a potential interest in research results, ranging from individuals and interest groups within organizations to the communities and societies within which organizations are embedded.

Rather than use sentence-by-sentence references, we would like to refer the reader to a small number of key references that support the thinking presented in this chapter. They include: Argyris, *Inner Contradictions of Rigorous Research* (New York: Academic Press, 1980); Emery, F. E., and Trist, E. L., *Towards a Social Ecology* (London: Plenum, 1972); Lewin, K., *Field Theory in Social Science* (New York: Harper and Row, 1951); Mitroff, I. I. *The Subjective Side of Science* (Amsterdam: Elsevier, 1974); and Watzlawick, P., Beavin, J., and Jackson, D. *Pragmatics of Human Communication* (New York: Norton. 1967).

Stakeholders judge the relevance of organizational research according to its perceived usefulness in contributing to valued outcomes. Stakeholder values define whether research findings are useful or useless; more implicitly, those values determine the initial choice of subject matter and methodology of research. Stakeholders in the research community typically derive their values from science, and they attempt to maximize those values through research that is scientifically rigorous and contributes to a body of fundamental knowledge. Within those overarching values, however, there is considerable diversity among researchers and disciplines as to the preferred form and content of research and the manner in which research should be used. Stakeholders in the user community generally derive their values from the social groups to which they belong and are committed, and research is supported and judged useful to the extent that it promotes those groups' values. To the extent that there is a diversity of stakeholder groups within organizations and their task environments, there are likely to be divergent judgments about whether research is useful or useless. Similarly, differences in stakeholder values between the research and user communities can be expected to generate conflict over the utility of research findings.

Useful for What?

In organizations, research can be considered useful if it contributes to learning. Generally, research findings promote organizational learning in two major ways: by helping organizational members gain a better understanding of the existing situation, and by providing information to guide organizational change. This suggests a distinction between research that is aimed at depicting the current state of organizations and research that is concerned with action. Moreover, action-oriented research can further be differentiated in terms of its relation to the existing situation or status quo. It can essentially accept the status quo and provide information to improve or refine it; alternatively, it can reject the current state and generate knowledge to transform it, or more generally, to learn how to change status quos. This latter distinction is of logical levels, where learning how to change states requires a higher level of knowledge than that needed to change from one organizational state to another.

The above discussion suggests that research can contribute to organizational learning in four distinct ways, which are illustrated in Figure 33.1. These contributions of organization research imply different research content, methodology, and usage patterns, as well as differences in the underlying values for judging the utility of research results. Perhaps most important, the four learning contributions suggest a wide diversity of research can be useful to organizations depending on the kind of organizational learning desired. Research that is competently conducted in any of the four

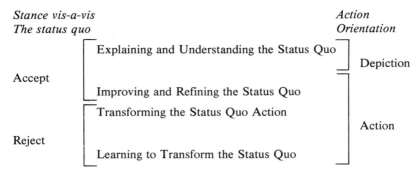

FIGURE 33.1. Useful for What?

categories is potentially useful to organizational stakeholders that share the orientation of the research.

WHY RESEARCH INFORMATION IS SEEN AS USEFUL

Most organizational researchers can locate their research efforts within one of the four usage patterns shown in Figure 33.1. Presumably, much of this research is competently executed, at least from a scientific perspective. Why, then, is there so much concern with usefulness? Apparently, organizations and concerned researchers do not perceive the products of organizational research as contributing to organizational learning. We propose that research will be useful to the extent that it is accepted by organizational members. To understand the linkage between acceptance and perceived utility, it is helpful to consider commonly voiced protests about academic research from organizational users. These protests typically embody several themes:

The legitimacy, competence, and intent of the researcher are questioned. Researchers are described as naive, ignorant of the "real world," biased by their own theories, and unaware of the trouble they cause.
The findings are discounted. They are perceived as ambiguous, overly negative, or irrelevant to the particular organization.
The importance of the study is questioned. Researchers are accused of examining unimportant issues, ignoring important variables, and discovering the obvious.
The presentation of the findings is attacked. It is seen as boring, full of jargon, poorly written, or too technical.

TABLE 33.1. Factors Affecting the Acceptance of Information

A. Attributes of the information itself
   1. Salience of Subject to User
   2. Credibility of Source
   3. Credibility of Data (Perceived Validity)
   4. Clarity of Presentation
   5. Value Congruence

B. Attributes of the feedback process
   6. Solicited
   7. Responsive to Perspective of Users
   8. Contains Ideas for How to Change
   9. Provides Choce

These criticisms clearly suggest that where usefulness is involved, research is judged on more than its technical scientific quality. Users do not look at the scientific adequacy of the research and then decide whether or not to use it.

Acceptance of research information is influenced by attributes of the information itself as well as by attributes of the communication process between researcher and user. Table 33.1 lists these factors. Five distinct attributes of the information are factors in user acceptance. The *salience of the content* to the user will determine whether the user is motivated to attend to the research results. Users generally are not aware of what the "hot" research issues are, and thus may not find the same research topics interesting as do researchers. *Source credibility* also has an impact on attention to information. The credibility of academics in the eyes of potential users is determined by the track record of the particular researcher and by the level of credibility attributed to academics in general. *Credibility of the data* and *clarity of presentation* can affect user willingness to accept research findings. Credibility and clarity must be judged relative to the sophistication of the user and the kind of information that is expected and valued. Sophisticated statistical treatment of quantified data may be compelling to certain audiences; however, other audiences may find it a distraction from the qualitative aspects of a situation. Audiences may judge validity using standards different from those used by the scientific community. Finally, people are more likely to attend to information that is *congruent with their values*. The orientation of the research to the status quo and its implied definition of effectiveness may conflict or fit with the values of major stakeholders in ways that directly determine acceptance of the research results.

The nature of the communication process between researcher and user can also impact user acceptance of research findings. Information provided by research may be experienced by organizational members as feedback about how the researchers have experienced the organization. Such data feedback can be expected to evoke defensive reactions similar to those evoked by interpersonal feedback unless it is presented skillfully. Organizational members are more likely to attend to research that is solicited, is sensitive to the way they view their world, provides ideas for change, and gives the receiver a sense of choice.

Much organizational research provides users with accounts of what organizations do wrong from an academic perspective, and suggests solutions abstractly from unclear implications for practice. Furthermore, much social science research is embedded in methodology and theory that views people as being reactive—as the recipients of social influence processes rather than as the initiators of change. Research is typically designed to preclude intentional subject influence over results; it also tends to utilize theory that views behavior as deterministic. Organizational researchers often depict organizational behavior as reactive, while judging it against rational, problem-solving standards. The implication is that researchers are able to exercise choice and solve problems, but subjects are not. This approach to research not only makes people appear foolish, but also leads researchers to view the utilization of "their knowledge" as a social influence challenge. Researchers are then faced with the dilemma: "How can we get organizations to solve problems utilizing the knowledge we have generated?"

In examining the characteristics of organizational research that can affect user acceptance of research information, only the first attribute in Table 33.1, "salience of the research topic," pertains to the actual content of research. The other characteristics relate to the values underlying the information and to the relationship between researcher and user. This suggests strongly that the reactivity of the research information itself has a major impact on whether that information is accepted as useful by organizations. So far, considerable attention has been directed at the reactivity of research methods in the social sciences, with relatively little concern for the reactivity of the research results. Because such reactivity is embedded in the relationship between researcher and user, the nature of that relationship impacts both the conduct of organizational research and whether the research findings are subsequently accepted as useful by organizational members.

ORGANIZATIONAL RESEARCH AS TEMPORARY INTERSYSTEM LINKAGE

Producing useful organizational knowledge often involves members of one organization (a university or research center) operating within another organization (a host or subject organization). To the extent that research requires cooperation between two or more organizations, intersystem linkages must be created and maintained. Within the context of those linkages, the relationship between the researcher, subject, and ultimate consumer of knowledge is defined, and the purpose and nature of the research are determined.

Temporary intersystem linkages established for organizational research have two major aspects: a *content* component that involves the specific research subject, methodology, and task, and a *relationship* aspect that includes the structures and processes that are necessary to create and sustain the social linkage between researcher and user organizations. Traditionally, researchers tend to focus on the content aspect of the linkage, particularly on the requirements for rigorous, publishable research. It is assumed that research that is not publishable cannot be disseminated, and information that is not disseminated is not useful. Concentration on content, however, cannot proceed independently of concern with the relationship part of the intersystem linkage. The very entry of researchers into an organization requires some negotiation, often done implicitly, about how the research will proceed and what is expected from both parties. Unfortunately, the criteria for such relationship decisions are often rather narrow, typically favoring the research organization. Research relationships are generally designed to disrupt minimally the host organization and to promote maximally the scientific integrity of the research content. It is not uncommon to find in such situations that many relationship issues are resolved superficially or simply ignored.

Failure to attend to the relationship aspect of organizational research can have negative consequences on both the research content and the subsequent utilization of the research by the user organization. It can result in incomplete exchange of information that may be vital to the researcher's understanding of the research content, and to an inadequate grasp by the researcher of the interests and needs of the host organization with respect to the study. Insufficient communication with organizational members can result in invalid and incomplete data; organizational members may not provide the researcher with open and complete information in the absence of a relationship based on mutual understanding and trust. Ill will, unmet expectations, and institutional stereotyping may result from a poor or ambiguous relationship between the researcher and host organization, leading to involuntary alterations in the research content or early termination of the research relationship.

Attention to the relationship aspect of organizational research can benefit both the research and organizational communities by contributing to scientific knowledge and by yielding practical learnings. Organizations are more likely to provide privileged and sensitive data and to commit the time and energy of organizational members if they feel they are receiving benefits in return. This requires a professional relationship between the researcher and the host organization, where the researcher provides services in return for privileged access to organizational data. Valid and complete information can be expected to the extent that organizational members trust that the researcher is acting in their interests. When trust is not present, organizational members generally feel that the researcher is mainly interested in publishing results, and by implication exposing organizational shortcomings. The anxiety inherent in that kind of relationship can be expected to conflict with the researcher's need to collect valid data.

Maintaining and nurturing the relationship part of research linkages is difficult for several reasons. First, the temporary nature of the intersystem leads both parties to try to minimize the time spent on the difficult process of establishing trust, common goals, and commitment. Second, research relationships generally include diverse values and interests. The institutional need of the research community to contribute to the larger, scientific body of knowledge may conflict with the need of the organization to obtain knowledge that can be put to immediate use. The career needs of the researcher—who is concerned with professional advancement—and of the user—who is concerned with organizational advancement—often conflict not only with each other, but also with the maximization of output of the temporary research system. These political issues tend to be smoothed over or ignored in organizational research. A third reason that intersystem linkages are difficult to maintain is that both researchers and organizational members tend to focus on the research content as the implicit "figure" in their linkage, with research relationship serving as the "ground." There is little precedent for reversing that perception and viewing the relationship aspect of organizational research as the key variable, even though it contributes heavily to research failures. The long-term maintenance of the interorganizational relationship may require as much or more time and attention than the research content of the linkage. Accepting this constitutes a significant redefinition of the researcher's tasks.

In summary, many of the critiques of organizational research result from the historical tendencies of researches and users to give insufficient attention to the intersystem context of their work.

Content Issues

Research content concerns the substantive and purposive component of the intersystem linkage—that is, its primary task or mission. Two questions asked earlier concern the two major dimensions of research content: For whom? For what? The answers to these questions affect directly the researcher and user relationship needed for providing useful knowledge, and must be dealt with early in the research process.

For Whom?

Despite the existence of multiple stakeholders in any research endeavor, most research is conducted to satisfy limited interests. Within the research community, basic researchers have generally pursued research to meet their own scientific needs, while applied researchers have conducted research to meet the needs of client organizations. Some of that applied research has included multiple stakeholders, with the post-World War II action research projects and the government-sponsored social science research of the 1960s being prime examples. In general, as more stakeholders become acknowledged and involved in organizational research, these efforts become more complex and consequently have greater need for supporting structures and processes to manage the relationship among stakeholders. The reasons for this are multiple and include the fact that different stakeholders often vary in their commitment to the research, the uses they wish to make of it, and even the topics they wish to cover. Thus, a successful multiple stakeholder research project must build a system that resolves conflicts among the stakeholders.

For What?

It was suggested earlier that research varies in its orientation toward action and toward the status quo; four research orientations were illustrated in Figure 33.1. Research designed to depict the status quo can often be conducted within a relatively short time frame and with relatively low psychological intensity in the relationship between the researcher and subject. However, explanation-oriented research that involves causal time-series analyses and/or investigates dynamic processes and stage theories generally requires a long time commitment, although the level of psychological intensity remains low because behavioral change is not implied.

Research efforts designed to help refine the status quo imply changes in behavior. Change always involves temporal commitment between researcher and user, and introduces psychological intensity because one party is suggesting needed behavior change for the other.

Research conducted with transforming organizational states into new forms based on different assumptions and guiding principles entails a sharp escalation in both time and intensity of researcher and user linkages, and is a much more complex type of research to carry out. Here, organizations are considering novel forms, testing innovative approaches, and trying out different assumptions, while researchers are participating in the exploration of uncharted waters. The risk of failure and the importance of the stakes are magnified for both parties.

Finally, organizational research aimed at how an organization can learn to transform itself implies fundamental changes not only in organizational form and processes, but also in the definition of an organization. Researcher

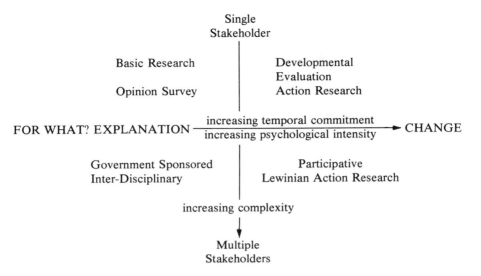

FIGURE 33.2. For Whom?

and organizational members are together attempting to transcend thinking about organizational forms as discrete entities, and are building the capacity for self-directed evolution of form and function. This type of research is rarely done, probably because extreme time and intensity are involved in such research efforts. The roles of researcher and of organizational members become blurred, and the intersystem linkage reaches further into the core activities of the organization and involves a more varied set of researcher activities.

In summary, as research proceeds from a concern with explanation of the status quo to learning how to transform organizational systems, both temporal commitment and psychological intensity between researcher and user increase.

Relationship Issues

Research content determines the level of complexity, temporal commitment, and psychological intensity of the intersystem linkages needed for organizational research. Those dimensions in turn place certain demands on the relationship aspect of the linkage—that is, the structures and processes required to maintain the social linkage between researcher and user organizations. We can identify particular relationship issues by simultaneously examining the answers to our content questions: For whom? For what? Figure 33.2 depicts these two continua as intersecting axes. The vertical axis represents "for whom" and varies from a single to multiple stakeholders; complexity of linkage increases as research includes greater numbers of stakeholders. The horizontal axis signifies "for what" and varies from explanation of organizations to changing them; temporal commitment and psychological intensity increase as research becomes more change oriented.

The upper left quadrant in Figure 33.2 represents research for a single stakeholder that is intended to explain the organizational status quo. Much basic research and such applied research as opinion surveys and market surveys are intended to meet the needs of one party, either the researcher or the organization. Here, research findings are likely to be rejected because of the nature of the information, including low salience, lack of credibility, and lack of clarity of presentation. Organizations are liable to discount basic research for these reasons, and researchers are likely to discount applied research for the same reasons. A solution to these problems is to involve multiple stakeholders in the research process, in an effort to create research findings that both contribute to scientific knowledge and are used by organizations for learning. Much government-funded research of the 1960s tried to stimulate research that meets the needs of multiple stakeholders, as shown in the lower left quadrant of Figure 33.2.

The upper right quadrant is action-oriented research performed for a single stakeholder. Developmental and evaluation research and much of what passes for action research fall into this quadrant. The beneficiary may be the organization, as in the case of research/consulting, or the researcher. Research in this quadrant is often rejected by organizations for reasons that involve the feedback variables presented in this chapter. Organizational members are likely to discount developmental and evaluation research if they have not solicited the information or do not find it helpful in addressing their problems. In order to gain acceptance of research findings, it is necessary to move toward a multiple stakeholder research model, where various interested parties have a role in determining the nature of the research. This shift would take us into the lower right quadrant, where action-oriented research is fully participative, involving multiple stakeholders.

In examining Figure 33.2, a clearer distinction can be made about the differential usefulness of various types of organizational research. Research that lies in the top half of Figure 33.2 might be explained as research "for" organizations; however, there is a high probability that the findings will be rejected by organizational members because they have not participated in the definition of the research. The bottom half of Figure 33.2 represents research "with" organizations. In this case, both organizational and researcher interests are addressed, and both are likely to see the research as useful.

Further, the left side of Figure 33.2 illustrates research concerning the organizational status quo. Because there is no explicit concern with action, organizations will likely see the findings as irrelevant or as not suggesting how things could be done differently. User complaints that a study has told them what they already know exemplify this failure to transcend the status quo.

The implication of this analysis is that if there is a serious concern that the research be useful for both practice and theory, research will gravitate to the lower right quadrant of Figure 33.2. This research allows multiple stakeholders to influence the content and conduct of the research. It is also concerned with action, and is likely to contribute to the understanding of causation. Knowledge of causal relationships is of interest both to practitioners who hope to make their organizations more effective, and to researchers who wish to make their theories more accurate.

In the lower right quadrant, the complexity, commitment, and psychological intensity of researcher and user linkages are high, and it is necessary to design relationship structures and processes to manage those characteristics. Specifically, action-oriented research involving multiple stakeholders requires shared control and decision making among the parties. This need for jointly determined research can better be understood in contrast to the more traditional researcher-controlled organizational inquiry.

The behavioral sciences have generally modeled the physical sciences in the stressing of tightly controlled research. The researcher designs the study to reduce error, insure validity, and enhance the power of the measurement devices to detect variance and relationships. The natural events and idiosyncratic social definitions within the research site are important to the researcher because they have the potential to interfere with the design and measurement system. Consequently, subjects are typically kept unaware of the intent and underlying hypotheses of the study in order to minimize response biases.

Researcher-defined research is generally useful from the researcher's viewpoint, assuming that subject compliance can be secured. Usefulness to organizations, however, depends on the salience of the research topic, the practical significance of the theoretical framework within which the research is conducted and the variables are defined, and the quality of data collected. The researcher has the responsibility to translate and interpret the findings using language that conveys meaning within the organizational setting.

We propose that researcher-controlled inquiry may be an impractical model for organizational research both because of the poor quality of data collected when such a framework is used and because organizations will be increasingly reluctant to cooperate with such researchers. If researchers are seriously concerned about the interests of multiple stakeholders, an alternative approach is required involving the joint definition and control of research by all parties involved. Issues must be partially field-determined, with the social scientist reinterpreting field events, concerns, and definitions into a theoretical framework, taking care to capture the richness and the variety of meanings in the field. When this is done, the issues will be of high salience to the practitioner because organizational members will have a key role in their definition. Moreover, the research findings will have high relevance to researchers because the richness and quality of data will contribute to a more realistic and practical body of knowledge. Clearly, considerable time and attention are needed to establish a jointly controlled relationship and to define and guide the study.

CONCLUSION

The case has been made that if organizational research is to be useful, researchers and organizational members must become partners in the research effort. Such research should be action oriented, jointly controlled, and involve relevant stakeholders from both researcher and user communities. Attention must be directed at the transactional context of the research. This will require explicit concern both for the subject matter and methodology of the research content, and for the structures and processes that are needed to create and sustain the social relationship between researcher and user organizations. Management of such research system linkages requires multiple roles. The scientific expertise of the researcher is no longer sufficient. It must be supplemented with skills for managing the linkage, coordinating the research, and working out the political and exchange aspects of the research relationship.

The institutions that can conduct such research must be sanctioned at a level high enough to resolve the conflicting interests of the divergent parties and to enlist the services of diverse participants. This scenario implies considerable alteration in the prevalent concept of organizational research and in the way it is conducted. It is beyond the scope of this chapter to describe in any detail what this type of research system might look like. Indeed, there is probably no one best way to create it. Research is needed on the effectiveness of different approaches in creating these intersystem linkages. It is hoped that this chapter makes the direction of the change toward useful research clearer, and the path easier to travel.

34

ON CONSIDERATION FOR THE USER: EXECUTIVE WORRIES IN RAPIDLY GROWING HIGH TECHNOLOGY COMPANIES

André L. Delbecq and James M. Kouzes

There is an old saying that whenever you ask four academics the same question you get five answers. This chapter is about that *fifth* answer to the question of producing useful knowledge for organizations. It is about the user's perspective.

We cannot adequately consider usefulness without considering the user. In defining the characteristics of knowledge that foster usefulness and in redesigning academic institutions to assure the development of useful knowledge, we must ask "Useful to whom?" In our opinion, the true test of the usefulness of knowledge is its acceptance by the user.

FACTS OF LIFE IN THE SILICON VALLEY

The focus of our study is the high-technology companies that populate the 60-mile stretch of Northern California from San Francisco to San Jose, popularly known as Silicon Valley. In this fertile area, where fruit orchards once blossomed, electronics companies now emerge and proliferate.

These organizations are of particular concern to us at the University of Santa Clara. They supply over 70 percent of our MBA students and over 80 percent of the participants in our executive programs. As a primary provider of university-based management education for companies in this area, we are concerned that the knowledge we produce is applicable to their organizational problems.

It is our perception that the conditions of business life for young high-technology companies are distinct from those faced by the more mature manufacturing and service organizations. While their problems are not necessarily unique, in high-technology firms the problems are being played out in a manner that is no longer congruent with traditional career and developmental cycles of the older, established businesses.

The Fast Lane

Alan F. Shugart, president and founder of Seagate Technology, located in Scotts Valley, California, recently spoke to the Kenna Club at the University of Santa Clara. The title he gave his talk was "Entrepreneurship in the Fast Lane." His company's story is representative of what many others are experiencing.

Shugart established Seagate's headquarters in December 1979. The company unveiled its first product—a mini-floppy disk-drive—in May 1980. It shipped 50 units in July 1980, and by October Seagate was shipping ten units a day or 200 units a month. In its first full year it had revenues of $12 million, and made $1.8 million in profit. In the first *quarter* of its second year it had $25 million in revenues and made $4.3 million in profit after taxes. This represents a 400 percent annual rate of growth. By 1984 Seagate projects it will be a $100 million company (Shugart, 1982).

Seagate's story is phenomenal, but not unusual in the Silicon Valley. The compounded annual average rate of sales growth from 1977 to 1981 for Apple Computer, for example, was 356 percent. For ASK Computer Systems it was 156 percent, for Tandem Computers 128 percent, and for Dysan 93 percent.

The *San Jose Mercury News* recently reported the quarterly earnings and sales for 66 high-technology companies in the Santa Clara area. Of the 66, 20 had sales increases over last year's quarter of greater than 40 percent; 32 had increases greater than 30 percent (July 5, 1982, p. 50).

Shortened Life-Cycles

Common high-technology wisdom has it that the product life-cycle is only two years for their products. This is juxtaposed against a four-year development cycle. This unprecedented rate of technological change shortens the available period of time for entry into the market. The windows are becoming narrower and narrower due to competition. *Business Week* (August 2, 1982) reports that a decade ago the minicomputer business spawned 40 new companies. Since 1977 at least 140 new companies have been added to the list (p. 53).

> Startup fever is sweeping the information processing industry for the second time in 15 years. . . . Lured by a ready supply of venture capital and a new, more cost-effective technology, these entrepreneurs are now offering low-cost computers that can more economically do the jobs once

handled only by the pricier models from the minicomputer producers. (*Business Week*, August 2, 1982, p. 53).

In addition, the computer giants have recently entered the macro-war over the minis and micros, heating up even more the competition in this young industry. The phenomenon of growth is already a fight for survival.

Scarcity Amid Growth

High-technology companies are, at present, engineering-driven, and there is a shortage of engineers to do the driving. Experienced, skilled engineers are at a premium. This strong demand for talented engineers has fostered a highly mobile technical workforce, who, it is said, can over lunch get a better paying job at a company across the street. The demand has also created a major salary escalation and compression problem in many companies. While the recession has slowed the mobility, it has not curtailed it, nor has it dampened the desire of talented engineers to start their own companies.

The shortage of skilled professionals is compounded by decreasing national mobility. Housing costs in Northern California are so high that they create a significant barrier to importing talent from outside the state. Individuals cannot afford the monthly payments, and companies cannot afford sufficient mortgage differentials and other incentives to attract people from other parts of the country. Thus, the national resource pool is relatively inaccessible to Silicon Valley firms. Companies are finding it necessary to open new plants in the southwest, where labor and the cost of living are cheaper and the life-style attractive.

Coupled with the shortage of engineers and other technical professionals is a great shortage of experienced managers. Engineers with no training or background in management find themselves, within four years of startup, being advanced into middle management positions. They are frequently unable to perform these jobs with the same competency they exhibited as technical contributors. Companies must lure experienced managers from the successful, established firms in the industry. Often the result is a culture clash between founders and newcomers or between experienced managers who bring with them the norms and expectations of their former employers.

A New Economic Order

The young, growing companies are developing at a time when the economic order for high technology has been profoundly altered. Much of the change has spawned rapid growth. The expansion of available venture capital, for example, is a direct result of change in economic policy. At the same time, the entry of so many new companies overcrowds the market and threatens the survival of any single company.

The prolonged recession also alters the growth pattern of many startups and young companies. Sales are now growing at a slower rate, and in some cases flattening or declining. While the recession impacts all businesses, small high-technology companies may not have the assets or managerial expertise to survive a lengthy recessionary seige. Add to these economic factors the development of nontraditional distribution patterns (such as Sears) and the global nature of the modern economy, and the pressures on young companies intensify.

These are the basic facts of business life for the high-technology firms that provide us with the majority of our MBA students and participants in our executive programs. They face the challenges of rapid growth, unprecedented technological change, a scarce and mobile workforce, and an altered economic order. The challenge to us is to produce useful knowledge that will help them function in this environment and solve the attendant problems.

BACKGROUND OF OUR STUDY

In August 1981 we began a study of the critical issues facing high-technology firms. The purpose of our investigation was diagnostic. We wanted to gather data that would better enable us to plan for the education of local managers and executives. We wanted to determine the emphasis appropriate for both executive development programs and modification to the content of our MBA program.

At the outset, we offer a caveat about our study. Ours was not an orderly research strategy, but rather a process of discovering converging themes from a sample of knowledgeable informants. Our confidence in reporting them here is due to the surprising consensus on the key issues, rich in redundancy and exemplification.

Participants

The initial sample of informants consisted of 17 local executives from high-technology firms or their direct support organizations. Eight were presidents: four of high-technology firms, three of executive search firms that recruit senior officers for high-technology companies, and one of a public relations firm for several major electronics manufacturers. Five of the interviewees were vice-presidents, and three were division general managers from high-technology firms. One was a venture capitalist who was formerly the president of a large peripherals manufacturer.

The initial sample was expanded to include: six corporate officers who were members of the Advisory Board of the University of Santa Clara and were associated with the industry; seven general managers who served on a special task force; six persons from the Dean's CEO Roundtable; and four senior officers who sat on a special panel convened by the director of the Executive Development Center.

Procedure

The original 17 participants were interviewed for an hour and a half. Each was asked two general open-ended questions and several follow-up probing questions. The two key questions were:

> What are the critical issues that high-technology executives are facing right now?
> What would it take to attract high-technology executives to a series of seminars that dealt with these issues?

Responses to these questions were recorded and analyzed. The items were sorted into clusters of issues relating to a similar theme. A mix of diagnostic methods was used to gather data from the other key informants. Four were asked to prepare brief presentations.

The Nominal Group Technique was used with seven, six were interviewed as a group, and six took part in a modified Delphi survey (Delbecq, Van de Ven, and Gustafson, 1975). Each informant responded to the question on critical issues, while only 24 responded to the question of program design.

THE CRITICAL ISSUES IN HIGH-TECHNOLOGY COMPANIES

Analysis of the data yielded 15 clusters of issues. Of the 15, four were considered crucial, receiving support from 50 percent or more of the informants. The four that were of highest priority are:

> What are the appropriate systems, structures, strategies, etc., for the different stages of corporate growth?
> How do we establish, maintain, and communicate a unique corporate culture—one based on a clear philosophy that provides an internal compass for employees?

What can be done to attract, motivate, and retain our employees? What can we do to develop a cadre of general managers who have an understanding of the firm as a whole?

The following is a brief description of each of these major issues.

Managing Rapid Growth

Not surprisingly, the central concern of the high-technology executives we surveyed was how to manage rapid growth. Here are a few quotes from the executives that we grouped into the cluster.

> How do we organize as we grow?
> As you grow, as you go through stages and phases, the issues usually are dramatic changes in systems, e.g., finance, engineering documentation systems, marketing control systems, etc.
> A common theme is the fourth year of operations, that is, after startup and into early maturity.
> There's the issue of founders staying or leaving after a period of time.
> How do you make transitions from one phase of growth to another?
> The most basic fact of life is "total uncertainty." You don't know if such and such will happen. You "can't predict" and "don't know."
> Another issue is managing change with the growth rate as it is. What will we trip over?
> How does one control fast growth? We are adding gobs and gobs of engineers monthly.
> The market is growing faster than the capacity to supply it. The dimension of rapid growth is something we don't understand. What does high growth mean?
> To dedicate oneself to this, one needs to consider over 30 percent growth per year!
> How do I control the engineering department when we grow so fast and things move so rapidly that we can't keep up?
> How do principals handle technical and engineering changes when they are beyond the scope of the officers to keep up with?

As one CEO put it, "We're playing high stakes poker here every-day. . . . You can blow it all with one bad decision." The shortened product life-cycles, investor pressures for quick profits, and the sheer intensity of the numbers all create a pressure-cooker work environment. This situation is only exacerbated by the propensity to shoot from the hip and the struggle to keep a unique corporate culture alive while growth seems to dilute it.

While these issues may suggest that executives need only to learn how to manage the "traditional" life-cycles challenges, they strongly indicate that these competencies must be acquired much more rapidly. These executive users of our business knowledge feel they must get up the learning curve much more quickly than is the norm in university settings.

Developing Corporate Culture

The founders of many young high-technology companies worked in large, mature organizations earlier in their careers. There they experienced the effects of size and the corporate policies and procedures that come with it. When they started their own companies, they were determined not to become like their former bureaucratic employers.

One founder of a rapidly growing high-technology company, when asked recently about the origin of his unique management philosophy, remarked: "It started when I was a researcher in 'Company X' [a very large multinational]. The way they managed was like emotional rape. I never want that to happen in my organization."

There is an intense, almost religious, drive to create unique and distinctive corporate cultures in many of the new high-technology companies. The recent articles about Tandem Computers, Inc. in *Fortune* (June 28, 1982) is but one very public example of many private efforts. Here are a few quotes executives made to us during our research on the corporate culture issue:

> A critical issue is establishing, communicating, and maintaining your company culture so people instinctively know what to do.
>
> In a company that is growing—doubling every year—at any given time employees are only there a year. It is very difficult to have a consistent culture. You can't do it from a policy manual; it is impractical.
>
> One of the key processes is developing and communicating a culture. You don't know if you're losing it if you don't know what it is.
>
> We'd like to develop a set of guidelines as opposed to rule books. Values are the key.
>
> Identification and definition of the philosophy of the company makes constraint dynamics clear.
>
> You have to have clear values and a non-threatening environment. You have to model the behavior that says we live the values.
>
> But the major concern is how to maintain a family feeling as we grow so fast!
>
> The successful companies have succinct and understandable mission statements and superordinate goals.
>
> We need to know how to create an environment in which employees want to stay and contribute; in which he'll feel proud and happy with the company.

How do we maintain small company closeness in a large company framework?

The whole focus is "What does the human system really mean?"

Attracting, Motivating, and Retaining Good People

The turnover rate in Silicon Valley high-technology firms for 1980 was 51 percent for nonexempt and 30 percent for exempt (Radford, 1981). While the recession has dampened turnover to 41 percent for nonexempt and 25 percent for exempt, the prediction is that the rate will climb once the economy improves. The demand for highly skilled technical people is exceptionally strong, and the need to find creative ways to manage it is equally intense.

Here is what a few of our executive informants had to say:

How do I attract good people, retain them, and reward them?

How companies handle people as they grow, how they reward them, nonfinancially, is a noble topic.

The key to the whole thing is companies taking care of their people. Companies want a special type of talent, and they need to know how to keep them.

Reducing turnover is also an issue.

We ask "What is that 'product mix' that a company offers to cause employees to identify with the company?" The product mix here means benefits, training, management style, etc.

How can we prevent movement from one company to another?

We can be a growth-oriented company in all senses of the phrase.

Valley participants are particularly retarded in executive compensation. One thing that separates the industry from others is equity participation (stock options, prerequisites, etc.). These are subsets of the management continuity issue, the golden handcuffs theme where distribution of money is deferred.

There is an important paradox to consider. The unique character of the Valley is built on small, startup companies founded by individualists who have left another company. Yet, in turn, they must maintain some degree of continuity among big talents who are likewise capable of leaving and in turn "venturing" in a startup. What is the balance between continuity and innovation?

Developing General Managers

As one executive put it, "Silicon Valley companies have no managerial bench strength. They are always playing their first-string, and if anyone gets hurt or leaves, the team suffers."

High-technology firms initially are design-driven and concerned about how to get the prototype out the door. But as soon as the prototype succeeds, enormous pressure builds to expand market share in order to meet founder and venture capitalist expectations for return on their investments.

Growth requires simultaneous attention to all functional departments. The earlier intensity of focus on design was the initial strength, but as the firm grows this develops into a general management weakness. Particularly absent are the interpersonal skills necessary to appreciate and integrate the conflicting interests of the diverse functional areas. Thus, the development of general managers who have a broad view and integrative skills has become a critical concern among high-technology executives. Again, here are examples of how they put it to us:

> Immature managers may not be able to withstand the pressures of venture capitalists.
>
> The level of managers here is close to being the least sophisticated in the U.S., because of their immaturity and youth.
>
> Will there ever be a crop of managers to pick from in this Valley? Housing is so costly. The lack of training inhibits getting experienced managers into Northern California. How do we attract these experienced people?
>
> What does it take to prepare a guy to be a general manager?
>
> The lack of a general manager pool is associated with the unbelievable rate of growth and uncertainty. Because of it [growth] you have diversification and differentiation in a short period of time. Therefore, you have a hell of a time developing general managers.
>
> How do you convert people from an obvious technical bent to management?
>
> The fickle nature of the Silicon Valley workforce raises the question of management stability. How do you provide for stability of management and continuity of management? Continuity of management is needed for growing companies.

NEEDED: A WHOLE NEW DIMENSION OF SKILLS

As one executive remarked in our interviews, "You couldn't find a better audience than high-technology companies for management development. We need a whole new dimension of management skills." One gets the distinct impression from our sample of high-technology executives that there are needs out there waiting to be filled. There is a desire to learn new ways to lead and manage, and the internal and external pressures to do so have never been greater than they are today.

The issues that seem most to concern local executives are those of maintaining the institutional viability of their growing corporations. They are concerned with framing the policies and strategies that will enable their firms to prosper over time.

One senses a deep searching among high-technology executives for a new model of organizational leadership. They seem to be engaged in a reexamination of the concept of the corporation and their assumptions about it. They are aware that a turnover rate of 50 percent, for example, is a symptom of an industry context much larger than compensation and benefits. Underlying their concerns, there appears to be a struggle to define a new corporate philosophy.

Researchable Questions

Our preliminary study of the concerns of high-technology executives has yielded many exciting questions for the organizational researcher who wishes to produce useful knowledge to help solve the problems of America's "third wave" industries. Promising items on the agenda of practically minded researchers might include these questions:

What are the models of organization appropriate for the situation where the organization mutates more rapidly than the traditional developmental careers of entrepreneurs and engineers?

How can early efficiencies be developed in young product lines?

What systems are useful in coordinating decentralized multiple venture units with the overall business plan?

What are the organizational systems and structures that offer, simultaneously, a flexible, creative atmosphere for innovation and a tight, controlled approach to operating efficiency?

What are the elements of corporate culture, and what is the content of some exemplary corporate cultures? How can culture be enacted in youthful enterprises?

How does one avoid creating a culture that is both time-bound and personality restrictive?

What is the unique role of corporate leadership in sustaining and transmitting culture?

What are the natural forces that diminish culture and fragment organizations?

When does loyalty become servitude and challenge become usurpation?

At what point does mobility as a mechanism for stimulating startups and innovation become mobility as a form of opportunistic narcissism?

How far should a company go in catering to young technical elites?

What is the ideal psychological contract between the corporation and the professional in high-technology companies? How "golden" should the handcuffs be?

What are the unique motivational characteristics of innovative engineers as a subpopulation among professionals?

How does one establish career paths for engineers that do not put artificial ceilings on technical careers and still offer adequate incentives to attract skilled engineers into general management?

What are the alternatives to developing general managers other than the MBA or traditional executive programs?

What are the necessary competencies for general managers in high-technology companies? How are they different from and similar to the competencies for managers in other organizational settings?

Designing Education for Executives

As we indicated earlier, the original purpose of our study was to collect data on the critical issues faced by executives in high-technology companies. We wanted to know what executives most wanted to know, so that we could develop useful educational programs for them and their organizations.

Their responses to the question "What would it take to attract high-technology executives to a series of seminars . . . ?" are testimony to the necessity to design perceived practicality in the programs. Here are few of their quotes about the need for relevance:

> The issues must be real to me.
> Keep them as practical as possible.
> They will ask, "How will it benefit me right now?"
> Practical solutions are needed.
> We want meat, not global generalities. Be very practical and nitty-gritty.
> It must be relevant. It must be of real value.
> Offer current themes of relevance.
> I have to feel I'll *gain* something from the experience.
> Offer new insights on the issues, an interesting perspective, a way of approaching problems to be addressed now and in the future.
> Select a provocative issue that looks like it would enable people to learn something practical.

In addition to stressing relevance and practicality, the executives we surveyed were also explicit about scheduling, design, and selection of participants. Time had an extremely positive valence, and they did not want to see it wasted.

> My time is of great value. Don't fool around.
> I am short on time and preoccupied. Err on the side of brevity.

To accommodate the work schedules of these executives of rapidly growing companies, there was a strong preference for scheduling events in such a way as to allow them to put in work at the office either before or after a program.

> At the onset, make them half-day. A full day is too much.
> You are not going to get people for two days. You may not get them for one day. You'll definitely get people for ½ day.
> If you do "whole day" seminars, think about 1 p.m. to 8 p.m.

Entrepreneurial high-technology executives want to associate with other executives with comparable experience, status, and ability. In fact, it was their major design recommendation.

> It is a very entrepreneurial group—rather self-sufficient and autonomous.
> They want to believe participants are at least as knowledgeable and competent as they are. This implies that you may want to break participation down by size and growth rate.
> Make it an elite group.
> Be selective as to whom you'd like to have.
> They like to feel it is exclusive in cost and location as well as people.

Our executive informants wanted to hear what their executive colleagues were doing about the problems they faced. While recognized academic experts could offer observations from research and consulting, these executives felt they could also learn from the ways their peers were managing.

> I want an opportunity to talk with peers—those who have been there.
> It helps to know how others have solved key issues in these companies.
> Let's share experience with successful others.
> If there are people who have had successes or failures, get that shared.

In response to this expressed need for useful knowledge to apply to critical problems, we created the *Executive Seminars in Corporate Excellence* in the fall of 1981. This educational venture is designed with two goals in mind. First, we want to provide a forum for disseminating the latest organizational research and theory that directly addresses the issues raised by high-technology executives. Equally important, we want this forum to enable executives to share and discuss their own practices that have led them to achieve organizational excellence.

The first *Executive Seminar in Corporate Excellence* was held on June 2, 1982. The theme was "Developing Corporate Culture in High-Technology Firms." The design of the day incorporated the previously cited design recommendations. We selected the material for its practicality and usefulness. The program was designed to allow for maximum exchange among participants. A case example of a successful company program that developed corporate culture was presented.

The program began 1:00 p.m. and ended at 8:00 p.m. to accommodate executives' schedules. Executives were personally invited to attend the executive seminar by the dean. A limited number of the senior executives were invited to participate. A mass mail approach was not used. Participation was limited to 30 executives in order to maximize exchange.

The response to the initial seminar was extremely positive. Three other *Executive Seminars in Corporate Excellence* were held in the first year. Three more are planned for the second year. What began as an experiment in university executive education evolved into an important new strategy for building a partnership in business problem-solving. But just what did we learn from this experiment?

PRODUCING USEFUL KNOWLEDGE FOR UNIVERSITIES

The chapters in this volume all address the question of "producing useful knowledge for organizations." This chapter also focuses on the critical issue of producing *useful knowledge for universities*. It is a case study of how a business school listened to its end users and itself benefitted from the knowledge it gained.

As we stated at the outset, our study was intended to be diagnostic. We had three ideal outcomes. First, we hoped to gather information that would lead to theoretical insights into the organizational world of high technology. Second, we hoped to discover topics and opportunities for faculty research. Finally, we sought information useful in improving our MBA curriculum and our executive programs.

To date, our first objective has not been realized, for reasons we shall discuss shortly. However, the project exceeded our expectations in the other two areas. The surveys and seminars proved to be extremely effective means of uncovering avenues for research. They also enabled us to learn much more about our local executives and establish a closer relationship with them.

Research Benefits to the School

Faculty research considerations have already been stimulated by the executive seminars in several ways. First, faculty who taught in the first two seminars have been intrigued by the excitement and provoked by the dialogue to conceptualize potential research projects. Second, faculty who are to teach in subsequent seminars have sat in the earlier seminars as observers. Third, a developmental program has been undertaken by the Executive Development Center to brief faculty who are to instruct in the seminars on issues associated with high-technology businesses. Finally, at a faculty retreat the entire faculty was given a briefing on the results of the interviews and dialogue with executives. Subsequently, each functional department formulated the following list of tentative researchable topics appropriate for both within department and interdepartmental research efforts.

Management

- Factors relating to the development of high performing work teams, with particular emphasis on the mix of "old" workers and "new" workers.
- Factors relating to the selection and retention of high performers. This would include studies relating to recruiting and selection strategies as well as studies in turnover.
- Special problems of project managers dealing with shortened time frames in matrix structures.
- Study of the strategic planning and strategy development processes in high-tech firms.
- Study of governmental regulation and its effect on high-tech firms.
- Investigation of the national debate with respect to an industrial policy to encourage and protect high-tech firms.
- Studies of the issues surrounding the piracy of ideas and unfair competition.

Accounting

- Investigation of a practical accounting definition of research and development.
- Surveying capitalization practices in software development firms (determining components of costs for computer software programs).
- Development of case studies in the budgeting and control of research and development expenditures.
- Examination of tax incentives that aid in the retention of key personnel.

Decision Sciences

- The manufacturing process selection (a technological choice of vital importance to the high-technology firm).

- The unique production planning and scheduling problems associated with semiconductor and computer-related equipment.
- The use of industrial robots and the mathematical models necessary for configuring robotics connected with computer hardware.
- The examination of computer softwares that will be effective for microcomputers.
- The examination of "office of the future."

Economics

- Product-pricing problems for uncertain and short life-cycles.
- The examination of the economics of inventory problems for "perishable software."
- An examination of comparative historical perspectives of other industries that went through periods of rapid growth and cost reductions.
- The theoretical and empirical investigation of the consequences of rapid growth on a geographic limited area.
- A study of the effects of capital substitution for labor across skill levels and key manufacturing areas.
- The effect of business cycles on high-technology firms.

Marketing

- Definition and conceptualization of what high-tech marketing means.
- Channel issues in high-tech markets.
- Alternative approaches to market segmentation in high-tech markets.
- Marketing high-tech intangibles.
- International marketing issues in high-tech products.
- Pricing and the experience curve.
- Organizational linkages among marketing, engineering, and R&D.

Finance

- The role of venture capital.
- The nature of the contract between venture capitalist and entrepreneurs.
- The role of investment bankers.
- The role of the financial function in the high-technology firm.
- The interaction between finance and other functions, for example, R & D and production.
- Changes in the finance function as the firm matures.
- Risk analysis and investment in high-technology.

A schoolwide faculty committee has been formed to study these potential research areas. Special seminars are under development that focus on feasibility studies with industry executives relative to these areas.

Lessons about Executive Learning Styles

One of the original intentions of our study was to enage high-technology executives in a conceptual dialogue about the management of their firms. We hoped that by bringing together executives, scholars, and leading consultants we would jointly produce new knowledge useful to managing high-technology firms.

Such was not the case. So far our efforts to engage high-technology executives in the formulation of new knowledge has been unsuccessful. We have learned from our executive seminars that a major contributing factor to our lack of success in this area is a natural disjunction between the learning styles of executives and academics.

Research on the daily behavior of general managers (see, for example, Kotter, 1982 and Mintzberg, 1973) indicates that they spend most of their time in conversation with others covering a very broad range of topics. Their discussions tend rarely to be planned in advance in any detail, and they usually are quite short and disjointed. Superior executives also tend to ask a great many questions. This daily pattern of activity tends to produce a highly stylized approach to learning. In our experience, executives favor brief presentations that summarize the facts, offer anecdotes and examples, and prescribe actions. Their questions are intended to clarify the facts, seek out exemplification, and get the opinions or recommendations of others.

High-technology executives approach our seminars in much the same way as they approach their daily agendas. They prefer faculty to be brief, practical, anecdotal, and prescriptive.

Academics, on the other hand, have their own stylized approach to learning. They prefer to be hypothetical, contingent, conditional, and causal. In their presentations, whether to executives or MBA students, academics reflect these preferences.

There is a natural and dynamic tension between the executive and academic approaches to learning. Just as with the "town versus gown" dilemma, it is a tension that is likely always to be there. The *Executive Seminars in Corporate Excellence* have taught us, however, that optimum learning occurs (on the part of both academics and executives) when this tension is consciously and conscientiously managed. (For example, one strategy we have used with some success is to have an academic and an executive present on the same topic. The academic presents data and concepts, the executive speaks of practice and example.)

We have learned that a focus on the *production* of useful knowledge is insufficient for increasing the usefulness of the organizational sciences. How useful, after all, is unused knowledge? Equally important to increasing usefulness is paying attention to the process of communicating that knowledge to executives. Consequently, our main efforts now are directed at finding ways of enabling academics and executives to accommodate the styles of the other.

CONCLUSIONS

Peters and Waterman (1982) have concluded from their study of 62 U.S. firms that "the excellent companies are not only better on service, quality, reliability, and finding a niche. They are also better listeners. . . . The customer is truly in a partnership with the effective companies, and vice versa." We believe this to be true of outstanding business schools as well.

The success of the *Executive Seminars in Corporate Excellence* is due primarily to the fact that we listened to our local business executives. The topics we selected and the format we designed were in direct response to their needs. It demonstrates that a "market-driven" strategy can enable a business school to build linkages with local corporations and generate extensive research opportunities. Listening to the user—in interviews, surveys, and seminars—is certainly one means of increasing the probability that the knowledge produced out of the organizational sciences will be useful to organizations.

At the same time, we have found that listening and producing are by themselves insufficient. A third element in the usefulness quotient is communicating the knowledge to the end user. Linking producer and consumer requires, among other things, learning to manage the natural tension between the learning styles of academics and executives. This is perhaps an even greater challenge than either discovering or producing useful knowledge.

REFERENCES

Delbecq, A. L ., Van de Ven, A. H., and Gustafson, D. H. *Group techniques for program planning: a guide to nominal group and delphi processes.* Glenview, Ill.: Scott, Foresman, 1975.

How local companies fared in the latest quarter. *San Jose Mercury News*, July 5, 1982, p. 50.

The incredible explosion of startups. *Business Week*, August 2, 1982, pp. 53–54.

Ketchum, B. W., Jr. The 1982 Inc. 100. *Inc.*, May 1982, pp. 49–58.

Kotter, J. P. *The general managers.* New York: Free Press, 1982.

Magnet, Myron. Managing by mystique at Tandem Computers. *Fortune,* June 28, 1982, pp. 84–91.

Mintzberg, H. *The nature of managerial work.* New York: Harper and Row, 1973.

Peters, T. J. and Waterman, R. H., Jr. *In search of excellence: Lessons from America's best run companies.* New York: Harper and Row, 1982.

Radford, S. Personal communication, April 30, 1981.

Shugart, A. *Entrepreneurship in the fast lane.* Speech to the Kenna Club, University of Santa Clara, May 1982.

35

THE MARKETING OF ACADEMIC RESEARCH:
AN EXAMPLE FROM ACCOUNTING

Jacob G. Birnberg, Lawrence Turopolec, and S. Mark Young

Research in academic institutions often fails to produce useful knowledge for private organizations. The lack of relevant research is due primarily to the inadequate matching of the product of academic institutions with the needs of private organizations. In this chapter, we offer an explanation of why this phenomenon occurs and illustrate our position with a specific example from auditing research.

Recent work in management studies contends that organizations vary continuously on a scale that anchors purely technical types on one end, and purely institutional types on the other (Meyer and Rowan, 1977; Boland, 1982).[1] Technical organizations are those whose structures are geared for rational control of complex relational networks, and whose control is gained by a focus on productive efficiency and effectiveness with concrete output criteria that are open for inspection. An institutional organization is characterized by a loosely coupled system of shared beliefs whose survival depends on adherence to institutional rules. Productive efficiency and effectiveness are not major concerns for participants as evaluation criteria are vague and subject to redefinition.

These different forms of culture and control are reflected in the types of research in which each organization engages. The technical organization—in line with its rational, production-oriented philosophy—tends to value practical problem-solving research. This kind of research is defined as that needed for solving immediate organizational problems. In contrast, academic institutions operate in a culture that is philosophically less concerned with productive efficiency. Their research is heavily concentrated on developing theories and integrating knowledge that can be generalized to many different settings rather than on practical problem-solving research.

	TECHNICAL	INSTITUTIONAL
PRACTICAL PROBLEM SOLVING	Day to day firm operations CELL 1	Consulting CELL 2
THEORY CONSTRUCTION/ MODELING	Firm Research and Development CELL 3	Academia CELL 4

FIGURE 35.1. Types of Auditing Research

Two dimensions on which we base our analysis of the relationship between practice and academe clearly emerge from the previous discussion. The two dimensions are type of organization—technical or institutional—and type of research—practical problem solving or theory construction/ modeling. Figure 35.1 links the two dimensions. Within each cell of the figure, we observe a different kind of research occurring.

Cell 1 research is typically the kind of day-to-day problem solving that results in improving on such techniques as linear programming or modifying a software package to fit certain needs. This work, usually done by practitioners, is often not published. When it is published, it appears in practitioner-oriented sections of journals such as the *Journal of Accountancy*. In cell 2, the research is not unlike consulting in its orientation. In this research the author often provides a solution to a problem of importance to the practitioner. The results of this work often comes out in the form of case analyses or applied articles, such as those appearing in *Management Accounting*. The kind of research that falls into cell 3 may best be characterized under the heading of research and development. This research initiates the application of new and novel techniques to longer-range problems of the firm. Such research often is published in research monographs. An example of this is Ashton's monograph, which was started while he was in residence at Peat, Marwick, Mitchell, and Company (Ashton, 1982). Finally, cell 4 encompasses pure academic research that occurs within the confines of universities (and perhaps think tanks) where practical relevance may not be an immediate goal. The results of this research are typically published in scholarly academic journals.

Figure 35.1 constitutes a framework of research and research issues that may be likened to focusing on separate aspects in a large-scale problem-solving domain. Kilmann and Mitroff (1979) have developed a problem-solving model that they adapt to the intervention process. In relation to their framework, academe has traditionally focused its efforts on the sensing and defining of problems with an emphasis on theoretical work. In accordance with their technical efficiency orientation, practitioners' main focus lies in deriving, implementing, and legitimizing solutions to their immediate problems.

These differences in organizational form and perspectives on research and problem solving create contrasting operating environments (see cells 1 and 4 of Figure 35.1) that form a substantial barrier for academe in producing useful knowledge. Each group works in its domain and there is little incentive for changing, especially for academics to engage in applied research.

KNOWLEDGE TRANSFER

The framework identified in Figure 35.1 suggests that different types of research activity occur in accordance with the culture and research orientation of the organization. These contrasting perspectives create problems when transferring knowledge from cell 4 to cell 1.[2]

Cell 4 research focuses on developing fairly complex theories and integrating knowledge that can be generalized to related problem areas. This type of research is often not compatible with organizational needs. The technical organization, in line with its production-oriented philosophy, requires research that is less complex and more specifically related to the problems facing its immediate environment.

The research developed by academe typically does not meet these organizational criteria. Academics are accused by practitioners of committing what Mitroff and Featheringham (1974) refer to as a type three error: solving the wrong problem. This apparent mismatch between the product of academe and the needs of practitioners implies that the transfer of knowledge is not a direct route from cell 4 to cell 1. The model in Figure 35.1 suggests that concerned parties must meet in cells 2 and 3 to transfer knowledge in a form that is compatible with the objectives of the users in cell 1. Such a transfer may be facilitated by intermediary organizations. These organizations may subsequently provide feedback that is useful for participants in both cells 1 and 4.

The use of intermediaries provides a potential bridging mechanism for transferring academic research into practice. In the accounting profession, as we will note later, this function has been served by auditing firms among others. In the various fields of marketing, finance, and organizational development, two forms of such intermediaries are consultants and the research and development departments of the technical organizations (cells 2 and 3 of Figure 35.1). As many consultants and research staff are from academe or have close ties with it, they form a potential connecting link between academe and the technical organization. They are in a position to match the product of academic research with specific organizational needs. Conversely, they could direct the attention of the academic community to issues that are of concern to practitioners. However, obstacles exist that can limit the usefulness of these mechanisms for channeling information.

The central focus of the consulting and research groups has been directed by the problems of the technical organization. Being employed by the private firms, these intermediary groups are mainly interested in solving the organization's problems. They are not as much concerned with finding an outlet for academic research. To the extent that research exists that is suitable to the immediate problem and is advantageous for the intermediaries to utilize, then the potential exists for transfer of the applicable knowledge.

The problem is further complicated by the nature of the linking units. They are loosely coupled groups with limited contact. There are few professional bodies serving as intermediaries that can forge a useful link with academe. Should such a network form, it could serve the dual purposes of informing academe of organizational needs and channeling academic research to these firms. But the problem of coordinating the activities of such a large-scale network poses an obstacle to its creation and effectiveness.

Since the problems dealt with by the intermediaries in cells 2 and 3 are typically generated by the experience of practitioners in cell 1, the linkage between cell 1 and cells 2 and 3 appears to be quite strong. Thus, academics must take this orientation as a given in the short run. Consequently, for substantial transfer to occur, a shift is needed by cell 4 researchers into these other research domains. However, the assessment process in academe is such that doing cell 1-related research can involve considerable risk for a researcher.

In summary, it would appear that the transfer of academic research directly to the users of cell 1 is difficult. The transfer occurs, presumably in cells 2 and 3, when the focus of academic research is better matched with the needs of the organization in cell 1. Such an exchange may be accomplished through a shift in orientation by academic researchers. This may be facilitated by the use of intermediary organizations. We will examine this process below in the context of auditing firms.

KNOWLEDGE TRANSFER—AN EXAMPLE FROM AUDITING

The intent here is to illustrate the applicability of our earlier discussion in a particular area of research: auditing. We will examine the mechanisms facilitating knowledge transfer in the auditing area and the conditions that led to their development. It is hoped that through this discussion we will achieve some useful insights into the area of researcher-practitioner cooperation in the area of knowledge use. Our concern is in the understanding and facilitation of joint involvement in auditing research by academic accounting researchers and CPA firms.

CPA Firms

Traditionally, the CPA profession has consisted of a small number of very large firms that opened offices as needed to service old clients and acquire new ones. They were partnerships with the partners being active in both the management and the practice of the firm. While the history of these firms has been chronicled elsewhere (see Montagna, 1974), today there exist eight major firms that operate internationally with their offices (or those of related firms) located throughout the world.

The original function of such firms was the attest (or audit) function. Over time they have branched out into related activities such as tax preparation and planning, management consulting, and less obvious areas such as executive searches. However, despite the growth of the other areas, these firms consider themselves primarily engaged in the practice of auditing. It is this function that is foremost in their view of their activities.

A second important characteristic of large CPA firms is their organization. Each firm has a head or home office and numerous branch offices. The former functions as the headquarters and is separate from the latter, who perform the audits, and so forth. In a firm's headquarters city (such as New York), a firm typically will have both a headquarters office and one or more operating branches. The headquarters office will have little if any operating activities and, geography aside, its relationship with those offices in the same metropolitan area will be similar to its relationship with offices in other areas.

This differentiation of function is similar to that found in other profit-seeking organizations where top management's function is that of strategic planning and policy making. It differs in the linkage between operations and top management. In the CPA firm the headquarters' link to operations is even more remote than in, say, an industrial firm's. Thus, while the various branches are clearly cell 1 situations, the headquarters of a large CPA firm may be characterized as being extensively concerned with issues that are cell 2 and 3 in nature as well as cell 1.

Thus, the headquarters of a CPA firm shares many of the qualities that Meyer and Rowan associated with institutions. Indeed, the objectives of the headquarters place a significant amount of emphasis on professional development and the legitimization of current practice. The last item to a CPA firm is the R&D of the accounting profession.

Finally, the headquarters has available a significant amount of resources that it can expend to achieve its goals of improved practice and professionalism within the firm. It is these resources that provide the critical link between the academic accountant willing to consider auditing research and the members of the headquarters' staff interested in improving auditing in the long run.

Academic-Practitioner Auditing Research: The Forms of Interaction

To be sure, there is no obvious form for this interaction to take; the form must to some degree be dictated by the needs of both parties. Thus, some consultancy does exist in the sense that academics will be hired to solve or assist in the solution of a currently pressing problem. However, our focus is on those interactions whose origins are rooted less in the currently vexing problem of the practitioner/auditor and more in the headquarters' perception of the need to improve the firm's general level of efficiency. These programs may take many forms. However, the most popular of these are faculty residencies and faculty research grant programs.

Faculty Residencies

In this case, the residencies are not in the firm's branch offices performing staff services. Rather, they are in the firm's headquarters working on projects of mutual interest. Since the firm usually seeks out the faculty member, there is an a priori basis for assuming receptivity on the firm's part. Additionally, the presence of the researcher in the firm's headquarters carries with it the availability of data in its multitude of forms (past audit records, auditors, policy directives, and so forth). Thus, the residency typically leads to research with "real" data and/or ease of access to practitioners that facilitates the researcher's performing research of mutual interest often with members of the firm's professional staff.

The outputs of these projects probably are different from what the researcher would perform given the same amount of release time but confined to his university office. The researcher will bring his expertise to bear on problems that often are identified for him by the CPA firm as "important" problems. This usually implies a high level of cooperation from the firm and its members. This is true for two reasons. Even those members who are oriented toward the firm's technical goals see the relevance of such studies. Additionally, the firm probably has been working on the problem and already has assembled a data base. Such cooperation facilitates the academic researcher's work and (for better or worse) assures visibility within the firm for the results.

A variety of examples of this can be identified from the authors' ·knowledge of the work of various faculty residents. No formal data collection about these activities was possible; however, the residents have worked in areas such as statistical sampling, audit planning, and analysis of internal control while on faculty residencies. Discussions with the residents suggest that it is their perception that their work was considered potentially useful and some felt that it affected practice. To the extent that these activities find their way into practice, they are examples of cell 2 research.

Similarly, the researcher often serves to begin the diffusion process. Because the headquarters office feels less constrained in the short term by criteria of effectiveness and efficiency and places greater emphasis on the need for professionalism than the branches, it will be willing to have a faculty resident whose research may be different from the firm's perception of its immediate needs. Such research can best be characterized as cell 3 research. What is being researched is the application of global knowledge to a particular problem. The work of Mock and Turner (1981) provides an excellent example of such an effort. While Mock and numerous other researchers have investigated the nature of expert judgment of various users of accounting data (such as bank loan officers), their subjects in those studies were selected because they were representative of informed users. The intent of the researchers was to understand how users (in general) utilized financial accounting inputs, while Mock and Turner's work focused on the judgment problem in an audit setting.

What the long-run impact of this research will be is difficult to evaluate. Much of it has been oriented toward the process by which the auditor performs his task. In the spirit of our earlier discussion, it is "problem sensing." Most researchers would welcome the opportunity to identify interesting research problems. The ability to study auditors in their natural habitat provides such an opportunity.

Whether these studies will lead to problem solving is dependent not only on the results of these studies, but also on the receptivity of the firm's work force (the audit staff at all levels) to accept them. The failure to observe any impact may tell us as much about the firm as about the research. However, if one assumes that the work has the potential to assist the firm in its operations, then its development within the firm should facilitate its diffusion. Not only is it perceived to be more relevant by the practitioner, often a firm member is a part of the research project. That individual can assist in its interpretation and dissemination after the resident leaves. Research conducted outside the firm has no such built-in change agent.

Research Grant Programs

While many CPA firms have research grant programs, the Research Opportunities in Auditing (ROA) undertaken by Peat, Marwick, Mitchell,

TABLE 35.1. Length of Time Until Implementation (percent)

Length	Percentage	Cumulative
Less than two years	19	19
Two to five years	46	65
More than five years	35	100

Source: PMM (1982) adapted

and Company (PMM) is probably the best known, most extensively funded, and its reports are most freely available. Thus, we have chosen ROA as the basis for our discussion. As PMM noted at the outset of its 1982 report:

> This report records the progress of Research Opportunities in Auditing's sixth year. The year's progress supports the Foundation's conviction that ROA research benefits the academic community, the auditing profession and the public. Participation by the academic community has been broad and diverse, and the output of published research has established new frontiers of knowledge. Less quantifiable, but no less important, is the impact of the research in the future. Moreover, ROA has continued to be, in the true meaning of the word, a partnership between practicing accountants and the academic community. The partnership has been characterized by cooperation, shared goals, and welcomed achievements. The Foundation looks forward to continuing the productive collaboration between the academic community and Peat Marwick that has characterized ROA. (PMM, 1982, p. 1)

Translated into the framework of this chapter, the PMM report was highlighting the need of the two groups to find a common ground (cells 2 and 3).

Table 35.1 summarizes PMM's assessment of the prospective time horizon before the project's results can be expected to be implemented in practice. The firm's estimates, which may be optimistic, clearly indicate that the bulk (81 percent) of the projects will require two years or more before implementation. Since changes in practice come slowly, this is not surprising. Table 35.2 summarizes, according to our framework, the authors' classification of the 65 projects either completed or in progress. While the PMM estimates of the length of time for a project to be implemented were not available by project, it would appear that, on the average, those projects classified in cell 2 have a shorter implementation time than those found in cell 3.

Overall, the PMM data would support the contention made earlier that the home office is willing to undertake projects that do not immediately affect the audit process. Unfortunately, no data are available on the extent to which completed projects (39 of the 65) have had an effect on practice within PMM or any other firm. Nor has there been sufficient time to ascertain the extent to which this research has led to new projects that are even closer to the firm's day-to-day activities.

While Table 35.2 does not show it, the vast majority of the cell 2 projects had been completed. If completion is a valid surrogate for the chronological order in which the grants were made (and it may not be), then it would appear that there is a shift from problem-solving projects to problem-sensing or problem-defining projects. It would be interesting to discuss this point with PMM's ROA board to see if there is any perceived basis for this. It is possible that the explanation simply is that all of the easy projects were done first.

One effect, however, is quite clear. The extent to which accounting researchers are investigating audit-related problems is increasing significantly. Thus, while financial resources undoubtedly are a factor, the availability of cooperation from the firm in the form of data, research sites, and subjects has caused researchers to formulate their research projects in an auditing context. Moreover, if casual empiricism has any merit, it has had effects far beyond the projects funded by PMM.

Implications of the Reward Structure

Up to this point our focus has been primarily on the organization rather than the individual. However, even an informal analysis of the Meyer-Rowan typology suggests that the form of the incentive scheme and the nature of the criteria by which the organization dispenses rewards are important to its members. Thus, before proceeding further it is worthwhile to look at the effect of the incentive systems on the likelihood of cooperation between academics and practitioners.

The differing nature of the organizational environments within which

TABLE 35.2. Classification of Projects by Cell

	Number	Percent
Cell 2	23	35.4
Cell 3	34	52.3
Attitude Surveys	8	12.3
Total	65	100

Source: Compiled from summaries in PMM (1982)

academics and practitioners exist dictates that the criteria against which they are measured differ. Practitioners perceive that they are being evaluated against a set of performance criteria that stress cost effectiveness constrained by the need to minimize the risk of any exposure to legal liability. Thus, they value the academic research that reflects the greatest benefits to them in the short run (see Tomassini & Karen, 1982). In contrast, academics value those items that will enhance their academic stature (that is, with their academic rather than practitioner peers) and their perceived value to the organization. The criteria involved reflect the research typically found in cells 2, 3, or 4.

Even a casual analysis of what is found in the academic journals will convince the reader that it reflects exactly the opposite point of view from that of the practitioner. For example, while the auditor judgment-oriented research has been quite popular with accounting researchers (see Ashton, 1982), such research ranked at the bottom of this list when auditing practitioners were asked to indicate what research, if any, was of value to them (Tomassini and Karen, 1982). Clearly, the interests of the two groups do not intersect. Thus, one group cannot attend to the interests of the other without a significant risk of being negatively evaluated by peers and superiors. Without one or both of the parties being willing to accept some amount of risk, no mutually satisfactory bargain can be struck, and knowledge transfer and use will be impeded. The willingness of each of the parties to share a part of the risk is a sine qua non of the knowledge utilization we seek. Such risk sharing occurs in cells 2 and 3. When the two parties cooperate on a cell 1 or a cell 4 project, one of the two parties bears the risk of an unfavorable evaluation.

One way for the risk to be reduced is for the academic to gain insight into those projects that are currently being accepted. The residencies and grant programs reveal the practitioner's criteria to the researcher in the form of accepted projects. The accepted project applications become a revealed preference function to the prospective applicants. This leads to another set of proposed projects that reflect what appear to be the selection committee's criteria. Researchers must decide how close they are willing to come to the committee's perceived preferences. The committee, in turn, must decide if it is willing to move further away from cell 1 when an interesting, but less directly relevant, project is proposed.

From the firm's perspective, academic research provides a basis for legitimizing their professional activities. Providing legitimacy is a concern for auditing firms for they are often exposed to legal liability during the course of their audits. Their participation in research that does not enhance organizational efficiency involves some risk sharing for them, but may serve to decrease their exposure. Thus, the managers are willing to expend monetary resources and in this manner bear some of the risk.

The Relevance to Other Disciplines

Whether there is a lesson in the auditing-academic accounting experience that is transferable is an interesting question. However, it is important to highlight those aspects of this relationship that appear to be critical to its evolution. These six aspects are:

The existence of a subset of practitioners with an interest in the creation of new knowledge for whatever reason.

The recognition by these practitioners that the knowledge in its initial form may not result in implementation or problem solving in the short run.

A willingness on the part of these practitioners to accept some of the cost because of their belief in the potential benefits to their organizations.

The recognition that practitioners are in a position to act as promoters when they believe the new developments are at a point where they have merit (that is, will enhance the organization's efficiency and effectiveness).

The existence of an identifiable group of researchers who are ready and willing to engage in projects of mutual interest.

The willingness of the academics to participate because the potential benefits more than offset the costs involved.

In other areas, some organizations exist that may serve as intermediaries to facilitate cooperation between practitioners and academe. These organizations, such as the National Science Foundation and the Stanford Research Institute, perform functions that are analogous to those of the headquarters of CPA firms. They fund research projects and can act as intermediaries to help transfer knowledge between academies and practitioners. Whether the nature and extent of the relationship of these institutions to practitioners is as effective as that of auditing firms is not easily determined as each has characteristics unique to its own situation. Unfortunately, an in-depth analysis of their similarity to auditing firms is beyond the scope of this chapter.

However, in one form or another the six conditions cited above may exist in other areas. Such settings provide the opportunities for a limited exchange of preference functions. Many of the institutions are in a position to give serious consideration to the innovations academics would very much like to see implemented in the real world. However, consonant with the above criteria, they are not free to implement *any* new idea of the academic. The practitioner is shopping and, if academics wish to have an effect, they must take the customer into consideration.

Thus, all research is not necessarily "salable," even if the academic feels it is potentially beneficial to the practitioner. Rather, the academic has to tailor the research either to a real world problem already identified by the practitioners, or to one where it would appear possible that the potential merit of the new knowledge is demonstrable to practitioners in their terms. Just as much of the accounting research of potential value to practitioners is ignored because practitioners feel it "isn't auditing," research in other areas may be destined for a much more circuitous route before it affects practice—if it affects practice at all.

With these considerations in mind and given the nature of the jobs of those practitioners with whom academic researchers interact, the individual desiring to have "a visible effect" on the practice of management may find that it can be achieved only at the cost of some of our valued freedom to pursue those topics that interest us! To those of us who have considered utilizing the PMM ROA program as a vehicle to have behaviorally oriented accounting research affect practice, this has not been an onerous price—if it has been a cost at all. Overall, it would appear that the difference between the setting in which accounting finds itself and many other possible relationships may be a mixed blessing. The structure is there to facilitate the knowledge development-transfer-utilization cycle. However, concurrent with it is a rather narrow range of practitioner interests relative to the range of research ongoing in academe.

NOTES

1. In this chapter, we use the term "organizational type" to refer to the same aspects of organizations that other participants in this conference have labeled "organizational culture" (see, for example, Serpa, this volume).

2. The focus of this section is on the transfer of knowledge and is not concerned with specific user-related problems (such as resistance and understanding of knowledge) that are dealt with in the intervention (Argyris, 1970) and knowledge utilization literature (Zaltman, 1979).

REFERENCES

Argyris, Chris. 1970. Intervention Theory and Method. Reading, MA: Addison-Wesley.

Ashton, Robert H. 1982. Human Information Processing in Accounting-Studies in Accounting Research #17. Sarasota, FL: American Accounting Association.

Boland, Richard J., Jr. 1982. "Myth and Technology in the American Accounting Profession." Journal of Management Studies, 19:109–127.

Kilmann, Ralph H., and Ian I. Mitroff. 1979, "Problem Defining and the Consulting/Intervention Process." California Management Review, 22:26–33.

Meyer, John., and B. Rowan. 1977. "Institutionalized Organizations: Formal Structure as Myth and Ceremony." American Journal of Sociology, 18:340–363.

Mock, Ted J., and Jerry L. Turner. 1981. Internal Accounting Control Evaluation and Auditor Judgment. Auditing Research Monograph, No. 3. New York, NY: American Institute of Certified Public Accountants.

Montagna, P. D. 1974. Certified Public Accounting. Houston, TX: Scholars Book Company.

Mitroff, Ian I., and T. R. Featheringham. 1974. "On Systematic Problem Solving and the Error of the Third Kind." Behavioral Science, 19: 383–393.

Otley, David T. 1982. "Management Accounting and Organization Theory: A Review of Their Interrelationship." Working Paper, University of Lancaster.

Peat, Marwick, Mitchell Foundation. 1982. Research Opportunities in Auditing Program Interim Report.

Rhenman, Eric. 1973. Organization Theory for Long Range Planning. New York, NY: Wiley.

Tomassini, Larry, and Karen, V. 1982. "The Perceived Usefulness of Behavioral Science Knowledge." Working Paper, University of Texas.

Zaltman, G. 1979. "Knowledge Utilization as Planned Social Change." Knowledge: Creation, Diffusion, Utilization, 1:82–105.

36

WHERE THEORY AND PRACTICE COALESCE: AN ACADEMIC MODEL THAT PROMOTES USEFUL KNOWLEDGE AND ITS UTILIZATION OR HOW WE WON THE BATTLE AND LOST THE WAR

Sue M. Gordon

That practitioners such as Koch, Freud, and Pasteur produced some of the most practically useful knowledge as well as some of the most theoretically interesting has been pointed out by several authors, including Ben-David (1971), Gilfilla (1935), and Gouldner (1957). This production of knowledge appears to occur for several reasons: first, the concerns of the workaday life focus the practitioner into areas of inquiry that have relevance; second, the pressures of these problems goad the practitioner in the setting to find innovative solutions (Gordon and Marquis, 1962); and third, having the relevant knowledge, practitioners familiar with the organization know how to get it assimilated for adoption. Thus, it was felt that with the right program, deliberately structuring the interaction between practitioners and theoreticians on campus might provide a catalyst for producing useful knowledge and having it used.

For the past five years Boston University has been offering a Ph.D. program specifically designed for human service professionals who continue working full-time while going to school full-time. The program aims at blending theory and practice with the expectation that these practitioners would use the knowledge to make their own organizations more effective and would serve as gatekeepers for their colleagues.

The program has been highly successful in terms of both traditional academic criteria and its impact on human service organizations. The 70 students in the program have displayed overall excellence in meeting degree requirements. They have won a large number of research grants and fellowships, and their publication rate has been high. The attrition rate has been exceptionally low—less than 15 percent. Each year the number of inquiries and applications has increased. Graduate Record scores for entering students have constantly risen, with the mean of those entering most recently above 1250. Students in the program feel good about the program. They report that the knowledge learned has been very useful and has led to significant changes both in their professional activities and their organizations. The faculty find the students interesting to teach and thought provoking.

Despite the successes of the program in terms of these and other criteria, the program has failed institutionally; it is no longer accepting students. In this chapter we will examine how the nature and structure of the program led to its successes and at the same time resulted in its failure. In order to understand the reasons for this paradox, it is necessary to compare in some detail the assumptions and structure of the program with the assumptions and structure of traditional graduate education.

VARIATIONS IN TRADITIONAL AND OLDER STUDENT GRADUATE EDUCATION

In order to stimulate the promotion of useful knowledge and its utilization, it was felt necessary that the students be in situations whereby they had sufficient expertise, organization position, and power both to test the knowledge learned and to bring a rich experiential background to the classroom. This meant that the program would have to be oriented toward "older" learners. Attempts at graduate education for older learners have met with limited success. We felt that the reasons for this were at least partially due to the fact that colleges are structured to meet the need of unemployed younger students. Consequently, it was felt a new model was required that would meet the needs, strengths, and life pressures of fully employed older students.

Traditional graduate education is based on the model of the undergraduate major who continues directly on full-time into graduate school. Supported by a teaching or research assistantship, this student is fully immersed academically on campus for an indefinite period of time. Past training and current involvement lead to a focus on the issues involving disciplinary paradigms. The traditional graduate student tends to have had relatively little life experience and to have few demands other than academic ones. This enables complete academic immersion; the student is available to work on faculty research, engage in departmental activities, and participate in informal discussions. Clearly in a subordinate position, the student looks to the faculty as role models. Their lead is followed in structuring a career path including the choice of problems on which to work.

The academic structure that has emerged in most universities reflects the life conditions of traditional students. A basic assumption of most programs is that students have little or no time pressures outside of academe. As a consequence, it is expected that for a while at least graduate students will be intellectual dilettantes sampling a wide range of intellectual pursuits. Structure is minimal, for the most part leaving students to design their own curriculum. The assumption is that by trial and error they will obtain a program fitted to their own intellectual needs. It is expected that students are versed in the byways and norms of the university and that only minimal socialization and social support are necessary. The minimal external time pressures on students have enabled graduate programs to use the master-apprentice relationship as the core of the academic experience. This relationship provides students with close supervision and state-of-the-art learning in areas of concern to them. It provides faculty members with helping hands and stimulation in their intellectual endeavors. The structure, when working well, benefits both students and faculty. However, for the structure to work, students must have time, be well socialized, and be willing to accept the role of the apprentice. Even when students can meet these conditions there is no certainty that mishaps will not occur. The folklore of the university abounds with tales of ten-year Ph.Ds., master-apprentice conflict, and a large number of ABDs. When students cannot meet these conditions, the chances for a successful graduate experience are considerably reduced.

For the most part, these conditions for intellectual development are not present when dealing with older learners. Being older, they tend to be responsible for a number of individuals besides themselves (children, aging parents). Typically, they have both work and family obligations. Given these diverse pressures, time is restricted, resulting in less time for intellectual interaction on campus including involvement with faculty and participation in departmental activities. Already on a career path, older students' role models are outside of academe. Outside pressures create a need and desire not only to restrict the time spent on campus on a weekly basis, but also in terms of time until receipt of degree. Older students feel pressured to make each moment on campus count and to structure interactions to meet their time schedules. The result is a less leisurely academic immersion. Also, with the variety of external involvements in which older students are engaged, the problems they face are frequently broad and cross-disciplinary and their approach pragmatic. With their greater maturity and life experience, the older graduate students are used to taking a superior role and to directing their own activities. Nevertheless, having been out of academe for some time, they feel apart from the ongoing process and somewhat hesitant to resume a student role.

Given the differences between traditional and older learners, it is not surprising that older learners are frequently dissatisfied with their graduate education. They criticize universities because:

Many offerings have a vocational or narrow discipline focus.

The timing of classes leads to a course of study taken on a catch-as-catch-can basis chosen to fit the learner's time schedule rather than an intellectual agenda.

Most part-time academic experience involves a lengthy commitment during which it is difficult to maintain a sense of continuity of content.

A diffused, segmentalized experience makes it difficult to find self-fulfillment and intellectual understanding, which studies on adult learners have found are important motivators for returning to school (Parelius, 1979).

Adults who can afford to go to school full-time frequently find themselves in programs geared for younger students. Therefore, it is not surprising that the aspirations of many older graduate learners have been undercut, which in turn has led to a plethora of incompleted courses of study.

Thus, one of the challenges in adult graduate education is simultaneously to maintain quality and limit attrition.

The major differences between traditional and working older graduate students are noted below:

Traditional Students	*Older Students*
younger	older
work on campus	work off campus
full academic involvement	fragmented academic involvement
discipline orientation	applied orientation
discipline major identity	profession (job) major identity
time open	time limited
accept apprentice role	reject apprentice role
unfocused interests	focused interests

In sum, to give older, fully employed graduate students in-depth social science knowledge, a new graduate education model was needed. The model should reflect the life-cycle, interests, strengths, and social-psychological needs of older learners. In addition, to meet the goal of developing a program that was aimed at knowledge use, it was necessary to develop an action orientation throughout the program's curriculum. Given the time pressure on the students, it also was necessary to accomplish this learning under fairly sharp time constraints.

PROGRAM MODEL

To meet these criteria, the following five goals guided the formation of the new model:

A melding of theoretical and practical expertise to create a learning environment that is both intellectually stimulating and capitalizes on and integrates work experience;

A student structure that is supportive intellectually, socially, and psychologically;

A transition structure that reduces the alienation of the student role and facilitates the student through the variety of rites of passage;

An interdisciplinary experience that cross-cuts rigid and artificial department and discipline borders in order to relate to the complex issues faced on the job; and

Administrative support to allow students to devote as much time as possible to their academic pursuits.

Building on these goals, the Center for Applied Social Science with the Department of Sociology and the Social Psychology Program in the Department of Psychology designed the Programs in Applied Social Science (PASS) to enable full-time employed older learners holding a master's degree to obtain a Ph.D. The human service professionals to whom the programs are geared earn the regular discipline Ph.D. in either Sociology or in Psychology (Social), and therefore meet all the requirements and standards for the department in which they are registered. Applicants followed the normal department admissions procedures. Students admitted to PASS were selected by Center faculty from among the PASS applicants whom the departments determined met their criteria. The program is administered through the Center by a faculty Coordinator who spends full-time administering and teaching two courses in the program. An Executive Committee representing the three cosponsoring bodies and the students provides guidance. Currently there are 70 students enrolled, ranging in age from 29 to 61 with a mean age of 40.

In designing the program for these students, the five goals mentioned above received special attention. We will now focus on each of these goals, indicating the philosophy behind them and how they were implemented.

Theory and Application Combined

The rationale for combining theory and practice comes from the findings mentioned earlier of the key role practitioners have had in the production of useful knowledge (Ben-David, 1971; Gilfilla, 1935; Gouldner, 1957).

Several approaches were taken to coalesce theory and practice. Both degree programs stress a firm grounding in social science theory and methods, coupled with specialized courses reflecting the unique aspects of applied activities. Class assignments may require the applicability of a theory or concept to understanding social problems, or the work setting may be used as a means of testing the relevance of a just-learned theory. For example, in the course Formal Organizations, each student becomes a consultant in another student's organization.

Another way in which the gap between practitioner and academician is bridged is by intertwining PASS with existing departmental programs. Each group of students takes half of the 12-course curriculum together in courses that are specially focused for the applied students. The other half of the curriculum is taken with traditional department students. This mingling offers traditional students the opportunity to learn about the practitioners' world while offering practitioners insight into the problems and concerns of academically oriented students.

Student Support (Cohort) Structure

The program started each year in May. The "cohort," or group of students entering, was structured to be used as the basic building block of the program. Fostering an active cohort enables members to profit from each other's experiences as well as from the more formal aspects of the program. Since they proceed through the academic curriculum at the same pace and have similar interests, study groups are a logical outgrowth of the cohort structure. The study groups form an important function as they help students gain independence and broaden their intellectual horizons. The cohort buffers some of the strangeness and difficulties of returning to school and being a graduate student. It is also important in providing social and psychological support. For individuals whose lives are fragmented, the cohort structure provides a sense of belonging and a feeling of continuity. Special events such as an orientation retreat are arranged to develop and foster a supportive cohesion within and between cohorts.

Transition Structure

Recognizing that adult learners frequently have not coped with student status for a long while, every attempt is made to orient them to and support them in the student role. In addition to the orientation retreat, during the first summer there was a workshop designed to introduce the language of the social sciences as well as to strengthen group cohesion. At the start of the second year another retreat was held for the purpose of evaluating their experiences, and to discuss the second year curriculum and the qualifying exams. A similar meeting is held with students when they finish their coursework. Furthermore, recognizing that after coursework an anomic situation occurs that often results in an ABD, some structure is imposed. The process toward the dissertation is begun during the last semester of coursework in a field research course. Continuity and continued structure is provided by two noncredit offerings: a continuing student workshop for those working toward their oral exams and a dissertation seminar for those at that stage.

It should be noted that to facilitate a cohesive and timely academic experience, a sequential and cumulative curriculum was developed. By using one summer session each year, the 12-course curriculum is completed in two years. Because the courses must be passed in a specified sequence and at a specified time, academic pressures are deliberately created to compete with and, it is hoped, take precedence over some of the external pressures that often result in unfinished courses of study.

Interdisciplinary Structure

The complex social problems of interest to the students require a broad interdisciplinary approach. To gain this breadth, both faculty and students were selected to expand perspective. Each cohort of students was deliberately chosen to represent various academic backgrounds (such as nursing, law, social work) and a variety of administrative levels and sectors of human services. The cohort courses required of all students are taught by Center faculty with appointments in Sociology or Psychology. In addition to the sponsoring departments, the curriculum draws upon the resources of the departments of Political Science, Economics, the School of Management, and other relevant departments and centers throughout the university.

Administrative Support

Every attempt is made to create an environment in which busy people can devote as much time as possible to their academic pursuits. For example, arrangements are made to expedite registration and to acquire library assignments. Desk space and a study lounge have been set aside to facilitate individual and group study. To see that these facilitations occur, the Program Coordinator, in addition to handling administrative details, tries to maintain a constant awareness of the students' academic status and needs, and so is frequently able to act as ombudsman to make accommodations that benefit the students. Having someone as a focal point of the program ensures that both problems and achievements are noted and appropriate changes rapidly made.

Even from this brief description it may be seen that the program model does not require extensive resources and only moderate structural change. Therefore, it is potentially adoptable by a wide variety of academic institutions. For these reasons, it is particularly important to evaluate its success.

PROGRAM OUTCOMES

We did find that one of the advantages of bringing practitioners into the classroom is that there is a direct and rapid communication between the theorists and the appliers of knowledge. Students have frequently approached faculty and related how last week's lecture or last night's reading helped them deal with a problem in which they were involved. In a survey in which the students were asked if their academic involvement had led to any practical consequences for their work, every single student gave an affirmative response. Examples of job enlargement, job enrichment, new outlooks, and organization changes implemented were frequent. Typical of the responses were the following two statements:

> I have been approached to work on an NIMH grant because people know what I was doing in the program. Also I have redesigned a number of the monitoring instruments we are using for contracted programs. I've initiated a number of things in our office drawing on some course material. I am trying to get us to face issues which we have not been facing.

> I have a better understanding and use of evaluation. Translating class discussions and assignments into my own organization has changed my leadership as a policy maker and in evaluating my organization. The evaluation aspects are helping me write a grant for an Alcohol Task Force with which I work. Just looking at the assumptions we work with—how you define delinquency—helps give you a new perspective on the problems you are dealing with.

These quotes highlight the important fact that students' leadership roles in their organizations enable them to influence others and effect change so that the knowledge learned has an impact beyond the individual student. Many students also act both as translators of knowledge and promoters or disseminators of useful knowledge for organizations by writing papers and giving presentations. Thirty-five out of the 58 second-year-and-above students have presented or written professional papers thus far. Some of this year's examples are: "Professionalization: Quality or Control?" (American Public Health Association Annual Meeting); "The Impact of Science upon the Occupational Therapy Profession" (Annual Occupational Therapy

Conference); "Survival in the Eighties—New Initiatives for Human Service Organizations" (National Association for Social Works Annual Conference); and "Social and Economic Policy in Cuba for Disabled Children" (World Federation of Occupational Therapy, Hamburg Germany).

That many faculty find these students stimulating is evident by the fact that several faculty each year ask the Program Coordinator specifically to be sure PASS students know about their classes. Faculty opinion was more systematically sought last year by a visiting faculty member on sabbatical, who conducted a questionnaire survey of PASS student instructors and advisors. In one series of questions, they were asked to compare "traditional" department students with PASS students. Overall, the findings show the 12 advisors (52 percent return) and nine instructors (69 percent return) "rate PASS students' performance as generally comparable to that of regular students" (Rosenthal, 1981).

The evaluation report continues with the finding that the instructors rate PASS students compared to traditional department students as: "having more applied and less theoretical interests, as being equal or superior in preparation, attendance and participation in class, having somewhat less prior exposure to the subject matter of the courses, and as being somewhat less timely in completing class assignments." Performance of PASS students was also rated as similar in class, on course examinations, and in quality of papers and class projects. The report stated that the advisors rated PASS students as:

> equal or superior to regular department students in clarity of academic goals, understanding the demands of a Ph.D. program, scholarly interest, and in applying knowledge to social problems. Regular students were rated slightly higher on disciplinary identification. The only problem area which this respondent group thought was particularly bothersome for PASS than regular students was in the area of "managing competing demands of job and family." A sizeable proportion of PASS students themselves point out a tension between school and family (50 percent) and school and social life (56 percent). That this type of problem should arise for individuals working full-time and carrying what averages close to a full-time academic load is not surprising. What is surprising is that in spite of this tension, advisors do not feel that PASS students have any more difficulty than regular students in "meeting academic performance standards." (Rosenthal, 1981:10–11)

These findings fit with our earlier description of the traditional and the older student. They indicate that given a supportive program it is possible for older students to achieve up to the level of students in a traditional program. These findings are supported by the fact that despite the experimental nature of the program, of the 45 students who finished coursework by 1981, four have graduated, nine are completing their dissertations, and ten are working on their prospectuses.

Knowledge useful for organizations is produced as early as during the coursework; application of the principles and methods learned have produced information leading to organization change. For example, a consultant's report done in the course "Formal Organizations" led to the reorganization of a law firm. A group project done in the "Evaluation and Social Policy" course led to the restructuring of a hospital service when the evaluation revealed a "nonprogram."

Recognition of students' abilities has come from a number of outside sources. For example, one student was appointed a White House Fellow; three have received scholarship funds outside of departmental funding; and seven have received research funds from various organizations (National Center for Health Research, the American Occupational Therapy Foundation, American· Nursing Association, the State Department of Youth Services, and universities).

Also, it should be noted that the reputation of the programs spread, leading to increased inquiries and applications. Over half of the last entering cohort learned about the program from a friend. Even though there was no program announcement last year, there were over 130 inquiries.

A major concern of this conference, while not stated explicitly, was what would help academics produce more useful organization knowledge. It is, of course, difficult to pinpoint the influences that lead one to a new theoretical concept. Given a multitude of inputs it would be presumptuous to expect that during their education any students would be credited with the generation of new theory. Nevertheless, the question remains: Did the PASS students have an impact on the faculty's production of useful organization knowledge? Despite the relative newness of the program, we see indications that there are two ways in which PASS students may help generate more useful knowledge for organization theorists. One way is by bringing "unusual" cases to the theorists' attention. The second way is by improving the research data base. An example of the first way are the observations of one noted theoretician. When asked if PASS students had had any impact on his research and/or conceptualizations he commented:

> Being more rich in personal experience, PASS students [compared to more traditional students] are not as easily made happy by the formulations I bring them. When working with [advisee's name] my organization theory had to accommodate a different kind of organization. I had to figure out what organization framework applied to it. It started me thinking of social movements and the meaning of social problems.

Other faculty have commented that PASS students' organizational contacts have given them a broader sense and more cases on which to test their concepts. The research the students undertake is enhanced by their organizational status, which gives them access to data that are not always available or known to outsiders. They not only know where the data are, they have the means to evaluate the data's reliability and validity. Familiarity with opinion leaders and gatekeepers of other organizations leads to effective supporting documents and contacts that further increase access and enhance return rates. For example, a recent female graduate's dissertation has the unusual data base of interviews six months apart with 53 men incarcerated in a maximum security prison. With more students just now reaching the final stages of their academic program, the impact of the students' research and its effect on the faculty and on the field is just beginning to be seen. Nevertheless, early indications are that there is potential for increasing the production of more useful knowledge.

Thus, in terms of many different criteria it appears the program is successful. How then is it possible that the program has been discontinued? To answer this question we will turn once more to the goals of the program to see how the major compenents that were felt to be the fundamental strengths of the educational success of the model were at the same time disadvantages institutionally.

PROGRAM DISSONANCE

Theory and Practice

By capitalizing on the theoretical and disciplinary strength of the academicians and the practice background of the students, the program expectation was that there would be an educational advantage to both the discipline-oriented and the applied students. The practitioners are expected to gain by learning how to use social science concepts, perspectives, and methods in order to analyze and deal in new ways with the problems they are facing. On the other hand, it was expected that the relevance of the knowledge produced by the theoreticians would increase due to the increased contact with the potential appliers of the knowledge.

One of the advantages of this contact has been that regular students have taken advantage of the ready access of a variety of organizations for field work. In the classroom we often find that theory and practice do coalesce, creating a synergy that is productive for the participants. However, we also find that Dewey was correct in his statement that:

> Human beings as individuals tend to devote themselves to the practice of knowing or to the practice of a professional business, social or anesthetic art. Each takes the other half of the circle for granted. Theorists and

practitioners, however, often indulge in unseemly wrangles as to the importance of their respective tasks. Then the personal difference of calling is hypostatized and made into an intrinsic difference of knowledge and practice. (1929:37–38)

These differences in orientation are visible in the program. One of the struggles with PASS students from the time they enter graduate school through their dissertation research is getting them to think in abstract frameworks. On the other hand, some nonprogram students view questions of application as irrelevant, and there have even been charges of "watering down" courses.

The assumed practitioner advantage of being concerned with relevant problems also has its drawbacks. Hardly a PASS student entered the program who did not have a dissertation topic in mind. The tendency to relate all subject matter to this topic area is helpful in organizing the information learned, but limiting in the opportunity to wonder and wander intellectualy. The converging effect of this applied focus is felt to be exacerbated by the PASS students' not having either master's training in the same discipline or the ability to spend long hours on campus. The fact that they nevertheless can successfully meet the degree requirements may call into question some of the assumptions upon which traditional programs are based, and in that sense may challenge long held notions about doctoral training.

Another aspect of the practitioner—the boundary spanning and gate-keeping roles that PASS students hold—appears to be effective in getting the knowledge learned directly and quickly into their organizations. Indeed, this appeared to be one of the most successful aspects of the program. However, by virtue of retaining these roles, coupled with the earlier education in another field, PASS students are reluctant to reject these loyalties and identities to make their professional identification solely that of the discipline. With many years in their professions of orientation and for the most part expecting to continue the career path they are on, the students prefer to add the discipline hat to that of their ongoing career to become a "nurse-sociologist" or "manager-social-psychologist." (Nevertheless, by the end of the degree experience the titles are sometimes reversed.) The reluctance to wear only the disciplinary hat reflects: an initial lack of understanding about what the discipline represents (an understanding that is gained as the students progress in their training); the relatively low status of the social sciences and particularly sociology in the nation today; a desire to apply social science concepts to the discipline of orientation rather than become an academician; and the utility of the discipline identification in their work area. Whatever the reason may be, the lack of desire to embrace fully the discipline is discordant to some who have made such a commitment.

The differences regarding identity raise the issue of the acceptance of the boundary spanner. For a decade applied sociologists have been trying to have their needs and interests receive the official sanction and support of the American Sociological Association. Though some major changes have taken place recently, at the December 1981 American Sociological Association Workshop on Applied Sociology, there were many expressions of feelings of rejection from "applied sociologists" who received the traditional training but had chosen not to work in the university. The problem for the "practitioner-sociologist" may be even greater. The question is how to create an environment that is neither so hostile that the applied scientist chooses to withdraw, nor so conducive that the applied scientist becomes co-opted.

Interdisciplinary Approach

There are two aspects of this interdisciplinary component of the model that are important: the structural aspect required by cross-department cooperation and intellectual integration.

Program Structure

The joint sponsorship of the program, with its administration out of a nondepartment unit of the university, meant that the program acted as a constraint to insure maintenance of an interdisciplinary perspective and concern with application. Nevertheless, while important to the vitality of the program, the coordination by the Center resulted in severe jurisdiction problems and feelings of exploitation.

As an anomalous structure, the external unit is tenuous in that its performance depends on the commitments and support of other units in the organization. For this reason external programs rarely have unadulterated champions. The external program's members are pulled by commitments in two directions. Because the university reward structure is based on disciplinary review, time and commitment to extradisciplinary involvement may suffer. Campbell points out that part of the organizational constraints come from the "ethnocentrism of disciplines." He notes that the specialists emphasizing the central focus of a discipline have more departmental allies than peripheral specialists whose more natural allies may be in other departments. Decision making therefore tends to favor the central specialties and to lead to the elimination of peripheral specialties (1969).

Such a trend is especially noticeable regarding staff changes. Discontinuities in staffing are especially troublesome for not only are staff lost, but the external unit is dependent on the priorities of the central units for hiring. The likelihood of replacements for the original staff having as much commitment to the program as the founders is especially slight. Particularly if the core faculty is small, changes in the participants may critically change a program's conceptual framework.

At the University of Pittsburgh, the Program for the Study of Knowledge Use started as an applied program in the Sociology Department. However, for many of the same philosophical reasons we have mentioned, it now has an external unit structure that reports to a dean. It is interesting to note that the major problem recently reported for this program was staffing difficulties, particularly with regard to finding faculty who could maintain a "dialectic equilibrium between openness and closedness" (Fisher et al., 1981:15).

Replacement of the loss of some of the original Center faculty for PASS courses was a catalyst in raising controversial interunit issues of control, teaching qualifications, and resource allocation. A precipitating incident such as a loss of faculty helps points out that despite the fact that an attempt is made to spell out responsibilities before the cooperating units establish their initial agreement, with changing environmental conditions there are always situations that were not originally anticipated that raise questions of jurisdiction.

In a relatively stable environment where the conditions of the initial organizing agreement hold, one would expect external units to endure longer than in a turbulent environment. Unfortunately, during the life of PASS the available university resources have been dwindling and priorities changing, moving us out of a relatively stable period. However, it is our contention that the allocation of resources and other administrative problems might have been settled to everyone's benefit if it were not for the discordant notes in the philosophical areas that were highly charged but below the surface, making it difficult to work on the nuts-and-bolts issues.

Finally, it should be noted that not being in the regular organization structure can enable greater freedom in that there is no organizational history or precedent that dictates behavior. On the other hand, one must be aware of the constraints of the dominant structure so as not to jeopardize one's position by running into conflict with the procedures or priorities of the central organization. Thus, freedom can be enjoyed as long as there is a low profile—as long as the external unit is neither clearly failing or successful, or as long as it remains small and is therefore nonthreatening.

Intellectual Interaction

At the level of the broadening horizons, by bringing in a heterogeneous group of students both in terms of academic background and work experience, an interdisciplinary approach was found to be intellectually stimulating. Unfortunately, on the department level we never created a truly interdisciplinary program. Because of scheduling limitations and the curricular requirements of other departments such as Economics and Political Science, we did not obtain the breadth of interdisciplinary orientation desired. Even the interaction between the Psychology and Sociology students was curtailed by the ongoing pull of meeting departmental requirements and participation in departmental activities. Despite a broad spectrum of speakers and a variety of formats, the program's colloquium series never coalesced. A jointly taught course was felt to be a solution—a solution that had faculty load, funding, and scheduling problems and would have required adjustments in the course sequencing of both departments. Nevertheless, given a future, we would have worked hard to obtain this type of course.

Cohort Structure

Great care was taken to stimulate interaction between the members of each cohort so that they would share intellectually and develop a supportive network. The cohort structure has proved highly successful in helping students both generalize and question their experience. It has proved supportive of the students' psychosocial needs. It has also proved a thorn in the side of the regular programs, epitomizing the threats of the external unit to the traditions of graduate education. First, the very identity of a group of students as a unit heightens the visibility of the program and enables invidious comparisons. Second, this unit identification is in direct opposition to the tradition of independent scholars. Third, the students' strong identification with the cohort and PASS is one more way the identification with the discipline is eroded. Fourth, already structured, the cohort may be viewed as a potential force to be used in opposition to the central organization. Finally, the cohort is viewed as exclusionary.

Though other programs may not use the cohort structure, some of the issues mentioned will still be raised depending on the ratio of the critical mass of the new program to the existing program(s). When in one department the number of PASS students began to equal that of the regular program, questions of the mission and image of the department were naturally raised. These are serious questions for any organization. Especially in a time of declining resources, changes in priorities threaten level of existence as well as existence itself.

Transition Structure

The transition structure is a means of providing group socialization into the expectations and requirements of graduate education. As with regular students, every PASS student is assigned a department advisor. Department faculty always participate in orientations. While group orientations may save individual faculty time, they also remove the individuality of the experience, putting it at different points in time in the hands of one or a few individuals rather than the colleagues as a whole. Despite an attempt to welcome nonprogram students to many of these activities (such as the Continuing Student Workshop and Dissertation Seminar), the activities gave a sense of privilege for one group and nonprivilege for the other.

The large number of required courses and their mandated sequential organization were also deliberately done to orient and support the student role. However, these structures may be seen as creating further instances in which PASS students miss important learning experiences. An evaluation of the program done by one department stated:

> The individual is shepherded and protected so that a more sheltered and buffered educational experience is provided, one which is not subjected to the usual rigors of graduate school education. One consequence is that students are not allowed to develop sufficient independence, flexibility and self-reliance and may encounter particular difficulties when the relatively structured first two years are completed.

Individuals who have successfully made their way up an organization ladder would generally be thought to be independent and self-reliant, and therefore not in need of acquiring these traits in school. As noted earlier, the courses taken by PASS students are taken with regular students or, in the case of cohort courses, are similar to departmental offerings except for their applied orientation. Thus, the statement may refer to the lack of freedom in selecting courses and their timing. In any event, the statement reflects the strength of belief in the assumptions of the traditional graduate model of the freedom and responsibility of individual students to find their way through the discipline.

The difficulties in reconciling the different education models are underscored by the fact that one department was pleased with the program to the extent that it fought to have the program completely under its aegis. At the same time, the department plan for the program entailed eliminating the cohort structure and some of the other program components mentioned that we and the students feel have been essential to the program's success.

Administrative Support

The administrative support offers services that ideally all students could enjoy (for example, registration is done before a class). The services are well appreciated by the students and save them a great deal of time. Thus, there is some jealousy over the availability of these services.

The fact that there is a program administrator also raises the feeling that one group of students has a spokesperson while the rest of the students must fend for themselves. It is felt that this gives unfair advantage to the students with the spokesperson. Once again, it contradicts the tradition of the student striving independently through the system.

We would like to point out that we do not think that Boston University is unusually recalcitrant to change or adverse to applied interests. Indeed, we feel that applied interests are a concern of most of the faculty and that this is one of the strengths of the university. Thus, we see the demise of both the Programs in Applied Social Science and the earlier developed Community Sociology Program, reported on so hopefully by Gelfand (1976), as representing a genuine desire on the part of the faculty to foster applied programs. At the same time, these experiences are indicative of the strength of the traditions, structure, and assumptions to which many of the faculty have been socialized.

CONCLUSION

Our experience with PASS has demonstrated that by bringing practitioners and academicians together on campus, theory and practice can coalesce to produce useful knowledge and its utilization. Based on our experience, we have learned several lessons. One is the organizational lesson that having the program in an anomalous unit outside the regular university structure allowed it to be hostage to the related departments' needs. Therefore, we would recommend that any such program should operate independently and be degree granting.

We have also learned as we meet older graduate students in other programs that our PASS experience is not unique. Practitioners in other departments, including schools of management and other professional schools, do not want to be clients of the university in the old medical model sense whereby they accept what the doctor tells them. Rather, they are seeking more of a business consultant relationship whereby they are recognized as having information and needs that figure into the solution. It is our feeling that we will waste fewer resources and have happier students in many areas on campus if we begin to recognize and actively seek ways to capitalize on the experience these students bring to class. Techniques that have worked for us are having students apply principles by acting as consultants in each other's organizations and, where possible, having students develop or work with data from their own organizations.

The most striking lesson, however, is the extent to which differences in the expectations and values of the traditional graduate model and the PASS older student model makes the coexistence of two such programs difficult.

Since for decades the traditional model has successfully produced competent scholars, the issue is not to change or eliminate that model but rather how to create an environment and structure in which more than one type of student can receive the intellectual stimulation and graduate degree desired.

Thus, we need to recognize that in creating models to meet the needs of students and to produce useful organization knowledge we are faced with two distinct challenges: first, to create a model that intellectually does the job, and second, to create a model that will be compatible with the ongoing university system. Only when both these criteria have been met can we claim success. We do not see any easy answers to these challenges, but we think a critical starting point is to surface the strategic assumptions underlying different views of graduate education. It will then be possible to work with faculty to develop views of graduate education that are alternatives to the one they have been socialized to accept.

Both the needs of society and demographic changes require a broader perspective than the traditional view of graduate degrees as primarily roads to teaching and research. We believe that if social science knowledge is to be more effectively used in the broader society, it will be necessary to supplement the traditional view with one that reflects the needs and strengths of the practitioner. If this resocialization occurs, it will not only benefit society at large but will also stimulate the development of the social sciences.

BIBLIOGRAPHY

Ben-David, Joseph
1971   The Scientist's Role in Society. Englewood Cliffs, N.J.: Prentice-Hall.
Campbell, Donald
1969   "Academic Ethnocentrism and the Fish-Scale Model of Omniscience" in Muzafer and Carolyn Sherif, Interdisciplinary Relationships in the Social Sciences. Chicago, Aldine
DeMartini, Joseph
1979   "Applied Sociology: An Attempt at Clarification and Assessment." Teaching Sociology, 6:4:331–354.
Dewey, John
1929   The Quest for Certainty. New York: Macmillan. Quoted in R. D. Mason and I. I. Mitroff, Challenging Strategic Planning Assumptions. New York, 1981.
Fisher, Evelyn, Burkart Holzner, and William Dunn
1981   "Bringing Social Science to Bear on Practical Problems: The University of Pittsburgh Program for the Study of Knowledge." Paper presented at the American Sociological Association Workshop on Applied Sociology. Washington, D.C.
Gelfand, Donald E.
1976   "Sociological Education and Sociological Practice." Teaching Sociology, 3:2:148–159.

Gilfillan, S. C.
1935   The Sociology of Invention, Chicago: Follett Publishing Company.
Gordon, Gerald and Sue Marquis
1962   "Freedom and Control in Four Scientific Settings." American Behavioral Scientist. 6:4:39.
Gouldner, Alvin W.
1957   "Theoretic Requirements of the Applied Social Sciences." American Sociological Review. 22:1:92–102.
Parelius, Ann P.
1979   "Age Inequality in Educational Opportunity: The Needs of Adult Students in Higher Education." Adult Education, spring.
Rosenthal, Stephen
1981   Report written for: Evaluation of Program, Boston University. (May).

37

CURRENT AND PROSPECTIVE ROLES FOR LINKING ORGANIZATIONAL RESEARCHERS AND USERS

Janice M. Beyer and Harrison M. Trice

In modern societies, scientific research is an important source of new knowledge. A basic requirement for the utilization of new knowledge derived from research is that it reach persons who can use it in a form that is useful to them. The transfer of knowledge from researchers to potential users is impeded, however, by the social separation of researchers from users. The two belong to different communities with few shared activities or sentiments and little social interaction (Homans, 1950). This chapter will focus upon problems involved in the transfer of new knowledge from organizational researchers to managers or other potential users. In focusing on this topic we made two assumptions: first that research on organizations is presently being conducted and will continue to be conducted as part of scientific inquiry; and second, that at least some of the knowledge produced by such scientific research is potentially useful. Our primary aim is to address the practical questions of how to achieve successful and persistent transfer of knowledge based on scientific organizational research from researchers to users. An ancillary question is how to transfer information that might make research more useful from users to organizational researchers.

In discussing factors inhibiting utilization of social science, many writers have pointed to differences in goals, values, and ideologies between research and user communities (Dunnette and Brown, 1968; Glaser and Taylor, 1973; Duncan, 1974b; Caplan, 1977; Dunlop, 1977; Dunn, 1980; Rothman, 1980). Others have suggested that language barriers are created between these two communities by the abstract theoretical terminology and quantitative techniques used in some research (Van de Vall et al., 1976), making translation necessary before findings can be communicated to users (Rothman, 1980). In a widely cited review of the literature, Havelock and his colleagues (1969) diagrammed researcher and practitioner communities as separated by a knowledge gap, thus implying that differences are so great that no overlap exists.

The most commonly advocated solutions for bridging the gap are various kinds of linking roles (Likert and Lippitt, 1953; Thompson, 1956; Guetzkow, 1959; Bennis, 1963; Lundberg, 1966; Havelock et al., 1969; Van de Vall, 1976; Sundquist, 1978; Rothman, 1980; Rossi, 1980). Titles given have varied over time from social engineer (Hauser, 1946; Likert and Lippitt, 1953:587; Thompson, 1956) to the currently popular "applied social scientist" (Van de Vall, 1976; Rossi, 1980). Although many of these writers envision creation of new roles, it seems clear to us that existing occupations and roles already provide some linkage between organizational researchers and users. Thus, one purpose of this chapter is to assess the performance of existing linking roles in bridging the gap between organizational researchers and potential users of their research. A second purpose is to assess the viability of designs for new linking roles. Our third purpose is to offer some suggestions on how the performance of the linking function might be improved through role redesign, new curriculum, and other supports that can be provided by universities.

SIZING UP THE GAP

Before assessing the performance of existing linking roles, it may be useful to examine the evidence for the presumed gap between organizational researchers and users. Research results on the two-communities' theory indicate that the breadth and depth of the presumed gap depends on which dimensions of the gap and what kinds of researchers and users are involved. In empirical studies that investigated the presumed gap, investigators have tended to look for disparities in values (sentiments) more than for lack of social contacts (interaction) or of shared activities and experiences. The results that seem most relevant to the field of organizations were obtained by Duncan (1974a), who found that practitioners from the American Society of Training Directors had some significantly different values about management knowledge and theory than members of the Academy of Management— who are primarily academic researchers. Both groups agreed that practicality and usefulness were the most important criteria, but practitioners valued empirical validity and logical preciseness less, and profitability and applicability to specific situations more than did researchers. The practitioners and users studied by Duncan probably fit the description of two separate communities in that they rarely shared activities or interacted socially. Yet, they shared some values toward research and its utilization. Further, his data showed considerable overlap in the distributions of the two communities on those values on which there were significant differences. Thus, to speak of a gap in values may be an exaggeration—at least for some researchers and some potential users.

Furthermore, as Glaser and Taylor (1973) suggested, social contact is likely to decrease further the differences in values. Weiss and Weiss (1981:845) found relatively few significant differences between mental health administrators and social scientists who had served as principal investigators or grant reviewers of mental health research about what makes some studies more useful than others. Their results are not surprising because the two groups had similiar educational backgrounds and various "shared experiences." Nor is it surprising that Baker (1981) found more areas of agreement than disagreement between attitudes of directors and evaluation specialists toward evaluation research; not only had the specialists been selected by directors as respondents, but the two sets of respondents worked in the same mental health centers. Clearly, the presumed gap in values between researchers and users has not been detected when the two groups had similar educational backgrounds and work experiences, and when there was extensive contact, mobility, and overlapping membership between them.

Results are sparse on whether and how differences in values that exist among researchers and users affect utilization. Caplan (1977:194) found that such differences best accounted for bureaucrats' failure to use research. However, Rich (1977:208) found more receptivity to research among practitioners than the two communities' theory suggests, and expressed doubt that the gap was "salient" in explaining utilization.

Unfortunately, the empirical research testing the two-communities' theory has tended to concentrate on values held toward research itself or its use, rather than toward more general issues like power equalization or distribution of resources. Thus, it is not clear that past studies have tapped into those value differences most likely to impede actual utilization. When Taguiri (1965) investigated differences in more general sets of values held by scientists, research managers, and executives, however, he also found more similarities than differences between these groups. Furthermore, when he asked members of each group to estimate the values of other groups, each tended to exaggerate differences between themselves and others, indicating that the values gap is perceived by practitioners and scientists to be wider than it actually is. Some researchers (Duncan, 1974a; Weiss and Weiss, 1981; Baker, 1981) assessed values relative to hypothetical use (inclination to use or intent to use); others (Caplan, 1977; Rich, 1977) assessed values relative to actual use of research. It seems likely that differences between researchers and users will become more evident when actual use has been attempted.

Although not designed to document and investigate the gap, various other studies provide pertinent data. A key issue is the amount and type of interaction that occurs between organizational researchers and potential users, and how it affects information flows and subsequent utilization. Glaser and Coffey (1967) found that diffusion of findings was enhanced when potential users visited sites where research was already in use or attended conferences where they could talk with researchers and current users. In Rothman's (1980:41) study, structural connections between researchers and planners facilitated utilization. But for the vast bulk of organizational research, such interactions or connections do not occur. Thus, when Dunnette and Brown (1968:180–183) surveyed executives perceived to be "acutely attuned to contributions by behavioral scientists," they found that "only a small portion" of them had even heard of many of the studies nominated by industrial psychologists as "most significant." The utilized researchers had made at least indirect contacts with users: the research reported as used by the largest numbers of their respondents had been diffused by its authors through publications widely read by executives, as well as in scientific and technical journals. Other means of indirect contact are suggested by Duncan's (1974a:731) work. He reported that both researchers and managers ranked textbooks and small group sessions, in addition to applied journals, as very important media for transforming theory and research into practice.

We found no data that specifically assessed the amount of shared activities between researchers and users. However, many writers on research utilization conclude that user participation in research—which must, by definition, generate shared activities between researchers and users—is positively related and perhaps essential to its utilization (Likert and Lippitt, 1953; Bennis, 1963; Gershinowitz, 1972; Coleman, 1972). Repeatedly, researchers report that users who participate in earlier phases of research are favorably disposed toward subsequent results (Mann and Likert, 1952; Flanagan, 1961; Glaser and Taylor, 1973; Alkin et al., 1979; Rothman, 1980). Participation can also facilitate utilization for other reasons,[1] but bringing the values, goals, and priorities of researchers and users closer together is undoubtedly an important product of the shread activities that go into planning, designing, and perhaps executing research together.

HOW CAN LINKING ROLES BRIDGE THE GAP?

At this point, we should be able to be more specific about what expectations should be attached to linking roles. Ideally, what should linkers do to facilitate the utilization of organizational research?[2]

The gap between researchers and potential users has at least three dimensions, and so a variety of activities are required to bridge it. The knowledge gap—the differences between what researchers and practitioners know—can be bridged by what we usually call boundary-spanning activities, especially carrying information about research developments to users and information about user needs to researchers. Bridging the practice gap—the differences between what practitioners do and what researchers have determined works best—can involve a wide range of activities, including especially: doing applied research incorporating ideas and methods from basic organizational research for user organizations; developing products, procedures, or services that are based on the findings of organizational research and that are useful to organizations; applying techniques or knowledge derived from organizational research to concrete problems of practitioners. These three levels of practice fit our usual conceptions of the roles of applied scientists, development engineers, and technicians, respectively. Bridging the culture gap—the differences in values, beliefs, customs, and language—seems to require the activities of what we usually call integrators: persons who can maintain a social position, hold values and beliefs somewhere in the middle between the groups to be integrated, and who know and can use the language and customs of each group.

SIZING UP EXISTING ROLES

A variety of existing roles and occupations have potential for linking organizational researchers and users. We will consider the four that seem most promising: personnel specialists, inside researchers and change agents, outside consultants and change agents, and extension specialists.

Personnel Specialists

Three features of staff roles in personnel departments make them suitable to provide linkages between organizational researchers and potential users. First, during most of the twentieth century, personnel specialists have enjoyed close relationships with line managers (Miller and Coghill, 1964). In addition, as labor relations specialists have joined personnel departments, close relationships with labor unions have also developed. These roles are therefore well-established within the formal and informal social structures of a large proportion of U.S. work organizations. Second, personnel specialists have been associated over the decades with the application of the social sciences to the workplace. Traditional industrial psychology (Dunnette and Bass, 1963) was imported through techniques used in personnel testing, wage and salary administration, and selection and training. Although less often, personnel specialists have also served as outlets for sociological and anthropological studies of workplaces (Whyte and Hamilton, 1964; Whyte, 1969a), including those in the human relations tradition. A study by the

Industrial Conference Board among its members showed that personnel managers were most often designated by management as the persons who coordinate or supervise the application of social science findings (Rush and Wikstrom, 1969). Complementing this finding was the reported high interest of personnel people in such research. Third, members of the personnel occupations have repeatedly sought professional status (Patten, 1968; Odiorne, 1979), which requires knowledge of both systematic bodies of research and techniques for its application. Recent efforts to generate a uniform series of guidelines for accrediting persons for the personnel occupations illustrate one aspect of these attempts to professionalize (Yoder and Heneman, 1978).

Other features of personnel occupations make them less suitable to provide linking functions. Historically, much of the emphasis within these roles was upon activities that bore little, if any, relation to the use of research in the workplace. In the early part of the century they were much involved in "welfare work," a form of paternalism widely approved by employers (Miller and Coghill, 1964) and still in evidence today. In a study of English personnel managers, Watson (1977) found that two-thirds were unable to identify a basic body of knowledge or theory underlying their work. A casual perusal of U.S. textbooks on personnel administration provided no evidence to contradict these findings. Few devote any space to pointing out the linking aspects of personnel jobs, even when writing about the future (Odiorne, 1981).

In addition, these occupations are viewed, in part at least, as "dumping grounds" for managers who fail in other parts of the organization (Foulkes and Morgan, 1977), as "trash cans" into which a wide variety of miscellaneous, trivial tasks are thrown, and as "fire fighters" or short-term problem solvers (Ritzer and Trice, 1969). Personnel managers report that many of their assigned tasks are dry, dull, technique-bound, clerical tasks or relatively meaningless fun-and-games activities.[3] Thus, much of the time of personnel specialists is probably taken up with activities unrelated to acting as linking agents for the application of organizational research findings.

Finally, the personnel occupations have relatively low status. The better professional-degree students, who might make effective linkers, have unfavorable images of personnel work (Carroll, 1974). Recent attempts to quantify the benefits of the personnel function (Schmidt et al., 1982) can be seen as efforts to enhance the relatively low organizational status of these occupations by demonstrating their practical value.

In sum, members of personnel occupations are unlikely to be very effective as boundary spanners for new organizational research because their current training does not encourage it. Their closeness to the managerial community also makes it unlikely that they will be able to stay as well-connected to sources of research information outside the organization as effective boundary-spanning requires (Tushman and Scanlon, 1981), and prevents them from being very effective as integrators. They are more likely to provide linkage with organizational research through some of their activities, where they may be able to apply specific techniques or findings derived from research in a very concrete way. But they are unlikely to engage in applied research or development activities unless they have also assumed the roles of internal researcher and change agent.

Inside Researchers-Change Agents

Another way that organizational researchers can be linked with users is by researchers or change agents located inside user organizations. One distinct advantage of the inside research role for performing this linking function is that occupants have usually been trained similarly to other researchers—that is, they have earned or worked toward a Ph.D. degree. They should thus be able to understand better than practitioners what outside researchers are saying and doing and why. They should also share at least some of the values of other researchers. Also, if they interact with other researchers and share some activities with them through participation in professional associations like the Academy of Management, the knowledge and values they share with other researchers will be reinforced, and they will be able to keep informed about new developments in knowledge and shifts in values within the field.

But these advantages cannot compensate for other characteristics of the inside research role that militate against its being an effective linking role for organizational research. Most obvious is the relative scarcity of inside social science researchers; only large organizations are likely to feel they can afford to hire social science Ph.D.s as in-house researchers. When they do, such researchers are often employed in a wide variety of fairly nitty-gritty projects—many of which will have nothing to do with *organizational* research per se (Klein, 1976). They are unlikely to have a free hand in deciding what research to do, and whether or not they initiate research, they are unlikely to end up doing what they choose because of time and cost pressures, pressures to be practical and inevitable pressures to design the research to make other people look good.

When inside researchers evaluate and try to change organizational practices, they become change agents. Because change can create new political power, it endangers existing distributions of power (Pettigrew, 1975) and threatens existing power holders. Persons consistently responsible for making changes can hardly avoid acquiring some enemies who have a stake in seeing them discredited in order to undo some results they have achieved. Often, when management seeks knowledge to apply to important organizational problems, outside consultants—who can be chosen so they have no history with organizational participants to overcome—are favored over inside researchers or change agents. Outsiders can preserve confidentiality better, they are usually recognized (and thus legitimated) experts on the issues of concern, and they have an outside power base to help them to deal with insiders' attempts to co-opt them (Zaltman and Duncan, 1977).

Klein's (1976) account of her experiences at Esso in England illustrates many of these points, but especially the political vulnerability of the inside researcher role. When her new boss chose to ignore her work, she lacked access to other communication channels to gain a hearing. When outside consultants were hired by top-level management to do organizational research she felt she could have done, she lacked any authority to force them to incorporate her ideas, and was unsuccessful in persuading them. Pettigrew (1975) argued that inside consultants need group support from colleagues in the research or consultant unit to have effective power. Turf battles between them can easily be exploited by clients who seek to control them. Also, if internal consultants become identified with particular organizational subunits (Margulis, 1971), their integrative role is hampered.

In his analysis of structural factors conducive to research utilization, Rothman (1980) emphasized that internal research units need to have top-level support and access to top-level planners and line managers. Sundquist (1978) identified the lack of such access by persons familiar with research as an impediment to utilization in federal executive departments. Unfortunately, inside social science researchers and change agents often report to middle levels of management, and thus lack such access. Klein (1976) was apparently able to gain access to top management only by resigning.

Whyte's (1969a) case studies of other internal research programs came to the same rather negative conclusions, but for different reasons. In one instance, the researchers produced a valuable piece of research, but their energies were soon diverted toward counselling programs that had little relationship to the research. Another internal research project had a somewhat similar fate: the researchers became so involved in applying their results that they were lost to further research; unfortunately, no one else replaced them as researchers. Another internal research project got caught up in a power struggle between two ambitious managers; the one who favored the research lost. The fourth program, which Whyte judged to be most successful, attracted a manager who served as an "interpreter of the research"—that is, as an internal linker between the research unit and management. More recently, Whyte (1982) observed a second instance in which the presence of inside facilitators (who were not researchers) helped to achieve utilization of research results.

All of these analyses of the roles of internal researchers and change agents suggest that they must focus considerable time, attention, and effort on maintaining the viability of their positions with practitioners within their organizations. Being able to find the time and energy to maintain contacts as well with the outside research community must be exceedingly difficult and often impossible. Thus, it seems unlikely that they can be very effective in performing boundary-spanning or integrating functions for organizational research. Inside researchers and change agents undoubtedly carry some sorts of information between different segments of organizations and from outside to inside the organization; in this sense, they are linkers (Menzel, 1975:288). But it is far from clear that the information they transfer includes knowledge gleaned from organizational research. They are probably best in bridging the practice gap—by putting research into practice, by incorporating some of it into their own applied research, and by basing developmental activities and programs for change upon it.[4] However, to the degree that they get caught up in implementing applications, they stop doing research. Whyte's observations suggest that if some other internal linking agent becomes attached to the research, the researchers can continue being researchers.

Outside Consultants-Change Agents

Although consultants and change agents from outside are less dependent on practitioners than those inside, there is still some dependency. Not only do consultants desire and perhaps need the business of practitioners, but they also derive their status from them (Becker and Stern, 1973). Furthermore, practitioners have the relative advantage of belonging to a pre-existing power structure that is likely to dwarf the average consulting firm. Consultants or change agents based in universities and affiliated with professional associations may gain some power from these memberships, but probably gain the most power from being freer to terminate the relation (Steele, 1969) because they have other assured income and other sources of status. Thus, lack of power is also a problem for outside consultants and change agents, making them vulnerable to co-optation by practitioners. Organizational development consultants may be especially vulnerable because of their espoused ideology that people should participate in decisions that affect them. Tichy (1975) found that OD-type change agents, more than other types of change agents, emphasized working on issues and problems that clients feel are important and not those they themselves feel are important. Thus, OD consultants, more than other types of change agents, exhibited inconsistencies between what they do—usually working to make the organization more efficient and productive—and the goals of democratic participation they espouse (Tichy, 1974).

Managers believe in intuition, not scientific principles (Goode, 1969: 288). Also, they value practical knowledge more than theory (Duncan, 1974a). They are likely to evaluate and hire consultants according to these beliefs and values. Thus, consultants who appear to be very scientific are not likely to be in great demand.

Consultants have other reasons to emphasize their experience over their scientific expertise. Scientific theories and knowledge are in the public domain, and thus all consultants have access to them. Experiential knowledge is exclusive. Becker and Stern (1973:241) found that only 16 percent of the consultants they studied mentioned a social science theory they espoused, and pointed out that "if the firms sold only applications of popular theories, the impression of special competence would be more difficult to convey." So consultants sell their experience as superior to that of other consultants. Also, outside change agents tend to filter information during diagnosis to fit their intervention strategies (Tichy, 1975). If they carry any scientific research results into organizations, it will be a highly selected portion of those results.

In sum, it seems clear that most consultants are not likely to be good boundary spanners. Nor is it clear that what they actually do includes putting research results into practice or helping others to do so. We suspect that consultants vary somewhat in the degree to which they provide an integrating function. Those affiliated with academic institutions can probably do so. Those wholly or very substantially dependent on consulting income for their livelihood probably end up espousing management values, talking management language, and accepting management goals. Thus, after a while, they are too far on one side to be good integrators. Like inside researchers, however, outside consultants may be good in developing new technologies and programs, some of which may be based in research theories or results, especially when the outside consultant is also an academic researcher.

Extension Specialists

The county agent and extension specialist in agriculture[5] have provided the models for a variety of linking roles in other areas of knowledge. Both roles provide linkages between university-based researchers and farmers, with extension specialists providing linkages in specialized areas, and county agents providing general linkages with farmers. A third role—located within state agricultural colleges—provides linkages between typical academic researchers and the specialists and agents in the field. Applied researchers, especially those who work in agricultural experiment stations, carry out experiments and demonstrations on the practical implications of more basic research. These researchers also travel and diffuse their results to extension specialists and field agents through periodic meetings around the state. State agricultural colleges have permanent professional positions designated for such applied research and dissemination activities. In addition, various administrative positions are provided to support this system. The whole is called the cooperative extension program because it is supported by a combination of federal, state, and county funds.[6]

Of course, farmers have other sources of information, including the media, commercial agents of various kinds, and other farmers. Wilkening (1956) found that county agents are most frequently used to find out how to put something into practice, and only secondarily to decide whether to put something into practice. In their study of extension specialists, Brown and Deekens (1958:267) found that the largest percentage saw their role as liaison and communicator: "to take the results of research out over the state to farmers, so they can better their lot." When asked what difficulties they encountered in doing this, they most often mentioned inadequate or not enough research results, and inadequate communications between them and researchers (Brown and Deekens, 1958:271). Communication flows primarily from college to county, and not vice versa. Yet the grass-roots doctrine that provides legitimation for their activities encourages the extension specialists to orient themselves toward user groups, adjusting their efforts to local areas, and encourages the county units to develop autonomous power bases in their counties. Thus, extension administrators located at the colleges have relatively little control or influence over extension programs.

Brown and Deeken's (1958) data also suggested role conflict. Although the extension specialists most often mentioned the liaison-communicator role as what they did, they rated the student role as most important and the one on which they would like to spend more time. Apparently, these extension specialists felt they should be spending more time learning from researchers about their research.

A variety of roles designed to facilitate knowledge transfer have been established in the field of education over the years. Louis and Sieber (1979:9) studied a federal program designed to create a network of local educational extension agents who were supposed to be "free-floating, full-time generalists . . . to serve as the vital link between research and practice." The program differed from the agricultural model in several important ways (Louis and Sieber, 1979:120), one of the most basic being that communication was initiated by users, who requested information from the extension agents. They were then expected to find relevant information in their own files or with the help of state people, get it back to the users, and engage in follow-up activities to assist users.[7] Louis and Sieber's users in those local areas where there were field agents reported more use of information than was reported by users in areas lacking them. The way the program was set up, however, the only contact between researchers and extension specialists was indirect—apparently through publications provided by the state office or found in some other way by the extension specialists.

Louis and Sieber discovered that many of the agents soon experienced role overload, which they solved by spending less time with individual users—concentrating their efforts instead on opinion leaders and highly motivated clients. This turned out to be a good solution, because the time spent interacting with clients was positively correlated with utilization only for the more motivated clients.

Trice et al. (1981) obtained similar results for a linking role set up to bring information about job-based alcoholism programs to industry and other employers. The occupation program consultants (OPCs)

> learned not to waste their time and energies on reluctant organizations, and to concentrate instead on those that were already receptive—because of prior knowledge, compatible values and ideologies, and similar other programs—to the innovation they sought to introduce. . . . by the end of the second year . . . they were reaching many potential client organizations and succeeding in influencing many of them to establish alcoholism programs. (p. 331)

The inherent role difficulties identified by Trice et al. for the OPC role apply to other linking roles: role ambiguity, strains resulting from linking diverse organizations, lack of legitimacy, financial insecurity, and lack of power. Havelock and his colleagues (1969:7–34) emphasized overload and marginality as endemic problems in linking roles.

Like occupants of other existing linking roles, extension specialists tend to be pulled more often into the orbit of users than that of researchers. They seem to enjoy their contacts with users more than those with researchers (Brown and Deekens, 1958), perhaps because their lesser formal education makes them feel inadequate in dealing with researchers who do not accord them equal status (Beyer and Trice, 1982). These and other factors mentioned make them ripe for co-optation by users. Their boundary-spanning function is damaged if only users define the information to be transmitted, and their integrating function is damaged if they feel too alienated from researchers.

The agricultural extension model probably works as well as it does because researchers and specialists in university settings largely determine the information to be transmitted, thus balancing off the tendencies of local agents to be co-opted and respond solely to user needs. Also, agricultural extension specialists are directly linked to the research community and provide effective indirect linkages for field agents.

The OPC program followed the top-down communication pattern of the agriculture model in that the OPCs knew in advance what information they would be disseminating to potential users. Nevertheless, they were initially co-opted by users and by the local organizations with which they were affiliated toward individual counselling and other activities inconsistent with program goals. In the New York State program studied, however, they also had access to researchers through training programs carried out as part of evaluative research on the program (Trice et al., 1981). The researchers took an action-research approach and used training sessions to redefine and reinforce original program goals, to set up closer ties between OPCs, and generally to encourage resistance to local efforts to co-opt them.

The educational extension role, however, was set up so occupants not only allowed users to initiate information flows, but also had very indirect links with the research community. Louis and Sieber (1979:197) express reservations about "a fully client-based dissemination and utilization system," wondering about the quality of information transmitted in such a system. We also wonder about the content and suspect little of the information transmitted is based on research; much of it is probably based on experience.

Extension specialists do not bridge the practice gap, except indirectly. They do not do applied research, development activities, or apply knowledge or techniques to specific problems. But they can assist users in development and application by advising them from their knowledge of research and the experience of other users. Unfortunately, many of these roles may be too temporary to permit much accumulation of such knowledge. Louis (1982) says that educational extension roles are temporary occupational roles that people enter on their way from one place to another—for example, from teaching to retirement. Occupants view the role as a career bridge, not as a career. The OPC role was also temporary for many of its occupants because federal funding that supported the role disappeared after three years. Agricultural extension agents are much more secure, with a regular place in state budgets. Thus, occupants in that role can afford to view it as a career.

HOW VIABLE ARE NEW LINKING ROLES?

If existing roles do not effectively bridge the three gaps identified, an obvious alternative—often suggested—is to design new roles to link organizational researchers and users. Unfortunately, those who make such suggestions do not specify the contents of such roles or analyze the many obstacles to their successful implementation. We think there are almost insurmountable obstacles to the establishment of such roles and will discuss two: the need for a social mandate to establish and support new roles, and the need for occupants of linking roles to deal with marginality.

Our foregoing analyses of existing roles suggested that any new role would need substantial autonomy in order to maintain its position in the middle and avoid the problem of co-optation encountered in existing roles. Autonomy requires, at a minimum, a substantial degree of occupational mandate and perhaps even full-fledged professionalization.

Mandate

An occupational mandate occurs when society assigns to occupants of a role exclusive rights to perform specific tasks (Hughes, 1958). Wilensky's (1964) study of 18 occupations showed that such exclusive jurisdiction comes about after occupational roles have passed through certain stages, and that degrees of mandate accumulate as these stages accrue. First, occupants of a given role begin to carry out certain tasks on a full-time basis. Second, the content of this role is then systematized, and training schools—usually in colleges and universities—are set up to train persons to fill the role. Such specific training confers a modest amount of mandate. Third, role occupants form an occupational association to promote and strengthen their claims to exclusive rights to perform certain tasks. Fourth, occupants begin persistent political agitation to secure recognition of their mandate through formal licensure of the occupation. When licensure is achieved, mandate has been granted. Fifth, rules are devised by members of the occupation to eliminate the unqualified and the unscrupulous, and a formal code of ethics emerges. This last stage—with its emphasis on the "service ideal"—constitutes professionalization.

Even if occupational roles have mandate, they do not automatically have autonomy when they are incorporated into formal work organizations. Typically, negotiation occurs between members of the occupation and those who hold power in the organizations (Stewart and Cantor, 1974). Most often, these negotiations result in some reduction in autonomy. Those occupations with greater amounts of mandate are usually more successful in retaining substantial autonomy. A well-developed and active occupational association is helpful in reinforcing mandate and resisting dilution of autonomy (Strauss, 1963). Any given level of mandate will confer more autonomy if the tasks performed are central and crucial for the organizations involved—for example, if the tasks reduce important sources of organizational uncertainty (Crozier, 1964). Thus, occupations with equal mandate do not have the same autonomy in all organizations. For example, doctors have more autonomy in hospitals than in industrial settings.

Existing linking roles already discussed may have certain modest mandates, but none of them has exclusive rights to perform the tasks involved in bridging any of the gaps between organizational researchers and potential users. It seems highly unlikely that any new roles could be devised that would capture such exclusive rights. One complication, of course, is the sheer number of expectations (and hence tasks) attached to linking roles. In order to achieve reasonable autonomy, new linking roles would have to start performing some coherent subset of these expected tasks, set up training schools and an occupational association, and thereby win social consensus that they alone should perform these tasks. Since existing occupational groups and roles currently claim many linking tasks, just gaining access to a relevant subset of tasks is a problem. Even if such access—followed by full-time employment, training, and a strong occupational association—were achieved, competition from other occupations would probably block social consensus on the issue of exclusivity. Thus, a strong mandate for a new role seems most unlikely.

Furthermore, organizations would need to be convinced that the tasks to be performed in the new linking roles were central and crucial to their functioning, or they would not grant occupants much autonomy. Unfortunately, organizations in the United States have not yet evinced the kind of interest in organizational research that would suggest that such linking roles could achieve a central and crucial status.[8]

Marginality

A new social role cannot be deliberately created unless people are attracted to the role, perform in it, persist in it, and prosper sufficiently in it to be able to recruit other qualified persons to perform the role. All other things being equal, roles that make unusual or difficult demands on their occupants are going to be harder to fill than ones with ordinary and easy demands. Presumably this is why society rewards more demanding roles more highly than less demanding ones.

All roles make emotional demands on their occupants. To perform in a given role with reasonable competence, persons in it must not only have certain abilities, training, and skills, they must also have temperaments that match the emotional demands of the role well enough to cope with them. In railroading, split-second timing is a pervasive demand that comes to permeate all other aspects of railroaders' lives (Cottrell, 1939). Underground miners (Fitzpatrick, 1980) and policemen (Manning, 1977) must adapt themselves emotionally to ever-present dangers. Nightwatchmen (Trice, 1961) must cope with isolation from human interaction.

Thus, different occupational roles make different temperamental demands on people. Linking roles require that people have a high tolerance—perhaps even a taste—for marginality. This is because linkers can better provide bridges between the research communities and user communities by maintaining only weak ties in each (Granovetter, 1973). People with predominantly strong ties to others tend to have ties with fewer people because strong ties take more time and effort to build and maintain than weak ones. Marginal people have only weak ties and therefore can maintain large numbers of ties, are likely to be tied in to a larger number of groups, and are consequently valuable in providing linkages between different groups.

Boundary-spanning roles are especially subject to various stresses and strains (Kahn et al., 1964), including those associated with marginality. Integrator roles also involve marginality in that persons in them must maintain positions somewhere "between two or more groups with different values, goals, and norms" (Cotton, 1977:133). Maintaining this marginal position is a necessary feature of effective functioning in these roles, and thus the experienced marginality cannot be removed from them. Ziller et al. (1969:488) argued that people with certain personality characteristics are more satisfied with the positive aspects of marginal roles and better able to cope with their negative aspects.

What personality traits fit the temperamental role demands of marginality? First and foremost, linkers should have low affiliation needs; if their affiliation needs were high, they would be inclined to join one community or the other, since it is impossible to belong in both. Maintaining a middle ground can be lonely, even if social interaction levels are high. Ziller et al. (1969:494) mention being able to accept "the detachment and objectivity required." Second, linkers should have a high tolerance for ambiguity. Conflicting expectations are likely to be received from a multitude of role senders located in the two communities. Reconciling them may be impossible, and thus no clear set of role expectations can be settled upon in roles characterized by marginality. Other features of the role also help to create ambiguity. Ambiguity, of course, is highest for completely new roles. Few precedents exist for such roles, meaning that neither role senders nor role occupants may have clear models to follow for what linkers should be doing (Louis and Sieber, 1979). The lack of social mandate for such roles also indicates that there is no social consensus for what role occupants should be doing, how they should be trained, what skills they should cultivate, and so on.

Other personality traits are desirable to deal with marginality—including open-mindedness, adaptability (Ziller et al., 1969:487), empathy, independence, good communication skills, and friendliness. We have discussed affiliation needs and tolerance for ambiguity because they are some of the more negative temperamental demands that make linking roles so difficult to fill.

SUGGESTIONS FOR ROLE REDESIGN

After reviewing the literature on linking roles, we have concluded it is ridiculous to think in terms of a single linking role. Successful performance of the linking function—as occurs in agriculture—seems to require a minimum of two roles, as Guetzkow (1959) first suggested, and perhaps a whole series of roles (Lundberg, 1966; Havelock, 1969; Cherns, 1972). One of these roles should be located within user organizations in order to be readily available to users and to be able to make timely responses. A second should be located within organizations where organizational research is done—

schools of management, public administration, business, and industrial relations in research-oriented universities—to keep in touch with current research developments, and to provide some measure of independence from users. There is certainly room for a third role located somewhere between user organizations and universities, but no existing organizations provide a ready-made home for such a role. We doubt whether such an in-between role is viable without ongoing organizations that will welcome and support it.

Three of the existing roles analyzed earlier—the personnel specialist, the inside researcher-change agent, and the extension specialist—have potential for role redesign to better fulfill linking functions for the field of organizations. We agree with Becker and Stern (1973) that the outside consultant-change agent role is often too dependent on selling unique experience and skills and too vulnerable to co-optation to provide a reliable link between organizational research and practice. Those relatively few consultants who have the personal status, skills, and organizational base needed to resist co-optation and to carry out usable research competently provide models that few others have the resources to imitate. What we are seeking are linking mechanisms that can be widely implemented and institutionalized.

Personnel/Human Resources Specialists

Several difficulties must be overcome if personnel specialists are going to link users with organizational researchers. First and perhaps foremost, the accepted content of the personnel occupations must be enlarged to include expertise on organizational issues. Clearly, the new rubric of human resources management already incorporates some broadening of the definition of the traditional personnel functions. Such enlargements, of course, involve alterations in role expectations not only of occupants, but also of other managers and other members of organizations.

Changing how personnel or human resources specialists are trained is not easy, but should be possible. Such training occurs primarily in schools that include organizational researchers as faculty. What would seem to be necessary is for organizational faculty to align themselves more closely with faculty in the fields of personnel and human resources.[9] Only then can organizational faculty become more influential in determining the curriculum for those students who intend to enter these occupations.

Organizational research can be made more prominent in the personnel/human resources curriculum in a variety of ways, from designing elective courses to attract such students, to offering special sections of required courses to teach applications of organizational research that are relevant to the personnel function.[10] The most difficult part in changing the curriculum will be to find room for new topics. Since personnel and human resource curricula already include considerable emphasis on industrial/organizational psychology, the main difficulty will be to introduce more macro topics like organizational design and interorganizational relations. Scholars with these interests will have to become persuasive salespersons and will probably have to devote more time than they do at present to thinking about teaching how macro research can be applied. Any curricular changes are likely to be incremental, and organizational scholars can begin by doing a better job of convincing their students to appreciate the importance of organizational research (Lippett and Lippett, 1978). Without such convictions in the user community, linkages with researchers will not be sought, and attempts to provide such linkages will be greeted with apathy or hostility. Also, personnel specialists who are familiar with organizational research and how it is done can better convey the research needs of their organizations to inside or outside researchers.

Authors of organizational textbooks could also make the connection between organizational research and the personnel function more evident. Current texts are written to teach the general management student about organizations; new texts could add some recognition that personnel specialists are a resource that other managers can turn to for special expertise and new knowledge on how to deal with organizational problems. Personnel specialists can also be encouraged by the way texts are written and courses are taught to seek out researchers to communicate to them what kinds of research are needed, and generally to provide feedback from practice to research.

Finally, organizational researchers should infiltrate all of the relevant professional associations, like the Personnel and Human Resources Division of the Academy of Management. Organizational researchers should also seek opportunities to interact with relevant practitioner associations, like the American Society for Personnel Administration—especially the local college chapter to which their own students belong. These occupational associations are important in helping members to maintain and develop professional norms and to resist co-optation. Organizational scholars should be interested in helping to strengthen these associations, and in helping to develop norms and values within them that favor a relatively broad definition of the occupation.

Inside Researchers-Change Agents

Tichy (1978) suggested that the specialty of organizational development is in a stage of crisis, and that absorption into human resource management is the most viable option for the future of O.D. We would like to expand his recommendation to include all types of inside organizational researchers and change agents.

Bill Whyte (1982) recently reiterated to us his earlier idea (Whyte, 1969a) that social science research units should be fitted into research and development departments, rather than located in personnel departments. He may be right, but we do not think organizational research fits into the R&D function very well. Most conventional research and development is concerned with developing new products, improving existing products, or discovering more efficient ways to produce them. It is not clear that the self-conscious examination of internal, interpersonal processes fits with this orientation. Marketing research is done as part of the marketing function. Similarly, we think organizational research—which has an underlying orientation toward the people connected with the organization—should be located in the personnel or human resources function.

Inside researchers can be especially important in providing linkages that communicate user needs and reactions to other researchers. They can do this through membership in the same professional associations, and by playing liaison roles between members of their organization and outside researchers who seek entry or have been hired to execute specific research projects within their organizations.

It is true that some case studies of organizational research and researchers that were located in the personnel function (Whyte, 1969b; Klein, 1976) have documented a variety of difficulties in achieving utilization. But there also are case studies with more positive outcomes (Lippett, 1961; Flanagan, 1961; Wilson, 1961; Whyte and Hamilton, 1964), even if it is not always clear how personnel departments were involved in these cases. Although it seems to be the conventional wisdom, we do not believe that there are enough hard data yet to conclude that organizational research cannot prosper within the personnel function. What is needed is a more systematic and careful assessment of the factors that inhibit the execution and utilization of organizational research within personnel departments, followed by an analysis of how such inhibiting factors can be overcome. For example, perhaps the industrial relations component of the personnel function reinforces conservative tendencies. Structural changes, in particular, can disturb unions as well as managers; union officials could lose power as a result of change, and thus prefer the status quo. Winning the support of relevant union officials for contemplated structural changes involves lots of hard work for IR specialists, who may therefore be hard to convince that change is desirable.

Further assessment of other inhibiting factors and how to overcome them is beyond the scope of this chapter. It seems likely, however, that definitions of the personnel occupations can be broadened to include more receptivity to organizational research by involving personnel students in doing such research as part of their required coursework, teaching them some of the research skills needed to do organizational research, and generally encouraging perspectives and skills compatible with organizational research. Also, if personnel specialists felt that they would gain power and status from having organizational research carried on within their function, they would be more welcoming.

Faculty Extension Specialists

Some schools that have programs in organizational behavior also have extension programs. The New York State School of Industrial and Labor Relations at Cornell is the example we know best; some of the analysis that follows is based on our observations of that extension program. State funding and regular budget lines are devoted to the support of such programs. They have fairly extensive staffs, some of whom are administrators and others of whom are faculty who engage full-time in applied research and teaching for the extension program. Academic faculty may teach in the extension program, but are far from the backbone of such programs. Many schools of business and management have extensive executive development activities, and others have some form of applied research center, but such activities are largely self-supporting. Thus, their full-time staff includes only an administrative component and they are dependent on regular academic faculty or outsiders they hire for teaching—usually on a voluntary, overload basis. Academic reward systems at most universities discourage extensive involvement by faculty members in executive development and applied research work because such activities (although they often pay well) take time away from publishable research, which is the primary criterion used for promotion—especially to tenured status. Thus, only the senior ranks of the faculty can afford to spend much time on these activities, and these senior faculty tend to be burdened with the administrative duties of their schools.

We believe that the extension-program model provides a better base from which to link researchers and users in a meaningful way. Without some full-time persons with faculty status devoted full-time to exploring possible applications of research, it is hard to see how that job is going to get done. Regular academic faculty have other values and interests, supported by strong reward systems. It is naive to expect to lure any members of regular faculty into applied activities for the university unless a different role and reward system is built to support those activities, and the faculty recruited to that role are relieved of other academic duties. If faculty members have a bent for such work, they can easily do it now—at higher pay—as a consultant. But these scattered consulting activities seldom cumulate in any sustained and systematic programs of applications. When they do, it is probably because the organizations involved were very receptive, and—as

Whyte (1982) reported to us—happened to have persons in them who helped to carry the applications forward.

It is important to locate such extension programs in research-oriented universities and to give them regular budgeted lines for administrators, faculty, and some support staff. They must be located in a large, prestigious, and independent institution to help their staffs to resist complete co-optation by users. Marginality is not such a problem if the linker belongs to an independent institution that is strong and accepted (Havelock et al., 1969). Regular, budgeted faculty lines connote an established status within the university community, and even more important, provide the basis for personal careers. Such positions might be able to attract regular faculty whose research is too applied to win complete approval when evaluated by solely academic standards, but care must be exercised so that extension faculty positions are not viewed as dumping grounds for misfits from the regular faculty.

When such roles and programs already exist, some redesign is needed to improve the linking function—which does not now seem to be as explicit as it is in the agricultural extension programs. Roles in current industrial relations extension programs seem to have grown without much conscious attention as how best to communicate and translate research to users, and how to learn about and convey user needs and interests to researchers. There is no consensus over role content, and thus no clear role identity. People in these roles tend to shape them to their own goals, talents, and inclinations. Some gravitate toward and identify with the academic faculty; they then try to sustain academic values. Others gravitate toward user groups, and get co-opted to do the kind of training users want.

As presently constituted, the role of faculty extension specialist has too little mandate and too much marginality. In order for this role to be an effective linking role, it must be strengthened. Useful first steps to think about include recruitment and selection, clarifying role expectations, and training people for the role.

Persons recruited to extension faculty roles should be able to tolerate and thrive under conditions of marginality. In order to do their job well, they must recognize that they cannot belong to either the researcher or user community. They should be trained to accept and deal with this marginality. They should also be encouraged to develop a professional lore and norms for dealing with marginality and other strains inherent in their roles.

The training suitable for extension roles should be reassessed. Perhaps some Ph.D. candidates with applied inclinations and what appear to be the other relevant qualifications should be alerted to this role as a possible career opportunity. Perhaps the traditions and values of some Ph.D. programs will need to be changed to accommodate students with more applied interests and programs of study. Research methods courses could consider the criteria of the practical usefulness of research and how it can be achieved. Ph.D. dissertations could reflect some consideration of possible applications of the findings. Students can be trained to monitor the user community through management-oriented magazines and newspapers for leads on interesting and useful topics and questions for research. Above all, students with applied interests can be encouraged to interact in every way possible with practitioners, so that they can learn firsthand the language, values, and interests of the user community.

Also, the expectations for the faculty extension specialist role need to be clarified. Should these persons all do both research and teaching—like academic faculty—but in a more applied mold? How much time should they spend seeking out users? How can they best link up with personnel roles inside companies? How much of that linkage should be forged before students graduate, and how much after they graduate and attain certain roles in personnel departments? Should faculty extension specialists see themselves as conveyers of research information they have decided is worth knowing and applying, or as searchers for information responsive to users' expressed needs? These are just some of many issues that need to be clarified.

Federal programs that supported the educational extension specialist and occupational program consultant programs already discussed were recent attempts to design and establish new roles in other areas of knowledge. Both were at least partially successful in that the roles survived the cessation of federal funding in some places. Also, it appears that some users profited from and used information provided through these roles. However, it is not clear that the information transmitted by these two roles originated in the research community. Neither followed the earlier agricultural model in that neither set up a role *within* the research community—that is, in colleges and universities—to provide information to the extension agents. Instead, both relied upon persons located in state bureaucracies—state education departments or state bureaus on alcoholism—to provide the first stage of translation and dissemination of knowledge. It is not clear how well the persons located in the state bureaucracies linked up with the research community.

Most basic of all, financial support must be won from somewhere to establish extension specialist roles where they do not currently exist. It is not clear to us why federal and state tax monies should be spent on linking farmers, educators, and union people—but not managers of business concerns and other organizations—to university researchers. Perhaps if those subunits within management schools under which training and applied research activities are currently carried out could be merged, full-time extension-type faculty lines could be developed and tried out. Perhaps such trials are necessary to establish a climate in which permanent funding can be won.

CONCLUSION

Current linking roles are not linking organizational researchers with users, nor users with researchers very well. Although new roles are often proposed, it is not clear how viable new roles can be created, nor where they would be located. We suggest instead that three existing roles could be redesigned to provide better linkages between organizational researchers and users. The personnel/human resources occupations could be enlarged to provide more specifically the three linking functions of boundary spanning, integrating, and developing practical ways to put organizational research results into practice. To reinforce further this new enlarged conception of the personnel function, internal organizational research and development activities could be moved into the personnel or human resources function. Faculty extension roles could be developed within universities to link organizational researchers with managerial and other users, but especially to link researchers with personnel/human resources specialists and researchers.

Future analysts may arrive at different conclusions about how linking roles do and do not work, may recommend different configurations of linking roles, and may advance different prescriptions for the content of roles. Such developments will not dismay us. The major purpose of this chapter will be fulfilled if it helps to provide a more concrete basis for future discussions and analyses of linking roles.

NOTES

1. These include commitment to the decision and the opportunity to co-opt the researcher (Beyer and Trice, 1982).

2. Various authors have developed role descriptions for a range of linking roles, or have derived empirically based taxonomies of what persons in linking roles do. See, for example Guetzkow (1959), Lundberg (1966), Havelock et al. (1969), Tichy (1974), and Sundquist (1978). Many other authors who have written on utilization have also suggested specific activities or functions that persons in linking roles should perform in order to enhance utilization.

3. These descriptions came from unpublished qualitative data collected by James Belasco and the second author; analyses of other portions of the same data set were published in Trice et al., 1969.

4. They also probably put a small portion of organizational research into practice by applying it to their own conduct as change agents.

5. A similar structure exists in home economics, but users are easier to study and identify in agriculture.

6. We are indebted to George Steffins, a researchers with the U.S. Department of Agriculture who was visiting Cornell this past year, for giving us a lucid account of how the agricultural extension program works.

7. In the agricultural model, as already mentioned, communication tends to be initiated by new results from researchers. Thus, the organizational problem in the agricultural model is one

of deciding whether the client fits the pattern of service; in the educational extension program, the problem was to decide how the organization's expertise could be adapted to the client (Louis and Sieber, 1979:10).

8. U.S. firms have not historically given high status to those who deal with "people problems." This is not an inevitable feature of industrialization, however. Ouchi (1981:30) reports that Japanese organizations give highest status and most power to the personnel function, but in U.S. firms personnel is rarely powerful and has one of the lowest statuses.

9. This may involve a rapprochement with faculty from whom organizational scholars not too long ago took pains to separate themselves.

10. At SUNYAB, Cindi Fukami just designed a new course of this sort for MBA students taking the human resources option. The course focuses on general aspects of application such as diagnosis, evaluating change, socialization, and quality of work life, as well as specific techniques such as task design, MBO, behavior modification, and so forth.

REFERENCES

Alkin, Marvin C., Richard Daillak, and Peter White
1979   Using Evaluations. Beverly Hills: Sage Publications.
Baker, Frank
1981   "Similarities and differences in perspectives of administrators and evaluators: results of a national study." Paper presented at Symposium on Program Evaluation: A Tool for Health Care Administrators, Hofstra University, July 16.
Becker, Theodore M. and Robert N. Stern
1973   "Professionalism, professionalization, and bias in the commercial human relations consulting operation: a survey analysis." Journal of Business, 46:230–257.
Bennis, Warren G.
1963   "A new role for the behavioral scientist: effecting organizational change." Administrative Science Quarterly, 8:125–165.
Beyer, Janice M. and Harrison M. Trice
1978   Implementing Change: Alcoholism Policies in Work Organizations. New York: Free Press.
1982   "The utilization process: a conceptual framework and synthesis of empirical findings." Administrative Science Quarterly, forthcoming, December.
Brown, Emory J. and Albert Deekens
1958   "Roles of the extension subject-matter specialist." Rural Sociology, 23:263–276.
Caplan, Nathan
1977   "A minimal set of conditions necessary for the utilization of social science knowledge on policy formulation at the national level." In Carol H. Weiss (ed.), Using Social Research on Public Policy-Making: 183–197. Lexington, MA: Lexington Books.
Carroll, Stephen J.
1974   "Graduate student attitudes toward personnel management and the future development of the field." In W. Clay Hamner and Frank L. Schmidt (eds.), Contemporary Problems in Personnel. Chicago: St. Clair Press.
Cherns, Albert B.
1972   "Models for the use of research." Human Relations, 25:25–33.
Coleman, James S.
1972   Policy Research in the Social Sciences. Morristown, NJ: General Learning Press.
Cotton, Chester C.
1977   "Marginality—a neglected dimension in the design of work." Academy of Management Review, 2:133–138.

Cottrell, W. E.
1939   "Of time and the railroader." American Sociological Review, 4:190–198.
Crozier, Michael
1964   The Bureaucratic Phenomenon. Chicago: University of Chicago Press.
Duncan, W. Jack
1974a   "Transferring management theory to practice." Academy of Management Journal, 17:724–738.
1974b   "The researcher and the manager: a comparative view of the need for mutual understanding." Management Science, 20:1157–1163.
Dunlop, John T.
1977   "Policy decisions and research in economics and industrial relations." Industrial and Labor Relations Review, 30:275–283.
Dunn, William N.
1980   "The two-communities metaphor and models of knowledge use." Knowledge: Creation, Diffusion, Utilization, 1:515–536.
Dunnette, Marvin D. and Bernard M. Bass
1963   "Behavioral scientists and personnel management." Industrial Relations, 2:115–130.
Dunnette, Marvin D. and Zita Marie Brown
1968   "Behavioral science research and the conduct of business." Academy of Management Journal, 11:177–187.
Fitzpatrick, John S.
1980   "Adapting to danger: a participant observer study of an underground mine." Sociology of Work and Occupations, 7:131–158.
Flanagan, John C.
1961   "Case of the utilization of behavioral science research." In Charles Y. Glock (ed.), Case Studies in Bringing Behavioral Science into Use: Studies in the Utilization of Behavioral Science, Vol 1:36–46. Stanford, CA: Stanford University, Institute for Communications Research.
Foulkes, Fred K. and Henry M. Morgan
1977   "Organizing and staffing the personnel function." Harvard Business Review, 55:142–154.
Gershinowitz, Harold
1972   "Applied research for the public good—a suggestion." Science, 1976:380–386.
Glaser, Edward M. and Hubert S. Coffey
1967   Utilization of Applicable Research and Demonstration Results. Final Report to Vocational Rehabilitation Administration, Department of H.E.W., Project RD-1263-G. Los Angeles: Human Interaction Research Institute.
Glaser, Edward M. and Samuel H. Taylor
1973   "Factors influencing the success of applied research." American Psychologist, 28:140–146.
Goode, William J.
1969   "The theoretical limits of professionalization." In Amitai Etzioni (ed.), The Semi-professions and Their Organization: 266–314. New York: Free Press.
Granovetter, Mark
1973   "The strength of weak ties." American Journal of Sociology, 78:1360–1380.
Guetzkow, Harold
1959   "Conversion barriers in using the social sciences." Administrative Science Quarterly, 4:68–81.
Hauser, Philip M.
1946   "Are the social sciences ready?" American Sociological Review, 11:379–384.
Havelock, Ronald G. and colleagues
1969   Planning for Innovation: A Comparative Study of the Literature on the Dissemination

and Utilization of Scientific Knowledge. Ann Arbor, MI: Center for Research on Utilization of Scientific Knowledge, Institute for Social Research, July.

Homans, George C.
1950   The Human Group. New York: Harcourt.

Hughes, Everett C.
1958   Men and Their Work. Glencoe, IL: Free Press.

Kahn, Robert L., Donald M. Wolfe, Robert P. Quinn, and J. Diedrick Snoek
1964   Organizational Stress. New York: Wiley.

Klein, Lisl
1976   A Social Scientist in Industry. New York: Wiley.

Likert, Rensis and Ronald Lippitt
1953   "The utilization of social science." In Leon Festinger and Daniel Katz (eds.), Research Methods in the Behavioral Sciences: 581–646. New York: Holt and Rinehart.

Lippett, Gordon and Ronald Lippett
1978   The Consulting Process in Action. La Jolla, CA: University Associates, Inc.

Lippitt, Ronald
1961   "Two case studies of utilization of the behavioral sciences." In Charles Y. Glock (ed.), Case Studies in Bringing Behavioral Science Into Use: Studies in the Utilization of Behavioral Science, Vol. I: 20–35. Stanford, CA: Stanford University, Institute for Communications Research.

Louis, Karen Seashore
1982   Personal communication to the first author.

Louis, Karen Seashore and Sam Dixon Sieber
1979   Bureaucracy and the Dispersed Organization: The Educational Extension Agent Program. Norwood, NJ: Ablex.

Lundberg, Craig C.
1966   "Middlemen in science utilization: some notes toward clarifying conversion roles." American Behavioral Scientist, 9:11–14.

Mann, Floyd and Rensis Likert
1952   "The need for research on the communication of research results." Human Organization, 11:15–20.

Manning, Peter K.
1977   Police Work. Cambridge, MA: MIT Press.

Margulies, Newton
1971   "Implementing organizational change through an internal consulting team." Training and Developmental Journal, 25:26–33.

Menzel, Robert K.
1975   "A taxonomy of change agent skills." Journal of European Training, 4:283–295.

Miller, Frank B. and Mary Ann Coghill
1964   "Sex and the personnel manager." Industrial and Labor Relations Review, 18:32–44.

Odiorne, George S.
1981   "Personnel management for the 80's." In Davis Keith and John Newstrom, (eds.) Organizational Behavior: Readings and Exercises. New York: McGraw-Hill. pp. 380–396.

Ouchi, William G.
1981   Theory Z: How American Business Can Meet the Japanese Challenge. New York: Avon.

Patten, Thomas H.
1968   "Is personnel administration a profession?" Personnel Administration, March-April:39–48.

Pettigrew, Andrew M.
1975   "Toward a political theory of organizational intervention." Human Relations, 28:191–208.
Rich, Robert F.
1977   "Use of social science information by federal bureaucrats: knowledge for action vs. knowledge for understanding." In Carol H. Weiss (ed.), Using Social Science in Public Policy-Making: 199–233. Lexington, MA: Lexington-Heath.
Ritzer, George and Harrison Trice
1969   An Occupation in Conflict: A Study of the Personnel Manager. Ithaca, NY: School of Industrial and Labor Relations.
Rossi, Peter H.
1980   "The presidential address: the challenge and opportunities of applied social research." American Sociological Review, 45:889–904.
Rothman, Jack
1980   Using Research in Organizations: A Guide to Successful Application. Beverly Hills: Sage Publications.
Rush, Harold M. F. and Walter S. Wikstrom
1969   "The reception of behavioral science in industry." Conference Board Record, 9:45–54.
Schmidt, Frank L., John E. Hunter, and Kenneth Pearlman
1982   "Assessing the economic impact of personnel programs on work force productivity." Personnel Psychology, 35:333–347.
Steele, Fred I.
1969   "Consultants and detectives." Journal of Applied Behavioral Science, 5:187–202.
Stewart, Phyllis and Muriel G. Cantor
1974   Varieties of Work Experiences. New York: Wiley.
Strauss, George
1963   "Professionalism and occupational associations." Industrial Relations, 2:7–30.
Sundquist, James L.
1978   "Research brokerage: the weak link." In Laurence E. Lynn, Jr. (ed.), Knowledge and Policy: The Uncertain Connection: 126–144. Washington: National Academy of the Sciences.
Taguiri, Renato
1965   "Value orientations and the relationship of managers and scientists." Administrative Science Quarterly, 10:39–51.
Thompson, James D.
1956   "On building an administrative science." Administrative Science Quarterly, 1:102–111.
Tichy, Noel M.
1974   "Agents of planned social change: congruence of values, cognitions, and actions." Administrative Science Quarterly, 19:164–182.
1975   "How different types of change agents diagnose organizations." Human Relations, 28:771–799.
1978   "Demise, absorption, or renewal for the future of organization development." In W. Warner Burke (ed.), The Cutting Edge: Current Theory and Practice in Organization Development: 70–81. La Jolla, CA: University Associates.
Trice, Harrison M.
1961   "Nightwatchmen: a study of an isolated occupation." Industrial and Labor Relations Research, 10:3–9.
Trice, Harrison M., James Belasco, and Joseph Alutto
1969   "The role of ceremonials in organizational behavior." Industrial and Labor Relations Review, 23:40–51.

Trice, Harrison M., Janice M. Beyer, and Cynthia Coppess
1981   "Sowing seeds of change: how work organizations in New York State responded to occupational program consultants." Journal of Drug Issues, 11:311–336.

Tushman, Michael L. and Thomas J. Scanlan
1981   "Boundary-spanning individuals: their role in information transfer and their antecedants." Academy of Management Journal, 24:289–305.

Van de Vall, Mark, Cheryl Bolas, and Tai S. Kang
1976   "Applied social research in industrial organizations: an evaluation of functions, theory, and methods." Journal of Applied Behavioral Science, 12:158–177.

Watson, Tony J.
1977   The Personnel Managers. London: Routledge and Kegan Paul.

Weiss, Janet A. and Carol H. Weiss
1981   "Social scientists and decision-makers look at the usefulness of mental health research." American Psychologist, 36:837–847.

Whyte, William F.
1969a   "On the application of behavioral science research to management problems." Indian Journal of Industrial Relations, 5:3–28.
1969b   Organizational Behavior: Theory and Application. Homewood, IL: Richard Irwin.
1982   Personal communication to the authors.

Whyte, William F. and Edith L. Hamilton
1964   Action Research for Management. Homewood, IL: Richard D. Irwin and Dorsey Press.

Wilensky, Harold L.
1964   "The professionalization of everyone?" American Journal of Sociology, 70:137–158.

Wilkening, Eugene A.
1956   "Roles of communicating agents in technological change in agriculture." Social Forces, 34:361–367.

Wilson, Elmo C.
1961   The Application of Social Research Findings. In Charles Y. Glock (ed.), Case Studies in Bringing Behavioral Science Into Use: Studies in the Utilization of Behavioral Science, Vol. 1: 47–58. Stanford, CA: Stanford University, Institute for Communications Research.

Yoder, Dale and Herbert G. Heneman, Jr.
1978   PAIR Jobs, Qualifications, and Careers, Chapter VIII, Official Handbook of the American Society for Personnel Administration. Washington, D.C.: Bureau of National Affairs.

Zaltman, Gerald and Robert Duncan
1977   Strategies for Planned Change. New York: Wiley.

Ziller, R. C., B. J. Stack, and H. O. Pruden
1969   "Marginality and integrative management positions." Academy of Management Journal, 12:487–493.

38

EXTENDING THE EXTENSION MODEL:
NEW INSTITUTIONAL FORMS FOR
USEFUL KNOWLEDGE

James C. Petersen and Dan Farrell

Education in the United States is currently facing demands that may require modifications in its internal structures and in its relationships to the rest of the society. According to the National Commission on Research:

> there is widespread and serious concern among leaders in government, the universities, and industry over the erosion of U.S. hegemony in science, technology, and rates of productivity. Much of this concern focuses on lagging innovation, on the idea that the U.S. has not maintained the innovative characteristics which fueled its earlier scientific and economic success. (1980)

The needs of small businesses are especially prominent. Such firms typically lack extensive research facilities and, therefore, must turn to universities for research and technical assistance. Advances in technology and accompanying changes in labor requirements are producing demands for new curricula and degree programs. Recently the Massachusetts High Technology Council (MHTC) asked MIT to develop new programs to permit currently employed professionals to earn graduate degrees. The rate of technological change also poses problems for voluntary associations and citizens groups. As these groups attempt to make their voice heard in such technical controversies as waste management, nuclear power, and land use management, they require technical assistance in conducting research or in translating available research literature (Petersen and Kaufman, 1981).

The demands on higher education are being aggravated by diminished resources resulting from economic malaise and administrative policy.

We wish to thank Jack S. Wood for his suggestions and assistance in the development of this paper.

Inasmuch as research in the United States is centered in universities rather than national research centers, increases in all areas of operating costs and reductions in federal support have made it difficult to fulfill current commitments, let alone meet new challenges. In 1980 the National Commission on Research concluded that "it is in the national interest for industry to increase its participation in the national basic research enterprise" (p. 11).

This chapter proposes several forms and institutional arrangements designed to restructure the ways in which higher education relates to industry and other social sectors. These innovations are designed to increase the production and diffusion of useful knowledge by universities. A key feature of our approach is that it builds upon one of the most successful models in higher education: the land-grant colleges and universities. The extension work at these institutions traditionally emphasized two themes: the transfer of technical information from the university to members of society, and the transmission of research needs from the public to the university. While the extension approach is normally associated with agriculture, it contains great potential for application to a wider range of problems.

THE LAND-GRANT EXPERIENCE

As a reaction against an excessive focus on classic studies in church-related colleges and universities, the Morrill Act of 1862 sought to establish a system of state-controlled colleges and universities focusing on agricultural, mechanical, and military studies. Each state was to set aside acreage from its public lands to provide "a perpetual fund, the capital of which shall remain forever undiminished" (Eddy, 1956:33). The initial land-grant schools were distinctive in their values: democratization of education, mission-oriented research, and services rendered directly to the people. Improved access for nonelites and for women was provided by the land grants along with reduced social distance between students and faculty. The applied research emphasis, a major appeal of the initial legislation, resulted in research directed toward solving economic and social problems. Influenced by the American Lyceum Movement and the Chautauqua system, and their programs of community instruction, from the beginning land-grant schools offered lectures, institutes, and other locally oriented instruction.

The down-to-earth beginnings of the land-grant colleges had laid the groundwork for the direct practical application of knowledge to the problems and interests of the people. "The new colleges had brought learning out of the 'Ivory Tower'. It was only the organization which delayed extending it beyond the campus to the communities and farms of the people themselves" (Eddy, 1956:78). While there were early efforts at "Farmers' Institutes"

(Eddy, 1956:78), it was the Hatch Act of 1887 that authorized the establishment of agricultural experiment stations. The purpose of this act was "to aid in acquiring and diffusing among the people of the United States useful and practical information on subjects connected with agriculture, and to promote scientific investigation and experiment respecting the principles and applications of agricultural science" (Sanders, 1966:26).

In time, the sheer volume of activities suggested the need for a separation of agricultural research from extension services. With the passage of the Adams Act (1906), experimental stations began to concentrate on genuine research and left to extension staffs the institutes, correspondence courses, lectures, and demonstration work. Comprehensive national organization was brought to agricultural extension work with the passage of the Smith-Lever Act in 1914. This legislation also provided a permanent appropriation base for extension services and attempted to coordinate the extension work of land-grant colleges and the Department of Agriculture. Subsequent legislation adjusted funding formulas and established some interorganizational linkages to establish today's Cooperative Extension Service.

Reasons for Success

The land-grant universities have not merely met the goals set forth in the founding legislation; they have been so "spectacularly successful" (Anderson, 1976:326) as to warrant close attention. They have been a major force behind the dramatic increases in agricultural productivity through the development of hybrid plants, herbicides, pesticides, and the improvement of animal stocks. In cooperation with engineering faculty, the agriculture staff of land-grants also produced agricultural machinery including the first spray machinery, mechanical harvesting equipment, and other now standard farm implements. The diffusion of plant innovations throughout the world has produced the "green revolution" for which land-grant-trained Norman Borlaug received the 1970 Nobel Peace Prize.

Four factors seem especially significant in explaining this pattern of success: outreach, demonstration, identification, and personalization. Drawing a lesson from popular education of the day, such as the Lyceum Movement, the land-grant colleges organized to bring information to the people. If they did not reach each and every farm, the early extension programs tried to reach every small rural community. The Seed Corn Gospel Train programs in Iowa, for example, traveled over 10,000 miles in 1904 and 1905, stopped 1,235 times, and reached 150,000 people (Eddy, 1956:132). Such local programs overcame the public's reluctance to go on campus. Having a presence in the community also allowed for an aggressive stance toward the dissemination of knowledge.

Extension work traditionally relied heavily on demonstration techniques as in agricultural shows, demonstration plots, and field days. So central was demonstration to early extension that official job titles included the word demonstration, as in home-demonstration agent. Being a multisensory technique, the demonstration has great impact and is more effective than printed material in transmitting new information. The demands of demonstration insured that researchers pushed their research ideas beyond the laboratory. Thus, the extension demonstrations provided a bridge between research and implementation.

Despite the frequency with which demonstrations were given, care was normally taken to tailor content to fit local conditions. Dr. Seaman Knapp established the principle in a pioneering boll weevil project. Recognizing the resistance of farmers, Knapp arranged for a properly indemnified local farm to be the site for a demonstration of insect control and improved crop management. Agricultural experiment stations were also used to ensure locally oriented research. For example, Michigan State University's experiment station at South Haven specialized in the development of new fruit varieties for the lake-shore climate.

The central role of the extension agents in conducting demonstrations and in meeting local citizens guaranteed a personalization of contact that has been absent in most techniques for transferring information. Negative stereotypes of university intellectuals and a distrust of book-learning are widespread among the public. Nothing is more effective in breaking down these barriers to learning than face-to-face contact with an extension agent. Research on extension service effectiveness (Kelsey and Hearne, 1963:270) showed direct correlations between numbers of personal contacts and farm family adoption of innovations. The importance of knowing the extension worker personally was emphasized by studies showing that people who had personal contacts with extension workers used four times as many innovative practices as people who had no contact (Kelsey and Hearne, 1963:271).

TECHNOLOGY TRANSFER PROGRAMS

As has been shown, the first half of this century saw one of the most successful periods of U.S. education. Land-grant schools and farmers joined together for a period of unparalleled improvement in agricultural techniques. In more recent years, extension-like programs have been developed to bring existing knowledge to other sectors of the economy. Nearly all of these new programs are pure technology transfer programs that provide existing information in a useful form to business, public agencies, and to individuals expressing need. There are, however, a handful of technology transfer programs that also possess a capability for generating new knowledge.

Programs to Transfer Existing Knowledge

On September 14, 1965, President Lyndon Johnson signed Public Law 89–102, the State Technical Service (STS) Act. The objectives of this legislation were: first, to promote commerce and encourage economic growth through the support of state and interstate programs; and second, to give U.S. enterprise the results of scientific research (Venett, 1981:44). The purpose of this act was to foster information transfer similar to that provided by the Agricultural Extension Service. Chronic uncertainty about funding plagued the programs from the beginning, making the recruitment and retention of well-qualified field staff difficult. The best programs "appeared in those states where the commitment for continuity existed such as in Pennsylvania and Georgia" (Robbins, 1977:3). Where the state-level commitment was absent, the programs failed, and as Robbins observed, "STS was out of business before most of the stake-holders knew it existed" (1977:5).

Technology transfer programs have also run into trouble when the problems brought to them lacked a common focus or the technologies applied were too diverse. A constant difficulty with STS programs was that the most urgent problem of each business tended to be unique. NASA's technology utilization program, despite good public support, failed for similar reasons. Robbins (1977:1) described it as a case where "a finite number of technologies was chasing after an infinite number of problems." Recognizing this difficulty, some urban technology transfer programs, such as the Urban Consortium, spent large amounts of time and effort to aggregate needs so as to permit common technological solutions. The more successful technology transfer program run by the Law Enforcement Assistance Administration (LEAA) operated in a context in which communities with similar problems were supplied with a limited range of technologies.

As part of the design of a national energy extension service, Robbins (1977) identified factors leading to the success or failure of technology transfer programs. In his judgment, four principles are characteristic of the successful programs: mere access to information is not sufficient; information must be translated before it is useful; face-to-face assistance is essential; solutions must be adapted to specific problems. Numerous programs operate on the assumption that all that is needed is to make the information available, usually in printed form. Virtually all users need some translation and there is no substitute for personal assistance in this process.

Founded in 1965, the Pennsylvania Technical Assistance Program (PENNTAP) has developed a national reputation for success in technology transfer. Business journalist Louis Rukeyser has described PENNTAP as the most sophisticated state program of its type, and one that other states should emulate. PENNTAP's visibility in Pennsylvania has developed to the point that annual requests for assistance exceed 2,000. Access to PENNTAP is gained by contacting the PENNTAP office at the main campus of the Pennsylvania State University or any of the 24 continuing education offices located throughout Pennsylvania. PENNTAP has an advisory board composed of engineers, business executives, and other individuals appointed by the president of the university. The core of the program consists of the full-time technical specialists who provide the interface between clients and elements of the university. These technical specialists are located in appropriate academic departments in order to improve their own ability to keep abreast of new developments and to improve access to other university specialists. All technical specialists are supported by the PENNTAP Library Information System. Other technical specialists assigned directly to the PENNTAP Library Information System supply information directly to users in the form of technical articles.

The PENNTAP program centers around the transmission of existing knowledge in both reactive and proactive modes. The technical specialists, who are the core of the program, respond to questions such as what government standards apply to cellulosic insulation or what gasoline additives are effective for improving mileage in school bus fleets. In addition, when new developments emerge with potential benefits for commonwealth organizations or businesses, the technical specialists contact and notify potential users. They offer to translate technologies and may arrange on-site demonstration. The human contact provided by the technical specialist is a necessary element in the process of tailoring technical solutions to the special situations of users.

The PENNTAP program provides for followups of the contacts as well as assistance for users in evaluating benefits of the new approaches. In addition, the PENNTAP program itself has been the subject of evaluation to determine the economic benefit to the citizens of Pennsylvania. The benefits to users are of two types: direct economic benefits such as increases in productivity or reduced costs, and indirect benefits such as improvements in quality of work life or planning assistance. Dollar benefits are calculated for both these benefits for one-time, one-year use. Even with this conservative approach, most suggestions prove to be helpful. When these calculations are applied to the PENNTAP program, the dollars expended to operate the service return in a 14 to 1 ratio (Venett, 1981).

There is a substantial demand for programs like PENNTAP from small businesses, public school administrators, service agency personnel, and citizens. In 1981 when Western Michigan University established its Office of Public Service (WESTOPS), a technology transfer program patterned after PENNTAP, it received nearly 225 requests for assistance in its first eight months of operation. This is even more dramatic when it is realized that the public announcement of the service was delayed until mid-September of that year. Even highly specialized assistance programs receive numerous requests. Virginia Polytechnic Institute's Center for Volunteer Development limits its service to volunteer groups and organizations using volunteers. Still, it received 96 requests for assistance in its first year of operation.

Joint Industry/University Research Projects

In some industries that are characterized by rapid technological change, the pressure for technical progress is such that full, or nearly full, utilization of available technology already exists. In other industries, specialization is so great that innovation requires carefully tailored, mission-oriented research. In such cases, industrial concerns have joined with universities as a means of fostering new research. These joint programs hold obvious attraction for both parties as the costs of research increase. At the same time, such joint ventures are an effective means for industry to bring research needs to the attention of academic researchers.

Since the early 1970s, the National Science Foundation has been a promoter of university/industry cooperative research projects. NSF-funded cooperative center research programs on technology for producing furniture and technology for New England's electrical utility industry have been widely viewed as failures. Lacking a coherent focus, they failed to attract continued industrial support. The NSF-backed polymer center at MIT, however, has been described as "an unqualified success" (Kiefer, 1980:43), and no longer requires NSF support. Building on this success, NSF has agreed to provide seed money to establish a Center of University of Massachusetts-Industry Research on Polymers. Generally, the center will conduct basic research on preparation and solid properties of polymers. The specific research projects will be determined by a steering committee with the advice of a board drawn from the sponsoring industrial firms, including: Allied Chemical, Alcoa, Arco, Celanese, Dow Chemical, Du Pont, Exxon, General Electric, Kendall Co., Eastman Kodak, Monsanto, Union Carbide, and Westinghouse.

Another example of the consortium approach to funding research is the Silicon Structures Project at the California Institute of Technology. In this case, cooperating companies send researchers to the university to work on the project for specified periods of time. These researchers then become the source of transfer back to the sponsoring firm. A disadvantage of this approach in industry's view is that research results are shared among the sponsoring firms. A mechanism that overcomes this drawback is the exclusive partnership between a firm and a university. Notable examples of this type include the Monsanto-Harvard project in modern biology, the studies of membrane reactors done jointly by the University of Pennsylvania and General Electric, and an examination of hydrosulfurization catalysts being carried out by Cornell University and Atlantic Richfield.

DESIGNING ORGANIZATIONS TO PRODUCE
USEFUL KNOWLEDGE

The successful technology transfer programs demonstrate that the basic features of the agricultural extension model can be extended to other technical fields. Universities are quite capable of generating and disseminating useful knowledge, however, and even greater potential for the creation of useful knowledge exists in these institutions. Many features of this approach are applicable to other areas of knowledge, including the social and organizational sciences. Developing and implementing a paradigm for generating useful knowledge will not only serve the needs of society, but can also serve academic disciplines searching for greater social support (Fishman and Neigher, 1982).

Technological transfer is simplified when there are concrete products such as new plant varieties or machinery to be disseminated. The products of much social and organizational research are frequently softer, often conceptual in nature, but this difference need not be a barrier to the transfer of information. Such extension principles as demonstration and personalization can be applied to the transfer of organizational and social science knowledge through techniques including computer simulation, role-playing, gaming, and video presentations.

A possible barrier to the transmission of organizational and behavioral science knowledge may be financial. Agricultural extension had the advantage of a substantial base of federal funding. New knowledge transfer programs that emulate the personalized character of extension will be expensive. Certainly the social and behavioral sciences have not fared well in the allocation of research funds by the current administration. Perhaps an emphasis on application, especially to business, might make extension-like programs more attractive to the federal government. The alternative is to fund services from contracts and user fees.

In surveying the land-grant programs and the recent extensions of the approach in spheres beyond agriculture, it is quite clear that these programs have been limited by largely one-way channels of communication. Better mechanisms must be found to influence university researchers, rather than leaving them in the position of deciding what the public in general or some specific client needs. The joint ventures between universities and industrial firms are steps in the direction of providing significant input into the process of problem selection in academic research.

Rapid change and continued uncertainty in the environment of contemporary organizations require that new institutional forms be developed to transfer technological innovations and to ensure that organizational needs have a greater impact on research priorities. Four innovations based on successful aspects of the land-grant experience and technology transfer programs are proposed: field laboratories, technical extension agents, an office of information services, and new university membership roles for clients and information users.

Field Laboratories

The agricultural experiment stations were one of the most successful components of the land-grant approach. Analogues to these institutions should be established to serve clients in nonagricultural sectors. Field laboratories performing activities for industry have clear potential and a ready clientele. In general, these laboratories are expected to conduct mission-oriented research and to work on the application of basic research conducted in academic units. More specifically, the activities of the field laboratories would include demonstrations, pilot programs, prototype development, modeling, and simulations.

The experiences of the agricultural stations and the technology transfer programs suggest other structural parameters as well. By definition, the stations established and funded by the Adams Act were confined to agricultural or engineering activities. The history of these stations and the reported difficulties of some technology transfer programs indicate that such laboratories must have a restricted scope of activities. Associating a laboratory with a regionally dominant industry such as paper making, textiles, or transportation seems to be a constructive approach. Field laboratories must also be structured so as to maintain close ties to the parent university. Excessive autonomy in such programs breaks the feedback linkage to academic units and reduces the input of applied needs on basic research.

The most difficult problem for a field laboratory is the question of the financial relationship with users and clients. The current trend of prestige universities establishing exclusive arrangements with large firms may not be a socially beneficial arrangement. At a minimum, it is an approach that excludes small business and other segments of society that cannot afford such expensive ties. While there is a need for industrial support of research, philanthropy, consortia, project-by-project support, and short duration contracts keep such laboratories from becoming captives of a single firm. The social responsibilities of universities require development of knowledge on bases other than current ability to pay. Field laboratories could be an effective mechanism for colleges and universities to meet the needs of small business and those citizens and citizen groups who want to be more effective in the policy-formation process.

Technical Extension Agents

The land-grant experience and the technology transfer programs also suggest the necessity of face-to-face personalized contact to bridge the gap between knowledge producers and knowledge consumers. In the future, extension agent roles must take on a more fully developed boundary-spanning character. In addition to providing information, translating technical information, and organizing demonstrations, technical extension agents must have as part of their job duties the task of conducting needs assessments. Agricultural extension and technical transfer programs both are subject to the criticism of being too top-down oriented. A centralized bureaucratic approach to technological problems is not sufficiently adaptive to cope with highly uncertain environments. Needs assessments are one means of increasing the flow of communication from users of knowledge to appropriate elements of the university.

Special care must also be taken regarding the job specifications and reward structures for technical extension agents. Unlike other professional positions in the university, the technical extension agents must have prior external experience as well as academic educational credentials. Translating technological innovations to industrial users requires a knowledge of manufacturing procedures and the constraints of labor relations. At the same time, these individuals must have the confidence and respect of their academic colleagues. During times of retrenchment administrators operating from traditional academic values might try to fill new extension roles by reassigning unproductive department members to such duties. Such actions would guarantee failure since such individuals normally lack external experience and are disdained by productive academic researchers. In order to ensure success, universities must seek individuals with a different mix of experience than the traditional academic. Universities must also give a clear message of support to applied work by altering reward systems to take account of success in the application of ideas.

Office of Information Services

The Pennsylvania Technical Assistance Program has shown that universities may fill a utilitarian role by opening the doors of their information storage facilities. The services provided by PENNTAP's Library Information System should be seen as a beginning point for direct transfer of information to users who wish to translate themselves or who only require minimal assistance in translating technical data for their own use. Reporting to the director of continuing education or the head of other units charged with external services, an office of information services could provide access to information and tools without duplicating private sector activities.

The potential of an office of information services is greatly expanded by the coming proliferation of cheap, easy-to-use computer terminals. Terminals capable of rapid and simple communication with university libraries and computer centers are now priced in the hundreds of dollars and are therefore likely to be in the hands of small businesses and many individuals. Furthermore, advances in terminal and modem technology and the development of user-friendly software are making communication through computers even easier. Without unduly overloading their own resources, universities should be able to offer access to computerized card catalogues, assist outside users with on-line bibliographic searches, provide highly specialized software, open public domain data banks, and provide self-instructional courses for adult education.

New Membership Roles

An area of difficulty and considerable agonizing for universities has been membership roles for outsiders. Universities claim to seek guidance from such persons, but, in truth, usually hope for benefits without the cost of loss of control. As higher education faces a more uncertain environment, it must be willing to accept greater input from those who use its services.

Client involvement may range from a simple advisory role to more penetrating involvements. Advisory boards must be continued in the areas of technical assistance programs, as with PENNTAP and several consortia-type research centers. More emphasis on applied activities will occur when clients are allowed to participate in research funding decisions within the university. The history of research in U.S. universities indicates that control over funding clearly shapes the selection of research problems. It also seems reasonable to assume that the criticism of research and scholarship should include an applied perspective. Within universities, informal reviews are done by colleagues in departmental colloquia and in special seminars. Related professionals from outside organizations should regularly be brought into the informal review process. Universities with a deep commitment to applied studies may also wish to involve clients in the curriculum-planning process. Business leaders and other practitioners would seem to be a unique source of insight into the long-range training needs of future workers in their fields.

CONCLUSION

The American public often views higher education as preoccupied with the arcane or esoteric. When someone describes an argument or a distinction as "academic," that person is asserting that it is irrelevant. Our society can no longer afford institutions of higher education that are supremely isolated from real world problems. Resources have grown too scarce and problems have become too pressing to permit such squandering of intellectual skills. Universities and colleges simply must be made to yield more socially useful knowledge.

Luckily, there are excellent models that can be followed and adapted. The land-grant tradition and a number of technology transfer programs stand as ready examples. The features that made these programs successful have been identified and can guide our structuring of new programs and our redesign of institutions of higher education. At the same time, substantial resistance from colleges and universities must be expected. Academic institutions revere tradition and change only with great pain. Values that denigrate the applied and the small scale are firmly entrenched in universities. The current budget problems of higher education, however, open up opportunities for change that may not have existed in more affluent days. Universities will now consider establishing relationships with industry and other segments of society as a way of gaining needed research resources.

One of the strengths of U.S. higher education has been its pluralist character. Institutions vary widely in terms of size, mission, facilities, resources, and visibility. While opportunities for the creation and diffusion of useful knowledge will exist everywhere, not all colleges and universities may wish to move in this direction. Some schools may view it as a distraction from their traditional teaching function. Others searching for new missions, however, would do well to consider adapting the extension model of the land-grant schools to meet new social needs.

REFERENCES

Anderson, G. Lester (ed.)
1976   Land Grant Universities and Their Continuing Challenge. East Lansing, Michigan: Michigan State University Press.
Eddy, Edward Danforth
1956   Colleges for Our Land and Time: The Land-Grant Idea in American Education. New York: Harper & Brothers.
Fishman, Daniel B., and William D. Neigher
1982   "American psychology in the eighties." American Psychologist, 37:533–546.
Kelsey, Lincoln David, and Cannon Chiles Hearne
1963   Cooperative Extension Work. Ithaca, New York: Comstock Publishing Associates.
Kiefer, David M.
1980   "Forging new and stronger links between university and industrial scientists." Chemical and Engineering News, 58:38–51.
National Commission on Research
1980   Industry and the Universities: Developing Cooperative Research Relationships in the National Interest. Washington, D.C.: National Commission on Research.

Petersen, James C., and Robert W. Kaufman
1981   "Public service science centers." Citizen Participation, 2:20–21, 23.
Robbins, Martin D.
1977   Factors Leading to the Success and Failure of Complex Technology Transfer Programs. Report prepared for Energy Research and Development Administration.
Sanders, H. C. (ed.)
1966   The Cooperative Extension Service. Englewood Cliffs, New Jersey: Prentice-Hall.
Venett, Anthony J.
1981   "Technology transfer for industry and business through the university library." Special Libraries, 72:44–50.

AUTHOR INDEX

SUBJECT INDEX

About the Editors

Ralph H. Kilmann is a Professor of Business Administration and Coordinator of the Organizational Studies Interest Group in the Graduate School of Business, University of Pittsburgh. In 1972, he received his Ph.D. from the University of California, Los Angeles. Some of his research activities focus on: organizational design; organizational strategy, structure, culture, and productivity; conflict management; and organizational development.

Kenneth W. Thomas is an Associate Professor of Business Administration in the Graduate School of Business, University of Pittsburgh. He received his Ph.D. in Administrative Sciences from Purdue University in 1971. His major research interests have involved organizational conflict and its management, research usefulness, and managerial power.

Dennis P. Slevin is an Associate Professor of Business Administration and Director of Executive Development Programs in the Graduate School of Business, University of Pittsburgh. He received his Ph.D. in Business Administration from Stanford University in 1969. Some of his research activities focus on: organizational innovation, leadership, designing effective organizations, and implementing organizational change.

Raghu Nath is an Associate Professor of Business Administration and the Coordinator of International Interest Group. He received his Ph.D. from Massachusetts Institute of Technology in 1964. His areas of interest are international corporate strategy, management of system change, design of integrating structures, development of flexitime and quality circles, human resource planning, assessment of organization climate and culture, cross-cultural and comparative management.

S. Lee Jerrell is an Assistant Professor of Business Administration in the Graduate School of Business, University of Pittsburgh. He received his Ph.D. in Business Administration from Stanford University in 1978. His current research concerns the advisory process at the strategic level, especially around CEO's; this includes functions, processes, and characteristics of advisors and advisees, and the networks in which advising takes place.